About Pearson

Pearson is the world's learning company, with presence across 70 countries worldwide. Our unique insights and world-class expertise comes from a long history of working closely with renowned teachers, authors and thought leaders, as a result of which, we have emerged as the preferred choice for millions of teachers and learners across the world.

We believe learning opens up opportunities, creates fulfilling careers and hence better lives. We hence collaborate with the best of minds to deliver you class-leading products, spread across the Higher Education and K12 spectrum.

Superior learning experience and improved outcomes are at the heart of everything we do. This product is the result of one such effort.

Your feedback plays a critical role in the evolution of our products and you can contact us – reachus@pearson.com. We look forward to it.

D1194848

10th EDITION

Strategic Compensation
A Human Resource Management Approach

Joseph J. Martocchio
University of Illinois at Urbana-Champaign

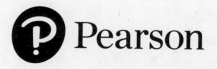
Pearson

Original edition, entitled *Strategic Compensation: A Human Resource Management Approach*, 10th Edition, by Martocchio, Joseph J. published by Pearson Education Limited, Copyright © 2019.

Indian Subcontinent Reprint

ISBN 978-93-539-4594-7

First Impression, 2020
Second Impression, 2022

This edition is manufactured in India and is authorized for sale only in India, Bangladesh, Bhutan, Pakistan, Nepal, Sri Lanka and the Maldives. Circulation of this edition outside of these territories is UNAUTHORIZED.

Published by Pearson India Education Services Pvt. Ltd, CIN: U72200TN2005PTC057128.

Head Office: 15th Floor, Tower-B, World Trade Tower, Plot No. 1, Block-C, Sector-16, Noida 201 301, Uttar Pradesh, India.

Registered Office: 7th Floor, SDB2, ODC 7, 8 & 9, Survey No.01 ELCOT IT/ ITES - SEZ, Sholinganallur, Chennai - 600119, Tamilnadu, India. Phone: 044-66540100
Website: in.pearson.com, Email: companysecretary.india@pearson.com

Printed in India at Sai Printo Pack Pvt Ltd, New Delhi.

Brief Contents

v

Contents

Chapter 12   Compensating the Flexible Workforce: Contingent Employees and Flexible Work Schedules   293

Preface

NEW TO THIS EDITION

Strategic Compensation: A Human Resource Management Approach, Tenth Edition, contains substantial new content and changes, including the following:

● Three new features appear in each chapter that enable students to integrate knowledge and valuable skills regardless of whether they are choosing a career in the compensation profession or other business functions in smaller or larger organizations.

■ **Ethics Dilemma.** Ethics is the discipline dealing with what is good and bad, right and wrong, or with moral duty and obligation. Most executives, managers, and professionals believe that integrity and ethical values have an important place in business and should form the foundation of a company's culture. Ethics focuses on individual decision making and behavior as well as the impact of ethical choices on employee welfare. The *Ethics Dilemma*, presented in the end-of-chapter material, will keep these important matters in the forefront as you move ahead in your career.

> ### Case 2: Ethics Dilemma: Pay for Performance Disconnect
> You are the new vice president for HR of a company that has not been performing well, and everyone, including yourself, has a mandate to deliver results. The pressure has never been greater. Shareholders are angry after three years of a tough market that has left their company stock losing value every day. Many shareholders desperately need stock performance to pay for their retirement. Working for you is a 52-year-old manager with two kids in college. In previous evaluations, executives told him he was doing fine, when he clearly was not, and his performance is still far below par. At the same time, the executives awarded him impressive annual pay raises.
> If you are to show others in the company that you are willing to make tough decisions, you feel you must fire this individual. The question is, who is going to suffer—the firm and, ultimately, the shareholders, whose retirements are in jeopardy—or a nice guy who's been lied to for 20 years?
>
> **Questions:**
> 3-9. What would you do?
> 3-10. What factor(s) in this ethical dilemma might influence a person to make a less-than-ethical decision?

> **☛ FYI**
> Both private-sector companies and the federal government are competing for cyber security talent; however, the difference in annual pay between the government and private sector is staggering, particularly for chief information officer jobs:
> • Private-sector: $500,000 to $2,000,000
> • Federal government: $123,175 to $185,100[14]

■ **FYI.** This feature provides tidbits of information from survey research and extensive databases (e.g., employment statistics) that illustrates trends, opinions, and the use of specific compensation practices.

> ### Working Together: Team Exercise
> In small groups of three or four, come up with specific answers to the following questions. Talk through your perspectives and come up with a team response. Be prepared to share your ideas with the class.
> We studied competency models in this chapter and viewed the U.S. Department of Labor competency model framework (Figure 5-1). The Department of Labor has the Competency Model Clearinghouse that contains several competency models across industries. As a group, review some of these competency models available on the *Careeronestop* website (https://www.careeronestop.org/CompetencyModel/) after clicking on the industry models link. Select a competency model from two industries.
>
> **Questions:**
> 5-14. Summarize the information available on your chosen models. What are some of the similarities?
> 5-15. What are some of the differences in occupation- and industry-competencies between your chosen models?

■ **Working Together.** This feature offers opportunities for students to collaborate through sharing ideas, listening to others' ideas, and coming up with a cohesive team response to the assignment.

● Other major updates to the tenth edition include:

■ Extend coverage of evolving compensation practices, statistics, and business professionals' perspectives. For instance, Chapter 3 (Traditional Bases for Pay: Seniority and Merit) includes a section on trends in performance appraisal practice. In a nutshell, some companies are providing performance feedback more frequently and as needed on a less structured basis rather than putting off providing feedback until structured annual reviews are given. This section also addresses the pros and cons of this more contemporary thinking as well the same for longstanding approaches to provide students a balanced view.

■ Chapter 15 has been converted into an Epilogue. It includes many important topics not covered in previous editions and makes significant updates to other topics. Some of the topics are the compensation productivity gap, the gender pay gap, and pay transparency.

■ Fifty percent of the Cases and nearly fifty percent of the Crunch the Numbers features are new.

SOLVING TEACHING AND LEARNING CHALLENGES

Increasingly, students expect to see the applicability of their coursework to life and work after graduation. When the connection is not clear to students, many may lose interest and, perhaps, choose to do as little as possible to earn a good enough grade on quizzes and exams. The choice of pedagogical features and the writing style in this text would pique interest in the subject matter and enhance learning and development of seven critical employability skills, which have been discussed in the 'Developing skills for your career' section in this textbook.

Strategic Compensation: A Human Resource Management Approach provides the foundation for building compensation systems in a variety of work organizations. The content of this textbook establishes the structure and design elements of compensation systems in a *forward-looking framework* that addresses decision making that supports companies' strategic plans. This approach, therefore, positions compensation practice as essential and compensation professionals as business partners. Individuals who pursue careers outside the compensation field will understand how to interact with compensation professionals for promoting effective recruitment, motivation, and retention of talent. This textbook is *readable* with a conversational tone and clear explanations for concepts and practices. It conveys the *relevance* of compensation system design overall as well as individual topics for organizations and aspiring professionals; and, this textbook takes on *contemporary topic coverage* in every chapter.

I approach the study of compensation in a realistic, practical, interesting, and stimulating manner. I focus on showing how compensation is practiced in the real world. Throughout the book, you will see examples of how organizations practice compensation management. In explaining a concept, I often quote compensation professionals and other business professionals, yet all compensation discussion is based on sound theoretical concepts and practice. Where appropriate, the strategic role of compensation is apparent, particularly in Chapter 1. In addition, I show how compensation practices are related to other Human Resource Management (HRM) topics. For instance, a firm that emphasizes recruiting top-quality candidates but neglects to provide satisfactory compensation is wasting time, effort, and money. If a firm's compensation system pays below-market wages, the firm will always be hiring and training new employees only to see the best leave for a competitor's higher wages. Besides this one example, the interrelationship of compensation practices set in a dynamic business environment will become more obvious as these topics are addressed throughout the book. These interrelationships are also shown to be important as organizations operate within the global environment. I included several features that appear in the textbook.

Crunch the Numbers Exercises

Crunch the Numbers provide an excellent opportunity to sharpen problem solving skills through the analysis of numerical data, creating the foundation for quantifying compensation concepts and practices. There are data-driven exercises in every chapter. Answers are found in the Instructors Manual.

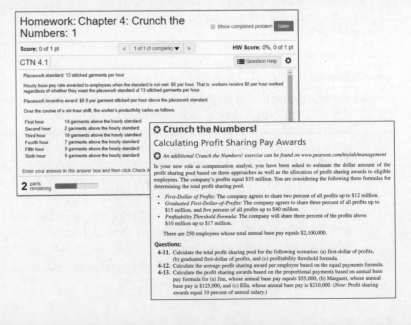

Compensation in Action

Compensation in Action explains how compensation professionals and managers throughout an organization work together to address important workplace issues. This feature highlights some of the specific connections between managers and compensation professionals, and the reality that compensation activities are never performed in isolation.

PREPARING FOR MY CAREER

Compensation in Action

Employee compensation will ultimately be a managerial decision. As a line manager, your focus will be on the broader issues of production, revenue, and competition; however, the rate at which employees are paid—and why—will be an important factor in sustaining high levels of production, revenue, and competitive advantage. In making these decisions, line managers and HR (and in many cases the compensation specialist within the HR department) must work together in order to reward employees on measurable accomplishments and effectively communicate how the measured performance led to the resulting compensation decision.

Working Together Exercises

As noted earlier, *Working Together* offers opportunities for students to collaborate through sharing ideas, listening to others' ideas, and coming up with a cohesive team response to the assignment. If assigned by the instructor, students may make brief oral presentations of their ideas to the class, creating an additional opportunity for working together.

DEVELOPING EMPLOYABILITY SKILLS

For students to succeed in a rapidly changing job market, they should be aware of their career options and how to go about developing a variety of skills. In this book, students will have the opportunity to develop seven important skills based on various learning features that are summarized in the matrix (given on the following page) and subsequently illustrating some of the connections between employability skills and learning features:

	Communication	Critical Thinking	Collaboration	Knowledge Application and Analysis	Business Ethics and Social Responsibility	Information Technology and Computing Skills	Data Literacy
FYI				✓			✓
Compensation in Action	✓		✓	✓			
Case (end-of-chapter)		✓		✓	✓		
Ethics Dilemma		✓		✓	✓		
Crunch the Numbers!		✓		✓		✓	✓
Working Together: Team Exercise	✓		✓	✓			

INSTRUCTOR TEACHING RESOURCES

Strategic Compensation comes with the following teaching resources.

Supplements available to instructors at *www.pearsoned.co.in/prc/home*	Features of the Supplement
Instructor's Manual authored by Lori Long	• Chapter-by-chapter summaries • Examples and activities not in the main book • Teaching outlines • Solutions to all questions and problems in the book
Test Bank authored by Angela Boston	More than 650 multiple-choice, true/false, short-answer, and graphing questions with these annotations: • Difficulty level (1 for easy, 2 for moderate, 3 for difficult) • Type (Multiple-choice, true/false, short-answer, essay) • Topic (The term or concept the question supports) • Learning objective • AACSB learning standard (Written and Oral Communication, Ethical Understanding and Reasoning; Analytical Thinking; Information Technology; Diverse and Multicultural Work; Reflective Thinking; Application of Knowledge; Interpersonal Relations and Teamwork)
Computerized TestGen©	TestGen allows instructors to: • Customize, save, and generate classroom tests • Edit, add, or delete questions from the Test Item Files • Analyze test results • Organize a database of tests and student results.
PowerPoints authored by Patricia Buhler	Slides include many of the figures and tables in the textbook PowerPoints meet accessibility standards for students with disabilities. Features include, but are not limited to: • Keyboard and Screen Reader access • Alternative text for images • High color contrast between background and foreground colors

ACKNOWLEDGMENTS

I thank the multitude of course instructors and students who have used past editions of my book. Their invaluable insights and constructive feedback has helped me to improve both the instructor's teaching and students' learning experiences.

At Pearson, I wish to thank my editor, Neeraj Bhalla for championing this edition and providing support throughout the revision process. Many others at Pearson provided expert advice and project management oversight, including my content producers, Shweta Jain and Sugandh Juneja. At SPi Global, I thank Bhanuprakash Sherla and his colleagues for their expert oversight of the process and keen eye for details.

ABOUT THE AUTHOR

Joseph J. Martocchio

My interest in the human resource management field began while I was a junior at Babson College and in compensation, particularly, while I was a first-year graduate student at Michigan State University. I found myself wanting to practice in the field as well as to become a university professor and researcher. I pursued both professional desires starting with employment at Cameron and Colby (a reinsurance company) in Boston and General Electric's Aerospace business group in Valley Forge, Pennsylvania.

I advanced my education in the human resource management (HRM) field by earning a master's degree and Ph.D. degree at Michigan State University. My master's degree enabled me to build an even stronger foundation in practice and my doctoral degree provided me with the skills to conduct scholarly research and teach college-level courses. Since earning my graduate degrees, I have been a professor in the School of Labor and Employment Relations at the University of Illinois, Urbana–Champaign and assumed administrative roles as a Provost Fellow, Associate Dean for Academic Affairs, and Interim Dean. All the while, I have taught a variety of courses in the HRM field. These include compensation systems, employee benefits, employment systems (HRM and labor relations), HR planning and staffing, and statistics. I also teach the compensation and statistics courses online. For many years, I served as the faculty advisor to the student chapter of the Society for Human Resource Management at the University of Illinois during which time students earned Merit Awards and Superior Merit awards on multiple occasions.

As a researcher, I have studied a variety of topics that include employee absenteeism, employee training and development, compensation systems, employee benefits, and generational diversity. My work appears in leading scholarly journals such as *Academy of Management Journal*, *Academy of Management Review*, *Journal of Applied Psychology*, *Journal of Management*, and *Personnel Psychology*. I received the Ernest J. McCormick Award for Distinguished Early Career Contributions from the Society for Industrial and Organizational Psychology (SIOP), and I was subsequently elected as a Fellow in both the American Psychological Association and SIOP. Following the attainment of this recognition, I served as the Chair of the HR Division of the Academy of Management as well as in various other leadership roles within that organization.

In 2018, a study in the *Academy of Management Learning and Education* revealed that I am in the top one percent of the most influential HRM authors out of a total of 9,744. Besides writing scholarly articles and *Strategic Compensation: A Human Resource Management Approach*, I have two additional sole-authored textbooks: *Human Resource Management* (Pearson Higher Education), 15th edition, and *Employee Benefits: A Primer for Human Resource Professionals* (McGraw-Hill), 6th edition.

SETTING THE STAGE FOR STRATEGIC COMPENSATION

1

Strategic Compensation
A Component of Human Resource Systems

Through the early twentieth century, manpower planning was the predecessor to contemporary human resource (HR) management. Manpower planning focused on the effective deployment of employees in factories to achieve the highest manufacturing output per employee per unit of time. That is, management sought to increase productivity (such as the number of handmade garments per hour) while also maintaining or lowering employee compensation costs. All else equal, higher employee productivity while maintaining or lowering employee compensation costs contributed to higher profitability for the firm.

Through the decades, mounting government regulation involving payroll taxes and laws centered on ensuring a minimum wage, prevailing wage, equal pay for equal work; and, equal employment opportunity later gave rise to the personnel management function, of which compensation was a component. Legal compliance necessitated that personnel management take on the role of an administrative, support function to maintain compliance with the myriad details of employment laws (e.g., determining prevailing wages in localities). Personnel management departments also engaged in transactions (e.g., payroll administration) with an eye toward administrative efficiency. Administrative efficiency is essential because it can *indirectly* contribute to company success through cost control.

Since the early 1980s, there has been growing widespread recognition that managing employees or human resources can contribute *more directly* to competitive advantage. **Competitive advantage** describes a company's success when the company acquires or develops capabilities that facilitate outperforming the competition. For example, Walmart is a successful retailer, in part, because its sheer size enables it to negotiate lower prices with suppliers (e.g., of clothing) than smaller retailers. In turn, Walmart can sell products at a price advantage relative to most competitors. Other resources may include the employment of highly skilled employees who can operate and troubleshoot problems with sophisticated robotic equipment, which can increase the pace of production while also maintaining quality.

Designing HR practices with competitive advantage in mind casts HR as a strategic function rather than as one that focuses exclusively on conducting transactions. In a strategic role, HR professionals proactively put forth forward-looking principles and ideas, and they play an important role in contributing to successful business outcomes by attracting, motivating, and retaining highly qualified employees.

DEFINING STRATEGIC COMPENSATION

"What is strategic compensation?" Answering this question requires that we first answer the question, "What is compensation?"

1-1. Define strategic compensation.

What Is Compensation?

Compensation represents both the intrinsic and extrinsic rewards employees receive for performing their jobs and for their membership as employees. Together, both intrinsic and extrinsic compensation describe a company's total compensation system, which we will look at more closely in this chapter, and, in even greater detail throughout the remainder of this textbook.

Intrinsic compensation reflects employees' psychological mind-sets that result from performing their jobs, for example, experiencing a great feeling from the belief that one's work matters in the lives of others. Perhaps it is easy to imagine that many health care providers feel this way. **Extrinsic compensation** includes both monetary and nonmonetary rewards. Organizational development professionals promote intrinsic compensation through effective job design. Compensation professionals are responsible for extrinsic compensation, which is the focus of this textbook.

Compensation professionals work with high-level managers to determine the best compensation plans that will contribute to recruitment, employee job performance, and retention. Then, compensation professionals use their expertise to establish monetary compensation programs to reward employees according to their job seniority, performance levels, or for learning job-related knowledge or skills. Some describe this exchange as a pay-effort bargain. As we will discuss shortly, monetary compensation represents **core compensation**. Nonmonetary rewards include protection programs (e.g., health insurance), paid time off (e.g., vacations), and services (e.g., day care assistance). Most compensation professionals refer to nonmonetary rewards as **employee benefits**. Employees receive some or all of these offerings as part of an employment arrangement. Rarely do employers base employee benefits on job performance. Employee benefits are becoming an increasingly important element of compensation packages. Since the so-called Great Recession (2007–2009) ended, many companies now offer lower pay increases (from an average 3.8 percent annual increase to less than 3 percent)[1] to better control costs and build cash reserves for a "rainy day." Another reason for lower pay increases is the rising cost of health care coverage, which employers are required to provide full-time employees under the Patient Protection and Affordable Care Act of 2010, or else pay a substantial monetary penalty.

Both monetary and nonmonetary compensation represents costs to companies. In the case of core compensation, employers pay an hourly wage or salary. In the case of employee benefits, employers pay some or the entire cost for employees to have health insurance coverage rather than providing dedicated monetary payments, apart from wage or salary, to pay for health care coverage and contributions to a retirement savings plan, among others.

What Is Strategic Compensation?

Defining strategic compensation requires that we place the relevance and importance of compensation practices in a broader context where compensation practices are linked to competitive business strategy, as shown in Figure 1-1. **Competitive business strategy** refers to the planned use of company resources—financial capital, equipment capital, and human capital—to promote and sustain competitive advantage. The time horizon for strategic decisions may span multiple years. For example, Netflix company leadership maintains that "Now internet entertainment— which is on-demand, personalized, and available on any screen—is replacing linear TV."[2] Netflix's success is largely due to its ability to capitalize on changing technology and consumer preferences as well as produce popular content. The company has been highly successful. In the last three months of 2017 alone, Netflix added 8.3 million subscribers globally.[3]

Human resource executives collaborate with company executives to develop human resource strategies. **Human resource strategies** specify the use of multiple HR practices to reinforce competitive business strategy. These statements are consistent with a company's competitive strategy. For example, Samsung emphasizes the essential role of its employees as it endeavors "to create a better world full of richer digital experiences, through innovative technology and products: For this, we dedicate our efforts to creativity and innovation, shared value with our partners, and our great people [employees]."[4]

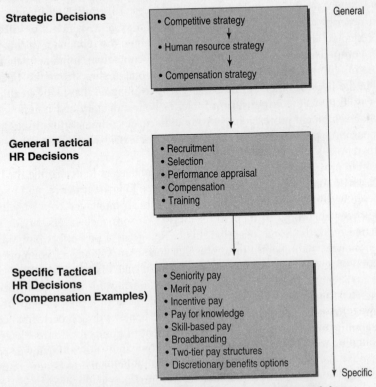

Strategic Decisions

- Competitive strategy
  ↓
- Human resource strategy
  ↓
- Compensation strategy

**General Tactical
HR Decisions**

- Recruitment
- Selection
- Performance appraisal
- Compensation
- Training

**Specific Tactical
HR Decisions
(Compensation Examples)**

- Seniority pay
- Merit pay
- Incentive pay
- Pay for knowledge
- Skill-based pay
- Broadbanding
- Two-tier pay structures
- Discretionary benefits options

General

Specific

**FIGURE 1-1 Relationship between Strategic Decisions
and Compensation Practices**

Within the context of competitive business strategy and human resource strategy, compensation professionals practice strategic compensation. **Strategic compensation** refers to the design and implementation of compensation systems to reinforce the objectives of both HR strategies and competitive business strategies. Compensation and benefits executives work with the lead HR executive and the company's chief financial officer (CFO) to prepare total compensation strategies. For example, pharmaceutical manufacturer Eli Lilly is well known for offering a balanced compensation and benefits program which recognizes employee contributions and embraces employees through recognition of their needs outside the workplace.[5]

COMPENSATION AS A STRATEGIC BUSINESS PARTNER

As noted earlier, personnel administration in the 1980s was transformed from a purely administrative function, engaged in transactions such as payroll processing, to a competitive resource in many emerging companies. Technological advances (e.g., the use of robotics in manufacturing), global competition (e.g., increased imports of Japanese and South Korean automobiles), and shifts in the composition of the workforce (e.g., a gap in leadership as many baby boom era employees retire) have contributed greatly to the need for a strategic approach.[6] As a strategic business partner, HR and compensation professionals today need to think like the chief executive officer (CEO) to become a strategic partner in achieving organizational plans and results.[7] Essentially, they must know more than just HR work.[8] For example, GE's Human Resources Leadership Program (HRLP)[9] is an exemplar of these ideas. The HRLP provides participants with opportunities to learn HR competencies, global leadership skills, and business acumen through formal training and rotational assignments in areas such as compensation, staffing, and employment relations. Participants also receive exposure to GE executives and HR leaders to put their work in the context of strategic issues facing the company. In doing so, they understand the production and service sides of the business and help to determine the strategic capabilities of the company's workforce, both today and in the future. For example, increasing sales and building brand loyalty are important goals of soft drink companies such as Coca-Cola and PepsiCo. Increasing sales requires hiring highly dedicated and motivated sales employees whose success is rewarded through innovative sales incentive arrangements.

Compensation professionals can give the CEO and CFO a powerful understanding of the role that employees play in the organization and the way it combines with business processes to expand or shrink shareholder value. Compensation professionals are integrating the goals of compensation with the goals of the organization and focusing on expanding its strategic and high-level corporate participation with an emphasis on adding value.

Perhaps a useful way to better understand *how* HR functions serve as a strategic business partner is to think about the role of capital for value creation. **Capital** refers to the factors that enable companies to generate income, higher company stock prices, economic value, strong positive brand identity, and reputation. There is a variety of capital that companies use to create value, including financial capital (cash) and capital equipment (state-of-the-art robotics used in manufacturing). Employees represent a specific type of capital called human capital. **Human capital**, as defined by economists, refers to sets of collective skills, knowledge, and abilities that employees can apply to create value for their employers. Companies purchase the use of human capital by paying employees an hourly wage or salary and providing benefits such as paid vacation and health insurance.

Compensation professionals can help leverage the value of human capital in a variety of ways. For example, well-designed merit pay programs reinforce excellent performance by awarding pay raises commensurate with performance attainments. The use of incentive pay practices is instrumental in changing the prevalent entitlement mentality U.S. workers have toward pay and in containing compensation costs by awarding one-time increases to base pay once work objectives have been attained. Pay-for-knowledge and skill-based pay programs are

1-2. Summarize the role of compensation as a strategic business partner.

key to giving employees the necessary knowledge and skills to use new workplace technology effectively. Management can use discretionary benefit offerings to promote employee behaviors that have strategic value. For example, employees who take advantage of tuition reimbursement programs gain knowledge and skills that directly add value to the work they do. In line with these ideas, Bosch offers a unique program to individuals who are pursuing PhD degrees at well-respected universities.[10] The company hires doctoral candidates on a limited-term basis while these students undertake dissertation work under the auspices of Bosch scientists who are working on pressing company matters of scientific importance. This arrangement is a win–win situation because students have direct access to research facilities and Bosch benefits from individuals who are gaining state-of-the-art knowledge and skills in their doctoral programs.

STRATEGIC COMPENSATION DECISIONS

1-3. Explain strategic compensation decisions.

Compensation professionals provide a strategic contribution to the company when they can answer *yes* to the following three questions:

- Does compensation strategy fit well with the objectives of competitive business and HR strategies?
- Does the choice and design of compensation practices fit well to support compensation strategy?
- Does the implementation of compensation practices effectively direct employee behavior to enhance job performance that supports the choice of compensation practices?

Companies base strategy formulation on environmental scanning activities. Discerning threats and opportunities is the focus of environmental scanning. A threat suggests a negative situation in which loss is likely and over which an individual has relatively little control. An opportunity implies a positive situation in which gain is likely and over which an individual has a fair amount of control.[11]

For instance, small specialty coffee shops are facing several *threats*, four of which are noted here. First, prices tend to be higher in small shops than in large-chain shops such as Dunkin' Donuts and Starbucks whose large sizes enable them to purchase coffee beans at a lower cost. Second, competition from unlikely sources has emerged in recent years. Gas stations have jumped into this market space by offering premium coffees at substantially lower prices than specialty coffee shops. Third, the rise in work-from-home arrangements has contributed to a decline in coffee shop patronage. Fourth, further pressures include a rising minimum wage rate throughout many cities and states, and soaring rental rates for retail space in prime locations.[12]

Government regulation provides U.S. pharmaceutical companies with the *opportunity* to recoup research and development costs as well as generate profits from the sale of products for which they have U.S. patent protection. For a limited period of a few to several years, the U.S. government grants these companies exclusivity. That is, no other company may manufacture or sell the product during this period. Without exclusivity provisions, pharmaceutical companies such as Wyeth Pharmaceuticals would be placed at a competitive disadvantage because other companies would manufacture and distribute a therapeutically equivalent product at a lower cost. For example, Wyeth Pharmaceuticals developed Protonix, a product which treats gastro esophageal reflux disease. The company enjoyed exclusivity protection for several years. The expiration of an exclusivity clause poses a threat for, in this case, Wyeth Pharmaceuticals; yet, an opportunity for more pharmaceutical companies to compete for market share. For example, Teva Pharmaceuticals has been selling pantoprazole, a therapeutically generic version of Protonix, at a lower price. These so-called generic alternatives are less expensive because companies that manufacture and distribute them do not have research and development costs to recoup. Adding to the threat to brand names, most health insurance companies refuse to provide coverage for brand name products where less expensive generic alternatives are available.

Competitive Business Strategy Choices

Companies use a variety of terms to describe competitive business strategy choices. These choices fundamentally focus on attaining competitive advantage either by achieving lowest cost or product (service) differentiation. Most companies pursue strategies that contain elements of both.

LOWEST-COST STRATEGY The **cost leadership** or **lowest-cost strategy** focuses on gaining competitive advantage by being the lowest-cost producer of a product or service within the marketplace, while selling the product or service at a price advantage relative to the industry average. Lowest-cost strategies require aggressive construction of efficient-scale facilities and vigorous pursuit of cost minimization in areas such as operations, marketing, and HR.

IKEA, a low-cost furniture manufacturer, is an excellent illustration of an organization that pursues a lowest-cost strategy because its management successfully reduced operations costs. Three noteworthy decisions have contributed to IKEA's goals. First, IKEA sources its products to countries where labor costs are low. Second, the company provides a low level of service to consumers. For example, IKEA does not assemble furniture. It also does not deliver furniture to people's homes. Instead, IKEA sends orders to warehouses where the customer is responsible for picking up purchases. Customers are willing to make significant efforts to retrieve and assemble furniture because prices are much lower than full-service manufacturers and retailers. The third point also illustrates threats to maintaining strategic objectives. Rising raw material costs has prompted IKEA to consider the use of alternative lower cost material, including bamboo, without compromising the quality of their products.

DIFFERENTIATION STRATEGY Companies adopt **differentiation strategies** to develop products or services that are unique from those of their competitors. Differentiation strategy can take many forms, including design or brand image, technology, features, customer service, and price. Differentiation strategies lead to competitive advantage through building brand loyalty among devoted consumers. Brand-loyal consumers are probably less sensitive to price increases, which enables companies to invest in research and development initiatives to further differentiate themselves from competing companies.

Apple Computer relies on a differentiation strategy to increase market demand and loyalty. Apple's products are successful, in large part, because they have always been designed to be on the leading edge compared to the competition. Even in the face of strong competition, Apple continually excels in creating demand for its products such as iPhones, iPads, and iPods, enabling them control over pricing through product differentiation, innovative advertising, and creative publicity prior to unveiling products.

Compensation Decisions that Support the Firm's Strategy

Compensation professionals support strategic initiatives through the design and implementation of compensation systems. Two broad elements are the basis for compensation professionals' work. These include basic building blocks and structural design elements, which we will introduce later in this chapter. For example, compensation professionals make decisions about whether to use (and how to design) pay-for-performance practices, whether to set pay levels that exceed typical market pay rates, and whether to create a pay mix that emphasizes long-term over short-term incentives. The totality of choices should fit well with cost or differentiation objectives and with an eye toward rewarding behaviors that support these objectives.

Employee Roles Associated with Competitive Strategies

Common wisdom and experience tell us that HR professionals must decide which employee roles are instrumental to the attainment of competitive strategies. Knowledge of these required roles should enable HR professionals to implement HR practices that encourage enactment of these roles. Of course, compensation professionals are responsible for designing and implementing compensation practices that elicit strategy-consistent employee roles.

For the lowest-cost strategy, the imperative is to reduce output costs per employee. The desired employee roles include repetitive and predictable behaviors, a relatively short-term focus, primarily autonomous or individual activity, high concern for quantity of output, and a primary concern for results. Successful differentiation strategies depend on employee creativity, openness to novel work approaches, and willingness to take risks. Design thinking has recently received much attention and is appropriate in companies that pursue a differentiation strategy. It has been described as "approaching management problems as designers approach design problems."[13] PepsiCo embraces the importance of design thinking. For example, the company designers created the Pepsi Spire, which is a high-tech beverage dispensing machine with a futuristic design. PepsiCo CEO Indra Nooyi had this to say about the company's design approach: "Other companies with dispensing machines have focused on adding a few more buttons and combinations of flavors. Our design guys essentially said that we're talking about a fundamentally different interaction between consumer and machine."[14] In addition, differentiation strategies require longer time frames to provide sufficient opportunity to yield the benefits of these behaviors.

BUILDING BLOCKS AND STRUCTURE OF STRATEGIC COMPENSATION SYSTEMS

1-4. Identify and discuss the building blocks and structural elements of strategic compensation systems.

As we discussed previously, extrinsic compensation includes both monetary (core compensation) and nonmonetary rewards (employee benefits). Figure 1-2 lists the main compensation building blocks. The building blocks are embedded within a system of three structural elements that ultimately support compensation strategies. These structural elements include internally consistent job structures, market competitive pay structures, and structures that recognize employee contributions.

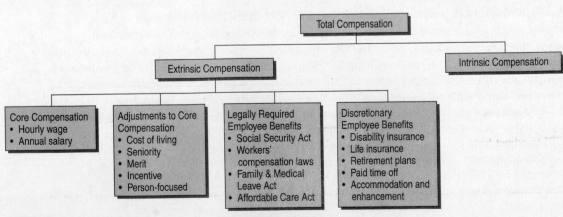

FIGURE 1-2 Compensation System Building Blocks

TABLE 1-1 Elements of Core Compensation

Base Pay
- Hourly pay
- Annual salary

How Base Pay Is Adjusted over Time
- Cost-of-living adjustments
- Seniority pay
- Merit pay
- Incentive pay
- Person-focused pay or competency-based pay: pay-for-knowledge, skill-based pay

Building Blocks: Core Compensation and Employee Benefits

CORE COMPENSATION There are two categories of core compensation: base pay and base pay adjustments over time. The specific practices associated with each category are listed in Table 1-1.

Employees receive **base pay**, or money, for performing their jobs (Chapter 7). Base pay is recurring; that is, employees continue to receive base pay as long as they remain in their jobs. Companies disburse base pay to employees in one of two forms: **hourly pay or wage**, or as **annual salary**. Employees earn hourly pay for each hour worked. Salaried employees earn salaries for performing their jobs, regardless of the actual number of hours worked throughout the year. Companies measure salary on an annual basis. The Fair Labor Standards Act (FLSA) (Chapter 2) established criteria for determining whether employees should be paid hourly or by salary. In 2017, the average hourly rate for workers was $24.33.[15] On an annual basis, this figure translates to $50,620.

Companies typically set base pay amounts for jobs according to the level of skill, effort, and responsibility required to perform the jobs and the severity of the working conditions. Compensation professionals refer to skill, effort, responsibility, and working condition factors as **compensable factors** because they influence pay level (Chapters 2 and 6). Courts of law use these four compensable factors to determine whether jobs are equal per the Equal Pay Act of 1963 (EPA). According to the EPA, it is against the law to pay women less than men for performing equal work though there are exceptions, which we will discuss in Chapter 2. Compensation professionals use these compensable factors to help meet three pressing challenges, which we will introduce later in this chapter: internal consistency (Chapter 6), market competitiveness (Chapter 7), and recognition of employee contributions (Chapter 8).

Over time, employers adjust employees' base pay to recognize increases in the cost of living, differences in employees' performance, or differences in employees' acquisition of job-related knowledge and skills. We will discuss these core compensation elements next.

Cost-of-living adjustments (COLAs) represent periodic base pay increases that are founded on changes in prices as recorded by the Consumer Price Index (CPI). In recent years, the typical COLA equaled approximately 2 to 3 percent annually. COLAs enable workers to maintain their purchasing power and standard of living by adjusting base pay for inflation. COLAs are most common among workers represented by unions. Union leaders fought hard for these improvements to maintain their members' loyalty and support. Many employers use the CPI to adjust base pay levels for newly hired employees.

Seniority pay systems reward employees with periodic additions to base pay according to employees' length of service in performing their jobs (Chapter 3). These pay plans assume that employees become more valuable to companies with time and that valued employees will leave if they do not have a clear idea that their wages will progress over time. This rationale comes from **human capital theory**,[16] which states that employees' knowledge and skills (human capital) add value. Employees can develop such knowledge and skills from formal education and training, including on-the-job experience. Over time, employees presumably refine existing skills or acquire new ones that enable them to work more productively. Seniority pay rewards employees for acquiring and refining their skills as indexed by length (years) of employment.

Merit pay programs assume that employees' compensation over time should be determined, at least in part, by differences in job performance as judged by supervisors or managers (Chapter 3). Employees earn permanent increases to base pay according to their performance. Merit pay rewards excellent effort or results, motivates future performance, and helps employers retain valued employees.

Incentive pay or **variable pay** rewards employees for partially or completely attaining a predetermined work objective. Incentive pay is defined as compensation (other than base wages or salaries) that fluctuates according to employees' attainment of some standard based on a pre-established formula, individual or group goals, or company earnings (Chapter 4).

Person-focused pay or **competency-based pay** rewards employees for specifically learning new curricula. **Pay-for-knowledge** plans reward managerial, service, or professional workers for successfully learning specific curricula (Chapter 5). **Skill-based pay**, used mostly for employees who perform physical work, increases these workers' pay as they master new skills (Chapter 5). Both skill- and knowledge-based pay programs reward employees for the range, depth, and types of skills or knowledge they are capable of applying productively to their jobs. This feature distinguishes pay-for-knowledge plans from merit pay, which rewards employees' job performance. Said another way, pay-for-knowledge programs reward employees for their potential to make meaningful contributions on the job.

EMPLOYEE BENEFITS Earlier, we noted that employee benefits represent nonmonetary rewards. Employee benefits include any variety of programs that provide paid time off, employee services, and protection programs. Companies offer many benefits on a discretionary basis. We refer to these as **discretionary benefits** (Chapter 9). In addition, the U.S. government requires most employers to provide sets of benefits to employees. We refer to these as **legally required benefits** (Chapter 10). Different forces led to the rise of legally required and discretionary employee benefits.

The first signs of contemporary discretionary benefits were evident in the late 1800s when large companies such as American Express offered pension plans to employees. Most of the development in employee benefits practice for the next few decades resulted from government legislation, as previously noted. Discretionary benefits offerings became more prominent in the 1940s and 1950s due in large part to federal government restrictions placed on increasing wage levels. Employee benefits were not subject to those restrictions.

Discretionary benefits fall into three broad categories: protection programs, paid time off, and services (Chapter 9). **Protection programs** provide family benefits, promote health, and guard against income loss caused by such catastrophic factors as unemployment, disability, or serious illness. Not surprisingly, **paid time off** provides employees with pay for time when they are not working (e.g., vacation). **Services** provide such enhancements as tuition reimbursement and day care assistance to employees and their families.

Legally required benefits historically provided a form of social insurance. Prompted largely by the rapid growth of industrialization in the United States during the late nineteenth and early twentieth centuries as well as the Great Depression of the 1930s, initial social insurance programs were designed to minimize the possibility of destitution for individuals who were unemployed or became severely injured while working. In addition, social insurance programs aimed to stabilize the well-being of dependent family members of injured or unemployed individuals. Further, early social insurance programs were designed to enable retirees to maintain subsistence income levels. These intents of legally required benefits remain intact today. The U.S. government has established programs to protect individuals from such catastrophic events as disability and unemployment. Legally required benefits are exclusively protection programs that attempt to promote worker safety and health, maintain the influx of family income, and assist families in crisis. Many of the key legally required benefits are mandated by the Social Security Act of 1935, various state workers' compensation laws, the Family and Medical Leave Act of 1993, and the Patient Protection and Affordable Care Act of 2010 (PPACA). All provide protection programs to employees and their dependents (Chapter 10). It especially should be noted that until the passage of PPACA, employers offered health insurance as a discretionary benefit. Not only does this law require that employers provide health insurance, but it also exerts influence on the design of health insurance arrangements (Chapter 10).

Employers typically spend substantial amounts to pay employees and provide benefits. Table 1-2 lists these costs.[17] This table also includes the cost of wages and salaries based on a sample of occupations and industry types. The costs are expressed on an hourly basis per employee. For example, in September 2017, employers characteristically spent $35.64 per employee per hour worked, including wages and salaries as well as benefits. Of this figure, $24.33 was spent on wages and salaries and $11.31 was spent on benefits ($2.63 for legally required benefits and $8.68 for discretionary benefits). All employee benefits costs account for 31.7 percent of total compensation costs.

Fundamental Compensation System Design Elements

Compensation professionals promote effective compensation systems by meeting three important goals: internal consistency, market competitiveness, and recognition of individual contributions, which corresponds to three important compensation system design elements.

INTERNAL CONSISTENCY Internally consistent compensation systems clearly define the relative value of each job among all jobs within a company. This ordered set of jobs represents the job structure or hierarchy. Companies rely on a simple, yet fundamental, principle for building internally consistent compensation systems: Employees in jobs that require greater qualifications, more responsibilities, and more complex job duties should be paid more than employees whose jobs require lesser qualifications, fewer responsibilities, and less-complex job duties. Internally consistent job structures formally recognize differences in job characteristics, which therefore enable compensation managers to set pay accordingly. For example, let's consider two related HR jobs that differ in job characteristics. According to the *Occupational Outlook Handbook*, the work of Human Resources Specialists and Labor Relations Specialists is described in the following manner:

> Human resources specialists recruit, screen, interview, and place workers. They often handle other human resources work, such as those related to employee relations, payroll and benefits, and training. Labor relations specialists interpret and administer labor contracts regarding issues such as wages and salaries, employee welfare, healthcare, pensions, and union and management practices.[18]

A Human Resources Manager's work is described in the following way:

> Human resources managers plan, direct, and coordinate the administrative functions of an organization. They oversee the recruiting, interviewing, and hiring of new staff; consult with top executives on strategic planning; and serve as a link between an organization's management and its employees.[19]

A comparison shows similarities (jobs that are focused on HR functions) and differences. The specialist roles are transactional (e.g., conducting job interviews) while the managerial roles include strategic considerations based on consultations with executives. The median annual pay for a specialist is $59,180[20] and $106,910 for the manager.[21] The pay difference can be attributed, in large part, to the noted dissimilarities between the jobs and the roles they play relative to competitive strategy attainment.

TABLE 1-2 Employer Costs per Hours Worked for Employee Compensation, Civilian Workers[a]

	Total Compensation	Wages and Salaries	All Benefits	Paid Leave	Supplemental Pay	Insurance	Retirement and Savings	Legally Required Benefits
			Cost per hour worked (in dollars)					
Civilian Workers	35.64	24.33	11.31	2.51	1.10	3.11	1.96	2.63
Occupational Group								
Management, professional, and related	59.42	40.19	19.23	4.82	2.11	4.82	3.83	3.65
Sales and office	25.57	17.95	7.62	1.70	0.61	2.44	0.95	1.91
Natural resources, construction, and maintenance	36.35	24.30	12.05	1.97	1.05	3.38	2.20	3.45
Production, transportation, and material moving	28.48	18.78	9.70	1.71	1.00	3.01	1.35	2.63
Industry Group								
Goods-producing	40.00	26.51	13.49	2.59	1.49	3.74	2.34	3.32
Service	34.87	23.95	10.92	2.49	1.03	3.00	1.90	2.51

[a] Includes workers in the private nonfarm economy excluding households and the public sector excluding the federal government.

Source: U.S. Bureau of Labor Statistics (December 15, 2017). *Employer costs for employee compensation, September 2017* (USDL: 17-1646). Available: *https://www.bls.gov/news. release/pdf/ecec.pdf*, accessed January 3, 2018.

☛ **FYI**

The increase in hourly compensation costs between 2007 and 2017 varied by compensation component:

- Total Compensation: 23.4%
- Wages and Salaries: 24.4%
- Employee Benefits: 33.5%[22]

Compensation professionals use job analysis and job evaluation to achieve internal consistency. **Job analysis** is a systematic process for gathering, documenting, and analyzing information to describe jobs. Job analyses describe content or job duties, worker requirements, and sometimes the job context or working conditions. For example, aerospace engineers design aircraft, spacecraft, satellites, and missiles. In addition, they test prototypes to make sure that they function according to design.[23] Aerospace engineers possess at least a bachelor's degree in aerospace engineering or another field of engineering or science related to aerospace systems. While some aerospace engineers work on projects that are related to national defense and thus require security clearances, others are employed in industries whose workers design or build aircraft, missiles, systems for national defense, or spacecraft.

Compensation professionals systematically use **job evaluation** to recognize differences in the relative worth among a set of jobs and to establish pay differentials accordingly. Whereas job analysis is almost purely descriptive, job evaluation partly reflects the values and priorities that management places on various positions. Based on job content differences (e.g., job analysis results) and the firm's priorities, managers establish pay differentials for virtually all positions within the company.

MARKET COMPETITIVENESS **Market-competitive pay systems** play a significant role in attracting and retaining the most qualified employees. Compensation professionals build market-competitive compensation systems based on the results of compensation surveys.

Compensation surveys collect and then analyze competitors' compensation data. Compensation surveys traditionally focused on competitors' wage and salary practices. Now, employee benefits are also a target of surveys because benefits are a key element of market-competitive pay systems. Compensation surveys are important because they enable compensation professionals to obtain realistic views of competitors' pay practices. In the absence of compensation survey data, compensation professionals would have to use guesswork to build market-competitive compensation systems.

RECOGNIZING EMPLOYEE CONTRIBUTIONS **Pay structures** represent pay rate differences for jobs of unequal worth and the framework for recognizing differences in employee contributions. No two employees possess identical credentials or perform the same jobs equally well. Companies recognize these differences by paying individuals according to their credentials, knowledge, or job performance. When completed, pay structures should define the boundaries for recognizing employee contributions. Well-designed structures should promote the retention of valued employees.

Pay grades and pay ranges are structural features of pay structures. **Pay grades** group jobs for pay policy application. Human resource professionals typically group jobs into pay grades based on similar compensable factors and value. These criteria are not precise. In fact, no single formula determines what is sufficiently similar in terms of content and value to warrant grouping into a pay grade. **Pay ranges** build upon pay grades. Pay ranges include minimum, maximum, and midpoint pay rates. The minimum and maximum values denote the acceptable lower and upper bounds of pay for the job's pay grades. The midpoint pay value is the halfway mark between the minimum and maximum pay rates.

Alternative Pay Structure Configurations

There are alternative pay structure configurations, which we will explore in this book. Each structure comes with its own set of challenges. These structures include:

- Merit pay plans (Chapter 8)
- Sales compensation plans (Chapter 8)
- Broadband structures (Chapter 8)
- Two-tier wage structures (Chapter 8)
- Executive compensation (Chapter 11)
- Contingent worker compensation (Chapter 12)
- Expatriate compensation (Chapter 13)
- Compensation structures in countries other than the United States (Chapter 14)

FITTING THE COMPENSATION FUNCTION IN AN ORGANIZATION'S STRUCTURE

1-5. Describe the fit of the compensation function in organizations.

Understanding compensation professionals' goals requires knowing the role of HR within companies and specific HR practices, particularly how HR professionals fit into the corporate hierarchy, and how the compensation function fits into HR departments.

How HR Professionals Fit into the Corporate Hierarchy

Line function and staff function broadly describe all employee functions. **Line employees** are directly involved in producing companies' goods or delivering their services. Assembler, production worker, and salesperson are examples of line jobs. **Staff employees** support those responsible for the line functions. Human resource professionals and accountants are examples of staff employees. Human resource professionals are staff employees because they offer a wide variety of support services for line employees. In a nutshell, HR professionals promote the effective use of all employees in companies. Effective use means attaining work objectives that fit with the overall mission of the company. According to Jay Hannah, BancFirst Corp. executive vice president of financial services, "The HR department is the source and keeper of critical information, which is key in today's workplace. With the information they provide, we in turn can build and design strategies to hire and retain the best workforce possible. And this may sound cliché, but it's very true—the real competitive advantage is our company's human resources."[24]

Human resource professionals design and implement a variety of HR practices that advance this objective. In addition to compensation determination, HR practices include:

- Recruitment
- Selection
- Performance appraisal
- Training
- Career development
- Labor–management relations
- Employment termination
- Managing HR within the context of legislation

Most company structures include an HR department. Traditionally, HR departments were thought of as an administrative or support function for the company because the financial or market value of HR was not as readily apparent as sales, manufacturing, or marketing functions. Some practitioners and researchers are suspect about the future of internal HR functions.

The Compensation Profession

Various designations are used within the human resource profession, in general, and in compensation, specifically. Among these are compensation executives, generalists, and specialists. An **executive** is a top-level manager who reports directly to the corporation's CEO or to the head of a major division. A **generalist**, who may be an executive, performs tasks in a variety of HR-related areas. The generalist is involved in several, or all, of the compensation functions such as building job structures, market competitive pay systems, and merit pay structures. A **specialist** may be an HR executive, manager, or non-manager who is typically concerned with only one of the areas of compensation practice. According to the *Occupational Outlook Handbook*, compensation and benefits managers do the following:

> Compensation managers plan, direct, and coordinate how much an organization pays its employees and how employees are paid. Benefits managers plan, direct, and coordinate retirement plans, health insurance, and other benefits that an organization offers its employees.[25]

Performance standards are established by members of the profession rather than by outsiders. Most professions also have effective representative organizations that permit members to exchange ideas of mutual concern. Several well-known organizations serve the profession. Among the more prominent for compensation professionals are the Society for Human Resource Management (*http://www.shrm.org*), the International Foundation of Employee Benefit Plans (*http://www.ifebp.org*), and WorldatWork (*http://www.worldatwork.org*).

Opportunities for employment as compensation and benefits managers are projected to grow at an annual rate of 5 percent through 2026.[26] The median annual compensation for Compensation and Benefits Managers was $116,240,[27] which is more than double the median annual earnings for all jobs. The salary levels vary on a few factors, including relevant work experience, educational credentials, and industry. For example, annual compensation was lowest in local government ($95,850) settings and highest in the insurance industry ($126,940).

 FYI

Additional jobs with compensation responsibilities and duties—Median Annual Pay and Projected Employment Growth/Decline (2016–2026):

- HR Specialists: $59,180; 7% growth
- Compensation, Benefits and Job Analysis Specialists: $62,080; 9% growth
- Labor Relations Specialists: $62,310; 8% decline (due to decline in unionization)[28]

How the Compensation Function Fits into HR Departments

Human resource practices do not operate in isolation. Every HR practice is related to others in different ways. For example, as an employer, U.S. federal government agencies publicly acknowledge the relationships between incentive compensation and other HR practices, including recruitment, relocation, and retention:

Recruitment: An agency may pay a recruitment incentive to a newly appointed career executive if the agency has determined that the position is likely to be difficult to fill in the absence of an incentive. A recruitment incentive may not exceed 25 percent of the executive's annual rate of basic pay in effect at the beginning of the service period multiplied by the number of years (including fractions of a year) in the service period (not to exceed 4 years).

Relocation: An agency may pay a relocation incentive to a current career executive who must relocate to accept a position in a different geographic area if the agency determines that the position is likely to be difficult to fill in the absence of an incentive. A relocation incentive may be paid only when the executive's rating of record under an official performance appraisal or evaluation system is at least "fully successful" or equivalent. A relocation incentive may not exceed 25 percent of the executive's annual rate of basic pay in effect at the beginning of the service period multiplied by the number of years (including fractions of a year) in the service period (not to exceed 4 years).

Retention: An agency may pay a retention incentive to a current career executive if (1) the agency determines that the unusually high or unique qualifications of the executive or a special need of the agency for the executive's services makes it essential to retain the executive, and that the executive would be likely to leave the Federal service in the absence of a retention incentive, or (2) the agency has a special need for the employee's services that makes it essential to retain the employee in his or her current position during a period of time before the closure or relocation of the employee's office, facility, activity, or organization and the employee would be likely to leave for a different position in the Federal service in the absence of a retention incentive. A retention incentive may be paid only when the executive's rating of record under an official performance appraisal or evaluation system is at least "fully successful" or equivalent. A retention incentive rate, expressed as a percentage of the executive's rate of basic pay, may not exceed 25 percent.[29]

Let's consider additional relationships between compensation and each of the HR practices.

COMPENSATION, RECRUITMENT, AND SELECTION Job candidates choose to work for companies for many reasons, including career advancement opportunities, training, the company's reputation for being a "good" place to work, location, and compensation. Companies try to spark job candidates' interest by communicating the positive features of the core compensation and employee benefits programs. As we will discuss in Chapter 7, companies use compensation to compete for the very best candidates. In addition, companies may offer such inducements as one-time signing bonuses to entice high-quality applicants. It is common for signing bonuses to amount to as much as 20 percent of starting annual salaries. Signing bonuses are useful when the supply of qualified candidates falls short of companies' needs for these candidates.

The next three sections will address performance appraisal, training, and career development. Before discussing these issues, however, let's first look at how the U.S. federal government explicitly acknowledges the relationship between compensation and these HR practices:

Chapter 43 of Title 5, United States Code, provides for performance management for the Senior Executive Service (SES), the establishment of SES performance appraisal systems, and appraisal of senior executive performance. Agencies establish performance management systems that hold senior executives accountable for their individual and organizational performance to improve the overall performance of Government by:

- Expecting excellence in senior executive performance;
- Linking performance management with the results-oriented goals of the Government Performance and Results Act of 1993;
- Setting and communicating individual and organizational goals and expectations;
- Systematically appraising senior executive performance using measures that balance organizational results with customer, employee, or other perspectives; and
- Using performance results as a basis for pay, awards, development, retention, removal and other personnel decisions.

Agencies develop performance management systems subject to Office of Personnel Management (OPM) regulations and approval.

The supervisor establishes performance elements and requirements in consultation with the executive and consistent with the goals and performance expectations in the agency's strategic planning initiatives. The supervisor proposes the initial summary rating, based on both individual and organizational performance, and considering customer satisfaction and employee perspective.[30]

COMPENSATION AND PERFORMANCE APPRAISAL Accurate performance appraisals are integral to effective merit pay programs. For merit pay programs to succeed, employees must know that their efforts toward meeting production quotas or quality standards will lead to pay raises. Job requirements must be realistic, and employees must be prepared to meet job goals with respect to their skills and abilities. Moreover, employees must perceive a strong relationship between attaining performance standards and receiving pay increases. Merit pay systems require specific performance appraisal approaches. Administering successful merit pay programs depends as much on sound performance appraisal practices as it does on the compensation professional's skill in designing and implementing such plans.

COMPENSATION AND TRAINING Successful pay-for-knowledge plans depend on a company's ability to develop and implement systematic training programs. When training is well designed, employees should be able to learn the skills needed to increase their pay, as well as the skills necessary to teach and coach other employees at lower skill levels. Companies implementing pay-for-knowledge plans typically increase the amount of classroom and on-the-job training. Pay-for-knowledge systems make training necessary rather than optional. Companies that adopt pay-for-knowledge systems must accordingly ensure that all employees have equal access to the training needed to acquire higher-level skills.

COMPENSATION AND CAREER DEVELOPMENT Most employees expect to experience career development within their present companies. Employees' careers develop in two different ways. First, some employees change the focus of their work—for example, from supervisor of payroll clerks to supervisor of inventory clerks. This change represents a lateral move across the company's hierarchy. Second, others maintain their focus and assume greater responsibilities. This change illustrates advancement upward through the company's hierarchy. Advancing from payroll clerk to manager of payroll administration is an example of moving upward through a company's hierarchy. Employees' compensation changes to reflect career development.

COMPENSATION AND LABOR-MANAGEMENT RELATIONS Collective bargaining agreements describe the terms of employment (e.g., pay and work hours) reached between management and the union. Compensation is a key topic. Unions have fought hard for general pay increases and regular COLAs to promote their members' standard of living. In Chapter 2, we will review the role of unions in compensation, and in Chapter 3, we indicate that unions have traditionally bargained for seniority pay systems in negotiations with management. More recently, unions have been willing to incorporate incentive pay systems. For example, unions appear to be receptive to behavioral encouragement plans because improving worker safety and minimizing absenteeism serve the best interests of both employees and employers.

COMPENSATION AND EMPLOYMENT TERMINATION Employment termination takes place when an employee's agreement to perform work is terminated. Employment terminations are either involuntary or voluntary. The HR department plays a central role in managing involuntary employment terminations. Companies initiate involuntary terminations for a variety of reasons, including poor job performance, insubordination, violation of work rules, reduced business activity due to sluggish economic conditions, and plant closings. Discharge represents involuntary termination for poor job performance, insubordination, or gross violation of work rules. Involuntary layoff describes termination under sluggish economic conditions or because of plant closings. In the case of involuntary layoffs, HR professionals typically provide outplacement counseling to help employees find work elsewhere. Companies may choose to award **severance pay**, which usually amounts to several months' pay following involuntary termination and, in some cases, continued coverage under the employer's medical insurance plan. Employees often rely on severance pay to meet financial obligations while they search for employment. In the past, companies commonly offered a year or more of severance pay. Severance benefits today tend to be less generous. For example, as part of Delta Air Lines' closure of its Boston reservation center, the company offered only 6 weeks of severance pay regardless of seniority with the company.

Employees initiate voluntary terminations, most often to work for other companies or to retire. In the case of retirement, companies sponsor pension programs. **Pension programs** provide income to individuals throughout their retirement. Companies sometimes use **early retirement programs** to reduce workforce size and trim compensation expenditures. Early retirement programs contain incentives designed to encourage highly paid employees with substantial seniority to retire earlier than they had planned. These incentives expedite senior employees' retirement eligibility and increase their retirement income.

COMPENSATION AND LEGISLATION Employment laws establish the bounds of both acceptable employment practices and employee rights. Federal laws that apply to compensation practices are grouped according to four themes:

- Income continuity, safety, and work hours
- Pay discrimination
- Medical care and the accommodation of disabilities and family needs
- Prevailing wage laws

The federal government enacted income continuity, safety, and work hour laws (e.g., the Fair Labor Standards Act of 1938) to stabilize individuals' incomes when the individuals became unemployed because of poor business conditions or workplace injuries, as well as to set pay minimums and work-hour limits for children. The civil rights movement of the 1960s led to the passage of key legislation (e.g., the Equal Pay Act of 1963 and the Civil Rights Act of 1964) designed to protect designated classes of employees and to uphold their individual rights against discriminatory employment decisions, including matters of pay. Congress enacted legislation, namely, the Patient Protection and Affordable Care Act of 2010, the Pregnancy Discrimination Act of 1978, the Americans with Disabilities Act of 1990, and the Family and Medical Leave Act of 1993 to provide medical care and accommodate employees with disabilities and pressing family needs. Prevailing wage laws (e.g., the Davis–Bacon Act of 1931) set minimum wage rates for companies that provide paid services—such as building maintenance—to the U.S. government. We will review these laws in Chapter 2.

STAKEHOLDERS OF THE COMPENSATION SYSTEM

1-6. Identify the stakeholders of the compensation function and summarize their stakes in the work compensation professionals perform.

The HR department provides services to stakeholders within and outside the company. These include:

- Employees
- Line managers
- Executives
- Unions
- U.S. government

The success of HR departments depends on how well they serve various stakeholders. "Each constituency [stakeholder] has its own set of expectations regarding the personnel department's activities; each holds its own standards for effective performance; each applies its own standards for assessing the extent to which the department's activities meets its expectations;

and each attempts to prescribe preferred goals for the subunit or presents constraints to its sphere of discretion. Multiple stakeholders often compete directly or indirectly for the attention and priority of the personnel department."[31] Our focus is on some of the ways compensation professionals serve these stakeholders.

Employees

As we discussed earlier, successful pay-for-knowledge programs depend on a company's ability to develop and implement systematic training programs. Compensation professionals must educate employees about their training options and how successful training outcomes will lead to increased pay and advancement opportunities within the company. These professionals should not assume that employees will necessarily recognize these opportunities unless they are clearly communicated. Written memos and informational meetings conducted by compensation professionals and HR representatives are effective communication media.

Discretionary benefits provide protection programs, paid time off, and services. As compensation professionals plan and manage employee benefits programs, they should keep these functions in mind. There is probably no single company that expects its employee benefits program to meet all these objectives. Compensation professionals as representatives of company management, along with union representatives, must therefore determine which objectives are the most important for their workforce.

Line Managers

Compensation professionals use their expert knowledge of the laws that influence pay and benefits practices to help line managers make sound compensation judgments. For example, the Equal Pay Act of 1963 (discussed in Chapter 2) prohibits sex discrimination in pay for employees performing equal work, so compensation professionals should advise line managers to pay the same hourly pay rate or annual salary for men and women hired to perform the same job.

Line managers turn to compensation professionals for advice about appropriate pay rates for jobs. Compensation professionals oversee the use of job evaluation to establish pay differentials among jobs within a company. In addition, they train line managers in how to evaluate jobs properly.

Executives

Compensation professionals serve company executives by developing and managing sound compensation systems. Executives look to them to ensure that the design and implementation of pay and benefits practices comply with pertinent legislation. Violation of these laws can lead to substantial monetary penalties to companies. Executives also depend on compensation professionals' expertise to design pay and benefits systems that will attract and retain the best-qualified employees.

Unions

As noted earlier, collective bargaining agreements describe the terms of employment reached between management and the union. Compensation professionals are responsible for administering the pay and benefits policies specified in collective bargaining agreements. They mainly ensure that employees receive COLAs and seniority pay increases on a timely basis.

U.S. Government

The U.S. government requires that companies comply with all employment legislation. Compensation professionals apply their expertise regarding pertinent legislation to design legally sound pay and benefits practices. In addition, since the passage of the Civil Rights Act of 1991, compensation professionals have applied their expertise to demonstrate that alleged discriminatory pay practices are a business necessity. As we will discuss in Chapter 2, the burden of proof to demonstrate that alleged discriminatory pay practices are not discriminatory rests with compensation professionals.

DEVELOPING SKILLS FOR YOUR CAREER

1-7. Explore essential skills for developing your career in compensation or any other career path.

If you are not an HRM or business major, or you do not plan to take an assignment in the compensation function in the foreseeable future, you may be thinking that this section isn't relevant to you. Let me assure you, it is. Whether you plan on a career in the compensation field, the lessons you learn in this course will help you in business and in your life. Also, it is only through the aggregate of your educational experience that you will have the opportunity to develop many of the skills that employers have identified as critical to success in the workplace. In this course, and, specifically in this text, you'll have the opportunity to develop and practice seven important skills in the following ways: communication, critical thinking, collaboration, knowledge application and analysis, business ethics and social responsibility, information technology application and computing skills, and data literacy.

Communication

Communication is defined as effective use of oral, written, and nonverbal skills for multiple purposes (e.g., to inform, instruct, motivate, persuade, and share ideas); effective listening; using technology to communicate; and being able to evaluate the effectiveness of communication efforts—all within diverse contexts. The *Working Together* feature offers opportunities to collaborate through sharing ideas, listening to others' ideas, and coming up with a cohesive team response to the assignment. If assigned by your instructor, you may make brief oral presentations, creating an additional opportunity for working together. All the while, you will gain insight into your and your group members' strengths and weaknesses pertaining to communication (and collaboration) skills. Never pass up an opportunity to hone these skills.

Critical Thinking

Critical thinking involves purposeful and goal-directed thinking used to define and solve problems and to make decisions or form judgments related to a situation or set of circumstances. The *Discussion Questions* and *Crunch the Numbers* provide you with an excellent opportunity to think through concepts and their applications. *Crunch the Numbers* will also give you the chance to analyze quantitative data to facilitate problem solving. Analysis of the *Cases*, which depict realistic scenarios that you will likely encounter in the workplace, requires your interpretation and an actionable response. Similarly, you will have the chance to think through and discuss your responses to common *Ethics Dilemmas*. More about the ethics dilemmas shortly. Critically thinking about situations is just one part of the story.

Collaboration

Collaborative learning takes place in a situation in which individuals actively work together on a task, constructing meaning and knowledge as a group through dialogue and negotiation resulting in a final product reflective of joint, interdependent actions. I've already made the case for *Working Together*. Your professor may similarly ask you to analyze *Cases* in small groups. Another feature, *Compensation in Action*, explains how HR professionals and managers throughout the organization work together to address important workplace issues. This feature highlights the connections between managers and compensation professionals, and the reality that work is rarely performed in isolation.

Knowledge Application and Analysis

Knowledge application and analysis is defined as the ability to learn a concept and then appropriately apply that knowledge in another setting to achieve a higher level of understanding. All the activities discussed in this section provide you with multiple opportunities to think through solutions to specific problems and generalize these processes to other situations you will likely encounter in the future. Two additional features further help you develop this skill. *Try It* directs you to mini simulations and, in *Watch It*, you will review video clips that require a response to important workplace challenges. If your instructor assigns it, the accompanying *Building Strategic Compensation Systems* case will enable you to determine the best strategic compensation design for company success.

Business Ethics and Social Responsibility

Business ethics are sets of guiding principles that influence the way individuals and organizations behave within the society that they operate. Two additional issues require everyone's attention. The first, corporate social responsibility, is the implied, enforced, or felt obligation of managers, acting in their official capacity, to serve or protect the interests of groups other than themselves. Second, corporate sustainability focuses on the possible future impact of an organization on society, including social welfare, the economy, and the environment. Both issues are like ethics; however, ethics also focuses on individual decision making and behavior as well as the impact of ethical choices on employee welfare. The *Ethics Dilemma,* presented in the end-of-chapter material, will keep these important matters in the forefront as you move ahead in your career.

Information Technology Application and Computing Skills

Information technology application and computing skills are defined as the ability to select and use appropriate technology to accomplish a given task. The individual is also able to apply computing skills to solve problems. *Crunch the Numbers* gives you the opportunity to develop these skills. Also, if your instructor chooses to have you complete the accompanying *Building Strategic Compensation Systems Case*, you will have the opportunity to become familiar with the power of Microsoft Excel for analyzing copious amounts of compensation data.

Data Literacy

Data literacy is the ability to access, assess, interpret, manipulate, summarize, and communicate data. Throughout this book, the newly created feature titled *FYI* provides tidbits of information from survey research and extensive databases (e.g., weekly pay statistics) that illuminate trends, opinions, and the use of specific compensation practices. Also, particularly in Chapters 6, 7, and 8, you will be challenged to quantify and interpret the value of jobs based on the knowledge, skills, and abilities required to perform them, analyzing and interpreting market pay rates to establish pay ranges, and merit pay increase grids to determine the appropriate pay increase based on performance as well as the budgetary implications of your choices. You also can build your data literacy by completing the *Crunch the Numbers* exercises and the *Building Strategic Compensation Systems* case. Altogether, these data should enable you to translate quantitative information for placement into the employment context. Further, you can expand this skill by thinking through when and how to create new policies or modify existing ones.

In summary, you will find opportunities throughout this book to develop several critical skills that provide a foundation of success on any career path that you follow. As you learn about compensation systems, consider how you can generalize these skills to other workplace situations. Best of luck whether you are preparing for the start of your career or are in the process of changing career paths!

PREPARING FOR EXAMS/QUIZZES

Chapter Summary by Learning Objectives

Learning Objective 1-1. *Define strategic compensation.* Strategic compensation refers to the design and implementation of compensation systems to reinforce the objectives of both HR strategies and competitive business strategies. The building blocks of strategic compensation include extrinsic compensation (monetary compensation or core compensation as well as nonmonetary compensation or employee benefits).

Learning Objective 1-2. *Summarize the role of compensation as a strategic business partner.* Compensation professionals must think like the Chief Executive Officer (CEO) to become a partner in achieving organizational plans and results. Compensation professionals help leverage the value of employees (human capital) for competitive advantage based on the design and use of various compensation practices, including merit pay and incentive pay.

Learning Objective 1-3. *Explain strategic compensation decisions.* Compensation professionals design compensation systems to meet the imperatives of two competitive business strategy types: lowest cost strategy and differentiation strategy. Success comes with being able to answer *yes* to each of three questions: (1) Does compensation strategy fit well with the objectives of competitive business and HR strategies? (2) Does the choice and design of compensation practices fit well to support compensation strategy? (3) Does the implementation of compensation practices effectively direct employee behavior to enhance job performance that supports the choice of compensation practices?

Learning Objective 1-4. *Identify and discuss the building blocks and structural elements of strategic compensation systems.* The building blocks of compensation systems include core compensation and employee benefits. The elements of compensation systems focus on achieving internally consistent job structures, market-competitive pay systems, and alternative pay structures that recognize employee contributions.

Learning Objective 1-5. *Describe the fit of the compensation function in organizations.* Fitting compensation into an organization's structure requires consideration of how compensation professionals fit into the corporate hierarchy, how compensation fits into HR departments, and the relationship between compensation practice and other HR functions (e.g., recruitment and training).

Learning Objective 1-6. *Identify the stakeholders of the compensation function and summarize their stakes in the work compensation professionals perform.* The HR department provides services to the several stakeholders: employees, line managers, executives, unions, and the U.S. government. Compensation professionals serve these stakeholders in different ways. For example, compensation professionals educate employees about their training options and how successful training outcomes will lead to increased pay and advancement opportunities.

Learning Objective 1-7. *Explore essential skills for developing your career in compensation or any other career path.* Whether you are embarking on a career in compensation or another path, there are seven essential skills needed for success: communication, critical thinking, collaboration, knowledge application and analysis, business ethics and social responsibility, information technology application and computing skills, and data literacy.

Key Terms

competitive advantage   3
compensation   3
intrinsic compensation   3
extrinsic compensation   3
core compensation   3
employee benefits   3
competitive business strategy   4
human resources strategies   4
strategic compensation   5
capital   5
human capital   5
cost leadership (lowest-cost
    strategy)   7
differentiation strategies   7
base pay   9
hourly pay or wage   9
annual salary   9

compensable factors   9
cost-of-living
    adjustments   9
seniority pay   9
human capital theory   9
merit pay   10
incentive pay   10
variable pay   10
person-focused pay   10
competency-based pay   10
pay-for-knowledge   10
skill-based pay   10
discretionary benefits   10
legally required benefits   10
protection programs 10
paid time off   10
services   10

internally consistent compensation
    systems   11
job analysis   13
job evaluation   13
market-competitive pay systems   13
compensation surveys   13
pay structures   13
pay grades   13
pay ranges   13
line employees   14
staff employees   14
executive   15
generalist   15
specialist   15
severance pay   18
pension programs   18
early retirement programs   18

Discussion Questions

1-1. What are the main building blocks of compensation systems? Briefly describe each one.

1-2. How can compensation professionals serve as strategic business partners?

1-3. Are the three main structural elements of compensation systems—internal consistency, market competitiveness, and recognizing employee contributions—equally important, or do you believe that they differ in importance? Explain.

1-4. The compensation profession is expected to grow at a healthy pace through the year 2026. Based on your understanding of how the chapter material blends together, what might be some reasons for this anticipated growth? Explain.

1-5. Stakeholder expectations pose challenges for compensation professionals. At times, there may be conflict among the expectations of different stakeholders. For two stakeholders, how do compensation professionals meet their expectations?

1-6. How are the seven employability skills relevant regardless of your career aspirations?

PREPARING FOR MY CAREER

Compensation in Action

Consistent, innovative, and fair compensation practices are central to ensuring the success of both human resource strategies and overall company competitive strategies. While it is HR's role to decide what kind of people are critical to fill roles that will lead to successful execution of competitive strategies, compensation professionals must align practices that will enable attraction, appropriate job placement, and development of these individuals. Many companies have moved from the personnel management model to the HR business partner model; however, some still look to HR to guarantee that policies are being enforced and the company mitigates legal risk. Depending on the company where you are employed—and whether you are a line manager or HR professional—you may find yourself able to understand the competitive strategy of the business and align compensation practices with the strategic thrust of the business.

Action checklist for line managers and HR—aligning compensation with strategy

HR takes the lead

- Work with line managers to fully understand which roles and types of employees will best support the execution of company strategy.
- Collaborate with compensation specialists to run analysis of market factors (competitors, industry standards, local labor market) to get indicators of compensation norms and standards to keep your company's compensation practices competitive.
- Create, together with line managers, pay structures wherein roles are placed into appropriate pay grades. Each grade will have a corresponding range that will serve as the basis for assigning pay rates for roles.

Line managers take the lead

- Educate staff positions, along with other business leaders, for all to understand what strategy is being employed to achieve specific company objectives.
- Educate HR on certain aspects of roles (e.g., autonomy, skill variety, task significance, etc.) that, when enhanced, could improve intrinsic motivation, thus leading to benefits for employees and employers. HR works on ways to couple the intrinsic compensation with the identified plan for the core compensation plan.
- Work together with HR to implement a plan that ties the compensation plan to a successful recruitment, training, and development plan, ensuring that the company is retaining the talent that is critical to the implementation and delivery of the strategic objectives.

Cases

Case 1: Competitive Strategy at Sportsman Shoes

Sportsman Shoes has been a leader in the shoe industry for more than 30 years. Sportsman manufactures and sells athletic shoes for all types of sports. The company has pursued a low-cost strategy to sustain its success. It sells a limited number of shoe designs and has held costs low through manufacturing efficiency and standardized operations. However, the past years have been a struggle at Sportsman. The shoe market has seen a rise in the availability of low-cost imported shoes that has threatened Sportsman's competitive position. As a result, company executives have decided it is time for a strategy shift.

Sportsman executives have done extensive market research and determined that many niche athletic shoe markets exist where athletes are willing to pay more for shoes designed to meet the unique needs of their sport. There are very few competitors in these niche athletic shoe markets, and most do not have Sportsman's experience in keeping control of manufacturing costs. Sportsman has determined that, with talented shoe designers in place, they can manufacture athletic shoes to meet the needs of the niche markets using their current manufacturing facilities and employees. By designing shoes that have features that differ from competitors and meet the specific needs of a new group of customers, Sportsman believes the company can create a competitive advantage. Further, while their shoes will not be as low cost as they were in the past, they will likely be able to sell their shoes for less than market competitors and still make a healthy profit.

Therefore, Sportsman has decided to shift from its current low-cost strategy to a differentiation strategy and will begin production to make specialty athletic shoes. Sportsman must now make many tactical decisions in various functional areas of the company to support its decision to shift its overall business strategy.

Its priority is to restructure the product development function. As it will need to understand the needs of the niche markets and design shoes to meet those needs, it will need to hire and retain talented shoe designers. The company will also need to hire operations specialists to transition its manufacturing operations to produce the new shoe designs. Beyond hiring new staff, Sportsman also must consider the implications for current employees to help them successfully transition to their new work requirements. Therefore, there are several considerations the company must address in human resource management.

Questions:

1-7. Following Sportsman's shift in competitive strategy, what are some considerations for the company's human resource management practices?

1-8. What kinds of challenges will Sportsman face specifically in compensation?

Case 2: Ethics Dilemma: Profits at Any Cost

Since 2006, more than 5,000 Wells Fargo bank employees opened 2 million bank accounts for customers who did not request them. The bank's leadership claimed that the employees acted on their own volition, and they were subsequently fired. Many current and past employees claimed that Wells Fargo raised daily sales goals to unrealistic levels, creating a high-pressure environment in which to earn their sales commissions and keep their jobs. Other employees talked about how managers regularly asked them about their progress, focusing exclusively on the number of accounts opened rather than discussing appropriate sales techniques that could help employees legitimately meet their quotas. When goals were not met, many employees alleged that they were threatened with formal written warnings and termination.

Indeed, many employees used fraudulent sales tactics to meet their sales quotas out of fear of receiving a bad employment reference. Others expressed that they could not afford to earn less sales commission (essentially, a pay cut) let alone be unemployed even for a brief time. Apparently, employees who called the company's ethics line to report their concerns were punished or fired. Even branch managers felt the pinch. Allegedly, high-ranking bank officials ordered employees to shred documents before auditor inspections.

Questions:

1-9. As a compensation professional, what would you do?

1-10. What factor(s) in this ethical dilemma might influence a person to make a less-than-ethical decision?

Crunch the Numbers!

Calculating the Costs of Increasing the Total Compensation Budget at Butcher Enterprises

Butcher Enterprises has experienced substantial employee turnover among its office workers. During exit interviews, more than 80 percent stated that low pay was the top reason for resigning. The company conducted a survey of local companies' pay practices to confirm whether this concern is valid. Indeed, Butcher Enterprises' average hourly pay rate for total compensation falls well below the market. The compensation survey showed an average hourly rate of $23 for total compensation. Of this amount, wages are $16 per hour and benefits are $7 per hour. In comparison, Butcher Enterprises spends an average hourly rate of $19 for total compensation. Of this amount, 70 percent is allocated for wages.

Questions:

1-11. On an average hourly basis, how much does Butcher Enterprises spend on wages and benefits, respectively, in dollars?

1-12. How much does the company spend on wages and benefits over the course of one year for 100 office workers? Assume that each worker provides 2,080 hours of service each year.

1-13. How much additional money does the company need to match the market rates for this group of 100 employees?

Working Together: Team Exercise

In small groups of three or four, come up with specific answers to the following questions. Talk through your perspectives and come up with a team response. Be prepared to share your ideas with the class.

As a group, think about retailers from which you make purchases for products or services (for example, purchasing an iPhone or Apple Music streaming service). Select two retailers—one that you believe follows a lowest cost strategy and another that follows a differentiation strategy that sell iPhones. In addition, conduct some research to identify what you believe to be one threat or one opportunity for each company. Please do not use the companies included as examples in this chapter.

Questions:

1-14. What is the rationale for the companies you chose? Explain. *(Hint: Compare your choices with alternative retailers to help formulate your rationale.)*

1-15. In what way is the opportunity or threat that you identified for each company likely to affect competitive advantage? Explain.

Endnotes

1. WorldatWork, "2017-2018 Top-Level Results," *WorldatWork Salary Budget Survey* (July 11, 2017), accessed January 4, 2018, http://worldatwork.org; Nancy E. Day, "Transforming the Role of Money in the New Economy: Removing Pay as the Star of the Show," *WorldatWork Journal* (Fourth Quarter, 2013): 7–20.

2. "Netflix's View: Internet TV Is Replacing Linear TV," (2018), accessed January 31, 2018, https://ir.netflix.com/netflixs-view-internet-tv-replacing-linear-tv.

3. Elizabeth Winkler, "Netflix Says Catch Me If You Can," *The Wall Street Journal* (January 22, 2018), accessed January 31, 2018, http://www.wsj.com.

4. *Samsung: What We Believe*, accessed January 5, 2017, http://www.samsung.com/us/aboutsamsung/vision/vision2020/.

5. *Careers: U.S. & Canada*, accessed January 4, 2018, https://careers.lilly.com/why-lilly.

6. Dow Scott, Tom McMullen, and Erik Larson"The Future of Work and Rewards: Forward Thinking from the C-suite and Total Rewards Leaders." *WorldatWork Journal* (First Quarter, 2017): 13–24.

7. "Attorney Urges HR Professionals to Think Like the CEO," *HR Focus* 89 (April 2012): 10.

8. "HR in 2020 Should Understand Clearly All Aspects of Business," *HR Focus* 90 (February 2013): 8–9.

9. GE (2018). *GE Careers: Human Resources Leadership Program (HRLP)*, accessed January 4, 2018, https://www.ge.com/careers/working-at-ge/human-resources-leadership-program.

10. Bosch, *Careers at Bosch | PhDs*, (2015), accessed January 4, 2018, http://your.bosch-career.com/en/web/us/us/joining_bosch_us/graduates_us/phds_us/phds.

11. Jane E. Dutton and Susan E. Jackson, "The Categorization of Strategic Issues by Decision Makers and Its Links to Organizational Action," *Academy of Management Review* 12, (1987): 76–90. http://dx.doi.org/10.2307/257995.

12. Julie Jargon, "Too Much Caffeine? Coffee Shops Face a Shakeout," *The Wall Street Journal* (November 7, 2017), accessed December 1, 2017, http://www.wsj.com.

13. David Dunne and Roger Martin, "Design Thinking and How It Will Change Management Education: An Interview and Discussion," *Academy of Management Learning & Education* 5, (December 2006): 512, http://www.jstor.org/stable/40214410.

14. Adi Ignatius, "How Indra Nooyi Turned Design Thinking into Strategy," *Harvard Business Review* (September 2015): 4.

15. U.S. Bureau of Labor Statistics, *The Employment Situation—December 2017* (USDL 18-0024), (2018), accessed January 6, 2018, http://www.bls.gov.

16. Gary S. Becker, *Human Capital* (New York: National Bureau of Economic Research, 1976).

17. U.S. Bureau of Labor Statistics, *Employer Costs for Employee Compensation, September 2017* (USDL: 17-1646), (December 15, 2017), accessed January 3, 2018, http://www.bls.gov.

18. U.S. Bureau of Labor Statistics, *Occupational Outlook Handbook,* Human resource specialists and labor relations specialists, (2018), accessed January 6, 2018, https://www.bls.gov/ooh/management/financial/human-resources-specialists-and-labor-relations-specialists.htm.

19. U.S. Bureau of Labor Statistics, *Occupational Outlook Handbook,* Human Resources Managers, (2018), accessed January 6, 2018, https://www.bls.gov/ooh/management/human-resources-managers.htm.

20. U.S. Bureau of Labor Statistics, *2016 Wage Data*, (2018), accessed January 6, 2018, http://www.bls.gov/oes.

21. Ibid.

22. U.S. Bureau of Labor Statistics, *Employer Costs for Employee Compensation Historical Listing: March 2004 – September 2017*, (2018), accessed January 8, 2018, https://www.bls.gov/web/ecec/.ececqrtn.pdf.

23. U.S. Bureau of Labor Statistics, *Occupational Outlook Handbook.* Aerospace Engineers, (2018), accessed January 6, 2018, http://www.bls.gov/ooh/architecture-and-engineering/aerospace-engineers.htm.

24. Quotation excerpted from B. Leonard, "Straight Talk: Executives Sound Off on Why They Think HR Professionals Lost Strategic Ground, and What They Can Do to Earn a Place 'At the Table,'" *HRMagazine*, January 2002, Vol. 47, No. 1, 48, accessed March 10, 2013, http://www.shrm.org.

25. U.S. Bureau of Labor Statistics, *Occupational Outlook Handbook,* Compensation and Benefits Managers, (2018), accessed January 6, 2018, https://www.bls.gov/ooh/management/compensation-and-benefits-managers.htm.

26. U.S. Bureau of Labor Statistics, 2016–2026 Employment Projections (USDL-17-1429), (2017), accessed January 6, 2018, https://www.bls.gov/news.release/pdf/ecopro.pdf.

27. U.S. Bureau of Labor Statistics, 2016 Wage Data, (2018), accessed January 6, 2018, http://www.bls.gov/oes.

28. U.S. Bureau of Labor Statistics, *Occupational Outlook Handbook*, (2018), accessed January 7, 2018, https://www.bls.gov/ooh/.

29. U.S. Federal Government, Performance & Compensation: Incentive Payments, accessed January 12, 2018, http://www.opm.gov/ses/performance/incentive.asp.

30. U.S. Federal Government, Performance, accessed January 12, 2018, http://www.opm.gov/ses/performance/index.asp.

31. Anne S. Tsui, "Personnel Department Effectiveness: A Tripartite Approach," *Industrial Relations 23,* (1984): 187.

2 Contextual Influences on Compensation Practice

Learning Objectives

When you finish studying this chapter, you should be able to:

2-1. Discuss the reasons for interindustry wage differentials.

2-2. Explain the factors that contribute to pay differentials based on occupational characteristics.

2-3. Summarize the reasons for the occurrence of geographic pay differentials.

2-4. Discuss the role of labor unions in setting compensation.

2-5. Identify and discuss key employment laws pertinent to compensation practice.

In Chapter 1, we discussed strategic compensation. That discussion revealed that compensation professionals plan, develop, and implement compensation practices to help achieve competitive advantage. From this perspective, it is imperative that compensation professionals understand the broader context in which compensation decisions are rendered. Compensation professionals should understand the patterns of pay differentials outside their companies to help make informed decisions about fair and competitive pay practices. Also, with these data, they may make compelling requests to the Chief Financial Officer (CFO) for monetary resources necessary to appropriately fund compensation programs for competitive advantage. These factors include interindustry wage differentials, occupational pay differentials, geographic pay differentials, and the role of labor unions. We will present basic statistical information to illustrate these differentials as well as discuss possible explanations for them.

Besides these various patterns of pay differentials, compensation professionals make decisions within the scope of pertinent employment and labor relations laws to maintain compliance with government mandates, and, in doing so, protecting the welfare of employees and serving the interests of company shareholders. Employment and labor relations laws are essential to maintain a balance of power between employers and employees. In a nutshell:

The freedom to contract is crucial to freedom of the market; an employee may choose to work or not to work for a given employer, and an employer may choose to hire or not to hire a given applicant. As a result, the employment relationship is regulated in some important ways. Congress tries to avoid telling employers how to manage their employees. . . . However, Congress has passed employment-related laws when it believes that the employee is not on equal footing with the employer. For example, Congress has passed laws that require employers to pay minimum wages and to refrain from using certain criteria, such as race or gender, in arriving at specific employment decisions. These laws reflect the reality that employers stand in a position of power in the employment relationship. Legal protections granted to employees seek to make the power relationship between employer and employee one that is fair and equitable.[1]

In this regard, compensation professionals strive to establish and maintain a fair pay-effort bargain (that is, appropriate pay for performing work according to standard), and to collaborate with managers and supervisors to ensure that employee performance is appropriately rewarded over time.

It should be noted that compensation professionals operate in a global context in which compensation practices may require modification to attract and retain employees on important international assignments. Also, it is necessary to understand the role governments and cultural values in other countries play in compensation practices. The global stage presents an important contextual factor. We will address those issues in Chapters 13 and 14.

INTERINDUSTRY WAGE DIFFERENTIALS

Are equivalent workers performing similar work paid more in some industries than in others? Most often, the answer is *yes*. In a competitive labor market, companies attempt to attract and retain the best individuals for employment partly by offering lucrative wage and benefits packages. Some companies are unable to compete with companies in other industries based on wage and benefits because of persistent interindustry wage differentials. **Interindustry wage differentials** represent the pattern of pay and benefits associated with characteristics of industries. Interindustry wage differentials can be attributed to many factors, including the industry's product market, the degree of capital intensity, the profitability of the industry, and unionization of the workforce.[2] The basis for interindustry wage differentials will be explained shortly. Table 2-1 displays the average weekly earnings in various industries for select years between 2009 and 2017. Utilities and mining establishments generally pay the highest wages; retail trade and leisure and hospitality establishments generally pay the lowest wages. In 2016, for instance, general office clerks who were employed in the coal mining industry earned an hourly wage, on average, of $18.39. In the full-service restaurant industry, the average hourly wage was $14.56.[3]

2-1. Discuss the reasons for interindustry wage differentials.

Companies that operate in product markets where there is relatively little competition from other companies tend to pay higher wages because these companies generally exhibit substantial profits. This phenomenon can be attributed to factors such as higher barriers to enter into the product market and virtually have no influence of foreign competition. Government regulation and extremely expensive heavy or robotic equipment represent entry barriers. The U.S. defense industry and the public utilities industry have high entry barriers and virtually no threats from foreign competitors.

Capital intensity refers to the extent to which companies' operations are based on the use of large-scale equipment. Capital intensity also explains pay differentials between industries. The amount of average pay varies with the degree of capital intensity. On average, capital-intensive industries (e.g., manufacturing) pay more than industries that are less capital intensive (e.g., retail). Capital-intensive businesses require employees who have the aptitude to learn how to use complex physical equipment such as casting machines and robotics. Workers usually receive on-the-job training, sometimes including employer-sponsored technical instruction. In addition, some employers may require specialized training or an associate's degree for the most skilled assembly and fabrication jobs. Employment settings include automotive assembly, aircraft engine assembly, and ship building.

TABLE 2-1 Average Weekly Earnings by Industry Group, Select Years 2009–2017

Industry	2009 ($)	2011 ($)	2013 ($)	2015 ($)	2017 ($)[a]
Utilities	1,366	1,385	1,474	1,530	1,649
Mining	1,180	1,276	1,276	1,365	1,492
Construction	911	988	1,010	1,049	1,149
Manufacturing	885	969	976	1,022	1,161
Retail trade	478	506	516	541	572
Leisure and hospitality	329	338	348	372	410

[a] 2017 figures are for December.

Source: U.S. Bureau of Labor Statistics. *The Employment Situation—December 2017*. Available: http://www. bls.gov, accessed January 8, 2018; U.S. Bureau of Labor Statistics. *Employment, Hours, and Earnings*. Data Retrieval. Available: *www.bls.gov/webapps/legacy/cesbtab3.htm*, accessed February 13, 2015.

Service industries such as retail are not capital intensive, and most have the reputation of paying low wages. The operation of service industries depends almost exclusively on employees with relatively common skills. Most retail sales workers receive on-the-job training, which usually lasts a few days to a few months.

Furthermore, companies in profitable industries tend to pay higher compensation, on average, than companies in less profitable industries. Employees in profitable industries presumably receive higher pay because their skills and abilities contribute to companies' success and are more productive; however, as more companies have failed to meet financial goals over the past few years, they have struggled with how best to pay for performance.

As we will discuss shortly, companies in highly unionized industries tend to pay higher wages, on average, than do companies in lesser unionized industries. In general, the power of collectively negotiating employment terms, including pay, is greater than the negotiating power of a single individual. Employees' right to strike could cripple not only their employer, but also hurt companies that rely on receiving raw materials or finished goods.

For instance, in 2016, 36,000 Verizon employees walked off the job after negotiations with management failed. Outsourcing jobs was one of the main reasons for workers' decision to strike. At the time, the U.S. Bureau of Labor Statistics indicated that the Verizon strike was the largest number of employees to strike in a single company. A strike halts production, resulting in lost customers and revenue, which the union hopes will force management to submit to its terms. In Korea, Hyundai workers conducted 21 partial strikes in 2016 that caused a production loss of about 117,000 vehicles, costing the company more than $2.5 billion.[4]

Some strikes can have far-reaching consequences for other firms and their customers. For example, when port workers on the west coast went on strike, many cargos ships were prohibited from reaching port and thousands of empty transport trucks remained empty. Many firms ranging from car dealers to retail companies experienced dwindling inventories of imported goods and the inability to serve all customer demand. The following Watch It! video briefly describes the Los Angeles port strike and its effects.

At the same time, most highly unionized industries (e.g., manufacturing, construction, and mining) are capital intensive, requiring employees with the aptitude to learn and use complex production technology such as the cranes and hoists for loading and unloading massive cargo containers.

PAY DIFFERENTIALS BASED ON OCCUPATIONAL CHARACTERISTICS

An **occupation** is a group of jobs, found at more than one company, in which a common set of tasks are performed or are related in terms of similar objectives, methodologies, materials, products, worker actions, or worker characteristics.[5] File clerk, clerk typist, administrative clerk, staff secretary, and administrative secretary are jobs in the office support occupation. Compensation analyst, training and development specialist, recruiter, and benefits counselor are jobs in the human resources management occupation. Considerable variation in pay *between occupations* can be explained by the complexity of knowledge, skills, and abilities (KSAs) that define jobs (for example, surgeons and building service workers). Another important factor is the labor market dynamics of the supply and demand for qualified employees.

2-2. Explain the factors that contribute to pay differentials based on occupational characteristics.

Pay variations can also be observed *within occupations*, based on the complexity of KSAs associated with different jobs that define an occupation, and we will look at some examples shortly. It should be noted that references to differences in KSAs or relative worth of different jobs are based exclusively on job content and demand for individuals who possess the required KSAs. These references *do not* convey value judgments about the worth of these jobs in society or to the value placed on the people who hold different jobs. The same applies to pay level references.

KNOWLEDGE, SKILLS, AND ABILITIES In Chapter 6, we will address the role of *job analysis* to provide detailed descriptions of jobs based on differing combinations of KSAs. Typically, jobs that are based on knowledge and skills, which are developed based on formal education (vocational education, college education) or early job experiences such as internships or apprenticeships (for example, in the cases of medical doctors or plumbers, respectively) are highly valued as measured by pay levels. Jobs with less specialized or complex KSAs are typically paid much less.

Let's consider one job from the health care practitioners and technical operations occupation and one from the office and administrative support occupation. According to the *Occupational Outlook Handbook*,[6] anesthesiologists focus on the care of surgical patients and on pain relief. They also work outside of the operating room, providing pain relief in the intensive care unit, during labor and delivery, and for those who suffer from chronic pain. Anesthesiologists work with other physicians and surgeons to decide on treatments and procedures before, during, and after surgery. Preparation for becoming an anesthesiologist requires advanced training that includes completion of medical school, internships, residencies, and attaining medical board certification. In May 2016, the average annual salary was $269,600.[7]

According to the *Occupational Outlook Handbook*,[8] secretaries and administrative assistants usually answer telephones and take messages or transfer calls, schedule appointments and update event calendars, arrange staff meetings, handle incoming and outgoing mail and faxes, draft routine memos, billing, or other reports, and maintain databases and filing systems. Typically, high school graduates who have basic office and computer skills qualify for entry-level positions. Most secretaries learn their job in several weeks. In May 2016, the average annual salary was $40,330.[9]

Pay differences are also evident within occupations because of different job requirements. Let's consider pharmacist and pharmacist technician jobs, which are part of the health care occupation. According to the *Occupational Outlook Handbook*,[10] pharmacists possess advanced training to give them the knowledge and skills to safely fill prescriptions, verify instructions from physicians on the proper amounts of medication to give to patients, check whether the prescription will interact negatively with other drugs that a patient is taking or any medical conditions the patient has, instruct patients on how and when to take a prescribed medicine, and inform them about potential side effects they may experience from taking the medicine. Pharmacy technicians support the work of pharmacists while under their supervision. For example, technicians take the information needed to fill a prescription from customers or health professionals, measure amounts of medication for prescriptions, package and label prescriptions, and organize inventory. Pharmacy technicians do not require advanced education; most of their training takes place on the job. Average annual pay reflects these differences. In 2016, pharmacists earned $120,270 while pharmacy technicians earned $32,170.[11]

SUPPLY AND DEMAND Companies' demand for qualified individuals for jobs relative to supply often influences compensation. There are upward pressures to raise starting pay when the demand for qualified workers jobs is greater than supply. These market dynamics require that companies compete for limited numbers of qualified workers. This appears to be the case for information security analysts. According to the *Occupational Outlook Handbook,*[12] demand for information security analysts is expected to be much higher than supply. The Center for Cyber Safety and Education estimates that there will be 1.8 million unfilled jobs by 2022, which represents a 20 percent rise from the 1.5 million unfilled jobs in 2015.[13] Cyberattacks have grown in frequency and sophistication over the last few years, and many organizations are behind in their ability to detect these attacks. For instance, the credit bureau Experian experienced a breach of their databases that contained customers' information to determine credit worthiness. Nearly 150 million records were unlawfully accessed by the hackers. Thus, analysts will be needed to come up with innovative solutions to prevent hackers from stealing critical information or creating havoc on computer networks. Also, the federal government is expected to greatly increase its use of information security analysts to protect the nation's critical information technology (IT) systems. Further, as the health care industry expands its use of electronic medical records, ensuring patients' privacy and protecting personal data are becoming more important. More information security analysts are likely to be needed to create the safeguards that will satisfy patients' concerns.

☞ **FYI**

Both private-sector companies and the federal government are competing for cyber security talent; however, the difference in annual pay between the government and private sector is staggering, particularly for chief information officer jobs:

- Private-sector: $500,000 to $2,000,000
- Federal government: $123,175 to $185,100[14]

Two major factors are contributing to a shortage of commercial airline pilots—airlines' increasing the size of their fleets and an expected 42 percent of current pilots are expected to retire by 2027.[15] The shortage of commercial airline pilots is expected to swell to 20,000 by 2022[16] and more than 30,000 by 2034.[17] This trend weighs heavily on most airlines. Greg Muccio, a senior manager at Southwest Airlines Company lamented: "That is one of the things in my job I get to worry about every day and when I got to bed at night."[18] And he sees an overall lack of interest in becoming a commercial pilot as a key problem: "That's what puts us in the most jeopardy."[19] There are many factors that may be contributing to this lack of interest. Most commercial pilots spend the first several years working for regional airlines where annual pay has been traditionally quite low—in the $20,000 range. Eventually, many of these airlines doubled starting pay. Still, raising pay has done little to move the needle. The cost of flight-training is quite high, surpassing the $100,000 mark after factoring in the cost of tuition and living expenses. And, recent tighter government regulation requires substantially more flight hours and other experience, typically, at lower paying jobs, before becoming eligible for co-pilot positions at commercial airlines.

A common assumption is that high demand for workers applies only to highly skilled jobs. But, that assumption is not necessarily correct. In 2017, wages for low-skilled jobs increased at a higher rate (2.3 percent) than more highly skilled jobs requiring a college degree.[20] Large retailers are finding it increasingly more difficult to hire well-qualified workers at lower pay rates, particularly since the unemployment rate has declined. In 2017, retailer Target announced that it would raise the pay for all its U.S. employees to at least $11 per hour, rising to $15 per hour by 2020, which would exceed the federal minimum wage level by $3.75 and $7.75 per hour (based on $7.25 per hour in 2018).[21] In part, Target was responding to Wal-Mart's higher starting hourly pay rates, $9 and $10 in 2015 and 2016, respectively. As a side note, in 2018, only the District of Columbia and three states—California, Massachusetts, and Washington mandated an hourly minimum wage equal to or higher than $11. This move would raise the pay of thousands of the company's more than 300,000 workers. Further punctuating the intensity of competition, Wal-Mart soon followed target's announcement with other enhancements to its compensation.[22] Specifically, Wal-Mart reported that it would raise its starting hourly wage to $11. Also, the company plans to award one-time cash bonuses to some part- and full-time workers, ranging from $250 to $1,000 based on seniority. Further, Wal-Mart announced that it will offer full-time employees 10 weeks of paid maternity leave and six weeks of paid parental leave. This phenomenon can be seen in the elevator repair jobs. These jobs, which require a high school diploma, are in high demand and pay well (at least $75,000 annually) because of the rapid growth in completed skyscrapers and planned development of office buildings and high-rise residences.[23]

These examples illustrate a labor shortage based on high company demand. Of course, there are situations where labor surpluses occur based on declining company demand. For instance, there is a trend of coal and nuclear power plants, used to generate electricity, shutting down. These older plants are being replaced by more efficient ones that rely on natural gas, wind, and solar power for generating electricity.[24] Then, why is there a growing surplus of power plant workers? Coal plants require people and machines to deliver rocks and prepare them to be ground into mist, which fuels the power generating boilers. Natural gas is transported through pipelines and wind and solar farms do not have raw materials that workers must first process as in coal-burning plants. Logically, then, less competition for plant workers negatively influences wage growth.

GEOGRAPHIC PAY DIFFERENTIALS

Overall, there are relative pay differentials between geographic areas. Most typically, these are focused on comparisons between the nation and small geographic areas such as city or state. Based on the most recent comprehensive analysis published by the U.S. Bureau of Labor Statistics, all Los Angeles, California area employees were paid, on average, 20 percent more than the national average.[25] In Lincoln, Nebraska, employees were paid 3 percent less than the national average. This is an example of *relative pay differentials*.

We can also consider *pay rate differentials* (expressed in dollars as hourly or annual pay) for occupations based on geographic regions (for instance, Massachusetts, and the city of Boston) and the United States, overall. On a day-to-day basis, compensation professionals focus on pay rates and pay rate differentials. It is important to note that pay rate differentials do not fully match relative pay differentials because relative pay differential measures control for the influence of various variables, and pay rate differentials do not, which we will discuss shortly. Nevertheless, we generally observe consistency in the direction of the relative pay and pay rate differentials. For instance, both statistics show that typical pay rates in the San Francisco area are higher than the national average. However, the magnitude of the differences captured by these statistics is most often different. For example, the relative pay differential for installation workers employed in the San Francisco area was 17 percent higher than in the United States, overall.[26] However, the pay rate difference was 33 percent.[27]

2-3. Summarize the reasons for the occurrence of geographic pay differentials.

These disparities are partly based on the calculation methods. Compared to relative rate differences, the relative pay differential calculation considers (controls for) other factors that can explain pay differences within a defined area. The idea is to present a clearer picture of regional-based pay differences. For example, as we have learned, interindustry wage differentials represent an important factor. Other control factors include the union status of the workforce, which we will discuss shortly, and whether employees work on a full- or part-time basis, which we will also discuss in Chapter 12. Additional control factors include occupational type, work level, whether firms operate on a profit or not-for-profit basis, and skill-level differences between employees who are performing the same job.[28] Thus, it is important for compensation professionals to consider both types of statistics when evaluating geographic differences in compensation decisions.

Cost-of-living differences between geographic locations also provide an additional explanation. Compensation professionals sometimes consider cost-of-living differences between locations. For example, let's assume that a company was to offer starting pay to two equally qualified individuals who have been hired to perform the same job, but placed in different cities—Boston, Massachusetts and Fargo, North Dakota. If a differential was to be considered, it might be based on the cost of housing. Housing costs are among the largest financial obligations most individuals assume. The median home price in Boston was $464,000, and only $214,000 in Fargo.[29] The company may consider offering the Boston-based employee a higher salary to help offset some of the difference in cost-of-living. The idea is to help employees in similar jobs to maintain comparable standards of living, which will help with recruitment and retention of qualified employees. Other spending categories include food, utilities, transportation, and health care. Oftentimes, companies consider all the spending categories when setting pay rates. Cost-of-living comparison calculators (for example, one furnished by CNN, *http://money.cnn.com/calculator/pf/cost-of-living/*) may be useful. Based on this calculator, a $50,000 salary in Fargo is equivalent to a $74,622 salary in Boston.

☛ **FYI**

Cost-of-living comparison calculators (for example, CNN's calculator) incorporate five categories as a basis for determining pay comparability between two locations:

- Groceries
- Housing
- Utilities
- Transportation
- Healthcare

LABOR UNIONS

2-4. Discuss the role of labor unions in setting compensation.

Since the passage of the **National Labor Relations Act of 1935 (NLRA)**, the federal government requires private-sector employers to enter good-faith negotiations with workers over the terms of employment. Workers join unions to influence employment-related decisions, especially when they are dissatisfied with job security, wages, benefits, and supervisory practices.

NATIONAL LABOR RELATIONS ACT OF 1935 The purpose of this act was to remove barriers to free commerce and to restore equality of bargaining power between employees and employers. Employers denied workers the rights to bargain collectively with them on such issues as wages, work hours, and working conditions. Employees consequently experienced poor working conditions, substandard wage rates, and excessive work hours. Section 1 of the NLRA declares the policy of the United States to protect commerce:

> . . . by encouraging the practice and procedure of collective bargaining and by protecting the exercise by workers of full freedom of association, self-organization, and designation

of representatives of their own choosing for the purpose of negotiating the terms and conditions of employment. . . .

Sections 8(a)(5), 8(d), and 9(a) are key provisions of this act. Section 8(a)(5) provides that it is an unfair labor practice for an employer " . . . to refuse to bargain collectively with the representatives of his employees subject to the provisions of Section 9(a)."

Section 8(d) defines the phrase "to bargain collectively" as the "performance of the mutual obligation of the employer and the representative of the employees to meet at reasonable times and confer in good faith with respect to wages, hours, and other terms and conditions of employment. . . ."

Section 9(a) declares:

Representatives designated or selected for the purposes of collective bargaining by the majority of employees in a unit appropriate for such purposes shall be the exclusive representatives of all the employees in such unit for the purposes of collective bargaining in respect to rates of pay, wages, hours of employment, or other conditions of employment. . . .

A **collective bargaining agreement** is a written document that describes the terms of employment approved by management and employees during negotiations. It codifies the terms and conditions of employment regarding rates of pay and pay adjustments, and hours of work or other working conditions of employees. Collective bargaining agreements are put in place for multiple years, most typically three or four years.

The National Labor Relations Board (NLRB) oversees the enforcement of the NLRA. The president of the United States appoints members to the NLRB for five-year terms. The National Labor Relations Act covers most private-sector employers. Left out from coverage under the NLRA are public-sector employees, agricultural and domestic workers, independent contractors, employees of air and rail carriers covered by the Railway Labor Act, and supervisors.

COMPENSATION ISSUES IN COLLECTIVE BARGAINING Union and management negotiations usually center on pay raises and employee benefits. Unions fought hard for general pay increases and regular COLAs. COLAs, or cost-of-living adjustments, represent automatic pay increases that are based on changes in prices, as recorded by the consumer price index (CPI). COLAs enable workers to maintain their standards of living by adjusting wages for inflation. Union leaders also fought hard for these improvements to maintain the memberships' loyalty and support.

Unions generally secured high wages for their members through the early 1980s. In fact, it was common for union members to earn as much as 30 percent more than their nonunion counterparts. Unions also improved members' employee benefits. The establishment of sound retirement income programs was most noteworthy. Unions' gains also influenced nonunion companies' compensation practices. Many nonunion companies offer higher compensation than they would if unions were nonexistent. This phenomenon is known as a **spillover effect** because management of nonunion firms generally offered somewhat higher wages and benefits to reduce the chance that employees would seek union representation.[30] In 2017, the average weekly pay for all union workers (both private- and public sectors) was $1,041 and $829 for all nonunion workers.[31] For union workers employed in the private sector, pay was $984 and it was $816 for nonunion workers. In the public sector, union workers earned $1,104 compared to $917 for nonunion workers. However, the decline in unionization, which we discuss next, has weakened the spillover effect to some extent.[32]

Notwithstanding unions' gains over the years, their influence has been in decline. Since 1954, when union representation was at its highest (28.3 percent of the U.S. labor force),[33] the percentage of U.S. civilian workers in both the public and private sectors represented by unions has declined steadily. In 1983, the representation rate was 20.1 percent.[34] In 2017, the union representation rate was 10.7 percent. Union representation will probably continue to decline in the future. There are five noteworthy reasons for the continued decline in unionization.

First, in decades past, unions often intimidated workers to become members even if they did not care to do so. Unions used such tactics to boost their membership, thus, their power to negotiate with employers over terms of employment. Quite simply, it is more difficult to ignore the voices of the many rather than the few. Over time, legislation outlawed unions' use of intimidation, after which the prevalence of unions began to decline.

Second, historically, unions provided a voice to protect the rights of disadvantaged groups, including women, older workers, and racial minorities. However, starting in the 1960s, antidiscrimination laws such as Title VII of the Civil Rights Act instituted protections. The array of legislation lessened the role of unions.

Third, globalization of business is believed to have contributed substantially to the decline in unionization in a variety of ways. For example, higher quality automobile imports (such as Toyota and Honda automobiles) required that U.S. automobile manufacturers make greater investments in quality control and workforce flexibility, which unions tend to resist. Unions resist giving management too much discretion over employee assignments and pay out of concern that they would treat them unfairly; however, the survival of companies required that unions accept flexibility. Unions' willingness to permit greater management discretion raised questions about their ability to protect workers.

Globalization through offshoring activities threatens unionization. Offshoring refers to the migration of all or a significant part of the development, maintenance, and delivery of services to a company located in another country. With rare exception, employees do not move with the jobs. Traditionally, the reason given for offshoring is to reduce costs. Moreover, the absence of or less restrictive labor laws (for example, minimum wage laws) in other countries generally permit U.S. companies to lower employment costs.

Fourth, large companies such as Boeing, which have highly unionized workforces, are establishing new manufacturing facilities in states where unionization rates are low. German automobile manufacturer Volkswagen built a state-of-the-art factory in Tennessee, which possess right-to-work laws. **Right-to-work laws** prohibit management and unions from entering into agreements requiring union membership as a condition of employment.[35] The prevalence of unions' influence on wages varies tremendously by state based on whether there are right-to-work laws in place. In right-to-work states, union influence is less potent than in other states. Currently, 28 states have right-to-work laws in place. Historically, most were found in southern states. Increasingly, northern states are adopting these laws. Michigan, which has a substantial population of union employees, recently adopted right-to-work laws. Employees in right-to-work states earned 16.6 percent less than employees in non right-to-work-states (median hourly wage, $18.40 vs. $15.79).[36] These differences have been one contributing factor that has led many manufacturing businesses to relocate in right-to-work states where employment costs are lower, further weakening unions' influence.

Fifth, unionization is substantially higher in the public or government sector than in the private sector. In 2017, the unionization rate of government workers was 34.4 percent, compared to 6.5 percent among private sector employees.[37] Still, public sector unionization is being challenged throughout the country. Traditionally, there was much less resistance to unionize in the public sector than in the private sector. But the tide is changing. For example, that began to change when Wisconsin Governor Scott Walker signed a law in 2011 that eliminated most union rights for government workers. The state lost nearly 50,000 public sector union members between 2011 and 2013. In Indiana, a right-to-work law took effect in 2012 where it lost about 52,000 union members in both the private and public sectors. Michigan lawmakers approved a right-to-work law a few months later, losing approximately 40,000 union members in both the private and public sectors.

EMPLOYMENT LAWS PERTINENT TO COMPENSATION PRACTICE

The **federal constitution** forms the basis for employment laws. The following four amendments of the Constitution are most applicable:

> **Article I, Section 8**. "The Congress shall have Power . . . to regulate Commerce with foreign Nations, and among the several States, and with the Indian Tribes. . . . "
>
> **First Amendment**. "Congress shall make no law respecting an establishment of religion, or prohibiting the free exercise thereof; or abridging the freedom of speech, or of the press; or the right of the people peaceably to assemble, and to petition the Government for a redress of grievances."
>
> **Fifth Amendment**. "No person shall . . . be deprived of life, liberty, or property, without due process of law. . . . "
>
> **Fourteenth Amendment, Section 1**. " . . . No State shall make or enforce any law which shall abridge the privileges or immunities of citizens of the United States, nor shall any State deprive any person of life, liberty, or property without due process of law; nor deny any person within its jurisdiction the equal protection of the laws."

2-5. Identify and discuss key employment laws pertinent to compensation practice.

Government in the United States is organized at three levels roughly defined by geographic scope. A single **federal government** oversees the entire United States and its territories. The clear majority of laws that influence compensation were established at the federal level. Next, individual **state governments** enact and enforce laws that pertain exclusively to their respective regions (e.g., Illinois and Michigan). Most noteworthy are differences in state minimum wage laws, which we will discuss shortly. Finally, **local governments** enact and enforce laws that are most pertinent to smaller geographic regions (e.g., Champaign County in Illinois and the City of Los Angeles). Many of the federal laws have counterparts in state and local legislation. State and local legislation may be concurrent with federal law or may exist in the absence of similar federal legislation. Wherever inconsistencies in federal, state, or local laws exist, the law that provides individuals the greatest benefit generally prevails. For example, in addition to federal minimum wage legislation, many states also have minimum wage laws. In cases where an employee is subject to both the state and federal minimum wage laws, the employee is entitled to the higher of the two minimum wages.

Federal laws that apply to compensation practices are grouped according to four key themes. Table 2-2 lists the laws associated with each theme:

- Income continuity, safety, and work hours
- Pay discrimination
- Accommodating disabilities and family needs
- Prevailing wage laws

Income Continuity, Safety, and Work Hours

Three factors led to the passage of income continuity, safety, and work hours legislation. The first factor was the **Great Depression**, the move from family businesses to large factories, and divisions of labor within factories. During the Great Depression, which took place in the 1930s, scores of businesses failed, and many workers became chronically unemployed. Government enacted key legislation designed to stabilize the income of an individual who became unemployed because of poor business conditions or workplace injuries. The **Social Security Act of 1935 (Title IX)** provided temporary income to workers who became unemployed through no fault of their own. **Workers' compensation** programs granted income to workers who were unable to work because of injuries sustained on the job. Supporting

TABLE 2-2 Laws that Influence Compensation Practice

Income Continuity, Safety, and Work Hours

Fair Labor Standards Act of 1938

Portal-to-Portal Act of 1947

Equal Pay Act of 1963

Work Hours and Safety Standards Act of 1962

McNamara–O'Hara Service Contract Act of 1965

Pay Discrimination

Equal Pay Act of 1963

Lilly Ledbetter Fair Pay Act (2009)

Civil Rights Act of 1964, Title VII

Bennett Amendment (1964)

Age Discrimination in Employment Act of 1967 (amended in 1978, 1986, and 1990)

Civil Rights Act of 1991

Accommodating Disabilities and Family Needs

Pregnancy Discrimination Act of 1978

Americans with Disabilities Act of 1990 (amended in 2008)

Family and Medical Leave Act of 1993

Prevailing Wage Laws

Davis–Bacon Act of 1931

Walsh–Healey Public Contracts Act of 1936

workers during these misfortunes promoted the well-being of the economy: These income provisions enabled the unemployed to participate in the economy as consumers of essential goods and services. We will defer a more detailed discussion of the Social Security Act of 1935 and workers' compensation laws until Chapter 10 because these laws instituted legally required employee benefits.

Second, the main U.S. economic activities prior to the twentieth century were agriculture and small family businesses that were organized along craft lines. Workers began to move from their farms and small family businesses to capitalists' factories for employment. The character of work changed dramatically with the move of workers to factories. An individual's status changed from owner to employee. This status change meant that individuals lost control over their earnings and working conditions.

Third, the factory system also created divisions of labor characterized by differences in skills and responsibilities. Some workers received training, whereas others did not. This contributed greatly to these differences. Workers with higher skills and responsibilities did not necessarily earn higher wages than workers with fewer skills and responsibilities. Paying some workers more than others only increased costs, which is something factory owners avoided whenever possible.

In sum, factory workers received very low wages and worked in unsafe conditions because factory owners sought to maximize profits. Offering workers high wages and providing safe working conditions would have cut into factory owners' profits. These conditions led to the passage of the **Fair Labor Standards Act of 1938 (FLSA)**. The FLSA addresses major abuses that intensified during the Great Depression and the transition from agricultural to industrial enterprises. These include substandard pay, excessive work hours, and the employment of children in oppressive working conditions.

FAIR LABOR STANDARDS ACT OF 1938 The FLSA addresses three broad issues:

- Minimum wage
- Overtime pay
- Child labor provisions

The FLSA establishes minimum wage, overtime pay, recordkeeping, and youth employment standards affecting employees in the private sector and in federal, state, and local governments. The U.S. Department of Labor enforces the FLSA.

Minimum Wage The purpose of the minimum wage provision is to ensure a minimally acceptable standard of living for workers. The original minimum wage was 25 cents per hour. Since the act's passage in 1938, the federal government has raised the minimum wage several times. In 2007, Congress passed an increase in the federal minimum wage from $5.15 in increments to $7.25 in 2009. Since then, the U.S. Congress has not raised the minimum wage. The main argument against raising the minimum wage centers on a higher cost burden on companies, particularly on small businesses.

According to the U.S. Department of Labor, as of January 2018, 45 states plus the District of Columbia had minimum wage requirements.[38] There were 2 states with minimum wage rates set lower than the federal minimum wage. There were 29 states plus the District of Columbia with minimum wage rates set higher than the federal minimum wage. There were 14 states that have a minimum wage requirement that is the same as the federal minimum wage requirement. The remaining 5 states do not have an established minimum wage requirement. As of January 2018, the District of Columbia had the highest minimum wage at $12.50 per hour while the states of Georgia and Wyoming had the lowest minimum wage ($5.15 per hour) of the 45 states that have a minimum wage requirement.

In general, federal minimum wage law supersedes state minimum wage laws where the federal minimum wage is greater than the state minimum wage. In those states where the state minimum wage is greater than the federal minimum wage, the state minimum wage rate prevails. Specific FLSA exemptions, however, permit employers to pay some workers less than the minimum wage. For instance, students employed in retail or service businesses, on farms, or in institutions of higher education may be paid less than the minimum wage with the consent of the Department of Labor. With explicit permission from the Department of Labor, employers can pay less than the minimum wage for trainee positions or to prevent a reduction in the employment of mentally or physically disabled individuals.

Even though the federal and some state governments raise the minimum wage from time to time, most workers who earn the minimum wage argue that it is insufficient to afford the necessities. In the summer of 2013, fast food workers across the United States walked off their jobs to protest what they believe is insufficient pay. Workers were concerned about the minimum wage level and the collective response of restaurant owners to their concerns. Many other protests followed, including a massive strike on Labor Day in 2017.

It is worth noting that fast food workers' continued protests may have contributed to increases in their minimum wage. For example, company-operated McDonald's stores announced that it would increase pay at least $1 more per hour than the local minimum wage. In 2017, New York instituted a minimum wage law requiring fast food restaurants to pay workers at least $13.50 in New York City (NYC) and $11.75 in the rest of the state.[39] The NYC rate rose to $15 at the end of 2018 and it will rise to the same level in the remainder of the state by 2021.

Overtime Provisions The FLSA requires employers to pay workers at a rate at least equal to time and one-half for all hours worked more than 40 hours within a period of 7 consecutive days. For example, a worker's regular hourly rate is $10 for working 40 hours or less within a 7-day

TABLE 2-3 FLSA Exemption Criteria

- *Test 1: Salary Level*

  The employee must be paid at least $455 per week or $910 biweekly or $1,971.66 monthly or $23,660 annually.
- *Test 2: Salary Basis*

  Employee must receive a predetermined, fixed salary that is not subject to reduction due to variations in quality or quantity of work performed.
- *Test 3: Job Duties*

  Employee must meet all the criteria specified in one or more of the following exemptions:

  - Executive
  - Administrative
  - Education Establishments and Administrative
  - Professional – Learned
  - Professional – Artistic
  - Computer-Related

Source: U.S. Department of Labor.

period. The FLSA requires the employer to pay this employee $15 per hour for each additional hour worked beyond the regular 40 hours within this 7-day period.

The overtime provision does not apply to all jobs. Table 2-3 summarizes the three tests used to determine whether an employer must pay the overtime rate for hours worked more than 40 hours within a period of 7 consecutive days. Satisfying all three tests indicates that a job is **exempt** from the overtime pay provision. Most other jobs are **nonexempt**. Nonexempt jobs are subject to the FLSA overtime pay provision.

The U.S. Department of Labor introduced revised guidelines known as the **FairPay Rules** in August 2004. Under the FairPay Rules, workers earning less than $23,660 per year—or $455 per week—are guaranteed overtime protection (as of January 2018). The U.S. Department of Labor provides extensive information regarding the FairPay Rules, including instructional videos and a "frequently asked questions" section (www.dol.gov). A federal rule was put in place by the Obama presidential administration to double the annual salary threshold in 2016; however, a U.S. District Judge banned implementation of the rule after a coalition of businesses and 21 states maintained that the U.S. Department of Labor overstepped its authority in issuing the new rule. These groups expressed concerns that higher compensation and overhead costs would be excessively burdensome. At the time of this revision, the U.S. Department of Labor was writing proposed rules to modify the salary test pertaining to overtime pay exemption status.

The federal government broadened the scope of the FLSA twice since 1938 through the passage of two acts:

- Portal-to-Portal Act of 1947
- Equal Pay Act of 1963

The **Portal-to-Portal Act of 1947** defines the term *hours worked* that appears in the FLSA. Table 2-4 lists the compensable work activities. For example, time spent by state correctional officers caring for police dogs at home is compensable under the FLSA (*Andres v. DuBois*).[40] The care of dogs, including feeding, grooming, and walking, is indispensable to maintaining dogs as a critical law enforcement tool, it is part of officers' principal activities, and it benefits the corrections department; however, this court ruled that time spent by state correction canine handlers transporting dogs between home and correctional facilities is not compensable under FLSA.

In a 2012 lawsuit, the judge found a Subway franchisee in Ohio to be in violation of labor laws after it refused to pay employees for the work they completed during the nightly closing routine.[41] For example, the company might say a worker's shift stopped when the store closed even when it took another half hour to shut the restaurant down and clean up.

TABLE 2-4 Compensable Work Activities

Waiting Time: Whether waiting time is hours worked under the act depends upon the circumstances. Generally, the facts may show that the employee was engaged to wait (which is work time), or the facts may show that the employee was waiting to be engaged (which is not work time). For example, a secretary who reads a book while waiting for dictation or a fireman who plays checkers while waiting for an alarm is working during such periods of inactivity. These employees have been "engaged to wait."

On-Call Time: An employee who is required to remain on call on the employer's premises is working while "on call." An employee who is required to remain on call at home, or who can leave a message where he/she can be reached, is not working (in most cases) while on call. Additional constraints on the employee's freedom could require this time to be compensated.

Rest and Meal Periods: Rest periods of short duration, usually 20 minutes or less, are common in industry (and promote the efficiency of the employee) and are customarily paid for as working time. These short periods must be counted as hours worked. Unauthorized extensions of authorized work breaks need not be counted as hours worked when the employer has expressly and unambiguously communicated to the employee that the authorized break may only last for a specific length of time, that any extension of the break is contrary to the employer's rules, and that any extension of the break will be punished. Bona fide meal periods (typically 30 minutes or more) generally need not be compensated as work time. The employee must be completely relieved from duty for eating regular meals. The employee is not relieved if he or she is required to perform any duties, whether active or inactive, while eating.

Sleeping Time and Certain Other Activities: An employee who is required to be on duty for less than 24 hours is working even though he or she is permitted to sleep or engage in other personal activities when not busy. An employee required to be on duty for 24 hours or more may agree with the employer to exclude from hours worked bona fide regularly scheduled sleeping periods of not more than 8 hours, provided adequate sleeping facilities are furnished by the employer and the employee can usually enjoy an uninterrupted night's sleep. No reduction is permitted unless at least five hours of sleep is taken.

Lectures, Meetings, and Training Programs: Attendance at lectures, meetings, training programs, and similar activities need not be counted as working time only if four criteria are met, namely: It is outside normal hours, voluntary, not job related, and no other work is concurrently performed. In other words, the time spent in employer-mandated training counts as compensable time.

Travel time: The principles that apply in determining whether time spent in travel is compensable time depends upon the kind of travel involved.

- **Home-to-work travel:** An employee who travels from home before the regular workday and returns to his or her home at the end of the workday is engaged in ordinary home-to-work travel, which is not work time.

- **Home-to-work travel on a special one-day assignment, including employer-mandated training, in another city:** An employee who regularly works at a fixed location in one city is given a special one-day assignment, including employer-mandated training, in another city and returns home the same day. The time spent in traveling to and returning from the other city is work time, except that the employer may deduct/not count that time the employee would normally spend commuting to the regular work site.

- **Travel that is all in a day's work:** Time spent by an employee in travel as part of his or her principal activity, such as travel from job site to job site during the workday, is work time and must be counted as hours worked.

- **Travel away from home community:** Travel that keeps an employee away from home overnight is travel away from home. Travel away from home is clearly work time when it cuts across the employee's workday. The time is not only hours worked on regular working days during normal working hours but also during corresponding hours on nonworking days. As an enforcement policy, the U.S. Department of Labor will not consider as work time that time spent in travel away from home outside of regular working hours as a passenger on an airplane, train, boat, bus, or automobile.

Source: Adapted from U.S. Department of Labor. (2011). Compliance Assistance—Fair Labor Standards Act (FLSA). Available: *http://www. dol.gov*, accessed February 19, 2013.

In 2014, the U.S. Supreme Court ruled on the issue whether security screenings at the workplace constitutes a compensable work activity (*Integrity Staffing Solutions, Inc. v. Busk et al.*).[42] The Supreme Court heard this case on appeal from the company after a lower court ruled that workplace screening constitutes a compensable work activity. Integrity Staffing Solutions, Inc. employs workers (paid on an hourly basis) whose jobs it is to retrieve products from warehouse shelves and package them for delivery to Amazon.com customers. The company mandated these workers to undergo a security screening before leaving the warehouse each day. Former employees claimed that they were entitled to compensation under the FLSA for the roughly 25 minutes each day that they spent waiting to undergo those screenings. They also claimed that the company could have substantially reduced wait times by adding more screeners or staggering shift terminations, and security screenings were conducted to prevent employee theft for the sole benefit of the employers and their customers.

The court concluded that the security screenings at issue here are not compensable activities because the screenings were not the principal activity which the employee is employed to perform. Integrity Staffing employed individuals to retrieve products from warehouse shelves and package those products for shipment to Amazon.com customers, not to undergo security screenings. In addition, the court ruled that the security screenings were not integral and indispensable to the employees' duties as warehouse workers. In other words, the screenings were not a necessary step for retrieving products from warehouse shelves or packaging them for shipment.

The **Equal Pay Act of 1963** prohibits sex discrimination in pay for employees performing equal work. We will discuss the Equal Pay Act of 1963 later in this chapter.

Child Labor Provisions The FLSA child labor provisions protect children from being overworked, working in potentially hazardous settings, and having their education jeopardized due to excessive work hours. The restrictions vary by age:

- Children under age 14 usually cannot be employed.
- Children ages 14 and 15 may work in safe occupations outside school hours if their work does not exceed 3 hours on a school day (18 hours per week while school is in session). When school is not in session, as in the summer, children cannot work more than 40 hours per week.
- Children ages 16 and 17 do not have hourly restrictions; however, they cannot work in hazardous jobs (e.g., the use of heavy industrial equipment or exposure to harmful substances).

Pay Discrimination

The civil rights movement of the 1960s led to the passage of key legislation designed to protect designated classes of employees and to uphold their rights individually against discriminatory employment decisions. Some of these laws, such as the **Civil Rights Act of 1964**, apply to all employment-related decisions (e.g., recruitment, selection, performance appraisal, compensation, and termination). Other laws, such as the Equal Pay Act of 1963, apply specifically to compensation practices. These laws limit employers' authority over employment decisions.

EQUAL PAY ACT OF 1963 Congress enacted the Equal Pay Act of 1963 to remedy a serious problem of employment discrimination in private industry: "Many segments of American industry [have] been based on an ancient but outmoded belief that a man, because of his role in society, should be paid more than a woman even though his duties are the same."[43] The Equal Pay Act of 1963 is based on a simple principle: Men and women should receive equal pay for performing equal work.

The Equal Employment Opportunity Commission (EEOC) enforces the Equal Pay Act of 1963. The EEOC possesses the authority to investigate and reconcile charges of illegal discrimination. The Act applies to all employers and labor organizations. In particular,

No employer . . . shall discriminate within any establishment in which such employees are employed, between employees on the basis of sex by paying wages to employees in such establishment at a rate less than the rate at which he pays wages to employees of the opposite sex . . . for equal work on jobs the performance of which requires equal skill, effort, and responsibility, and which are performed under similar working conditions . . . [29 USC 206, Section 6, paragraph (d)]

The Equal Pay Act of 1963 pertains explicitly to jobs of equal worth. Companies assign pay rates to jobs according to the skill, effort, responsibility, and working conditions required. Skill, effort, responsibility, and working conditions represent **compensable factors**. The U.S. Department of Labor's definitions of these compensable factors are listed in Table 2-5.

How do we judge whether jobs are equal? The case *EEOC v. Madison Community Unit School District No. 12*[44] sheds light on this important issue. The school district paid female athletic coaches of girls' sports teams less than it paid male athletic coaches of boys' teams. The judge concluded:

The jobs that are compared must be in some sense the same to count as "equal work" under the Equal Pay Act of 1963; and here we come to the main difficulty in applying the Act; whether two jobs are the same depends on how fine a system of job classification the courts will accept. If coaching an athletic team in the Madison, Illinois, school system is considered a single job rather than a [collection] of jobs, the school district violated the Equal Pay Act prima facie by paying female holders of this job less than male holders. . . . If, on the other hand, coaching the girls' tennis team is considered a different job from coaching the boys' tennis team, and if coaching the girls' volleyball or basketball team is considered a different job (or jobs) from coaching the boys' soccer team, there is no prima facie violation. So, the question is how narrow a definition of job the courts should be using in deciding whether the Equal Pay Act is applicable. We can get some guidance from the language of the Act. The act requires that the jobs compared have "similar working conditions," not the same working conditions. This implies that some comparison of different jobs is possible . . . since the working conditions need not be "equal," the jobs need not be completely identical. . . . Above the lowest rank of employee, every employee has a somewhat different job from every other one, even if the two employees being compared are in the same department. So, if "equal work" and "equal skill, effort, and responsibility" were taken literally, the Act would have a minute domain. . . .

TABLE 2-5 U.S. Department of Labor Definitions of Compensable Factors

Factor	Definition
Skill	Experience, training, education, and ability as measured by the performance requirements of a job.
Effort	The amount of mental or physical effort expended in the performance of a job.
Responsibility	The degree of accountability required in the performance of a job.
Working conditions	The physical surroundings and hazards of a job, including dimensions such as inside versus outside work, heat, cold, and poor ventilation.

Source: U.S. Department of Labor, *Equal pay for equal work under the Fair Labor Standards Act* (Washington, DC: U.S. Government Printing Office, December 31, 1971).

The courts have thus had to steer a narrow course. The cases do not require an absolute identity between the jobs, but do require substantial identity.

Pay differentials for equal work are not always illegal. Pay differentials between men and women who are performing equal work are acceptable where

> . . . such payment is made pursuant to (i) a seniority system; (ii) a merit system; (iii) a system which measures earnings by quantity or quality of production; or (iv) a differential based on any other factor other than sex: Provided, that an employer who is paying a wage rate differential . . . shall not . . . reduce the wage rate of any employee. [29 USC 206, Section 6, paragraph (d)]

☛ FYI

According to the Equal Employment Opportunity Commission, in 2017, there were 966 charges of illegal sex discrimination based on the Equal Pay Act. This figure represents 1.2 percent of all charges of illegal discrimination filed with the EEOC in 2017.[45]

It is important to acknowledge that a pervasive pay gap exists between men and women. There are a variety of statistics about this gap as well as theories for them. Some include illegal discrimination while others point to pervasive social biases. We will take up the complexities of the gender pay gap in Epilogue.

Civil Rights Act of 1964

The Civil Rights Act of 1964 is a comprehensive piece of legislation. **Title VII** of the Civil Rights Act is the most pertinent to compensation. Legislators designed Title VII to promote equal employment opportunities for underrepresented minorities. According to Title VII:

> It shall be an unlawful employment practice for an employer—(1) to fail or refuse to hire or to discharge any individual, or otherwise to discriminate against any individual with respect to his compensation, terms, conditions, or privileges of employment, because of such individual's race, color, religion, sex, or national origin; or (2) to limit, segregate, classify his employees or applicants for employment in any way which would deprive or tend to deprive any individual of employment opportunities or otherwise adversely affect his status as an employee, because of such individual's race, color, religion, sex, or national origin. (42 USC 2000e-2, Section 703)

The courts have distinguished between two types of discrimination covered by Title VII: disparate treatment and disparate impact. **Disparate treatment** represents intentional discrimination, occurring whenever employers intentionally treat some workers less favorably than others because of their race, color, sex, national origin, or religion. Applying different standards to determine pay increases for blacks and whites may result in disparate treatment. For example, choosing to award a high-performing African American employee a smaller pay raise than a lower-performing Caucasian employee could be considered disparate treatment.

Disparate impact represents unintentional discrimination. It occurs whenever an employer applies an employment practice to all employees, but the practice leads to unequal treatment of protected employee groups. Awarding pay increases to male and female production workers according to seniority could lead to disparate impact if females had less seniority, on average, than males.

Title VII protects employees who work for all private sector employers; local, state, and federal governments; and educational institutions that employ 15 or more individuals. Title VII also applies to private and public employment agencies, labor organizations, and joint labor management committees controlling apprenticeship and training.

It had become more difficult to sue employers for pay discrimination under Title VII. Title VII imposes a statute of limitation period, typically 180 days, after which employees may file claims of illegal discrimination against employers. In 2007, the U.S. Supreme Court rendered a very strict interpretation as to when the statute of limitations period begins for women to sue their employers for discrimination in pay. In *Ledbetter v. Goodyear Tire & Rubber Co.*,[46] a female employee named Lilly Ledbetter sued Goodyear Tire & Rubber Co. after she learned that some male employees with the same job had been paid substantially more than her over a period of several years. Ledbetter claimed that the statute of limitation period began when each discriminatory pay decision was made and communicated to her. She argued that multiple pay decisions were made over the years each time Goodyear endorsed each paycheck, making each paycheck a separate act of illegal pay discrimination. The Supreme Court rejected Ledbetter's allegation that each paycheck (following the initial paycheck when the pay disparity first existed) represented an intentionally discriminatory act by the employer. Instead, any act of discrimination occurred each time pay raise decisions were made. In Ledbetter's case, the court argued that any discriminatory decisions literally occurred years prior to raising her concerns with the EEOC. The later effects of past discrimination do not restart the clock for filing an EEOC charge, making Ledbetter's claim an untimely one. Not all the judges agreed with this ruling, noting that given pay secrecy policies in most companies many employees would have no idea within 180 days that they had received a lower raise than others. In addition, an initial disparity in pay may be small, leading a woman or minority group member not to make waves to try to succeed.

In 2009, the *Ledbetter* court decision was overturned with the passage of the **Lilly Ledbetter Fair Pay Act**, a key initiative in closing the pay gap between men and women. This Act restores the law as it was prior to the narrowly decided (5–4) Supreme Court *Ledbetter* decision in 2007. That decision tossed aside long-standing prior law and made it much harder for women and other workers to pursue pay discrimination claims—stating a pay discrimination charge must be filed within 180 days of the employer's initial decision to pay an employee less. The bill restores prior law—providing that a pay discrimination charge must simply be filed within 180 days of a discriminatory paycheck. The **Paycheck Fairness Act** is a second key initiative in closing the pay gap between men and women. This bill bolsters the Equal Pay Act of 1963 by strengthening the remedies available to put sex-based pay discrimination on par with race-based pay discrimination. That is, employers are now required to justify unequal pay by showing that the pay disparity is not sex based, but, rather, job related. This act also prohibits employers from retaliating against employees who share salary information with their coworkers.

BENNETT AMENDMENT The **Bennett Amendment** is an amendment to Title VII and allows female employees to charge employers with Title VII violations regarding pay only when the employer has violated the Equal Pay Act of 1963. The Bennett Amendment is necessary because lawmakers could not agree on the answers to the following questions:

• Does Title VII incorporate both the Equal Pay Act of 1963's equal pay standard and the four defenses for unequal work [(i) a seniority system; (ii) merit system; (iii) a system which measures earnings by quantity or quality of production; or (iv) a differential based on any other factor other than sex]?
• Does Title VII include only the four exceptions to the Equal Pay Act of 1963 standard?

Some lawmakers believed that Title VII incorporates the equal pay standard (i.e., answering *yes* to the first question and *no* to the second question); however, other lawmakers believed that Title VII does not incorporate the equal pay standard (i.e., answering *no* to the first question and *yes* to the second question). If Title VII did not incorporate the equal pay standard, then employees could raise charges of illegal pay discrimination (based on race, religion, color, sex, or national origin) for unequal jobs. Pay differentials based on different or unequal jobs fit with the foundation for effective compensation systems—internal consistency and market competitiveness, which we will address in Chapters 6 and 7, respectively.

AGE DISCRIMINATION IN EMPLOYMENT ACT OF 1967 (AS AMENDED IN 1978, 1986, AND 1990) Congress passed the **Age Discrimination in Employment Act of 1967 (ADEA)** to protect workers aged 40 and older from illegal discrimination. This act provides protection to a large segment of the U.S. population known as the **baby boom generation** or "baby boomers." The baby boom generation was born roughly between 1946 and 1964 and represented a swell in the American population. Some members of the baby boom generation reached age 40 in 1986, and all baby boomers are now over age 50.

A large segment of the population will probably continue to work beyond age 67, which is the retirement age for receiving Social Security retirement benefits, because many fear that Social Security retirement income (Chapter 10) will not provide adequate support. The U.S. Census Bureau predicts that the number of individuals age 65 and older will increase from about 25 million in 2001 (12.4 percent of the population) to about 77 million (20.3 percent of the population) by 2050.[47]

The ADEA established guidelines prohibiting age-related discrimination in employment. Its purpose is "to promote the employment of older persons based on their ability rather than age, to prohibit arbitrary age discrimination in employment, and to help employers and workers find ways of meeting problems arising from the impact of age on employment." The ADEA specifies that it is unlawful for an employer:

(1) to fail or refuse to hire or to discharge any individual or otherwise discriminate against any individual with respect to his compensation, terms, conditions, or privileges of employment, because of such individual's age; (2) to limit, segregate or classify his employees in any way which would deprive or tend to deprive any individual of employment opportunities or otherwise adversely affect his status as an employee, because of such individual's age; or (3) to reduce the wage rate of any employee in order to comply with this act. (29 USC 623, Section 4)

The **Older Workers Benefit Protection Act (OWBPA)**[48]—the 1990 amendment to the ADEA—placed additional restrictions on employer benefits practices. When employers require that all employees contribute toward coverage of benefits, under circumstances, they can also require older employees to pay more for health care, disability, or life insurance than younger employees. This is the case because these benefits generally become costlier with age (e.g., older workers may be more likely to incur serious illnesses, thus, insurance companies may charge employers higher rates to provide coverage for older workers than younger ones). However, an older employee may not be required to pay more for the benefit *as a condition of employment*. Where the premium has increased for an older employee, the employer must provide three options to older workers. First, the employee has the option of withdrawing from the benefit plan altogether. Second, the employee has the option of reducing his or her benefit coverage to keep his or her premium cost the same. Third, an older employee may be offered the option of paying more for the benefit to avoid otherwise justified reductions in coverage.

Employers can legally reduce the coverage of older workers for benefits that typically become costlier as employees further age *only if* the costs for providing those benefits are significantly greater than the cost for younger workers. When costs differ significantly, the employer may reduce the benefit for older workers only to the point where it is paying just as much per older worker (with lower coverage) as it is for younger workers (with higher coverage). This practice is referred to as the equal benefit or equal cost principle.

The ADEA covers private employers with 20 or more employees, labor unions with 25 or more members, and employment agencies. The EEOC enforces this act.

CIVIL RIGHTS ACT OF 1991 The **Civil Rights Act of 1991** overturned several Supreme Court rulings. The reversal of the *Atonio v. Wards Cove Packing Co.* court decision is perhaps the most noteworthy.[49] The Supreme Court ruled that plaintiffs (employees) must indicate which employment practice created disparate impact and demonstrate how the employment practice created disparate impact. Since the passage of the Civil Rights Act of 1991, employers must show that the challenged employment practice is a business necessity. Thus, the Civil Rights Act of 1991 shifted the burden of proof from employees to employers.

Two additional sections of the Civil Rights Act of 1991 apply to compensation practice. The first feature pertains to seniority systems. As we will discuss in Chapter 3, public sector employers commonly make employment decisions based on employees' seniority. For example, public sector employers award more vacation days to employees with higher seniority than to employees with lower seniority. The Civil Rights Act of 1991 overturned the Supreme Court's decision in *Lorance v. AT&T Technologies*,[50] which allowed employees to challenge the use of seniority systems only within 180 days from the system's implementation date. Employees may now file suits claiming discrimination either when the system is implemented or whenever the system negatively affects them.

A second development addresses the geographic scope of federal job discrimination. Prior to the Civil Rights Act of 1991, the U.S. Supreme Court (*Boureslan v. Aramco*)[51] ruled that federal job discrimination laws do not apply to U.S. citizens working for U.S. companies in foreign countries. Since the act's passage, U.S. citizens working overseas may file suit against U.S. businesses for discriminatory employment practices.

The Civil Rights Act of 1991 provides coverage to the same groups protected under the Civil Rights Act of 1964. The 1991 act also extends coverage to Senate employees and political appointees of the federal government's executive branch. The EEOC enforces the Civil Rights Act of 1991.

Accommodating Disabilities and Family Needs

Congress enacted the Pregnancy Discrimination Act of 1978, the Americans with Disabilities Act of 1990, and the Family and Medical Leave Act of 1993 to accommodate employees with disabilities and pressing family needs, respectively. These laws protect a significant number of employees: In 2000, approximately 68 percent of employed women were responsible for children under the age of 18. The preamble to the Americans with Disabilities Act states that it covers 43 million Americans. Many employees will benefit from the Family and Medical Leave Act if they need substantial time away from work to care for newborns or elderly family members. Two trends explain this need. First, many elderly and seriously ill parents of the employed baby boom generation depend on their children. Second, both husbands and wives work full-time jobs now more than ever before, necessitating extended leave to care for newborns or for children who become ill.

PREGNANCY DISCRIMINATION ACT OF 1978 The **Pregnancy Discrimination Act of 1978 (PDA)** is an amendment to Title VII of the Civil Rights Act of 1964. The PDA prohibits disparate impact discrimination against pregnant women for all employment practices. Employers must not treat pregnancy less favorably than other medical conditions covered under employee benefits plans. In addition, employers must treat pregnancy and childbirth the same way they treat other causes of disability. Furthermore, the PDA protects the rights of women who take leave for pregnancy-related reasons. The protected rights include:

- Credit for previous service
- Accrued retirement benefits
- Accumulated seniority

AMERICANS WITH DISABILITIES ACT OF 1990 The **Americans with Disabilities Act of 1990 (ADA)** prohibits discrimination against individuals with mental or physical disabilities within and outside employment settings, including public services and transportation, public accommodations, and employment. It applies to all employers with 15 or more employees, and the EEOC is the enforcement agency. In employment contexts, there are two ADA requirements:

- [P]rohibits covered employers from discriminating against a "qualified individual with a disability" in regard to job applications, hiring, advancement, discharge, compensation, training or other terms, conditions, or privileges of employment.
- Employers are required to make "reasonable accommodations" to the known physical or mental limitations of an otherwise qualified individual with a disability unless to do so would impose an "undue hardship."[52]

Title I of the ADA requires that employers provide reasonable accommodation. Reasonable accommodation for disabled employees may include such efforts as making existing facilities readily accessible, restructuring the job, and modifying work schedules. Every "qualified individual with a disability" is entitled to reasonable accommodation. A qualified individual with a disability, however, must be able to perform the "essential functions" of the job in question. Essential functions are those job duties that are critical to the job. The act prohibits employers from offsetting the cost of providing reasonable accommodation by lowering pay.

On September 25, 2008, former president George W. Bush signed the Americans with Disabilities Act Amendments Act of 2008, making important changes to the definition of the term *disability*. These changes make it easier for an individual seeking protection under the ADA to establish that he or she has a disability within the meaning of the ADA.

The act retains the ADA's basic definition of *disability* as an impairment that substantially limits one or more major life activities, a record of such an impairment, or being regarded as having such an impairment. However, it changes the way that these statutory terms should be interpreted. For example, it expands the definition of "major life activities" by including two non-exhaustive lists.

The first list includes many activities that the EEOC has recognized (e.g., walking) as well as activities that EEOC has not specifically recognized (e.g., reading, bending, and communicating). The second list includes major bodily functions (e.g., "functions of the immune system, normal cell growth, digestive, bowel, bladder, neurological, brain, respiratory, circulatory, endocrine, and reproductive functions").

FAMILY AND MEDICAL LEAVE ACT OF 1993 The **Family and Medical Leave Act of 1993 (FMLA)** aimed to provide employees with job protection in cases of family or medical emergency. The basic thrust of the act is guaranteed leave, and a key element of that guarantee is the right of the employee to return to either the position he or she left when the leave began or to an equivalent position with the same benefits, pay, and other terms and conditions of employment. We will discuss this act in greater detail in Chapter 10 because compensation professionals treat such leave as a legally required benefit.

Prevailing Wage Laws

DAVIS-BACON ACT OF 1931 The **Davis–Bacon Act of 1931** establishes employment standards for construction contractors holding federal government contracts valued at more than $2,000. Covered contracts include highway building, dredging, demolition, and cleaning, as well as painting and decorating public buildings. This act applies to laborers and mechanics who are employed on site. Contractors must pay wages at least equal to the prevailing wage in the local area. The U.S. Secretary of Labor determines prevailing wage rates based on compensation surveys of different areas. In this context, "local" area refers to the general location where work is performed. Cities and counties represent local areas. The "prevailing wage" is the typical hourly wage paid to more than 50 percent of all laborers and mechanics employed in the local area. The act also requires that contractors offer fringe benefits that are equal in scope and value to fringe compensation that prevails in the local area.

WALSH-HEALEY PUBLIC CONTRACTS ACT OF 1936 This act covers contractors and manufacturers who sell supplies, materials, and equipment to the federal government. Its coverage is more extensive than the Davis–Bacon Act. The **Walsh–Healey Public Contracts Act of 1936** applies to both construction and nonconstruction activities. In addition, this act covers all the contractors' employees except office, supervisory, custodial, and maintenance workers who do any work in preparation for the performance of the contract. The minimum contract amount that qualifies for coverage is $10,000 rather than the $2,000 amount under the Davis–Bacon Act of 1931.

The Walsh–Healey Act of 1936 mandates that contractors with federal contracts meet guidelines regarding wages and hours, child labor, convict labor, and hazardous working conditions. Contractors must observe the minimum wage and overtime provisions of the FLSA. In addition, this act prohibits the employment of individuals younger than 16 as well as convicted criminals. Furthermore, this act prohibits contractors from exposing workers to any conditions that violate the **Occupational Safety and Health Act of 1970**. This act was passed to ensure safe and healthful working conditions for working men and women by authorizing enforcement of the standards under the act.

PREPARING FOR EXAMS/QUIZZES

Chapter Summary by Learning Objectives

Learning Objective 2-1. *Discuss the reasons for interindustry wage differentials.* Interindustry wage differentials represent the pattern of pay and benefits associated with characteristics of industries. Interindustry wage differentials can be attributed to many factors, including the industry's product market, the degree of capital intensity, the profitability of the industry, and unionization of the workforce.

Learning Objective 2-2. *Explain the factors that contribute to pay differentials based on occupational characteristics.* An occupation is a group of jobs, found at more than one company, in which a common set of tasks are performed or are related in terms of similar objectives, methodologies, materials, products, worker actions, or worker characteristics. Considerable variation in pay can be explained by the complexity of knowledge, skills, and abilities (KSAs) that define jobs (for example, surgeons and building service workers). Another important factor is the labor market dynamics of the supply and demand for qualified employees.

Learning Objective 2-3. *Summarize the reasons for the occurrence of geographic pay differentials.*

Many factors influence geographic pay differentials. Interindustry wage differentials represent an important factor. Other factors include the union status of the workforce, occupational type, work level, whether firms operate on a profit or not-for-profit basis, skill-level differences between employees who are performing the same job, and cost-of-living.

Learning Objective 2-4. *Discuss the role of labor unions in setting compensation.* Labor unions increase the bargaining power of employees by organizing into a collective to negotiate terms of employment with management. Wages in union settings, on average, are higher than wages in nonunion settings.

Learning Objective 2-5. *Identify and discuss key employment laws pertinent to compensation practice.* There are a variety of laws that were put in place to ensure a balance of power between employees and employers. For the purposes of compensation management, these laws can be categorized in four groups as income continuity, safety, and work hours; pay discrimination; accommodating disabilities and family needs; and prevailing wage laws.

Key Terms

interindustry wage differentials   29

occupation   31

National Labor Relations Act of 1935 (NLRA)   34

collective bargaining agreement   35

spillover effect   35

right-to-work laws   36

federal constitution   37

federal government   37

state governments   37

local governments   37

Great Depression   37

Social Security Act of 1935 (Title IX)   37

workers' compensation   37

Fair Labor Standards Act of 1938 (FLSA)   38

exempt   40

nonexempt   40

FairPay Rules   40

Portal-to-Portal Act of 1947   40

Equal Pay Act of 1963   42

Civil Rights Act of 1964   42

compensable factors   43

Title VII   44

disparate treatment   44

disparate impact   44

Lilly Ledbetter Fair Pay Act   45

Paycheck Fairness Act   45

Bennett Amendment   45

Age Discrimination in Employment Act of 1967 (ADEA)   46

baby boom generation   46

Older Workers Benefit Protection Act (OWBPA)   46

Civil Rights Act of 1991   46

Pregnancy Discrimination Act of 1978 (PDA)   47

Americans with Disabilities Act of 1990 (ADA)   47

Title I   48

Family and Medical Leave Act of 1993 (FMLA)   48

Davis–Bacon Act of 1931   48

Walsh–Healey Public Contracts Act of 1936   49

Occupational Safety and Health Act of 1970   49

Discussion Questions

2-1. Which contextual influence do you believe will pose the greatest challenge to companies' competitiveness? Explain your rationale.

2-2. Should the federal government raise the minimum wage? Explain your answer.

2-3. Do unions make it difficult for companies to attain competitive advantage? Explain your answer.

2-4. What are some pros and cons of adjusting pay based on cost-of-living differences from a company's perspective and an employee's perspective?

2-5. Some people argue that there is too much government intervention, while others say there is not enough. Based on the presentation of laws in this chapter, do you think there is too little or too much government intervention? Explain your answer.

PREPARING FOR MY CAREER

Compensation in Action

It is critical for HR and compensation professionals to have a working knowledge of legislative imperatives and organizational policies designed to oversee certain aspects of compensation and benefits. Together with the legal department, HR has the responsibility to educate line managers and other decision makers in the organization as to what should and should not be done in working with employees on compensation and benefits issues. While ultimately the administration of compensation and benefits will be the responsibility of HR, line managers must have enough awareness to make informed decisions which will both protect the company from certain liabilities as well as ensure the retention and engagement of employees critical to the success of the organization. The most successful line managers are often quite adept at explaining these nuances and are respected by their employees for their concern with the factors that influence the employee experience.

Action checklist for line managers and HR—understanding and applying the legal landscape

HR takes the lead

- Work with the legal department to conduct training sessions designed to educate line managers on some of the most important legislation that will govern employee-related actions (e.g., FLSA, Civil Rights Acts, ADEA, ADA, and FMLA).
- Conduct an audit to identify certain potential for disparate impact; disparate impact training is conducted to ensure that line managers and other decision makers are aware of some of the pitfalls.
- Consider private sector companies that hold government contracts to understand what additional standards may be placed on them because of their relationship with the federal government.
- Provide legal updates to line managers, with legislation changing quickly (particularly in these times). Many law firms provide this type of service via pro bono teleconferences. In-house employment lawyers could also provide these updates.
- Make sure that the legislative necessities create a starting point for establishing company policy and not merely the justification for doing the bare minimum.

Line managers take the lead

- Identify employees who fall into a group addressed specifically by law or company policy (e.g., ADA) which may be a new experience for you to work with as a manager (e.g., in most jobs, you will have more experience working with minority employees than disabled employees).

Cases

Case 1: Take It or Leave It

Both John Johnson and Martin LeBlanc are employed as systems software engineers for a budding social media company with offices in San Jose, California and Atlanta, Georgia. In fact, John and Martin studied at the same university and were in several courses together. Both were hired last year at about the same time, assigned to work in the Atlanta office. John accepted the company's salary offer of $65,000 and Martin negotiated a slightly higher starting salary. Both salaries were competitive with starting pay for software engineers employed in Atlanta.

After six months on the job, Martin's manager, Beth Liu, called him into her office to discuss his early job performance. Beth lavished Martin with praise, citing his technical skills prowess, for taking the initiative to recommend system improvements, and his demonstrated ability to work well with others. Of course, Martin was pleased and he expressed satisfaction in his role and he promised to make more impressive contributions to the company.

Beth said that she was pleased to hear Martin's thoughts and indicated that she looked forward to his further contributions. Then, she went on to say that a software engineer in the San Jose office left the company and asked him to fill the vacancy. Martin was excited to hear the news because he had hoped to work in the San Jose office one day.

Before leaving Beth's office, Martin asked her to confirm his new salary rate. Beth was puzzled by the question because Martin would be assuming the same role in San Jose. She reminded him of this fact and indicated that his salary would remain the same. Following company policy, Martin could expect to receive future pay increases based on performance or promotion into a higher-ranking job. His excitement turned to disappointment and he had second thoughts about moving to San Jose and began wondering whether he should take it or leave it.

Questions:

2-6. Why did Martin become disappointed?

2-7. Do you think that Beth's decision was reasonable? Why or why not?

2-8. What are some of the factors that Beth should consider when transferring employees from Atlanta to San Jose? From San Jose to Atlanta?

Case 2: Ethics Dilemma: Perpetuating the Gender Pay Gap at Safe Security Alarm Systems

Roberto Jiminez, compensation manager for Safe-Security Systems, is scheduled to meet Sally Brown, director of customer satisfaction, at 3 pm today. The purpose for meeting is to discuss the terms of job offers for two candidates who they hope will fill vacancies in the customer service department. One will oversee customer service based on purchasing experience, and the other will oversee post-service (for example, after a routine service check or repair) customer satisfaction. Other than these differences, the required skills, knowledge, abilities, education, and relevant work experience are the same. Roberto and Sally hope that candidate Jill Johnson will oversee post-sales activities and Sean Miller will oversee post-service activities.

In preparation for the meeting, Roberto reviewed annual salary survey information for customer service manager jobs in the local area, revealing a range of $50,000 to $75,000. He also compared Safe-Security's job descriptions and the competitors' job descriptions. Roberto concluded that the job descriptions are comparable and that salary offers of $60,000 were competitive.

Roberto explained his findings and recommendations to Sally who expressed that the market salary information was no longer useful. She already told each candidate that they would receive a salary offer that is 10 percent higher than their current pay. Jill earned $45,000, resulting in a salary offer equaling $49,500 and Sean earned $60,000, resulting in a salary offer of $66,000. Neither Jill nor Sean knew the other's starting pay rate, and both were satisfied with the 10 percent increase.

In an angry tone, Roberto asked Sally whether she considered the fact that both candidates possessed equally impressive credentials or the fact that both would be performing the same job. Sally acknowledged their equal credentials and agreed that the jobs were equal, save for difference in customer satisfaction focus. She added that she had asked Sean and Jill their previous salaries, which led to her decision to offer each a 10 percent higher starting salary. Sally ignored Roberto's anger and stated that the salary offers fit well within the departmental budget and she could not afford to pay anything more. She also went on to say that Jill expressed joy about her offer because she is desperate to leave her current position.

Questions:

2-9. As a compensation professional, what would you do?

2-10. What factor(s) in this ethical dilemma might influence a person to make a less-than-ethical decision?

Crunch the Numbers!

Comparison of Compensation and Benefits Costs in Union and Nonunion Settings

The management of nonunion companies strives to maintain nonunion status to keep employment costs low and to maintain tighter control over the terms of employment. It is against the law for companies to interfere with workers' attempts to unionize; however, companies that want to remain nonunion can adjust employment terms proactively to minimize workers' interest in unionizing. As we discussed in this chapter text, companies may choose to offer higher compensation than they would otherwise in the absence of a union threat. The following table shows hourly compensation costs for union and nonunion settings.

	Total compensation	Wages and salaries	Benefit costs					
			Total	Paid leave	Supplemental pay	Insurance	Retirement and savings	Legally required benefits
			Cost per hour worked					
Union	50.21	28.94	21.27	2.60	1.87	7.06	5.48	4.26
Nonunion	38.04	26.09	11.95	2.58	1.42	3.08	1.71	3.16

Questions:

2-11. As a percent of total compensation costs for union settings, how much do these companies spend to provide (a) wages and salaries and (b) total benefits? As a percent of total compensation costs in nonunion settings, how much do these companies spend to provide (c) wages and salaries and (d) total benefits?

2-12. By what percent are compensation costs in union settings higher than in nonunion settings for (a) wages and salaries and for (b) total benefits? If nonunion companies want to reduce the gap by 10 percent, how much will they pay to provide (c) paid leave, (d) supplemental pay, (e) insurance, and (f) retirement and savings benefits?

2-13. If costs were to increase by 5 percent in union settings, what would the new costs be for (a) wages and salaries and (b) total benefits? To maintain the 10 percent reduction (question 2-12), how much would nonunion companies spend on (c) wages and salaries and (d) total benefits?

Working Together: Team Exercise

In small groups of three or four, come up with specific answers to the following questions. Talk through your perspectives and come up with a team response. Be prepared to share your ideas with the class.

As a group, conduct a bit of research online about one of the topics discussed in this chapter. Look for information about the topic that was not mentioned in the chapter. To guide your research, if helpful, think about how your topic relates to an experience you or a close friend or family member has had in the workplace.

Questions:

2-14. What information in your research did you find most surprising? Explain.

2-15. What information in your research did you find least surprising? Explain.

Endnotes

1. Dawn D. Bennett-Alexander and Laura P. Hartman, *Employment Law for Business* (8th ed.,) (Burr Ridge, IL: McGraw-Hill/Irwin, 2014): 4.

2. Jane Osburn, "Interindustry Wage Differentials: Patterns and Possible Sources," *Monthly Labor Review*, (February, 2000): 34–46; Alan B. Krueger and Lawrence H. Summers, "Reflections on Inter-industry Wage Structure," in K. Lang & J. S. Leonard (Eds.), *Unemployment and the Structure of the Labor Market* (New York, NY: Basil Blackwell, 1987): 14–17.

3. U.S. Bureau of Labor Statistics, May 2016 National Industry-Specific Occupational Employment and Wage Estimates, (2018), accessed January 8, 2018, http://www.bls/oes.gov.

4. Frank Ahrens, "Hyundai Battles Striking Workers as Global Ambitions Surge," *Forbes* (October 5, 2016), accessed January 8, 2018, http://www.forbes.com.

5. U.S. Department of Labor, *The Revised Handbook for Analyzing Jobs* (Washington, DC: U.S. Government Printing Office, 1991)

6. U.S. Bureau of Labor Statistics, *Occupational Outlook Handbook*, Physicians and Surgeons, accessed January 8, 2018, http://www.bls.gov/ooh/healthcare/physicians-and-surgeons.htm.

7. U.S. Bureau of Labor Statistics, *Occupational Employment Statistics*, Data Retrieval, accessed January 8, 2018, http://data.bls.gov/oes/.

8. U.S. Bureau of Labor Statistics, *Occupational Outlook Handbook*, Secretaries and Administrative Assistants, accessed January 8, 2018, http://www.bls.gov/ooh/office-and-administrative-support/secretaries-and-administrative-assistants.htm.

9. U.S. Bureau of Labor Statistics, *Occupational Employment Statistics*, Data Retrieval, accessed January 8, 2018, http://data.bls.gov/oes/.

10. U.S. Bureau of Labor Statistics, *Occupational Outlook Handbook*, Pharmacists, accessed January 8, 2018, http://www.bls.gov/ooh/healthcare/pharmacists.htm and U.S. Bureau of Labor Statistics, *Occupational Outlook Handbook*, Pharmacy Technicians, accessed January 8, 2018, http://www.bls.gov/ooh/healthcare/pharmacy-technicians.htm.

11. U.S. Bureau of Labor Statistics, *Occupational Employment Statistics*, Data Retrieval, accessed January 8, 2018, http://data.bls.gov/oes/.

12. U.S. Bureau of Labor Statistics, *Occupational Outlook Handbook*, Information Security Analysts, accessed January 8, 2018, http://www.bls.gov/ooh/computer-and-information-technology/information-security-analysts.htm.

13. Angus Loten and Steven Norton, "The Government Needs More Cyber Talent—But So Does Everyone Else," *The Wall Street Journal* (September 27, 2017), accessed January 15, 2018, http://www.wsj.com.

14. Ibid.

15. Jon Ostrower, "The U.S. Will Face a Staggering Shortage of Pilots," *Money CNN* (July 31, 2017), accessed January 15, 2018, http://www.money.cnn.com.

16. "The Coming U.S. Pilot Shortage Is Real," *Aviation Week* online (February 16, 2015), accessed January 8, 2018, http://www.aviationweek.com.

17. Brian Prentice and Philippe Gouel, "Pilot Shortage Threatens to Slow U.S. Airline Growth," *Forbes* (January 28, 2016), accessed January 9, 2018, http://www.forbes.com.

18. Mary Schlangenstein and Michael Sasso, "Shrinking Pool of Future Pilots Keeps Major Airlines on Edge," *Bloomberg News* online (June 29, 2016), accessed January 9, 2018, http://www.bloomberg.com.

19. Ibid.

20. Sarah Chaney, "Less-Educated Workers See Biggest Weekly Pay Bumps," *The Wall Street Journal* (January 9, 2018), accessed March 16, 2018, http://www.wsj.com.

21. Matthew Boyle, "Target Will Raise Hourly Wage to $11 to Counter Wal-Mart", *Bloomberg* (September 25, 2017), accessed January 8, 2018, http://www.bloomberg.com.

22. Abha Bhattarai, "Walmart to Raise Starting Hourly Wage to $11, Offer Paid Parental Leave," *The Wall Street Journal* (January 11, 2018), accessed January 12, 2018, http://www.wsj.com.

23. Sarah Chaney, "Want Better Pay Than the Bosses? Get a Job in Elevator Repair," *The Wall Street Journal* (February 14, 2018), accessed March 16, 2018, http://www.wsj.com.

24. Russell Gold, "Utility Jobs Shrink as New Power Plants Need Fewer Workers," *The Wall Street Journal* (January 15, 2018), accessed January 15, 2018, http://www.wsj.com.

25. U.S. Bureau of Labor Statistics, *Occupational Pay Comparisons among Metropolitan Areas* (USDL: 09-0843), accessed January 8, 2018, http://www.bls.gov.

26. Ibid.

27. U.S. Bureau of Labor Statistics, *National Compensation Survey – Wages* (data retrieval), accessed January 8, 2018, http://www.bls.gov/ncs/ocs/data.htm.

28. U.S. Bureau of Labor Statistics, *Occupational Pay Comparisons among Metropolitan Areas* (USDL: 09-0843), accessed January 8, 2018, http://www.bls.gov.

29. National Association of Realtors, *Median Price of Existing Single-family Homes for Metropolitan Areas*, (2017), accessed January 8, 2018, https://www.nar.realtor/sites/default/files/documents/metro-home-prices-q3-2017-single-family-2017-11-02.pdf.

30. Loren M. Solnick, "The Effect of the Blue Collar Unions on White Collar Wages and Benefits," *Industrial and Labor Relations Review*, 38, no. 2 (1985): 23–35, https://doi.org/10.1177/001979398503800206.

31. U.S. Bureau of Labor Statistics, *Union Members—2017*. (USDL 18-0080), (2018), accessed March 15, 2018, http://www.bls.gov.

32. Jake Rosenfeld, Patrick Denice, and Jennifer Laird, *Union Decline Lowers Wages of Nonunion Workers* (August 30, 2016), Economic Policy Institute, accessed January 9, 2018, http://www.epi.org/112811.

33. Gerald Mayer, *Union Membership Trends in the United States*, (Washington, DC: Congressional Research Service, 2004).

34. U.S. Bureau of Labor Statistics, *Union Members—2017*. (USDL 18-0080) (2018), accessed March 15, 2018, http://www.bls.gov.

35. Sean Higgins, "Wages Lag but Unemployment Falls in Right-to-Work States," *Washington Examiner* (April 17, 2017), accessed January 15, 2018, http://www.washingtonexaminer.com.

36. Elise Gould and Will Kimball, *"Right-to-work" States Still Have Lower Wages* (August 22, 2015), accessed January 9, 2018, https://www.epi.org/files/pdf/82934.pdf.

37. U.S. Bureau of Labor Statistics, *Union Members—2017*, USDL 18-0080 (2017), accessed January 21, 2018, http://www.bls.gov, and, historical database of union membership.

38. U.S. Department of Labor, *Minimum Wage Laws in the States – January 1, 2018*, (2018), accessed January 15, 2018, https://www.dol.gov/whd/minwage/mw-consolidated.htm.

39. New York State Department of Labor, *Minimum Wage for Fast Food Workers: December 31, 2017 through December 30, 2018*, (2018), accessed January 9, 2018, https://labor.ny.gov/formsdocs/factsheets/pdfs/p716.pdf.

40. *Andres v. DuBois*, 888 F. Supp. 213 (D.C. Mass 1995), 2 WH Cases 2d 1297 (1995).

41. Annalyn Kurtz, "Subway Leads Fast Food Industry in Underpaying Workers," *CNNMoney* (May 1, 2014), accessed February 15, 2015, http://cnnmoney.com.

42. *Integrity Staffing Solutions, Inc. v. Busk et al.*, No. 13-433 (U.S. Supreme Court, December 9, 2014).

43. S. Rep. No. 176, 88th Congress, 1st Session, 1 (1963).

44. *EEOC v. Madison Community Unit School District No. 12*, 818 F. 2d 577 (7th Cir., 1987).

45. U.S. Equal Employment Opportunity Commission, *Charge Statistics (Charges Filed with the EEOC): FY 1997 through FY 2017*, accessed July 4, 2018, http://www.eeoc.gov.

46. *Ledbetter v. Goodyear Tire & Rubber Co.*, No. 05–1074 (U.S. Supreme Court, May 29, 2007).

47. U.S. Department of Commerce, (2004–2005), *Statistical Abstracts of the United States* (124th ed.), U.S. Department of Census (May 2001), Profile of general demographic statistics, Table DP–1, accessed February 12, 2011, http://www.census.gov.

48. Older Workers Benefit Protection Act of 1990, Pub. L. No.PL 101-433.

49. *Atonio v. Wards Cove Packing Co.*, 490 U.S. 642, 49 FEP Cases 1519 (1989).

50. *Lorance v. AT&T Technologies*, 49 FEP Cases 1656 (1989).

51. *Boureslan v. Aramco*, 499 U.S. 244, 55 FEP Cases 449 (1991).

52. Bureau of National Affairs, "Americans with Disabilities Act of 1990: Text and Analysis," *Labor Relations Reporter*, Vol. 134, No. 3, (Washington, DC: Author, 1990).

BASES FOR PAY

Where We Are Now:

PART I, SETTING THE STAGE FOR STRATEGIC COMPENSATION, explained what compensation is, strategic compensation concepts, compensation professionals' goals, employment laws that influence compensation practices, and the roles of unions and market forces in influencing compensation practices. Now, we turn to the methods for determining employee pay.

In **PART II, WE WILL COVER**

CHAPTER 3 TRADITIONAL BASES FOR PAY

CHAPTER 4 INCENTIVE PAY

CHAPTER 5 PERSON-FOCUSED PAY

3 Traditional Bases for Pay
Seniority and Merit

Learning Objectives

When you finish studying this chapter, you should be able to:

3-1. Describe seniority and longevity pay practices.

3-2. Explain the merit pay approach to compensation.

3-3. Explore a variety of performance appraisal methods.

3-4. Discuss how compensation professionals can strengthen the pay-for-performance link.

3-5. Summarize the possible limitations of merit pay programs.

For decades, companies have awarded raises to base pay according to employees' seniority or job performance. Many companies, such as IBM, tended to pay employees according to performance, but the system became one of entitlements. Changes in the global marketplace forced many companies to reconsider their approach to employee compensation. Fierce global competition requires that employees perform their jobs better than ever before to enable companies to offer the best possible products and services at the lowest cost. As a solution, many companies use compensation programs that emphasize rewards according to performance attainment. Still, traditional seniority and longevity pay plans, which do not tie compensation to performance, remain in use in particular settings, which we will explore in this chapter.

In this chapter, we will consider the traditional seniority and longevity approaches to compensating employees. We will then turn our attention to merit pay, which is a widely used form of performance-based pay in U.S. companies. In Chapter 4, we will take up a variety of incentive programs that also reward pay for performance.

SENIORITY AND LONGEVITY PAY

3-1. Describe seniority and longevity pay practices.

Seniority pay and **longevity pay** systems reward employees with periodic additions to base pay according to employees' length of service in performing their jobs. These pay plans *assume* that employees become more valuable to companies with time and that valued employees will leave if they do not have a clear idea that their salaries will progress over time.[1] This rationale comes from **human capital theory**,[2] which states that employees' knowledge and skills generate productive capital known as human capital. Employees can develop such knowledge and skills from formal education and training, including on-the-job experience. Over time, employees presumably refine existing skills or acquire new ones that enable them to work more productively. Thus, seniority pay rewards employees for acquiring and refining their skills as indexed by seniority.

Historical Overview

A quick look back into U.S. labor relations history can shed light on the adoption of seniority pay in many companies. President Franklin D. Roosevelt advocated policies designed to improve workers' economic status in response to the severely depressed economic conditions that had started in 1929. Congress instituted the National Labor Relations Act (NLRA) in 1935 to protect workers' rights, predicated on a fundamental, but limited, conflict of interest between workers and employers. President Roosevelt and other leaders felt that companies needed to be regulated to establish an appropriate balance of power between the parties. The NLRA established a collective bargaining system nationwide to accommodate employers' and employees' partially conflicting and partially shared goals.

Collective bargaining led to **job control unionism**,[3] in which collective bargaining units negotiate formal contracts with employees and provide quasi-judicial grievance procedures to adjudicate disputes between union members and employers. Union shops establish workers' rights and obligations and participate in describing and delineating jobs. In unionized workplaces, terms of collective bargaining agreements may determine the specific type of seniority system used, whereas seniority tends to be the deciding factor in nearly all job scheduling, transfer, layoff, compensation, and promotion decisions. Moreover, seniority may become a principal criterion for selecting one employee over another for transfer or promotion. Table 3-1 illustrates the rules for a seniority pay program contained in a collective bargaining agreement between the Board of Trustees of the University of Illinois and Local 698 of the American Federation of State, County, and Municipal Employees. That is, Table 3-1 shows the actual rates for job classification and seniority level.

Political pressures probably drive the prevalence of public sector seniority pay. Seniority-based pay systems essentially provide automatic pay increases. Performance assessments tend to be subjective rather than objective because accurate job performance measurements are very difficult to obtain. In contrast, employees' seniority is easily indexed because time on the job is a relatively straightforward and concrete concept. Implementing a system that specifies the amount of pay raise an employee will receive according to his or her seniority is automatic. Politically, "automatic" pay adjustments protect public sector employees from the quirks of election-year politics.[4] In addition, the federal, state, and local governments can avoid direct responsibility for pay raises so employees can receive fair pay without political objections.

TABLE 3-1 Hourly Wage Rates by Seniority Level

Classification Title	Start ($)	13 Months ($)	25 Months ($)	37 Months ($)
Staff Nurse I	23.19	24.47	25.77	27.03
Nursing Assistant	11.50	11.77	12.18	12.54
Medical Assistant	16.95	17.82	18.67	18.67
Medical Technologist	20.42	21.86	23.29	24.73

Source: Based on Agreement between the Board of Trustees of the University of Illinois and Local 698 of the American Federation of State, County, and Municipal Employees, AFL-CIO.

Who Participates?

Today, most unionized private sector and public sector organizations continue to base salary on seniority or length of employee service, though the number of these workplaces is steadily declining as described in Chapter 2. In 2017, the overall unionization rate was 10.7 percent of the civilian labor force with a 6.5 percent representation rate in the private sector and 34.4 percent rate in the public sector.[5] Members of union-bargaining units whose contracts include seniority provisions, usually rank-and-file as well as clerical workers, receive automatic raises based on the number of years they have been with the company. In the public sector, most administrative, professional, and even managerial employees receive such automatic pay raises. The use of seniority pay is more common in the public sector given the substantially higher unionization rate than in the private sector.

☞ FYI

The difference between union and nonunion weekly pay is substantial for the workforce overall and by sex, race, and ethnicity, with Asians earning the most and Hispanic/Latinos earning the least:

- Overall: $1,028 vs. $829 (union vs. nonunion)
- Men: $1,094 vs. $914
- Women: $954 vs. $746
- White: $1,076 vs. $829
- Black: $813 vs. $659
- Asian: $1,126 vs. $1,034
- Hispanic/Latino: $880 vs. $629[6]

Effectiveness of Seniority Pay Systems

Virtually no systematic research has demonstrated these pay plans' effectiveness nor is there any documentation regarding their prevalence in the private sector. Seniority or longevity pay plans are likely to disappear from for-profit companies in increasingly competitive markets. Such external influences as increased global competition, rapid technological advancement, and skill deficits of new and current members of the workforce necessitate a strategic orientation toward compensation. These influences will probably force companies to establish compensation tactics that reward their employees for learning job-relevant knowledge and skills and for making tangible contributions toward companies' quests for competitive advantage. Seniority pay meets neither goal.

Public sector organizations had, until the 1990s, faced less pressure to change these systems because they exist to serve the public rather than make profits. For example, the Internal Revenue Service (IRS) is responsible for collecting taxes from U.S. citizens. Paying taxes to the federal government is an obligation of virtually all U.S. citizens. The amount of taxes each citizen pays is based on established tax codes. The IRS is not in the business of finding new customers to pay taxes. It does not compete against any other businesses for taxpayers.

The federal government, however, has now raised questions about the effectiveness of its seniority pay system for white-collar workers—the General Schedule—because most employees receive raises regardless of how well they perform. Questions about the effectiveness of its seniority pay system are based on how the world of work has dramatically changed since the system's inception in 1949. The federal government has extensively considered the strategic importance of moving beyond seniority-based pay by studying the experience of private sector companies, though it has not made noteworthy modifications to its current pay system.[7]

Design of Seniority Pay and Longevity Pay Plans

Although seniority pay and longevity pay are similar, there are some important distinctions between them. The object of seniority pay is to reward job tenure or employees' time as members of a company explicitly through permanent increases to base salary. Employees begin

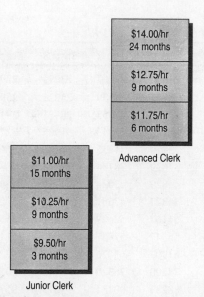

FIGURE 3-1 A Sample Seniority Policy for Junior and Advanced Clerk Jobs

their employment at the starting pay rate established for the particular jobs. At specified time intervals, which can be as short as three months and as long as three years, employees receive designated pay increases. These pay increases are permanent additions to current pay levels. Over time, employees will reach the maximum pay rate for their jobs. Companies expect that most employees will earn promotions into higher-paying jobs that have seniority pay schedules. Figure 3-1 illustrates a seniority pay policy for a junior clerk job and an advanced clerk job. Pay rates are associated with seniority. When employees reach the top pay rate for the junior clerk position, they are presumably qualified to assume the duties of the advanced clerk position.

If employees choose to remain in their job classifications or are not qualified to advance to the next level, longevity pay plans reward employees who have reached pay range maximums and who are not likely to move into higher grades. Longevity pay plans are used to help reward long-service employees for their continued contributions, without regularly paying more than the job is worth based on knowledge, skills, abilities, and other job-related requirements.

Most federal government employees are subject to longevity pay via the **General Schedule (GS)**, which is shown in Table 3-2. The General Schedule classifies federal government jobs into 15 classifications (GS-1 through GS-15) based on such factors as skill, education, and experience levels. The GS-1 category includes the lowest-level jobs and GS-15 includes the highest-level jobs. In addition, jobs that require high levels of specialized education (e.g., a physicist), influence public policy significantly (e.g., law judges), or require executive decision making are classified (the top executive in a U.S. government agency such as the U.S. Department of Labor) in separate categories: Senior Level (SL), Scientific and Professional (SP) positions, and the Senior Executive Service (SES).

The government typically increases all pay amounts annually to adjust for inflation. The 2018 schedule represents a 1.4 percent increase over 2017 rates. The federal government relies on a base schedule, shown in Table 3-2, to compensate employees in most locations. Additional schedules are published for particular geographic areas where the cost of living differs substantially from the national average. Examples include the greater Boston and Los Angeles areas. Table 3-2 shows that the annual salary for a job in Grade 15, Step 1 is $105,123. In Boston, the salary for the same job is $134,011, to reflect a 27.4 percent higher cost-of-living in Boston.

TABLE 3-2 Salary Table 2018-GS (Annual Rates by Grade and Step)

Grade	Step 1	Step 2	Step 3	Step 4	Step 5	Step 6	Step 7	Step 8	Step 9	Step 10	WGI
1	18785	19414	20039	20660	21285	21650	22267	22891	22915	23502	VARIES
2	21121	21624	22323	22915	23175	23857	24539	25221	25903	26585	VARIES
3	23045	23813	24581	25349	26117	26885	27653	28421	29189	29957	768
4	25871	26733	27595	28457	29319	30181	31043	31905	32767	33629	862
5	28945	29910	30875	31840	32805	33770	34735	35700	36665	37630	965
6	32264	33339	34414	35489	36564	37639	38714	39789	40864	41939	1075
7	35854	37049	38244	39439	40634	41829	43024	44219	45414	46609	1195
8	39707	41031	42355	43679	45003	46327	47651	48975	50299	51623	1324
9	43857	45319	46781	48243	49705	51167	52629	54091	55553	57015	1462
10	48297	49907	51517	53127	54737	56347	57957	59567	61177	62787	1610
11	53062	54831	56600	58369	60138	61907	63676	65445	67214	68983	1769
12	63600	65720	67840	69960	72080	74200	76320	78440	80560	82680	2120
13	75628	78149	80670	83191	85712	88233	90754	93275	95796	98317	2521
14	89370	92349	95328	98307	101286	104265	107244	110223	113202	116181	2979
15	105123	108627	112131	115635	119139	122643	126147	129651	133155	136659	3504

Source: U.S. Office of Personnel Management. Available: *https://www.opm.gov/policy-data-oversight/pay-leave/salaries-wages/salary-tables/18Tables/html/GS.aspx*, accessed January 17, 2018.

Employees are eligible for ten within-grade step pay increases, each increase amounts to about 3 percent of the employee's salary. Progression through the steps is based on an assumption that their job performance is acceptable. The increase from step to step equals the within-grade increase (WGI) amount. The waiting periods within steps are:

- Steps 1–3: 1 year
- Steps 4–6: 2 years
- Steps 7–9: 3 years

☞ FYI

At present, it takes employees 18 years to progress from Step 1 to Step 10 if they remain within a single GS grade.

Position descriptions usually indicate a series of GS ranges for which the job may be classified. For example, a Human Resources Assistant position[8] could fit within GS ranges 5 through 7. Determination of the grade depends upon the qualification level of the newly hired employee. For this position, an individual with the minimum acceptable qualifications would be placed in GS-5. An individual with one or more years of specialized experience would be placed in GS-6 if the experience were at least equivalent to GS-5 requirements. Placement in GS-7 would require at least one year of specialized experience fitting with GS-6 requirements. Employees could be eligible for promotions to classifications that are higher than advertised. For this job, movement to GS-8 would be based on competition under merit system principles, to be discussed in the next section. The pay increase associated with any promotion would typically be equal to at least two steps at the GS grade immediately before promotion. For this human resources assistant job, an employee whose classification is GS-7 (let's assume Step 6) could be promoted to GS-8 based on merit. Pay would increase from \$41,829 to at least \$44,219 based on the following calculation: (\$41,829 + [\$1,195 × 2 steps]) where \$1,195 is the WGI for Grade 7.

Advantages of Seniority Pay

Seniority pay offers a number of advantages to both employees and employers. Employees are likely to perceive they are treated fairly because they earn pay increases according to seniority, which is an objective standard. Seniority stands in contrast to subjective standards based on supervisory judgment. The inherent objectivity of seniority pay systems should lead to greater cooperation among coworkers.

Seniority pay offers two key advantages to employers. First, seniority pay facilitates the administration of pay programs. Pay increase amounts are set in advance, and employers award raises according to a pay schedule, much like the federal government's GS. A second advantage is that employers are less likely to offend some employees by showing favoritism to others because seniority is an objective basis for making awards. The absence of favoritism should enable supervisors and managers effectively to motivate employees to perform their jobs even in the absence of a formal performance appraisal system.

Fitting Seniority Pay with Competitive Strategies

Seniority pay does not necessarily fit well with the imperatives of competitive strategies because employees can count on receiving the same pay raises for average and exemplary performance, and this fact represents the greatest disadvantage of seniority pay systems. Employees who make significant contributions in the workplace receive the same pay increases as coworkers who make modest contributions. In addition, employees receive pay raises without regard to whether companies are meeting their competitive objectives. Employees clearly do not have any incentives to actively improve their skills or to take risks on the job because they receive pay raises regardless of any initiative they show. Finally, because seniority increases become a recurring part of base pay, the growing costs can become burdensome to employers. Besides, do pay raises earned years in the past continue to benefit the employer? Probably not. This especially would be the case if the employee were once a stellar performer and regressed to just an acceptable performer.

So, in light of increased external pressures on companies to promote productivity and product quality, will seniority or longevity pay be gradually phased out? With the exception of companies that are shielded from competitive pressures, it is likely that companies that intend to remain competitive will set aside seniority pay practices. Although seniority pay plans reflect employees' increased worth, they measure such contributions indirectly rather than based on tangible contributions or the successful acquisition of job-related knowledge or skills. Now more than ever, companies need to be accountable to shareholders, which will require direct measurement of employee job performance.

To illustrate the incompatibility of seniority pay structures with the attainment of competitive strategy further, Toyota, a manufacturer of automobiles, is reconsidering its use of seniority-based wage system in favor of a performance-based pay system. Traditional Japanese companies defined *seniority* as employee age, leaving substantial pay gaps between younger and older employees. These gaps are making it difficult to attract younger talent to the company.[9] Despite Toyota's worldwide reputation as a manufacturer of high-quality automobiles, company management continually adopts employment practices that encourage even better-quality products. Performance-based pay fits with Toyota's mission. Other Japanese companies, Hitachi, Panasonic, and Sony, are following suit.[10]

MERIT PAY

3-2. Explain the merit pay approach to compensation.

Merit pay programs assume that employees' compensation over time should be determined, at least in part, by differences in job performance.[11] Employees earn permanent merit increases based on their performance. The increases reward excellent effort or results, motivate future performance, and help employers retain valued employees. Merit increases are usually expressed as a percentage of hourly wages for nonexempt employees and as a percentage of annual salaries for exempt employees. In 2017, employees earned average merit increases of 3.0 percent across all industries, and the projected average increase for 2018 was 3.1 percent.[12] This average increase did not vary significantly across employee groups (exempt vs. nonexempt, nonunion vs. union); however, the average raise differed based on employee performance. High performers earned an average pay increase of 4.5 percent while average performers earned a 2.6 percent increase.[13] It's worth noting that the size of the average pay raise is much smaller after accounting for cost-of-living increases (higher prices). Based on a recent 2 percent annual increase in cost-of-living, a 3 percent raise, on average, increases spending power by only 1 percent (3 percent raise less 2 percent cost-of-living increase).[14]

Who Participates?

Merit pay is one of the most commonly used compensation methods in the United States. In 2017, a survey of *WorldatWork* members revealed that 65 percent of companies indicated that they use a rating system with a performance score that is tied to pay increases. The rates were 72 percent and 65 percent in 2014 and 2010, respectively.[15] Merit pay programs occur most often in the private for-profit sector of the economy rather than in such public sector organizations as local and state governments.

Exploring the Elements of Merit Pay

Managers rely on objective as well as subjective performance indicators to determine whether an employee will receive a merit increase and the amount of increase warranted. As a rule, supervisors give merit increases to employees based on subjective appraisal of employees' performance.[16] Supervisors periodically review individual employee performance to evaluate how well each worker is accomplishing assigned duties relative to established standards and goals. Thus, as we will discuss later in this chapter, accurate performance appraisals are key to effective merit pay programs.

For merit pay programs to succeed, employees must know that their efforts in meeting production quotas or quality standards will lead to pay raises. Job requirements must be realistic, and employees must have the skills and abilities to meet job goals. Moreover, employees must perceive a strong relationship between attaining performance standards and receiving pay increases.

Furthermore, companies that use merit programs must ensure that the funds needed to fulfill these promises to compensate employees are available. For now, we assume that adequate funding for merit pay programs is in place. We will address the ramifications of insufficient budgets for funding merit pay programs in Chapter 8.

Finally, companies should make permanent adjustments to base pay according to changes in the cost of living or inflation before awarding merit pay raises. Then, permanent merit pay raises should always reward employee performance rather than represent adjustments for inflation. Inflation represents rises in the cost of consumer goods and services (e.g., food and health care) that boost the overall cost of living. Over time, inflation erodes the purchasing power of the dollar. You've no doubt heard the comment, "It's harder to stretch a dollar these days." Employees are concerned about how well merit increases raise purchasing power. Compensation professionals attempt to minimize negative inflationary effects by making permanent increases to base pay, known as cost-of-living adjustments. For now, let's assume that inflation is not an issue. (As a side note, this principle also applies to seniority pay. Pay increases should reflect additional seniority after making specific adjustments for inflation.)

Although fairly common, merit pay systems are not appropriate for all companies. Compensation professionals should consider two factors—commitment from top management and the design of jobs—before endorsing the use of merit pay systems. Top management must be willing to reward employees' job performances with meaningful pay differentials that match employee performance differentials. Companies ideally should grant sufficiently large pay increases to reward employees for exemplary job performance and to encourage similar expectations about future good work.

The amount of a merit pay increase should reflect prior job performance levels and motivate employees toward striving for exemplary performance. The pay raise amount should be meaningful to employees. The concept of a **just-meaningful pay increase** refers to the minimum pay increase that employees will see as making a meaningful change in compensation.[17] The basic premise of this concept is that a trivial pay increase for average or better employees is not likely to reinforce their performance or to motivate enhanced future performance. In addition to top management's commitment to merit pay programs, HR professionals must design jobs explicitly enough that employees' performance can be measured accurately. Merit programs are most appropriate when employees have control over their performance and when conditions outside employees' control do not substantially affect their performance. Conditions beyond employees' control that are likely to limit job performance vary by the type of job. For sales professionals, recessionary economic spells generally lead consumers to limit spending on new purchases because they anticipate the possibility of layoffs. Sales professionals certainly do not create recessionary periods nor can they allay consumers' fears about the future. For production workers, regular equipment breakdowns will lead to lower output.

Furthermore, there must be explicit performance standards that specify the procedures or outcomes against which employees' job performance can be clearly evaluated. At Pratt & Whitney, HR professionals and employees worked together to rewrite job descriptions. The purpose was to define and put into writing the major duties of a job and to specify written performance standards for each duty to ensure that the job requirements provided a useful measurement standard for evaluation. The main performance standards included such factors as quality, quantity, and timeliness of work.

Table 3-3 displays a job description for a Transportation Security Officer (TSO) in the U.S. Department of Homeland Security. The description lists the activities the jobholder performs and qualifications necessary to perform the job at an acceptable level. For instance, a successful candidate must be able to operate various screening equipment and technology to identify dangerous objects in baggage.

PERFORMANCE APPRAISAL

Effective performance appraisals drive effective merit pay programs. Merit pay systems require specific performance appraisal approaches, as noted previously. Administering successful merit pay programs depends as much on supervisors' appraisal approaches as it does on the professionals' skills in designing and implementing such plans. The frequency of providing employees with performance feedback is critically important. The following Watch It! video describes The Weather Channel's performance appraisal process in which appraisals are recommended to be done on an ongoing, continual basis so that an employee always knows where he or she stands as far as what is expected and how well he or she is currently performing. This way, the employee can look forward to performance reviews in stead of dreading them; they will be an official confirmation of all of the progress that the employee has been making under the ongoing relationship of appraisal and feedback with the employee's manager. Many other companies have followed suit, including VMware Inc., Wayfair Inc., and the Boston Consulting Group, where they particularly instill the importance of celebrating small performance victories.[18]

3-3. Explore a variety of performance appraisal methods.

TABLE 3-3 Transportation Security Officer (TSO)

Job: Transportation Security Officer (TSO)

Agency/Department: Department of Homeland Security

Location: Denver, CO

Job Summary:

Transportation Security Officers (TSOs) provide security and protection of air travelers, airports, and aircraft in a courteous and professional manner.

Key Job Duties:

• Operating various screening equipment and technology to identify dangerous objects in baggage, cargo, and on passengers, and preventing those objects from being transported onto aircraft.

• Performing searches and screening, which may include physical interaction with passengers (e.g., pat-downs, search of property, etc.), conducting bag searches and lifting/carrying bags, bins, and property weighing up to 50 lbs.

• Controlling terminal entry and exit points.

• Interacting with the public, giving directions, and responding to inquiries.

• Maintaining focus and awareness while working in a stressful environment which includes noise from alarms, machinery, and people; crowd distractions; time pressure; and disruptive and angry passengers, in order to preserve the professional ability to identify and locate potentially life-threatening or mass destruction devices, and to make effective decisions in both crisis and routine situations.

• Engaging in continuous development of critical thinking skills, necessary to mitigate actual and potential security threats, by identifying, evaluating, and applying appropriate situational options and approaches. This may include application of risk-based security screening protocols that vary based on program requirements.

• Retaining and implementing knowledge of all applicable Standard Operating Procedures, demonstrating responsible and dependable behavior, and being open to change and adapting to new information or unexpected obstacles.

Qualifications Required:

Applicants must meet these qualifications in order to be further evaluated in the TSO hiring process:

• Have a high school diploma, General Educational Development (GED), High School Equivalency Test (HiSET), or Test Assessing Secondary Completion (TASC) credential **OR** at least one year of full-time work experience in the security industry, aviation screening, or as an x-ray technician.

• Be proficient in the English language (i.e., able to read, write, speak, and comprehend).

Source: Department of Homeland Security, Transportation Security Administration. Transportation Security Officer (TSO) (Announcement number DEN-F09-P001). Available: *https://www.usajobs.gov/GetJob/ViewDetails/404038500*, accessed January 17, 2018.

 FYI

In a survey commissioned by the Society for Human Resource Management:

• Nine out of ten companies reported using annual or semiannual performance reviews.
• Only three out of ten expressed that they conducted them well.[19]

Types of Performance Appraisal Plans

Performance appraisal methods fall into four broad categories:

- Trait systems
- Comparison systems
- Behavioral systems
- Goal-oriented systems

The four kinds of performance appraisal methods are next described in order.

TRAIT SYSTEMS Trait systems ask raters to evaluate each employee's traits or characteristics (e.g., quality of work, quantity of work, appearance, dependability, cooperation, initiative, judgment, leadership responsibility, decision-making ability, or creativity). Appraisals are typically scored using descriptors ranging from unsatisfactory to outstanding. Table 3-4 contains an illustration of a trait method of performance appraisal.

Trait systems are easy to construct, use, and apply to a wide range of jobs. They are also easy to quantify for merit pay purposes. Trait systems are increasingly becoming common in companies that focus on the quality of interactions with customers. For example, Leon Leonwood Bean, founder of L.L.Bean, made customer service the foundation of his business from its beginning in 1912. That focus translates into employee traits of dependability, friendliness, trustworthiness, and honesty.[20]

The trait approach does have limitations. First, trait systems are highly subjective[21] because they are based on the assumption that every supervisor's perception of a given trait is the same. For example, the trait "quality of work" may be defined by one supervisor as "the extent to which an employee's performance is free of errors." To another supervisor, quality of work might mean "the extent to which an employee's performance is thorough." Human resource professionals and supervisors can avoid this problem by working together in advance to specify the definition of traits clearly.

Another drawback is that systems rate individuals on subjective personality factors rather than on objective job performance data. Essentially, trait assessment focuses attention on employees rather than on job performance. Employees may simply become defensive rather than trying to understand the role that the particular trait plays in shaping their job performance and then taking corrective actions.

COMPARISON SYSTEMS Comparison systems evaluate a given employee's performance against that of other employees. Employees are ranked from the best performer to the poorest performer. In simplest form, supervisors rank each employee and establish a performance

TABLE 3-4 A Trait-Oriented Performance Appraisal Rating Form

Employee's Name:	Employee's Position:
Supervisor's Name:	Review Period:

Instructions: For each of the following traits, circle the phrase that best represents the employee.

1. Diligence

a. outstanding	b. above average	c. average	d. below average	e. poor

2. Cooperation with others

a. outstanding	b. above average	c. average	d. below average	e. poor

3. Communication skills

a. outstanding	b. above average	c. average	d. below average	e. poor

4. Leadership

a. outstanding	b. above average	c. average	d. below average	e. poor

5. Decisiveness

a. outstanding	b. above average	c. average	d. below average	e. poor

hierarchy such that the employee with the best performance receives the highest ranking. Employees may be ranked on overall performance or on various traits.

An alternative approach, called a **forced distribution** performance appraisal, assigns employees to groups that represent the entire range of performance. For example, three categories that might be used are best performers, moderate performers, and poor performers. A forced distribution approach, in which the rater must place a specific number of employees into each of the performance groups, can be used with this method. Table 3-5 displays a forced distribution rating form for an animal keeper job with five performance categories.

Many companies use forced distribution approaches to minimize the tendency for supervisors to rate most employees as excellent performers. This tendency usually arises out of supervisors' self-promotion motives. Supervisors often provide positive performance ratings to most of their employees because they do not want to alienate them. After all, their performance as supervisors depends largely on how well their employees perform their jobs.

Although used by some prestigious firms, the forced distribution system appears to be unpopular with many managers.[22] Some believe it fosters cutthroat competition, paranoia, and general ill will, and destroys employee loyalty.[23] For example, David Auerback, a former Microsoft employee, stated that this type of appraisal system had employees feeling helpless and "encouraged people to backstab their coworkers."[24] Many believe that a "rank-and-yank" system such as forced distribution is not compatible when a company encourages teamwork. In addition, critics of forced distribution contend that they compel managers to penalize a good, although not a great, employee who is part of a superstar team. Another reason employees are opposed to forced ranking is that they suspect that the rankings are a way for companies to rationalize terminations more easily.

Forced distribution approaches have drawbacks. The forced distribution approach can distort ratings because employee performance may not fall into these predetermined distributions. Let's assume that a supervisor must use the following forced distribution to rate her employees' performance:

- 15 percent well below average
- 25 percent below average
- 40 percent average
- 15 percent above average
- 5 percent well above average

TABLE 3-5 A Forced Distribution Performance Appraisal Rating Form

Instructions: You are required to rate the performance for the previous three months of the 15 workers employed as animal keepers to conform with the following performance distribution:

- *15 percent* of the animal keepers will be rated as having exhibited poor performance.
- *20 percent* of the animal keepers will be rated as having exhibited below-average performance.
- *35 percent* of the animal keepers will be rated as having exhibited average performance.
- *20 percent* of the animal keepers will be rated as having exhibited above-average performance.
- *10 percent* of the animal keepers will be rated as having exhibited superior performance.

Use the following guidelines for rating performance. On the basis of the five duties listed in the job description for animal keeper, the employee's performance is characterized as:

- *Poor* if the employee performs only one of the duties well.
- *Below average* if the employee performs only two of the duties well.
- *Average* if the employee performs only three of the duties well.
- *Above average* if the employee performs only four of the duties well.
- *Superior* if the employee performs all five of the duties well.

This distribution is problematic to the extent that the actual distribution of employee performance is substantially different from this forced distribution. If 35 percent of the employees' performance were either above average or well above average, then the supervisor would be required to underrate the performance of 15 percent of the employees. Based on this forced distribution, the supervisor can rate only 20 percent of the employees as having demonstrated above-average or well-above-average job performance. Management–employee relationships ultimately suffer because workers feel that ratings are dictated by unreal models rather than by individual performance.

A third comparative technique for ranking employees establishes **paired comparisons**. Supervisors compare each employee to every other employee, identifying the better performer in each pair. Table 3-6 displays a paired comparison form. Following the comparison, the employees are ranked according to the number of times they were identified as being the better performer. In this example, Allen Jones is the best performer because he was identified most often as the better performer, followed by Bob Brown (identified twice as the better performer) and Mary Green (identified once as the better performer).

Comparative methods are best suited for small groups of employees who perform the same or similar jobs. They are cumbersome for large groups of employees or for employees who perform different jobs. For example, it would be difficult to judge whether a production worker's performance is better than a secretary's performance because the jobs are substantively different. The assessment of a production worker's performance is based on the number of units he or she produces during each work shift; a secretary's performance is based on the accuracy with which he or she types memos and letters.

As do trait systems, comparison approaches have limitations. They tend to encourage subjective judgments, which increase the chance for rater errors and biases. In addition, small differences in performance between employees may become exaggerated by using such a method if supervisors feel compelled to distinguish among levels of employee performance.

BEHAVIORAL SYSTEMS **Behavioral systems** rate employees on the extent to which they display successful job performance behaviors. In contrast to trait and comparison methods, behavioral methods rate objective job behaviors. When correctly developed and applied, behavioral models provide results that are relatively free of rater errors and biases. The main types of behavioral systems are the critical incident technique (CIT) and behaviorally anchored rating scales (BARS).

The **critical incident technique (CIT)**[25] requires job employees and their supervisors to identify performance incidents (e.g., on-the-job behaviors and behavioral outcomes) that distinguish successful performance from unsuccessful ones. The supervisor then observes the employees and records their performance on these critical job aspects. Supervisors usually rate employees on how often they display the behaviors described in each critical incident. Table 3-7 illustrates a CIT form for an animal keeper job. Two statements represent examples of ineffective job performance (numbers 2 and 3), and two statements represent examples of effective job performance (numbers 1 and 4).

TABLE 3-6 A Paired Comparison Performance Appraisal Rating Form

Instructions: Please indicate by placing an X next to which employee of each pair has performed most effectively during the past year.

X	Bob Brown		X	Mary Green
	Mary Green			Jim Smith
X	Bob Brown			Mary Green
	Jim Smith		X	Allen Jones
	Bob Brown			Jim Smith
X	Allen Jones		X	Allen Jones

TABLE 3-7 A Critical Incidents Performance Appraisal Rating Form

Instructions: For each description of the following work behaviors, circle the number that best describes how frequently the employee engages in that behavior.

1. The employee removes manure and unconsumed food from the animal enclosures.

1	2	3	4	5
Never	Almost never	Sometimes	Fairly often	Very often

2. The employee haphazardly measures the feed items when placing them in the animal enclosures.

1	2	3	4	5
Never	Almost never	Sometimes	Fairly often	Very often

3. The employee leaves refuse dropped by visitors on and around the public walkways.

1	2	3	4	5
Never	Almost never	Sometimes	Fairly often	Very often

4. The employee skillfully identifies instances of abnormal behavior among the animals, which represent signs of illness.

1	2	3	4	5
Never	Almost never	Sometimes	Fairly often	Very often

The CIT tends to be useful because this procedure requires extensive documentation that identifies successful and unsuccessful job performance behaviors by both the employee and the supervisor. The CIT's strength, however, is also its weakness: Implementation of the CIT demands continuous and close observation of the employee. Supervisors may find the record keeping to be overly burdensome.

Behaviorally anchored rating scales (BARS)[26] are based on the CIT, and these scales are developed in the same fashion with one exception. For the CIT, a critical incident would be written as "the employee completed the task in a timely fashion." For the BARS format, this incident would be written as "the employee is expected to complete the task in a timely fashion." The designers of BARS write the incidents as expectations to emphasize the fact that the employee does not have to demonstrate the exact behavior that is used as an anchor in order to be rated at that level. Because a complete array of behaviors that characterize a particular job would take many pages of description, it is not feasible to place examples of all job behaviors on the scale. Experts therefore list only those behaviors that they believe are most representative of the job the employee must perform. A typical job might have eight to ten dimensions under BARS, each with a separate rating scale. Table 3-8 contains an illustration of a BARS for one dimension of an animal keeper job (i.e., cleaning animal enclosures and removing refuse from the public walkways). The scale reflects the range of performance on the job dimension from ineffective performance (1) to effective performance (7).

As with all performance appraisal techniques, BARS has its advantages and disadvantages.[27] Among the various performance appraisal techniques, BARS is the most defensible in court because it is based on actual observable job behaviors. In addition, BARS encourages all raters to make evaluations in the same way. Perhaps the main disadvantage of BARS is the difficulty of developing and maintaining the volume of data necessary to make it effective. The BARS method requires companies to maintain distinct appraisal documents for each job. As jobs change over time, the documentation must be updated for each job.

GOAL-ORIENTED SYSTEMS Management by objectives (MBO)[28] could be the most effective performance appraisal technique because supervisors and employees determine objectives for employees to meet during the rating period and employees appraise how well they have achieved their objectives. Management by objectives is used mainly for managerial and professional employees and typically evaluates employees' progress toward strategic planning objectives.

TABLE 3-8 A Behaviorally Anchored Rating Scale

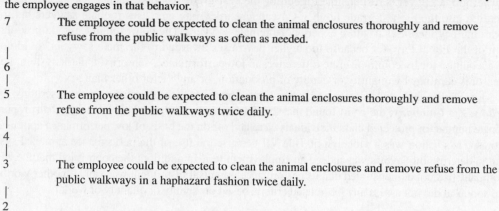

Instructions: On the following scale from 7 to 1, circle the number that best describes how frequently the employee engages in that behavior.

7   The employee could be expected to clean the animal enclosures thoroughly and remove refuse from the public walkways as often as needed.

|
6
|
5   The employee could be expected to clean the animal enclosures thoroughly and remove refuse from the public walkways twice daily.

|
4
|
3   The employee could be expected to clean the animal enclosures and remove refuse from the public walkways in a haphazard fashion twice daily.

|
2
|
1   The employee could be expected rarely to clean the animal enclosures or remove refuse from the public walkways.

Employees and supervisors together determine particular objectives tied to corporate strategies. Employees are expected to attain these objectives during the rating period. At the end of the rating period, the employee writes a report explaining his or her progress toward accomplishing the objectives, and the employee's supervisor appraises the employee's performance based on accomplishment of the objectives. Despite the importance of managerial employees to company success, it is often difficult to establish appropriate performance goals because many companies simply do not fully describe the scope of these positions. Management by objectives can promote effective communication between employees and their supervisors. On the downside, management by objectives is time-consuming and requires a constant flow of information between employees and employers. Moreover, its focus is only on the attainment of particular goals, often to the exclusion of other important outcomes. This drawback is known as a "results at any cost" mentality.[29] The role of automobile sales professionals historically was literally limited to making sales. Once these professionals and customers agreed on the price of a car, the sales professionals' work with customers was completed. Automobile salespeople today remain in contact with clients for as long as several months following the completion of the sale. The purpose is to ensure customer satisfaction and build loyalty to the product and dealership by addressing questions about the vehicle's features and reminding clients about scheduled service checks.

Goal-oriented systems are often a component of broader development programs that help employees achieve career goals.

Exploring the Performance Appraisal Process

Performance appraisals represent a company's way of telling employees what is expected of them in their jobs and how well they are meeting those expectations. Performance appraisals typically require supervisors to monitor employees' performance, complete performance appraisal forms about the employees, and hold discussions with employees about their performance. Companies that use merit pay plans must assess employee job performance, which serves as a basis for awarding merit pay raises. Awarding merit pay increases on factors other than job performance, except for four exceptions (a seniority system, a merit system, quality or quantity of production, and any factor besides sex), could lead some employees to level charges of illegal pay discrimination against the employer based on the Equal Pay Act of 1963.

One such violation of the Equal Pay Act involved two female employees of Cascade Wood Components Company, which remanufactures lumber products.[30] The job in question was the sawyer job; a sawyer is responsible for cutting the best-grade wood segments that will be manufactured into the highest-grade lumber. Cascade awarded pay increases to male sawyers before awarding pay increases to more experienced female sawyers. The court found Cascade in violation of the Equal Pay Act because the higher pay raises awarded to the male sawyers could not be accounted for by commensurate differences in job performance, seniority, a merit system that measures earnings by quantity or quality of production, or any factor other than sex.

Legislation and court decisions have subjected performance appraisals to close scrutiny. In **Brito v. Zia Company**, the court found that the Zia Company violated Title VII when a disproportionate number of protected class individuals were laid off on the basis of low performance appraisal scores. Zia's action was a violation of Title VII because the use of the performance appraisal system in determining layoffs was indeed an employment test. In addition, the court ruled that the Zia Company had not demonstrated that its performance appraisal instrument was valid. In other words, the appraisal did not assess any job-related criteria based on quality or quantity of work.[31]

FOUR ACTIVITIES TO PROMOTE NONDISCRIMINATORY PERFORMANCE APPRAISAL PRACTICES Since the *Brito v. Zia Company* decision, court opinions and compensation experts suggest the following four points to ensure nondiscriminatory performance appraisal practices and to protect firms using merit pay systems if legal issues arise.[32] Nondiscriminatory performance appraisal systems are key to effective merit pay systems because they accurately measure job performance.

1. **Conduct job analyses to ascertain characteristics necessary for successful job performance.**
   Companies must first establish definitions of the jobs and then discover what employee behaviors are necessary to perform the jobs. Job analysis is essential for the development of content-valid performance appraisal systems. Content validity displays connections between the measurable factors upon which the employee is being appraised and the job itself. For example, customer service associates' performance might be judged on the basis of courtesy and knowledge of the company's products or services, and these measures would be content-valid dimensions.

   Human resource and compensation experts must review performance appraisal tools regularly to ensure that the tools adequately reflect the key behaviors necessary for effective job performance. Jobholders, supervisors, and clients can often give the most relevant input to determine whether a performance appraisal system contains dimensions that relate to a particular job.

2. **Incorporate these characteristics into a rating instrument.**
   Although the professional literature recommends rating instruments that are tied to specific job behaviors (e.g., behaviorally anchored rating scales), the courts routinely accept such less-sophisticated approaches as simple graphic rating scales and trait ranges. Regardless of the method, HR departments should provide all supervisors and raters with written definitive standards, such as illustrated by the animal keeper job.

3. **Train supervisors to use the rating instrument properly.**
   Raters need to know how to apply performance appraisal standards when they make judgments. The uniform application of standards is extremely important. In addition, evaluators should be aware of common rater errors, which will be discussed later in this chapter.

4. **Several cases demonstrate that formal appeal mechanisms and review of ratings by upper-level personnel help make performance appraisal processes more accurate and effective.**
   Allowing employees to voice their concerns over ratings they believe to be inaccurate or unjust opens a dialogue between employees and their supervisors that may shed light on the performance appraisal outcomes. Employees may be able to point out instances of their performance that may have been overlooked in the appraisal process or explain particular

extreme instances as the result of extraordinary circumstances. For example, an ill parent in need of regular attention is the reason for an employee's absence.

SOURCES OF PERFORMANCE APPRAISAL INFORMATION Information for performance appraisal can be ascertained from five sources:

- Employee (i.e., the individual whose job performance is being appraised)
- Employee's supervisor
- Employee's coworkers
- Employee's supervisees
- Employee's customers or clients

More than one source can provide performance appraisal information. Although supervisory input is the most common source of performance appraisal information, companies are increasingly calling on as many sources of information as possible to gain a more complete picture of employee job performance. Performance appraisal systems that rely on many appropriate sources of information are known as **360-degree performance appraisals**. By shifting the responsibility for evaluation to more than one person, many of the common appraisal errors can be reduced or eliminated. Software is available to permit managers to give the ratings quickly and conveniently. Furthermore, including the perspective of multiple sources results in a more comprehensive and fair view of the employee's performance by minimizing biases resulting from limited views of performance.

In a survey of training participants, 84 percent said their 360-degree experience was useful. However, some managers believe that the 360-degree feedback method has problems. General Electric's (GE's) former CEO Jack Welch maintains that the 360-degree system in his firm had been "gamed" and that people were saying nice things about one another, resulting in all good ratings. Another critical view with an opposite twist is that input from peers, who may be competitors for raises and promotions, might intentionally distort the data and sabotage the colleague. Yet, because so many firms use 360-degree feedback evaluation, it seems that many firms have found ways to avoid the pitfalls.

Significant risks with 360-degree feedback are confidentiality and possible legal ramifications. Many firms outsource the process to make participants feel comfortable that the information they share and receive is completely anonymous. Information is very sensitive, and, in the wrong hands, could impact careers. In addition, Nesheba Kittling, an attorney at labor law firm Fisher & Phillips, states that "Employees' performance reviews are an employers' first line of defense against discrimination claims." Detailed documentation of job performance "provides support for an employer's contention that it had legitimate, non-discriminatory reasons" for adverse action against employee such as a demotion or termination.

ERRORS IN THE PERFORMANCE APPRAISAL PROCESS Almost all raters make **rating errors**. Rating errors reflect differences between human judgment processes versus objective, accurate assessments uncolored by bias, prejudice, or other subjective, extraneous influences.[33] Rating errors occur because raters must always make subjective judgments. Human resource departments can help raters to minimize errors by carefully choosing rating systems and to recognize and avoid common errors. Major types of rating errors include:[34]

- Bias errors
- Contrast errors
- Errors of central tendency
- Errors of leniency or strictness

Bias Errors Bias errors happen when the rater evaluates the employee based on a personal negative or positive opinion of the employee rather than on the employee's actual performance. Four ways supervisors may bias evaluation results are first-impression effects, positive and negative halo effects, similar-to-me effects, and illegal discriminatory biases. A manager biased by a **first-impression effect** might make an initial favorable or unfavorable judgment about an employee and then ignore or distort the employee's actual performance based on this impression. A **positive halo effect** or **negative halo effect** occurs when a rater generalizes an employee's good or bad behavior on one aspect of the job to all aspects of the job. A **similar-to-me effect** refers to the tendency on the part of raters to judge favorably employees whom they perceive as similar to themselves. "Similar-to-me" errors or biases easily can lead to charges of **illegal discriminatory bias,** wherein a supervisor rates members of his or her race, sex, nationality, or religion more favorably than members of other classes.

Contrast Errors Supervisors make **contrast errors** when they compare an employee with other employees rather than to specific, explicit performance standards. Such comparisons qualify as errors because other employees are required to perform only at minimum acceptable standards. Employees performing at minimally acceptable levels should receive satisfactory ratings, even if every other employee doing the job is performing at outstanding or above-average levels.

Errors of Central Tendency When supervisors rate all employees as average or close to average, they commit **errors of central tendency.** Such errors are most often committed when raters are forced to justify only extreme behavior (i.e., high or low ratings) with written explanations; therefore, HR professionals should require justification for ratings at every level of the scale and not just at the extremes.

Errors of Leniency or Strictness Raters sometimes place every employee at the high or low end of the scale, regardless of actual performance. With a **leniency error,** managers tend to appraise employees' performance more highly than they really rate compared with objective criteria. Over time, if supervisors commit positive errors, their employees will expect higher-than-deserved pay rates.

On the other hand, **strictness errors** occur when a supervisor rates an employee's performance lower than it would be if compared against objective criteria. If supervisors make this error over time, employees may receive smaller pay raises than deserved, lower their effort, and perform poorly. In effect, this error erodes employees' beliefs that effort varies positively with performance and that performance influences the amount of pay raises.

☞ **FYI**

Researchers maintain that 61 percent of an employee's rating is based on the manager's judgment of him/herself rather than on the employee.[35]

Are Traditional Performance Appraisal Methods Becoming Irrelevant?

Many companies have scrutinized the use of traditional formal performance appraisal practices in recent years. The scrutiny is based on many factors; for instance, reducing annual employee performance to a numeric rating. Some companies such as Adobe have set aside the use of traditional methods in favor of frequent informal check-ins. While there are advantages to informal performance appraisal approaches, there are also limitations. For example, how do companies use the information gleaned from check-ins to make fair and consistent pay raise decisions? We will consider this important question in Epilogue.

3-4. Discuss how compensation professionals can strengthen the pay-for-performance link.

STRENGTHENING THE PAY-FOR-PERFORMANCE LINK

Companies who don't consider these possible limitations ultimately weaken the relationship between pay and performance. Human resource managers can employ a number of approaches to strengthen the link between pay and job performance.

Link Performance Appraisals to Business Goals

The standards by which employee performance is judged should be linked to a company's competitive strategy or strategies. For example, each member of a product development team that is charged with the responsibility of marketing a new product might be given merit increases if certain sales goals are reached.

Analyze Jobs

Job analysis (Chapter 6) is vital to companies that wish to establish **internally consistent compensation systems**. As discussed earlier, job descriptions—a product of job analyses—can be used by supervisors to create objective performance measures. Job descriptions note the duties, requirements, and relative importance of a job within the company. Supervisors appraising performance can match employees' performance to these criteria. This approach may help reduce supervisors' arbitrary decisions about merit increases by clarifying the standards against which employees' performance is judged.

Communicate

For merit pay programs to succeed, employees must clearly understand what they need to do to receive merit increases and what the rewards for their performance will be. Open communication helps an employee develop reasonable expectations and encourages him or her to trust the system and those who operate it. Figure 3-2 illustrates worksheets both supervisors and employers may use to establish performance expectations.

Establish Effective Appraisals

During performance appraisal meetings with employees, supervisors should discuss goals for future performance and employee career plans. When performance deficiencies are evident, the supervisor and employee should work together to identify possible causes and develop an action plan to remedy these deficiencies. The performance standards listed within job descriptions should serve as the guides for establishing performance targets. For example, a company's job description for a secretary specifies that the job employee must be able to use one word processing software package proficiently. The supervisor should clearly explain what software usage proficiency means. Proficiency may refer to the ability to operate certain features of the software well, including the mail merge utility, the table generator, and the various outlining utilities, or proficiency may refer to the ability to operate all features of the software well.

Empower Employees

Because formal performance appraisals are conducted periodically—maybe only once per year—supervisors must empower their employees to make performance self-appraisals between formal sessions.[36] Moreover, supervisors need to take on a coach's role to empower their workers.[37] As coaches, supervisors must ensure that employees have access to the resources necessary to perform their jobs. Supervisors-as-coaches should also help employees interpret and respond to work problems as they develop. Empowering employees in this fashion should lead to more self-corrective actions rather than reactive courses of action to supervisory feedback and only to the criticisms addressed in performance appraisal meetings.

Differentiate Among Performers

Merit increases should consist of meaningful increments. If employees do not see significant distinctions between top performers and poor performers, top performers may become frustrated and reduce their levels of performance. When companies' merit increases don't clearly reflect differences in actual job performance, they may need to provide alternative rewards (e.g., employee benefits—additional vacation days or higher discounts on the company's product or service—can complement merit pay increases).

Supervisor's Performance Planning Worksheet

To be filled out by supervisor

Name of Employee: **Date**:

Employee Title: **Department**:

1. List what you consider to be the primary job duties or assignments at this time (list in order of priority):
2. Describe contributions, achievements, or improvements made by the employee during the past appraisal period:
3. Describe any specific change, improvements, or goals desired for the employee's performance in the next appraisal period:

_____ _____ _____ _____

Employee   **Date**   **Supervisor**   **Date**

Employee's Performance Planning Worksheet

To be filled out by employee

Name of Employee: **Date:**

Employee Title: **Department:**

1. List what you consider to be your primary job duties or assignments at this time (list in order of priority):
2. Describe contributions or achievements that indicate your success at improving your performance or exceeding job requirements during the past appraisal period:
3. Describe any specific changes or improvements you want to make in your performance in the next appraisal period. Describe obstacles to getting your job done and suggest possible solutions:

_____   _____

Employee Signature   Date

_____ (Initial) I have been given the opportunity to fill this out and choose not to do so.

FIGURE 3-2 Supervisor's and Employee's Performance Planning Worksheets

POSSIBLE LIMITATIONS OF MERIT PAY PROGRAMS

3-5. Summarize the possible limitations of merit pay programs.

Despite the popularity of merit pay systems, these programs are not without potential limitations, which may lessen their credibility with employees. If employees do not believe in a merit pay program, the pay system will not bring about the expected motivational impacts. Supervisors, HR managers, and compensation professionals must address the following nine potential problems with merit pay programs.

Failure to Differentiate among Performers

Employees may receive merit increases even if their performance does not warrant them because supervisors want to avoid creating animosity among employees. Poor performers, therefore, may receive the same pay increase as exemplary performers, and poor performers may come to view merit pay increases as entitlements. Superior performers consequently may question the value of striving for excellent performance.

Poor Performance Measures

Accurate and comprehensive performance measures that capture the entire scope of an employee's job are essential to successful merit pay programs. In most companies, employees' job performance tends to be assessed subjectively, based on their supervisors' judgments. As discussed, merit pay programs rely on supervisors' subjective assessments of employees' prior job performance. Developing performance measures for every single job unfortunately is both difficult and expensive.

Supervisors' Biased Ratings of Employee Job Performance

As we discussed earlier, supervisors are subject to a number of errors when they make subjective assessments of employees' job performance. These errors often undermine the credibility of the performance evaluation process. Performance evaluation processes that lack credibility do little to create the perception among employees that pay reflects performance.

Lack of Open Communication between Management and Employees

If managers cannot communicate effectively with employees, employees will not trust the performance appraisal processes. Trust is difficult to build when decisions are kept secret and employees have no influence on pay decisions. Thus, merit pay decision systems can cause conflict between management and employees. If mistrust characterizes the relationship, then performance appraisals will mean little to employees and could even lead to accusations of bias. In an environment of secrecy, employees lack the information necessary to determine if pay actually is linked to job performance.

Undesirable Social Structures

We acknowledged that relative pay grades can reflect status differentials within a company: Employees with lucrative salaries are usually granted higher status than lower-paid employees. Permanent merit increases may rigidify the relative pay status of employees over time.[38] Table 3-9 shows the permanence of the relative pay difference between two distinct jobs that each receives a 5 percent merit increase each year. Even though both employees performed well and received "equal" merit increases in percentage terms, the actual salary differentials prevail each year. Thus, where pay level is an indicator of status, permanent merit increases may reinforce an undesirable social structure. Lower-paid employees may resent never being able to catch up.

Mounting Costs

As is the case with seniority pay, merit pay presents an escalating cost burden to companies because pay increases are recurring, as illustrated in Table 3-9.

Factors Other than Merit

Merit increases may be based on factors other than merit, which will clearly reduce the emphasis on job performance. For example, supervisors may subconsciously use their employees' ages or seniority level as bases for awarding merit increases. Studies show that the extent to which

TABLE 3-9 The Impact of Equal Pay Raise Percentage Amounts for Distinct Salaries

At the end of 2018, Anne Brown earned $50,000 per year as a systems analyst and John Williams earned $35,000 per year as an administrative assistant. Each received a 5 percent pay increase every year until the year 2023.

	Anne Brown ($)	John Williams ($)
2019	52,500	36,750
2020	55,125	38,587
2021	57,881	40,516
2022	60,775	42,542
2023	63,814	44,669

supervisors like the employees for whom they are responsible determines the size of pay raises in a merit pay program.[39] In addition, company politics assumes that the value of an employee's contributions depends on the agenda, or goals, of the supervisor[40] rather than on the objective impact of an employee's contributions to a rationally determined work goal. For instance, an accounting manager wishes to employ accounting methods other than top management's accounting methods. She believes that she can gain top management support by demonstrating that the accounting staff agrees with her position. The accounting manager may give generally positive performance evaluations, regardless of demonstrated performance, to those who endorse her accounting methods.

Undesirable Competition

Because merit pay programs focus fundamentally on individual employees, these programs do little to integrate workforce members.[41] With limited budgets for merit increases, employees must compete for a larger share of this limited amount. Competition among employees is counterproductive if teamwork is essential for successfully completing projects. Thus, merit increases are best suited for jobs where the employee works independently (e.g., clerical positions) and many professional positions from job families (e.g., accounting).

Little Motivational Value

Notwithstanding their intended purpose, merit pay programs may not positively influence employee motivation. Employers and employees may differ in what they see as "large enough" merit increases really to motivate positive worker behavior. For example, increases diminish after deducting income taxes and contributions to Social Security, and differences in employees' monthly paychecks may be negligible.

PREPARING FOR EXAMS/QUIZZES

Chapter Summary by Learning Objectives

Learning Objective 3-1. *Describe seniority and longevity pay practices*. Seniority and longevity pay reward employees with periodic additions to base pay according to length of service. Whereas seniority pay increases become a part of base pay, longevity awards do not.

Learning Objective 3-2. *Explain the merit pay approach to compensation*. Merit pay rewards employees based on performance with periodic, recurring additions to base pay. Merit pay systems commonly incorporate subjective measures of employee performance.

Learning Objective 3-3. *Explore a variety of performance appraisal methods*. Performance appraisal is a mechanism that helps determine whether employees qualify for merit pay raises as well as the amount based on performance attainment. There are four types: trait systems, comparison systems, behavioral systems, and goal-oriented systems.

Learning Objective 3-4. *Discuss how compensation professionals can strengthen the pay-for-performance link*. Possible limitations of performance appraisal practices stand to weaken the pay-for-performance link, ultimately, undermining merit pay systems. With proper attention, compensation professionals can design performance appraisal methods that help to overcome these limitations.

Learning Objective 3-5. *Summarize the possible limitations of merit pay programs*. Merit pay programs have inherent limitations. With proper attention, compensation professionals can help minimize the impact of these limitations.

Key Terms

seniority pay   58
longevity pay   58
human capital theory   59
job control unionism   59
General Schedule (GS)   61
merit pay programs   64
just-meaningful pay increase   65
trait systems   67
comparison systems   67
forced distribution   68
paired comparisons   69

behavioral systems   69
critical incident technique (CIT)   69
behaviorally anchored rating scales
   (BARS)   70
management by objectives (MBO)   70
Brito v. Zia Company   72
360-degree performance
   appraisals   73
rating errors   73
bias errors   73
first-impression effect   74

positive halo effect   74
negative halo effect   74
similar-to-me effect   74
illegal discriminatory bias   74
contrast errors   74
errors of central tendency   74
leniency error   74
strictness errors   74
internally consistent compensation
   systems   75

Discussion Questions

3-1. Human capital theory has been advanced as a rationale underlying seniority pay. Identify an individual you know who has performed the same job for at least a few months. Ask them to describe the changes in knowledge and skills they experienced from the time they assumed their jobs to the present. What did you find most interesting in your discussion? Explain.

3-2. Subjective performance evaluations are subject to several rater errors, which makes objective measures seem a better alternative. Are there instances where subjective performance evaluations might be better (or more feasible) than objective ratings? Explain.

3-3. Consider a job that you have held. Write a brief job description. Then develop a behaviorally anchored rating scale (BARS). What are some of the strengths and weaknesses associated with BARS?

3-4. Merit pay plans appear to be the most common form of compensation in the United States. Based on your knowledge of merit pay systems, identify one job for which merit pay may be appropriate and another for which it may be inappropriate. What is the rationale for your choices?

3-5. Should companies abandon traditional performance appraisal methods in favor of frequent conversations about employee performance? Explain.

PREPARING FOR MY CAREER

Compensation in Action

Employee compensation will ultimately be a managerial decision. As a line manager, your focus will be on the broader issues of production, revenue, and competition; however, the rate at which employees are paid—and why—will be an important factor in sustaining high levels of production, revenue, and competitive advantage. In making these decisions, line managers and HR (and in many cases the compensation specialist within the HR department) must work together in order to reward employees on measurable accomplishments and effectively communicate how the measured performance led to the resulting compensation decision.

Action checklist for line managers and HR—accurately tying performance to compensation

HR takes the lead

- Work with line managers to design the performance appraisal plan that best fits the specific duties and responsibilities of particular roles.
- Consider implementing a training program wherein line managers are trained in two areas: (1) accurately assessing performance and (2) recording the assessment in a way that is lawful and easily understood by both the employer and employee.
- Review the final distribution allocation made by the managers and, after approving the complete plan, set in motion the discussions between managers and employees during which performance will be discussed and compensation increases will be communicated.

Line managers take the lead

- Determine performance criteria and accurate measurements to ensure that a specific output is the expectation of both the employee and employer.
- Work with HR to become educated on the subjective limitations of performance reviews. While certain roles may have very objective standards (e.g., sales numbers) by which employees are measured, supervisor judgment is subject to error.
- Use appraisals to accurately compensate employees. Working with HR, use the total annual increase to make compensation increases accordingly (e.g., if you are allotted a 5 percent increase to distribute among your employees, top performers may get an 8–10 percent increase, steady performers 5–6 percent, and underperformers 0–2 percent).

Cases

Case 1: The Dreaded Performance Appraisal

"There—at last, it's finished," thought Rajiv Chaudhry, as he laid aside the last of 12 PA forms. It had been a busy week for Rajiv, who supervises a road maintenance crew for the Georgia Department of Highways.

In passing through Rajiv's district a few days previously, the governor had complained to the area superintendent that repairs were needed on several of the highways. Because of this, the superintendent assigned Rajiv's crew an unusually heavy workload. In addition, Rajiv received a call from the HR office that week reminding him that the PAs were late. Rajiv explained his predicament, but the HR specialist insisted that the forms be completed right away.

Looking over the appraisals again, Rajiv thought about several of the workers. The PA form had places for marking *quantity of work*, *quality of work*, and *cooperativeness*. For each characteristic, the worker could be graded *outstanding*, *good*, *average*, *below average*, or *unsatisfactory*. As Rajiv's crew had completed all the extra work assigned for that week, he marked every worker *outstanding* in *quantity of work*. He marked Joe Blum *average* in *cooperativeness* because Joe had questioned one of his decisions that week. Rajiv had decided to patch a pothole in one of the roads, and Joe thought the small section of road surface ought to be broken out and replaced. Rajiv didn't include this in the remarks section of the form, though. As a matter of fact, he wrote no remarks on any of the forms.

Rajiv felt a twinge of guilt as he thought about Roger Short. He knew that Roger had been goofing off, and the other workers had been carrying him for quite some time. He also knew that Roger would be upset if he found that he had been marked lower than the other workers. Consequently, he marked Roger the same to avoid a confrontation. "Anyway," Rajiv thought, "these things are a pain, and I really shouldn't have to bother with them."

As Rajiv folded up the PAs and put them in the envelope for mailing, he smiled. He was glad he would not have to think about PAs for another six months.

Questions:

3-6. What weaknesses do you see in Rajiv's performance appraisals?

3-7. Should HR have the ability to insist that the forms be "completed right away"? Discuss.

3-8. Many managers would agree with Rajiv's beliefs that performance appraisals are a nuisance and unnecessary. What are the disadvantages in doing away with performance appraisals?

Case 2: Ethics Dilemma: Pay for Performance Disconnect

You are the new vice president for HR of a company that has not been performing well, and everyone, including yourself, has a mandate to deliver results. The pressure has never been greater. Shareholders are angry after three years of a tough market that has left their company stock losing value every day. Many shareholders desperately need stock performance to pay for their retirement. Working for you is a 52-year-old manager with two kids in college. In previous evaluations, executives told him he was doing fine, when he clearly was not, and his performance is still far below par. At the same time, the executives awarded him impressive annual pay raises.

If you are to show others in the company that you are willing to make tough decisions, you feel you must fire this individual. The question is, who is going to suffer—the firm and, ultimately, the shareholders, whose retirements are in jeopardy—or a nice guy who's been lied to for 20 years?

Questions:

3-9. What would you do?

3-10. What factor(s) in this ethical dilemma might influence a person to make a less-than-ethical decision?

Crunch the Numbers!

Determining Pay Increases in Job Classification Plans

The federal government's General Schedule (GS) (Table 3-2) is an example of a job classification plan in which pay rates are based, in part, on compensable factors such as knowledge and skills. Jobs are grouped into 15 classifications, ranging from GS level 1 through GS level 15 as well as the level or degrees of compensable factors (e.g., follow procedures vs. establishing procedures). Over time, employees receive pay increases according to length of service (Steps 1–10) and progression through the steps assumes a minimum of acceptable performance. The pay increase from step to step equals the within-grade increase (WGI) amount. The waiting periods within steps are:

- Steps 1–3: 1 year in each step
- Steps 4–6: 2 years in each step
- Steps 7–9: 3 years in each step

Refer to Table 3-2 when answering the following questions.

Questions:

3-11. Using the General Schedule, calculate the number of years it would take an employee to advance from her starting position in Grade 11 (Step 1) to Step 10 if she is demonstrating acceptable performance.

3-12. Another employee asked what his salary would likely be after completing two additional years of service. This employee just entered his first year in Grade 4 (Step 5). If he was to demonstrate acceptable performance, calculate the expected salary after completing two years of service.

3-13. All pay rates typically increase each year based on changes in the Consumer Price Index. Calculate the Grade 7 WGI amount based on an overall 3 percent increase.

Working Together: Team Exercise

In small groups of three or four, come up with specific answers to the following questions. Talk through your perspectives and come up with a team response. Be prepared to share your ideas with the class.

As a group, become familiar with *Careeronestop* (http://www.careeronestop.org). The U.S. Department of Labor sponsors Careeronestop, which is a valuable resource for career exploration, training, and job search. Also, become familiar with the different resources available on this website. Then, select a job of interest by clicking on the *job search* link at the top of the page. In the search boxes, enter a job title or keyword, and specify the location—city, state, or zip code. You are likely to see several results with jobs indicating the same or very similar job titles. Compare two or more of the results by reviewing the job descriptions.

Questions:

3-14. What are some of the tools available to users of Careeronestop? Which (one or two) resource(s) do you feel will be most helpful as you think about finding full-time employment after earning your degree? Explain.

3.15. Job descriptions for jobs with the same titles will vary somewhat because companies customize them to fit the situation. What are some similarities and differences that you found? Based on those differences, how likely are you to recommend different pay rates? Explain.

Endnotes

1. N. Joseph Cayer, *Public Personnel Administration in the United States* (New York: St. Martin Press, 1975).

2. Gary S. Becker, *Human Capital* (New York: St. Martin Press, 1975).

3. T. R. Kochan, H. C. Katz, and R. B. McKersie, *The Transformation of American Industrial Relations* (Ithaca, NY: ILR Press, 1994).

4. Cayer, *Public Personnel Administration.*

5. U.S. Bureau of Labor Statistics, *Union Members—2017*, (2017) USDL 18-0080, accessed January 21, 2018, http://www.bls.gov.

6. Ibid.

7. Kay Coles James, *A Fresh Start for Federal Pay: The Case for Modernization* (Washington, DC: U.S. Government Printing Office, April 2002).

8. U.S. Department of the Interior, Bureau of Land Management, *Human Resources Assistant* (GS-0203-06/07), accessed January 31, 2015, http://www.usa.jobs.gov.

9. Craig Trudell and Yuki Hagiwara, "Toyota Plans Overhaul to Seniority-based Pay," *BloombergBusiness* (January 26, 2015), accessed February 3, 2015, http://www.bloomberg.com.

10. Kana Inagaki, "Japan Inc Shuns Seniority Pay in Favour of Merit-based Pay," *The Financial Times* (January 27, 2015), accessed February 3, 2015, http://www.ft.com.

11. Charles Peck, *Pay and Performance: The Interaction of Compensation and Performance Appraisal* (Research Bulletin No. 155) (New York: The Conference Board, 1984).

12. WorldatWork, *WorldatWork Salary Budget Survey, Top-Level Results*, (2017), accessed January 17, 2018, http://www.worldatwork.org.

13. Sandra Block, "The Outlook for Pay Raises in 2018," *Kiplinger's Personal Finance* (November, 2017), accessed January 17, 2018, http://www.kiplinger.com.

14. Alanna Petroff, "Don't Expect a Big Pay Raise in 2018," *CNN Money* (December 12, 2017), accessed January 3, 2018, http://www.money.cnn.com.

15. WorldatWork, *Compensation Programs and Practices* (August, 2016), accessed January 17, 2018, http://www.worldatwork.org; WorldatWork, *Compensation Programs and Practices* (January, 2015), accessed February 25, 2016, http://www.worldatwork.org.

16. Gary P. Latham and Kenneth N. Wexley, *Increasing Productivity through Performance Appraisal* (Reading, MA: Addison-Wesley, 1982).

17. Linda A. Krefting and Thomas A. Mahoney, "Determining the Size of a Meaningful Pay Increase," *Industrial Relations* 16 (1977): 83–93, https://doi.org/10.1111/j.1468-232X.1977.tb00650.x.

18. Rachel Feintzeig, "Everything Is Awesome! Why You Can't Tell Employees They're Doing a Bad Job," *The Wall Street Journal* (February 10, 2015), accessed February 12, 2015, http://www.wsj.com.

19. Stephanie Taylor Christensen, "3 Ways Companies Are Changing the Dreaded Performance Review," *Fast Company* online (October 2, 2015), accessed January 21, 2018, http://www.fastcompany.com.

20. L. L. Bean, *Culture*, accessed January 21, 2015, https://llbeancareers.com/culture.htm.

21. H. John Bernardin and Richard W. Beatty, *Performance Appraisal: Assessing Human Behavior at Work* (Boston, MA: Kent, 1984).

22. Joshua Brustein, "Microsoft Kills Its Hated Stack Rankings. Does Anyone Do Employee Reviews Right?" *Bloomberg Businessweek* (November 13, 2013), accessed January 25, 2014, http://www.businessweek.com.

23. Liz Ryan, "Ten Management Practices to Throw Overboard in 2012," *BusinessWeek.com* (January 23, 2012): 1.

24. Joshua Brustein "Microsoft Kills Its Hated Stack Rankings."

25. Grave Fivars, "The Critical Incident Technique: A Bibliography," *JSAS Catalog of Selected Documents in Psychology* 5 (1975): 210.

26. Patricia Cain Smith and Lorne M. Kendall, "Retranslation of Expectation: An Approach to the Construction of Unambiguous Anchors for Rating Scales," *Journal of Applied Psychology* 47 (1963): 149–155, http://dx.doi.org/10.1037/h0047060.

27. Latham & Wexley, *Increasing Productivity*.

28. Bernardin & Beatty, *Performance Appraisal*.

29. Ibid.

30. *Coe v. Cascade Wood Components*, 48 FEP Cases 664 (W.D. OR. 1988).

31. *Brito v. Zia Company*, 478 F2d 1200, CA 10 (1973).

32. Gerald V. Barrett and Mary C. Kernan, "Performance Appraisal and Terminations: A Review of Court Decisions Since *Brito v. Zia Company* with Implication for Personnel Practices," *Personnel Psychology* 40 (1987): 489–503, https://doi.org/10.1111/j.1744-6570.1987.tb00611.x.

33. Milton L. Blum and James C. Naylor, *Industrial Psychology: Its Theoretical and Social Foundations* (New York: Harper & Row, 1968).

34. Bernardin & Beatty, *Performance Appraisal*.

35. Steffen Maier, "4 Unconscious Biases that Distort Performance Reviews," *Entrepreneur.com* (September 22, 2016), accessed January 5, 2018, http://www.entrepreneur.com/article/281919.

36. Raymond A. Noe, *Employee Training* (3rd ed.) (Burr Ridge, IL: McGraw-Hill, 2005).

37. Roger D. Evered and James C. Selman, "Coaching and the Art of Management," *Organizational Dynamics* 18 (1989): 16–33, https://doi.org/10.1016/0090-2616(89)90040-5.

38. Mason Haire, Edwin E. Ghiselli, and M. E. Gordon, "A Psychological Study of Pay," *Journal of Applied Psychology Monograph* 51 (Whole No. 636), (1967): 1–24.

39. Robert L. Cardy and Gregory H. Dobbins, "Affect and Appraisal: Liking as an Integral Dimension in Evaluating Performance," *Journal of Applied Psychology* 71, no. 4 (1986): 672–678, http://dx.doi.org/10.1037/0021-9010.71.4.672.

40. Kevin R. Murphy and Jeanette N. Cleveland, *Performance Appraisal: An Organizational Perspective*, (Boston, MA: Allyn & Bacon, 1991).

41. Edward E. Lawler and Susan G. Cohen, "Designing a Pay System for Teams," *American Compensation Association Journal* 1 (1992): 6–19.

4 Incentive Pay

As we will discuss momentarily, incentive pay places some portion of employee compensation at risk. When employees, groups of employees, or entire companies fail to meet preestablished performance standards (e.g., annual sales), they forfeit some or all their compensation. Expert incentive pay consultants argue that a critical element of successful incentive pay plans is the provision of regular, honest communication with employees. We will explore this issue and several others related to effective incentive pay design.

EXPLORING INCENTIVE PAY

4-1. Explore the incentive pay approach.

Incentive pay or **variable pay** rewards employees for partially or completely attaining a predetermined work objective. Incentive or variable pay is defined as compensation, other than base wages or salaries that fluctuate according to employees' attainment of some standard, such as a preestablished formula, individual or group goals, or company earnings.[1]

Effective incentive pay systems are based on three assumptions:[2]

- Individual employees and work teams differ in how much they contribute to the company, in what they do as well as in how well they do it.

- The company's overall performance depends to a large degree on the performance of individuals and groups within the company.
- To attract, retain, and motivate high performers and to be fair to all employees, a company needs to reward employees based on their relative performance.

Much like seniority and merit pay approaches, incentive pay augments employees' base pay, but incentive pay appears as a one-time payment. Employees usually receive a combination of recurring base pay and incentive pay, with base pay representing the greater portion of core compensation. More employees are presently eligible for incentive pay than ever before, as companies seek to control costs and motivate personnel continually to strive for exemplary performance. Companies increasingly recognize the importance of applying incentive pay programs to various kinds of employees as well, including production workers, technical employees, and service workers.

Some companies use incentive pay extensively. Lincoln Electric Company, a manufacturer of welding machines and motors, is renowned for its use of incentive pay plans. At Lincoln Electric, production employees receive recurring base pay as well as incentive pay. The company determines incentive pay awards according to five performance criteria: quality, output, dependability, cooperation, and ideas. The company has awarded incentive payments every year since 1934, through prosperous and poor economic times. In 2016, the average profit sharing payment per employee was $24,111.[3] Coupled with average base pay, total core compensation for Lincoln employees was $72,323. The company determines bonus amounts based on profitability and individual job performance. Similarly, Southwest Airlines has distributed profit sharing payments to employees every year for the past 40 years.[4] In 2017, Southwest announced that it would share $586 million in profits.[5] These profits translate into profit-sharing bonuses equal to approximately 13.2 percent of base pay.

Companies generally institute incentive pay programs to control payroll costs or to motivate employee productivity. Companies can control costs by replacing annual merit or seniority increases or fixed salaries with incentive plans that award pay raises only when the company enjoys an offsetting rise in productivity, profits, or some other measure of business success. Well-developed incentive programs base pay on performance, so employees control their own compensation levels. Companies can choose incentives to further business objectives. For example, the management of H. Lee Moffitt Cancer Center and Research Institute at the University of South Florida continually strives to improve patient care as well as control costs. Moffitt's incentives are usually tied to net income or operating surplus, quality of care measures, patient satisfaction scores, and operating efficiencies.

CONTRASTING INCENTIVE PAY WITH TRADITIONAL PAY

In traditional pay plans, employees receive compensation based on a fixed hourly pay rate or annual salary. Some companies use incentive pay programs that replace all or a portion of base pay to control payroll expenditures and to link pay to performance. Since 1998, there has been more than a 50 percent increase in the use of incentive pay programs. Companies use incentive pay programs in varying degrees for different kinds of positions.[6] Nowadays, most companies use a mix of traditional and incentive pay methods. The mix has steadily changed. In 1998, traditional pay increases totaled 4.2 percent of payroll while incentive pay increases amounted to 8.0 percent. In 2017, the amounts were 3.0 percent and 11.6 percent, respectively.[7]

As we discussed in Chapter 3, employees under traditional pay structures earn raises according to their length of service in the organization or to supervisors' subjective appraisals of employees' job performance. Again, both merit pay raises and seniority pay raises are permanent increases to base pay. Annual merit pay increase amounts usually total no more than a small

4-2. Describe the differences between incentive pay methods and traditional pay methods.

TABLE 4-1 Permanent Annual Merit Increases versus Annual Incentive Awards: A Comparison

(At the end of 2018, John Smith earned an annual salary of $35,000.)

Year	Increase Amount (%)	Annual Increase Cost (Total Current Salary: 2018 Salary Equals $35,000)		Total Annual Salary	
		Permanent Merit Increase ($): Percent Increase x Previous Year Salary	Incentive Award ($): Percent Increase x 2018 Salary	Permanent Merit Increase ($): (Percent Increase x Previous Year Salary) + Previous Year Salary	Incentive Award ($): (Percent Increase x 2018 Salary) + 2018 Salary
2019	3	1,050	1,050	36,050	36,050
2020	5	1,802	1,750	37,853	36,750
2021	4	1,514	1,400	39,367	36,400
2022	7	2,755	2,450	42,122	37,450
2023	6	2,527	2,100	44,649	37,100
Total Pay Increase: (2019 through 2023)		$9,648 (*recurring*)	$8,750 (*nonrecurring*)		

percentage of base pay (approximately 3 percent), but the dollar impact represents a significant cost to employers over time. Table 4-1 shows the contrast in rate of compensation increase between a traditional merit compensation plan and an incentive plan.

Companies use incentive pay to reward individual employees, teams of employees, or whole companies based on their performance. Incentive pay plans are not limited solely to production or nonsupervisory workers. Many incentive plans apply to such categories of employees as sales professionals, managers, and executives. Management typically relies on business objectives to determine incentive pay levels such as company profits and sales growth. Management then communicates these planned incentive levels and performance goals to managers. Although merit pay performance standards aim to be measurable and objective, incentive levels tend to be based on even more objective criteria, such as quantity of items an employee produces per production period or market indicators of a company's performance (e.g., an increase in market share for the fiscal year). Moreover, supervisors communicate the incentive award amounts in advance that correspond to objective performance levels. On the other hand, supervisors generally do not communicate the merit award amounts until after they offer subjective assessments of employees' performance.

Incentive pay plans can be broadly classified into three categories:

- *Individual incentive plans.* These plans reward employees whose work is performed independently. Some companies have piecework plans, typically for their production employees. Under piecework plans, an employee's compensation depends on the number of units she or he produces over a given period.
- *Group incentive plans.* These plans promote supportive, collaborative behavior among employees. Group incentives work well in manufacturing and service delivery environments that rely on interdependent teams. In gainsharing programs, group improvements in productivity, cost savings, or product quality are shared by employees within the group.
- *Company-wide incentive plans.* These plans tie employee compensation to a company's performance over a short time frame, usually from a one-month period to a five-year period.

Table 4-2 lists common performance measures used in individual, group, and company-wide incentive plans.[8]

TABLE 4-2 Typical Performance Measures for Individual, Group, and Company-wide Incentive Plans

Individual Incentive Plans

Quantity of work output

Quality of work output

Monthly sales

Work safety record

Work attendance

Group Incentive Plans

Customer satisfaction

Labor cost savings (through gainsharing plans)

Materials cost savings

Services cost savings (e.g., utilities)

Company-wide Incentive Plans

Operational Measures:

   Customer satisfaction

   Operational efficiency

   Service/quality

   Safety/occupational injury

Financial Measures:

   Revenue

   Earnings per company stock share

Operating income

Revenue growth

Note: Measures such as safety records and customer satisfaction can be measured on an individual, group, or company-wide basis according to a company's objectives.

INDIVIDUAL INCENTIVES

Individual incentive pay plans are most appropriate under three conditions. First, employees' performance can be measured objectively. Examples of objective performance measures include:

4-3. Explain the practice of individual incentive pay plans.

- Number of units produced—an automobile parts production worker's completion of a turn signal lighting assembly
- Sales amount—a CA Technologies sales professional's monthly sales revenue
- Reduction in error rate—a warehouse worker's reduction in product damage

Second, individual incentive plans are appropriate when employees have sufficient control over work outcomes. Factors such as frequent equipment breakdowns and delays in receipt of raw materials limit employees' ability to control their performance levels. Employees are not likely to be diligent when they encounter interference: Chances are good that employees who previously experienced interference will expect to encounter interference in the future. Employees' resistance threatens profits because companies will find it difficult to motivate people to work hard when problem factors are not present.

Third, individual incentive plans are appropriate when they do not create a level of unhealthy competition among workers that ultimately leads to poor quality. For example, a company may create unhealthy competition when it limits the number of incentive awards to only 10 percent of the employees who have demonstrated the highest levels of performance. If the company judges performance according to volume, then employees may sacrifice quality as they compete against each other to outmatch quantity. In addition, under an incentive plan that rewards quantity of output, those employees who meet or exceed the highest standard established by their employer may be subject to intimidation by workers whose work falls below the standard.[9] Unions may use these intimidation tactics to prevent plan standards from being raised.

Defining Individual Incentives

Individual incentive plans reward employees for meeting such work-related performance standards as quality, productivity, customer satisfaction, safety, or attendance. Any one of these standards by itself or in combination may be used. A company ultimately should employ the standards that represent work that an employee performs. For instance, take the case of telemarketers. Customer satisfaction and sales volume measures indicate telemarketers' performance. Tardiness would not be as relevant unless absenteeism was a general management problem.

Managers should also choose factors that are within the individual employee's control when they create individual performance standards. Furthermore, employees must know about standards and potential awards before the performance period starts. When designed and implemented well, individual incentive plans reward employees based on results for which they are directly responsible. The result should be that excellent performers receive higher incentive awards than poor performers.

Types of Individual Incentive Plans

There are six common types of individual incentive plans:

- Piecework plans
- Management incentive plans
- Behavioral encouragement plans
- Referral plans
- Spot bonuses
- Signing bonuses

PIECEWORK PLANS Companies generally use one of two **piecework plans**.[10] The first, which is typically found in manufacturing settings, rewards employees based on their individual hourly production against an objective output standard and are determined by the pace at which manufacturing equipment operates. For each hour, workers receive piecework incentives for every item produced over the designated production standard. Workers also receive a guaranteed hourly pay rate regardless of whether they meet the designated production standard. Table 4-3 illustrates the calculation of a piecework incentive.

Companies use piecework plans when the time to produce a unit is relatively short, usually less than 15 minutes, and the cycle repeats continuously. Piecework plans are usually found in such manufacturing industries as textiles and apparel.

Quality is also an important consideration. Companies do not reward employees for producing defective products. In the apparel industry, manufacturers attempt to minimize defect rates because they cannot sell defective clothing for the same price as nondefective clothing. Selling defective clothing at a lower price reduces company profits.

The second type of piecework incentive plan establishes individual performance standards that include both objective and subjective criteria. Units produced represent an objective standard. Overall work quality is a subjective criterion that is based on supervisors' interpretations and judgments. For example, supervisors may judge customer service representatives' performance to be higher when sales professionals emphasize the benefits of purchasing extended product warranties than when sales professionals merely mention the availability and price of extended product warranties.

Economists argue that there are two advantages to companies of using piecework plans in manufacturing settings known as the **incentive effect** and the **sorting effect**.[11] The incentive effect refers to a worker's willingness to work diligently to produce more quality output than

TABLE 4-3 Calculation of a Piecework Award for a Garment Worker

Piecework standard: 15 stitched garments per hour

Hourly base pay rate: Awarded to employees when the standard is not met: $4.50 per hour. That is, workers receive $4.50 per hour worked, regardless of whether they meet the piecework standard of 15 stitched garments per hour.

Piecework incentive award: $0.75 per garment stitched per hour above the piecework standard

	Guaranteed Hourly Base Pay ($)	Piecework Award (No. of Garments Stitched above the Piecework Standard × Piecework Incentive Award)	Total Hourly Earnings ($)
First hour	4.50	10 garments × $0.75/garment = $7.50	12.00
Second hour	4.50	Fewer than 15 stitched garments, thus piecework award equals $0	4.50

simply attending work without putting in the effort. To put this simply, employees earn much less under the piecework system than they would under a standard hourly pay system. Whereas employees are certainly expected to perform without an incentive (piece rate), research shows that incentives often are associated with higher employee performance.

The sorting effect addresses an employee's choice to stay versus leave his or her employer for another job, presumably one without an incentive pay contingency. Specifically, a hardworking, highly skilled employee is likely to choose to remain employed under an incentive system because both diligence and skill presumably contribute to higher quantity and quality of output—thus, higher pay.

MANAGEMENT INCENTIVE PLANS **Management incentive plans** award bonuses to managers when they meet or exceed objectives based on sales, profit, production, or other measures for their division, department, or unit. Management incentive plans differ from piecework plans in that piecework plans base rewards on the attainment of one specific objective, and management incentive plans often require multiple complex objectives. For example, management incentive plans reward managers for increasing market share or reducing their budgets without compromising the quality and quantity of output. The best-known management incentive plan is management by objectives (MBO).[12] In Chapter 3, MBO was presented as an outcome-oriented performance appraisal technique for merit pay systems. When MBO is used as part of merit pay systems, superiors make subjective assessments of managers' performance, and they use these assessments to determine permanent merit pay increases. When used as part of incentive programs, superiors communicate the amount of incentive pay managers will receive based on the attainment of specific goals. An example is the submission of the company's approved annual affirmative action plan by the Office of Federal Contract Compliance Programs based on timely submission.

BEHAVIORAL ENCOURAGEMENT PLANS Under **behavioral encouragement plans**, employees receive payments for specific behavioral accomplishments (e.g., good attendance or safety records). For example, companies usually award monetary bonuses to employees who have exemplary attendance records for a specified period. When behavioral encouragement plans are applied to safety records, workers earn awards for lower personal injury or accident rates associated with the improper use of heavy equipment or hazardous chemicals. Repeated employee violations of safety rules may require the employer to pay costly fines set by the Occupational Safety and Health Administration. In addition, frequent or serious workplace injuries could lead to workers' compensation insurance claims and subsequent payments to the injured (set by law). A pattern of workplace injuries will eventually lead to increases in the employer's cost to purchase workers' compensation insurance. Overall, the cost of safety incentives stands to be substantially lower than the prices of fines and rising workers' compensation insurance rates.

TABLE 4-4 A Sample Behavioral Encouragement Plan that Rewards Employee Attendance

At the end of each three-month period, employees with exemplary attendance records will receive monetary incentive awards according to the following schedule. Note that the number of days absent does not refer to such company-approved absences as vacation, personal illness, jury duty, bereavement leave, military duty, scheduled holidays, and educational leave.

Number of Days Absent	Monetary Incentive Award ($)
0 (perfect attendance)	250
1	200
2	100
3	50
4	25

Companies sometimes set absenteeism levels as a performance criterion. Table 4-4 contains an illustration of a sample behavioral encouragement plan that rewards employees for excellent attendance. Employees can earn $250 for perfect attendance during a three-month period. With perfect attendance for an entire year, employees can earn $1,000. Behavioral encouragement plans have the potential to save companies substantially more money than the cost of these awards. For example, frequent absenteeism in a company's workforce could disrupt production goals and quality. Customers may respond by choosing to make purchases for better quality products from other companies. Loss of customer bases will have a negative impact on profitability and reputation that prompts prospective customers to choose alternate sources from which to purchase products.

REFERRAL PLANS Employees may receive monetary bonuses under **referral plans** for referring new customers or recruiting successful job applicants. Companies commonly rely on referral bonuses to enhance recruitment of highly qualified employees, particularly when the supply of highly qualified individuals is low, or the company is experiencing substantially higher in demand for its products. Atlassian, the developer of project management and communication software, relies substantially on the work of talented software engineers and designers as well as account executives. In response to these supply and demand considerations, Atlassian offers up to a $10,000 bonus to employees whose referral becomes a successful employee.[13] Some companies, including Dell, post information about its employee referral bonus policy on their websites.[14]

A successful referral usually means that companies award bonuses only if hired referrals remain employed with the company in good standing beyond a designated period, often at least 30 days. Referral plans rely on the idea that current employees' familiarity with company culture should enable them to identify viable candidates for job openings more efficiently than employment agencies could because agents are probably less familiar with client companies' cultures. Employees are likely to make only those referrals they truly believe are worthwhile because their personal reputations are at stake.

☛ FYI

According to a WorldatWork survey, the use of referral bonuses is widespread in companies overall (74 percent). The use of referral plans varies by company size and industry:

- 72 percent for companies with fewer than 500 employees and 86 percent for companies of 40,000 or more employees
- 62 percent in utilities, oil, and gas, 87 percent in health care and social assistance, and 89 percent in finance and insurance[15]

SPOT BONUSES Many organizations today are providing *spot bonuses* for critical areas and talents. **Spot bonuses** are relatively small monetary gifts provided to employees for outstanding work or effort during a reasonably short period of time. If an employee's performance has been exceptional, the employer may reward the worker with a one-time bonus with an amount as low as $50. For certain professional jobs, it is not unheard of for a highly productive worker to receive $5,000 shortly after a noteworthy achievement. About 67 percent of companies have spot bonus programs.[16]

SIGNING BONUSES In Chapter 2, we discussed the influence of supply and demand on wage and salary levels. Besides raising starting base pay rates, companies can also consider offering signing bonuses. **Signing bonuses** are monetary awards given to promote recruitment and job offer acceptance. These bonuses are particularly effective when coupled with a competitive wage or salary offer. Focusing exclusively on wage and salary levels may trigger a bidding war raising wages and salaries that companies cannot sustain for extended periods. To preempt bidding wars, some companies use signing bonuses to entice individuals to join the firm. In 2016, 76 percent of companies surveyed used signing bonuses.[17] Even the military uses signing bonuses. For example, the U.S. Army Corps offers a signing bonus up to $40,000 for translators who speak certain Middle-Eastern languages and enlist as translator aides in the U.S. Army.[18]

Other skilled occupations with shortages include nurses and commercial airline pilots. In the case of nursing, many nurses who planned retirement around the time of the Great Recession (2007–2009) chose to delay doing so. Since then, improvement in the economy has seen a massive wave of nursing retirements, creating labor shortages, particularly as the health care industry grows. The competition is often so fierce in some areas that many hospitals pay signing bonuses of as much as $10,000 to fill large numbers of job vacancies.[19]

Advantages of Individual Incentive Pay Programs

There are four key advantages of individual incentive pay plans. First, individual incentive plans can promote the relationship between pay and performance. As discussed in Chapter 1, employees in the United States are highly motivated by earning money. Employees strive for excellence when they expect to earn incentive awards commensurate with their job performance.

Second, individual incentive plans promote an equitable distribution of compensation within companies (i.e., the amount employees earn depends on their job performance). The better employees perform, the more they earn. Equitable pay ultimately enables companies to retain the best performers. Paying better performers more money sends a signal that the company appropriately values positive job performance.

Third, well-designed incentive plans can instill an ownership mentality for employees who participate. An innovative approach entails educating employees about the costs of doing business (e.g., costs of liability insurance) relative to sales revenue. Leaving employees out of this loop typically leads most to expect generous merit pay raises. A company's willingness to provide generous performance incentives for having employees take ownership over reducing costs and boosting revenues translates this idea into measurable actions and outcomes. For instance, Wayne Automatic Fire Sprinklers awards branch managers with 10 percent of their branch's profits, which can amount to as much as a $300,000 annual incentive payment on top of annual base pay of $75,000.[20] The company also provides total salary incentives of $400,000 to regional managers, which is four times the national average.

A fourth advantage of individual incentive plans is their compatibility with such individualistic cultures as the United States. Because U.S. employees are socialized to make individual contributions and be recognized for them, the national culture of the United States probably enhances the motivational value of individual incentive programs.

Disadvantages of Individual Incentive Pay Programs

Although individual incentive plans can prove effective in certain settings, these programs also have serious limitations. Supervisors, human resource (HR) managers, and compensation professionals should know about three potential problems with individual incentive plans.

First, individual incentive plans possess the potential to promote inflexibility. Because supervisors determine employee performance levels, workers under individual incentive plans become dependent on supervisors for setting work goals. If employees become highly proficient performers, they are not likely to increase their performance beyond their reward compensation. For example, let's assume that management defines the maximum incentive award as $500 per month, which is awarded to employees whose productivity rates 15 percent above the performance standard. Employees who produce more than 15 percent above the production standard will not receive additional incentive pay beyond the $500. With this design, employees would not be motivated to further improve their performance.

Second, with merit pay systems, supervisors must develop and maintain comprehensive performance measures to properly grant incentive awards. Individual incentive programs pose measurement problems when management implements improved work methods or equipment. When such changes occur, it will take some time for employees to become proficient performers. Thus, it will be difficult for companies to determine equitable incentive awards, which may lead to employees' resistance to the new methods.

A third limitation of individual incentive plans is that they may encourage undesirable workplace behavior when these plans reward only one or a subset of dimensions that constitute employees' total job performance. Let's assume that an incentive plan rewards employees for quantity of output. If employees' jobs address such various dimensions as quantity of output, quality, and customer satisfaction, employees may focus on the one dimension—in this case, quantity of output—that leads to incentive pay and thereby neglect of the other dimensions. The Ethics Dilemma presented in Chapter 1 described the ill effects of an undesirable incentive pay program at Wells Fargo.

Our focus has been on financial incentive awards. Companies may provide nonfinancial incentives to employees, including companies such as hotels that operate in a low-paying industry. Hotel chain Joie de Vivre Hospitality does just that. Several times a year, employees are given the opportunity to stay in any of the company's hotels at no charge and to take full advantage of the amenities. By assuming the customer role, Joie de Vivre Hospitality employees can improve job performance because they gain a better understanding of their guests' needs.

GROUP INCENTIVES

4-4. Summarize the practice of group incentive plans.

U.S. employers are increasingly using teams to get work done. Two main changes in the business environment have led to an increased use of teams in the workplace.[21] First, in the 1980s, many more Japanese companies were conducting business in the United States, particularly in the automobile industry. A common feature of Japanese companies was the use of teams, which contributed to superior product quality. Second, team-based job design promotes innovation in the workplace.[22] At Newell Rubbermaid, a manufacturer of such plastic household products as snap-together furniture and storage boxes, product innovation has become the rule since the implementation of project teams. Team members represent various cross-functional areas, including research and development (R&D), marketing, finance, and manufacturing. Rubbermaid attributes the rush on innovation to the cross-fertilization of ideas that has resulted from the work of these diverse teams.[23]

Companies that use work teams need to change individualistic compensation practices so that groups are rewarded for their behavior together.[24] Team-based pay plans should accordingly emphasize cooperation between and within teams, compensate employees for additional responsibilities they often must assume in their roles as members of a team, and encourage team members to attain predetermined objectives for the team.[25] Merit, seniority, or individual incentives do not encourage team behaviors and may potentially limit team effectiveness. Experts suggest that traditional pay programs will undermine the ability of teams to function effectively.[26] Both merit- and seniority-based pay emphasize hierarchy among employees, which is incompatible with the very concept of a team.

Team-based organizational structures encourage team members to learn new skills and assume broader responsibility than is expected of them under traditional pay structures that are geared toward individuals. Rather than following specific orders from a supervisor, employees who work in teams must initiate plans for achieving their team's production. A pay plan for teams usually emphasizes cooperation and rewards its members for the additional responsibilities they must take on, as well as the skills and knowledge they must acquire. Chapter 5 will show how skill- and knowledge-based pay plans can address these additional responsibilities.

Defining Group Incentives

Group incentive programs reward employees for their collective performance, rather than for each employee's individual performance. Group incentive programs are most effective when all group members have some impact on achieving the goal, even though individual contributions might not be equal. Boeing utilizes a team-based approach to manufacture its model 787 Dreamliner.[27] More than 200 cross-functional teams contribute to the construction of each jet, and the contribution of everyone is clearly not equal. Installing such interior trim features as upholstery is not nearly as essential to the airworthiness of each jet as are the jobs of ensuring the aerodynamic integrity of each aircraft.

Well-designed group incentive plans ultimately reinforce teamwork, cultivate loyalty to the company, and increase productivity. For instance, The Morning Star Company, which processes tomato production, is based almost entirely on self-management principles: "We envision an organization of self-managing professionals who initiate communication and coordination of their activities with fellow colleagues, customers, suppliers, and fellow industry participants, absent directives from others."[28] Annually, each employee negotiates a Colleague Letter of Understanding with other employees who are most affected by his or her work.[29] Morning Star leadership believes that voluntary agreements among individuals can produce effective coordination.

Types of Group Incentive Plans

Companies use two major types of group incentive plans:

- *Team-based or small-group incentive plans.* A small group of employees shares a financial reward when a specific objective is met.
- *Gainsharing plans.* A group of employees, generally a department or work unit, is rewarded for productivity gains.

TEAM-BASED OR SMALL-GROUP INCENTIVE PLANS Team-based incentives are similar to individual incentives with one exception. Each group member receives a financial reward for the attainment of a group goal. There are many kinds of team incentive programs. Most companies define these programs based on the type of team.[30]

Work (process) teams refer to organizational units that perform the work of the organization on an ongoing basis. Membership is relatively permanent, and members work full time in the team. Customer service teams and assembly teams on production lines represent excellent examples of work teams. Work teams are effective when individuals are cross-trained to perform other team members' work when they are absent. The goal is to maintain consistency in performance quality (e.g., addressing customer concerns promptly even when one or more team members are absent) and output (e.g., in the case of assembly teams). Team members ultimately engage in performance sharing rather than focusing exclusively on one set of tasks. For instance, the company Blinds Direct, builds teams by having team members switch roles. The goal is to facilitate a better understanding of the complexities of each other's jobs and how they coordinate to maximize team effectiveness.[31] The knowledge and skill sets required to contribute effectively to the work of a process team can also be acquired with the assistance of person-focused pay, which we discuss in Chapter 5.

Project teams consist of a group of people assigned to complete a one-time project. Members usually have well-defined roles and may work on specific phases of the project, either full time or in addition to other work responsibilities of the team. Project teams usually work across such functions as engineering, product development, and marketing to ensure that the final product meets company specifications in terms of cost, quality, and responsiveness to market demands. Many automobile manufacturers rely on project teams for new product development. In the case of hybrid automobiles, many individuals collaborate to ensure the design, engineering, and production of cars that rely less on fossil fuels, demonstrate excellent gas mileage, and offer the same driving experience that people have come to expect of gasoline-powered automobiles.

Parallel teams, or task forces, include employees assigned to work on a specific task in addition to normal work duties. The modifier *parallel* indicates that an employee works on the team task while continuing to work on normal duties. Also, parallel teams or task forces operate on a temporary basis until their work culminates in a recommendation to top management. Task forces are used to evaluate existing systems and processes, to select new technology, and to improve existing products. There is some evidence that team interactions on complex tasks are likely to influence creativity more than individual efforts, and group incentive plans may foster creativity. This especially seems to be the case when incentive compensation is truly an add-on, and independent of employees' regular base pay.[32]

Teams or groups may ultimately receive incentive pay based on such criteria as customer satisfaction (i.e., customer service quality), safety records, quality, and production records. Although these criteria apply to other categories of incentive programs as well (individual, company-wide, and group plans), companies allocate awards to each worker based on the group's attainment of predetermined performance standards.

Human resource managers must devise methods for allocating incentives to team members. Although the team-based reward is generated by the performance of the team, the incentive payments are typically distributed to members of the team individually. Human resource experts allocate rewards in one of three ways:

- Equal incentive payments to all team members.
- Differential incentive payments to team members based on their contribution to the team's performance.
- Differential payments determined by a ratio of each team member's base pay to the total base pay of the group.

The first method—the equal incentives payment approach—reinforces cooperation among team members except when team members perceive differences in members' contributions or performance. The second method—the differential incentive payments approach—distributes rewards based to some extent on individual performance. Differential approaches obviously can hinder cooperative behavior. Some employees may focus on their own performance rather than on the group's performance because they wish to maximize their income. As a compromise, companies may base part of the incentive on individual performance, with the remainder based on the team's performance. The third disbursement method—differential payments by ratio of base pay—rewards each group member in proportion to her or his base pay. This approach assumes that employees with higher base pay contribute more to the company and so should be rewarded in accord with that worth.

GAINSHARING PLANS **Gainsharing** describes group incentive systems that provide participating employees with an incentive payment based on improved company performance for increased productivity, increased customer satisfaction, lower costs, or better safety records.[33]

Gainsharing was developed so that all employees could benefit financially from productivity improvements resulting from the suggestion system. In addition to serving as a compensation tool, most gainsharing reflects a management philosophy that emphasizes employee involvement. The use of gainsharing is most appropriate where workplace technology does not constrain productivity improvements. For example, assembly line workers' abilities to improve productivity may be limited. Increasing the speed of the conveyor belts may compromise workers' safety.

Most gainsharing programs have three components:[34]

- Leadership philosophy
- Employee involvement systems
- Bonuses

The first component—leadership philosophy—refers to a cooperative organizational climate that promotes high levels of trust, open communication, and participation. The second component—employee involvement systems—drives organizational productivity improvements. Employee involvement systems use broadly based suggestion systems. Anyone can make suggestions to a committee made up of both hourly and management employees who oversee the suggestion implementation. This involvement system also may include other innovative employee involvement practices (e.g., problem-solving task forces).

The bonus is the third component of a gainsharing plan. A company awards gainsharing bonuses when its actual productivity exceeds its targeted productivity level. The gainsharing bonuses are usually based on a formula that measures productivity that employees perceive as fair and the employer believes will result in improvements in company performance. Employees typically receive gainsharing bonuses monthly. Most bonuses range between 5 and 10 percent of an employee's base annual pay. A noteworthy exception to this norm is Ameristeel. On average, Ameristeel's gainsharing plan pays out between 35 and 45 percent of base pay.

Although many accounts of gainsharing use can be found in the practitioner and scholarly literature, no one has completed a comprehensive, soundly designed investigation of the effectiveness of gainsharing programs.[35] Meanwhile, gainsharing programs' success has been attributed to company cultures that support cooperation among employees.[36] Some gainsharing attempts have failed. Such organizational, external environmental and financial information factors, including poor communications within and across departments, highly competitive product markets, and variable corporate profits over time can inhibit effective gainsharing programs.[37] Poor communications will stifle the creativity needed to improve the efficiency of work processes when employees focus exclusively on their own work. Highly competitive product markets often require companies to make frequent changes to their production methods, as in the automobile industry, where such changes occur each year with the introduction of new models. When companies make frequent or sudden changes, employees must have time to learn the new processes well before they can offer productive suggestions. Companies that experience variable profits from year to year most likely do not use gainsharing because management sets aside as much excess cash as possible in reserve for periods when profits are down and excess cash is scarce.

The Scanlon, Rucker, and Improshare gainsharing plans are the most common forms used in companies, and they were also the first types of gainsharing plans developed and used by employers. These plans were adopted wholesale in the early days of gainsharing. Employers today generally modify one of these traditional plans to meet their needs or adopt hybrid plans.

THE SCANLON PLAN Joseph Scanlon first developed the gainsharing concept in 1935 as an employee involvement system without a pay element.[38] The hallmark of the **Scanlon plan** is its emphasis on employee involvement. Scanlon believed that employees will exercise self-direction and self-control if they are committed to company objectives and that employees will accept and seek out responsibility if given the opportunity.[39] Current Scanlon plans include monetary rewards to employees for productivity improvements. Scanlon plans assume that companies will be able to offer higher pay to workers, generate increased profits for stockholders, and lower prices for consumers. The *Scanlon plan* is a generic term referring to any gainsharing plan that has characteristics common to the original gainsharing plan devised by Scanlon. Scanlon plans have the following three components:[40]

- An emphasis on teamwork to reduce costs, assisted by management-supplied information on production concerns.
- Suggestion systems that route cost-saving ideas from the workforce through a labor–management committee that evaluates and acts on accepted suggestions.
- A monetary reward based on productivity improvements to encourage employee involvement.

Scanlon plan employee involvement systems include a formal suggestion program structured at two levels. Production-level committees, usually including a department foreman or supervisor and at least one elected worker, communicate the suggestion program and its reward features to workers. Production committee members encourage and assist workers in making suggestions and formally record suggestions for consideration. Production committees may also reject suggestions that are not feasible, but they must provide a written explanation of the reasons for the rejection to the worker who made the suggestion. Providing the written rationale under this circumstance is key to helping employees understand why the suggestions are not feasible and, thus, workers are not discouraged from making suggestions in the future. After employees' suggestions have been fully implemented, they typically receive bonuses monthly.

The production committee forwards appropriate suggestions to a company-wide screening committee. This committee also includes worker representatives, and it reviews suggestions referred by the production committees, serves as a communications link between management and employees, and reviews the company's performance each month.

Actual gainsharing formulas are designed to suit the individual needs of the company.[41] Formulas are usually based on the ratio between labor costs and **sales value of production (SVOP)**.[42] The SVOP is the sum of sales revenue plus the value of goods in inventory.

Smaller Scanlon ratios indicate that labor costs are lower relative to SVOP. Companies strive for lower ratios, as Table 4-5 illustrates. In addition, Table 4-5 shows the calculation for a bonus distribution under a Scanlon plan.

TABLE 4-5 Illustration of a Scanlon Plan

For the period 2016–2018, the labor costs of XYZ Manufacturing Company have averaged $44,000,000 per year. During the same three-year period, the sales value of XYZ's production (SVOP) averaged $83,000,000 per year. (As an aside, of the $83,000,000, $65,000,000 represents sales revenue and $18,000,000 represents the value of goods held in inventory.) The Scanlon ratio for XYZ Manufacturing Company is:

$$\$44,000,000/\$83,000,000 = 0.53$$

The ratio of 0.53 is the base line or standard. Any benefits that result from an improvement in production methods produce results. Labor cost savings are shared with workers. In other words, when improvements lead to a Scanlon ratio that is lower than the standard of 0.53, employees will receive gainsharing bonuses.

The operating information for XYZ Manufacturing Company for March 2019 was as follows:

Total labor costs	$3,100,000
SVOP	$7,200,000

The Scanlon ratio, based on March 2019 information was

$$\frac{\$3,100,000}{\$7,200,000} = 0.43$$

The Scanlon ratio for March 2019 was less than the standard of 0.53. For there to be a payout, labor costs for March 2019 must be less than $3,816,000 (i.e., 0.53 × $7,200,000); $3,816,000 represents allowable labor costs for March 2019 based on the Scanlon standard established for XYZ Manufacturing.

In summary, the allowable labor costs for March 2019 were $3,816,000. The actual labor costs were $3,100,000. Thus, the savings $716,000 ($3,816,000–$3,100,000) is available for distribution as a bonus.

THE RUCKER PLAN Similar to Scanlon's plan, the **Rucker plan** was developed by Allan W. Rucker in 1933. Both the Scanlon and Rucker plans emphasize employee involvement and now provide monetary incentives to encourage employee participation. The main difference lies in the formula used to measure productivity. Rucker plans use a **value-added formula** to measure productivity. Value added is the difference between the value of the sales price of a product and the value of materials purchased to make the product. The following example illustrates the concept of value added based on the sequence of events that eventually lead to selling bread to consumers. These events include growing the wheat, milling the wheat, adding the wheat to other ingredients to make bread, and selling the bread to consumers.

A farmer grows the wheat and sells it to a miller; the added value is the difference in the income the farmer receives for the wheat and the costs incurred for purchasing seed, fertilizer, fuel, and other supplies. The miller, in turn, buys the wheat from the farmer, mills it, and then sells it to a bakery. The difference in the cost of buying the wheat and the price it is sold for to the baker is the amount of "value" the miller "adds" in the milling processes. The same process is repeated by the baker, as the flour that was milled by the miller is mixed with other ingredients, baked, and sold as bread either to the consumer or to a retailer who in turn sells it to the consumer. The baker "adds value" by blending in the other ingredients to the flour and baking the bread. If the bread is sold to the consumer through a retailer, then the retailer also "adds value" by buying the bread from the bakery, transporting it to a store convenient for the consumer, displaying the bread, and selling it. The total of all the added values from each step along the way equals the total contribution to the overall economy from the chain of events.[43]

The following ratio is used to determine whether bonuses will be awarded under a Rucker plan:

$$\frac{\text{Value added}}{\text{Total employment costs}}$$

In contrast to the Scanlon ratio, companies prefer a larger Rucker ratio. A larger Rucker ratio indicates that the value added is greater than total employment costs. Table 4-6 illustrates the calculation for bonus distribution under the Rucker plan.

Invented by Mitchell Fein in 1973, **Improshare**—Improved Productivity through Sharing—measures productivity physically rather than in terms of dollar savings like those used in the Scanlon and Rucker plans. These programs aim to produce more products with fewer labor hours. Under Improshare, the emphasis is on providing employees with an incentive to finish products. The Improshare bonus is based on a **labor hour ratio formula**. A standard is determined by analyzing historical accounting data to find the number of labor hours needed to complete a product. Productivity is then measured as a ratio of standard labor hours and actual labor hours. Unlike the Rucker and Scanlon plans, employee participation is not a feature, and workers receive bonuses on a weekly basis.

In summary, the Scanlon, Rucker, and Improshare plans are among the best-known kinds of gainsharing programs that are used by companies. Although the principle underlying these different plans is the same (i.e., a group incentive system that provides all or most employees a bonus payment based on improved performance), they each rest on slightly different assumptions.

Advantages of Group Incentives

The use of group incentive plans has two advantages for companies. First, companies can more easily develop performance measures for group incentive plans than they can for individual incentive plans. There are obviously fewer groups in a company than individuals. Thus, companies generally use fewer resources (e.g., staff time) to develop performance measures. In addition, judging the quality of the final product makes the most sense because companies must deliver high-quality products to maintain competitiveness. During the late 1970s and early 1980s, U.S. automobile manufacturers lost substantial market share to foreign automobile manufacturers because foreign automakers marketed automobiles of substantially higher quality than U.S. automakers. The trend did not change until U.S. automakers manufactured high-quality vehicles on a consistent basis.

TABLE 4-6 Illustration of a Rucker Plan

Calculating the Standard:

For the 2015–2018 period, ABC Manufacturing Company generated average net sales of $7,500,000. The company paid $3,200,000 for materials, $250,000 for sundry supplies, and $225,000 for such services as liability insurance, basic maintenance, and utilities. Based on these data, average value added was $3,825,000 (i.e., net sales – costs of materials, supplies, and services rendered), for this example, $7,500,000 - ($3,200,000 + $250,000 + $225,000).

For the same period, average total employment costs were $2,400,000, which includes hourly wages for nonexempt workers, annual salaries for exempt employees, payroll taxes, and all benefit costs. Based on the Rucker formula, the ratio of value added to total employment costs was 1.59 ($3,825,000/$2,400,000).

If there are to be bonuses at the end of 2019, each dollar attributed to employment costs must be accompanied by creating at least $1.59 of value added.

Value added	$3,825,000
Total employment costs	$2,400,000

The Rucker ratio, based on this information, was:

$$\frac{\$3,825,000}{\$2,400,000} = 1.59$$

Applying the Standard to 2019 Performance:

The operating information for ABC Manufacturing Company for 2019 was as follows:

Value added	$670,000
Total employment costs	$625,000

The Rucker ratio, based on 2019 data, was:

$$\frac{\$670,000}{\$625,000} = 1.07$$

This Rucker ratio for 2019 was less than the standard of 1.59. For there to be a payout, value added for 2019 must be more than the standard, which would be $1,065,300 (1.59 × $670,000). However, based on the Rucker ratio obtained for this month (1.07), value added was only $716,900 (1.07 × $670,000). Therefore, employees of ABC Manufacturing will not receive any gainsharing bonuses based on 2019 performance.

Greater group cohesion is the second advantage associated with group incentive plans.[44] Cohesive groups usually work more effectively toward achieving common goals than do individual group members focusing on the specific tasks for which they are responsible. Working collaboratively is undoubtedly in group members' best interests to maximize their incentive awards.

Disadvantages of Group Incentives

The main disadvantage of group incentive compensation is employee turnover. Companies' implementation of group incentive programs may lead to turnover because of the **free-rider effect**. Some employees may make fewer contributions to the group goals because they possess lower ability, skills, or experience than other group members. In some groups, members may deliberately choose to put forth less effort, particularly when each group member receives the same incentive compensation regardless of individual contributions to the group goals. In any case, the free-rider effect initially leads to feelings of inequity among those who make the greatest contributions to the attainment of the group goal. Over time, members who make the greatest contributions are likely to leave.

Group members may feel uncomfortable with the fact that other members' performance influences their compensation level. Exemplary performers are more likely to feel this way when other group members are not contributing equally to the attainment of group goals. The lower performance of a few group members may lead to lower earnings for all members of the group. Discomfort with group incentive plans is likely to be heightened where incentive compensation represents the lion's share of core compensation.

COMPANY-WIDE INCENTIVES

The use of company-wide incentive plans can be traced to the nineteenth century. Companies instituted profit sharing programs to ease workers' dissatisfaction with low pay and to change their beliefs that company management paid workers substandard wages while earning substantial profits. Quite simply, management believed that workers would be less likely to challenge managerial practices if they received a share of company profits.

4-5. Describe the practice of company-wide incentive plans.

Defining Company-wide Incentives

Company-wide incentive plans reward employees when the company exceeds minimum acceptable performance standards (e.g., profits or the overall value of the company based on its stock price). As competitive pressures on companies increased, management sought methods to improve employee productivity. Companies presently use company-wide incentive programs to motivate employees to work harder for increased profits or increased company value to owners. Advocates of company-wide incentive plans believe that well-designed programs make workers' and owners' goals more compatible as workers strive toward increasing company profits or value.

Types of Company-wide Incentive Plans

Companies use two major types of company-wide incentive plans:

- *Profit sharing plans.* Employees earn a financial reward when their company's profit objective is met.
- *Employee stock option plans.* Companies grant employees the right to purchase shares of company stock.

PROFIT SHARING PLANS Profit sharing plans pay a portion of company profits to employees, separate from base pay, cost-of-living adjustments, or permanent merit pay increases. Two basic kinds of profit sharing plans are used widely today. First, **current profit sharing** plans award cash to employees, typically on a quarterly or annual basis. Current profit sharing represents a form of short-term incentive because of the frequency of payout potential. Second, **deferred profit sharing** plans place cash awards in trust accounts for employees. These trusts are set aside on employees' behalf as a source of retirement income, and can also be considered a long-term incentive. Ford offers current profit sharing plans to its 54,000 unionized (United Automobile Workers union) workers. In 2017, based on a net profit of $8.4 billion, each worker received a $7,500 profit sharing award.[45] In 2017, Delta Airlines awarded $1.1 billion in profit sharing awards to its 80,000 employees worldwide.[46]

☛ FYI

According to a WorldatWork survey, 22 percent of companies overall offer current profit sharing plans. Utilization varies by industry:

- The greatest prevalence is in the manufacturing industry (38 percent) and in the consulting, professional, scientific, and technical services industry (31 percent).
- The least prevalence is in the utilities, oil, and gas industry (10 percent) and the health care and social assistance industry (12 percent).[47]

Calculating Profit Sharing Awards HR professionals determine the pool of profit sharing money with any of three possible formulas. A fixed *first-dollar-of-profits* formula uses a specific percentage of annual profits, contingent upon the successful attainment of a company goal. For instance, a company might establish that the profit sharing fund will equal 7 percent of corporate profits; however, payment is contingent on a specified reduction in scrap rates.

Second, companies may use a *graduated first-dollar-of-profits* formula instead of a fixed percentage. For example, a company may choose to share 3 percent of the first $8 million of profits and 6 percent of the profits more than that level. Graduated formulas motivate employees to strive for extraordinary profit targets by sharing even more of the incremental gain.

Third, *profitability threshold* formulas fund profit sharing pools only if profits exceed a predetermined minimum level but fall below some established maximum level. Companies establish minimums to guarantee a return to shareholders before they distribute profits to employees. They establish maximums because they attribute any profits beyond this level to factors other than employee productivity or creativity (e.g., technological innovation).

After management selects a funding formula for the profit sharing pool, they must consider how to distribute pool money among employees. Companies usually make distributions in one of two ways: equal payments to all employees and proportional payments to employees based on annual base earnings. There is a third approach that, while it is based on sound logic, is difficult to operationalize. Some companies measure employee contributions to profits based on job performance; however, this approach is not feasible because it is difficult to isolate each employee's contributions to profits. For example, how does a secretary's performance (based on answering telephones, greeting visitors, and typing memos) directly contribute to company performance? The same can be said for employees throughout the ranks of the company. To what extent and by how much does an employee relations manager contribute to profits?

Equal payments to all employees reflect a belief that all employees should share equally in the company's gain to promote cooperation among employees; however, employee contributions to profits probably vary. Most employers accordingly divide the profit sharing pool among employees based on a differential basis.

Companies may disburse profits based on *proportional payments to employees based on annual base earnings*. As we will detail in Chapters 6 and 7, salary levels vary based on both internal and external factors; in general, the higher the salary, the more value the company assigns to a job. Higher-paying jobs presumably indicate more potential to influence a company's competitive position. For any given job, pay will differ according to performance or seniority. Chapter 3 notes that higher performance levels and seniority result in greater worth.

Advantages of Profit Sharing Plans The use of a profit sharing plan has two main advantages, one for employees and the other for companies. When properly designed, profit sharing plans enable employees to share in companies' fortunes. As employees benefit from profit sharing plans, they will be more likely to work productively to promote profits. The upshot of enhanced employee productivity obviously is greater profits for companies that use profit sharing plans.

Companies that use profit sharing programs gain greater financial flexibility. As we discussed, monetary payouts to employees vary with profit levels. During economic downturns, payout levels are significantly lower than they are during economic boom periods. This feature of profit sharing plans enables companies to use limited cash reserves where needed (e.g., for R&D activities).

Disadvantages of Profit Sharing Plans There are two main disadvantages associated with profit sharing plans. The first one directly affects employees; the second affects companies. Profit sharing plans may undermine the economic security of employees, particularly if profit sharing represents a sizable portion of direct compensation. Because company profits vary from year to year, so do employees' earnings. Thus, employees will find it difficult to predict their earnings, which will affect their saving and buying behavior. If there is significant variability in earnings, a company's excellent performers are likely to leave for employment with competitors. The turnover of excellent performers certainly represents a significant disadvantage to companies.

Employers also find profit sharing programs to be problematic under certain conditions. Profit sharing plans may fail to motivate employees because they do not see a direct link between their efforts and corporate profits. Hourly employees may have trouble seeing this connection because their efforts appear to be several steps removed from the company's performance. For instance, an assembly line worker who installs interior trim (e.g., carpeting and seats) in automobiles may not find any connection between his or her efforts and the level of company profits because interior trim represents just one of many steps in the production of automobiles.

EMPLOYEE STOCK OPTION PLANS Employee stock option plans represent a long-term company-wide incentive that provides employees with stock options. Under these plans, companies grant employees the right to purchase shares of company stock. **Company stock** represents total equity of a company. **Company stock shares** represent equity segments of equal value. Equity interest increases positively with the number of stock shares. **Stock options** describe an employee's right to purchase company stock. Employees do not actually own stock until they exercise the stock option rights. This is done by purchasing stock at a designated price after a company-chosen time lapses, usually no more than 10 years. Employee stock options provide an incentive to work productively, with the expectation that collective employee productivity will increase the value of company stock over time. Employees earn monetary compensation when they sell the stock at a higher price than they originally paid for it.

DESIGNING INCENTIVE PAY PROGRAMS

When designing an incentive pay plan, HR professionals and line managers should consider five key factors:

4-6. Summarize considerations when designing incentive pay programs.

- Whether the plan should be based on group or individual employee performance
- The level of risk employees will be willing to accept in their overall compensation package
- Whether incentive pay should replace or complement traditional pay
- The criteria by which performance should be judged
- The time horizon for goals—long term, short term, or a combination of both

Group versus Individual Incentives

Companies considering various design alternatives should choose a design that fits the structure of the company. Group incentive programs are most suitable where the nature of the work is interdependent and the contributions of individual employees are difficult to measure. In such situations, companies require cooperative behavior among their employees. Companies may be able to encourage team behavior by linking compensation to the achievement of department or division goals and eliminating from the pay determination process such factors that are outside the group's control as the late delivery of raw materials by an independent vendor.

On the other hand, individual incentive plans reward employees for meeting or surpassing such predetermined individual goals as production or sales quotas. The attainment of individual goals should be well within employees' grasp as is the case for group incentives. Moreover, goals for individual incentive programs should be based on independent work rather than interdependent work. For example, it would be appropriate to base an employee's incentive on typing accuracy because the work can be performed independently and there are few external constraints on an employee's ability to complete such work. At the group level, it would be reasonable to provide incentives to the individual members of a sales team. In the case of computer hardware and networks, the sale and implementation of these products involve a team of marketing professionals and technical experts who depend on the others' expertise to identify the appropriate configuration of hardware and networking equipment (i.e., meeting the client's needs) and to install the equipment in the client's company successfully.

Level of Risk

Careful consideration should be given to the level of risk employees are willing to accept. As mentioned previously, incentive pay may complement base salary or may be used in place of all or a portion of base salary. The level of risk clearly increases as incentive pay represents a greater proportion of total core compensation. The level of risk tends to be greater among higher-level employees than among those who are at the lower levels of a company's job structure. It is reasonable to infer that the attainment of a first-line supervisor's goal of maintaining a packing department's level of productivity above a predetermined level is less risky than the achievement of a sales manager's goal of increasing market share by 10 percent in a market where the competition is already quite stiff. Apart from an employee's rank, the level of risk chosen should depend on the extent to which employees control the attainment of the desired goal. The adoption of incentive pay programs makes the most sense when participants have a reasonable degree of control over the attainment of the plan's goals. Incentive programs logically are bound to fail when the goals are simply out of reach because they are too difficult or because extraneous factors are hampering employees' efforts to meet goals.

Complementing or Replacing Base Pay

When complementing base pay, a company awards incentive pay in addition to an employee's base pay and benefits. On the other hand, companies may reduce base pay by placing the reduced portion at risk in an incentive plan. For instance, if a company grants its employees 10 percent raises each year, the company could, instead, grant its employees a 4 percent cost-of-living increase and use the remaining 6 percent as incentive by awarding none of it to below-average performers, only half of it to employees whose performance is average, and the entire 6 percent to employees whose performance is above average. In this scenario, the 6 percent that was expected by the employees to become part of their base pay is no longer a guarantee because that potential salary has been placed at risk. By introducing risk into the pay program, employees have the potential to earn more than the 6 percent because poor performers will receive less, leaving more to be distributed to exemplary performers.

Companies in such cyclical industries as retail sales could benefit by including an incentive component in the core compensation programs they offer to employees. During slow business periods, the use of regular merit pay programs that add permanent increments to base pay can create budget problems. If incentive pay were used instead of permanent merit raises, then the level of expenditure on compensation would vary with levels of business activity. In effect, the use of incentive pay can lower payroll costs during lean periods and enhance the level of rewards when business activity picks up.

Performance Criteria

As seen in the discussion of performance appraisal in Chapter 3, the measures used to appraise employee performance obviously should be quantifiable and accessible. For incentive pay programs, common measures of employee performance are company profits, sales revenue, and number of units produced by a business unit. The measures chosen preferably should relate to the company's competitive strategy. For instance, if a company is attempting to enhance quality, its incentive plan would probably reward employees on the basis of customer satisfaction with quality.

More than one performance measure may be relevant. In such instances, a company is likely to employ all the measures as a basis for awarding incentives. The weighting scheme would reflect the relative importance of each performance criterion to the company's competitive strategy [e.g., company performance (10 percent), unit performance (40 percent), and individual performance (50 percent), incorporating all the organizational levels]. An employee clearly would receive an incentive even if company or departmental performance was poor. In effect, the relative weights are indicative of the degree of risk to an employee that is inherent in these plans. Compared with the previous example, the following plan would be quite risky: 50 percent company performance, 35 percent departmental performance, and 15 percent individual performance. Employees' earnings would depend mainly on company and departmental performance over which they possess less control than they do over their own performance.

Time Horizon: Short Term versus Long Term

A key feature of incentive pay plans is the time orientation. There are no definitive standards to distinguish between short term and long term. A general rule of thumb is that short-term goals generally can be achieved in five years or less and that long-term goals may require even longer. Most companies offer one or more short-term plans.[48] Among the most popular plans are spot awards, profit sharing, and team-based incentives.

On the other hand, incentive programs for professionals and executives also have a long-term orientation. Stock option plans are among the most commonly used.[49] For instance, rewarding an engineer's innovation in product design requires a long-term orientation because it takes an extended amount of time to move through the series of steps required to bring the innovation to the marketplace (e.g., patent approval, manufacturing, and market distribution). The incentives that executives receive are based on a long-term horizon because their success is matched against the endurance of a company over time.

 FYI

According to a WorldatWork survey, nearly all companies (94 percent) use short-term incentives, but only about half (53 percent) used long-term incentives.[50]

PREPARING FOR EXAMS/QUIZZES

Chapter Summary by Learning Objectives

Learning Objective 4-1. *Explore the incentive pay approach.* Incentive pay or variable pay is defined as compensation, other than base wages or salaries, which fluctuates according to employees' attainment of some standard, such as a preestablished formula, individual or group goals, or company earnings.

Learning Objective 4-2. *Describe the differences between incentive pay methods and traditional pay methods.* In traditional pay plans, employees receive compensation based on a fixed hourly pay rate or annual salary. Annual raises are added to base pay according to seniority or a supervisor's evaluation of past performance. In incentive plans, employees receive one-time payments that correspond to the level of performance attainment based on objective goals.

Learning Objective 4-3. *Explain the practice of individual incentive pay plans.* Individual incentive plans reward employees whose work is performed independently and can be quantified objectively such as by sales volume or number of units produced.

Learning Objective 4-4. *Summarize the practice of group incentive plans.* Group incentive plans promote supportive, collaborative behavior among employees. In general, members of a group or team receive the same incentive award for the group's performance.

Learning Objective 4-5. *Describe the practice of company-wide incentive plans.* Company-wide incentive plans tie employee compensation to a company's performance over a relatively short time frame, commonly, from three months to five years.

Learning Objective 4-6. *Summarize considerations when designing incentive pay programs.* Compensation professionals consider at least five important factors when designing effective incentive pay plans. These include: (a) group versus individual incentives, (b) level of risk, (c) compensating or replacing base pay, (d) performance criteria, and (e) a short- or long-term time horizon.

Key Terms

Discussion Questions

4-1. Do you agree with the following statement? Individual incentive plans are less preferable than group incentives and company-wide incentives. Explain your answer.

4-2. There is currently a tendency among business professionals to endorse the use of incentive pay plans. Identify an occupation for which individual incentive pay is appropriate and an occupation for which individual incentive pay is inappropriate. What is the rationale for your choices?

4-3. Critics of profit sharing plans maintain that these plans do not motivate employees to perform at higher levels. Under what conditions are profit sharing plans not likely to motivate employees?

4-4. Unlike individual incentive programs, group and company-wide incentive programs reward individuals based on group (e.g., cost savings in a department) and company-wide (e.g., profits) performance standards, respectively. Under group and company-wide incentive programs, it is possible for poor performers to benefit without making substantial contributions to group or company goals. What can companies do to ensure that poor performers do not benefit?

4-5. Opponents of incentive pay programs argue that these programs manipulate employees more than seniority and merit pay programs. Do you agree with this statement? Explain.

PREPARING FOR MY CAREER

Compensation in Action

The use of incentive pay by an employer can be an effective way to tie individual or team performance to compensation. Many of the items in the *Action Checklist* are critical to the proper formation and administration of an incentive pay program (i.e., accurate criteria and measurement along with ongoing and honest performance discussions). Once this critical foundation is established, line managers and HR and compensation specialists must ensure that the plan is understood by employees and they can see the link between their performance and the portion of pay at risk.

Action checklist for line managers and HR—establishing an incentive pay program

HR takes the lead

- Work with compensation specialists on your team to examine whether industry competitors use individual, group, or company-wide programs. The goal is to stay current with trends and ensure that the best employees are retained.
- Work with line managers, based on the chosen program (individual, group, or company-wide), to choose which types of plan are utilized.
- Hold roundtable discussions with employees to gather feedback on the proposed program and to identify potential areas where additional buy-in may be necessary.

Line managers take the lead

- Work with HR to identify the desired behavior(s) you want to tie to incentives—ensuring that the focus on these behaviors does not come at the expense of other desired outcomes.
- Seek the education of HR to understand limitations of the chosen plan and how to overcome some of the potential pitfalls; plan should be monitored and/or tailored if these obstacles lead to the wrong behaviors being rewarded.
- Provide proper information to HR so that a communication plan is created for rollout and implementation of the program—HR will form frequently asked questions (FAQs) and talking points that detail rationale for the change.

Cases

Case 1: Individual or Team Reward?

Jack Hopson has been making wood furniture for more than ten years. He recently joined Metropolitan Furniture and has some ideas for Sally Boston, the company's CEO. Jack likes working for Sally because she is very open to employee suggestions and is serious about making the company a success. Metropolitan is currently paying Jack a competitive hourly pay rate for him to build various designs of tables and chairs. However, Jack thinks that an incentive pay plan might convince him and his coworkers to put forth more effort.

At Jack's previous employer, a competing furniture maker, Jack was paid on a piece-rate pay plan. The company paid Jack a designated payment for every chair or table that he completed. Jack felt this plan provided him an incentive to work harder to build the furniture pieces. Sally likes Jack's idea; however, Sally is concerned about how such a plan would affect the employees' need to work together as a team.

While the workers at Metropolitan build most furniture pieces individually, they often need to pitch in and work as a team. Each worker receives individual assignments, but as a delivery date approaches for a preordered furniture set due to a customer, the workers must help each other complete certain pieces of the set to ensure on-time delivery. A reputation for on-time delivery differentiates Metropolitan from its competitors. Several companies that compete against Metropolitan have a reputation for late deliveries, which gives Metropolitan a competitive edge. Because their promise of on-time delivery is such a high priority, Sally is concerned that a piece-rate pay plan may prevent employees from working together to complete furniture sets.

Sally agrees with Jack that an incentive pay plan would help boost productivity, but she thinks that a team-based incentive pay plan may be a better approach. She has considered offering a team-based plan that provides a bonus payment when each set of furniture is completed in time for scheduled delivery. However, after hearing from Jack about the success of the piece-rate pay plan at his previous employer, she is unsure of which path to take.

Questions:

4-6. What are some advantages of offering a piece-rate pay plan to the furniture builders at Metropolitan Furniture?

4-7. What are some advantages of offering a team-based incentive pay plan?

4-8. What do you think Sally should do?

Case 2: Ethics Dilemma: Incentive Pay Gone Wrong

The U.S. Veteran Administration (VA) hospital in Phoenix awarded incentive payments to managers for increasing the efficiency of hospital operations. One measure was reduced time in the waiting room and this objective could be achieved by limiting the daily number of appointments. Not surprisingly, Veterans and their family members complained that the period between making an appointment and the appointment itself was growing. In many cases, veterans waited months before they could "get in" to see the doctor. In the interim, dozens died of their illnesses—with shorter wait times, several deaths could have been prevented. Public attention to the VA hospital situation prompted investigations to determine the reasons for lengthy wait times. Reviews of hospital records showed that wait times for an appointment were about two weeks, except, the hospital created a waiting list to control the number of patients at any one time. Fewer appointments increased the likelihood that doctors would stay on schedule. Unfortunately, wait times grew from two weeks to anywhere between 6 and 20 weeks.

Questions:

4-9. As a compensation professional, what would you do?

4-10. What factor(s) in this ethical dilemma might influence a person to make a less-than-ethical decision?

Crunch the Numbers!

Calculating Profit Sharing Pay Awards

In your new role as compensation analyst, you have been asked to estimate the dollar amount of the profit sharing pool based on three approaches as well as the allocation of profit sharing awards to eligible employees. The company's profits equal $35 million. You are considering the following three formulas for determining the total profit sharing pool.

- *First-Dollar of Profits*: The company agrees to share two percent of all profits up to $12 million.
- *Graduated First-Dollar-of-Profits*: The company agrees to share three percent of all profits up to $15 million, and five percent of all profits up to $40 million.
- *Profitability Threshold Formula*: The company will share three percent of the profits above $10 million up to $17 million.

There are 250 employees whose total annual base pay equals $2,100,000.

Questions:

4-11. Calculate the total profit sharing pool for the following scenarios: (a) first-dollar of profits, (b) graduated first-dollar of profits, and (c) profitability threshold formula.

4-12. Calculate the average profit sharing award per employee based on the equal payments formula.

4-13. Calculate the profit sharing awards based on the proportional payments based on annual base pay formula for (a) Jim, whose annual base pay equals $55,000, (b) Margaret, whose annual base pay is $125,000, and (c) Ella, whose annual base pay is $210,000. (*Note*: Profit sharing awards equal 10 percent of annual salary.)

Working Together: Team Exercise

In small groups of three or four, come up with specific answers to the following questions. Talk through your perspectives and come up with a team response. Be prepared to share your ideas with the class.

As a group, think about group class project teams on which you participated. Also, think about the project grade as an incentive. Most group members agree that a grade of *A* is the desired target. Unfortunately, some group members do not pull their weight (free riders), putting the attainment of a high grade in jeopardy. At one time or another, you were probably a member of a team in which one or more members held the group back.

Questions:

4-14. How did you handle free riders? Explain.

4-15. In situations where you experienced free riders, could the evaluation of student performance have been structured differently? Explain.

Endnotes

1. Charles Peck, *Variable Pay: Nontraditional Programs for Motivation and Reward* (New York: The Conference Board, 1993).
2. Luis R. Gómez Mejía and David B. Balkin, *Compensation, Organizational Strategy and Firm Performance* (Cincinnati, OH: South-Western, 1992).
3. Frank Koller, "2016 Ends at Lincoln Electric, No Layoffs for, Now, 68 Years and 83 Years of Amazing Profit-sharing Bonuses," (December 9, 2016), Frank Koller blog, accessed January 28, 2018, http://www.frankkoller.com.
4. Southwest Airlines, *WorkPerks*, (2015), accessed February 23, 2015, http://www.southwest.com.
5. Conor Shine, *Share the Love: Southwest Airlines to Give Employees $586 Million in Profit-share Bonuses* (February 9, 2017), accessed January 28, 2018, http://www.dallasnews.com.
6. WorldatWork and Vivient Consulting, *Incentive Pay Practices Survey: Publicly Traded Companies* (February, 2016), accessed January 29, 2018, http://www.worldatwork.org.
7. Stephen Miller, *Bonus Binge: Variable Pay Outpaces Salary* (August 11, 2016), accessed January 28, 2018, http://www.shrm.org.
8. WorldatWork and Vivient Consulting, *Incentive Pay Practices Survey: Publicly Traded Companies* (February 2016), accessed January 29, 2018, http://www.worldatwork.org.
9. Dubofsky Melvyn and Joseph A. McCartin, *Labor in America: A History*, (9th ed.) (New York: John Wiley & Sons, 2017).
10. Peck, *Variable Pay.*
11. Edward P. Lazear, *Personnel Economics for Managers* (New York: John Wiley & Sons, 1998).
12. Peter Drucker, *The Practice of Management* (New York: Harper, 1954).
13. Kristen Pope, (2015). *Refer a Friend: 15 Employee Referral Programs that Offer Serious Cash*, (Blog on Brazen.com), accessed January 29, 2018, http://www.brazen.com.
14. *Referral Rewards: Employee Referral Bonus Policy (2017)*, accessed January 29, 2018, https://dell.referrals.selectminds.com/info/rewards.
15. WorldatWork and Compdata Surveys & Consulting, *Inventory of Total Rewards Programs & Practices*, (January, 2017), accessed January 29, 2018, http://www.worldatwork.org.
16. Ibid.
17. WorldatWork, "Bonus Programs and Practices," A Report by WorldatWork (July 2016), accessed February 3, 2018, http://www.worldatwork.org/waw/adimLink?id=80398.
18. U.S. Army, "Bonuses," (February 2017), accessed February 3, 2018, https://www.goarmy.com/benefits/money/bonuses-earning-extra-money.html.
19. Jacob Mincer, "Short on Staff: Nursing Crisis Strains U.S. Hospitals," *Reuters*, (October 20, 2017), accessed January 4, 2018, http://www.reuters.com; M. Evans, "Nurses Are in Demand Again," *The Wall Street Journal*, (November 8, 2016), accessed January 8, 2018, http://www.wsj.com.
20. Steven Adams, "Paying Huge Incentives for Performance, Wayne Automatic Fire Sprinklers Makes Big Profits, Too," *Forbes*, (October 2, 2017), accessed February 3, 2018, http://www.forbes.com.
21. Susan E. Jackson, "Team Composition in Organizational Settings: Issues in Managing an Increasingly Diverse Workforce," in S. Worchel, W. Wood & J. A. Simpson (Eds.), *Group Process and Productivity* (Newbury Park, CA: Sage, 1992), 138–173.
22. Rosabeth Moss Kanter, "When a Thousand Flowers Bloom: Structural, Collective, and Social Conditions for Innovation in Organizations," in B. M. Staw & L. L. Cummings (Eds.), *Research in Organizational Behavior* (Vol. 10) (Greenwich, CT: JAI, 1988) 169–211.s

23. Newell Rubbermaid, Design Center, (2015), accessed January 31, 2015, http://design.newellrubber-maid.com/index.html.

24. Stephen Worchel, Wendy L. Wood, and Jeffry A. Simpson, (Eds.), *Group Process and Productivity* (Newbury Park, CA: Sage, 1992).

25. Jill Kanin-Lovers and Marsha Cameron, "Team-based Reward Systems," *Journal of Compensation and Benefits* (January–February, 1993): 55–60.

26. Jay R. Schuster and Patricia K. Zingheim, "Building Pay Environments to Facilitate High-performance Teams," *ACA Journal* 2, (1993): 40–51.

27. Dominic Gates, "Boeing Will Accelerate 787 Production to 14 Per Month," *Seattle Times* (September 13, 2017), accessed January 29, 2018, http://www.seattletimes.com.

28. "Our Vision" in the "Morning Star Colleague Guidelines," Used by permission from The Morning Star Company.

29. Colleague Principles (2017). The Morning Star Company, accessed January 29, 2018, http://www.morningstarco.com.

30. Joshua R. Greene, "Team Incentives," in D. Scott (Ed.), *Incentive Pay: Creating a Competitive Advantage* (Phoenix, AZ: WorldatWork Press, 2007).

31. "Real life examples of successful teamwork," *Active.collab* (blog) accessed January 29, 2018, http://www.activcollab.com.

32. Rachel E. Silverman, "How to Pay Employees for Great Ideas," *The Wall Street Journal* (December 4, 2014), accessed December 10, 2014, http://www.wsj.com.

33. John G. Belcher, Jr. "Gainsharing and Variable Pay: The State of the Art," *Compensation & Benefits Review*, (May–June, 1994): 50–60.

34. Robert J. Doyle, *Gainsharing and Productivity* (New York: American Management Association, 1983).

35. Peck, *Variable Pay*.

36. George T. Milkovich and Jerry M. Newman, *Compensation* (4th ed.) (Homewood, IL: Irwin, 1993).

37. Timothy L. Ross, "Why Gainsharing Sometimes Fails," in B. Graham-Moore & T. Ross (Eds.), *Gainsharing: Plans for Improving Performance* (Washington, DC: Bureau of National Affairs, 1990), 100–115.

38. M. H. Schuster, "Gainsharing: Research and Practice," *WorldatWork Journal* (Second Quarter, 2013): 30–39.

39. Frederick G. Lesieur, (Ed.), *The Scanlon Plan: A Frontier in Labor–Management Cooperation* (Cambridge, MA: MIT Press, 1958).

40. R. J. Bullock and Edward E. Lawler, "Gainsharing: A Few Questions and Fewer Answers," *Human Resource Management* 23, (1984): 18–20, https://doi.org/10.1002/hrm.3930230104.

41. Barrie T. Smith, "The Scanlon Plan Revisited: A Way to a Competitive Tomorrow," *Production Engineering* 33, (1986): 28–31.

42. Alan J. Geare, "Productivity from Scanlon Type Plans," *Academy of Management Review* 1, (1976): 99–108.

43. Donald W. Myers, *Compensation Management* (Chicago, IL: Commerce Clearing House, 1989).

44. Edward E. Lawler and Susan G. Cohen, "Designing a Pay System for Teams," *American Compensation Association Journal* 1 (1992): 6–19.

45. Phoebe Wall Howard, "Ford UAW Workers Will Get $7,500 Profit-sharing Checks," *Detroit Free Press* (January 24, 2018), accessed January 29, 2018, http://www.freep.com.

46. Dominic Gates, "Delta Air Employees Get Bonuses Averaging $13,000," *Seattle Times* (February 13, 2017), accessed January 29, 2018, http://www.seattletimes.com.

47. WorldatWork and Compdata Surveys & Consulting, *Inventory of Total Rewards Programs & Practices* (January, 2017), accessed January 29, 2018, http://www.worldatwork.org.

48. WorldatWork and Vivient Consulting, *Incentive Pay Practices Survey: Publicly Traded Companies* (February, 2016), accessed January 29, 2018, http://www.worldatwork.org.

49. Ibid.

50. WorldatWork and Compdata Surveys & Consulting, *Inventory of Total Rewards Programs & Practices* (January, 2017), accessed January 29, 2018, http://www.worldatwork.org.

Person-Focused Pay

Learning Objectives

When you finish studying this chapter, you should be able to:

5-1. Define person-focused pay.

5-2. Describe the usage of person-focused pay.

5-3. Name and explain the reasons companies adopt person-focused pay programs.

5-4. Summarize the varieties of person-focused pay programs.

5-5. Contrast person-focused pay with job-based pay.

5-6. Explain the advantages and disadvantages of person-focused pay plans.

Improved performance, the bottom-line purpose of training and development, is a strategic goal for organizations. Toward this end, many companies strive to become learning organizations. A learning organization is a firm that recognizes the critical importance of continuous performance-related training and development, and takes appropriate action. Learning organizations view learning and development opportunities in all facets of their business. In a learning organization, employees are rewarded for learning and are provided enriched jobs, promotions, and compensation. Person-focused compensation programs provide the basis for such rewards that are tightly coupled with strategic training and development activities.

DEFINING PERSON-FOCUSED PAY: PAY-FOR-KNOWLEDGE, SKILL-BASED PAY, AND COMPETENCY BASED PAY

Person-focused pay plans reward employees for acquiring job-related knowledge, skills, or competencies rather than for demonstrating successful job performance. Person-focused pay rewards employees for the promise of performance in the future; merit pay and incentive pay reward employees for the promise fulfilled (job performance). This approach to

5-1. Define person-focused pay.

compensating employees often refers to three basic types of person-focused pay programs: pay-for-knowledge, skill-based pay, and competency-based pay. Sometimes, companies combine person-focused pay programs with traditional merit pay programs by awarding pay raises to employees according to how well they demonstrate competencies on the job.

Knowledge-Based Pay and Skill-Based Pay

Pay-for-knowledge plans reward managerial, service, or professional workers for successfully learning specific curricula. **Skill-based pay**, a term used mostly for employees who do physical work, increases the workers' pay as they master new skills. For example, both unions and contractors who employ carpenters use skill-based pay plans. Carpenters earn additional pay as they master more advanced woodworking skills (e.g., cabinet making).

Both skill- and knowledge-based pay programs reward employees for the range, depth, and types of skills or knowledge they can apply productively to their jobs. This feature distinguishes pay-for-knowledge plans from merit pay, which rewards employees' job performance. Said another way, again, pay-for-knowledge programs reward employees for their potential to make meaningful contributions on the job.

Human resource (HR) professionals can design person-focused pay plans to reward employees for acquiring new horizontal skills, vertical skills, or a greater depth of knowledge or skills. Employees can earn rewards for developing skills in one or more of these dimensions based on the kind of skills the company wants to foster. **Horizontal skills** (or **horizontal knowledge**) refer to similar skills or knowledge. For example, clerical employees of a retail store might be trained to perform several kinds of record-keeping tasks. They may maintain employee attendance records, schedule salespeople's work shifts, and monitor the use of office supplies (e.g., paper clips and toner cartridges for laser printers) for reordering. Although focused on different aspects of a store's operations, all three of these tasks are based on employees' fundamental knowledge of record keeping.

Vertical skills (or **vertical knowledge**) are those skills traditionally considered supervisory (e.g., scheduling, coordinating, training, and leading others). These types of supervisory skills are often emphasized in person-focused pay plans designed for self-managed work teams because team members often need to learn how to manage one another.[1] Such work teams, which can be referred to as self-regulating work groups, autonomous work groups, or semi-autonomous work groups, typically bring employees together from various functional areas to plan, design, and complete one product or service. For example:

A manager of a food processing plant [who] wanted employees who were "a combination of self-reliant and resourceful." In this plant, good hiring systems and excellent training systems were critical, including systems for training operators in maintenance skills. Several plants had adopted interesting innovations to promote good training and certification. These innovations included:

- Several plants put all training on their intranet, so employees could access it at any time.
- One plant used hundreds of "One-Point Lessons" (OPLs—one-page sheets including a digital photograph of the appropriate equipment). Because each OPL focused on only one problem and its solution, OPLs were easy to search and use on the job.
- Several plants invested heavily in documentation of training and required practical skills demonstration.[2]

Depth of skills (or **depth of knowledge**) refers to the level of specialization or expertise an employee brings to a job. Some person-focused pay plans reward employees for increasing their depth of skills or knowledge. Human resource professionals may choose to specialize in managing an aspect of the HR function (e.g., compensation, benefits administration, training evaluation, or new employee orientation). To be considered a compensation specialist, HR professionals must develop depth of knowledge, perhaps by taking courses offered by WorldatWork on job evaluation, salary survey analysis, principles of person-focused pay system design, merit pay system design, and incentive pay system design, among others. The more compensation topics HR professionals master, the greater will be their depth of knowledge about compensation.

Competency-Based Pay and the Competency Model Clearinghouse

The term competency has become an increasingly important topic in HR practice because of the changing nature of work. Competencies build upon the use of knowledge, skills, and abilities, which we describe with job analysis. A **competency** refers to an individual's capability to orchestrate and apply combinations of knowledge and skills consistently over time to perform work successfully in the required work situations. Traditionally, as we have seen, work has been described by many dimensions including knowledge, skills, and abilities. Although this is largely still the case, HR and compensation professionals have embraced the ideas of competencies as the field has increasingly taken on strategic importance.

A competency model specifies and defines all the competencies necessary for success in a group of jobs that are set within an industry context. Changing and new technology and global competition, which we discuss later in this chapter, has led to changing skill needs. In response, a collaborative effort between the U.S. Department of Labor, Employment and Training Administration and industry partners created and maintain the Competency Model Clearinghouse (https://www.careeronestop.org/CompetencyModel/home.aspx). According to the website, this resource provides:

> . . . dynamic models of the foundational and technical competencies that are necessary in economically vital industries and sectors of the American economy. The goal of the Industry Competency Model Initiative is to promote an understanding of the skill sets and competencies that are essential to educate and train a globally competitive workforce. It does this by providing competency models for key industry sectors. There are currently 26 models in industries as diverse as the economy itself, including transportation, hospitality, cybersecurity, and engineering, to name just a few.[3]

Figure 5-1 shows the basic framework for the Department of Labor's competency model structure.

 FYI

The Competency Model Clearinghouse published competency models in ten industries:

- Accommodation and Services
- Construction
- Energy and Utilities
- Finance and Insurance
- Health Care and Social Assistance
- Information
- Manufacturing
- Professional, Scientific, and Technical Services
- Transportation and Warehousing
- Others (Entrepreneurship)[4]

FOUNDATIONAL COMPETENCIES At the base of the model, Tiers 1 through 3 represent competencies that provide the foundation for success in school and in the world of work. Foundational competencies are essential to many occupations and industries. Employers have identified a link between foundational competencies and job performance and have also discovered that foundational competencies are a prerequisite for workers to learn industry-specific skills.

Occupation-Related Competencies

Tier 9 – Management Competencies
Tier 8 – Occupation-Specific Requirements
Tier 7 – Occupation-Specific Technical Competencies
Tier 6 – Occupation-Specific Knowledge Competencies

Industry-Related Competencies

Tier 5 – Industry-Sector Technical Competencies
Tier 4 – Industry-Wide Technical Competencies

Foundational Competencies

Tier 3 – Workplace Competencies
Tier 2 – Academic Competencies
Tier 1 – Personal Effectiveness Competencies

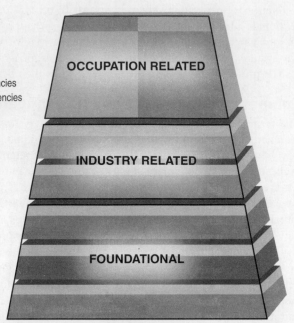

FIGURE 5-1 U.S. Department of Labor Competency Model

Source: U.S. Department of Labor Employment and Training Administration, "Competency Model General Instructions," *CareerOneStop* (2014). Online *http://www.careeronestop.org/ CompetencyModel/CareerPathway/CPWGenInstructions.aspx*. Accessed March 1, 2015.

INDUSTRY-RELATED COMPETENCIES The competencies shown on Tiers 4 and 5 are referred to as industry competencies and are specific to an industry or industry sector. Industry-wide technical competencies cut across industry sub-sectors making it possible to create career lattices where a worker can move easily across industry subsectors. Rather than narrowly following a single occupational career ladder, this model supports the development of an agile workforce.

OCCUPATION-RELATED COMPETENCIES The competencies on Tiers 6, 7, 8, and 9 are referred to as occupational competencies. Occupational competency models are frequently developed to define performance in a workplace, to design competency-based curriculum, or to articulate the requirements for an occupational credential such as a license or certification.

Figure 5-2 illustrates an example of a competency model, listing sample management competencies and occupation-specific competencies, for Solar Photovoltaic Installers who work in the renewable energy industry. The lower tiers, from personal effectiveness competencies through industry-sector technical competencies, apply to most jobs within the renewable energy industry. Hydroelectric production managers and wind engineers are examples of jobs within this industry. The top tiers, in this case, management competencies and occupation-specific competencies, apply to one or more, but not all, jobs within this industry.

USAGE OF PERSON-FOCUSED PAY PROGRAMS

5-2. Describe the usage of person-focused pay.

A wide variety of employers have established person-focused pay programs.[5] Some targeted studies and anecdotal information suggest that companies of various sizes use person-focused pay programs. Many of the companies known to be using this kind of pay system employ between approximately 150 and 2,000 employees and the average age of the companies is approximately 10 years.[6] This study also conjectures that hundreds of *Fortune 1,000* firms use skill-based pay for their manufacturing or production workers. There is limited published evidence regarding the effectiveness of person-focused pay plans. One study found that a

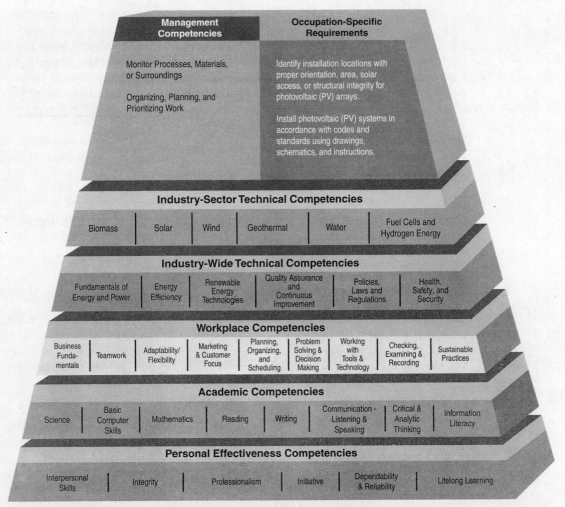

FIGURE 5-2 U.S. Department of Labor Competency Model

Source: U.S. Department of Labor Employment and Training Administration, "Renewable Energy," CareerOneStop. Online *http://www.careeronestop.org/CompetencyModel/pyramid.aspx?RE=Y*. Accessed February 4, 2018.

skill-based pay plan in a manufacturing setting increased plant productivity by 58 percent, lowered labor cost per part by 16 percent, and generated favorable quality outcomes (82 percent scrap reduction).[7] Another study demonstrated that participants in a skill-based pay program increased their skills, and maintained increased skill levels back on the job.[8] A more recent study examined attitudes among participants in a skill-based pay plan. The researchers found that these plans are perceived to produce superior work outcomes.[9]

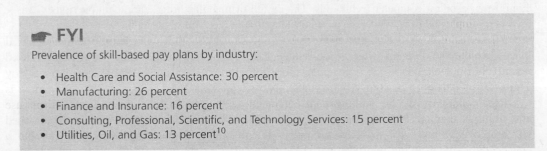

☛ **FYI**

Prevalence of skill-based pay plans by industry:

- Health Care and Social Assistance: 30 percent
- Manufacturing: 26 percent
- Finance and Insurance: 16 percent
- Consulting, Professional, Scientific, and Technology Services: 15 percent
- Utilities, Oil, and Gas: 13 percent[10]

These programs are most fitting for continuous process settings (e.g., manufacturing companies that use assembly lines where one employee's job depends on the work of at least one other employee).[11] At Bell Sports, a manufacturer of motorcycle safety helmets and auto racing helmets, the assembly process includes applying enamel and attaching visors to the helmets. Both tasks clearly require different sets of skills. Applying enamel requires the ability to use automated sprayers. This skill specifically demands that workers possess strong literacy skills so they can interpret readouts from the sprayers that suggest possible problems. Attaching visors to the helmets requires proficient motor skills that involve eye–hand coordination. When employees learn how to perform different jobs, they can cover for absent coworkers. In the event of absenteeism or turnover, Bell Sports benefits from having cross-trained employees because they are more capable of meeting its production schedules.

Person-focused pay programs that emphasize vertical skills work well at manufacturing companies that organize work flow around high-performance work teams in which employees are expected to learn both functional and managerial tasks (e.g., work scheduling, budgeting, and quality control). This means that groups of employees work together to assemble entire products.

REASONS TO ADOPT PERSON-FOCUSED PAY PROGRAMS

5-3. Name and explain the reasons companies adopt person-focused pay programs.

Person-focused pay programs represent important innovations in the compensation field. Person-focused pay systems imply that employees must move away from viewing pay as an entitlement. Instead, these systems treat compensation as a reward earned for acquiring and implementing job-relevant knowledge and skills. Advocates of person-focused pay programs offer two key reasons that firms seeking competitive advantage should adopt this form of compensation: technological innovation and increased global competition.[12]

TECHNOLOGICAL INNOVATION In an age of technological innovation in which robots, artificial intelligence, software, and lasers perform routine tasks, some skills have become obsolete.[13] Jobs, therefore, require new and different worker skills. The skills needed by automobile mechanics, for instance, have changed dramatically. Competent automobile mechanics previously were adept at manually assembling and disassembling carburetors. Now, electronic fuel injection systems, which are regulated by onboard computers, have replaced carburetors, necessitating that auto mechanics possess different kinds of skills. Auto mechanics, specifically, must now be able to use computerized diagnostic systems to assess the functioning of fuel injectors.

As technology leads to the automation of more tasks, employers combine jobs and confer broader responsibilities on workers. For example, the technology of advanced automated manufacturing (e.g., in the automobile industry) has required some employees to begin doing the jobs of other employees, including the laborer, the materials handler, the operator-assembler, and the maintenance person. A single employee now performs these tasks in a position called "manufacturing technician." The expanding range of tasks and responsibilities in this job demands higher levels of reading, writing, and computation skills than did its predecessor, which required strong eye–hand coordination. Most employees must possess better reading skills than before because they must be able to read the operating manuals and, when problems arise, the troubleshooting manuals of automated manufacturing equipment based on computer technology. The design of manufacturing equipment previously was relatively simple and easy to operate, based on such simple mechanical principles as pulleys.

These technological changes have fostered increased autonomy and team-oriented workplaces, which also demand different job-related skills than employees needed previously.[14] The manufacturing technician's job is generally more autonomous than that of his or her predecessor. Thus, technicians must be able to manage themselves and their time.

Employers now rely on working teams' technical and interpersonal skills to drive efficiency and improve quality. Today's consumers often expect customized products and applications, and employees must have sufficient technical skill to tailor products and services to customers' needs, as well as the interpersonal skills necessary to determine client needs and handle customer service.[15] Telecommunications service providers such as AT&T and Verizon seek competitive advantage by serving clients' present needs as well as by anticipating possible changes in customers' service needs.

Further dramatic advances in robotic technology have created machines that have taken on human-like qualities. For example, Google launched a specially equipped fleet of driverless cars, which safely traveled approximately 700,000 miles on California roads.[16] In addition, there are machines that can read human facial expressions and take initiative in interactions with workers.[17] The goal is not to replace workers, but rather to further enhance their productivity.[18] These advances will undoubtedly demand even more skill and knowledge sets that eclipse current workplace realities. In fact, a survey of 1,000 executives acknowledged that some jobs will be lost (ones focused on routine tasks), but many others are being created to interface with artificial intelligence technology. These changes have influenced the way companies hire and train employees to understand and work with artificial intelligence applications.[19] Finally, many experts believe that such technology will create new, yet-to-be imagined work.[20]

INCREASED GLOBAL COMPETITION Increased global competition has forced companies in the United States to become more productive. Now more than ever, to sustain competitive advantage, companies must provide their employees with leading-edge skills and encourage employees to apply their skills proficiently. Evidence clearly shows that foreign workers are better skilled and able to work more productively than U.S. employees in at least two ways.

First, employers in both the European Common Market and some Pacific Rim economies emphasize learning. In both cases, employers use classes and instruction as proactive tools for responding to strategic change. In Ireland, the private sector offers graduate employment programs to employees in such skill areas as science, marketing, and technology.[21] An example of a marketing skill is the application of inferential statistics to a market analysis. Marketing professionals use inferential statistics to draw conclusions about whether the level of satisfaction with Brand A athletic shoes among a small sample of Brand A athletic shoe owners represents the level of satisfaction among every person who has purchased Brand A athletic shoes.

Second, both Western European and some Pacific Rim cultures provide better academic preparation and continuing workplace instruction for the non-college-bound portions of their workforces. Although the United States is well regarded for the quality of education its colleges and universities provide to such skilled professionals as engineers, the Europeans are much better at educating the "vocational" segment of their workforces. Western European workplaces emphasize applied rather than theoretical instruction for vocational employees. The European apprenticeship structure mixes academic and applied learning both in "high schools" and in continuing education for employees. Success has been attributed to many reasons, mainly the collaborative efforts between schools and industry. According to Wilfried Porth, who oversees HR and labor relations at automobile manufacturer Daimler, "You need a school system which supports it. We have this tradition in Germany of being loyal to the company. We also have a technology focus here in Germany."[22]

Companies strive to market the highest quality of products and services in the face of increased global competition and the availability of new technology. To establish and maintain competitive advantage, companies should carefully consider person-focused pay systems. As discussed earlier, many companies already compensate employees on this basis because they have discovered the advantages of such plans. Of course, as companies consider adopting these pay systems, they must tailor compensation programs to the kinds of skills they wish to foster. Human resource professionals can guide employee development through a variety of person-focused pay systems.

Training lies at the heart of person-focused pay programs. Indeed, as technological advances occur at a break-neck pace and as competition among companies intensifies, companies must make many decisions, including whether to develop talent internally or to hire talent away from competitors.

VARIETIES OF PERSON-FOCUSED PAY PROGRAMS

5-4. Summarize the varieties of person-focused pay programs.

There are four varieties of common person-focused pay structures. The first, a **stairstep model** resembles a flight of stairs, much like the arrangement illustrated in Figure 5-3, for an assembly technician. The steps represent jobs from a job family that differ in terms of complexity. Jobs that require more skills are more complex than jobs with fewer skills. For example, an Assembly Technician 1 job requires employees to possess two skills: line restocking and pallet breakdown. An Assembly Technician 3 job requires employees to possess six skills: line restocking, pallet breakdown, burr removal, line jockey, major assembly, and soldering. In terms of the stairs, higher steps represent jobs that require more skills than lower steps. Compensation specialists develop separate stairstep models for individual job families (e.g., clerks or accountants). Thus, a company may have more than one stairstep model, each corresponding to a job family such as accounting, finance, or clerical. No stairstep model should include both clerical workers and skilled trade workers (e.g., carpenters, electricians, and plumbers).

How do employees earn increases in hourly pay based on a stairstep model? Using the model in Figure 5-3, Howard Jones wants to become an assembly technician. ABC Manufacturing Company hires Howard as an assembly technician trainee at $7 per hour. Howard starts by completing three core workshops designed for Assembly Technician 1: a company orientation, a safety workshop, and a quality workshop. After successfully completing all three courses, based on earning greater than the minimum scores on tests for each subject, he receives a $0.50 per hour pay increase, making his total hourly pay $7.50. In addition, Howard completes the core electives designated for his Assembly Technician 1 job: He learns how to restock lines and break down pallets. Upon successfully completing both courses, he receives a $0.65 per hour pay raise, making his total hourly pay $8.15 and earning him the Assembly Technician 1 title.

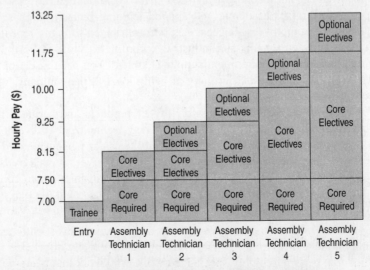

FIGURE 5-3 A Stairstep Model at ABC Company

Core Required

Employees must complete all three workshops.

1. Orientation Workshop: The goal of this workshop is to familiarize employees with ABC's pay schedule, offerings of employee benefits, work hours, holiday and vacation policies, and grievance procedures.
2. Safety Workshop: The goal of this workshop is to educate employees about the procedures for ensuring the health and safety of themselves and coworkers while using and being around the machinery.
3. Quality Workshop: The goal of this workshop is to acquaint employees with ABC's procedures for maintaining quality standards for parts assembly.

Core Electives

Employees must complete all core elective courses for the designated job before they assume the commensurate duties and responsibilities.

Assembly Technician 1:	a. Line restocking
	b. Pallet breakdown
Assembly Technician 2:	a. Core electives for Assembly Technician 1
	b. Burr removal
	c. Line jockey
Assembly Technician 3:	a. Core electives for Assembly Technician 2
	b. Major assembly
	c. Soldering
Assembly Technician 4:	a. Core electives for Assembly Technician 3
	b. Acid bath
	c. Final inspection
Assembly Technician 5:	a. Core electives for Assembly Technician 4
	b. Equipment calibration
	c. Training

Optional Electives

Employees may choose to complete up to two optional electives at each step.
Administrative procedures
Public relations
Group facilitation
Grievance resolution
Training
Marketing fundamentals (basic)
Marketing fundamentals (intermediate)
Finance fundamentals (basic)
Finance fundamentals (intermediate)
Accounting fundamentals (basic)
Accounting fundamentals (intermediate)
Human resource management fundamentals (basic)
Human resource management fundamentals (intermediate)

FIGURE 5-3 Continued

Howard may continue to learn more skills for an assembly technician by completing the curriculum for the Assembly 2 level. If he chooses to do so thereafter, Howard can complete the curricula to move to Level 3.

Training courses may be offered in-house by the company, at a local vocational school, or at a local community college or four-year university. Companies usually offer specialized courses in-house for skills that pertain to highly specialized work or to work that bears on a company's competitive advantage. Federal Express sponsors customer service training internally because the skills and knowledge required to be an effective Federal Express customer service employee distinguish its service from other express mail companies, including United Parcel Service (UPS). For more common skills or skills that do not influence competitive advantage, companies typically arrange to have their employees take training courses offered by such external agents as community colleges.

Careful planning and orchestration of training methods and systems is essential to achieving effective performance outcomes. The Watch It! video describes Wilson Learning's approach and philosophy. The company offers sales training, leadership training, and workforce development to help drive business results in organizations worldwide.

The second variety of person-focused pay plans is the skill blocks model. The **skill blocks model** also applies to jobs from within the same job family. Just as in the stairstep model, employees progress to increasingly complex jobs; however, in a skill blocks program, skills do not necessarily build on each other. Thus, an employee may progress two or more steps, earning the pay that corresponds with each step. Although similar, the stairstep model and the skill blocks model differ in an important way. The stairstep model addresses the development of knowledge or skills depth. Howard Jones could develop his skills depth as an assembly technician by mastering the five separate curricula. With the successful completion of each curriculum, Howard will enhance the depth of his skills as an assembly technician. As we will see shortly, the skill blocks model emphasizes both horizontal and vertical skills.

As shown in Figure 5-4, Pro Company hired Bobby Smith as a Clerk 1 because her employment tests demonstrated her proficiency in the skills and knowledge that she needs for this level job. These required skills correspond to Clerk 1 core requirements (i.e., filing, typing, and possessing a working knowledge of a word processing program). Moreover, Bobby knows transcription and shorthand, which are Level 1 core electives. During employee orientation for new clerical hires, an HR representative explained the pay-for-knowledge pay program available to this employee group. Bobby knows that she can advance to any level in the clerical pay structure by successfully completing the corresponding curriculum. To make her goal of becoming a Clerk 4, Bobby simply needs to complete the Level 4 curriculum. She need not take the curricula for the Clerk 2 and Clerk 3 jobs. Taking the Clerk 2, 3, or 4 curricula will enhance Bobby's horizontal skills. The Clerk 3 curriculum provides the knowledge required to successfully manage different types of ledgers. Taking the Clerk 5 curriculum will increase Bobby's vertical skills, including project scheduling and assigning personnel to projects.

The third variety is the job-point accrual model. A **job-point accrual model** encourages employees to develop skills and learn to perform jobs from different job families. A company would benefit if its employees were proficient in a small subset of jobs. Employees are generally not free to learn as many jobs as they would like. Companies limit the number of jobs employees are allowed to learn in order to avoid having them become "jacks-of-all-trades." Job-point accrual methods create organizational flexibility and promote company goals by assigning a relatively greater number of points to skills that address key company concerns (e.g., customer relations). The more points that employees accrue, the higher their core compensation level will be.

For example, let's assume that ZIP-MAIL is a new company that competes in express mail delivery service against established firms in the business (e.g., Federal Express and UPS). ZIP-MAIL couriers must meet their delivery promise of 7:30 A.M., which is at least a half hour earlier than some of the competitors. They must also convey a professional image and establish rapport with corporate clients to encourage individuals and representatives from client companies to

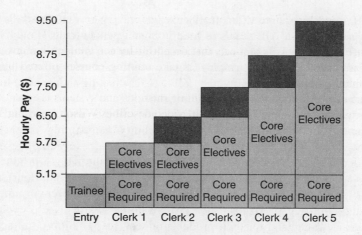

Core Required

All employees must be proficient in all of the following skills or take the necessary courses that are offered by Pro Company in order to become proficient.

Principles of filing

Typing skill, 40 words per minute minimum speed

Working knowledge of one word processing program such as Word or WordPerfect

---

Core Electives

Employees must complete all core elective courses for the designated job before they assume the commensurate duties and responsibilities.

Clerk 1:   a. Transcription
             b. Shorthand

Clerk 2:   a. Maintaining office supplies inventory
             b. Ordering office supplies from local vendor

Clerk 3:   a. Accounts receivable ledgers
             b. Accounts payable ledgers
             c. Working knowledge of one spreadsheet program, for example, Lotus 1-2-3
                or Excel

Clerk 4:   a. Payroll records
             b. Maintaining records of sick pay usage, vacation usage, and performance
                bonus awards based on company policy

Clerk 5:   a. Project scheduling
             b. Assigning personnel to projects

Optional Electives

Employees may choose to complete up to two optional electives at each step.

Public relations (basic, intermediate, advanced)

Supervisory skills

Resolving minor employee conflicts

Effective written communication skills (basic, intermediate, advanced)

Effective oral communication skills (basic, intermediate, advanced)

FIGURE 5-4 A Skill Blocks Model at Pro Company

choose ZIP-MAIL over other competitors. In other words, customer relations skills are essential to ZIP-MAIL's success. ZIP-MAIL stands to benefit from a person-focused pay program, particularly one that follows the job-point accrual model. Under this system, employees who successfully complete customer relations training courses would earn more points than they would earn by taking other kinds of training offered by ZIP-MAIL, creating an incentive for employees to learn customer relations skills over other kinds of skills.

The fourth variety of person-focused pay plans is the cross-departmental model. **Cross-departmental models** promote staffing flexibility by training employees in one department with critical skills they would need to perform effectively in other departments. If the shipping department experienced a temporary staffing shortage, a production department supervisor who has been trained in distribution methods can be "lent" to the shipping department. The cross-departmental model can help production environments manage sporadic, short-term staffing shortages. Such cross-training can also help companies meet seasonal fluctuations in demand for their products or services. The job-point accrual model and the cross-departmental model are similarly arranged, but the intended purposes of these programs differ. The job-point accrual model encourages employees to learn skills and acquire knowledge that bear directly on companies' attainment of competitive advantage, as in the case of ZIP-MAIL.

The holiday shopping rush represents an excellent context in which a company can benefit from cross-departmental training systems. Retail business activity varies widely, with enhanced volume during the holiday shopping season during the fall months. Business activity tends to subside dramatically. Let's consider a company that manufactures and distributes custom-made shoes. For weeks prior to the holidays, employees in the production department are working rapidly to complete all the telephone gift orders that must be shipped before Hanukkah and Christmas Day. Within a few days of the holidays, the company is likely to receive fewer orders because purchasers of custom-made shoes recognize that they need to place orders well in advance of the date they expect to receive their shoes. As orders drop off, many workers in both sales and production will be less busy than workers in the distribution department. Under the cross-departmental person-focused pay system, sales and production department workers will be rewarded for learning how to package shoes properly and how to complete express mail invoices so they can assist the shipping department during its peak activity periods.

CONTRASTING PERSON-FOCUSED PAY WITH JOB-BASED PAY

5-5. Contrast person-focused pay with job-based pay.

Companies institute job-based pay plans or person-focused pay plans based on very different fundamental principles and goals. Table 5-1 lists the key differences between these two pay programs. **Job-based pay** compensates employees for jobs they currently perform, and include seniority pay, merit pay, and incentive pay. Human resource professionals establish a minimum and maximum acceptable amount of pay for each job. Under seniority plans, employees receive automatic increases over time based on the assumption that they are further developing their capabilities, which translate into higher job performance. In the case of merit pay, managers evaluate employees based on how well they fulfilled their designated roles as specified by their job descriptions and periodic objectives. Managers then award a permanent merit addition to base pay, based on employee performance.

With incentive pay, managers award one-time additions to base pay. Pay raise amounts are based on the attainment of work goals, which managers communicate to employees in advance.

Person-focused pay compensates employees for developing the flexibility and skills to perform many jobs effectively. Moreover, these programs reward employees on their potential to make positive contributions to the workplace based on their successful acquisition of work-related skills or knowledge. Job-based pay plans reward employees for the work they have done

TABLE 5-1 Person-Focused and Job-Based Pay: A Comparison

Feature	Person-Focused	Job-Based
Pay level determination	Market basis for skill valuation	Market basis for job valuation
Base pay	Awarded on how much an employee knows or on skill level	Awarded on the value of compensable factors
Base pay increases	Awarded on an employee's gain in knowledge or skills	Awarded on attaining a job-defined goal
Job promotion	Awarded on an employee's skills base and proficiency on past work	Awarded on seniority or exceeding job performance standards
Key advantage to employees	Job variety and enrichment	Perform work and receive pay for a defined job
Key advantage to employers	Work scheduling flexibility	Easy pay system administration

as specified in their job descriptions or periodic goals (i.e., how well they have fulfilled their potential to make positive contributions in the workplace).

Finally, job-based pay programs apply to an organization-wide context because employees earn base pay rates for the jobs they perform. (We will address how management establishes these pay rates in Chapter 7.) Person-focused pay plans apply in a more limited context because not all jobs require complex skill or knowledge. Table 5-2 describes the duties that toll booth operators perform. This position would clearly not be appropriate in a person-focused pay system because the job is narrowly defined and the skills are very basic. Toll booth operators probably master the required skills and knowledge soon after assuming their responsibilities.

ADVANTAGES AND DISADVANTAGES OF PERSON-FOCUSED PAY PROGRAMS

Although no large-scale studies have clearly demonstrated these benefits, case studies suggest that employees and companies enjoy advantages from person-focused pay programs. Well-designed person-focused pay systems can provide employees and employers with distinct advantages over traditional pay systems. There are potential limitations of person-focused programs.

5-6. Explain the advantages and disadvantages of person-focused pay plans.

Advantages

Employees usually like person-focused pay systems for the following two reasons. First, they can provide employees with both job enrichment and job security. Job enrichment refers to a job design approach that creates more intrinsically motivating and interesting work environments.

TABLE 5-2 Job Description for a Toll Collector

Collects toll charged for use of bridges, highways, or tunnels by motor vehicles, or fare for vehicle and passengers on ferryboats. Collects money and gives customer change. Accepts toll and fare tickets previously purchased. At end of shift, balances cash and records money and tickets received. May sell round-trip booklets. May be designated according to place of employment as toll-bridge attendant (government service), or type of fare as vehicle-fare collector (motor trans.; water trans.). May admit passengers through turnstile and be designated turnstile collector (water trans.).

Source: Reprinted from *Dictionary of Occupational Titles*, Vol. 1, 4th ed. (Washington, DC: U.S. Government Printing Office, 1991).

Companies can enrich jobs by combining narrowly designed tasks so an employee is responsible for producing an entire product or service.[24]

At W. L. Gore, employees are required to demonstrate specific competencies to build a performance record by increasing their *depth* by becoming an expert in a certain specialized field, or by increasing their *breadth* by assuming broader responsibilities.[25] Employees are given opportunities through internal training, continuous learning, and external education. The company's learning and development team offers hundreds of workshops on topics including communications, computer skills, leadership, project management, sales training, safety, and technical skills.

So far, evidence does suggest that person-focused pay plans lead to increased employee commitment, enhanced work motivation, and improved employee satisfaction.[26] These results are probably due to the fact that well-designed, person-focused pay plans promote skill variety and autonomy. Some experts attribute these positive outcomes of person-focused pay programs to the fact that employees can increase their skills and be paid for it.[27]

The second advantage for employees is that, because person-focused pay programs create more flexible workers, these programs can represent better job security for employees. Rather than being laid off during periods of low product demand, employees can perform a variety of jobs that draw on the skills they have attained through person-focused pay programs. During periods of slow sales, many companies conduct inventories of their products. Customer service employees who have learned inventory accounting techniques are less likely to be laid off during periods of low sales than those who have not. Furthermore, employees who update their skills will also be more attractive applicants to other employers. Clerical employees who become proficient in the use of Windows-based computer software will have more employment opportunities available to them than clerical employees who have resisted learning these programs. Likewise, HR professionals who become familiar with important employment laws, such as the Fair Labor Standards Act, will probably have more employment opportunities available to them than will HR professionals who choose not to become familiar with these pertinent laws.

Employers like person-focused pay systems because, when properly designed and implemented, these programs can lead to enhanced job performance, reduced staffing, and greater flexibility. First, person-focused pay programs can influence both the quantity and the quality of an employee's work. Employees who participate in a person-focused pay program often exhibit higher productivity levels because employees who know more about an entire process may also be able to identify production shortcuts that result in increased productivity. For example, electrical wiring in an automobile runs along the vehicle's interior beneath the seats and carpeting. Members of auto assembly teams familiar with all aspects of the automobile manufacturing process could potentially identify and fix problems with the wiring before the seats and carpeting are installed. If such problems were identified after the seats and carpeting were installed, completion of the vehicle would be delayed, and fewer automobiles could be counted as finished.

Second, companies that use person-focused pay systems can usually rely on leaner staffing because multiskilled employees are better able to cover for unexpected absenteeism, family or medical leave, and training sessions that take individual employees away from their work. The successful operation of a restaurant depends on coordinated efforts from bus persons, waitstaff, chefs, and other food preparers. When one or two bus people are absent, the restaurant will not be able to serve its reservations customers on time. If employees are cross-trained in many jobs, fewer employees will have to be on hand to provide backup for absent bus people.

Third, person-focused pay systems provide companies with greater flexibility in meeting staffing demands at any time. Quite simply, because participants in person-focused pay plans have acquired a variety of skills, they can perform a wider range of tasks. This kind of staffing flexibility helps companies when unexpected changes in demand occur. After a tornado devastated a densely populated area in Illinois, the municipal water supply was not fit for drinking because area-wide power outages disabled the pumps that purify the water. As a result, residents living in the affected areas rushed to grocery stores to purchase bottled water. Because this sudden demand exceeded the normal inventories of bottled water in grocery stores, such wholesale distributors as SuperValu had to respond quickly by moving bottled water inventories from their warehouses to the retail grocery stores.

Disadvantages

Although person-focused pay programs present many advantages, they have four possible limitations. First, employers feel that the main drawback of person-focused pay systems is that hourly labor costs, training costs, and overhead costs can all increase. Hourly labor costs often increase because greater skills should translate into higher pay levels for most workers. Because training is an integral component of person-focused pay systems, training costs are generally higher than they are at companies with job-based pay programs. These costs can be especially high during initial start-up periods as HR professionals attempt to standardize employee backgrounds. This process begins with assessing the skill levels of employees. Federal Express tests its employees twice per year.[28] The company pays for four hours of study time and two hours of actual test time, which are bound to be quite expensive.

Second, person-focused pay systems may not mesh well with existing incentive pay systems.[29] When both person-focused and incentive pay systems are in operation, employees may not want to learn new skills when the pay increase associated with learning a new skill is less than some incentive award employees could earn based on skills they already possess. Employees often place greater emphasis on maximizing rewards in the short term rather than preparing themselves to maximize the level of rewards over time, which can be facilitated through person-focused pay programs.

An assembly-line worker chooses to focus on her work because she receives monetary incentives for meeting weekly production goals set by management rather than taking skills training in inventory control for which he or she will earn additional pay upon successful completion of the training. In the short term, this worker is earning a relatively large sum of money; in the long term, however, he or she may be jeopardizing earnings potential and job security. In the future, the company may experience reduced demand for its product, which would eliminate the incentive program. During such times, the company may also place production workers in other jobs (e.g., in the warehouse) until the demand for the product returns to normal. Without the skills required to work in the warehouse, this employee may be targeted for a layoff or a reduced work schedule, clearly leading to lower personal earnings.

Third, effective person-focused pay programs depend, in large part, on well-designed training programs. There is a lot at stake: Person-focused pay systems include costly training programs, and these systems award pay raises to employees who successfully complete training. These programs also require that employers bear the price of base pay and benefits while employees attend training during regular work hours. Companies must wait patiently before realizing a return on investment for training. Several months may pass before employees apply newly learned knowledge and skills to their jobs. After all, practice makes perfect, and training programs cannot anticipate all the circumstances employees face when performing their jobs.

Fourth, companies struggle with determining the monetary value of skill and knowledge sets. As we will discuss in Chapter 7, compensation surveys report the monetary value of entire jobs rather than individual skill sets. This fact is not surprising because most companies subscribe to job-based pay approaches as we described in Chapters 3 and 4, so it makes sense that surveys will focus on whole job value. In addition, knowledge and skill sets are usually company specific, which would make comparability difficult if surveys were common.

PREPARING FOR EXAMS/QUIZZES

Chapter Summary by Learning Objectives

Learning Objective 5-1. *Define person-focused pay*. Person-focused pay plans reward employees for acquiring job-related knowledge, skills, or competencies rather than for demonstrating successful job performance. Person-focused pay rewards employees for the promise of performance in the future; merit pay and incentive pay reward employees for the promise fulfilled (job performance).

Learning Objective 5-2. *Describe the usage of person-focused pay*. Some targeted studies and anecdotal information suggest that companies of various sizes use person-focused pay programs. Many of the companies known to be using this kind of pay system employ between approximately 150 and 2,000 employees, the majority operates in the manufacturing industry, and the average age of the companies is approximately ten years. There is grounded speculation that hundreds of *Fortune 1000* firms use skill-based pay for their manufacturing or production workers.

Learning Objective 5-3. *Name and explain the reasons companies adopt person-focused pay programs*. Advocates of person-focused pay programs offer two key reasons that firms seeking competitive advantage should adopt this form of compensation: technological innovation and increased global competition.

Learning Objective 5-4. *Summarize the varieties of person-focused pay programs*. There are four varieties of common person-focused pay structures: stair-step model, skill blocks model, job-point accrual model, and cross-departmental model.

Learning Objective 5-5. *Contrast person-focused pay with job-based pay*. Person-focused pay rewards employees for acquiring job-relevant knowledge, skills, and competencies. Job-based pay rewards employees for the work they perform. Seniority, merit, and incentive pay programs are forms of job-based pay.

Learning Objective 5-6. *Explain the advantages and disadvantages of person-focused pay plans*. Person-focused pay offers several advantages, including job enrichment, higher commitment, enhanced job performance, staffing flexibility, and leaner staffing. Disadvantages include higher labor costs and possible incompatibility with other types of compensation plans in use.

Key Terms

person-focused pay plans   109
pay-for-knowledge   110
skill-based pay   110
horizontal skills   110
horizontal knowledge   110

vertical skills   110
vertical knowledge   110
depth of skills   110
depth of knowledge   110
competency   111

stairstep model   116
skill blocks model   118
job-point accrual model   118
cross-departmental models   120
job-based pay   120

Discussion Questions

5-1. Person-focused pay plans are least preferable compared with individual incentive pay programs. Do you agree or disagree with this statement? Detail your arguments to support your position.

5-2. Person-focused pay is becoming more prevalent in companies; however, person-focused pay is not always an appropriate basis for compensation. Do you agree with this statement? Explain.

5-3. The use of drones has been proposed by retailers like Amazon.com as a method for package delivery. If drones eventually become a widely adopted technology for this purpose, some workers who are employed by delivery services or warehouses might become displaced. If the displaced workers were to become drone operators, what are some of the key knowledge and skill sets they could acquire in a person-focused pay program.

5-4. Do you agree with the following statement? Companies should not provide training to employees because it is the responsibility of individuals to possess the necessary knowledge and skills prior to becoming employed. Explain.

5-5. Person-focused pay programs are not suitable for all kinds of jobs. Based on your understanding, identify at least one job for which person-focused pay is inappropriate. Explain.

PREPARING FOR MY CAREER

Compensation in Action

Whether your company is considering the transition into a person-focused pay program or already has such a program in place, as a line manager or HR professional, you will have responsibilities to guide the process and keep critical features at the forefront. By clearly outlining the expectations and metrics of the program, you will be able to provide a program that equips the company with tools to deliver its strategy and employees who possess valuable skills that will help them internally as they perform and externally should they choose to test their marketability in other companies or organizations.

Action checklist for line managers and HR—keeping the focus in person-focused pay

HR takes the lead

- Work with line managers to ensure that the benefit of the program is measurable and can be easily explained to employees and members of senior management.
- Communicate with employees and line managers so they understand the long-term benefits of the approach and how it will allow both parties to achieve individual and shared objectives.
- Explore potential partnerships with local community colleges or universities that could provide the necessary training to enhance the identified competencies at a fraction of the cost, but with added benefit to the employees (e.g., college credit and degree completion).

Line managers take the lead

- Educate HR on the competencies that are critical to company strategy.
- Inform HR of jobs that have obvious potential for cross-training. Some jobs will lend themselves to cross-training, while others may require too much training with relatively little return.

Cases

Case 1: Person-Focused Pay at Mitron Computers

The technicians at Mitron Computers are integral to the company's success. Mitron builds custom personal computers for several office supply chains. The company's ability to build a quality product to specifications in an efficient manner allows Mitron to hold an advantage over competitors. However, recently the company has experienced some delays in shipments, and the plant manager is growing concerned.

Mitron works directly with the retail locations of the office supply chains to meet the needs of customers ordering computers with specific capabilities. A customer at a retail store orders a computer with certain components, and the order is sent to Mitron to be fulfilled within a specified time frame. The technicians work in teams to build the computers to the desired specifications. It is a complex process, and the technician's ability to build the computers efficiently has helped build Mitron's reputation as a quality producer of personal computers.

Depending on the specifications, building each computer can involve between 10 and 18 different steps. Most technicians have the knowledge and skills to complete one or two of the steps, but some technicians can complete multiple steps. The technicians that can complete multiple steps provide the company greater flexibility in scheduling and ensuring the computers are built on time. Each step in the building process involves intricate procedures, and a technician must take the initiative to attend training to learn each new step. However, there is little incentive for the technicians to attend the training.

The technicians work in teams to build the computers, and they are paid an hourly pay rate plus a team-based bonus payment for each computer that is built on time with no defects. The teams are composed of technicians that have complementary skills, but the company has had some delays when a team member with the skills to complete a certain step is absent or already working on another computer. This problem occurs often as few technicians have the skills to complete the higher-level steps in the building process. Most technicians do not want to take time away from their work to attend the training as they will likely lose some of their team-based bonuses.

Holly Turner, Mitron's human resource director, has been asked by the plant manager to examine the technician's pay structure to determine if a change in the structure could affect the technician's efficiency. Holly is confident that the more steps each technician can complete, the more efficient Mitron will be in building computers. Therefore, Holly is considering implementing a person-focused program that would tie the technician's pay to the steps in the building process that he or she is trained to complete. By doing so, Holly believes the technicians will be more likely to attend training and learn the new skills. With more technicians trained to complete the higher-level steps in the building process, the teams will be better prepared to meet shipping deadlines.

Questions:

5-6. What are some advantages of a person-focused pay system at Mitron?

5-7. What are some disadvantages?

5-8. What approach would you recommend for Holly to take in designing a person-focused pay system?

Case 2: Ethics Dilemma: Limiting Access to Training

Skill sets for manufacturing workers are changing rapidly as manual labor is being replaced with employee-assisted manufacturing robots. Rather than hire new workers, a company chooses to invest in a skill-based pay plan that will tie pay increases to successfully learning new skills. The cost of the training system is significantly higher than anticipated, causing the company to limit access to training. The company decides to limit participation to workers who joined the company upon completing high school (age 18) and who have fewer than 15 years with the company. This decision excludes a large segment of the workforce who have substantially higher seniority, particularly those with more than 25 years of seniority.

Questions:

5-9. What would you do? (*Hint: Review the material in Chapter 2, Learning Objective 2-5.*)

5-10. What factor(s) in this ethical dilemma might influence a person to make a less-than-ethical decision?

Crunch the Numbers!

Hiring a Mix of Entry-Level Workers and Skilled Candidates under a Skill-Based Pay Program

A product distribution company has recently adopted a highly complex automated operations management system with an artificial intelligence component that requires highly skilled workers. Company growth is strong and it is expected to increase through the next ten years, requiring it to build additional distribution centers. Initially, there were enough highly qualified job candidates with the necessary experience required to perform the job without requiring company investments in training. As growth continued, the supply of similar job candidates relative to the company's need was low. This labor market reality led the company to establish a skill-based pay system. The company's analysis of the labor market enabled them to project the mix of employees that will be available (those who are already fully qualified, needing little training, and those who have the potential to perform well, but who do not have the required skills to perform the jobs).

The company offers pay that is 10 percent above the market average hourly pay rate ($23.00) to entice the best qualified candidates to accept job offers. Those new hires are productive right from the start with little company training investment. The company offers the other new hires starting pay at 20 percent below the market average because of the extensive training needed before they can perform their jobs.

Finally, the company employs 500 workers of whom 40 percent are paid above the market average and 60 percent are paid below the market average. Over the next year, the company plans to hire 70 additional employees of whom 20 percent are expected to be paid above the market rate and 80 percent are expected to be paid below the market rate.

Questions:

5-11. What is the hourly pay rate for (a) highly skilled workers and (b) workers who are building skills through training?

5-12. Based on 160 monthly work hours, what is the total cost of monthly wages for current (a) highly skilled workers and (b) workers who are building skills through training?

5-13. Based on 160 monthly work hours, what will the total cost of monthly wages be for the newly hired workers (expected to be hired over the next year) who (a) are highly skilled and (b) will be building skills through training?

Working Together: Team Exercise

In small groups of three or four, come up with specific answers to the following questions. Talk through your perspectives and come up with a team response. Be prepared to share your ideas with the class.

We studied competency models in this chapter and viewed the U.S. Department of Labor competency model framework (Figure 5-1). The Department of Labor has the Competency Model Clearinghouse that contains several competency models across industries. As a group, review some of these competency models available on the *Careeronestop* website (https://www.careeronestop.org/CompetencyModel/) after clicking on the industry models link. Select a competency model from two industries.

Questions:

5-14. Summarize the information available on your chosen models. What are some of the similarities?

5-15. What are some of the differences in occupation- and industry-competencies between your chosen models?

Endnotes

1. Bureau of National Affairs, Skill-based pay. *BNA's Library on Compensation & Benefits CD* [CD-ROM] (Washington, DC: Bureau of National Affairs, 2002).
2. Gerald E. Ledford, "Factors Affecting the Long-term Success of Skill-based Pay," *WorldatWork Journal* (First Quarter, 2008): 6–17.

3. U.S. Department of Labor, *Overview of the Competency Model Clearinghouse*, accessed February 4, 2018, https://www.careeronestop.org/CompetencyModel/overview-of-cmc.aspx.

4. WorldatWork, *Compensation Programs and Practices* (January, 2017), accessed February 9, 2018, http://www.worldatwork.org.

5. G. Douglas Jenkins, Jr., Gerald E. Ledford, Jr., Nina Gupta and D. Harold Doty *Skill-Based Pay: Practices, Payoffs, Pitfalls, and Prescriptions* (Scottsdale, AZ: American Compensation Association, 1992).

6. Atul Mitra, Nina Gupta and Jason D. Shaw "A Comparative Examination of Traditional and Skill-based Pay Plans," *Journal of Managerial Psychology* 4, (2011): 278–296, http://dx.doi.org.library.capella.edu/10.1108/02683941111124827.

7. Brian Murray and Barry Gerhart, "An Empirical Analysis of a Skill-based Pay Program and Plant Performance Outcomes," *Academy of Management Journal* 41, (1998): 68–78.

8. Erich C. Dierdorff and Eric A. Surface, "If You Pay for Skills, Will They Learn? Skill Change and Maintenance under a Skill-based Pay System," *Journal of Management* 34, (2008): 721–743.

9. Atul Mitra, Nina Gupta and Jason D. Shaw, "A Comparative Examination of Traditional and Skill-based Pay Plans," *Journal of Managerial Psychology* 4, (2011): 278–296, http://dx.doi.org.library.capella.edu/10.1108/02683941111124827.

10. WorldatWork, *Compensation Programs and Practices* (January, 2017), accessed February 9, 2018, http://www.worldatwork.org.

11. Judy Canavan, "Overcoming the Challenge of Aligning Skill-based Pay Levels to the External Market," *WorldatWork Journal* (First Quarter, 2008): 18–25.

12. Jay R. Schuster and Patricia K. Zingheim, *The New Pay: Linking Employee and Organizational Performance* (New York: Lexington Books, 1992).

13. American Society for Training and Development, *Training America: Learning to Work for the 21st Century* (Alexandria, VA: American Society for Training and Development (ASTD), 1989).

14. Peter B. Doeringer, *Turbulence in the American Workplace* (New York: Oxford University Press, 1991).

15. Charles C. Manz and Henry P. Sims *Business without Bosses: How Self-Managing Work Teams Are Building High Performance Companies* (New York: John Wiley & Sons, 1993).

16. Joe Miller, "Google's Driverless Cars Designed to Exceed Speed Limit," *BBC* (August 19, 2014), accessed February 3, 2015, http://www.bbc.com.

17. Maha Salem, Stefan Kopp, Ipke Wachsmuth, Katharina Rohlfing and Frank Joublin (2012), "Generation and Evaluation of Communicative Robot Gestures," *International Journal of Social Robotics* 4, (2012): 201–217.

18. Sara Castellanos, "Technology Innovation Isn't Just for Tech Companies," *The Wall Street Journal* (December 5, 2017), accessed February 4, 2018, http://www.wsj.com.

19. Angus Loten, "AI-powered Tools Cutting Tasks, Not Jobs: Survey," *The Wall Street Journal* (January 23, 2018), accessed February 4, 2018, http://www.wsj.com.

20. Timothy Aeppel, "What Clever Robots Mean for Jobs," *The Wall Street Journal* (February 24, 2015), accessed February 25, 2015, http://www.wsj.com.

21. Anthony P. Carnevale and Janet W. Johnston *Training in America: Strategies for the Nation* (Alexandria, VA: National Center on Education and the Economy and the American Society for Training and Development, 1989).

22. Nigel Cassidy, "German Apprenticeships: A Model for Europe?" *BBC News* (December 13, 2011), accessed April 5, 2014, http://www.bbcnews.com.

23. "2017 Training Industry Report," *Training* (November/December, 2017), accessed February 9, 2018, https://trainingmag.com/trgmag-article/2017-training-industry-report.

24. Edward E. Lawler, *High Involvement Management* (San Francisco, CA: Jossey-Bass, 1986).

25. *Growth & Development at Gore*, accessed March 1, 2015, http://www.gore.com.

26. Nina Gupta, Timothy P. Schweizer and G. Douglas Jenkins, Jr., "Pay-for-knowledge Compensation Plans: Hypotheses and Survey Results," *Monthly Labor Review* 110, (1987): 40–43.

27. Shari Caudron, "Master the Compensation Maze," *Personnel Journal* 72, (1993): 64a–64o.

28. Diane Filipowski, "How Federal Express Makes Your Package Its Most Important," *Personnel Journal* 71, (1992): 40–46.

29. G. Douglas Jenkins, Jr. and Nina Gupta, "The Payoffs of Paying for Knowledge," *National Productivity Review* 4, (1985): 121–130, https://doi.org/10.1002/npr.4040040203.

DESIGNING COMPENSATION SYSTEMS

Where We Are Now:

PART II, BASES FOR PAY, explained the concepts and practices available to compensation professionals for setting base pay as well as for determining pay increases over time. After gaining an understanding of these basics, compensation professionals turn to using tools to determine the relative worth of jobs, set base pay, and award pay increases according to the chosen basis for pay. We therefore turn to methods for building internally consistent job structures, establishing market-competitive pay rates, and creating pay structures that recognize employee contributions according to the bases for pay concepts.

In **PART III, WE WILL COVER**

CHAPTER 6 BUILDING INTERNALLY CONSISTENT COMPENSATION SYSTEMS

CHAPTER 7 BUILDING MARKET-COMPETITIVE COMPENSATION SYSTEMS

CHAPTER 8 BUILDING PAY STRUCTURES THAT RECOGNIZE EMPLOYEE CONTRIBUTIONS

6 Building Internally Consistent Compensation Systems

Learning Objectives

When you finish studying this chapter, you should be able to:

6-1. Explain the concept of internal consistency.

6-2. Summarize the practice of job analysis.

6-3. Describe the practice of job evaluation.

6-4. Summarize various job evaluation techniques.

6-5. Explain how internally consistent compensation systems and competitive strategy relate to each other.

Job descriptions serve as a cornerstone in the development of internally consistent compensation systems as well as in describing selection standards and performance criteria in performance evaluation systems. Well-written job descriptions provide compensation professionals with sufficiently well-specified information about job duties and worker requirements so that they can begin making judgments about the relative worth of jobs based on differences in job content. With these judgments in hand, compensation professionals will be well positioned to survey market pay rates to establish competitive pay levels (Chapter 7) to attract and retain talented employees.

INTERNAL CONSISTENCY

6-1. Explain the concept of internal consistency.

Internally consistent compensation systems clearly define the relative value of each job among all jobs within a company. This ordered set of jobs represents the job structure or hierarchy. Companies rely on a simple, yet fundamental principle for building internally consistent compensation systems: Jobs that require higher qualifications and encompass more responsibilities and more complex job duties should be paid more than jobs that require lower qualifications and encompass fewer responsibilities and less-complex job duties. **Job structures** formally recognize differences in job characteristics that enable compensation managers to set pay accordingly. Figure 6-1 illustrates an internally consistent job structure for employee benefits professionals. As Figure 6-1 indicates, a benefits manager should earn substantially more than a benefits counselor I. Benefits

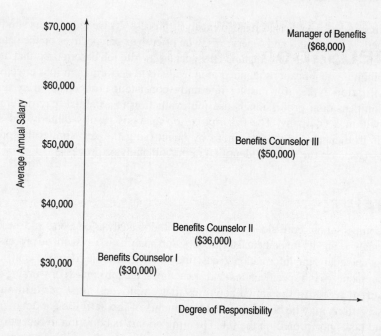

Benefits Counselor I

Provides basic counseling services to employees and assistance to higher-level personnel in more complex benefits activities. Works under general supervision of higher-level counselors or other personnel.

Benefits Counselor II

Provides skilled counseling services to employees concerning specialized benefits programs or complex areas of other programs. Also completes special projects or carries out assigned phases of the benefits counseling service operations. Works under general supervision from Benefits Counselor III or other personnel.

Benefits Counselor III

Coordinates the daily activities of an employee benefits counseling service and supervises its staff. Works under direction from higher-level personnel.

Manager of Benefits

Responsible for managing the entire benefits function from evaluating benefits programs to ensuring that Benefits Counselors are adequately trained. Reports to the Director of Compensation and Benefits.

FIGURE 6-1 Internally Consistent Compensation Structure

managers have far greater responsibility for ensuring effective benefits practices than does the entry-level counselor. The difference in average pay rates between benefits counselor II and benefits counselor I jobs should be far less than that between benefits manager and benefits counselor I jobs because the differences in responsibility between benefits counselor II and benefits counselor I are far less than the differences between benefits manager and benefits counselor I.

Compensation experts and HR professionals create internally consistent job structures through two processes—job analysis followed by job evaluation. **Job analysis** is almost purely a descriptive procedure; job evaluation reflects value judgments. Effective job analysis identifies and defines **job content**. Job content describes job duties and tasks as well as such pertinent factors as the skill and effort (i.e., compensable factors) needed to perform the job adequately.

Human resources specialists lead the job analysis process. As we will discuss shortly, they solicit the involvement of employees and supervisors, who offer their perspectives on the nature of the jobs being analyzed. Based on this information, HR specialists write job descriptions that describe the job duties and minimum qualifications required of individuals to perform their jobs effectively.

Job evaluation is key for casting internally consistent compensation systems as strategic tools. Compensation professionals use job evaluation to establish pay differentials among employees within a company. The descriptive job analysis results directly aid compensation professionals in their pay-setting decisions by quantifying the key similarities and differences between jobs based on the content identified in the job analysis process.

JOB ANALYSIS

6-2. Summarize the practice of job analysis.

Competent compensation professionals are familiar with job analysis concepts and the process of conducting job analysis and its fundamental techniques. Job analysis is a systematic process for gathering, documenting, and analyzing information to describe jobs. Job analyses describe content or job duties, worker requirements or job specifications, and, sometimes, the job context or working conditions.

Job content refers to the actual activities that employees must perform on the job. Job-content descriptions may be broad, general statements of job activities or detailed descriptions of duties and tasks performed on the job. Greeting clients is common to receptionist jobs. The job activity of greeting clients represents a broad statement. Describing the particular activities associated with greeting clients (e.g., saying "hello," asking the clients' names and using the telephone to notify the employees of their clients' arrivals) represents a detailed statement.

Worker requirements represent the minimum qualifications and the knowledge, skills, and abilities (KSAs) that people must have to perform a job. Such requirements usually include education; experience; licenses; permits; and specific abilities and skills such as typing, drafting, or editing. For example, HR managers must have knowledge of principles and procedures for recruitment, selection, training, compensation and benefits, labor relations and negotiations, and HR information systems. Active listening and critical thinking are two examples of many necessary skills for effective HR managers. Human resources managers must possess abilities such as oral comprehension and written comprehension.

Working conditions are the social context or physical environment within which work will be performed. For instance, social context is a key factor for jobs in the hospitality industry. Hospitality industry managers emphasize the importance of employees' interactions with guests. Hotel registration desk clerks should convey an air of enthusiasm toward guests and be willing to accommodate each guest's specific requests for a nonsmoking room or an early check-in time.

Physical environments vary along several dimensions, based on the level of bad conditions including noise and possible exposure to hazardous factors, including hazardous chemicals. Work equipment also defines the character of the physical environment. Nuclear power plant employees work in rather hazardous physical environments because of possible exposure to dangerous radiation levels. Accountants perform their jobs in relatively safe working environments because office buildings must meet local building safety standards.

Steps in the Job Analysis Process

The job analysis process has five main activities:

- Determining a job analysis program.
- Selecting and training analysts.
- Directing job analyst orientation.
- Conducting the study: data collection methods and sources of data.
- Summarizing the results: writing job descriptions.

DETERMINE A JOB ANALYSIS PROGRAM A company must decide between using an established system or developing its own system tailored to specific requirements. Both established and custom job analysis programs vary in the method of gathering data. The most typical methods for collecting job analysis information are questionnaires, interviews, observation, and participation. Administrative costs often represent a major consideration in selecting a job analysis method.

SELECT AND TRAIN ANALYSTS Job analysts generally must be able to collect job-related information through various methods, relate to a wide variety of employees, analyze the information, and write clearly and succinctly. A task force of representatives from throughout the company ideally conducts the analysis, and HR staff members coordinate it. Although some companies rely on HR professionals to coordinate and conduct job analysis, many use teams to represent varying perspectives on work because virtually all employees interact with coworkers and supervisors.

Before the task force embarks on a job analysis, members need to be taught about the basic assumptions of the model and the procedures they must follow. The training should include discussions of the study's objectives, how the information will be used, methodology overviews, and discussions and demonstrations of the information-gathering techniques. Analysts also should be trained to minimize the chance that they will conduct ineffective job analyses. For example, analysts should involve as many job incumbents as possible within the constraints of staff time to have representative samples of job incumbents' perceptions.

Finally, job analysts must be familiar with the structure of pertinent job data. Job analysis data are configured in levels, hierarchically from specific bits of information to progressively broader categories that include the prior specific pieces. Table 6-1 defines representative analysis levels and lists examples of each one. The most specific information is a job element, and the broadest element is an occupation.

The U.S. Office of Management and Budget published the 2018 *Standard Occupational Classification System (SOC)*, which identifies 23 major occupational groups. Table 6-2 lists these groups. These occupational group concepts are relevant for making compensation

TABLE 6-1 Units of Analysis in the Job Analysis Process

1. An element is the smallest step into which it is practical to subdivide any work activity without analyzing separate motions, movements, and mental processes involved. Setting font size and style as well as paragraph formatting are examples of a job element.

2. A task is one or more elements and is one of the distinct activities that constitute logical and necessary steps in the performance of work by the worker. A task is created whenever human effort, physical or mental, is exerted to accomplish a specific purpose. Keyboarding text into memo format represents a job task.

3. A position is a collection of tasks constituting the total work assignment of a single worker. There are as many positions as there are workers. John Smith's position in the company is clerk typist. His tasks, which include keyboarding text into memo format, running a spell-check on the text, and printing the text on company letterhead, combine to represent John Smith's position.

4. A job is a group of positions within a company that are identical, with respect to their major or significant tasks, and sufficiently alike to justify their being covered by a single analysis. There may be one or many persons employed in the same job. For example, Bob Arnold, John Smith, and Jason Colbert are clerk typists. With minor variations, they essentially perform the same tasks.

5. A job family is a group of two or more jobs that call for either similar worker characteristics or similar work tasks. The clerical job family would include positions such as file clerk, clerk typist, and administrative clerk because each job mainly requires employees to perform clerical tasks.

6. An occupation is a group of jobs, found at more than one establishment, in which a common set of tasks are performed or are related in terms of similar objectives, methodologies, materials, products, worker actions, or worker characteristics. Examples of office support occupation job titles include file clerk, clerk typist, administrative clerk, staff secretary, and administrative assistant. Human resources management occupation job titles include compensation analyst, training and development specialist, recruiter, and benefits counselor.

Source: U.S. Department of Labor (1991). *The Revised Handbook for Analyzing Jobs.* Washington, DC: U.S. Government Printing Office.

decisions. As we will see shortly, this classification system links to the Occupational Information Network (O*NET), which contains detailed information to facilitate compensation professionals making precise comparisons for pay-setting purposes.

☛ FYI

In addition to identifying 23 major occupations, the SOC also identifies 459 broad occupational groups and 97 minor groups. For instance:

- *Major occupational group*:   Architecture and engineering occupations
- *Minor group*:   Engineers
- *Broad occupational group*:   Industrial engineers
- *Detailed occupation*:   Health and safety engineers[1]

DIRECT JOB ANALYST ORIENTATION Before analysts start specific job analysis techniques, they must analyze the context in which employees perform their work to better understand influencing factors. In addition, analysts should obtain and review such internal information as organizational charts, listings of job titles, classifications of each position to be analyzed, job incumbent names and pay rates, and any instructional booklets or handbooks for operating equipment. Job analysts may also find pertinent job information in such external sources as *The Standard Occupational Classification System*, trade associations, professional societies, and trade unions.

TABLE 6-2 Major Occupational Groups of the Standard Occupational Classification

- Management
- Business and financial operations
- Computer and mathematical
- Architecture and engineering
- Life, physical, and social science
- Community and social service
- Legal
- Education, training, and library
- Arts, design, entertainment, sports, and media
- Health care practitioners and technical
- Health care support
- Protective service
- Food preparation and serving-related
- Building and grounds cleaning and maintenance
- Personal care and service
- Sales and related
- Office and administrative support
- Farming, fishing, and forestry
- Construction and extraction
- Installation, maintenance, and repair
- Production
- Transportation and material-moving
- Military-specific

Source: U.S. Bureau of Labor Statistics (2018). *2018 SOC User Guide*. Available: *www.bls.gov/soc/*, accessed February 4, 2018.

CONDUCT THE STUDY: DATA COLLECTION METHODS AND SOURCES OF DATA Once analysts have gathered and made sense of these preliminary data, they can begin gathering and recording information for each job in the company. Analysts should carefully choose the method of data collection and the sources of data. The most common methods are questionnaires and observation. Questionnaires direct job incumbents' and supervisors' descriptions of the incumbents' work through a series of questions and statements, for example:

- Describe the task you perform most frequently.
- How often do you perform this task?
- List any licenses, permits, or certifications required to perform duties assigned to your position.
- List any equipment, machines, or tools you normally operate as part of your position's duties.
- Does your job require any contacts with other department personnel, other departments, outside companies, or agencies? If yes, please describe.
- Does your job require supervisory responsibilities? If yes, for which jobs and for how many employees?

Observation requires job analysts to record perceptions they form while watching employees perform their jobs.

The most common sources of job analysis data are job incumbents, supervisors, and the job analysts. Job incumbents should provide extensive and detailed information about how they perform job duties. Experienced job incumbents will probably offer the most details and insights. Supervisors also should provide extensive and detailed information, but with a different focus. Supervisors specifically are most familiar with the interrelationships among jobs within their departments. They are probably in the best position to describe how employees performing different jobs interact. Job analysts also should involve as many job incumbents and supervisors as possible because employees with the same job titles may have different experiences.

For example, parts assembler John Smith reports that a higher level of manual dexterity is required than parts assembler Barbara Bleen reports. Parts assembler supervisor Jan Johnson indicates that assemblers interact several times a day to help each other solve unexpected problems, and supervisor Bill Black reports no interaction among parts assemblers. Including as many job incumbents and supervisors as possible will provide a truer assessment of the parts assembler job duties.

Of course, job analysts represent a source of information. In the case of observation, job analysts write descriptions. Job analysts, when using questionnaires, often ask follow-up questions to clarify job incumbents' and supervisors' answers. In either case, job analysts' HR expertise should guide the selection of pertinent follow-up questions.

Companies ultimately strive to conduct job analyses that meet reliability and validity criteria. A **reliable job analysis method** yields consistent results under similar conditions. For example, let's assume that two job analysts independently observe John Smith perform his job as a retail store manager. The method is reliable if the two analysts reach similar conclusions about the duties that constitute the retail store manager job. Although important, reliable job analysis methods are not enough. Job analyses also must be valid.

A **valid job analysis method** accurately assesses each job's duties or content. In this regard, we are referring to a validity—content validity. Unfortunately, neither researchers nor practitioners can demonstrate whether job analysis results are definitively accurate or content valid. At present, the *best* approach to producing valid job descriptions requires that results among multiple sources of job data (e.g., job incumbents, analysts, supervisors, and customers) and multiple methods (e.g., interview, questionnaire, and observation) converge.[2]

Reliable and valid job analysis methods are essential to building internally consistent compensation systems. The factors that describe a job should indeed reflect the actual work. Failure to match accurately compensable factors with the work employees perform may result in either inadequate or excessive pay rates. Both cases are detrimental to the company. Inadequate pay may lead to dysfunctional turnover (i.e., the departure of high-quality employees). Excessive pay represents a cost burden to the company that can ultimately undermine its competitive position. Moreover, basing pay on factors that do not relate to job duties leaves a company vulnerable to allegations of illegal discrimination.

What can compensation professionals do to increase the likelihood that they will use reliable and valid job analysis methods? Whenever time and budgetary constraints permit, job analysts should use more than one data collection method, and they should collect data from more than one source. Including multiple data collection methods and sources minimizes the inherent biases associated with any one. For example, job incumbents may view their work as having greater impact on the effectiveness of the company than does the incumbents' supervisor. Observation techniques do not readily indicate why an employee performs a task in a specific way, but the interview method provides analysts with an opportunity to make probing inquiries.

SUMMARIZE THE RESULTS: WRITING JOB DESCRIPTIONS Job descriptions summarize a job's purpose and list its tasks, duties, and responsibilities, as well as the KSAs necessary to perform the job at a minimum level. Effective job descriptions generally explain:

- What the employee must do to perform the job
- How the employee performs the job
- Why the employee performs the job in terms of its contribution to the functioning of the company
- Supervisory responsibilities, if any
- Contacts (and purpose of these contacts) with other employees inside or outside the company
- The skills, knowledge, and abilities the employee should have or must have to perform the job duties
- The physical and social conditions under which the employee must perform the job

Job descriptions usually contain four sections:

- Job title
- Job summary
- Job duties
- Worker specifications

Table 6-3 contains a job description for a training and development specialist.

Job titles indicate the name of each job within a company's job structure. In Table 6-3, the job title is training and development specialist. The **job summary** statement concisely summarizes the job with two to four descriptive statements. This section usually indicates whether the job incumbent receives supervision and by whom. The training and development specialist works under general supervision from higher-level training and development professionals or other designated administrators.

The **job duties** section describes the major work activities and, if pertinent, supervisory responsibilities. For instance, the training and development specialist evaluates training needs of employees and departments by conducting personal interviews, questionnaires, and statistical studies.

The **worker specifications** section lists the education, KSAs, and other qualifications individuals must possess to perform the job adequately. **Education** refers to formal training. Minimum educational levels can be a high school diploma or a general equivalency diploma (GED) through such advanced levels as masters' or doctoral degrees.

The **Equal Employment Opportunity Commission (EEOC)** guidelines distinguish among the terms *skill, ability,* and *knowledge.* **Skill** refers to an observable competence to perform a learned psychomotor act. Typing 50 words per minute is an example of a psychomotor act. Typing requires knowledge of the keyboard layout and manual dexterity. According to the EEOC, **ability** refers to a present competence to perform an observable behavior or a behavior

TABLE 6-3 Job Description: Training and Development Specialist

Job Title

Training and Development Specialist

Job Summary

Training and development specialists perform training and development activities for supervisors, managers, and staff to improve efficiency, effectiveness, and productivity. They work under general supervision from higher-level training and development professionals.

Job Duties

A training and development specialist typically:

1. Recommends, plans, and implements training seminars and workshops for administrators and supervisors, and evaluates program effectiveness.
2. Evaluates training needs of employees and departments by conducting personal interviews, and using questionnaires and statistical studies.
3. Researches, writes, and develops instructional materials for career, staff, and supervisor workshops and seminars.
4. Counsels supervisors and employees on policies and rules.
5. Performs related duties as assigned.

Worker Specifications

1. Any one or any combination of the following types of preparation:
   a. Credit for college training leading to a major or concentration in education or other fields closely related to training and development (such as human resources management or vocational education).

   —or—

   b. Two years of work experience as a professional staff member in a human resources management department.
2. Two years of professional work experience in the training and development area in addition to the training and experience required in item 1 above.

that results in an observable product. For example, possessing the competence to mediate a dispute between labor and management successfully reflects ability. **Knowledge** refers to a body of information applied directly to the performance of a function. Companies measure knowledge with tests, or they infer that employees have knowledge based on formal education completed. For instance, compensation professionals should know about the Fair Labor Standards Act's overtime pay requirements. Since these definitions were issued, the United States slightly modified the definitions of KSAs. These definitions are largely consistent with each other. We will work with the revised definitions when we review O*NET later in this chapter.

Legal Considerations for Job Analysis

The government does not require companies to conduct job analyses; however, conducting them increases the chance that employment decisions are based solely on pertinent job requirements. Under the Equal Pay Act (Chapter 2), companies must justify pay differences between men and women who perform equal work. Different job titles do not suffice as justification. Instead, companies must demonstrate substantive differences in job functions. Job analysis helps HR professionals discern whether substantive differences between job functions exist. Job analysis is also useful for determining whether a job is exempt or nonexempt under the Fair Labor Standards Act (FLSA). As we discussed in Chapter 2, failure to pay nonexempt employees an overtime hourly pay rate violates the FLSA.

Companies may perform job analyses to see if they comply with the Americans with Disabilities Act (ADA) and the Americans with Disabilities Act Amendments Act of 2008, also discussed in Chapter 2. The amendments emphasize that the definition of disability should be construed in favor of broad coverage of individuals to the maximum extent permitted by the terms of the ADA. If disabled applicants can perform the essential functions of a job with reasonable accommodation, companies must not discriminate against these applicants by paying them less than other employees performing the same job. Human resources professionals use job analysis to define essential job functions systematically.

Job Analysis Techniques

Human resources professionals can either choose from a variety of established job analysis techniques or custom-design them. Most companies generally choose to use established job analysis techniques because the costs of custom-made job analysis techniques often outweigh the benefits. Besides, many of the established job analysis techniques apply to a wide variety of jobs and both researchers and practitioners have already tested and refined them.

Choosing one established plan over another depends on two considerations: applicability and cost. Some job analysis techniques apply only to job families (e.g., managerial jobs), but others can be applied more broadly. In addition, some methods are proprietary, yet others are available to the public at no charge. Private consultants or consulting firms charge substantial fees to companies that use their methods, but the U.S. Department of Labor does not charge fees to use its job analysis resources. Next, we will review the U.S. Department of Labor's **Occupational Information Network (O*NET)**.

Occupational Information Network (O*NET)

O*NET is a database. The U.S. Department of Labor's employment and training administration spearheaded its creation for two reasons: First, it is designed to describe jobs in the relatively new service sector of the economy (e.g., wireless telecommunications). Second, O*NET more accurately describes jobs that evolved as the result of technological advances (e.g., software and hardware engineering).

O*NET is comprehensive because it incorporates information about both jobs and workers. The O*NET **Content Model** lists six categories of job and worker information. Job information contains the components that relate to the actual work activities of a job (i.e., information that HR professionals should include in the summary and duties sections of job descriptions). Worker information represents characteristics of employees that contribute to successful job performance. Figure 6-2 shows the six categories of the O*NET Content Model. According to the creators of O*NET, the Content Model was developed using research on job and organizational analysis. It embodies a view that reflects the character of occupations (via job-oriented descriptors) and people (via worker-oriented descriptors). The Content Model also allows occupational information to be applied across jobs, sectors, or industries (cross-occupational descriptors) and within occupations (occupational-specific descriptors). A description of each content area follows.

EXPERIENCE REQUIREMENTS Experience requirements include:

- Experience and training
- Licensing

Experience and training information describes specific preparation required for entry into a job plus past work experience contributing to qualifications for an occupation. **Licensing** information describes licenses, certificates, or registrations that are used to identify levels of skill that are required for entry and advancement in an occupation. Preferred education or training, and required apprenticeships will be documented by this part of the model. Table 6-4 lists the specific experience requirements.

OCCUPATIONAL REQUIREMENTS Occupational requirements include:

- Generalized work activities
- Organizational context
- Work context

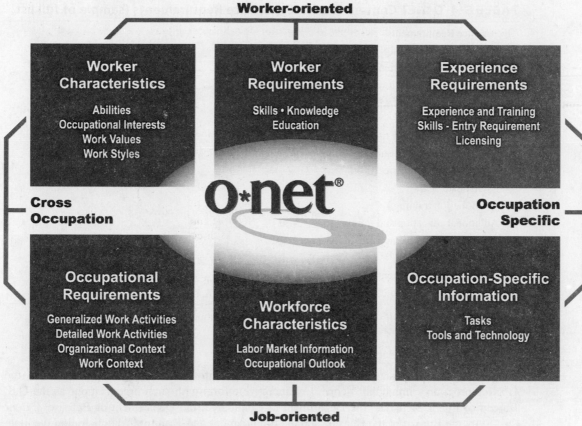

FIGURE 6-2 O*Net Content Model

The occupational requirements domain includes information about typical activities required across occupations. Identifying generalized work activities and detailed work activities summarizes the broad and more specific types of job behaviors and tasks that may be performed within multiple occupations. Using this framework makes it possible to use a single set of descriptors to describe many occupations. Contextual variables such as the physical, social, or structural context of work that may impose specific demands on the worker or activities are also included in this section.

Generalized work activities information describes general types of job behaviors occurring on multiple jobs. **Organizational context** information indicates the characteristics of the organization that influence how people do their work. **Work context** information describes physical and social factors that influence the nature of work. Table 6-5 lists examples of occupational requirements.

OCCUPATION-SPECIFIC INFORMATION REQUIREMENTS Occupation-specific information requirements detail a comprehensive set of elements that apply to a single occupation or a narrowly defined job family. These requirements are occupational skills, knowledge, tasks, duties, machines, tools, and equipment. This domain parallels other Content Model domains because it includes requirements such as work-related knowledge, skills, and tasks in addition to the machines, equipment, tools, software, and information technology workers may use in their workplace.

WORKFORCE CHARACTERISTICS Workforce characteristics refer to variables that define and describe the general characteristics of occupations that may influence occupational requirements. Organizations do not exist in isolation. They must operate within a broader social and economic structure. To be useful, an occupational classification system must incorporate global contextual characteristics. O*NET provides this information by linking descriptive occupational information to statistical labor market information. This includes compensation and wage data, employment

TABLE 6-4 O*NET Content Model: Experience Requirements (sample of full list)

Experience Requirements
- Experience and training
  - Related work experience
  - On-site or in-plant training
  - On-the-job training
- Licensing
- License, certificate, or registration required
- Education, training, examination or other requirements for license, certificate, or registration
  - Post-secondary degree
  - Graduate degree
  - On-the-job training
- Additional education and training
- Organization and agency requirements
  - Legal requirement
  - Employer requirement
  - Union, guild, or professional association requirement

Source: Occupational Information Network Consortium. Content model. Available: *www.onetcenter.org/content.html*, accessed February 4, 2018.

outlook, and industry size information. Much of this information is collected outside of the O*NET program's immediate scope. Collaborative efforts with such organizations as the U.S. Bureau of Labor Statistics, the Department of Commerce, the Department of Defense, Career One Stop, the Bureau of the Census, and the Employment and Training Administration facilitate these labor market information linkages. These characteristics include:

- Labor market information
- Occupational outlook

TABLE 6-5 O*NET Content Model: Occupational Requirements (sample of full list)

- Human resources systems and practices
  - Recruitment and selection
    - Recruitment operations
    - Reward system
  - Basis of compensation
  - Which of the following is part of your compensation package?
    - Profit sharing
    - Gainsharing
    - Knowledge/skill-based pay
    - Pay based on your individual performance
    - Pay based on the performance of your team
    - Pay based on customer satisfaction
    - Pay based on job tenure/seniority
    - Pay based on job attributes

Source: Occupational Information Network Consortium. Content model. Available: *www.onetcenter.org/content.html*, accessed February 4, 2018.

Labor market information describes current labor force characteristics of occupations. Occupational outlook describes future labor force characteristics of occupations.

WORKER CHARACTERISTICS **Worker characteristics** information includes:

- Abilities
- Interests
- Work styles

Abilities are enduring attributes of the individual that influence performance. **Interests** describe preferences for work environments and outcomes. **Work styles** are personal characteristics that describe important interpersonal and work style requirements in jobs and occupations. Table 6-6 lists a sample of worker characteristics.

Worker characteristics, such as interests and work styles, often rank highly in the employee selection process. Patagonia is a designer of outdoor clothing and gear for a variety of sports. The company strives to hire new employees whose interests and work styles are consistent with the company's mission and work culture. For example, Patagonia requires that new employees have a passion for and participate in outdoor activities as well as are fanatical about protecting the environment. The following video describes Patagonia's requirements.

TABLE 6-6 O*NET Content Model: Worker Characteristics (sample of full list)

- Abilities
- Cognitive abilities
  - Verbal abilities
    - Oral comprehension
    - Written comprehension
    - Oral expression
    - Written expression
  - Idea generation and reasoning abilities
    - Fluency of ideas
    - Originality
    - Problem sensitivity
  - Quantitative abilities
    - Mathematical reasoning
    - Number facility
  - Memory
    - Memorization
  - Perceptual abilities
    - Speed of closure
    - Flexibility of closure
    - Perceptual speed

Source: Occupational Information Network Consortium. Content model. Available: *www.onetcenter.org/content.html*, accessed February 4, 2018.

WORKER REQUIREMENTS Worker requirements include:

- Basic skills
- Cross-functional skills
- Knowledge
- Education

Worker requirements represent developed or acquired attributes of an individual that may be related to work performance such as work-related knowledge and skill. Knowledge represents the acquisition of facts and principles about a domain of information. Experience lays the foundation for establishing procedures to work with given knowledge. These procedures are more commonly known as skills. Skills may be divided further into basic skills and cross-functional skills. Basic skills (e.g., reading) facilitate the acquisition of new knowledge. Cross-functional skills (e.g., problem solving) extend across several domains of activities.

Basic skills information describes developed capacities that facilitate learning or the more rapid acquisition of knowledge. **Cross-functional skills** information indicates developed capacities that facilitate performance of activities that occur across jobs. Knowledge information describes organized sets of principles and facts applying in general domains. Education information details prior educational experience required to perform in a job. **Knowledge** refers to organized sets of principles and facts applying in general domains. **Education** refers to prior educational experience required to perform in a job. Table 6-7 lists a sample of worker requirements.

 FYI

There are seven different ways to search for jobs in O*NET (https://www.onetonline.org/find/):

- Bright Outlook (rapid job growth)
- Career Clusters (same field of work requiring similar skills)
- Green Economy Sector (e.g., solar energy)
- Industry (broad groups of businesses with similar activities, products, or services)
- Job Family (occupations grouped by work performed, skills, education, training, and credentials)
- Job Zone (occupational groups based on levels of education, experience, and training necessary to perform the occupation)
- STEM (occupations that require science, technology, engineering, and mathematics disciplines)

USING O*NET Human resources professionals use O*NET by consulting the **O*NET User's Guide** as well as the most current **O*NET database**.[3] They may find the latest O*NET information on the U.S. Department of Labor Employment and Training Administration's Web site (http://online.onetcenter.org).

JOB EVALUATION

6-3. Describe the practice of job evaluation.

Compensation professionals use job evaluation to systematically recognize differences in the relative worth among a set of jobs and to establish pay differentials accordingly. Whereas job analysis is almost purely descriptive, job evaluation partly reflects the values and priorities that management places on various positions. Based on job content and the firm's priorities, managers establish pay differentials for virtually all positions within the company.

Compensable Factors

Compensation professionals generally base job evaluations on **compensable factors**, which are the salient job characteristics by which companies establish relative pay rates. Most

TABLE 6-7 O*NET Content Model: Worker Requirements (sample of full list)

- Basic Skills
  - Content
    - Reading comprehension
    - Active listening
    - Writing
  - Process
    - Critical thinking
    - Active learning
    - Learning strategies
  - Cross-functional skills
    - Social skills
    - Social perceptiveness
    - Coordination
    - Persuasion
  - Complex problem-solving skills
    - Problem identification
    - Information gathering
    - Information organization

Source: Occupational Information Network Consortium. Content model. Available: *www.onetcenter.org/content.html*, accessed February 4, 2018.

companies consider skill, effort, responsibility, and working conditions, which were derived from the Equal Pay Act. These four dimensions help managers determine whether dissimilar jobs are "equal."

Skill, effort, responsibility, and working conditions are **universal compensable factors** because virtually every job contains these four factors. How, then, can meaningful distinctions regarding the value of jobs be made with such broad factors? Many companies break these general factors into more specific factors. For example, responsibility required could be further classified as responsibility for financial matters and responsibility for personnel matters.

Most jobs today can be described broadly in terms of KSAs given the evolution of jobs that require greater cognitive skills and mental (versus physical) effort. A working conditions compensable factor is most helpful when a company expects a substantial difference in working conditions for similar jobs. For example, a company may employ geologists, but while some of them are required to work in the field where possible dangers are greater, other geologists are required to work within the safe confines of a laboratory.

In any event, compensation professionals should choose compensable factors based on two considerations. First, factors must be job related. The factors that describe a job should indeed reflect the actual work that is performed.

Second, compensation professionals should select compensable factors that further a company's strategies. For example, companies that value product differentiation probably consider innovation to be an important compensable factor for research scientist and marketing manager jobs. Companies that distinguish themselves through high-quality customer relations are likely to place great value on such compensable factors as product knowledge and interpersonal skills. Lowest-cost strategies may emphasize different kinds of compensable factors (e.g., efficiency and timeliness).

The Job Evaluation Process

The job evaluation process entails six steps:

- Determining single versus multiple job evaluation techniques
- Choosing the job evaluation committee
- Training employees to conduct job evaluations
- Documenting the job evaluation plan
- Communicating with employees
- Setting up the appeals process

DETERMINING SINGLE VERSUS MULTIPLE JOB EVALUATION TECHNIQUES Compensation professionals must determine whether a single job evaluation technique is sufficiently broad to assess a diverse set of jobs. The decision is prompted by such questions as, "Can we use the same compensable factors to evaluate a forklift operator's job and the plant manager's job?" If the answer is *yes*, then a single job evaluation technique is appropriate. If not, then more than one job evaluation approach should be employed. Job evaluation plans are differentiated based on sets of compensable factors that are common to one set of jobs, but different from others. It is not reasonable to expect that a single job evaluation technique, based on one set of compensable factors, can adequately assess diverse sets of jobs (i.e., operative, clerical, administrative, managerial, professional, technical, and executive). A carpenter's job is clearly distinct from a certified public accountant's position because manual dexterity is an important compensable factor that describes carpentry work and is not nearly as central to an accounting position. Ultimately, compensation professionals will create as many job structures as there are job evaluation techniques that are appropriate for groups of like jobs. As described earlier, Figure 6-1 illustrates an internally consistent job structure for employee benefits professionals.

CHOOSING THE JOB EVALUATION COMMITTEE Human resources professionals help put together a committee of rank-and-file employees, supervisors, managers, and, if relevant, union representatives to design, oversee, and evaluate job evaluation results. The functions, duties, responsibilities, and authority of job evaluation committees vary considerably from company to company. In general, committees simply review job descriptions and analyses and then evaluate jobs. Larger companies with a multitude of jobs often establish separate committees to evaluate job classifications such as nonexempt, exempt, managerial, and executive jobs. The immense number of jobs in large companies would otherwise preclude committee members from performing their regular duties.

Job evaluation is an important determinant of a job's worth within many companies. All employees, regardless of their functions, wish to be compensated and valued for their efforts. All employees strive for a reasonable pay-effort bargain (i.e., a compensation level consistent with their contributions). Managers strive to balance employee motivation with cost control because they have limited resources for operating their departments. Union representatives strive to ensure that members enjoy a good standard of living. Therefore, unions try to prevent the undervaluation of jobs.

Job evaluation committees help ensure commitment from employees throughout companies. They also provide a checks-and-balances system. Job evaluation procedures are not scientifically accurate because these evaluation decisions are based on ordinary human judgment. Therefore, a consensus of several employees helps to minimize the biases of individual job evaluators.

TRAINING EMPLOYEES TO CONDUCT JOB EVALUATIONS Individuals should understand the process objectives. In addition to knowing company objectives, evaluators also should practice using the chosen job evaluation criteria before applying them to actual jobs. Similar to job analysis procedures, evaluators should base their decisions on sound job- and business-related rationales to ensure legal compliance.

DOCUMENTING THE JOB EVALUATION PLAN Documenting the job evaluation plan is useful for legal and training purposes. From an employer's perspective, a well-documented evaluation plan clearly specifies job- and business-related criteria against which jobs are evaluated. Well-documented plans can allow employees to understand clearly how their jobs were evaluated and the outcome of the process. In addition, well-documented plans provide guidelines for clarifying ambiguities in the event of employee appeals or legal challenges.

COMMUNICATING WITH EMPLOYEES Job evaluation results matter, personally, to all employees. Companies must formally communicate with employees throughout the job analysis and evaluation processes to ensure employees' understanding and acceptance of the job evaluation process and results. Information sessions and memoranda are useful media. Employers should share basic information, and employees should be given the opportunity to respond to what they believe are either unsatisfactory procedures or inaccurate outcomes of the job evaluation process.

SETTING UP THE APPEALS PROCESS Companies should set up appeals procedures that permit reviews on a case-by-case basis to provide a check on the process through reexamination. Such appeals reduce charges of illegal discrimination that would be more likely to occur if employees were not given a voice. Compensation professionals usually review employees' appeals. Companies increasingly process appeals through committees made up of compensation professionals and a representative sample of employees and supervisors. Grievants are more likely to judge appeal decisions as fair if committees are involved: Committee decisions should reflect the varied perspectives of participants rather than the judgment of one individual.

JOB EVALUATION TECHNIQUES

Compensation professionals categorize job evaluation methods as either market-based evaluation or job-content evaluation techniques. **Market-based evaluation** plans use market data to determine differences in job worth. Many companies choose market-based evaluation methods because they wish to assign job pay rates that are neither too low nor too high relative to the market. Setting pay rates too low will make it difficult to recruit talented candidates, whereas setting pay rates too high will result in an excessive cost burden for the employer. Compensation professionals rely on compensation surveys to determine prevailing pay rates of jobs in the relevant labor market. We will address that issue in Chapter 7.

6-4. Summarize various job evaluation techniques.

Job-content evaluation plans emphasize the company's internal value system by establishing a hierarchy of internal job worth based on each job's function in company strategy. Compensation professionals review preliminary structures for consistency with market pay rates on a representative sample of jobs known as benchmark jobs. Compensation professionals ultimately must balance external market considerations with internal consistency objectives. In practice, compensation professionals judge the adequacy of pay differentials by comparing both market rates and pay differences among jobs within their companies. They consult with the top HR official and chief financial officer when discrepancies arise, particularly if company pay rates are generally lower than the market rates. Upon careful consideration of the company's financial resources and the strategic value of the jobs in question, these executives decide whether to adjust internal pay rates for jobs with below-market pay rates.

Neither market-based nor job-content evaluation approaches alone enable compensation professionals to balance internal and external considerations. Most companies therefore rely on both approaches. The point method is the most popular job-content method because it gives compensation professionals better control over balancing internal and market considerations. Chapter 7 fully addresses how compensation professionals combine point method results with market approaches. Nevertheless, a brief overview will follow our discussion of the point method in this chapter.

The Point Method

The **point method** is a job-content valuation technique that uses quantitative methodology. Quantitative methods assign numerical values to compensable factors that describe jobs, and these values are summed as an indicator of the overall value for the job. The relative worth of jobs is established by the magnitude of the overall numerical value.

The point method evaluates jobs by comparing compensable factors. Each factor is defined and assigned a range of points based on the factor's relative value to the company. Compensable factors are weighted to represent the relative importance of each factor to the job. Job evaluation committees follow seven steps to complete the point method.

STEP 1: SELECT BENCHMARK JOBS Point method job evaluations use **benchmark jobs** to develop factors and their definitions to select jobs to represent the entire range of jobs in the company. Benchmark jobs, found outside the company, provide reference points against which jobs within the company are judged.

STEP 2: CHOOSE COMPENSABLE FACTORS BASED ON BENCHMARK JOBS Managers must define compensable factors that adequately represent the scope of jobs slated for evaluation. Each benchmark job should be described by those factors that help distinguish it from the value of all other jobs. In addition to the "universal" factors (e.g., skill, effort, responsibility, and working conditions), additional factors may be developed to the extent that they are job- and business-related.

Compensable factor categories may be broken down further into specific related factors or subfactors. For example, skill may include job knowledge, education, mental ability, physical ability, accuracy, and dexterity. Effort may include factors relating to both physical and mental exertion. Responsibility may include considerations related to fiscal, material, or personnel responsibilities. Working conditions may be unpleasant because of extreme temperatures or possible exposure to hazardous chemicals.

The number of compensable factors companies should use varies. Compensation professionals should select as many compensable factors as are needed to describe the range of benchmark jobs adequately.

STEP 3: DEFINE FACTOR DEGREES Although compensable factors describe the range of benchmark jobs, individual jobs vary in scope and content. Evaluators must therefore divide each factor into enough degrees to identify the level of a factor present in each job. To clarify this idea of factor degrees, it is helpful to think about a paint sample that can be found in any home improvement store. Specifying a color such as gray is not straightforward because there are various shades of gray. Likewise, a compensable factor is like a color. For example, the compensable factor *writing ability* can be described in degrees (shades of color) ranging from the ability to write simple sentences to the ability to write paragraphs of complex information.

Table 6-8 illustrates a factor definition for writing ability and its degree statements. Degree definitions should set forth and limit the meaning of each degree so evaluators can uniformly interpret job descriptions. It is generally helpful to include a few actual work examples as anchors.

The number of degrees will vary based on the comprehensiveness of the plan. For example, if the plan covers only a limited segment of jobs (e.g., clerical employees), fewer degrees will be required than if the plan covered every group of employees. Take education as an example. Only two degrees may be necessary to describe the educational requirements for clerical jobs (i.e., high school diploma or equivalent and an associate's degree). More than two degrees would be required to describe adequately the educational requirements for administrative, production, managerial, and professional jobs (i.e., high school diploma or equivalent, associate's degree, bachelor's degree, master's degree, and doctorate). Most analyses anchor minimum and maximum degrees, with specific jobs representing these points.

STEP 4: DETERMINE THE WEIGHT OF EACH FACTOR Weighting compensable factors represents the importance of the factor to the overall value of the job. The weights of compensable factors are

TABLE 6-8 Writing Ability: Factor Definition and Degree Statements

Definition	Capacity to communicate with others in written form.
First Degree	Print simple phrases and sentences, using normal work order and present and past tenses.
Sample Anchor	Print shipping labels for packages, indicating the destination and the contents of the packages.
Second Degree	Write compound and complex sentences, using proper end punctuation and adjectives and adverbs.
Sample Anchor	Fill requisitions, work orders, or requests for materials, tools, or other stock items.
Third Degree	Write reports and essays with proper format, punctuation, spelling, and grammar, using all parts of speech.
Sample Anchor	Type letters, reports, or straight-copy materials from rough draft or corrected copy.
Fourth Degree	Prepare business letters, expositions, summaries, and reports using prescribed format and conforming to all rules of punctuation, grammar, diction, and style.
Sample Anchor	Compose letters in reply to correspondence concerning such items as request for merchandise, damage claims, credit information, or delinquent accounts or to request information.
Fifth Degree	Write manuals or speeches.
Sample Anchor	Write service manuals and related technical publications concerned with installation, operation, and maintenance of electronic, electrical, mechanical, and other equipment.

usually expressed as percentages. Weighting is often done by management or by a job evaluation committee's decision. All the factors are ranked according to their relative importance, and final weights are assigned after discussion and consensus. For example, let's assume the relative importance of skill, effort, responsibility, and working conditions to ABC Manufacturing Corporation:

- Skill is the most highly valued compensable factor, weighted at 60 percent.
- Responsibility is the next most important factor, weighted at 25 percent.
- Effort is weighted at 10 percent.
- The working conditions factor is least important, weighted at 5 percent.

STEP 5: DETERMINE POINT VALUES FOR EACH COMPENSABLE FACTOR Compensation professionals set point values for each compensable factor in three stages. First, they must establish the maximum possible point values for the complete set of compensable factors. This total number is arbitrary, but it represents the possible maximum value jobs can possess. As a rule of thumb, the total point value for a set of compensable factors should be determined by a simple formula (e.g., the number of compensable factors times 250). ABC Manufacturing sets 1,000 (4 compensable factors x 250) as the possible maximum number of points.

Second, the maximum possible point value for each compensable factor is based on total weight as described in Step 4. Again, for ABC Manufacturing, skill equals 60 percent, responsibility 25 percent, effort 10 percent, and working conditions 5 percent:

- The maximum possible total points for skills equal 600 points (60 percent × 1,000 points).
- The maximum possible total points for responsibility equal 250 points (25 percent × 1,000 points).
- The maximum possible total points for effort equal 100 points (10 percent × 1,000 points).
- The maximum possible total points for working conditions equal 50 points (5 percent × 1,000 points).

Third, compensation professionals distribute these points across degree statements within each compensable factor. The point progression by degrees from the lowest to the highest point value advances arithmetically (i.e., a scale of even incremental values). This characteristic is essential for conducting regression analysis (a statistical analysis method that we will address in Chapter 7 in the discussion of integrating internal job structures—based on job evaluation points—with external pay rates for benchmark jobs).

How do compensation professionals assign point values to each degree? Let's illustrate this procedure by example, using the skill compensable factor. Let's also assume that the skill factor has five degree statements. Degree 1 represents the most basic skill level, and Degree 5 represents the most advanced skill level. The increment from one degree to the next highest is 120 points (600-point maximum divided by five degree statements).

- Degree 1 = 120 points (120 points × 1)
- Degree 2 = 240 points (120 points × 2)
- Degree 3 = 360 points (120 points × 3)
- Degree 4 = 480 points (120 points × 4)
- Degree 5 = 600 points (120 points × 5)

STEP 6: VERIFY FACTOR DEGREES AND POINT VALUES Committee members should independently calculate the point values for a random sample of jobs. Table 6-9 shows a sample job evaluation worksheet. After calculating the point values for this sample, committee members should review the point totals for each job. Committee members give careful consideration to whether the hierarchy of jobs makes sense in the context of the company's strategic plan, as well as to the inherent content of the jobs. For instance, sales jobs should rank relatively high on the job hierarchy within a sales-oriented company, such as the pharmaceuticals industry. Research scientist jobs ought to rank relatively high for a company that pursues a differentiation strategy. Messenger jobs should not rank more highly than claims analyst jobs in an insurance company. In short, where peculiarities are apparent, committee members reconsider compensable factor definitions, weights, and actual ratings of the benchmark jobs.

STEP 7: EVALUATE ALL JOBS Committee members evaluate all jobs in the company once the evaluation system has been tested and refined. Each job then is evaluated by determining which

TABLE 6-9 Sample Job Evaluation Worksheet

Job Title: _____

Evaluation Date: _____

Name of Evaluator: _____

Compensable Factor	Degree 1	2	3	4	5	Total
Skill						
Mental skill	60	120	180	240	(300)	300
Manual skill	60	(120)	180	240	300	120
Effort						
Mental effort	10	20	30	40	(50)	50
Physical effort	10	20	(30)	40	50	30
Responsibility						
Supervisory	25	50	(75)	100	125	75
Department budgeting	(25)	50	75	100	125	25
Working conditions						
Hazards	10	20	30	(40)	50	40
Total job value						640

degree definition best fits the job and by assigning the corresponding point factors. All points are totaled for each job, and all jobs are ranked according to their point values.

BALANCING INTERNAL AND MARKET CONSIDERATIONS USING THE POINT METHOD How do compensation professionals balance internal and market considerations with point method results? They convert point values into the market value of jobs through regression analysis, a statistical technique. As we will discuss in Chapter 7, regression analysis enables compensation professionals to set base pay rates in line with market rates for benchmark or representative jobs. Companies identify market pay rates through compensation surveys. Of course, a company's value structure for jobs based on the point method will probably differ somewhat from the market pay rates for similar jobs. Regression analysis indicates base pay rates that minimize the differences between the company's point method results and the market pay rates.

Alternative Job-Content Evaluation Approaches

Most other job-content approaches use qualitative methods. Qualitative methods evaluate entire jobs and typically compare jobs with each other or some general criteria. These criteria are usually vague (e.g., importance of jobs to departmental effectiveness). Four prevalent kinds of qualitative job evaluation techniques include:

- Simple ranking plans
- Paired comparisons
- Alternation ranking
- Classification plans

SIMPLE RANKING PLANS Simple ranking plans order all jobs from lowest to highest according to a single criterion (e.g., job complexity or the centrality of the job to the company's competitive strategy). This approach considers each job in its entirety, usually used in small companies that have relatively few employees. In large companies that classify many jobs, members of job evaluation committees independently rank jobs on a departmental basis. Different rankings will likely result. When this occurs, job evaluation committees discuss the differences in rankings and choose one set of rankings by consensus.

PAIRED COMPARISON AND ALTERNATION RANKING Two common variations of the ranking plan are paired comparison and alternation ranking. The **paired comparison** technique is useful if there are many jobs to rate, usually more than 20. Job evaluation committees generate every possible pair of jobs. For each pair, committee members assign a point to the job with the highest value, whereas the lowest-value job does not receive a point. After evaluating each pair, the evaluator sums the points for each job. Jobs with higher points are more valuable than are jobs with fewer points. The job with the most points is ranked the highest; the job with the fewest points is ranked the lowest.

The **alternation ranking** method orders jobs by extremes. Yet again, committee members judge the relative value of jobs according to a single criterion (e.g., job complexity or the centrality of the job to the company's competitive strategy). This ranking process begins by determining which job is the most valuable, followed by determining which job is the least valuable. Committee members then judge the next most valuable job and the next least valuable job. This process continues until all jobs have been evaluated.

Despite the simplicity of ranking plans, they exhibit three limitations. First, ranking results rely on purely subjective data; the process lacks objective standards, guidelines, and principles that would aid in resolving differences of opinion among committee members. Companies usually do not fully define their ranking criteria. For example, the criterion job complexity can be defined as level of education or as number of distinct tasks that the workers must perform daily.

Second, ranking methods use neither job analyses nor job descriptions, which makes this method difficult to defend legally. Committee members rely on their own impressions of the jobs.

Third, ranking approaches do not incorporate objective scales that indicate how different in value one job is from another. For instance, let's assume that a committee decides on the following ranking for training and development professionals (listed from most valuable to least valuable):

- Director of training and development
- Manager of training and development
- Senior training and development specialist
- Training and development specialist
- Training and development assistant

Rankings do not offer standards for compensation professionals to facilitate answering such questions as, "Is the director of training and development job worth four times as much as the training and development assistant job?" Compensation professionals' inability to answer such questions makes it difficult to establish pay levels according to job-content differences.

CLASSIFICATION PLANS Companies use **classification plans** to place jobs into categories based on compensable factors. Public sector organizations (e.g., civil service systems) use classification systems most prevalently. The federal government's classification system is a well-known example. As we discussed in Chapter 3, the General Schedule classifies federal government jobs into 15 classifications (GS-1 through GS-15) based on such factors as skill, education, and experience levels. In addition, jobs that require high levels of specialized education (e.g., a physicist), significantly influence public policy (e.g., law judges), or require executive decision making are classified in separate categories: Senior Level (SL) positions, Scientific and Professional (SP) positions, and the Senior Executive Service (SES).

Alternatives to Job Evaluation

Compensation professionals assign pay rates to jobs in numerous ways other than through the job evaluation process as previously defined. These alternate methods include reliance on market pay rates, pay incentives, individual rates, and collective bargaining. Many companies determine the value of jobs by paying the average rate in the external labor market. The procedures for assessing market rates are addressed fully in Chapter 7.

In addition to the market pay rate, pay incentives may also be the basis for establishing the core compensation for jobs. As we discussed extensively in Chapter 4, incentives tie part or all an employee's core compensation to the attainment of a predetermined performance objective. Next, both core and fringe compensation may be determined through negotiations between an individual and an employer. The employer typically uses the market rate as a basis for negotiations, agreeing to higher pay if the supply of talented individuals is scarce and the individual in question has an established track record of performance. Finally, when unions are present, pay rates are established through the collective bargaining process, which we already considered in Chapter 2.

INTERNALLY CONSISTENT COMPENSATION SYSTEMS AND COMPETITIVE STRATEGY

6-5. Explain how internally consistent compensation systems and competitive strategy relate to each other.

We established the importance of instituting internally consistent compensation systems. Tightly specified job descriptions that focus on work efficiency may be appropriate for companies that pursue a lowest cost strategy. There may be limitations, however, that hamper agility for companies that strive to differentiate themselves from their competition. For example, internally consistent pay systems may reduce a company's flexibility to respond to changes in competitors' pay practices because job analysis leads to structured job descriptions and job structures. In addition, job evaluation establishes the relative worth of jobs within the company. Responding to the competition may require employees to engage in duties that extend beyond what's written in their job descriptions whenever competitive pressures demand. In the process, the definitions of jobs become more fluid, which makes equity assessments more difficult.

Another potential limitation of internally consistent compensation structures is the resultant bureaucracy. Companies that establish job hierarchies tend to create narrowly defined jobs that lead to greater numbers of jobs and staffing levels.[4] Such structures promote heavy compensation burdens. Employees' core compensation depends on the jobs they perform, how well they perform their jobs, or the skills they possess. Employee benefits (Chapters 9 and 10), however, represent fixed costs that typically do not vary with employees' job performance or their skills. Employing a larger number of workers to staff a multitude of narrowly defined jobs contributes substantially to exorbitant fixed costs for employee benefits.

PREPARING FOR EXAMS/QUIZZES

Chapter Summary by Learning Objectives

Learning Objective 6-1. *Explain the concept of internal consistency.* Internal consistency is a characteristic of job structures that clearly define the relative value of each job among all jobs within a company.

Learning Objective 6-2. *Summarize the practice of job analysis.* Job analysis is a systematic process that describes job content.

Learning Objective 6-3. *Describe the practice of job evaluation.* Job evaluation is a systematic process that recognizes differences in the relative worth among a set of jobs and helps to establish pay differentials accordingly.

Learning Objective 6-4. *Summarize various job evaluation techniques.* There are a variety of job evaluation techniques. A clear distinction is made between two approaches: job-content evaluation and market-based evaluation. There are a variety of job-content job evaluation practices. The point method is among the most prominent.

Learning Objective 6-5. *Explain how internally consistent compensation systems and competitive strategy relate to each other.* Internally consistent compensation systems can facilitate lowest cost strategies by clearly defining job duties and responsibilities that focus on efficiency. On the other hand, internal consistency could create rigid job structures that limit flexibility.

Key Terms

internally consistent compensation systems   130
job structures   130
job analysis   131
job content   131
job evaluation   132
worker requirements   132
working conditions   132
reliable job analysis method   135
valid job analysis method   135
job descriptions   136
job titles   136
job summary   136
job duties   136

worker specifications   136
education   136
Equal Employment Opportunity Commission (EEOC)   136
skill   136
ability   136
knowledge   137
Occupational Information Network (O*NET)   138
Content Model   138
experience and training   138
licensing   138
occupational requirements   138
generalized work activities   139

organizational context   139
work context   139
occupation-specific information requirements   139
workforce characteristics   139
worker characteristics   141
abilities   141
interests   141
work styles   141
basic skills   142
cross-functional skills   142
O*NET User's Guide   142
O*NET database   142
compensable factors   142

Discussion Questions

6-1. What are some differences between job analysis and job evaluation? How do these practices help establish internally consistent job structures?

6-2. Write a draft job description (no longer than one page) for a job that you have had according to the principles described in this chapter. Which tasks and responsibilities were most challenging to express in writing? Explain.

6-3. This chapter provides rationale for conducting job analysis, and indicates some of the limitations. Do you support the use of job analysis? Provide convincing arguments for your position.

6-4. Many business leaders maintain that creating and maintaining internally consistent job structures is burdensome to companies. Do you agree or disagree? Explain.

6-5. Do you consider job evaluation to be an art or a science? Explain.

PREPARING FOR MY CAREER

Compensation in Action

Creating a clear expectation of performance and organizing employee roles in a way that aligns strategy, pay, and performance will benefit you as a line manager or HR professional. Line managers and HR should employ the help of those who know roles the best—the employees who fill those roles—to arrive at conclusions that are fair, informed, and consistent. Line managers will have insight in many cases to choose the right people to help in this process. HR will ensure that these individuals receive proper training and are equipped to assess roles and provide appropriate and objective recommendations. As a line manager or HR professional, your main responsibility in creating a system is to ensure that employee compensation is equitable internally and competitive externally.

Action checklist for line managers and HR—building an equitable and competitive system

HR takes the lead

- Capture the analysis provided by incumbents and create job descriptions for each role.
- Compare the newly created job descriptions with those found on O*NET to validate the decisions made based on the incumbent information.
- Compensation specialists work with HR professionals to identify the compensable factors within each job description; these factors will serve as the basis for pay differentials (the more critical these factors are to company strategy, the more they will be compensated).
- Work with compensation specialists to evaluate differentials across departments in the organization and compare them with similar jobs in other organizations (ideally competitors); consult with line managers and senior finance executives as discrepancies arise and adjustments appear to be necessary.

- Monitor the match of performance expectations and job descriptions to guard against role stagnation in the face of competition that could require jobs to flex and people to take on unexpected responsibilities—monitor equity carefully.

Line managers take the lead

- Partner with job incumbents to understand job content of their roles.
- Select workers to sit on committees that will be given the task of assessing the accuracy of the assigned pay differentials.

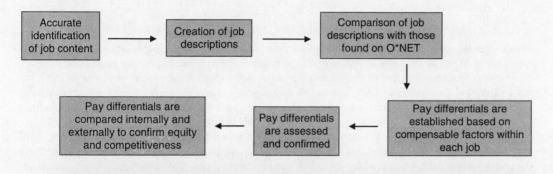

Cases

Case 1: Job Evaluation at Smith Upholstery

Smith Upholstery has been in business since 1970. The company started out hand upholstering the seats for luxury automakers. It built a reputation of excellence. In recent years, however, many luxury automobile companies established in-house upholstering shops, leading to a reduction in business. The company's founder, Robert Smith, anticipated these changes and actively sought contracts to upholster seats for the high-volume economy car market, using automated technology. Robert staffed the manufacturing line to oversee the operation of automated systems and troubleshoot problems that threatened to slow down the line.

Robert recognized that he needed help crafting job descriptions and job evaluation plans to help set pay rates. He hired Marco Colella following the completion of a master's degree in human resources. Robert met Marco shortly after he began his first day of work. He reviewed priorities with Marco and Robert asked him to lead the job description and job evaluation projects. They agreed to meet at the end of the week to discuss a plan for getting this work done.

Marco met with managers to understand current staffing and job structures. Also, he discussed anticipated staffing needs. Marco used the information that he gathered and what he learned about job descriptions and job evaluation in his degree program to develop a proposal for completing this project. He crafted alternatives for conducting job evaluation, including simple ranking, alternate ranking, and point method plans; and he estimated the time it would take to complete job evaluation with each method. Finally, Marco analyzed the pros and cons of each approach. Altogether, it would take two weeks to complete job evaluation with either simple or alternate ranking techniques and two months for the point method. Taking everything into account, Marco decided that the point method would provide the best information for building internally consistent job structures. Marco submitted his plan to Robert in anticipation of their upcoming meeting.

At the start of the meeting, Robert thanked Marco for his excellent plan and for the detailed rationale and timeline for each option. Although Marco recommended using the point method, Robert instructed him to conduct the job evaluations with the simple ranking method. He also asked Marco to conduct the ratings himself rather than involving multiple raters, indicating his desire to reduce the completion time from two weeks to one week. Marco respectfully asked Robert to reconsider his decision, but he would not. Instead, Robert also assigned Marco the task of completing the company's first affirmative action plan, which was already two weeks overdue.

Questions:

6-6. What are some of the advantages and disadvantages of the simple ranking, alternate ranking, and point method job evaluation techniques?

6-7. What problems may occur by following Robert's approach?

6-8. What do you recommend Marco do first? Why?

Case 2: Ethics Dilemma: Stop Complaining or Else

Margot Hemmings and Jeanette McBride created Sweet Indulgence Confectionary when they began making fudge in Margot's kitchen and selling it to local restaurants and bakeries. Twenty years later, the company sells product to restaurant chains nationwide, major airlines, and large grocery store chains and it has grown from two employees to 1,000 employees. Employees work in a variety of roles including baking, sales, and distribution. As the company has grown, new jobs have been created and staffed. Employee pay was largely based on negotiations with job finalists with little consideration to internal consistency.

Sweet Indulgence developed a reputation as a great place to work and has been included on a national magazine's list of desirable companies to work for. Recently, the tone of the workplace has changed. There have been complaints from many long-service workers about their pay, particularly those whose job duties have expanded and include more complex tasks. Others' jobs remained relatively unchanged. Manny Jenkins, Sweet Indulgence's compensation manager, became concerned as the number of complaints rose. He became particularly concerned when he realized that experienced supervisors and managers, especially those near retirement age (age 65), were doing more for less pay. Upon further investigation, he was alarmed that younger new hires in entry level jobs were making substantially more pay. Virtually all of them were content with their pay.

Manny informed Margot and Jeanette of his concerns, which they promptly rejected. He explained that it had been a few years since the company reviewed job descriptions and pay structure. Jeanette immediately dismissed Manny's concerns and those of the complainers, citing Sweet Indulgence's repeated national recognition as a great place to work. Margot added that unhappy employees should stop complaining or risk being fired.

Questions:

6-9. As a compensation professional, what would you do?

6-10. What factor(s) in this ethical dilemma might influence a person to make a less-than-ethical decision?

Crunch the Numbers!

Modifying a Job Evaluation Worksheet

This chapter discusses the principles of internally consistent compensation systems and the practices that establish them. The point method system assigns point values to jobs based on the degree of compensable factors that define them. When job evaluation is conducted correctly, jobs with higher point totals will be valued (in terms of average market pay rates) more highly than jobs with lower point totals. The following list shows five jobs and each job's point total.

Job Title	Job Evaluation Point Total
Management trainee	200 points
Assistant manager	310 points
Associate manager	450 points
Manager	525 points
Senior manager	700 points

Let's assume that the average market pay rate for the associate manager job is $50,000 and it is being used as the frame of reference for determining the rates for the remaining jobs on the list.

Questions:

6-11. What should the typical pay rate be for the following jobs: (a) management trainee, (b) assistant manager, (c) manager, and (d) senior manager? (*Hint*: Calculate the dollar value per job evaluation point to start based on the associate manager job and salary.)

6-12. What would the pay rates be for the remaining jobs if the associate manager job pay rate was increased by $10,000? (a) management trainee, (b) assistant manager, (c) manager, and (d) senior manager.

6-13. Assume that the associate manager job is valued at $50,000 (with a point total of 450 points), and we add 50 points to the total of the remaining jobs. What should the pay rates be for the (a) management trainee, (b) assistant manager, (c) manager, and (d) senior manager?

Working Together: Team Exercise

In small groups of three or four, come up with specific answers to the following questions. Talk through your perspectives and come up with a team response. Be prepared to share your ideas with the class.

As a group, use O*NET to select a job for further study. Start by browsing jobs in different occupations (www.onetonline.org/find/). Next, from the *find occupations* drop down list, select *job family*. There, you will see 23 unique job families (occupations). Then, select a job family (click on the link for the chosen job family). Finally, select a job from the chosen job family (click on the link for the chosen job) and review the information contained in the detailed report.

Questions:

6-14. What are three categories (e.g., one category is the job summary) contained in the detailed report? Explain.

6-15. What are some of the knowledge, skill, and ability factors listed in the report that you believe are most crucial for distinguishing this job from a job in another job family? Explain.

Endnotes

1. U.S. Bureau of Labor Statistics, *Standard Occupational Classification*, (2018), accessed February 4, 2018, http://www.bls.gov/soc/.
2. Wayne F. Cascio and Herman Aguinis, *Applied Psychology in Personnel Management* (7th ed.) (Upper Saddle River, NJ: Prentice Hall, 2011).
3. U.S. Department of Labor, Employment and Training Administration, *O*NET* (2018) Washington, DC: Government Printing Office, accessed February 3, 2018, http://www.onetcenter.gov.
4. Edward E. Lawler III, "What's Wrong with Point-factor Job Evaluation?" *Compensation and Benefits Review* 18, (1986): 20–28, http://dx.doi.org/10.1177/088636878601800502.

7 Building Market-Competitive Compensation Systems

Learning Objectives

When you finish studying this chapter, you should be able to:

7-1. Explain the concept of market-competitive compensation systems and summarize the four activities compensation professionals engage in to create these systems.

7-2. Discuss compensation survey practices.

7-3. Describe how compensation professionals integrate internal job structures with external market pay rates.

7-4. Explain the basic concepts of compensation policies and strategic mandates: pay level and pay mix.

Compensation surveys function as a cornerstone in the development of market-competitive compensation systems. Well-designed and executed surveys provide compensation professionals with sufficient data about other companies' pay rates and practices to begin establishing competitive pay policies that are focused on pay level and pay mix. With sound data in hand, compensation professionals will be well positioned to establish pay structures (Chapter 8) that fulfill strategic mandates and to effectively attract and retain talented employees.

7-1. Explain the concept of market-competitive compensation systems and summarize the four activities compensation professionals engage in to create these systems.

MARKET-COMPETITIVE PAY SYSTEMS: THE BASIC BUILDING BLOCKS

Market-competitive pay systems represent companies' compensation policies that fit the imperatives of competitive advantage. Market-competitive pay systems play a significant role in attracting and retaining the most qualified employees. Well-designed pay systems should promote companies' attainment of competitive strategies. Paying more than necessary can undermine lowest-cost strategies: Excessive pay levels represent an undue burden. In addition, excessive pay restricts companies' abilities to invest in other important strategic activities (e.g., research and development, training) because money is a limited resource. Companies that pursue differentiation strategies must strike a balance between offering sufficiently high salaries to attract and retain talented candidates and providing sufficient resources to enable them to be productively creative.

Compensation professionals create market-competitive pay systems based on four activities:

- Conducting strategic analyses
- Assessing competitors' pay practices with compensation surveys
- Integrating the internal job structure with external market pay rates
- Determining compensation policies

First, a **strategic analysis** entails an examination of a company's external market context and internal factors. Examples of external market factors include industry profile, information about competitors, and long-term growth prospects. Internal factors encompass financial condition and functional capabilities (e.g., marketing and human resources).

Second, **compensation surveys** involve the collection and subsequent analysis of competitors' compensation data. Compensation surveys traditionally focused on competitors' wage and salary practices. Employee benefits have more recently become a target of surveys because benefits are a key element of market-competitive pay systems. Compensation surveys are important because they enable compensation professionals to obtain realistic views of competitors' pay practices. In the absence of compensation survey data, compensation professionals would have to use guesswork to try to build market-competitive compensation systems, and making too many wrong guesses could lead to noncompetitive compensation systems that undermine competitive advantage.

Third, compensation professionals integrate the internal job structure (Chapter 6) with the external market pay rates identified through compensation surveys. This integration results in pay rates that reflect both the company's and the external market's valuations of jobs. Most often, compensation professionals rely on regression analysis, a statistical method, to achieve this integration.

Finally, compensation professionals recommend two sets of pay policy options that fit with their companies' standing and competitive strategies. As we discuss later in this chapter, compensation professionals must strike a balance between managing costs and attracting, motivating, and retaining the best-qualified employees. Top management ultimately makes compensation policy decisions after careful consideration of compensation professionals' interpretation of the data and strategic considerations.

Ideally, companies engage in these steps annually to ensure that their systems remain competitive as market pay rates generally rise over time. Changing business priorities sometimes influence expectations of employees. Companies would be well served by reconsidering pay mix policies as changes occur. These policies (and policy changes) are codified in compensation plans. **Compensation plans** represent the selection and implementation of pay level and pay mix policies over a specified period, usually one year.

 FYI

A survey of companies revealed that the frequency of compensation survey administration varies:

- Multiple times per year: 6 percent
- Once a year: 53 percent
- Once every two years: 15 percent
- Not consistently (as needed based on market conditions): 21 percent[1]

COMPENSATION SURVEYS

7-2. Discuss compensation survey practices.

Compensation surveys contain data about competing companies' compensation practices.

Preliminary Considerations

There are two important preliminary considerations compensation professionals take under advisement before investing time and money into compensation surveys:

- What companies hope to gain from compensation surveys
- Custom development versus use of an existing compensation survey

WHAT COMPANIES HOPE TO GAIN FROM COMPENSATION SURVEYS Clarifying what companies hope to gain from compensation surveys is critical to developing effective compensation systems. Compensation professionals usually want to learn about competitors' compensation practices and something about employees' preferences for alternative forms of compensation due to economic changes. Staying abreast of new developments in market surveys will enable compensation professionals to get the most out of surveys. Oftentimes, compensation professionals think about surveys as a translator.[2] Information to be learned about competitors' compensation offerings includes base pay levels and mix of total monetary compensation. We will discuss pay level policies and pay mix policies in more detail later in this chapter. For example, a company may choose to set base pay levels that exceed the average market pay rate by 5 percent. Pay mix can be described as the percentage of employer compensation costs applied to the components of core compensation (e.g., base pay, incentives, merit pay) and benefits. For example, 70 percent of an employee's total compensation may consist of core compensation, and 30 percent of employee benefits. Said another way, for every dollar that an employer spends on total compensation, $0.70 funds core compensation and $0.30 funds employee benefits.

Compensation professionals wish to make sound decisions about pay levels based on what the competition pays its employees. Sound pay decisions promote companies' efforts to sustain competitive advantage, and poor pay decisions compromise those efforts. Compensation surveys enable compensation professionals to make sound judgments about how much to pay employees. Offering too little will limit a company's ability to recruit and retain high-quality employees. Paying well above the competition represents opportunity costs. Excessive pay represents an opportunity cost because it is money companies could have spent on other important matters such as marketing or research and development.

CUSTOM DEVELOPMENT VERSUS USE OF AN EXISTING COMPENSATION SURVEY Managers must decide whether to develop their own survey instruments and administer them or rely on the results of surveys conducted by others. In theory, customized surveys are preferable because the survey taker can tailor the questions the survey asks and select respondent companies to provide the most useful and informative data. Custom survey development should enable employers to monitor the quality of the survey developers' methodologies.

In practice, companies choose not to develop and implement their own surveys for three reasons. First, most companies lack employees qualified to undertake this task. Developing and implementing valid surveys both require specialized knowledge and expertise in sound questionnaire design, sampling methods, and statistical methods.

Second, rival companies are understandably reluctant to surrender information about their compensation packages to competitors because compensation systems are instrumental to competitive advantage issues. If companies are willing to cooperate, the information may be incomplete or inaccurate. For example, rival companies may choose to report the salaries for their lowest-paid accountants instead of the typical salary levels. Such information may lead the surveying company to set accountants' salaries much lower than if they had accurate, complete information about typical salary levels. Setting accountants' salaries too low may hinder recruitment efforts. Thus, custom development is potentially risky.

Third, custom survey development can be costly. Although cost figures are not readily available, it is reasonable to conclude that most companies use published survey data to minimize such costs as staff salaries and benefits (i.e., for those involved in developing a compensation survey as well as analyzing and interpreting the data), distribution costs, and statistical packages for data analyses.

Using Published Compensation Survey Data

Companies usually rely on existing compensation surveys rather than creating their own. Using published compensation survey data starts with two important considerations:

- Survey focus: core compensation or employee benefits
- Sources of published compensation surveys

SURVEY FOCUS: CORE COMPENSATION OR EMPLOYEE BENEFITS Human resource professionals should decide whether to obtain survey information about base pay, employee benefits, or both. Companies historically competed for employees mainly based on base pay. Many companies offered similar, substantial benefits packages to employees without regard to the costs. Companies typically did not use benefits offerings to compete for the best employees.

Times have changed. Benefits costs are now extremely high, which has led to greater variability in benefits offerings among companies. As of September 2017, companies spent an average $18,000 per employee annually to provide discretionary benefits.[3] In 2017, discretionary benefits accounted for as much as 24.4 percent of employers' total payroll costs. When we factor in legally required benefit costs as well, total employee benefits account for 31.7 percent of total compensation costs. That is a huge cost to employers, one that has been rising rapidly,[4] but one that cannot be avoided. Benefits have become a basis for attracting and retaining the best employees, particularly as noted earlier in this chapter. As a result, employers are likely to use compensation surveys to obtain information about competitors' base pay and benefits practices so they can compete effectively for the best candidates.

SOURCES OF PUBLISHED COMPENSATION SURVEYS Companies can obtain published survey data from various sources such as professional associations, industry associations, consulting firms, and the federal government. Oftentimes, it makes sense to obtain multiple surveys because differences in survey methodology can lead to differences in results. Using multiple surveys should give compensation professionals a more accurate picture of market practices.[5] For example, as we discussed in Chapter 2, interindustry wage differentials explain some of the variation we observe in average pay rates for similar or identical jobs. In that chapter, we explained that capital intensive businesses tend to pay more highly than do service industry businesses. In this case, a survey of exclusively capital-intensive companies will show higher average pay rates than a survey of exclusively service industry companies.

Professional and industry associations survey members' salaries, compile the information in summary form, and disseminate the results to members. The survey data tend to be accurate because participants—as well as association members—benefit from the survey results. In addition, membership fees often entitle members to survey information at no additional cost.

For example, the Society for Industrial and Organizational Psychology's (SIOP) primary membership includes college and university faculty members and practitioners who specialize in such HR management-related fields as selection, training, performance appraisal, and career development. SIOP periodically provides members' salary information based on gender, age, employment status (i.e., part time versus full time), years since earning degree, and geographic region according to metropolitan area (e.g., Boston, San Francisco/San Jose, and Washington, DC). Employers use the survey results to judge whether they are paying employees too much or too little relative to the market and to determine how much to pay new hires. Employees use the survey results to judge the adequacy of job offers and to ask their deans for pay raises when their salaries fall below the market rates.

Professional associations that specialize in the field of compensation often conduct surveys that focus on broader types of employees and employers. WorldatWork collects comprehensive data on an annual basis.

Consulting firms are another source of compensation survey information. Some firms specialize in occupations (e.g., engineers) or industries (e.g., financial services). Examples of consulting firms that provide compensation services include:

- Aon (www.aon.com/human-capital-consulting/)
- Culpepper (www.culpepper.com)
- Frederic W. Cook & Company (www.fwcook.com)
- Korn Ferry - Hay Group (www.haygroup.com)
- Pearl Meyer & Partners (www.pearlmeyer.com)
- William M. Mercer (www.mercer.com)
- Willis Towers Watson (www.willistowerswatson.com)

You will find useful updates about compensation and benefits on these firms' Web sites. Clients may have two choices. First, consulting firms may provide survey data from recently completed surveys. Second, these firms may literally conduct surveys from scratch exclusively for a client's use. In most cases, the first option is less expensive to companies than the second option; however, the quality of the second option may be superior because the survey was custom-designed to answer a client's specific compensation questions.

The federal government is an invaluable source of compensation survey information. The U.S. Bureau of Labor Statistics (BLS) provides free salary survey results to the public. Highly qualified survey takers and statisticians are responsible for producing these surveys. Many factors contributed to the implementation of BLS pay and benefits surveys. The government began collecting compensation data in the 1890s to assess the effects of tariff legislation on wages and prices. The government's survey programs have been rooted in competitive concerns ever since.

The BLS publishes a large amount of information on the wages, earnings, and benefits of workers. Generally, this information is grouped in one or more of the following seven categories:

- Employment cost trends
- National compensation data
- Wages by area and occupation
- Earnings by demographics
- Earnings by industry
- County wages
- Employee benefits

The following summary of these programs was excerpted from the public domain U.S. Bureau of Labor Statistics Web site (www.bls.gov).

EMPLOYMENT COST TRENDS This program publishes quarterly statistics that measure change in labor costs (also called employment costs or compensation costs) over time; quarterly data measuring the level of costs per hour worked are also published. Indexes are available for total labor costs, and separately for wages and salaries and for benefit costs. Some information is available by region, major industry group, major occupational group, and bargaining status.

NATIONAL COMPENSATION DATA The National Compensation Survey (NCS) provides comprehensive measures of occupational earnings; compensation cost trends, benefit incidence, and detailed plan provisions. Detailed occupational earnings are available for metropolitan and non-metropolitan areas, broad geographic regions, and on a national basis. The index component of the NCS—Employer Cost Index (ECI)—measures changes in labor costs. Average hourly employer cost for employee compensation is presented in the Employer Costs for Employee Compensation (ECEC) feature.

WAGES BY AREA AND OCCUPATION Wage data are available by occupation for the nation, regions, states, and many metropolitan areas. Wage data by area and occupation are derived from the National Compensation Survey, Occupational Employment Statistics Survey, or the Current Population Survey.

EARNINGS BY DEMOGRAPHICS Data are available by demographic characteristics such as age, sex, race, and Hispanic or Latino ethnicity.

EARNINGS BY INDUSTRY The Current Employment Statistics survey is a monthly survey of the payroll records of business establishments that provides national estimates of average weekly hours and average hourly earnings for the private sector for all employees and for production and nonsupervisory employees. Average weekly overtime hours in manufacturing are also available. State and area estimates of hours and earnings from this survey are available for all employees as well as for production workers (in the goods-producing industries) and nonsupervisory workers (in the private service-providing industries).

COUNTY WAGES (QUARTERLY CENSUS OF EMPLOYMENT AND WAGES) Annual and quarterly wage data are available by detailed industry for the nation, states, and many metropolitan areas and counties.

EMPLOYEE BENEFITS The National Compensation Survey provides information on the share of workers who participate in specified benefits, such as health care, retirement plans, and paid vacations. These data also show the details of those benefits, such as health insurance deductible amounts and amounts of paid leave.

☛ **FYI**

There are many available compensation surveys and most companies consider whether to use more than one. Five questions for determining the appropriate number of surveys include:

- Do you have a broad array of jobs in many functional areas?
- Do you recruit locally, regionally, nationally, or internationally?
- Are your jobs unique to your industry or common across many industries?
- Is your company significantly larger or smaller than your competition?
- How much can you afford for survey purchases?[6]

Compensation Surveys: Strategic Considerations

Two essential strategic considerations are:

- Defining the relevant labor market
- Choosing benchmark jobs

DEFINING THE RELEVANT LABOR MARKET **Relevant labor markets** represent the fields of potentially qualified candidates for jobs. Companies collect compensation survey data from the appropriate relevant labor markets. Relevant labor markets are defined based on occupational classification, geography, and product or service market competitors.

As we discussed in Chapter 6, an occupation is a group of jobs found at more than one establishment, in which a common set of tasks are performed or are related in terms of similar objectives, methodologies, materials, products, worker actions, or worker characteristics. The U.S. Bureau of Labor Statistics' *Standard Occupational Classification System (SOC)* helps business professionals and government economists make proper occupational matches for collecting compensation data. As we noted in Chapter 6, the SOC links to the O*NET, a Web site containing detailed job description information to facilitate compensation professionals making precise comparisons for pay-setting purposes.

Companies that plan to hire accountants and auditors should consider data about accountants and auditors only, rather than individuals from such other job families as engineers. After all, the worker characteristics and work tasks are clearly different: Accountants and auditors prepare, analyze, and verify financial reports and taxes, as well as monitor information systems that furnish this information to managers in business, industrial, and government organizations. Engineers apply the theories and principles of science and mathematics to the economical solution of practical technical problems. For example, civil engineers design, plan, and supervise the construction of buildings, highways, and rapid transit systems.

Companies search over a wider geographical area for candidates for jobs that require specialized skills or skills that are low in supply relative to the demand. For instance, hospitals are likely to search nationwide for neurosurgeons because their specialized skills are scarce. Companies are likely to limit searches for clerical employees to more confined local areas because clerical employees' skills are relatively common, and their supply tends to be higher relative to companies' demand for them. For example, an insurance company based in Hartford, Connecticut, most likely restricts its search for clerical employees to the Hartford area.

Companies use product or service market competitors to define the relevant labor market when industry-specific knowledge is a key worker qualification and competition for market share is keen. For example, beverage companies probably prefer to lure marketing managers away from industry competitors rather than from such unrelated industries as software or medical and surgical supplies. Knowledge about the features of software has little to do with customers' preferences for soft drinks.

Occupational classification, geographic scope, and product or service market competitors are not necessarily independent dimensions. For example, a company uses product or service market competitors as the basis for defining the relevant labor market for product managers; however, this dimension overlaps with geographic scope because competitor companies are located throughout the country (e.g., Boston, San Francisco, Dallas, and Miami).

With many professional, technical, and management positions, all three factors (i.e., job family, geographic scope, and companies that compete based on product or service) can be applicable. For more information about relevant labor markets for various occupations, employers can consult professional and industrial associations and consulting firms.

CHOOSING BENCHMARK JOBS As we discussed in Chapter 6, benchmark jobs are key to conducting effective job evaluations. They also play an important role in compensation surveys. Human resource professionals determine the pay levels for jobs based on typical market pay rates for similar jobs. In other words, HR professionals rely on benchmark jobs as reference points for setting pay levels. Benchmark jobs have four characteristics:[7]

- The contents are well known, relatively stable over time, and agreed upon by the employees involved.
- The jobs are common across many different employers.
- The jobs represent the entire range of jobs that are being evaluated within a company.
- The jobs are generally accepted in the labor market for the purposes of setting pay levels.

Why are benchmark jobs necessary? Human resource professionals ideally would match each job within their companies to jobs contained in compensation surveys; however, one-to-one matches are not feasible for two reasons. First, large companies may have hundreds of unique jobs, making one-to-one matches tedious, time-consuming, and expensive because of the salary and benefits paid to staff members responsible for making these matches. Second, it is highly unlikely that HR professionals will find perfect or close matches between each of a company's jobs and jobs contained in the compensation surveys: Companies adapt job duties and scope to fit their situations. In other words, jobs with identical titles may differ somewhat in the degrees of compensable factors. Perfect matches are the exception rather than the rule. For example, Company A's Secretary I job may require only a high school education or GED equivalent. Company B's Secretary I job may require an associate's degree in office administration.

The following Watch It! video describes talent management at the *Weather Channel*. The company's executive vice president of human resources discusses the importance of job analysis and job descriptions in this practice. Compensation professionals contribute to talent management in a variety of ways. Related to this chapter's material, they determine the extent to which benchmark job duties and responsibilities match the company's job description so that they may accurately assess market pay rates. Failure to do so may result in setting pay rates too low, which would undermine efforts to recruit and retain talent.

Companies can make corrections for differences between their jobs and external benchmark jobs. These corrections are based on subjective judgment rather than on objective

**TABLE 7-1 Sample Compensable Factor and Point-Level Definitions:
Physical Environment**

Factor 4. Physical Environment

• Nonstrenuous with Low Risk (See definitions below.)	10 Points
• Moderately Strenuous with Low Risk or • Nonstrenuous with Moderate Risk (See definitions below.)	25 Points
• Strenuous with Low Risk or • Moderately Strenuous with Moderate Risk (See definitions below.)	40 Points
• Moderately Strenuous with High Risk or • Strenuous with Moderate Risk (See definitions below.)	70 Points
• Strenuous with High Risk (See definitions below.)	100 Points

Definition

Nonstrenuous—Primarily sedentary with some walking, standing, and carrying of light objects.

Moderately strenuous—Often lifts 30 to 50 pounds, walks over uneven surfaces, and/or stands for long periods.

Strenuous—Often lifts more than 50 pounds, climbs high, runs, or defends against physical attack.

Low risk—Adequately lighted, ventilated, and heated area where normal precautions must be observed.

Moderate risk—Requires special mitigating precautions and/or protective gear or clothing due to potential risk from such sources as moving machinery, chemicals, animals, or diseases.

High risk—Extreme temperatures, likelihood of physical attack, or potential exposure to smoke and fire.

Source: U.S. Bureau of Labor Statistics (2013) *National Compensation Survey: Guide for Evaluating Your Firm's Jobs and Pay* (revised, May). Available: http://www.bls.gov, accessed March 3, 2015.

criteria. This process is referred to as **job leveling**. There are a variety of job leveling approaches. Compensation professionals can adopt a point rating approach referred to as **point factor leveling**[8] to achieve the job leveling objective. Table 7-1 illustrates a physical environment factor. Participants will rate a job based on a standard set of compensable factors that have point values associated with each level of the factor, much like we accomplished with the point rating job evaluation approach (Chapter 6). Table 7-2 illustrates a rating sheet that shows the relevant compensable factors, point totals, and point ranges. Both job incumbents and supervisors should complete a rating form separately to achieve job leveling based on all the relevant factors. Independent ratings should help to minimize rater biases. Differences in ratings generally can be reconciled through discussion.

 FYI

Experts recognize the challenges of matching a company's jobs within a company with survey benchmark jobs. A rule of thumb:

- At least 80 percent of a company's job, based on job content, should match benchmark jobs.
- At least 60 percent of a company's jobs will spend at least 50 percent of the time specified in benchmark jobs.[9]

Compensation Survey Data

Compensation professionals should be aware of three compensation survey data characteristics. First, compensation surveys contain immense amounts of information. A perusal of every datum **point** would be mind-boggling even to the most mathematically inclined individuals. In addition, **there** is bound to be wide variation in pay rates across companies, making it difficult to

TABLE 7-2 Leveling Instructions and Points

After recording the level for each factor for a job, determine points associated with that level from the chart below. Sum the points to determine overall work level.

Points associated with each factor

Factor	Factor number								
Knowledge	50	200	350	550	750	950	1250	1550	1850
Job controls and complexity	100	300	475	625	850	1175	1450	1950	X
Contacts	30	75	110	130	280	X	X	X	X
Physical environment	10	25	40	70	100	X	X	X	X

Points range by work level

Level	Minimum points	Maximum points
1	190	254
2	255	454
3	455	654
4	655	854
5	855	1104
6	1105	1354
7	1355	1604
8	1605	1854
9	1855	2104
10	2105	2354
11	2355	2754
12	2755	3154
13	3155	3604
14	3605	4054
15	4055 and up	

Source: U.S. Bureau of Labor Statistics (2013) *National Compensation Survey: Guide for Evaluating Your Firm's Jobs and Pay* (revised, May). Available: http://www.bls.gov, accessed February 14, 2018.

build market-competitive pay systems. Thus, compensation professionals should use statistics to describe large sets of data efficiently. Second, compensation survey data are outdated because there is a lag between when the data were collected and when employers implement the compensation plan based on the survey data. Third, compensation professionals must use statistical analyses to integrate their internal job structures (based on job evaluation points; see Chapter 6) with the external market based on the survey data. We will discuss this matter in detail later in this chapter.

Table 7-3 contains sample salary information collected from a salary survey of 35 accounting jobs according to seniority. Accountant I incumbents possess less than two years of accounting work experience. Accountant II incumbents have two to less than four years of accounting work experience. Accountant III incumbents possess 4 to 6 years of work experience as accountants. Seven companies (A–G) from Atlanta participated in the survey, and most have more than one incumbent at each level. Company B has three accountant I incumbents, three accountant II incumbents, and two accountant III incumbents.

As a starting point, let's begin with basic tabulation of the survey data. Basic tabulation helps organize data, promotes decision makers' familiarization with the data, and reveals possible extreme observations (i.e., outliers). Table 7-4 displays a frequency table, and Figure 7-1 displays a histogram. Both indicate the number of job incumbents whose salaries fall within the

TABLE 7-3 Raw Compensation Survey Data for Accountants in Atlanta, Georgia

Company	Job Title	Annual Salary ($)
A	Accountant I	33,000
A	Accountant I	34,500
A	Accountant II	36,000
A	Accountant III	43,500
B	Accountant I	33,000
B	Accountant I	33,000
B	Accountant I	36,000
B	Accountant II	37,500
B	Accountant II	36,000
B	Accountant II	37,500
B	Accountant III	45,000
B	Accountant III	43,500
C	Accountant I	34,500
C	Accountant II	37,500
C	Accountant III	43,500
D	Accountant I	36,000
D	Accountant I	36,000
D	Accountant III	55,000
E	Accountant I	33,000
E	Accountant I	33,000
E	Accountant I	34,500
E	Accountant II	36,000
E	Accountant II	36,000
E	Accountant II	37,500
E	Accountant III	45,000
F	Accountant I	34,500
F	Accountant II	37,500
F	Accountant III	45,000
F	Accountant III	45,000
F	Accountant III	43,500
G	Accountant I	34,500
G	Accountant I	33,000
G	Accountant II	37,500
G	Accountant II	37,500
G	Accountant III	43,500

TABLE 7-4 Frequency Table for Accountants

Salary Interval ($)	Number of Salaries from Survey
30,000–35,000	11
35,001–40,000	14
40,000–45,000	9
45,000+	1

specified intervals. For example, 11 accountants' annual salaries range between $30,000 and $35,000. Only one job incumbent falls in the $45,001 and above interval, which suggests the possibility of an outlier. We'll discuss the importance of recognizing outliers shortly.

USING THE APPROPRIATE STATISTICS TO SUMMARIZE SURVEY DATA Two properties describe numerical data sets:

- Central tendency
- Variation

Central tendency represents the fact that a set of data clusters or centers around a central point. Central tendency is a number that represents the typical numerical value in the data set. What is the typical annual salary for accountants in our data set? Two types of central tendency measures are pertinent to compensation—arithmetic mean (often called mean or average) and median.

We calculate the **mean** annual salary for accountants by adding all the annual salaries in our data set and then dividing the total by the number of annual salaries in the data set. The sum of the salaries in our example is $1,337,500 based on 35 salaries. Thus, the mean equals $38,214.29 ($1,337,500 divided by 35). In this example, the mean informs compensation professionals about the "typical" salary or going market rate for the group of accountants I, II, and III. Compensation professionals often use the mean as a reference point to judge whether employees' compensation is below or above the market.

We use every data point to calculate the mean. As a result, one or more outliers can lead to a distorted representation of the typical value. The mean understates the "true" typical value when there is one or more extremely small value, and it overstates the "true" typical value when there is one or more extremely large value. The mean's shortcoming has implications for compensation professionals.

Understated mean salaries may cause employers to set starting salaries too low to attract the best-qualified job candidates. Overstated mean salaries probably promote recruitment efforts because employers may set starting salaries higher than necessary, a condition that creates a cost burden to companies.

The **median** is the middle value in an ordered sequence of numerical data. If there is an odd number of data points, the median literally is the middle observation. Our data set contains an odd number of observations. The median is $36,000. Table 7-5 illustrates the calculation of the median.

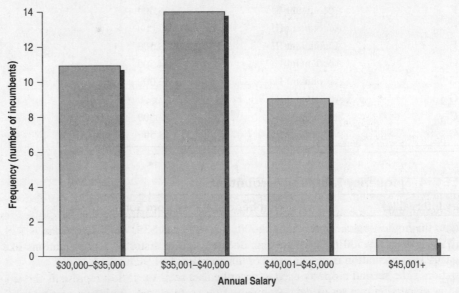

FIGURE 7-1 Histogram of Survey Data for Accountants

TABLE 7-5 Calculation of the Median for Accountant Survey Data

The salary data are arranged in ascending order. The median is $(n + 1)/2$, where n equals the number of salaries. The median is item 18 ([35 + 1]/2). Thus, the median value is $36,000.

1.	$33,000
2.	$33,000
3.	$33,000
4.	$33,000
5.	$33,000
6.	$33,000
7.	$34,500
8.	$34,500
9.	$34,500
10.	$34,500
11.	$34,500
12.	$36,000
13.	$36,000
14.	$36,000
15.	$36,000
16.	$36,000
17.	$36,000
18.	$36,000 ⟵ Median (Half of the salaries are less than the median value and half are higher than the median value.)
19.	$37,500
20.	$37,500
21.	$37,500
22.	$37,500
23.	$37,500
24.	$37,500
25.	$37,500
26.	$43,500
27.	$43,500
28.	$43,500
29.	$43,500
30.	$43,500
31.	$45,000
32.	$45,000
33.	$45,000
34.	$45,000
35.	$55,000

If there is an even number of data points, the median is the mean of the values corresponding to the two middle numbers. Let's assume that we have four salaries, ordered from the smallest value to the highest value: $25,000, $28,000, $29,500, and $33,000. The median is $28,750 (that is, [$28,000 + $29,500]/2). The median does not create distorted representations like the mean because its calculation is independent of the magnitude of each value.

Variation is the second property used to describe data sets. **Variation** represents the amount of spread or dispersion in a set of data. Compensation professionals find three measures of dispersion to be useful (standard deviation, quartile, and percentile).

Standard deviation refers to the mean distance of each salary figure from the mean (i.e., how larger observations fluctuate above the mean and how smaller observations fluctuate below the mean). Table 7-6 demonstrates the calculation of the standard deviation for our data set.

The standard deviation equals $5,074.86. Compensation professionals find standard deviation to be useful for two reasons. First, as we noted previously, compensation professionals often use the mean as a reference point to judge whether employees' compensations are below or above the market. The standard deviation indicates whether an individual salary's departure below or above the mean is "typical" for the market. For example, Irwin Katz's annual salary is $27,500. His salary falls substantially below the typical average salary: The difference between the mean salary and Katz's salary is $10,714.29 ($38,214.29 – $27,500). This difference is much greater than the typical departure from the mean because the standard deviation is just $5,074.86.

Second, the standard deviation indicates the range for most salaries. Most salaries fall between $33,139.43 ($38,214.29 – $5,074.86) and $43,289.15 ($38,214.29 + $5,074.86). Remember, $38,214.29 is the mean, and $5,074.86 is the standard deviation. Compensation professionals can use this range to judge whether their company's salary ranges are similar to the market's salary ranges. A company's salary ranges are not typical of the market if most fall below or above the market range. A company will probably find it difficult to retain good employees when most salaries fall below the typical market range.

Both quartiles and percentiles describe dispersion by indicating the percentage of figures that fall below certain points. Table 7-7 illustrates the use of quartiles and percentiles for our survey data. **Quartiles** allow compensation professionals to describe the distribution of data—in this case, annual base pay amount—based on four groupings. The first quartile is $34,500. In other words, 25 percent of the salary figures are less than or equal to $34,500. The second quartile is $36,000. Fifty percent of the salary figures are less than or equal to $36,000. The third quartile is $43,500. Seventy-five percent of the salary figures are less than or equal to $43,500. The fourth quartile is $55,000. One hundred percent of the salary figures are less than or equal to $55,000. There are one hundred **percentiles** ranging from the first percentile to the 100th percentile. For our data, the 10th percentile equals $33,000, and the 90th percentile equals $45,000.

Quartiles and percentiles complement standard deviations by indicating the percentage of observations that fall below particular figures. Compensation professionals' reviews of percentiles and quartiles can enhance their insights into the dispersion of salary data. For example, compensation professionals want to know the percentage of accountants earning a salary level or less. If $33,000 represents the 10th percentile for accountants' annual salaries, then only 10 percent earn $33,000 or

TABLE 7-6 Calculation of the Standard Deviation (S.D.) for Accountant Survey Data

$$S.D. = \sqrt{\frac{\sum_{i=1}^{n} X_i^2 - nM^2}{n - 1}}$$

Where

$\sum_{i=1}^{n} X_i^2 =$ the sum of the squares of the individual salary observations.

$nM^2 =$ the sample size (n; i.e., 35 salaries) multiplied by the square of the mean for the 35 salaries.

$$S.D. = \sqrt{\frac{(\$33,000^2 + \$33,000^2 + \cdots + \$55,000^2) - 35(\$38,214.92^2)}{35 - 1}}$$

$$S.D. = \sqrt{\frac{51,987,260,000 - 51,111,618,000}{34}}$$

$$S.D. = \$5,074.86$$

TABLE 7-7 Percentile and Quartile Ranks for Accountant Survey Data

$55,000	⟵ 4th quartile (maximum value)
$45,000	
$45,000	⟵ 90th percentile
$45,000	
$45,000	
$43,500	
$43,500	
$43,500	⟵ 3rd quartile
$43,500	
$43,500	
$37,500	
$37,500	
$37,500	
$37,500	
$37,500	
$37,500	
$36,000	⟵ 2nd quartile (also, the 50th percentile or median)
$36,000	
$36,000	
$36,000	
$36,000	
$36,000	
$36,000	
$34,500	
$34,500	
$34,500	⟵ 1st quartile
$34,500	
$34,500	
$33,000	
$33,000	
$33,000	⟵ 10th percentile
$33,000	
$33,000	
$33,000	

less. Compensation professionals are less likely to recommend similar pay for new accountant hires. Although paying at this level represents a cost savings, companies are likely to experience retention problems because 90 percent of accountants earn more than $33,000.

It is important to keep in mind that statistics of a given type (e.g., central tendency) provide consistent information for a given set of data. As we discussed, the mean and median are measures of central tendency. The mean and median are often different for a given set of data points. When the distribution of data are skewed to the left (i.e., there is a higher frequency of larger values than smaller values), the mean will be less than the median. On the other hand, when the distribution of data are skewed to the right (i.e., there is a lower frequency of larger values than smaller values), the mean will be greater than the median.

Let's look at an example. The mean hourly wage rate for production workers in Company A is $8.72. The union in Company A is demanding that management grant pay raises to production workers because the mean hourly pay rate for production workers in Company B is higher—$9.02. The mean value for Company B is based on the following survey of its production workers:

Hourly Wage Rates of Production Workers						
$8.15	$8.39	$8.51	$8.55	$8.60	$10.25	$10.72

Company A's management is unwilling to raise production workers' pay: Company A's production workers earn a higher mean hourly wage ($8.72) than the median hourly wage rate of Company B's production workers ($8.55).

Updating the Survey Data

Compensation professionals must rely on historical salary data to build market-competitive pay systems. Obviously, it is impossible to obtain future salary data for an upcoming compensation plan. Changes in the cost of living tend to make survey data obsolete quickly. Over time, the average cost of goods and services usually increases. Failure to adjust pay rates could lead to a situation where real compensation falls below nominal compensation. **Real compensation** measures the purchasing power of a dollar while **nominal compensation** is the face value of a dollar. Increases in the costs of goods and services cause nominal pay to be less than real pay. For example, let's assume that an employee accepted a job at $10 per hour. This figure—$10 per hour—represents nominal pay. At the same time, $10 also represents real pay. However, over one year, let's assume that the price of goods and services increased, on average, 5 percent. At the end of the year, nominal pay remains at $10. Real pay, on the other hand, declined by 5 percent, or $0.50. In other words, $10 purchases only $9.50 worth of goods and services. In this example, $9.50 represents real pay.

To remain competitive, companies therefore update salary survey data with the **Consumer Price Index**, the most commonly used method for tracking cost changes, or consumer inflation, throughout the United States. CPI data are available on the U.S. BLS Web site (www.bls.gov). Table 7-8 provides descriptive information about the CPI as well as how to calculate cost changes between two periods. The *Crunch the Numbers!* feature illustrates how to update salary survey data. It is important to note that the CPI does not permit for comparison between locations (e.g., cost of living differences between Chicago and Seattle); rather, it only allows for a comparison of cost of living differences over time within a single location.

Several additional factors play an important role in updating. The most influential could be the supply relative to demand for labor as we discussed in Chapter 2. We noted that there tend to be pressures to raise starting pay when the demand for qualified workers is greater than supply. These market dynamics require that companies compete for limited qualified workers. This appears to be the case for information security analysts. According to the *Occupational Outlook Handbook*,[10] demand for information security analysts is expected to be very high because cyberattacks have grown in frequency and sophistication.

INTEGRATING INTERNAL JOB STRUCTURES WITH EXTERNAL MARKET PAY RATES

7.3. Describe how compensation professionals integrate internal job structures with external market pay rates.

In Chapter 6, we discussed that compensation professionals use job evaluation methods to establish internally consistent job structures. In other words, companies value jobs that possess higher degrees of compensable factors (e.g., ten years of relevant work experience) than jobs with fewer degrees of compensable factors (e.g., one year of relevant work experience). These valuation differences ultimately should correspond to pay differences based on compensation survey data.

Earlier, we indicated that paying well below or well above the typical market rate for jobs can create a competitive disadvantage for companies. Thus, it is important that companies set pay rates by using market pay rates as reference points. To this end, we use **regression analysis**, which is a

TABLE 7-8 The Consumer Price Index: Basic Facts and Interpretation Issues

Basic Facts

The CPI indexes monthly price changes of goods and services that people buy for day-to-day living. The index is based on a representative sample of goods and services. The BLS gathers price information from thousands of retail and service establishments. Thousands of landlords provide information about rental costs, and thousands of home owners give cost information pertaining to home ownership.

The CPI represents the average of the price changes for the representative sample of goods and services *within* each of the following areas:

- Urban United States
- Four geographic regions (sometimes called census regions): Northeast, Midwest, South, and West
- Three population-size classes: large metropolitan areas, small metropolitan areas, and nonmetropolitan urban places
- Selected region-size classes—regions cross-classified by population size (for example, large metropolitan areas in the Northeast)
- Selected metropolitan areas (e.g., St. Louis, MO-IL)

The BLS publishes CPI for two population groups: a CPI for All Urban Consumers (CPI-U) and the CPI for Urban Wage Earners and Clerical Workers (CPI-W). The CPI-U represents the spending habits of 88 percent of the population of the United States. The CPI-U covers wage earners; clerical, professional, managerial, and technical workers; short-term and self-employed workers; unemployed persons; retirees; and others not in the labor force. The CPI-W represents the spending habits of 28 percent of the population, and it applies to consumers who earn more than one-half of their income from clerical or wage occupations. The distinction between the CPI-U and CPI-W is important because the CPI-U is most representative of all consumers, whereas unions and management use the CPI-W during negotiations to establish effective cost-of-living adjustments; most unionized jobs are clerical or wage jobs rather than salaried professional, managerial, or executive jobs.

CPI data are both available as not seasonally adjusted and seasonally adjusted. Seasonal adjustment removes the effects of recurring seasonal influences from many economic series, including consumer prices. For example, changing climatic conditions, production cycles, model changeovers, and holidays can cause seasonal variation in prices. Automobile makers often discount car prices for current model year vehicles in preparation for incoming new model year vehicles.

The BLS also computes a chained CPI-U (C CPI-U). It is based on the idea that when prices go up for some goods, consumers will substitute the higher priced goods with lower priced goods. For example, increases in the price of beef may lead many consumers to choose a less expensive alternative such as chicken. Compared to the CPI-U, the C CPI-U shows a slower cost increase rate than the CPI-U because of the substitution effect.

Interpreting the CPI: Percentage Changes versus Point Changes

The span from 1982 to 1984 is the base period for the CPI-U and CPI-W, which is 100. For example, how much did consumer prices increase in Atlanta between the base period and December 2014?

The CPI database indicates that the 2014 CPI-U for Atlanta was 218.05. We know that the base period CPI is 100. Consumer prices in Atlanta increased 118.05 percent between December 2014 and the base period. We determine price change with the formula:

$$\frac{(\text{Current CPI} - \text{Previous CPI})}{\text{Previous CPI}} \times 100\%$$

For this example:

$$\frac{(218.05 - 100)}{100} \times 100\% = 118.05\%$$

Compensation professionals are most concerned with annual CPI changes because they are updating recently collected survey data. The same formula yields price changes between periods other than the base period. How much did prices increase in Atlanta between December 2013 and December 2014? The CPI database indicates that the December 2013 CPI-U for Atlanta was 216.01, and we know that the December 2014 average is 218.05

$$\frac{(218.05 - 216.01)}{216.01} \times 100\% = 0.94\%$$

Consumer prices in Atlanta increased approximately **0.94** percent between December 2013 and December 2014.

Source: Based on U.S. Bureau of Labor Statistics. Consumer Price Index (Chapter 17, revised February 14, 2018). *BLS Handbook of Methods.* Available: https://www.bls.gov/opub/hom/pdf/homch17.pdf, accessed February 14, 2018.

statistical analysis technique. Regression analyses enable compensation professionals to establish pay rates for a set of jobs that are consistent with typical pay rates for jobs in the external market.

We'll apply regression analysis to determine pay rates for the accountant I, accountant II, and accountant III jobs listed in Table 7-3. Before presenting the regression analysis technique, we need two sets of information: the job evaluation point totals for each accountant job based on job evaluation and the updated salary survey data. In this sample, the accountant jobs have the following job evaluation points: accountant I (100 points), accountant II (500 points), and accountant III (1,000) points.

Regression analysis enables decision makers to predict the values of one variable from another. A compensation professional's goal is to predict salary levels for each job based on job evaluation points. Why not simply "eyeball" the list of salaries in the survey to identify the market rates? There are two reasons. First, companies pay different rates to employees who are performing the same (or very similar) jobs. Our salary survey indicates that accountant III pay rates vary between $43,500 and $55,000. "Eyeballing" the typical rate from the raw data are difficult when surveys contain large numbers of salaries.

Second, we wish to determine pay rates for a set of jobs in a company (e.g., accountant I, accountant II, and accountant III) based on their relative worth to typical market pay rates for the corresponding jobs contained in the salary survey. Our focus is on pricing a job structure in the market pay context, not pricing one job in isolation.

How does regression analysis work? Regression analysis finds the best-fitting line between two variables. Compensation professionals use job evaluation points assigned to benchmark jobs (based on the matching process discussed earlier) and the salary survey data for the benchmark jobs. They refer to the best-fitting line as the **market pay line**. The market pay line is representative of typical market pay rates, expressed as a mean or median, relative to a company's job structure. Pay levels that correspond with the market pay line are market-competitive pay rates. Figure 7-2 displays the regression results.

The following equation models the prediction.

$$\hat{Y} = a + bX$$

$\hat{Y}$ = predicted salary

X = job evaluation points

a = the Y intercept (This is the Y value at which $X = 0$)

b = the slope

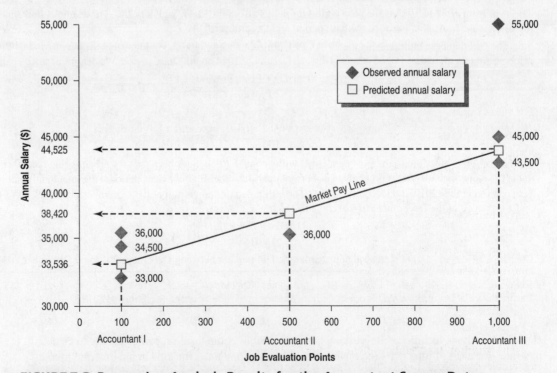

FIGURE 7-2 Regression Analysis Results for the Accountant Survey Data

The slope represents the change in Y for every one unit change in job evaluation points. In other words, the slope represents the dollar value of each job evaluation point. For example, let's assume that the slope is 26. A job consisting of 301 job evaluation points is worth $26 more than a job consisting of 300 job evaluation points.

For our data, the equation is:

$$\hat{Y} = \$32,315.66 + \$12.21X$$

Thus, this market policy line indicates the following market pay rates:

- Accountant I: $33,536.66

  $\hat{Y} = \$32,315.66 + (\$12.21 \times 100 \text{ job evaluation points})$

- Accountant II: $38,420.66

  $\hat{Y} = \$32,315.66 + (\$12.21 \times 500 \text{ job evaluation points})$

- Accountant III: $44,525.66

  $\hat{Y} = \$32,315.66 + (\$12.21 \times 1,000 \text{ job evaluation points})$

The regression analysis provides an additional important statistic known as R^2. This statistic tells us how well the variation in the company's valuation of jobs based on job evaluation points explains the variation in market pay rates from the compensation survey. The R^2 statistic can range in numerical value between 0 and 1. When R^2 equals 0, none (0 percent; i.e., 0.0×100 percent) of the variation in market pay rates can be explained by the company's job structure. When R^2 equals one, this means that all (100 percent) of the variation in market pay rates can be explained by the company's job structure. Just one more example—when R^2 equals 0.52, 52 percent (i.e., 0.52×100 percent) of the variation in market pay rates can be explained by the company's job structure. As you can see, we interpret R^2 in this context as the percentage variation in y values (market pay rates) that can be explained by x values (job evaluation points).

By now, you may be asking how to describe the difference between an R^2 equal to 1.0 and, for example, an R^2 equal to 0.71 in this situation. The difference (0.29) refers to the percentage of variation in market pay rates that cannot be explained by the company's job structure. In this illustration, 29 percent of the variation is unexplained. Discrepancies often exist between the job duties of the jobs specified in the compensation survey (i.e., the benchmark jobs) and the company's job definitions.

Your HR colleagues are likely to ask you to interpret your conclusion even further because they will want to know whether the obtained R^2 value represents a small, medium, or large amount. As a rule of thumb, R^2 values between 0.0 and 0.30 represent a small amount; between 0.31 and 0.70 represent a medium amount; and between 0.71 and 1.0 represent a large amount.

COMPENSATION POLICIES AND STRATEGIC MANDATES

Compensation policies refer to choices that compensation professionals make to promote competitive advantage. Broadly, choices are made about pay level policies and pay mix policies.

7.4. Explain the basic concepts of compensation policies and strategic mandates: pay level and pay mix.

Pay Level Policies

Companies can choose from three pay level policies:

- Market lead
- Market lag
- Market match

The **market lead policy** distinguishes a company from the competition by compensating employees more highly than most competitors. Leading the market denotes pay levels that place in the area above the market pay line (Figure 7-2). The **market lag policy** also distinguishes a company from the competition, but by compensating employees less than most competitors. Lagging the market indicates that pay levels fall below the market pay line (Figure 7-2). The **market match policy** most closely follows the typical market pay rates because companies pay according to the market pay line. Thus, pay rates fall along the market pay line (Figure 7-2). Most often, market lead policies are set to the third quartile (75th percentile) ranking in the salary survey. Similarly, market match policies are set to the second quartile (50th percentile or median) ranking, and market lag policies are set to the first quartile (25th percentile) ranking.

The market lead policy is clearly most appropriate for companies that pursue differentiation strategies. A company may choose a market lead pay policy for its accountants because the company needs the very best accountants to promote its competitive strategy of being the top manufacturer of lightest-weight surgical instruments at the lowest possible cost by 2025.

The market lag policy appears to fit well with lowest-cost strategies because companies realize cost savings by paying lower than the market pay line. Paying well below the market will yield short-term cost savings; however, these short-term savings will probably be offset by long-term costs. Companies that use the market lag policy may experience difficulties in recruiting and retaining highly qualified employees. Too much turnover will undercut a company's ability to operate efficiently and to market goods and services on a timely basis. Thus, companies that adopt market lag policies need to balance cost savings with productivity and quality concerns.

The market match policy represents a safe approach for companies because they generally are spending no more on compensation (per employee) than competitors. This pay policy does not fit with the lowest-cost strategy for obvious reasons. It does fit better with differentiation strategies. This statement appears to contradict previous ones about differentiation strategies (i.e., pay "high" salaries to attract and retain the best talent). Some companies that pursue differentiation strategies follow a market match policy to fund expensive operating or capital needs that support differentiation (e.g., research equipment and research laboratories).

Pay Mix Policies

Pay mix policies refer to the combination of core compensation and employee benefits components that make up an employee's total compensation package. In Chapter 1, we identified and briefly described the various elements of core compensation and employee benefits; then we discussed core compensation elements fully in Chapters 3, 4, and 5. We will review the main elements of employee benefits in Chapters 9 and 10.

Pay policy mix may be expressed in dollars (or other currency as relevant) or as a percentage of total dollars allocated for an employee's total compensation. The following is an example of a pay policy mix:

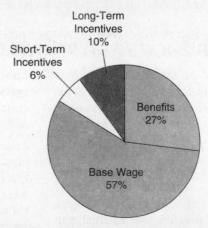

This example indicates that base pay accounts for 57 percent of the money allocated to an employee's total compensation. Let's assume that the company spends $200,000 annually to fund an employee's total compensation package. Of the total, an employee receives base pay in the amount of $114,000 (that is, $200,000 × 57 percent).

What is an appropriate pay mix? For policy purposes, it makes sense to consider guidelines for jobs within a structure (for example, managerial, administrative, or sales) because of the common job content and worker requirements of jobs within a structure. For example, in a technology company, a greater portion of bonus compensation might be allocated to engineers than to administrative staff. Engineers possess crucial skills relating to the company's ability to find innovative applications of technology, and bonus incentives throughout the year may promote innovation initiatives. On the other hand, the administrative staff, though important to the company, may not play as important a role in determining the company's profitability or objectives. Therefore, less of their total compensation would likely be devoted to bonus funds. Also, with some job structures, such as sales, employees may receive most of their compensation in the form of bonuses. To motivate a sales force to continually exceed quarterly targets, quarterly bonuses equal to or exceeding their annual base salaries might be used.

Companies emphasize some elements relative to others in formulating pay mix. For instance, the majority include merit pay and short-term incentives focused on individual performance.[11] Fewer than half include long-term incentives such as stock options or long-term performance awards

The types of employee benefits have become an increasingly important element of pay mix as we will discuss in Chapter 9. Companies may choose to offer a combination of benefits that are likely to attract and retain employees.[12] One consideration is the composition of the relevant labor force and an understanding of the benefits members are likely to value. For instance, student loan repayment assistance benefits may boost recruitment and retention of recent college graduates. Or, generous paid parental or family leave policies will be helpful to employees who are starting families or are caring for elderly relatives. Another consideration for determining the level of benefits is what competitors are offering and, certainly, this is where compensation surveys become most valuable to companies. For example, companies may be interested in offering a more substantial matching contribution to retirement plans than offered by the competition.

PREPARING FOR EXAMS/QUIZZES

Chapter Summary by Learning Objectives

Learning Objective 7-1. *Explain the concept of market-competitive compensation systems and summarize the four activities compensation professionals engage in to create these systems.* Market-competitive pay systems represent companies' compensation policies that fit the imperatives of competitive advantage. Compensation professionals create market-competitive pay systems based on four activities: Conducting strategic analyses, conducting compensation surveys, integrating the internal job structure with external market pay rates, and determining compensation policies.

Learning Objective 7-2. *Discuss compensation survey practices.* Compensation surveys involve the collection and subsequent analysis of competitors' compensation data.

Learning Objective 7-3. *Describe how compensation professionals integrate internal job structures with external market pay rates.* Integrating internal job structures with external market pay rates is based on statistical analysis; most often, regression analysis. Regression analyses enable compensation professionals to establish pay rates for a set of jobs that are consistent with typical pay rates for jobs in the external market.

Learning Objective 7-4. *Explain the basic concepts of compensation policies and strategic mandates: pay level and pay mix.* Compensation professionals develop two types of compensation policies. *Pay level* is the relationship between the company's pay rates and the market pay rates for corresponding jobs. A company can choose to match, lead, or lag the market. *Pay mix* refers to the combination of core compensation and employee benefits components that make up an employee's total compensation package.

Key Terms

market-competitive pay systems   156
strategic analysis   157
compensation surveys   157
compensation plans   157
relevant labor markets   161
job leveling   163
point factor leveling   163
central tendency   166

mean   166
median   166
variation   167
standard deviation   168
quartiles   168
percentiles   168
real compensation   170
nominal compensation   170

consumer price index (CPI)   170
regression analysis   170
market pay line   172
market lead policy   173
market lag policy   173
market match policy   174

Discussion Questions

7-1. You are a compensation analyst for a pharmaceuticals company, which is in Los Angeles, California. What is the scope of the relevant labor markets for chemists and for data entry clerks? Describe the rationale for your definitions.

7-2. Can companies easily develop compensation that is both internally consistent and market competitive? What are some of the challenges to this goal? Explain.

7-3. Which do you believe is most important for a company's competitive advantage: internal consistency or market competitiveness? Explain.

7-4. Refer to the regression equation presented in this chapter. When $b = 0$, the market pay line is parallel to the x-axis (i.e., job evaluation point scale). What does this result indicate?

7-5. Refer to Table 7-3. Cross out salaries for Company F and Company G. What is the mean and median for the set of Companies A through E?

PREPARING FOR MY CAREER

Compensation in Action

What employees are paid internally can have a significant impact on what happens externally. As with any business function, an overemphasis on the activities within the firm can blind decision makers to the activities outside the firm, which could undermine competitive advantage. Paying too little for top talent will ensure that those highly sought-after individuals go elsewhere for employment; paying too much could come at the cost of investing additional capital into resources that are critical to the execution and delivery of company strategy. By measuring the right variables and seeking data that will lead to informed and up-to-date decisions, you, as line managers, HR professionals, and compensation specialists, will work together in providing a system that is in line with the needs of the organization and the objectives of the individual.

Action checklist for line managers and HR—staying current and attracting the right employees

HR takes the lead

- Work with compensation specialists to access compensation *and* benefits data from other firms to find out what they are offering employees; how this data will be collected—customized survey, professional organization, or compensation consultant—will depend on budget, relationships with competitors, and expertise of staff.
- Together with line managers, compare internal roles with external roles to create job matches that, although subjective, will allow a side-by-side comparison to see how compensation matches up.
- Compensation specialists analyze data using appropriate statistics to identify consistencies with competitors and areas of high discrepancy.

Line managers take the lead

- Identify the types of resources necessary to carry out company strategy; if talent is the top priority, HR will seek to establish a compensation system that will lead competitors; if other resources are deemed a higher priority (e.g., infrastructure and research), the sought-after compensation system will be lower than the industry standard (this will be the context within which the data are assessed).
- Lead the identification of the internal employee market (e.g., marketing professionals, accountants, and finance managers in China) that needs to be assessed.
- Partnering with HR, recommendations are made to members of senior management based on the data that are revealed and the assessment of these data in relation to the strategy of the firm.

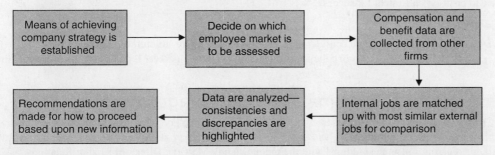

In summary, a "one size fits all" approach to pay policy selection is inappropriate. Most companies use more than one pay policy simultaneously. For example, companies generally use market match or market lead policies for professional and managerial talent because these employees contribute most directly to a company's competitive advantages. Companies typically apply market match or market lag policies to clerical, administrative, and unskilled employees (e.g., janitorial). Companies' demands for these employees relative to supply in the relevant labor markets are low, and these employees' contributions to attainment of competitive advantage are less direct. Companies are likely to apply different pay policy mixes to jobs in different structures given differences in the level of strategic importance placed on jobs as well as to promote desired behaviors as previously discussed.

Cases

Case 1: Nutriment's New Hires

With the demand for more nutritional food options growing, Nutriment Biotech is positioned to become a leader in agricultural biotechnology. Nutriment is a start-up biotech company that is working to develop genetically engineered food crops that offer enhanced nutrition along with easier production for farmers. Emily Hart and Harold James established Nutriment as a research organization through national grant funding five years ago. Nutriment is one of only a few agricultural biotechnology companies focused on enhancing nutrition in food crops. The company currently has an edge over competitors as its research has led to some scientific discoveries that now position them to grow their company significantly. As a result, Nutriment is ready to start hiring staff to get operations started.

Emily and Harold have hired Jack Stewart, an HR management consultant, to help them determine how to hire the most talented staff to grow their business. Jack works mostly with start-up technology-based companies and plans to help Nutriment implement a recruiting and hiring plan and establish its preliminary HR management practices such as its pay structure.

Nutriment has secured additional funding to allow it to ramp up full operations quickly. An analysis of its projected workload suggests it will need to hire approximately 15 new employees to get started. It will need to hire not only ten new scientists but also administrative staff members including a receptionist, an office manager, a lab manager, a marketing professional, and an accountant.

As an experienced recruiter, Jack is confident that he will be able to quickly identify strong candidates for the administrative staff positions. The current labor market works in Nutriment's favor, and, therefore, Jack will be able to easily generate a pool of qualified applicants. The scientists, on the other hand, will be challenging to find as they need specific expertise related to agricultural biotechnology and genetic engineering. The number of scientists with this combination of skills is limited, and the scientists are in demand by competitors. However, Nutriment is in a geographic area rich with research universities and other biotech firms, so Jack is confident that it can attract a good pool of talent if it is able to offer an opportunity that is attractive to the scientists.

To start the recruiting process, Jack must first establish a pay structure. Before he starts researching market rates, Jack plans to meet with Emily and Harold to establish pay level policies and discuss other strategic aspects of determining the compensation structure for the new employees. Nutriment must offer a pay package that will allow it to attract and retain both the administrative staff members and the scientists. Establishing the right pay practices will help ensure that the recruitment process allows it to put talent in place to position Nutriment for success.

Questions:

7-6. What are some strategic considerations in establishing a pay structure at Nutriment?

7-7. Should Jack suggest a pay policy to lead, lag, or match the market? Explain your recommendation.

Case 2: Ethics Dilemma: A Slanted Wage Proposal

In Chapter 2, we learned that management is obligated to engage in good faith bargaining with unions over terms of employment. Setting wage and salary levels is a mandatory subject of bargaining. Johnson Auto Parts is preparing for its negotiations with the union. Mandy Mattson, Director of Labor Relations, asked Roberta Robinson, lead compensation analyst, for a market wage analysis to bring to the bargaining table. Roberta prepared the following material to discuss with Mandy. The report shows the current wage rates and proposed rates based on the market mean and median.

	Current	Proposed	
	Wage ($)	Mean Wage ($)	Median Wage ($)
Entry-level Assembler	15	16	20
Associate Assembler	20	21	25
Assembler	25	29	34
Senior Assembler	30	33	41

Roberta explained the methodology for surveying the market rates and calculating the market mean and median for each job. Mandy asked why Roberta proposed two rates rather than one. Roberta indicated that she wanted to provide a fuller picture of the market rates and discussed that the mean is less than the median when there are only a few outliers. In this case, the outliers are substantially lower wage rates than the majority reported in the survey. She went on to tell Mandy that she recommends sharing all the information with the union negotiators and to demonstrate good faith by explaining the reasoning for these differences. Mandy abruptly dismissed Roberta's recommendation, saying that full information will likely lead to higher wage costs. Presenting the mean rates exclusively will keep labor costs down and that will make the shareholders happy. Roberta urged Mandy to reconsider this approach after a further inspection of the data revealed that some companies were unlawfully paying employees less than the lawful state minimum wage rate. The inappropriately low wage rates resulted in lower means than would otherwise be the case.

Questions:

7-8. As a compensation professional, what would you do?

7-9. What factor(s) in this ethical dilemma might influence a person to make a less-than-ethical decision?

Crunch the Numbers!
Updating Salary Survey Data

As a newly hired compensation analyst, you've been asked by the Director of Compensation to assist with the preparation of next year's compensation plan for accounting jobs. The period for the compensation plan is January 1–December 31, 2018. Your assignment is to update salary survey data using the CPI-U to estimate new salary information. Also, assume that it is July 1, 2017, and you have been asked to submit your analysis within the next two days. The salary survey data were current through the end of 2016, and the *initial average salary* reported for accountant jobs in the survey was $50,000. The salary data will be 12 and 24 months old at the pay plan's implementation (on January 1, 2018) and end (December 31, 2018), respectively. You have been provided with national CPI-U data, which were obtained from the U.S. Bureau of Labor Statistics website.

Year	Jan	Feb	Mar	Apr	May	Jun	Jul	Aug	Sep	Oct	Nov	Dec
2012	227.84	228.32	228.80	229.18	228.71	228.52	228.59	229.91	231.01	231.63	231.24	231.22
2013	231.67	232.93	232.28	231.79	231.89	232.44	232.90	233.45	233.54	233.66	234.10	234.71
2014	235.34	235.52	235.95	236.46	236.86	237.18	237.48	237.43	237.45	237.44	237.04	236.27
2015	234.83	235.27	235.95	236.16	236.95	237.61	237.99	237.98	237.46	237.76	238.07	237.82
2016	237.99	237.53	238.02	238.84	239.43	240.07	240.05	240.56	241.01	241.66	242.08	242.78
2017	244.02	244.10	243.71	244.08	243.91	244.03						

Questions:

7-10. By what percent did the cost of goods and services change between December 2016 and June 2017?

7-11. (a) By what percent might you expect the average cost of goods and services to change over the second 6-month period of 2017? *Hint:* First, calculate the percentage cost change for the period July through December for each of the previous years: 2012 through 2016. Second, take the average of these five figures. This calculation gives us the *average percent cost change*. Estimates based on multiple years gives us a more stable picture of percent cost changes.

(b) What is the estimated average salary for December 31, 2017? *Hint:* [(initial average salary × average percent cost change) + initial average salary].

7-12. (a) By what percent might you expect the average cost of goods and services to change between January 1, 2018 and December 31, 2018? *Hint:* First, calculate the percent cost change for the period January through December for each of the previous years: 2012 through 2016. Second, take the average of these five figures to calculate the average percent cost change.

(b) What is the estimated average salary for December 31, 2018? *Hint:* [(December 2017 average salary × average percentage cost change) + December 2017 average salary].

Working Together: Team Exercise

In small groups of three or four, come up with specific answers to the following questions. Talk through your perspectives and come up with a team response. Be prepared to share your ideas with the class.

In this chapter, we identified seven survey program areas published by the U.S. Bureau of Labor Statistics (http://www.bls.gov) and brief summaries of the surveys were included. There is much more to know about these surveys beyond the summaries. A good place to find more information is in the FAQ section for National Compensation survey respondents (https://www.bls.gov/respondents /ncs/faqs.htm#related). As a group, explore the FAQ section, thinking about the questions asked and answered.

Questions:

7-13. What are two questions that you found most interesting and what recommendations do you have for clarifying answers to those questions? Explain. (*Note: Answer these questions from the perspective of a possible first-time survey participant.*)

7-14. FAQs usually don't cover every possible question. As a prospective survey participant, what is an additional question or two you'd like to see included in the FAQ section? Explain.

Endnotes

1. WorldatWork. *Compensation Programs and Practices Survey*, (Scottsdale, AZ: WorldatWork, 2016).

2. Robert. J. Greene, "Compensation Surveys: The Rosetta Stones of Market Pricing, *WorldatWork Journal*, First Quarter (2014): pp. 23–31.

3. U.S. Bureau of Labor Statistics, *Employer Costs for Employee Compensation—September 2017*, (USDL-17-1646). (2017), accessed February 14, 2018, http://www.bls.gov.

4. U.S. Bureau of Labor Statistics, *Employer Costs for Employee Compensation Historical Listing— March 2004 – March 2017*, (2017), accessed February 21, 2018, www.bls.gov.

5. Theodore. E. Weinberger, "Incremental Market Intelligence: Does It Make Sense to Purchase That Additional Salary Survey?," *WorldatWork Journal* (First Quarter, 2013): 6–18.

6. Kerry Chou, "How Many Salary Survey Sources Is the Right Number?," *Workspan* (February, 2017), accessed February 21, 2018, http://www.worldatwork.org.

7. George T. Milkovich and Jerry M. Newman, *Compensation*, 5th ed. (Homewood, IL: Irwin, 1996).

8. U.S. Bureau of Labor Statistics, *National Compensation Survey: Guide for Evaluating Your Firm's Jobs and Pay*, (revised, May, 2013), accessed February 15, 2018, www.bls.gov.

9. Brock Meyer, "Good Operation Practices for Utilizing Salary Surveys" (October 17, 2016). *Compensation Focus*, accessed February 21, 2018, http://www.worldatwork.org.

10. U.S. Bureau of Labor Statistics, "Information Security Analysts," *Occupational Outlook Handbook*, accessed February 14, 2018, http://www.bls.gov/ooh/computer-and-information-technology/ information-security-analysts.htm.

11. WorldatWork, *Inventory of Total Rewards Programs & Practices* (Scottsdale, AZ: WorldatWork, 2017).

12. Joseph J. Martocchio, *Employee Benefits: A Primer for the Human Resource Professional*, 6th ed. (Burr Ridge, IL: Irwin/McGraw-Hill, 2018).

Building Pay Structures That Recognize Employee Contributions

Learning Objectives

When you finish studying this chapter, you should be able to:

8-1. Explain the concept of pay structures and the five steps necessary to construct pay structures.

8-2. Discuss the components of merit pay systems.

8-3. Summarize the features of sales compensation plan design.

8-4. Describe the essentials of person-focused pay program design.

8-5. Summarize pay structure variations.

Pay structures assign different pay rates for jobs of unequal worth and provide the framework for recognizing differences in individual employee contributions. No two employees possess identical credentials, nor do they perform the same jobs equally well. Companies recognize these differences by paying individuals according to their credentials, knowledge, or job performance. When completed, pay structures should define the boundaries for recognizing employee contributions. Employee contributions in this context correspond to the pay bases that we addressed in previous chapters (i.e., seniority, merit, incentive, and person-based pay). Pay structures also have strategic value. Well-designed structures should promote the retention of valued employees.

In this chapter, we will address how companies structure these pay bases, apart from seniority, which we addressed in Chapter 3. We will start out by considering the fundamental process of constructing pay structures. Then we will move on to specific pay structures, including merit pay, sales incentive pay, person-focused pay, broadbanding, and two-tier structures.

CONSTRUCTING A PAY STRUCTURE

Compensation specialists develop pay structures based on five steps:

- Deciding on the number of pay structures
- Determining a market pay line

8-1. Explain the concept of pay structures and the five steps necessary to construct pay structures.

- Defining pay grades
- Calculating pay ranges for each pay grade
- Evaluating the results

Step 1: Deciding on the Number of Pay Structures

Most companies establish more than one pay structure, depending on market rates and the company's job structure.[1] Common pay structures include exempt and nonexempt structures, pay structures based on job families, and pay structures based on geography. A large-scale survey estimates that approximately 29 percent of companies establish pay structures based on job exemption criteria, 48 percent based on job families, and 60 percent based on geographic scope. (Note: The sum is greater than 100 percent because some companies have multiple structures, which are based on more than one category.)[2]

EXEMPT AND NONEXEMPT PAY STRUCTURES   As you will recall, these categories reflect a distinction in the Fair Labor Standards Act (FLSA). Exempt jobs are not subject to the overtime pay provisions of the act. Core compensation terms for these jobs are usually expressed as an annual salary. Nonexempt jobs are subject to the overtime pay provision of the act. The core compensation for these jobs is therefore expressed as an hourly pay rate. Companies establish these pay structures for administrative ease. Some broadly consistent features distinguish exempt from nonexempt jobs: Exempt jobs, by the definition of the Fair Labor Standards Act, are generally supervisory, professional, managerial, or executive jobs that contain a wide variety of duties. Nonexempt jobs are generally nonsupervisory in nature, and the duties tend to be narrowly defined.

PAY STRUCTURES BASED ON JOB FAMILY   Executive, managerial, professional, technical, clerical, and craft jobs represent distinct job families. Pay structures are also defined based on job family, each of which shows a distinct salary pattern in the market. For example, the Davis–Bacon Act requires contractors and subcontractors to pay wages at least equal to those prevailing in the area where work is performed. This act applies only to employers with federal or federally financed contracts worth more than $2,000 for the construction, alteration, or repair of public works or buildings. Moreover, the Davis–Bacon Act also applies only to laborers and mechanics, excluding clerical, professional, and managerial employees. Thus, companies holding federal contracts meeting these criteria have limited latitude for setting pay for certain jobs; however, the latitude for setting pay rates for other jobs is greater.

PAY STRUCTURES BASED ON GEOGRAPHY   Companies with multiple, geographically dispersed locations such as sales offices, manufacturing plants, service centers, and corporate offices may establish pay structures based on going rates in different geographic regions because local conditions may influence pay levels. As we discussed in Chapter 2, the cost of living is an important consideration. Cost of living varies considerably between broad regions (e.g., the Northeast versus the Southeast) and more narrowly focused areas (e.g., Boston, Massachusetts, versus Fargo, North Dakota). Cost-of-living comparison calculators (for example, one furnished by CNN, http://money.cnn.com/calculator/pf/cost-of-living/) may be useful. Based on this calculator, a $50,000 salary in Fargo was equivalent to a $74,622 salary in Boston as of early 2018. Among companies that deploy geographic-based pay structures, most do so according to U.S. city or metropolitan area.

 FYI

The number of pay structures established by companies varies:

- Two: 60 percent
- Three: 24 percent
- Four: 3 percent
- Five or more: 12 percent[3]

Step 2: Determining a Market Pay Line

In Chapter 7, we discussed that companies rely on surveys to help establish pay policy levels and mixes. Our focus here will be on pay level policy considerations. We also discussed how to determine the market pay line in Chapter 7. Again, the market pay line is representative of typical market pay rates relative to a company's job structure. Pay levels that correspond with the market pay line are market-competitive pay rates. It is important to recall that surveys can provide a plethora of information pertaining to competitors' full range of compensation practices, including base pay levels, types and value of incentives, and employee benefits. Approximately 80 percent of companies establish their competitive pay-level position (matching, leading, or lagging the market) on base pay.[4]

Figure 8-1 illustrates a market pay line for a series of clerical jobs. Pay rates that fall along the market pay line represent competitive pay rates based on the company's selection of a relevant labor market, and these rates promote internal consistency because pay rates increase with the value of jobs based on a company's systematic job evaluation. The clerk I job has the least complex and demanding duties, and it has fewer worker requirements than do the remaining clerk jobs (clerk II, clerk III, and chief clerk).

Step 3: Defining Pay Grades

Pay grades group jobs for pay policy application. Human resource (HR) professionals typically group jobs into pay grades based on similar compensable factors and value. These criteria are not precise. In fact, no one formula determines what is sufficiently similar in terms of content and value to warrant grouping jobs into a pay grade.

Job groupings are ultimately influenced by such other factors as management's philosophy. Wider pay grades (i.e., grades that include a relatively larger number of jobs) minimize hierarchy and social distance between employees. Narrower pay grades tend to promote hierarchy and social distance. Figure 8-2 illustrates pay grade definitions, based on the jobs used in Figure 8-1.

Human resource professionals can develop pay grade widths as either "absolute" job evaluation point spreads or as percentage-based job evaluation point spreads. When absolute point spreads are used, grades are based on a set number of job evaluation points for each grade. For example, a compensation professional establishes pay grades equal to 200 points each. Grade 1 includes jobs that range from 1 to 200 job evaluation points, Grade 2 contains jobs that range from 201 to 400 points, and so on.

Companies may choose to vary the "absolute" point spread by increasing the point spread as they move up the pay structure, in recognition of the broader range of skills that higher pay grades represent. For example, certified public accounting jobs require a broader range of skills (e.g., knowledge of financial accounting principles and both state and federal tax codes) than do mailroom clerk jobs. Companies often assign trainee positions to the lower, narrower pay grades because trainees generally have limited job-relevant skills. For instance, Grade 1 may contain trainee positions with job evaluation scores that range from 1 to 150, Grade 2 may contain basic jobs beyond traineeships with scores of 151–400, and Grade 3 may include advanced jobs with scores of 401–1,000.

Step 4: Calculating Pay Ranges for Each Pay Grade

Pay ranges build upon pay grades. Pay grades represent the horizontal dimension of pay structures (i.e., job evaluation points). **Pay ranges** represent the vertical dimension (pay rates). Pay ranges include midpoint, minimum, and maximum pay rates. The minimum and maximum values denote the acceptable lower and upper bounds of pay for the jobs within pay grades. Figure 8-3 illustrates pay ranges.

Human resource professionals establish midpoints first, followed by minimum and maximum values. The **midpoint pay value** is the halfway mark between the range minimum and maximum rates. Midpoints generally match values along the market pay line, representing the competitive market rate determined by the analysis of compensation survey data. Thus, the midpoint may reflect the market average or median (Chapter 7).

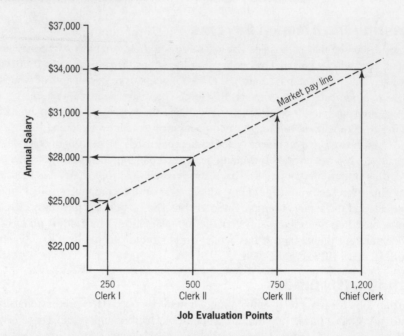

Clerk I

Employees receive training in basic office support procedures, the operation of office equipment, and the specific activities of the unit. Tasks assigned are simple and repetitive in nature and are performed in accordance with explicit instructions and clearly established guidelines. Sample duties include: files materials in established alphabetical order and prepares new file folders and affixes labels. Clerk Is must possess a high school diploma or equivalent.

Clerk II

Employees work under general supervision in support of an office. They perform routine office support tasks that require a knowledge of standard office procedures and the ability to operate a variety of office equipment. Sample duties include: prepares simple factual statements or reports involving computations such as totals or subtotals and composes memos requesting or transmitting factual information. Clerk IIs must possess a high school diploma or equivalent and 1 year work experience performing simple clerical tasks.

Clerk III

Employees work under general supervision in support of an office. They perform office support tasks requiring knowledge of general office and departmental procedures and methods and ability to operate a variety of office equipment. Sample duties include: reconciles discrepancies between unit records and those of other departments and assigns and reviews work performed by Clerks I and II. Clerk IIIs must possess a high school diploma or equivalent, 2 years work experience performing moderately complex clerical tasks, and completed coursework (five in all) in such related topics as word processing and basic accounting principles.

Chief Clerk

Employees work under direction in support of an office. They perform a wide variety of office support tasks that require the use of judgment and initiative. A knowledge of the organization, programs, practices, and procedures of the unit is central to the performance of the duties. Chief clerks must possess a high school diploma or equivalent, 4 years work experience performing moderately difficult clerical tasks, and an associate's degree in office management.

FIGURE 8-1 Pay Structure for Clerk Jobs

A company sets the midpoints for its pay ranges according to its competitive pay policy, as discussed in Chapter 7. If the company wants to lead the market with respect to pay offerings (market lead policy), it sets the midpoint of the ranges higher than the average for similar jobs at other companies. Companies wanting to pay according to the market norm (market match policy)

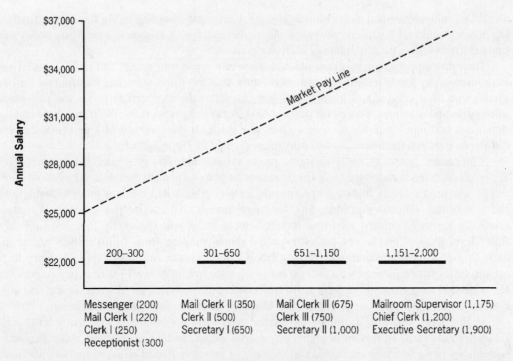

FIGURE 8-2 Pay Grade Definitions

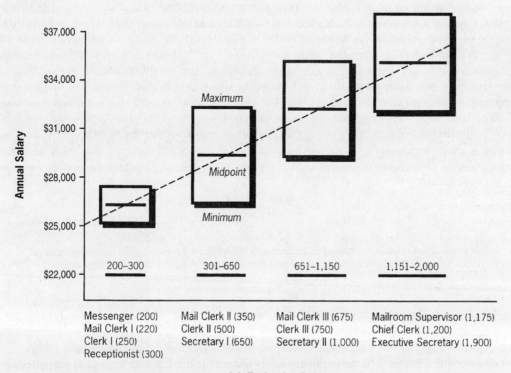

FIGURE 8-3 Pay Range Definitions

should set midpoints equal to the market average. Companies wanting to lag the market (market lag policy) would set the midpoints below the market average. A company's base-pay policy line graphically connects the midpoints of each pay grade.

How do compensation professionals calculate pay grade minimums and maximums? They may fashion pay grade minimums and maximums after the minimums and maximums for pay grades that their competitors have established. An alternate approach is to set the pay grade minimums and maximums based on range spread. A **range spread** is the difference between the maximum and minimum pay rates of a given pay grade. It is expressed as a percentage of the difference between the minimum and maximum divided by the minimum.

Companies generally apply different range spreads across pay grades. Most companies apply range spreads that vary typically between 20 percent and 80 percent.[5] They most commonly use progressively higher range spreads for pay grades that contain more valuable jobs in terms of the companies' criteria. Smaller range spreads characterize pay grades that contain relatively narrowly defined jobs that require simple skills with generally low responsibility. Entry-level clerical employees perform limited duties ranging from filing folders alphabetically to preparing file folders and affixing labels. These jobs presumably represent entry-level opportunities for employees who will probably advance to higher-level jobs as they acquire the skills needed to perform these jobs proficiently. Advanced clerical employees review and analyze forms and documents to determine the adequacy and acceptability of information.

Higher-level jobs afford employees greater promotion opportunities than entry-level jobs. Employees also tend to remain in higher pay grades longer, and the specialized skills associated with higher pay grade jobs are considered valuable. It therefore makes sense to apply larger range spreads to these pay grades. The following are typical range spreads for different kinds of positions:[6]

- 20–50 percent: hourly employees
- 45–75 percent: salaried (nonexecutives)
- 45–85 percent: executive

After deciding on range spread, compensation professionals calculate minimum and maximum rates. Figure 8-4 illustrates the calculation of minimum and maximum rates based on knowledge of the pay grade midpoint (as discussed earlier in Step 1) and the chosen range spread. Table 8-1 illustrates the impact of alternative range spread values on minimum and maximum values. This approach is typically applied when a company chooses to base the minimum and maximum rates on budgetary constraints; we will discuss budgeting issues later in this chapter. Pay range spread percentage amounts can be calculated with knowledge of a pay range's minimum and maximum values: (maximum rate – minimum rate)/minimum rate.

Adjacent pay ranges usually overlap with other pay ranges so that the highest rate paid in one range is above the lowest rate of the successive pay grade. Figure 8-5 illustrates how to calculate pay range overlap. Overlapping pay ranges allow companies to promote employees to the next level without

	Steps	
1. Identify the midpoint:	$20,000	Maximum = $23,333.33
2. Determine the range spread:	40%	
3. Calculate the minimum:		Range spread = 40%
$\dfrac{\text{midpoint}}{100\% + (\text{range spread}/2)}$	$= \dfrac{\$20,000}{100\% + (40\%/2)}$	
	$= \$16,666.67$	Midpoint = $20,000
4. Calculate the maximum: minimum + (range spread × minimum)	$= \$16,666.67 + (40\% \times \$16,666.67)$	
	$= \$23,333.33$	Minimum = $16,666.67

FIGURE 8-4 Calculation of Range Spread

TABLE 8-1 The Impact of Alternative Range Spreads on Pay Range Minimum and Maximum Values, with Midpoint of $25,000

	Range Spread ($)			
	20%	50%	80%	120%
Minimum: $\dfrac{\text{midpoint}}{100 + (\text{range spread}/2)}$	$22,727	$20,000	$17,857	$15,625
Maximum: minimum + (range spread × minimum)	$27,272	$30,000	$32,143	$34,375
Difference between maximum and minimum values	$4,545	$10,000	$14,286	$18,750

adding to their pay. Approximately 36 percent of companies that responded to a large-scale survey indicate that they promote employees to higher pay grades without pay increases.[7] For those that offer pay increases based on job promotions, the average increase was 7.6 percent for nonexempt employees, 8.8 percent for exempt employees, and 10.1 percent for officers/executives. Nonoverlapping pay ranges require pay increases for job promotions. Compensation professionals express overlap as a percentage. In this example, the degree of overlap between pay range A and pay range B is about 33 percent.

PAY COMPRESSION The minimum pay rate for a range usually is the lowest pay rate that the company will pay for jobs that fall within that pay grade. In theory, newly hired employees receive pay that is at or near the minimum. In practice, new employees often receive well above

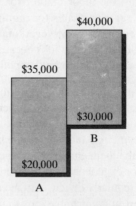

$$100\% \times \frac{(\text{max. rate for A } - \text{ min. rate for B})}{(\text{max. rate for A } - \text{ min. rate for A})}$$

$$100\% \times \frac{(\$35,000 - \$30,000)}{(\$35,000 - \$20,000)}$$

The overlap between range A and range B is 33.33%

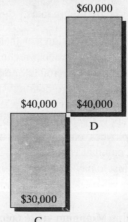

$$100\% \times \frac{(\text{max. rate for C } - \text{ min. rate for D})}{(\text{max. rate for C } - \text{ min. rate for C})}$$

$$100\% \times \frac{(\$40,000 - \$40,000)}{(\$40,000 - \$30,000)}$$

The overlap between range C and range D is 0%

FIGURE 8-5 Calculating Pay Range Overlap

minimum pay rates, sometimes only slightly below or even higher than the pay moderately tenured employees receive. **Pay compression** occurs whenever a company's pay spread between newly hired or less qualified employees, and more qualified job incumbents is small.[8]

Two situations result in pay compression. The first is a company's failure to raise pay range minimums and maximums. Companies that retain set range maximums over time limit increase amounts. For example, let's assume that the entry-level starting salaries for newly minted certified public accountants have increased 7 percent annually for the past 5 years. Tax-It, a small accounting firm, did not increase its pay range minimums and maximums for entry-level accountants during the same period because of lackluster profits. Nevertheless, Tax-It hired several new accountants at the midpoint pay rate. Failure to pay competitive pay rates would hinder Tax-It's ability to recruit talented accountants. As a result, many of the Tax-It accountants with 5 or fewer years' experience have lower salaries (or slightly higher salaries at best) than newly hired accountants without work experience. The second situation that results in pay compression is a scarcity of qualified candidates for jobs. When the supply of such candidates falls behind companies' demand, wages for newly hired employees rise, reflecting a bidding process among companies for qualified candidates.

Pay compression can threaten companies' competitive advantage. Dysfunctional employee turnover is a likely consequence of pay compression. Dysfunctional turnover represents high-performing employees' voluntary termination of their employment. High-performing employees will probably perceive their pay as inequitable because they are receiving lower pay relative to their positive contributions (i.e., experience and demonstrated performance) than newly hired employees who are receiving similar pay.

How can companies minimize pay compression? Maximum pay rates represent the most that a company is willing to pay an individual for jobs that fall in that range. Maximum pay rates should be set close to the maximum paid by other companies in the labor market for similar jobs. Setting competitive maximum rates enables a company to raise pay rates for high-quality employees who may consider employment opportunities with a competitor; however, maximum rates should not exceed maximum rates offered by competitors for comparable jobs because high maximums represent costs to the company over and above what are needed to be competitive.

GREEN CIRCLE PAY RATES Employees sometimes receive below-minimum pay rates for their pay ranges, especially when they assume jobs for which they do not meet every minimum requirement in the worker specification section of the job description. Below-minimum pay range rates are known as **green circle rates**. The pay rates of employees who are paid at green circle rates should be brought within the normal pay range as quickly as possible, which requires that both employer and employee take the necessary steps to eliminate whatever deficiencies in skill or experience that warranted paying below the pay range minimum. In addition, companies should regularly review current employees' pay relative to the starting pay rates for newly hired employees in comparable jobs to plan for necessary pay adjustments before current employees' pay falls below the minimum rates.[9]

RED CIRCLE PAY RATES On occasion, companies must pay certain employees greater than maximum rates for their pay ranges. Known as **red circle rates**, these higher pay rates help retain valued employees who have lucrative job offers from competitors. On the other hand, exemplary employees may receive red circle rates for exceptional job performance, particularly when a promotion to a higher pay grade is not granted. For these exemplary performers, companies may provide lump sum pay awards that are not added to regular base pay.[10] Red circle rates also apply to employees who receive job demotions to pay grades with lower maximum rates than the employees' current pay. Companies usually reduce demoted employees' pay over time until they receive pay that is consistent with their new jobs. In this case, red circle rates allow employees a chance to adjust to pay decreases.

Step 5: Evaluating the Results

After compensation professionals establish pay structures according to the previous steps, they must evaluate the results. They must specifically analyze significant differences between the company's internal values for jobs and the market's values for the same jobs. If discrepancies are evident, the company must reconsider the internal values they have placed on jobs. If their valuation of jobs exceeds the market's valuation of the same jobs, they must decide whether higher-than-market pay rates will undermine attainment of competitive advantage. If a company undervalues jobs relative to the market, managers must consider whether these discrepancies will limit the company's ability to recruit and retain highly qualified individuals.

Compensation professionals must also consider each employee's pay level relative to the midpoint of the pay grade. Again, the midpoint represents a company's competitive stance relative to the market. **Compa-ratios** index the relative competitiveness of internal pay rates based on pay range midpoints. Compa-ratios are calculated as follows:

$$\frac{\text{Employee's pay rate}}{\text{Pay range midpoint}}$$

Compa-ratios are interpreted as follows: A compa-ratio of 1 means that the employee's pay rate equals the pay range midpoint. A compa-ratio less than 1 means that the employee's pay rate falls below the competitive pay rate for the job. Companies with market lag policies strive for compa-ratios of less than 1. A compa-ratio that is greater than 1 means that an employee's pay rate exceeds the competitive pay rate for the job.

Human resource professionals also can use compa-ratios to index job groups that fall within a pay grade. Compa-ratios may be specifically calculated to index the competitive position of a job—by averaging the pay rates for each job incumbent. Moreover, compa-ratios may be calculated for all jobs that comprise a pay grade, departments, or such functional areas as accounting.

Compa-ratios provide invaluable information about the competitiveness of companies' pay rates. Compensation professionals can use compa-ratios as diagnostic tools to judge the competitiveness of their companies' pay rates. Compa-ratios that exceed 1 tell compensation professionals that pay is highly competitive with the market. Compa-ratios that fall below 1 tell them that pay is not competitive with the market and that they should consider another course of action to increase pay over a reasonable period.

☛ FYI

The frequency of pay structure adjustments varies across companies:

- Once a year: 60%
- Less than once every two years: 3%
- Once every two years: 12%
- Multiple times per year: 1%[11]
- Not consistently (as needed based on market conditions): 24%

We've reviewed the elements of pay structures and the steps compensation professionals follow to construct them. Next, we will consider three popular pay structures that should be familiar to compensation professionals:

- Merit pay structure
- Sales incentive compensation structure
- Person-focused structure

DESIGNING MERIT PAY SYSTEMS

As we noted in Chapter 3, companies that use merit pay systems must ensure that employees see definite links between pay and performance. We also reviewed the rationale for using merit pay systems, as well as the possible limitations of this kind of pay system. Establishing an effective merit pay program that recognizes employee contributions requires avoiding such pitfalls as

8-2. Discuss the components of merit pay systems.

ineffective performance appraisal methods and poor communication regarding the link between pay and performance. In addition to these considerations, managers interested in establishing a merit pay system must determine merit increase amounts, timing, and the type of merit pay increase (i.e., permanent or recurring increases versus one-time or nonrecurring additions to base pay). They must also settle on base-pay levels relative to the base pay of functionally similar jobs.[12]

Merit Increase Amounts

Merit pay increases should reflect prior job performance levels and motivate employees to perform their best. As managers establish merit increase amounts, they must consider both past performance levels and establish rates that will motivate employees even after the impact of inflation and payroll deductions. Updating compensation survey data should account for increases in consumer prices (Chapter 7). As we noted in Chapter 3, "just-meaningful pay increases" refers to the minimum amounts employees will see as making a meaningful change in their compensation.[13] Trivial pay increases for average or better employees will not reinforce their performance or motivate them.

No precise mathematical formula determines the minimum merit increase that will positively affect performance; managers must consider three research findings.[14] First, boosting the merit increase amount will not necessarily improve productivity because research has shown diminishing marginal returns on each additional dollar allocated to merit increases.[15] In other words, each additional merit increase amount was associated with a smaller increase in production.

Second, employees' perceptions of just-meaningful differences in merit increases depend on their cost of living, their attitudes toward the job, and their expectations of rewards from the job. For employees who value pay for meeting economic necessity, a just-meaningful difference in pay increase tends to depend on changes in the cost of living. On the other hand, for employees who value pay as a form of recognition, the size of the expected pay raise (versus cost of living) affects a just-meaningful difference.[16]

Third, for the pay increase to be considered meaningful, the employee must see the size of the increase as substantive in a relative sense as well as in an absolute sense.[17] **Equity theory** suggests that an employee must regard his or her own ratio of merit increase pay to performance as similar to the ratio for other comparably performing people in the company. In practical terms, managers should award the largest merit pay increases to employees with the best performance, and they should award the smallest increases to employees with the lowest acceptable performance. The difference between these merit increases should be approximately equal to the differences in performance.

It is also essential that compensation professionals design plans that reinforce employees' motivation to perform well, with just-meaningful pay increases and merit increase percentages that clearly distinguish among employees based on their performance; however, the best-laid plans don't always lead to the desired results. Well-designed merit pay structures (and others that we discuss shortly) will fail without adequate funding.

Compensation budgets are blueprints that describe the allocation of monetary resources to fund pay structures. Compensation professionals index budget increases that fund merit pay programs in percentage terms. For example, a 10 percent increase for next year's budget means that it will be 10 percent greater than the size of the current year's budget. This value is often an indicator of the average pay increase employees will receive. It is obvious that the greater the increase in the compensation budget, the more flexibility compensation professionals will have in developing innovative systems with substantial motivating potential.

The magnitude of the increases in compensation budgets in recent years has unfortunately been just about the same as cost-of-living increases. For example, the average annual earnings in the United States increased only 2.7 percent between May 2015 and May 2016.[18] Although this value varies by occupation, industry, and region of the country, it does reflect a trend in the United States of stagnant growth in compensation budgets. The picture becomes less positive because the increase in cost of living for the same period was 1.0 percent.[19] This means that, on average, annual merit pay raises were slightly above the rise in cost of living by 1.7 percent, likely taking the motivational value out of pay increases.

Timing

The clear majority of companies allocate merit increases, as well as cost-of-living and other increases, annually. At present, companies typically take one of two approaches in timing these pay raises. Companies may establish a **common review date** or **common review period** so that all employees' performances are evaluated on the same date or during the same period (e.g., the month of June, which immediately follows a company's peak activity period). Best suited for smaller companies, common review dates reduce the administrative burden of the plan by concentrating staff members' efforts to limited periods.

On the other hand, companies may review employee performance and award merit increases on the **employee's anniversary date** (i.e., the day on which the employee began to work for the company). Most employees will thus have different evaluation dates. Although these staggered review dates may not monopolize supervisors' time, this approach can be administratively burdensome because reviews must be conducted regularly throughout the year.

Recurring versus Nonrecurring Merit Pay Increases

Companies have traditionally awarded merit pay increases permanently, and permanent increases are sometimes associated with some undesirable side effects (e.g., placing excessive cost burdens on the employer). In terms of costs, U.S. companies are increasingly concerned with containing costs as just one initiative in their quest to establish and sustain competitive advantage in the marketplace. Companies may advocate **nonrecurring merit increases** (i.e., lump sum bonuses), which lend themselves well to cost containment and have recently begun to gain some favor among unions, including the International Brotherhood of Electrical Workers.[20] Lump sum bonuses strengthen the pay-for-performance link and minimize costs because these increases are not permanent, and subsequent percentage increases are not based on higher base-pay levels.

The Watch It! video discusses the performance appraisal process at Hautelook. The HR director discusses that informal performance appraisals may take place multiple times during a year; however, decisions about permanent pay increases, bonuses, and promotions take place annually during the formal performance appraisal process. This video also discusses the company's performance appraisal process and possible limitations, some of which we addressed in Chapter 3.

Present Level of Base Pay

Pay structures specify acceptable pay ranges for jobs within each pay grade. Thus, each job's base-pay level should fall within the minimum and maximum rates for its respective pay grade. In addition, compensation professionals should encourage managers to offer similar base pay to new employees performing similar jobs unless employees' qualifications (i.e., education and relevant work experience) justify pay differences. This practice is consistent with the mandates of several laws (Chapter 2) such as Title VII of the Civil Rights Act of 1964 and the Equal Pay Act of 1963. Of course, employees' merit pay increases should vary with their performance.

Rewarding Performance: The Merit Pay Grid

Table 8-2 illustrates a typical merit pay grid that managers use to assign merit increases to employees. Managers determine pay raise amounts by two factors jointly: employees' performance ratings and the position of employees' present base-pay rates within pay ranges. Pay raise amounts are expressed as percentages of base pay. For instance, let's say that two employees will each receive a 5 percent merit pay increase. One employee is paid on an hourly basis, earning $8.50 per hour, and the other is paid on an annual basis, earning $32,000. The employee whose pay is based on an hourly rate (usually nonexempt in accord with the Fair Labor Standards Act; one who must be paid overtime for time worked more than 40 hours per week) receives a pay raise of $0.44 per hour, increasing her hourly pay to $8.94. The employee whose pay is based on an annual rate (typically exempt from the Fair Labor Standards Act provisions) receives a pay increase of $1,600, boosting her annual pay to $33,600.

In Table 8-2, employees whose current annual salary falls in the second quartile of the pay range and whose performance rates an average score receive a 6 percent merit pay increase. Employees whose current annual salary falls in the first quartile of the pay range and whose job performance is excellent receive a 12 percent merit pay increase. The term *cell* (as in spreadsheet software programs such as *Microsoft Excel*) is used to reference the intersection of quartile ranking and performance rating. Table 8-2 contains 20 cells.

EMPLOYEES' PERFORMANCE RATINGS Merit pay systems use performance appraisals to determine employees' performance rating. Where merit pay systems are in place, an overall performance rating guides the pay raise decision. In Table 8-2, an employee receives any one of five performance ratings ranging from "Poor" to "Excellent." As you can see when we hold position in pay range constant, pay raise amounts increase with level of performance. This pattern fits well with the logic underlying pay-for-performance principles—it recognizes higher performance with greater rewards.

EMPLOYEES' POSITIONS WITHIN THE PAY RANGE Employees' positions within the pay range are indexed by quartile ranking, which, in Chapter 7, we described as a measure of dispersion. Again, quartiles allow compensation professionals to describe the distribution of data (in this case, hourly or annual base-pay amount) based on four groupings. In Table 8-2, the first quartile is the point below which 25 percent of the salary data lie (and above which 75 percent of the salary data are found), which is $25,000. In this example, 25 percent of the salary figures are less than or equal to $25,000 and 75 percent of these figures are greater than $25,000. The second quartile is the point below which 50 percent of the salary data lie (and above which 50 percent of the salary figures are found), which is $40,000 for this example. The third quartile is the point below which 75 percent of the salary figures lie (and above which 25 percent of the salary figures are found), which is $55,000 for this example. The fourth quartile is the point below which all the salary data lie, which is $70,000. The lower a person's pay falls within its designated pay grade (e.g., the first quartile versus the third quartile), the higher the percentage pay raise, all else being equal. Along those lines, the higher a person's pay within its grade, the lower the percentage pay raise, all else being equal.

Holding performance ratings constant, compensation professionals reduce merit pay increase percentages as quartile ranks increase to control employees' progression through their

TABLE 8-2 Merit Pay Increase Grid

		Performance Rating				
		Excellent (%)	Above Average (%)	Average (%)	Below Average (%)	Poor (%)
Q4 ⇒	$70,000					
	$65,000	5	3	1	0	0
	$60,000					
Q3 ⇒	$55,000					
	$50,000	7	5	3	0	0
	$45,000					
Q2 ⇒	$40,000					
	$35,000	9	7	6	2	0
	$30,000					
Q1 ⇒	$25,000					
	$20,000	12	10	8	4	0
	$15,000					

pay ranges. Pay grade minimums and maximums reflect corporate criteria about the value of various groups of unlike jobs and may be dictated by budgeting. We'll look at the issue of budgeting shortly. Let's take the case of two employees whose performance ratings are identical but whose base pay places them in different quartiles of the pay grade (one in the third quartile and the other in the first quartile). If these employees were to receive the same pay raise percentage, the base-pay rate for the employee in the third quartile likely would exceed the maximum pay rate for the range more quickly than would the base-pay rate for the employee in the first quartile.

Merit Pay Increase Budgets

Now that we've considered the design principles for merit pay grids, we'll take a closer look at budgetary considerations. Budgets limit the merit pay increase percentages in each cell. A **merit pay increase budget** is expressed as a percentage of the sum of employees' current base pay. For instance, let's assume that a company's top financial officers and compensation professionals agree to a 5 percent merit pay increase budget. Let's also assume that the sum of all employees' current base pay is $10 million based on an employee population of 350. A 5 percent merit pay increase budget for this example equals $500,000, that is, 5 percent of the sum of all employees' current base pay totaling $10,000,000 (5 percent × $10,000,000). In other words, the company will distribute $500,000 to increase the current base pay of its employees. As described earlier, merit pay increases awarded to individual employees will vary according to performance level and position in the pay range; however, the total of the individual pay increases must not exceed the allotted merit pay increase budget, again, $500,000 in this example. As an aside, the typical merit pay increase budget today ranges between 2 and 3 percent for the small proportion of companies that even have awarded pay increases in the past few years. This range is much lower than the average 4 percent increase in recent past years.

Compensation professionals begin plans for setting the merit increase pay grid within the estimated merit increase pay budget with the following six steps:

1. Compensation professionals ask managers and supervisors to indicate the percentage of employees who they expect will fall in each of the performance categories in the performance appraisal instrument. Managers will often use the actual distribution of employees based on recent past years as an estimate for budget planning. The sample merit pay grid illustrated in Table 8-2 lists five performance categories. For illustrative purposes, let's assume the following performance distribution for employees:

   • Excellent: 10 percent
   • Above average: 20 percent
   • Average: 40 percent
   • Below average: 25 percent
   • Poor: 5 percent

2. Compensation professionals rely on position in the pay range to determine the percentage of employees whose pay falls into each pay quartile. For example, let's assume the following distribution of employees in each pay quartile:

   • Q4: 20 percent
   • Q3: 25 percent
   • Q2: 40 percent
   • Q1: 15 percent

   In other words, 20 percent of employees earn pay that falls in the range from $55,000 to $70,000 (fourth quartile) in Table 8-2. Similarly, 25 percent of the employees earn pay that falls in the range from $40,000 to $55,000 (third quartile). The same rationale applies to the first and second quartiles.

3. Compensation professionals combine both sets of information to determine the percentage of employees who fall into each cell. The percentage of employees whose performance

rating is excellent and whose base pay falls in the fourth quartile equals 2 percent (10 percent × 20 percent). The sum of the cell percentages totals 100 percent.

	Excellent (%)	Above Average (%)	Average (%)	Below Average (%)	Poor (%)
Q4	10 × 20 = 2	20 × 20 = 4	40 × 20 = 8	25 × 20 = 5	5 × 20 = 1
Q3	10 × 25 = 2.5	20 × 25 = 5	40 × 25 = 10	25 × 25 = 6.25	5 × 25 = 1.25
Q2	10 × 40 = 4	20 × 40 = 8	40 × 40 = 16	25 × 40 = 10	5 × 40 = 2
Q1	10 × 15 = 1.5	20 × 15 = 3	40 × 15 = 6	25 × 15 = 3.75	5 × 15 = 0.75

4. Next, compensation professionals calculate the expected number of employees who fall into each cell. It is important to remember that this is the expected (versus actual) number of employees because managers provide only an estimate of employees' performance distribution. For this example, let's assume that the company employs 350 people. The number of employees whose performance rating is excellent and whose base pay falls in the fourth quartile equals 7 (350 people × 2 percent).

	Excellent (%)	Above Average (%)	Average (%)	Below Average (%)	Poor (%)
Q4	350 × 2 = 7	350 × 4 = 14	350 × 8 = 28	350 × 5 = 17.5	350 × 1 = 3.5
Q3	350 × 2.5 = 8.75	350 × 5 = 17.5	350 × 10 = 35	350 × 6.25 = 21.875	350 × 1.25 = 4.375
Q2	350 × 4 = 14	350 × 8 = 28	350 × 16 = 56	350 × 10 = 35	350 × 2 = 7
Q1	350 × 1.5 = 5.25	350 × 3 = 10.5	350 × 6 = 21	350 × 3.75 = 13.125	350 × 0.75 = 2.625

5. Compensation professionals now distribute the merit increase budget amount ($500,000) to each cell based on the following formula:

$$\text{Expected number of employees in cell} \times \text{Desired pay increase for cell } \%$$
$$\times \text{Current median pay level for the current quartile}$$

We calculated the expected number of employees in each cell in the previous step. The desired pay increase amount is an estimate that we made (see Table 8-2). Compensation professionals usually specify these percentage amounts initially on pay-for-performance and equity considerations as described earlier (i.e., holding performance constant, individuals in higher pay quartiles receive smaller percentage increases than employees in lower pay quartiles). We calculate the median values as described in Chapter 7. Let's assume for this example that the medians for each quartile are:

- Q4: $65,000
- Q3: $50,000
- Q2: $35,000
- Q1: $20,000

	Excellent	Above Average	Average	Below Average	Poor
Q4	7 × 5% × $65,000 = $22,750	14 × 3% × $65,000 = $27,300	28 × 1% × $65,000 = $18,200	17.5 × 0% × $65,000 = $0	0.5 × 0% × $65,000 = $0
Q3	8.75 × 7% × $50,000 = $30,625	17.5 × 5% × $50,000 = $43,750	35 × 3% × $50,000 = $52,500	21.875 × 0% × $50,000 = $0	4.375 × 0% × $50,000 = $0
Q2	14 × 9% × $35,000 = $44,100	28 × 7% × $35,000 = $68,600	56 × 6% × $35,000 = $117,600	35 × 2% × $35,000 = $24,500	7 × 0% × $35,000 = $0
Q1	5.25 × 12% × $20,000 = $12,600	10.5 × 10% × $20,000 = $21,000	21 × 7% × $20,000 = $29,400	13.125 × 4% × $20,000 = $10,500	2.625 × 0% × $20,000 = $0

The sum of expected merit pay increases equals $523,425.

6. Compensation professionals check whether the expected merit increase total fits within the actual budgeted amount. In this example, the sum of expected increases exceeds the budgeted amount by $23,425 ($523,425 – $500,000). When the expected increase amount exceeds the budgeted amount, compensation professionals adjust the percentages in the cells with the following considerations in mind: lowering costs, recognizing performance differences, and considering equity.

Pay structures based on merit differ from sales compensation in at least two key ways. First, whereas sales compensation programs center on incentives that specify rewards an employee will receive for meeting a preestablished—often objective—level of performance, merit pay programs generally base an employee's reward on someone else's (most often the employee's supervisor's) subjective evaluation of the employee's past performance. Second, in most instances, a sales employee's compensation is variable to the extent that it is composed of incentives. Under a merit pay system, an employee earns a base pay appropriate for the job (as discussed earlier in this chapter) that is augmented periodically with permanent pay raises or one-time bonuses.

DESIGNING SALES INCENTIVE COMPENSATION PLANS

Compensation programs for salespeople rely on incentives.[21] Sales compensation programs can help businesses meet their objectives by aligning the financial self-interest of sales professionals with the company's marketing objectives.[22] By extension, sales compensation programs can help companies achieve strategic objectives by linking sales professionals' compensation to fulfilling customer needs or other marketing objectives (e.g., increasing market share). Thus, sales compensation plans derive their objectives directly from strategic marketing objectives, which, in turn, are derived from company competitive strategy. Sales objectives include:[23]

8-3. Summarize the features of sales compensation plan design.

*   *Improve sales productivity*: More volume and profit from current investment in sales resources.
    *   New-customer sales volume
    *   New-product sales volume
    *   New balanced product-line sales
    *   Reduced "churn" among current customers

*   *Improve sales coverage of current customers*: Regardless of industry, customers want flexibility, customization, faster response, and personalized service. To meet these requirements, market-leading companies improve the coverage of their current customers. This often means investments in new ways to interact with customers.
    *   Overall account volume
    *   Greater share of the account's business
    *   Achievement of customer objectives
    *   More lines of business sold
    *   Account profitability

*   *Grow sales overall*: Track the percentage of sales realized from the following:
    *   New direct customers
    *   New distribution channels
    *   New products

Alternative Sales Compensation Plans

Companies usually use one of five kinds of sales incentive plans. The type of plan appropriate for any given company will depend on the company's competitive strategy. The order of presentation roughly represents the degree of risk (from lowest to highest) to employees.

*   Salary-only plans
*   Salary-plus-bonus plans

- Salary-plus-commission plans
- Commission-plus-draw plans
- Commission-only plans

SALARY-ONLY PLANS Under **salary-only plans**, sales professionals receive fixed base compensation, which does not vary with the level of units sold, increase in market share, or any other indicator of sales performance. From the employees' perspective, salary-only plans are relatively risk-free because they can expect a certain amount of income. From a company's perspective, salary-only plans are burdensome because the company must compensate its sales employees regardless of their achievement levels. Thus, salary-only plans do not fit well with the directive to link pay with performance through at-risk pay. Nevertheless, salary-only plans may be appropriate for such kinds of selling situations as:

- Sales of high-priced products and services or technical products with long lead times for sales
- Situations in which sales representatives are primarily responsible for generating demand, but other employees close the sales
- Situations in which it is impossible to follow sales results for each salesperson (i.e., where sales are accomplished through team efforts)
- Training and other periods when sales representatives are unlikely to make sales on their own

SALARY-PLUS-BONUS PLANS **Salary-plus-bonus plans** offer a set salary coupled with a bonus. Bonuses usually are single payments that reward employees for achievement of specific, exceptional goals. For a real estate agent, generating more than $2 million in residential sales for a 1-year period may mean earning a bonus totaling several thousand dollars.

SALARY-PLUS-COMMISSION PLANS **Commission** is a form of incentive compensation based on a percentage of the selling price of a product or service. **Salary-plus-commission plans** spread the risk of selling between the company and the sales professional. The salary component presumably enhances a company's ability to attract good employees and allows a company to direct its employees' efforts to deter employees from undertaking tasks that do not lead directly to commissions (e.g., participating in further training or servicing accounts). The commission component serves as the employees' share in the gains they generated for the company.

COMMISSION-PLUS-DRAW PLANS **Commission-plus-draw plans** award sales professionals with subsistence pay or draws—money to cover basic living expenses—yet provide them with a strong incentive to excel. This subsistence pay component is known as a **draw**. Unlike salaries, however, companies award draws as advances, which are charged against commissions that sales professionals are expected to earn.

Companies use two types of draws. **Recoverable draws** act as company loans to employees that are carried forward indefinitely until employees sell enough to repay their draws. **Nonrecoverable draws** act as salary because employees are not obligated to repay the loans if they do not sell enough. Nonrecoverable draws clearly represent risks to companies because these expenses are not repaid if employee sales performance is lackluster. Companies that adopt nonrecoverable draws may stipulate that employees cannot continue in the employment of the company if they fail to cover their draw for a specified number of months or sales periods during the year. This arrangement is quite common among car salespeople.

COMMISSION-ONLY PLANS Under **commission-only plans**, salespeople derive their entire income from commissions. Three types of commissions warrant mention. **Straight commission** is based on a fixed percentage of the sales price of the product or service. For instance, a 10 percent commission would generate a $10 incentive for a product or service sold that is priced at $100 and $55 for a product or service sold that is priced at $550.

Graduated commissions increase percentage pay rates for progressively higher sales volume. For example, a sales professional may earn a 5 percent commission per unit for sales volume up to 100 units, 8 percent for each unit from 101 to 500 units, and 12 percent for each unit more than 500 sold during each sales period.

Finally, **multiple-tiered commissions** are similar to graduated commissions, but with one exception. Employees earn a higher rate of commission for all sales made in each period if the sales level exceeds a predetermined level. For instance, employees might earn only 8 percent for each item if total sales volume falls short of 1,000 units. If total sales volume exceeds 1,000 units, however, then employees might earn a per-item commission equal to 12 percent for every item sold. Evidence encourages the use of multiple-tiered commissions because a pattern of higher performance was achieved prior to the use of these structures.[24] Commission-only plans are well suited for situations in which:

- The salesperson has substantial influence over the sales.
- Low-to-moderate training or expertise is required.
- The sales cycle—the time between identifying the prospect and closing the sale—is short.

In contrast to salespeople on salary-only plans, commission-only salespeople shoulder all the risk: Employees earn nothing until they sell. Despite this risk, potential rewards are substantial, particularly with graduated and multiple-tiered commission plans.

Although commissions may fit well with cost-cutting measures, these incentives are not always the best tactic for compensating sales professionals. In fact, commission structures probably suffer from many of the same limitations of individual incentive plans that we discussed in Chapter 4 (e.g., competitive behaviors among employees). Moreover, some sales experts argue that commissions undermine employees' intrinsic motivation to sell (i.e., their genuine interest for the challenge and enjoyment that selling brings). These experts argue that once salespeople have lost that intrinsic motivation, commissions act essentially as controls to maintain sales professionals' performance levels. Said another way, such professionals may simply go through the motions to earn money without regard to quality and customer satisfaction.[25] In addition, the younger generation appears to be more risk averse than older generations, which is making it difficult for companies to fill sales positions because members of the younger generation prefer higher certainty associated with earning base pay.[26]

For any sales compensation plan, it is critical that companies establish realistic total sales targets and individual performance standards. Beyond reasonable limits, it is possible that sales compensation plans will backfire. Consequences of such backfire include lower employee motivation, unprofessional behavior, and compromised profits.

 FYI

A survey revealed that companies inadvertently make inaccurate payments (variable pay based on sales). Respondents indicated the following accuracy rates:

- Less than 80 percent accurate: 3 percent of companies
- 80 to 90 percent accurate: 16 percent
- 91 to 95 percent accurate: 36 percent
- 96 to 100 percent accurate: 45 percent[27]

Sales Compensation Plans and Competitive Strategy

Sales plans with salary components are most appropriate for differentiation strategies. Under salary-based sales plans, employees can count on receiving income. By design, salary plans do not require employees to focus on attaining sales volume goals or other volume indicators (e.g., market share). Sales professionals who receive salaries can turn their attention to addressing clients' needs during the presale and servicing phases of the relationship. Salary-based sales compensation applies to the sale and servicing of such technical equipment as computer networks, including the hardware (e.g., the individual computers and network server) and the software (e.g., applications programs such as *Microsoft Excel* or the *Microsoft Windows* operating system).

Commission-oriented sales compensation plans are best suited for lowest-cost strategies because compensation expenditures vary with sales revenue. As a result, only the most productive employees earn the best salaries. Commissions essentially represent rewards for "making the sale." For example, real estate sales agents' earnings depend on two factors: number of houses sold and their selling price. New-car salespersons' earnings similarly depend on the number of cars sold and their selling price. In either situation, customers are likely to have questions and concerns following sales transactions. Many real estate sales companies employ real estate assistants at low salaries who mediate such buyers' queries of the sellers as, "What grade of rock salt is most appropriate for the water softener apparatus?" Real estate assistants are often training to be full-fledged real estate agents, and they view low pay as a necessary trade-off for learning the ropes.

Regardless of competitive strategy, rapidly growing companies, including ones that acquire new businesses, run the risk of undermining competitive advantage. Cisco Systems faced this problem in its sales function because sales approaches and strategies within the company were decentralized. Communication across the businesses was poor and concerns about undermining sales performance increased. Cisco Systems implemented a sales center of excellence (COE) to help remedy this problem.[28] COEs are established to serve as a capability center for a specific area or focus. It allows management to maximize leverage and create alignment and consistency in how systems, methodologies, and business processes are developed and communicated.

Determining Fixed Pay and the Compensation Mix

Managers must balance fixed and incentive pay elements to directly affect employee motivation. The mix depends mainly on three factors:

- Influence of the salesperson on the buying decision
- Competitive pay standards within the industry
- Amount of nonsales activities required

INFLUENCE OF THE SALESPERSON ON THE BUYING DECISION For the most part, the more influence sales professionals have on "buying" decisions, the more the compensation mix will emphasize incentive pay. Salespeople's influence varies greatly with the specific product or service marketed and the way these are sold. Many sales professionals assume an order-taker role, with little influence over purchase decisions. For example, salespeople in such large department stores as Best Buy have little influence over the merchandise for sale because these stores send their buyers to manufacturers to purchase lines of products that will be sold in their stores throughout the United States and beyond. Product display and promotional efforts are determined by store management.

On the other end of the spectrum, some employees serve as consultants to the client. For instance, when a company decides to invest in computerizing its entire worldwide operations, it may approach a computer manufacturer such as Dell to purchase the necessary equipment. Given the technical complexity of computerizing a company's worldwide operations, the client would depend on Dell to translate its networking needs into the appropriate configuration of hardware and software. These Dell sales professionals ultimately influence the purchaser's decision to buy.

COMPETITIVE PAY STANDARDS WITHIN THE INDUSTRY A company's compensation mix must be as enticing as that offered by competitors if the company wants to recruit high-quality sales professionals. Industry norms and the selling situation are among the key determinants of compensation mix. For instance, competitive standards may dictate that the company must give greater weight to either incentive or fixed pay, which we addressed earlier. Incentive (commission) pay weighs heavily in highly competitive retail industries, including furniture, home electronics, and auto sales. Salary represents a significant pay component in such high entry-barrier industries as pharmaceuticals. In the case of pharmaceuticals, barriers to entry include the U.S. Food and Drug Administration regulations on testing new products that significantly extend the time from product conception through testing to marketing for general use. Salary is an appropriate compensation choice because pharmaceutical companies face little risk of new competition.

AMOUNT OF NONSALES ACTIVITIES REQUIRED In general, the more nonsales duties salespeople have, the more their compensation package should tend toward fixed pay. Some companies and products, for instance, require extensive technical training or customer servicing activities. An excellent example is again the pharmaceuticals industry. Sales professionals employed by such companies as Bristol-Myers Squibb, Eli Lilly and Company, and Merck & Company must maintain a comprehensive understanding of their products' chemical compositions, clinical uses, and contraindications.

DESIGNING PERSON-FOCUSED PROGRAMS

As indicated in Chapters 3 and 4, merit pay and incentive pay represent job-based approaches to compensating employees. In Chapter 5, we discussed the importance of person-focused pay that many companies recognize. For this discussion, we use the terms *knowledge* and *skills* interchangeably, as the design features for both structures are virtually the same. In their purest form, person-focused programs reward employees for the acquisition of job-related knowledge (or skills, in the case of skill-based pay plans). In practice, companies are concerned with how much employees' performance improves because of their newly acquired knowledge. Our focus in this section is on the latter.

8-4. Describe the essentials of person-focused pay program design.

A fundamental issue in person-focused programs is whether investments in training provide measurable payoffs to companies. The Association for Talent Development, a premier professional organization of training and development professionals, offered some insight. Based on a research study involving approximately 2,500 companies, training investments are positively related to future total stockholder return, gross profit margin, and income per employee.[29] In addition, executives within and outside the training function at IBM maintain that training programs have strategic value for companies.[30]

Establishing Skill Blocks

Skill (knowledge) blocks are sets of skills (knowledge) necessary to perform a specific job (e.g., typing skills versus analytical reasoning) or group of similar jobs (e.g., junior accounting clerk, intermediate accounting clerk, and senior accounting clerk). Table 8-3 contains an example of a knowledge block—building market-competitive compensation systems—discussed in the accompanying companion casebook *Building Strategic Compensation Systems*.

The number of skill blocks included in a person-focused structure can range from two to several. The appropriate number of blocks depends on the variety of jobs within a company. The development of skill blocks should occur with three considerations in mind.

First, the company must develop job descriptions, which we discussed in Chapter 6. Job descriptions should be treated as blueprints for the creation of a person-focused system. Well-crafted job descriptions should facilitate the identification of major skills, the training programs employees need to acquire horizontal and vertical skills, and accurate measures of performance.

Second, individual jobs should be organized into job families, or groups of similar jobs such as clerical, technical, and accounting. The information conveyed within a job description should enable the plan developers to identify skills that are common to all jobs in the family and skills that are unique for individual jobs in the family. Based on these groupings, all tasks necessary to perform the jobs in a job family should be listed to facilitate the identification of the skills necessary to perform the tasks.

TABLE 8-3 Knowledge Block: Building Market-Competitive Compensation Systems

I. Strategic analyses
   A. External market environment
   B. Internal capabilities

II. Compensation surveys
   A. Using published compensation survey data
   B. Compensation surveys: Strategic considerations
   C. Compensation survey data: Summary, analysis, and interpretation

Third, skills should be grouped into blocks. There are no hard-and-fast rules compensation professionals can follow to determine skill blocks. A general guideline is that the blocked knowledge should relate to specific job tasks and duties. Referring again to Table 8-3, knowledge about the external environment and a company's internal capabilities—two distinct sets of knowledge—together form the foundation of strategic analyses.

Transition Matters

A few initial considerations arise in the transition from using job-based pay exclusively to using person-focused programs as well. These issues include assessment of skills, alignment of pay with the knowledge structure, and access to training.[31]

SKILLS ASSESSMENT The skills assessment issue centers on who should assess whether employees possess skills at levels that justify a pay raise, on what basis assessments should be made, and when assessments should be conducted. Gaining employee trust is critical during the transition period because employees may view new systems as threats to job security. Some combination of peer and self-assessments, as well as input from known "experts" such as supervisors, therefore, might be essential. The important ingredients here are employee input and the expertise of supervisors and managers.

Having established who should conduct assessments, on what basis should assessments be made? During the transition, companies use conventional performance measures that reflect employees' proficiency in skills use, complemented by employees' self-assessments. The use of both types of data is likely to increase an employee's understanding of the new system as well as build faith in it, particularly when testimony and the more conventional performance measures converge.

A final assessment matter concerns timing. During transition phases, managers should assess employees' performance more frequently to keep employees informed of how well they are doing under the new system. In addition, more frequent assessments should reinforce the key aim of pay for knowledge (i.e., to encourage employees to learn more). Performance feedback is essential for this process.

ALIGNING PAY WITH THE KNOWLEDGE STRUCTURE One of the most difficult tasks that managers face as they guide employees toward a person-focused system is aligning pay with the knowledge structure.[32] This is often the case because most compensation surveys price whole jobs (e.g., surgeons) rather than specific knowledge or skill sets that make up jobs, such as jobs that require manual dexterity. (See the article by Judy Canavan listed in endnote 32, which addresses strategies for pricing skills.) Still, upon implementation of pay for knowledge, employees' core compensation must reflect the knowledge or skills they have that the company incorporates into its person-focused structure. If employees' actual earnings are more than what the person-focused system indicates, managers must develop a reasonable course of action so that employees can acquire skills that are commensurate with their current pay. If employees are underpaid, the company must provide pay adjustments as quickly as possible. The length of time required to make these necessary adjustments will depend on two factors: the number of such employees and the extent to which they are underpaid. With limited budgets, companies will obviously require more extended periods as either the number of underpaid employees or the pay deficit increases.

ACCESS TO TRAINING A final transition matter is access to training. Person-focused systems make training necessary, rather than optional, for those employees who are motivated for self-improvement. Companies that adopt pay for knowledge must therefore ensure that all employees have equal access to the needed training for acquiring higher-level skills. They must do so both to meet the intended aim of person-focused programs (i.e., to reward employees for enhancing their skills) and to address legal imperatives. Restricting access to training can lead to a violation of key laws (e.g., Title VII of the Civil Rights Act of 1964 and the Age Discrimination in Employment Act of 1967; see Chapter 2). Companies must also educate employees about what their training options are and how successful training will lead to increased pay and advancement opportunities within the company. In other words, employers should not assume that employees will necessarily recognize the opportunities that are available to them unless they are clearly communicated. Written memos, e-mails, and informational meetings conducted by HR representatives are effective communication media.

Training and Certification

Successful person-focused programs depend on a company's ability to develop and implement systematic training programs. For many of the reasons cited in earlier chapters (e.g., intense domestic and global competition, rapid technological advancement, and educational deficits of new workforce entrants), progressive companies in the United States have adopted a continuous learning philosophy, which, like person-focused pay programs, encourages employees to take responsibility for enhancing their skills and knowledge.[33] Training clearly represents a key venue for continuous learning.

Because employees are required to learn new skills constantly, training becomes an ongoing process. Companies implementing pay for knowledge typically increase the amount of classroom and on-the-job training.[34] When training is well designed, employees should be able to learn the skills needed to increase their pay as well as the skills necessary to teach and coach other employees at lower skill levels. Accurate job descriptions are useful in determining training needs and focusing training efforts.

Employers must make necessary training available to employees so they can progress through the person-focused system. A systematic method for ensuring adequate training coverage involves matching training programs with each skill block. Accessibility does not require that employers develop and deliver training themselves. Training that is developed and delivered by an agency not directly affiliated with the company (e.g., community college, vocational training institute, university, or private consultant) can be just as accessible when the employer integrates the offering of these other sources with its person-focused program.

In-House or Outsourcing Training

The following criteria should be used to determine whether to develop and deliver training within the workplace or to outsource.[35]

Expertise Specialized training topics require greater expertise, and more generic topics require less expertise. Employers generally turn to in-house resources if they can draw on existing expertise. If in-house expertise is lacking, employers often seek an outside provider either to fill the need directly or to train individuals who become instructors. Employers usually rely on in-house expertise for employer- and product-specific training. Such training is governed by employer philosophies and procedures and is, therefore, not readily available in the external market.

Timeliness Employers often seek outside services if the in-house staff does not have adequate time to develop and deliver the program within the time frame requested. For example, Oracle, a business applications software development company, trains its clients on how to use the systems it installs. Over time, client companies experience turnover, which often includes the departure of employees who are well trained to use installed Oracle systems. To maintain effective business operations, client companies require training on demand. PeopleSoft offers training on demand to its clients through different forms of media.

Size of the Employee Population to be Trained Employers typically rely on in-house resources for larger groups of employees. The major impetus behind this decision is economics. If there is a large demand for training, the program is more likely to be delivered more than once, resulting in economies of scale.

Sensitivity or Proprietary Nature of the Subject Matter Sensitive or proprietary training is defined as training used to gain a competitive advantage or training that gives access to proprietary, product, or strategic knowledge. Employers rarely issue security clearances to outside resources to provide training of this nature. If the area of the training is sensitive or proprietary, the training is likely to be done in-house regardless of the other factors just discussed.

Certification and Recertification Certification ensures that employees possess at least a minimally acceptable level of skill proficiency upon completion of a training unit. If employees do not have an acceptable degree of skill, then the company quite simply wastes any skill-based compensation expenditure. Supervisors and coworkers, who are presumably most familiar with the intricacies of their work, usually certify workers. Certification methods can include work samples, oral questioning, and written tests.

Recertification, under which employees periodically must demonstrate mastery of all the jobs they have learned or risk losing their pay rates, is necessary to maintain the workforce flexibility offered by a person-focused plan.[36] The recertification process typically is handled by retesting employees, retraining employees, or requiring employees to occasionally perform jobs that use their previously acquired skills.

For example, the Society for Human Resource Management (SHRM) offers two types of professional certification: the SHRM-CP (CP: certified professional) and the SHRM-SCP (SCP: senior certified professional). Individuals with at least one year of HR work experience earn certification when they pass a comprehensive examination of knowledge in the HR domain. Because the field of HR knowledge changes over time, individuals with certification must periodically earn continuing education credits to maintain certification. Credits are earned through a wide variety of activities, including course and/or conference attendance, membership in professional organizations, leadership with the association, teaching, speaking, writing, and projects completed on the job. This updating process is known as recertification.

PAY STRUCTURE VARIATIONS

8-5. Summarize pay structure variations.

The principles of pay structure development reviewed previously apply to the majority of established pay structures in companies throughout the United States. Broadbanding and two-tier pay structures represent variations to those pay structure principles.

Broadbanding

THE BROADBANDING CONCEPT AND ITS ADVANTAGES Companies may choose **broadbanding** to consolidate existing pay grades and ranges into fewer, wider pay grades and broader pay ranges.[37] Figure 8-6 illustrates a broadbanding structure and its relationship to traditional pay grades and ranges. Broadbanding represents the organizational trend toward flatter, less hierarchical corporate structures that emphasize teamwork over individual contributions

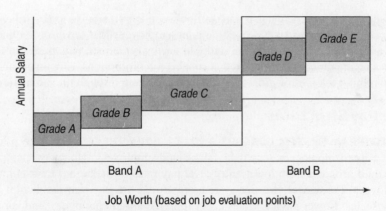

FIGURE 8-6 Broadbanding Structure and Its Relationship to Traditional Pay Grades and Ranges

alone.[38] Some federal government agencies, including the Navy, the General Accounting Office, and the Central Intelligence Agency, began experimenting with the broadbanding concept in the 1980s to introduce greater flexibility to their pay structures. Some private sector companies began using broadbanding in the late 1980s for the same reason. General Electric's former plastics business is a noteworthy adopter of broadbanding.

Broadbanding uses only a few large salary ranges to span levels within the organization previously covered by several pay grades. Thus, HR professionals place jobs that were separated by one or more pay grades in old pay structures into the same band under broadbanding systems. For example, condensing three consecutive grades into a single broadband eliminates the hierarchical differences among the jobs evident in the original, narrower pay grade configuration. Employees holding jobs in a single broadband now have equal pay potential, unlike employees in a multiple pay grade configuration. In addition, elimination of narrow bands broadens employees' job duties and responsibilities.

Some companies establish broadbands for distinct employee groups within the organizational hierarchy (e.g., upper management, middle management, professionals, and staff). This approach reduces management layers dramatically, and it should promote quicker decision-making cycles. Other companies create broadbands based on job families (e.g., clerical, technical, and administrative). Job family–based bands should give employees broader duties within their job classes. Still others may set broadbands according to functional areas, collapsing across job families. For example, a broadband may be established for all HR specialists (i.e., training, compensation, recruitment, and performance appraisal). These bands should encourage employees to expand their knowledge and skills in several HR functions.

Broadbanding shifts greater responsibility to supervisors and managers for administering each employee's compensation within the confines of the broadbands. Because broadbands include a wider range of jobs than narrowly defined pay grades, supervisors have greater latitude in setting employees' pay according to the tasks and duties they perform. Under traditional pay grades, employees receive pay and pay increases based on a limited set of duties stated in their job descriptions.

LIMITATIONS OF BROADBANDING Notwithstanding the benefits of broadbanding, it does possess some limitations. Broadbanding is not a cure-all for all compensation-related dysfunction within companies. For instance, broadbanding changes how compensation dollars are allocated, but not how much is allocated. Managers often think that flatter organizational structures reduce costs. To the contrary, broadbanding may lead to higher compensation expenses because managers have greater latitude in assigning pay to their employees. In fact, the federal government's limited experience showed that broadbanding structures were associated with more rapid increases in compensation costs than traditional pay structures.[39]

Broadbanding also necessitates a trade-off between the flexibility to reward employees for their unique contributions and a perception among employees that fewer promotional opportunities are available. This transition from multiple narrowly defined pay grades to fewer broadbands reduces organizational hierarchies that support job promotions. Employers and employees alike need to rethink the idea of promotions as a positive step through the job hierarchy.

Two-Tier Pay Structures

THE TWO-TIER PAY SYSTEM CONCEPT AND ITS ADVANTAGES Two-tier pay structures reward newly hired employees less than established employees. Under the temporary basis, employees could progress from lower entry-level pay rates to the higher rates enjoyed by more senior employees. Permanent two-tier systems reinforce the pay-rate distinction by retaining separate pay scales: Lower-paying scales apply to newly hired employees, and current employees enjoy higher-paying scales. Although pay progresses within each scale, the maximum rates to which newly hired employees can progress are always lower than more senior employees' pay scales. Table 8-4 illustrates a typical two-tier wage structure.

Two-tier wage systems are more prevalent in unionized companies. For example, at Ford Motor Company, a two-tier wage structure compensated new hires substantially less than other employees, including an hourly base rate that is $10 less than earned by the established employees.[40]

Labor representatives reluctantly agreed to two-tier wage plans as a cost-control measure. In exchange for reduced compensation costs, companies promised to limit layoffs. These plans represent a departure from unions' traditional stance of single base-pay rates for all employees within job classifications. The U.S. auto industry implemented two-tier wage structures to help make it more competitive with foreign car companies. Largely operating without unions in the U.S., foreign automakers' labor costs are substantially lower than U.S. automakers' union rates. Also, the so-called Great Recession (2007–2009) and the slow economic recovery threatened the economic viability of the companies because fewer people were buying passenger cars and trucks.

Two-tier pay structures also enable companies to reward long-service employees while keeping costs down by paying lower rates to newly hired employees who do not have an established performance record within the company. As senior employees terminate their employment (taking jobs elsewhere or retiring), they are usually replaced by workers who are compensated according to the lower-paying scale.

TABLE 8-4 Two-Tier Wage Structures

Typical Base Rate		
	Assembler ($)	Tool & Die ($)
Base Rate—Contract End	26.86	31.52
COLA Fold-In	1.19	1.19
New Agreement Base	28.05	32.71
Beginning COLA Float	1.06	1.06
Base Rate Plus COLA	29.11	33.77
Lump Sum Examples		
	Assembler ($)	Tool & Die ($)
October 2014 Settlement Bonus	3,000	3,000
September 2015 Performance Bonus (3%)	2,171	2,534
September 2016 Performance Bonus (4%)	2,894	3,377
September 2017 Performance Bonus (3%)	2,170	2,533

Note: Based on a standard 2,080-year, plus 10 percent overtime, with projected COLA adjustments based on inflation averaging 2.44 percent.

In 2015, Ford Motor Company's management decided to hire approximately 1,500 new hourly employees because of increased business demand.[41] The collective bargaining agreement between the company and the United Auto workers, set to expire at the end of 2015, limited the number of employees who can be paid at the lower-tier wage to 20 percent of the unionized hourly workforce. As a result, the company has been moving hundreds of workers from lower-tier (entry) wages to a higher pay rate. Ford eliminated the use of two-tier wage structures in its collective bargaining agreement with the United Auto Workers, which was ratified at the end of 2015 (and set to expire in 2019).

LIMITATIONS OF TWO-TIER PAY STRUCTURES A potentially serious limitation of two-tier plans is that the lower pay scale applied to newly hired workers may restrict a company's ability to recruit and retain the most highly qualified individuals. Resentment can build among employees on the lower tier toward their counterparts on the upper tier, which may lead to lower-tier employees' refusal to perform work that extends in any way beyond their job descriptions. Such resentment may lead employees on the upper tier to scale back their willingness to take on additional work to the extent that they perceive pay premiums are not sufficiently large to compensate for extra duties. In addition, opponents of two-tier wage systems contend that pay differentials cause lower employee morale. Finally, conflict between the tiers may lead to excessive turnover. When high performers leave, then the turnover is dysfunctional to the company and can have long-term implications for productivity and quality. For many of these reasons, Ford as well as Fiat Chrysler and General Motors no longer use two-tier wage structures. Over time, employees hired on the lower-tier will advance to higher-tier pay.

PREPARING FOR EXAMS/QUIZZES

Chapter Summary by Learning Objectives

Learning Objective 8-1. *Explain the concept of pay structures and the five steps necessary to construct pay structures.* Pay structures assign different pay rates for jobs of unequal worth and provide the framework for recognizing differences in individual employee contributions. Compensation professionals develop pay structures based on five steps: deciding on how many pay structures, determining the market pay line, defining pay grades, calculating pay ranges for each pay grade, and evaluating the results.

Learning Objective 8-2. *Discuss the components of merit pay systems.* Merit pay systems reward employees for past performance. The key considerations include merit increase amounts, timing of increases, recurring versus nonrecurring increases, present level of base pay, merit pay grid design, and merit pay increase budget.

Learning Objective 8-3. *Summarize the features of sales compensation plan design.* The main components of sales incentive compensation plans are the choice of commission, bonus, salary, and the mix of these elements.

Learning Objective 8-4. *Describe the essentials of person-focused pay program design.* Person-focused pay programs require consideration of skill blocks establishment, transition matters from job-based plans, and training and certification.

Learning Objective 8-5. *Summarize pay structure variations.* Two common pay structure variations include broadbanding and two-tier pay structures. Broadbanding consolidates existing pay grades and ranges into fewer, wider pay grades and broader pay ranges. Two-tier pay structures reward newly hired employees less than established employees.

Key Terms

Discussion Questions

8-1. Respond to the following statement: Pay grades limit a company's ability to achieve competitive advantage. Do you agree? Explain.

8-2. Two employees perform the same job, and each received exemplary performance ratings. Is it fair to give one employee a smaller percentage merit increase because his pay falls within the third quartile but give a larger percentage merit increase to the other because his pay falls within the first quartile? Explain your answer.

8-3. Describe some ethical dilemmas sales professionals may encounter. How can sales compensation programs be modified to minimize ethical dilemmas?

8-4. What are your reactions to the following statement? Merit pay grids have the potential to undermine employee motivation. Discuss your views.

8-5. Compression represents a serious dysfunction of pay structures. What are some of the major ramifications of compression? Also, how can companies minimize or avoid these ramifications?

PREPARING FOR MY CAREER

Compensation in Action

As a line manager or HR manager, you will be faced with the challenge of determining which pay structures best suit the employee populations you serve. Regardless of the specifics of the plan (several specific plans are covered in this chapter), there are general guidelines that should be followed to build the link between the pay structure and the successful recognition of employee contributions. As you are educated by compensation specialists, you will provide senior executives with recommendations that appropriately identify correct incentives and produce desired behaviors.

Action checklist for line managers and HR—keeping the focus on employees as structures are built

HR takes the lead

- Assess the organization, and identify factors that will determine the pay structures within the organization (e.g., hourly versus salaried and geographic location). Line managers help in this assessment and provide additional insight to identify the correct factors.

- Partner with compensation specialists to group employees into pay grades that are determined by some similarity in the work they produce; corresponding ranges will also be established for each grade.
- Compensation specialists conduct market analyses to certify that current employees are being compensated at the right levels and that offers are being made to prospective employees that are comparable to the offers made by competitors (retain and attract top talent).

Line managers take the lead

- Communicate with HR regarding behaviors in employee population—HR and line managers work together to ensure that the compensation and benefits incentives are continuing to target the correct behaviors. HR carefully considers subtle changes to the system in the face of market pressures or new leadership and direction within the company.
- Employees will continue to progress within the grade in which they have been placed, receiving pay increases (as determined by line manager in consultation with HR) commensurate with their individual performance—compensation specialists will work with HR to ensure that, with these merit increases, equity still exists in the grade and that the percentage increases in pay correspond with superior levels of performance.

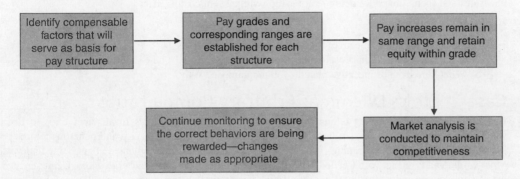

Cases

Case 1: A New Sales Representative

After 10 years in business, John Shurtman has determined that it is time to hire a sales representative. As the founder and president of United Fleet Service (UFS), John has been the main driver of new business sales for the company. However, as UFS has grown, John has found that he must spend more time on planning and administration, leaving little time to generate new sales leads or call on potential customers.

UFS provides maintenance, mechanical repair services, and body repair services to organizations that maintain fleets of large vehicles. UFS customers include mostly school districts that own bus fleets and municipalities that own fleets of fire and police vehicles. While UFS has a strong hold on these public-sector organizations, John sees many opportunities for expansion through targeting other potential customers such as utility companies and commercial trucking companies.

UFS has several competitors in its geographic area, but none provide as comprehensive a service as UFS. For example, several competitors provide mechanical repair services, but do not provide body repair services; on the other hand, several competitors provide body repair services, but do not provide mechanical repair services. UFS also has a reputation for high-quality repairs and fast turnaround times on service. With these strengths in mind, John is convinced that an effective sales representative that can take the time to contact and develop relationships with potential customers can help lead the organization to expansion.

John has experienced steady growth over the past 10 years, acquiring just two or three new customers each year. Leads on potential new customers have come primarily through referrals from current customers. John personally called on the leads to secure sales. Once a target was established as a customer, John handed the customer account over to a service advisor. The service advisor's role is to process incoming vehicles and communicate work progress with customers. Service advisors are also encouraged to generate new sales from current customers by suggesting add-on services or establishing ongoing maintenance schedules. Due to increased volume growth, the service advisors have had little time to develop more significant relationships with customers. Because of this, UFS has missed out on many add-on sales opportunities.

Therefore, John plans to hire a new sales representative to both call on new customers and develop better relationships with current customers. Cultivating new customers will require cold-calling on potential customers as well as following up on referrals from current customers. Because most companies that have vehicle fleets establish contractual relationships with mechanical service providers, some new customers may take a long time to acquire. That is, the sales representative may have to interact with a potential new customer over an extended period until the company's contract with another service provider expires.

Working with current customers will require significant interaction with the service advisors to understand each customer's history of services and identify opportunities to increase the number and frequency of services provided. Growing business from current customers will also require spending time developing relationships with each customer.

Before he begins recruiting for this position, John must determine how to compensate the new sales representative. He's researched market rates for sales representatives in his industry and has a targeted salary range, but he wants to make sure that the compensation plan provides enough incentive to both secure new sales and spend time developing relationships with current customers.

Questions:

8-6. What are the sales objectives for the new sales representative?

8-7. What role will the compensation design play in motivating the new sales representative?

8-8. What kind of sales incentive plan do you recommend? Why?

Case 2: Ethics Dilemma: Arbitrary Compa-ratios

Buy-From-Home is a growing online retailer, selling a range of products from paper clips to luxury watches. The company's success is largely based on its quality customer service and generous returns policy. Recently, some high-performing customer service employees have complained about being underpaid. Most wrote emails or met with Cecile McBride, Director of HR, to share their grievances. Cecile created a list of complainers and noncomplainers (of all high-performing customer service employees). She handed the list to Joseph Barelli, Buy-From-Home's compensation analyst, instructing him to determine whether there is a significant pay difference between high-performing complainers and noncomplainers.

After preparing this analysis, Joseph reported that there were no significant pay differences between the two groups. Cecile then asked Joseph to calculate the compa-ratios for all high-performing employees, instructing him to use different midpoint pay rates in his calculations. Joseph was puzzled and asked Cecile to clarify her request: For the complaining high performers, use pay range midpoint rates that were in place when the company began operations several years ago; and, for the noncomplainers, use anticipated midpoints set 5 percent higher than the current midpoint rates. Joseph realized that this approach would lead to substantially higher compa-ratios for the complainers. Soon, these compa-ratios will be used to determine market pay adjustments.

Questions:

8-9. As a compensation professional, what would you do?

8-10. What factor(s) in this ethical dilemma might influence a person to make a less-than-ethical decision?

Crunch the Numbers!

Calculating Pay Range Minimums, Maximums, and Pay Range Overlap

You have been assigned to calculate the pay range minimum and maximum values for two pay grades as well as the overlap between these two pay ranges.

Questions:

8-11. *Pay Range A*: For a pay range midpoint equal to $47,500, calculate the minimum and maximum pay values for a 15 percent range spread.

8-12. *Pay Range B*: For a pay range midpoint equal to $53,750, calculate the minimum and maximum pay rates for a 25 percent range spread.

8-13. What is the overlap between pay range A and pay range B?

Working Together: Team Exercise

In small groups of three or four, come up with specific answers to the following questions. Talk through your perspectives and come up with a team response. Be prepared to share your ideas with the class.

The issue of pay transparency—whether to widely communicate pay information within a company—continues to get a lot of attention in the news. As a group, conduct an internet search for articles or blog posts that address pay transparency. Consider the arguments for and against transparency based on a company's and employee's perspective, respectively.

Questions:

8-14. From each perspective, what are some of the arguments for and against pay transparency practices?

8-15. What do you believe companies should do? Explain.

Endnotes

1. WorldatWork, *Compensation Programs and Practices* (August, 2016), Scottsdale, AZ: WorldatWork.
2. Ibid.
3. Ibid.
4. WorldatWork and Deloitte Consulting LLP, *Salary Structure Policies and Practices* (October, 2012), Scottsdale, AZ: WorldatWork.
5. Ibid.
6. WorldatWork, *Compensation Programs and Practices* (August, 2016), Scottsdale, AZ: WorldatWork.
7. WorldatWork, *Promotional Guidelines* (January, 2015), Scottsdale, AZ: WorldatWork.
8. Linda Ulrich, Money talks: Identifying, Preventing and Alleviating Systemic Salary Compression Issues. *Workspan*, November, (2008): 43–46.
9. Rebecca Manoli, Addressing salary compression in any economy. *Workspan* (December, 2009): 54–57.
10. Andrew L. Klein, Alisa McMillan, & George Reiter, The Mixed Value of Using Lump Sums in Lieu of Putting Merit Pay into Base Pay. *WorldatWork Journal*, First Quarter, (2010): 49–57.
11. WorldatWork, *Compensation Programs and Practices Survey* (August, 2016). Scottsdale, AZ: WorldatWork.
12. Robert L. Heneman, *Merit Pay: Linking Pay Increases to Performance*, (Reading, MA: Addison-Wesley, 1992).
13. Linda A. Krefting and Thomas A. Mahoney, Determining the Size of a Meaningful Pay Increase. *Industrial Relations*, 16 (1977): 83–93, https://doi.org/10.1111/j.1468-232X.1977.tb00650.x.
14. Heneman, *Merit Pay*.
15. William W. Rambo and John N. Pinto, Employees' Perceptions of Pay Increases. *Journal of Occupational Psychology*, 62, (1989): 135–145, https://doi.org/10.1111/j.2044-8325.1989.tb00484.x.
16. Linda A. Krefting, Jerry M. Newman, and Frank Krzystofiak, What is a Meaningful Pay Increase? In D. B. Balkin & L. R. Gómez-Mejía (Eds.), *New Perspectives on Compensation*, (Upper Saddle River, NJ: Prentice Hall, 1987)

17. Heneman, *Merit Pay*.

18. U.S. Bureau of Labor Statistics. *Occupational Employment Statistics*, accessed February 14, 2018, www.bls.gov.

19. U.S. Bureau of Labor Statistics. *Consumer Price Index*, accessed February 14, 2018, www.bls.gov.

20. Christopher L. Erickson and Andrea C. Ichino, Lump-sum Bonuses in Union Contracts. *Advances in Industrial and Labor Relations, 6*, (1994): 183–218.

21. James F. Carey, *Complete Guide to Sales Force Compensation*, (Homewood, IL: Irwin, 1992).

22. David C. Kuhlman, Implementing business strategy through sales compensation. In William Keenan Jr. (Ed.), *Commissions, Bonuses, & Beyond*, (Chicago, IL: Probus Publishing, 1994).

23. Jerome A. Colletti and Mary S. Fiss, Designing Sales Incentive Plans for Competitive Advantage. In D. Scott (Ed.), *Incentive Pay*, (Scottsdale, AZ: WorldatWork, 2007): 43–56.

24. Thomas Steenburgh and Michael Ahearne, Motivating Salespeople: What Really Works. *Harvard Business Review* (July, 2012), accessed February 28, 2015, http://www.hbr.org.

25. William Keenan, Jr. (Ed.), The Case Against Commissions. In *Commissions, Bonuses, & Beyond*, (Chicago, IL: Probus Publishing, 1994).

26. Lauren Weber, Why it's so Hard to Fill Sales Jobs. *The Wall Street Journal* (February 4, 2015), accessed March 2, 2015, http://www.wsj.com.

27. Xactly and WorldatWork, *2017 Sales Compensation Administration Best Practices Survey*, 2017, accessed February 21, 2018, https://go.xactlycorp.com/2017-Comp-Survey-Report.html.

28. Joseph Dimisa and Parvin Jahanbakhsh, How to Build a Sales Compensation Center of Excellence. *Workspan* (November, 2013): 43–46.

29. American Society for Training and Development, *Profiting from Learning: Do Firms' Investments in Education and Training Pay Off?*, 2000, accessed July 7, 2002, www.astd.org/virtual—community /research/PFLWhitePaper.pdf.

30. American Society for Training and Development, *C-Level Perceptions of the Strategic Value of Learning Research Report*, (January, 2006), accessed June 19, 2007, www.astd.org/astd/research /research.

31. Barbara J. Dewey, Changing to Skill-Based Pay: Disarming the Transition Landmines. *Compensation & Benefits Review, 26*, (1994): 38–43. https://doi.org/10.1177/088636879402600107.

32. Judy Canavan, Overcoming the challenge of aligning skill-based pay levels to the external market. *WorldatWork Journal* (First Quarter, 2008): 18–25.

33. Jerome M. Rosow and Robert Zager, *Training: The Competitive Edge*, (San Francisco, CA: Jossey-Bass, 1988).

34. G. Douglas Jenkins, Jr., and Nina Gupta, The payoffs of paying for knowledge. *National Productivity Review, 4*, (1985): 121–130, https://doi.org/10.1002/npr.4040040203.

35. Raymond A. Noe, *Employee Training and Development* (5th ed.), (Burr Ridge, IL: McGraw-Hill Higher Education, 2010).

36. Jenkins, G. Douglas, Jr., Gerald E. Ledford Jr., Nina Gupta, and D. Harold Doty. Skill-Based Pay: Practices, Payoffs, Pitfalls and Prescriptions, (Scottsdale, AZ: American Compensation Association, 1992).

37. Elizabeth Dougherty, You Want Me to Talk About *What?* Broadbanding? *Workspan* (March, 2010), 69–72.

38. Howard H. Risher and Robert J. Butler, Salary banding: An Alternative Salary-Management Concept. *ACA Journal, 2* (1993–1994): 48–57.

39. Brigitte Wittkamp Schay, K. Craig Simons, Evelyn Guerra and Jacqueline Caldwell, *Broad-Banding in the Federal Government—Technical Report* (Washington, DC: U.S. Office of Personnel Management, 1992).

40. Frank Giancola, Ford Motor Company's 58 Years of Experience with a Cost-of-Living Allowance Plan, *WorldatWork Journal*, Third Quarter, (2009): 37–46.

41. Mike Ramsey and John D. Stoll, Ford to move hundreds of entry-level workers to higher pay rate. *The Wall Street Journal* (February 4, 2015), accessed February 6, 2015, http://www.wsj.com.

Where We Are Now:

PART III, DESIGNING COMPENSATION SYSTEMS, explained the concepts and methods to build compensation systems that meet important goals of compensation professionals, including internal consistency, market competitiveness, and recognition of employee contributions. Our focus was on core compensation issues. We do know that employee benefits represent an important component of total compensation. Now we turn to the myriad employee benefits—discretionary benefits as well as legally-required benefits. We also give attention to designing and planning the benefits program in the discretionary benefits chapter.

In **PART IV, WE WILL COVER**

CHAPTER 9   DISCRETIONARY BENEFITS

CHAPTER 10 LEGALLY REQUIRED BENEFITS

9

Discretionary Benefits

Today, discretionary benefits represent a significant cost to companies. In 2018, on average, companies spent nearly $18,000 per employee.[1] For the same period, discretionary benefits accounted for nearly 25 percent of employers' total payroll costs.

As the term implies, discretionary benefits are offered at the will of company management. Discretionary benefits fall into three broad categories: protection programs, paid time off, and services. Protection programs provide family benefits, promote wellness, and guard against income loss caused by such catastrophic factors as disability, serious illness, or death. Retirement plans assist employees to accumulate wealth to serve as an income source throughout retirement. Paid time off, not surprisingly, provides employees time off with pay for such events as vacations. Services provide such enhancements as tuition reimbursement and day care assistance to employees and their families. Understanding which benefits are most important to employees is critically important. A recent survey revealed that 60 percent consider employee benefits as a major factor when deciding whether to accept a job offer.[2]

ORIGINS OF DISCRETIONARY BENEFITS

9-1. Discuss the origins of discretionary benefits.

In the past several decades, firms have offered a tremendous number of both legally required and discretionary benefits. In Chapter 10, we will discuss how the growth in legally required benefits from a select body of federal and state legislation developed out of social welfare philosophies. Quite different from these reasons are several factors that have contributed to the rise in discretionary benefits.

The rise of retirement plans, particularly pension plans, appeared as one of the first signs in the use of discretionary benefits. According to the Employee Benefit Research Institute,[3] the first pension plan in the United States was established in 1759 to benefit widows and children of Presbyterian ministers. In 1875, the American Express Company established a formal pension plan. From that point until World War II, pension plans were adopted primarily in the railroad, banking, and public utility industries. The most significant growth occurred after the favorable tax treatment of pensions was established through the passage of the Revenue Act of 1921, and government-imposed wage increase controls during World War II in the early 1940s led more companies to adopt discretionary employee benefits.

Because of the government-imposed wage freezes, companies invested in expanded discretionary benefits offerings as an alternative to pay hikes as a motivational tool. As a result, many companies began to offer **welfare practices**. Welfare practices were "anything for the comfort and improvement, intellectual or social, of the employees, over and above wages paid, which is not a necessity of the industry nor required by law."[4] Moreover, companies offered employees welfare benefits to promote good management and to enhance worker productivity.

The opportunities for employees through welfare practices varied. For example, some employers offered libraries and recreational areas, and others provided financial assistance for education, home purchases, and home improvements. In addition, employers' sponsorships of medical insurance coverage became common, which, until the Patient Protection and Affordable Care Act of 2010, was made on a discretionary basis.

Quite apart from the benevolence of employers, employee unions also directly contributed to the increase in employee welfare practices through the National Labor Relations Act of 1935 (NLRA), which legitimized bargaining for employee benefits. Even today, union workers tend to have greater access to discretionary benefits than do nonunion employees.[5] Table 9-1 illustrates some of the differences in benefits between nonunion and union employees as well as by major occupational groups, and full- and part-time work status.

Unions also indirectly contributed to the rise in discretionary benefits offerings in nonunion settings. As we discussed in Chapter 2, nonunion companies often fashion their employment practices after union companies as a tactic to minimize the chance that their employees will seek union representation[6] and may offer their employees benefits that are comparable to the benefits received by employees in union shops.

Through many decades, discretionary benefit offerings were based on a relatively homogeneous workforce, characterized by males who were the sole bread winners and provided for

TABLE 9-1 Percentage of Workers with Access to Selected Employee Benefits in Private Industry: March 2017

Worker Characteristics	Vacation	Sick Leave	Retirement Plans	Employee-Assistance Plans	On-site and Off-site Child Care	Wellness Programs	Flexible Workplace
Total	76	68	66	51	10	39	7
Management occupations	88	88	82	67	20	56	20
Production, transportation, and material-moving occupations	82	62	71	50	4	38	4
Service occupations	52	46	42	33	7	22	7
Full-time	91	81	77	57	13	45	8
Part-time	36	35	38	35	4	24	8
Union	89	79	92	74	17	52	3
Nonunion	75	67	64	49	9	38	7

Source: Based on U.S. Bureau of Labor Statistics. (2017). *National Compensation Survey: Employee Benefits in the United States, March 2017* (Bulletin 2787). Available: *http://www.bls.gov*, accessed February 14, 2018.

their wives and children. In recent decades, the labor force has become more diverse in terms of age, gender, race, ethnicity, and definition of families based on same-sex civil unions and marriage.[7] Increasing diversity has given rise to flexible benefit plans, which we discuss later in this chapter. According to the U.S. Bureau of Labor Statistics, labor force diversity will continue to increase. A standardized, one-size-fits-all employer-sponsored benefits program is most effective when the workforce is relatively similar in terms of needs and preferences.

For example, let's assume a company's workforce has 60 percent women and 40 percent men. Most of the women are of child-bearing age and most of the men range in age between their 50s and 60s. One could reasonably expect that there will be substantial differences in the needs and preferences for benefits. Chances are that most of the women in this example may place a high value on day care benefits while most of the men will not have a need for such benefits because their children are likely to be near or at adulthood.

CATEGORIES OF DISCRETIONARY BENEFITS

9-2. Explain the three categories of discretionary benefits.

Several benefits practices fall into the category of discretionary employee benefits. We can explore these practices by recognizing the three broad goals employers hope to achieve when offering discretionary benefits: protection, paid time off, and services to enhance work and life experiences.

Protection Programs

Three important discretionary protection programs include disability insurance, life insurance, and retirement programs. Until recently, employer-sponsored health insurance benefits were offered on a discretionary basis, falling into the protection category. Since the passage of the Patient Protection and Affordable Care Act of 2010, the government has imposed an employer mandate for health insurance. As such, we will review health insurance as a legally required benefit in Chapter 10.

DISABILITY INSURANCE Disability insurance replaces income for employees who become unable to work because of sicknesses or accidents. Employees unfortunately need this kind of protection. At all working ages, the probability of being disabled for at least 90 consecutive days is much greater than the chance of dying while working; one of every three employees will have a disability that lasts at least 90 days.[8]

Employer-sponsored or group disability insurance typically takes two forms. The first, **short-term disability insurance** provides benefits for a limited time, usually less than 6 months.[9] Approximately 41 percent of private sector workers had access to employer-sponsored short-term disability plans in 2018.[10] Access was greater in more hazardous work environments, such as manufacturing, where approximately 63 percent of workers had access. The second, **long-term disability insurance** provides benefits for extended periods between 6 months and life. Approximately 33 percent of private sector workers had access to employer-sponsored long-term disability plans in 2018.[11] Access was greater in more hazardous work environments, such as manufacturing, where approximately 46 percent of workers had access.

Disability criteria differ between short- and long-term plans. Short-term plans usually consider disability as an inability to perform any and every duty of the disabled person's occupation. Long-term plans use a more stringent definition, specifying disability as an inability to engage in any occupation for which the individual is qualified because of training, education, or experience.

Short-term disability plans classify **short-term disability** as an inability to perform the duties of one's regular job. Manifestations of short-term disability include the following temporary (short-term) conditions:

- Recovery from injuries
- Recovery from surgery
- Treatment of an illness requiring any hospitalization
- Pregnancy—the Pregnancy Discrimination Act of 1978 mandates that employers treat pregnancy and childbirth the same way they treat other causes of disability (Chapter 2)

Most short-term disability plans pay employees 60 to 70 percent of their pretax salary on a monthly or weekly basis.[12] Many companies set a maximum benefit amount. In 2018, the typical maximum weekly benefit amount was $2,500.

Three additional features of short-term disability plans include the preexisting condition clause, two waiting periods, and exclusions of health conditions. A **preexisting condition** is a mental or physical disability for which medical advice, diagnosis, care, or treatment was received during a designated period preceding the beginning of disability insurance coverage. The designated period is usually any time prior to employment and enrollment in a company's disability insurance plan. Insurance companies impose preexisting conditions to limit their liabilities for disabilities that predate an individual's coverage.

Two waiting periods include the preeligibility period and an elimination period. The **preeligibility period** spans from the initial date of hire to the time of eligibility for coverage in a disability insurance program. Once the preeligibility period has expired, an **elimination period** refers to the minimum amount of time an employee must wait after becoming disabled before disability insurance payments begin. Elimination periods exclude insignificant illnesses or injuries that limit a person's ability to work for just a few days.

Short-term disability plans often contain exclusion provisions. **Exclusion provisions** list the health conditions that are ineligible for coverage. Disabilities that result from self-inflicted injuries are almost always excluded. Short-term disability plans often exclude most mental illnesses or disabilities due to chemical dependencies (e.g., addictions to alcohol or illegal drugs). Many employers support addicted workers through employee assistance programs, which we will discuss shortly.

Long-term disability insurance provides a monthly benefit to employees who, due to illness or injury, are unable to work for an extended period. Payments of long-term disability benefits usually begin after three to six months of disability and continue for a specified number of months. Payments generally equal a fixed percentage of pre-disability earnings, most typically, 50 to 60 percent.[13]

Long-term disability insurance companies rely on a two-stage definition for long-term disability. **Long-term disability** initially refers to illnesses or accidents that prevent an employee from performing his or her "own occupation" over a designated period. The term *own occupation* applies to employees based on education, training, or experience. After the designated period elapses, the definition becomes more inclusive by adding the phrase "inability to perform any occupation or to engage in any paid employment." The second-stage definition is consistent with the concept of disability in workers' compensation programs (Chapter 10). There are four types of disabilities: temporary total, permanent total, temporary partial, and permanent partial.

Full benefits usually equal 50 to 70 percent of monthly pretax salary, subject to a maximum dollar amount. The monthly maximum may be as high as $15,000. Long-term benefits are generally subject to a waiting period of anywhere from 6 months to 1 year and usually become active only after an employee's sick leave and short-term disability benefits have been exhausted.

Long-term disability plans also include preexisting condition and exclusion clauses. These are similar to the provisions in short-term disability plans. Long-term plans impose two waiting periods: preeligibility period and elimination period. The preeligibility periods for short- and long-term plans are usually identical. When companies offer both plans, the elimination period expires upon the exhaustion of short-term benefits. As discussed earlier, long-term plans become effective immediately following the end of short-term benefit payments, making the elimination period virtually nonexistent. When companies offer long-term plans only, the elimination period runs three to six months following a disability.

Both short- and long-term disability plans may duplicate disability benefits mandated by the Social Security Act and state workers' compensation laws (Chapter 10). These employer-sponsored plans generally supplement legally required benefits. Employer-sponsored plans do not replace disability benefits mandated by laws—workers' compensation and disability benefits through the Social Security Act of 1935.

LIFE INSURANCE Employer-provided **life insurance** protects employees' families by paying a specified amount to an employee's beneficiaries upon the employee's death. Most policies pay a fixed multiple of the employee's salary. Customarily, the multiple equals one to two times an employee's annual salary. Employer-sponsored life insurance plans also frequently include accidental death and dismemberment claims, which pay additional benefits if death was the result of an accident or if the insured incurs accidental loss of a limb. In 2018, approximately 55 percent of private sector employees had access to employer-sponsored life insurance protection.[14]

There are three kinds of life insurance: term life insurance, whole life insurance, and universal life insurance. **Term life insurance**, the most common type offered by companies, provides protection to employees' beneficiaries only during a limited period based on a specified number of years (e.g., 5 years) subject to a maximum age (e.g., 65 or 70). After that, insurance protection automatically expires. Neither the employee nor his or her beneficiaries receives any benefit upon expiration.

Whole life insurance pays an amount to the designated beneficiaries of the deceased employee, but unlike term policies, whole life plans do not terminate until payment is made to beneficiaries. As a result, whole life insurance policies are substantially more expensive than are term life policies, making the whole life insurance approach an uncommon feature of employer-sponsored insurance programs. From the employee's or his or her beneficiary's perspective, whole life insurance policies combine insurance protection with a savings (or cash accumulation) plan. That is, a portion of the money paid to meet the policy's premium will be available in the future. The amount will be augmented with a low fixed annual interest rate of usually no more than two or three percent. **Universal life insurance** combines features of term life insurance and whole life insurance. The insured may shift money between the insurance and savings components of the policy, making this a more flexible alternative to whole life insurance.

RETIREMENT PROGRAMS **Retirement programs** provide income to employees and their beneficiaries during some or all their retirement. Individuals may participate in more than one program simultaneously where employers offer this option. Companies establish retirement or pension plans following one of three design configurations: a defined benefit plan (commonly referred to as **pension plan**), a defined contribution plan, or hybrid plans that combine features of traditional defined benefit and defined contribution plans. According to the U.S. Bureau of Labor Statistics, nearly 55 percent of workers employed in the private sector participated in at least one company-sponsored retirement plan from 1992–1993.[15] In 2017, access has increased to approximately 66 percent as displayed in Table 9-1.[16] However, there has been a noticeable decrease in access to defined benefit plans over the past several years. In 1992–1993, 32 percent of private sector employees had access to at least one defined contribution plan, and slightly fewer had access to at least one defined benefit plan.[17] In 2017, 62 percent had access to at least one defined contribution plan, but only 18 percent had access to at least one defined benefit plan.[18]

Defined benefit plans guarantee retirement benefits specified in the plan document. This benefit is usually expressed in terms of a monthly sum equal to a percentage of a participant's preretirement pay multiplied by the number of years he or she has worked for the employer. Employees typically forfeit their benefits if they leave their employer before meeting a minimum age and years of service requirement. Although the benefit in these plans is fixed by a formula, the level of required employer contributions fluctuates from year to year. The level depends on the amount necessary to make certain that benefits promised will be available when participants and beneficiaries are eligible to receive them. One reason for the decline in defined benefit plans is increasing longevity. On average, a 65-year old man will live to be 86.6 years old and a 65-year-old woman will live to be 88.8 years old.[19] Longevity increases an employer's contribution necessary to ensure that these plans have sufficient funds.

Annual benefits are usually based on age, years of service, and final average wages or salary. Retirement plan formulas specify annual retirement benefits as a percentage of final average salary. Table 9-2 illustrates these percentages for one retirement plan based on age and years of service. Looking at this table, let's assume Mary retires at age 59 with 35 years of service. Let's also assume her final average salary is $52,500. Mary multiplies $52,500 by the annual percentage of 68.20 percent. Her annual benefit is $35,805.00 ($52,500 × 68.20 percent).

Under defined contribution plans, employees have the option to make regular contributions to separate accounts in their names, based on a formula contained in the plan document. Formulas typically call for employers to contribute a given percentage of compensation annually with these funds automatically deducted from pay in equal amounts. Employers invest these funds on behalf of the employee, choosing from a variety of investment vehicles such as company stocks, diversified stock market funds, or federal government bond funds. Most often employees are given a choice of investment vehicles based on the guidelines established by the employer.

Oftentimes, employers contribute money to defined contribution plans in the form of a **company match**. A recent survey revealed that 92 percent of companies made matching contributions to defined contribution plans. Three common company match approaches include: full match, fixed dollar match, and variable dollar match. Companies typically use the variable dollar match approach. The matching contribution decreases as an employee's contribution increases. For instance, an employer might deposit $1 for every $1 on the first 3 percent of pay contributed by the employee, and 50 cents per dollar on the next 3 percent of pay, contributing up to a limit, oftentimes, 6 percent of employee pay. These approaches challenge employees to save as much as possible. The *Crunch the Numbers* feature at the end of the chapter provides an opportunity to calculate matching contributions under the full match, fixed dollar match, and variable dollar match approaches.

Defined contribution plans specify rules for making contributions. Unlike defined benefit plans, defined contribution plans do not guarantee benefit amounts. Participants bear the risk of possible investment gain or loss. Account balances mainly depend on several factors, including contribution amounts, company matches, and investment performance. Compared to defined benefit plans, defined contribution plans are portable. That is, an employee can take the balance of the account from employer to employer after fulfilling the vesting requirement, which we discuss later in the chapter.

The Internal Revenue Code (IRC), which is the body of tax regulation in the United States, sets annual contribution amounts to these plans on a pretax basis. That is, contributions are not subject to income tax. **Annual addition** refers to the annual maximum allowable

TABLE 9-2 Annual Retirement Benefits for a Defined Benefit Plan

Years of Service	Age					
	60	59	58	57	56	55
5	...	...	...	...	...	...
6	...	...	...	...	...	...
7	...	...	...	...	...	...
8	13.36	12.56	11.76	10.96	10.15	9.35
9	15.03	14.13	13.23	12.32	11.42	10.52
10	16.70	15.70	14.70	13.69	12.69	11.69
.						
.						
.						
35	68.20	68.20	68.20	68.20	68.20	68.20
36	70.50	70.50	70.50	70.50	70.50	70.50
37	72.80	72.80	72.80	72.80	72.80	72.80
38	75.10	75.00	75.00	75.00	75.00	75.00
39	77.40	75.00	75.00	75.00	75.00	75.00
40	79.70	75.00	75.00	75.00	75.00	75.00
+40	80.00	75.00	75.00	75.00	75.00	75.00

contribution to a participant's account in a defined contribution plan. In 2018, annual additions were limited to the lesser of $55,000, or 100 percent of the participant's compensation mainly based on the sum of employer and employee contributions.[20] Of the annual addition, an employee's contribution was limited to $18,500 ($24,500 for employees age 50 or above) or 100 percent of salary, whichever is less. Withdrawals in retirement are taxed.

There are a variety of defined contribution plans. The most common are 401(k) plans, Roth 401(k) plans, and deferred profit sharing plans. **Section 401(k) plans** are retirement plans named after the section of the IRC that created them. Following the previous description of defined contribution plans, 401(k) plans enable employees and employers to defer part of employee compensation to an employee's account. Only private sector employers are eligible to sponsor 401(k) plans. The IRC established **Roth 401(k) plans** in 2006. These plans are similar to 401(k) plans, but there are two noticeable differences. First, employee contributions are taxed at the individual's income tax rate. Second, upon retirement, employee withdrawals are not taxed. Roth 401(k) plans are becoming an increasingly popular offering to help employees manage the uncertainty of possible changes in future income tax rates. For example, it is difficult to predict what income tax rates will be when an individual retires. The rates could be equal to, lower than, or greater than current income tax rates. Higher future income tax rates would require greater withdrawal amounts to meet retirees' needs. Higher withdrawal rates would lower the value of a 401(k) plan more quickly, affecting the number of years in which available funds will provide income. Similar to 401(k) plans are **Section 403(b) plans** and **Section 457 plans**. Section 403(b) plans may be offered to employees of government and tax-exempt groups, such as schools, hospitals, and churches. Section 457 plans apply to state government employees.

☞ **FYI**

Company matching contributions to 401(k) plans, measured as a percentage of employee pay, have been on the rise in recent years:

- 2009: 3.0 percent
- 2015: 3.9 percent
- 2017: 4.7 percent[21]

Companies set up **profit sharing plans** to distribute money to employees. Companies choose between offering a current profit sharing plan as an incentive or a deferred profit sharing plan for retirement savings. Current profit sharing plans award employees with a share of the company's profits, usually on an annual basis. Alternatively, **deferred profit sharing plans** set aside money in employee accounts for use in retirement. For deferred plans, employees do not pay taxes until they make withdrawals in retirement. In 2018, companies could take a tax deduction for their contributions not to exceed 25 percent of each participant's compensation or $55,000, whichever is the lesser amount.[22]

Table 9-3 summarizes selected differences between defined benefit and defined contribution plans.

Hybrid plans combine features of traditional defined benefit and defined contribution plans. The cash–balance plan is the most common hybrid plan. **Cash–balance plans** are structured as "defined benefit plans that define benefits for each employee by reference to the amount of the employee's hypothetical account balance."[23] Cash–balance plans are a relatively new phenomenon compared to traditional defined benefit and defined contribution plans. Many companies have chosen to convert their defined benefit plans to cash balance plans for two key reasons. First, cash balance plans are less costly to employers than defined benefit plans. Second, these plans pay benefits in a lump sum instead of a series of payments. Companies are presumably in a better position to recruit more mobile workers. Under a traditional defined benefit plan, an employee who leaves employment prior to qualifying for a retirement annuity (a series of monthly payments for the rest of one's life) will forfeit the annuity.

TABLE 9-3 Selected Differences between Defined Benefit and Defined Contribution Plans

Characteristics	Defined Benefit Plan	Defined Contribution Plan
Benefit formula	Determines pension due at normal retirement age.	Determines amount regularly contributed to individual account.
Form of benefit expressed by formula	An annuity—a series of payments beginning at the plan's normal retirement age for the life of the participant.	A single lump sum distribution at any time.
Funding	Annual funding is based on an actuarial formula subject to strict limits set by the IRC and is not equivalent to annual increases in pension benefits.	Annual contributions and investment earnings are held in an individual account.
Investment risk/profit	Employee is guaranteed benefits regardless of investment returns on trust. Employer is responsible for ensuring sufficient funding to pay promised benefit.	Employee bears the investment risk, which can result in higher investment returns or the loss of previously accumulated pension benefits.

Source: U.S. General Accounting Office (2000). *Cash Balance Plans: Implications for Retirement Income*, GAO/HEHS-00-207. Washington, DC: General Accounting Office, pp. 9–10.

Paid Time Off

The second type of discretionary benefit is paid time off. This category is relatively straightforward. As the name implies, paid time off policies compensate employees when they are not performing their primary work duties as defined by the Portal-to-Portal Act (Chapter 2). The major types of paid time off benefits follow (we will consider some in this chapter):

- Holidays
- Vacation
- Sick leave
- Personal leave
- Jury duty
- Funeral leave
- Military leave
- Clean-up, preparation, or travel time
- Rest period "break"
- Lunch period
- Integrated paid time off policies
- Parental leave
- Sabbatical leave
- Volunteerism

Companies offer most paid time off as a matter of custom, particularly paid holidays, vacations, and sick leave. In unionized settings, the collective bargaining agreement specifies the terms of paid time off benefits. The paid time off practices that are most typically found in unionized settings are jury duty, funeral leave, military leave, clean-up, preparation, travel time, rest period, and lunch period.

For employees and employers, paid time off benefits are significant. These benefits provide employees the opportunity to balance work and nonwork interests and demands. Companies stand to gain from sponsoring these benefits. Employees may legitimately take time off from scheduled work without incurring loss of pay and benefits, which should help reduce unapproved absenteeism from work. By keeping absenteeism in check, overall productivity and product or service quality should be higher. These benefits also contribute toward positive employee attitudes and commitment to the company, particularly for employees with longer lengths of service. The length of paid time off, such as vacation time, can increase to several weeks with years of service.

Vacation refers to paid time off for reasons other than illness, holidays, parental leave, or formally designated paid time off. Vacation benefits are a common benefit in most companies, and the amounts vary by seniority. For example, after one year, employees are eligible to take two weeks of vacation, three weeks after five years, and so forth, usually up to five weeks after 20 years of service. Some companies deviate from this norm. A standout example of paid vacation policy can be found at the internet company FullContact. Not only do employees receive their pay while on vacation, which is standard, but the founder of this company also provides each employee with $7,500 cash to spend on their vacation on one condition.[24] To qualify, employees may not use company e-mail or perform any work. Other companies have followed suit with similar policies, including Airbnb.[25] The following Watch It! video describes this unique approach to paid vacations and the company's rationale for offering this generous benefit.

Sick leave benefits compensate employees for a specified number of days absent due to personal illness. Sick leave policies are separate from disability leave policies because the focus is on occasional minor illness or injury. Sometimes, these policies permit employees paid time off to care for an ill child, spouse, or parent. Although beneficial to employees, sick leave plans can be disruptive when other employees are off from work. As we will discuss in Chapter 10, some cities and states have recently passed laws that mandate paid sick leave.

As previously shown in Table 9-1, most workers received paid time off benefits in 2017. There have been three developments in paid time off offerings: integrated paid time off policies, sabbatical leave, and volunteerism. We will discuss each of these practices in turn, highlighting the benefits of such paid time off practices to employers.

Private-sector employers usually follow the **holiday** time-off practices for federal government employees. Federal law established 12 paid holidays for federal government employees such as Martin Luther King Jr. Day, Independence Day, Thanksgiving, and Christmas Day. Companies must pay attention to the treatment of religious holidays, which, except for Christmas, are not included on any list of federal or state public holidays. Title VII of the Civil Rights Act prohibits illegal discrimination in employment practices based on sex, religion, color, race, and national origin. The Equal Employment Opportunity Commission (EEOC) established guidelines that encourage companies to honor employee wishes to observe religious holidays, unless doing so would cause undue hardship to both the company and some employees. It is imperative that companies treat the observance of religious holidays uniformly as paid or unpaid time off. Employees who feel that they are being discriminated against on religious grounds may file a complaint at the nearest EEOC field office (www.eeoc.gov/offices.html).

It is common for holidays to overlap with scheduled vacation time or sick leave time. Companies must decide whether to count such instances of paid holidays as a paid vacation day or sickness day. Most often, companies choose to recognize holidays as separate from vacation or sick leave. Thus, when overlap occurs, the employer provides an additional day of paid time off.

Integrated paid time off policies or **paid time off banks** combine holiday, vacation, sick leave, and personal leave policies into a single paid time off policy. Such policies do not distinguish among reasons for absence as do specific policies. The idea is to provide individuals the freedom to schedule time off without justifying the reasons. This freedom should presumably substantially reduce the incidence of unscheduled absences that can be disruptive to the workplace because these policies require notice unless sudden illness is the cause (e.g., you went to sleep one evening feeling fine and then wake up the next morning on a scheduled work day with a stomach virus). Integrated paid time off policies have become an increasingly popular alternative to separate holiday, vacation, sick leave, and personal leave plans because they are more effective in controlling unscheduled absenteeism than other types of absence control policies.[26] In 2017, approximately 35 percent of private sector employees had access to a paid time off bank arrangement.[27] Integrated policies also relieve the administrative burden of managing separate plans and the necessity to process medical certifications in the case of sick leave policies.

Paid time off banks do not incorporate all types of time off with pay. Bereavement and funeral leave are stand-alone policies because the death of a friend or relative is typically an unanticipated event beyond an employee's control. Integrating funeral leave into paid time off banks would also likely create dissatisfaction among workers because it would signal that grieving for a deceased friend or relative is equivalent to a casual day off. Jury duty and witness leave, military leave, and nonproduction time are influenced by law, and nonproduction time is negotiated as part of a collective bargaining agreement. Sabbatical leaves are also not included in paid time off banks because these are extended leaves provided as a reward to valued, long-service employees.

As we will discuss in Chapter 10, the Family and Medical Leave Act of 1993 mandates that most companies provide employees up to 12 weeks of unpaid leave for family reasons. In recent years, many companies voluntarily instituted paid parental leave policies. Paid **parental leave** compensates new-parent employees following the birth, adoption, or foster placement of a child.[28] Many companies are instituting paid parental leave policies. Some include Amazon. com Inc., Microsoft Corp., Netflix Inc., and Blackstone Group LP. Netflix offers one of the most generous family benefits, where employees may take up to one year of paid leave to care for a child. (As a side note, in Chapter 10, we will review recent legally mandated paid parental leave policies.) Approximately 38 percent of companies offer paid parental leave and, of the companies that offer it, nearly two-thirds are mandated to do so by local or state laws.[29]

Paid family leave traditionally benefited female workers because they played the role of primary caregiver. Increasingly, companies are working diligently to legitimize paternity leave. There continues to be a social stigma that is associated with fathers who choose to take time off (paid or unpaid) following the birth or adoption of a child. Unfortunately, a prevalent corporate norm devalues men who take such time off, in part, characterizing those men as not being committed to their careers or interested in advancement. Facebook's CEO Mark Zuckerberg set an example to legitimize paternity leave by taking extended leave after the birth of his first child. Currently, Facebook offers its employees up to four weeks of paid parental leave. Overall, there appears to be a trend toward offering paid parental leave programs, and, most recently, well-known companies are giving legitimacy to paternity leave.

 FYI

A survey of paid parental leave policies revealed differences in pay amounts and duration of pay:

- Full pay during the entire leave period: 80 percent
- Full pay for the initial part of the leave period and partial pay for the remainder: 16 percent
- Partial pay during the entire leave period: 4 percent[30]

Sabbatical leaves are paid time off for such professional activities as a research project or curriculum development. These practices are common in college and university settings and apply most often to faculty members. Most universities grant sabbatical leaves to faculty members who meet minimum service requirements (e.g., 3 years of full-time service) with partial or full pay for up to an entire academic year. The service requirement is applied each time, which limits the number of leaves taken per faculty member.

Outside academia, sabbatical leaves are usually limited to professional and managerial employees who stand to benefit from intensive training opportunities outside the company's sponsorship. Sabbatical leaves are most suitable for such employees as computer engineers whose standards of knowledge or practice are rapidly evolving. Companies establish guidelines regarding qualification, length of leave, and level of pay. An important guideline pertains to minimum length of employment following completion of a sabbatical. For example, companies require employees to remain employed for a minimum of 1 year following the sabbatical or repay part or all of one's salary received during the sabbatical. This provision is necessary to protect a company's invest-ment and to limit moves to competitors. For example, Capterra, which maintains a comprehensive catalog of business software, offers a 5-week, fully paid sabbatical every five years to each of its employees.[31] According to Capterra's CEO, the cost of a sabbatical equals a 10 percent reduction in productivity on an annual basis, but only 2 percent over a 5-year period. He maintains that the benefit to the company and the employee's health and personal growth is a worthwhile expense.

Previously, only large companies were known for offering employees sabbatical leaves. Among them are General Mills, which provides a sabbatical leave after serving the company for seven years. Upon returning from a sabbatical, a 25-year veteran of General Mills said, "I had all the energy and strength and endurance that I wanted."[32] Nowadays, smaller companies have begun offering sabbati-cal leaves. According to the WorldatWork survey, about 20 percent of companies with an employee base of up to 2,500 offer sabbatical leave benefits. For example, law firm Perkins Cole offers a two-month sabbatical after 10 years for exempt staff and after 13 years for nonexempt staff.

Volunteerism refers to giving of one's time to support a meaningful cause. More and more companies are providing employees with paid time off to contribute to causes of their choice. In 2017, approximately 20 percent of companies offered paid time off for volunteer activities, trend-ing up since 2007.[33] Companies favor providing paid time off for volunteer work for three reasons. First, volunteer opportunities allow employees to balance work and life demands. In many instances, companies tout this benefit as a form of work–life balance and a mechanism for the betterment of the community. Brokerage company Charles Schwab provides employees with eight paid hours per year for this purpose. Managers have the discretion to provide additional paid time off for volunteer activities.[34] Second, giving employees the opportunity to promote charitable causes on company time shows a company's commitment to social responsibility, thus enhancing the company's over-all image in the public eye. Third, paid time off to volunteer is believed to help promote retention. Employees are likely to feel that the employer shares similar values, possibly boosting commitment to the company. For younger employees, company-sponsored volunteer benefits can help with recruitment. According to Sales Foundation's Suzanne DiBiana, "In Silicon Valley young gradu-ates and employees are accepting jobs depending upon whether a company has a CSR [corporate social responsibility initiative] in place."[35] It's not surprising that companies with volunteer benefits regularly appear on the *Fortune* magazine annual rankings of the 100 best companies to work for.

Services

EMPLOYEE ASSISTANCE PROGRAMS **Employee assistance programs (EAPs)** help employ-ees cope with such personal problems that may impair their job performance as alcohol or drug abuse, domestic violence, the emotional impact of AIDS and other diseases, clinical depression, and eating disorders. In 2017, approximately 51 percent of private-sector employees and 78 percent of government employees had access to an EAP.[36]

Companies offer EAPs because many employees are likely to experience difficulties that interfere with job performance. Although EAP costs are substantial, the benefits seem to outweigh the costs. For example, the annual cost per employee of an EAP is approximately $50 to $60. Anecdotal evidence, however, indicates that employers' gains outweigh their out-of-pocket expenses for EAPs: savings from reduced employee turnover, absenteeism, medical costs, unemployment insurance rates, workers' compensation rates, accident costs, and disability insurance costs. Most important, many employees who take advantage of EAP resources benefit; unfortunately, large-scale evaluation studies are virtually nonexistent.

Depending on the employer, EAPs provide a range of services and are organized in various ways. In some companies, EAPs are informal programs developed and run on-site by in-house staff. Other employers contract with outside firms to administer their EAPs, or they rely on a combination of their own resources and help from an outside firm.

FAMILY ASSISTANCE PROGRAMS **Family assistance programs** help employees provide elder care and child care. Elder care programs provide physical, emotional, or financial assistance for aging parents, spouses, or other relatives who are not fully self-sufficient because they are too frail or disabled. Child care programs focus on supervising preschool-age dependent children whose parents work outside the home. Many employees now rely on elder care programs because of their parents' increasing longevity and the growing numbers of dual-income families. Child care needs arise from the growing number of single parents and dual-career households with children.

A variety of employer programs and benefits can help employees cope with their family responsibilities. The programs range from making referrals to on-site child care or elder care centers to company-sponsored day care programs, and they vary in the amount of financial and human resources needed to administer them. The least expensive and least labor-intensive programs are generally referral services. Referral services are designed to help workers identify and take advantage of available community resources, conveyed through such media as educational workshops, videos, employee newsletters and magazines, and EAPs.

Flexible scheduling and leave allows employees the leeway to take time off during work hours to care for relatives or react to emergencies. Flexible scheduling, which includes compressed work weeks (e.g., 10-hour days or 12-hour days), flextime, and job sharing, helps employees balance the demands of work and family. In addition to flexible work scheduling, some companies allow employees to extend their legally mandated leave sanctioned by the Family and Medical Leave Act (see Chapter 10). Under extended leave, employers typically continue to provide such employee benefits as insurance and promise to secure individuals comparable jobs upon their return.

Day care is another possible benefit. Some companies subsidize child or elder day care in community-based centers. Elder care programs usually provide self-help, meals, and entertainment activities for the participants. Child care programs typically offer supervision, preschool preparation, and meals. Facilities must usually maintain state or local licenses.

EDUCATIONAL BENEFITS Educational assistance includes advance payments for tuition, fees, and similar expenses, books, supplies, and equipment. The payments may be for either undergraduate- or graduate-level courses and do not have to be for work-related classes. McDonald's pays a portion of full- or part-time restaurant employees' tuition up to $2,500 each year (up to $3,000 for managers).[37] As an alternative, companies may choose to offer educational benefits such as **tuition reimbursement programs**. Under a tuition reimbursement program, an employer fully or partially reimburses an employee for expenses incurred for education or training. There is substantial variability in the percentage of tuition an employer reimburses. Some companies base the percentage on the relevance of the course to the companies' goals or the grades employees earn. Starbucks Coffee is an example of a company that offers generous tuition reimbursement, which is named the "College Achievement Program." In 2015, the company announced that it would pay for most employees (currently, about 140,000 out of 238,000) to earn a bachelor's degree from Arizona State University's online course offerings.

Neither educational benefit is synonymous with pay-for-knowledge programs (Chapter 5). Instead, educational assistance or reimbursement programs fall under the category of employee benefits. Under these benefits programs, employees choose the courses they wish to take when they want to take them. In addition, employees may enroll in courses that are not directly related to their work. As we discussed in Chapter 5, pay-for-knowledge is one kind of core compensation. Companies establish set curricula that employees take, and they generally award pay increases to employees who successfully complete courses within the curricula. Pay increases are not directly associated with tuition reimbursement programs.

TRANSPORTATION SERVICES Some employers sponsor **transportation services**, programs that help bring employees to the workplace and back home again by using more energy-efficient forms of transportation. They may sponsor public transportation or vanpools: employer-sponsored vans or buses that transport employees between their homes and the workplace.

Employers provide transit subsidies to employees working in metropolitan and suburban areas served by mass transportation (e.g., buses, subways, and trains). Companies may offer transit passes, tokens, or vouchers. Practices vary from partial subsidy to full subsidy.

Many employers must offer transportation services to comply with the law. Local and state governments increasingly request that companies reduce the number of single-passenger automobiles commuting to their workplace each day because of government mandates for cleaner air. The Clean Air Act Amendments of 1990 require employers in large metropolitan areas such as Los Angeles to comply with state and local commuter-trip reduction laws. Employers may also offer transportation services to recruit individuals who do not care to drive in rush-hour traffic. Furthermore, transportation services enable companies to offset deficits in parking space availability, particularly in congested metropolitan areas.

Employees obviously stand to benefit from these transportation services. For example, using public transportation or joining a vanpool often saves money by eliminating such commuting costs as gas, insurance, car maintenance and repairs, and parking fees. Moreover, commuting time can be quite lengthy for some employees. By leaving the driving to others, employees can use the time more productively by reading, completing paperwork, or "unwinding."

OUTPLACEMENT ASSISTANCE Some companies provide technical and emotional support through **outplacement assistance** to employees who are being laid off or terminated. They do so with a variety of career and personal programs designed to develop employees' job-hunting skills and strategies and to boost employees' self-confidence. A variety of factors leads to employee termination. Those best suited to outplacement assistance programs include:

- Layoffs due to economic hardship
- Mergers and acquisitions
- Company reorganizations
- Changes in management
- Plant closings or relocation
- Elimination of specific positions, often the result of changes in technology

Outplacement assistance provides such services as personal counseling, career assessments and evaluations, training in job search techniques, résumé and cover letter preparation, interviewing techniques, and training in the use of such basic workplace technology as computers. Although beneficial to employees, outplacement assistance programs hold possible benefits for companies as well. They can promote a positive image of the company among those being terminated, as well as their families and friends, by helping these employees prepare for employment opportunities.

WELLNESS PROGRAMS In the 1980s, employers began sponsoring **wellness programs** to promote and maintain employees' physical and psychological health. Wellness programs vary in scope. They may emphasize weight loss only, or they may emphasize a range of activities such as weight loss, smoking cessation, and cardiovascular fitness. Programs may be offered on- or off-site. Although some companies invest in staffing professionals for wellness programs, others contract with such external vendors as community health agencies or private health clubs. An important goal besides promoting employee health is containing health care costs. The evidence appears to be mixed.[38] Nowadays, nearly 90 percent of employers offer financial incentives or prizes to employees who strive for better health.[39] For example, Johnson & Johnson employees pay $500 less for their annual health insurance premium if they complete a health profile, which the company uses to recommend wellness activities. Some employers, on the other hand, impose penalties for employees who do not engage in at least three wellness activities (for example, completing a health assessment). For instance, Houston, Texas, municipal employees take a $25 monthly pay reduction for failure to complete designated wellness activities.

Companies need to ensure that participation in wellness programs is not a condition of employment. Recently, the U.S. Equal Employment Opportunity Commission charged that Orion Energy violated the Americans with Disabilities Act by requiring an employee to submit to medical exams and inquiries that were not job-related or of business necessity.[40] This employee refused to participate in the wellness program. In response, the company deducted the entire cost of the health insurance premium from this employee's pay, and, ultimately, terminated her employment. The disposition of the case was not reached by the time this edition of the book went to press.

FYI

Companies realize tangible benefits associated with wellness program offerings:

- Medical costs fall by about $3.27 for every dollar invested in wellness program offerings.
- Absenteeism costs decline by $2.73 for every dollar invested in wellness program offerings.[41]

Smoking cessation, stress reduction, nutrition and weight loss, exercise and fitness activities, and health-screening programs are the most common workplace wellness programs. One poll revealed that smoking can be both disruptive and costly to companies. It estimated that the cost of absenteeism attributed to smoking-related health conditions amounted to $218.5 billion, and companies incurred an additional $59.4 billion in health-care costs.[42] Smoking cessation plans range from simple campaigns that stress the negative aspects of smoking to intensive programs directed at helping individuals to stop smoking. Many employers offer courses and treatment to help and encourage smokers to quit. Other options include offering nicotine replacement therapy (e.g., nicotine gum and patches) and self-help services. Many companies sponsor such antismoking events as the Great American Smoke-Out, during which companies distribute T-shirts, buttons, and literature that discredit smoking.

An alarming statistic indicates that workplace stress contributes to 120,000 deaths per year. Also, the health-care costs related to stress were estimated to be $48 billion due to significant work demands and $24 billion due to work-family conflict.[43] **Stress management** programs can help employees cope with many factors inside and outside work that contribute to stress. For instance, job conditions, health and personal problems, and personal and professional relationships can make employees anxious and therefore less productive. Symptoms of stressful workplaces include low morale, chronic absenteeism, low productivity, and high turnover rates. Employers offer stress management programs to teach workers to cope with conditions and situations that cause stress. Seminars focus on recognizing signs of stress and burnout, as well as on how to handle family- and business-related stress. Stress reduction techniques can improve quality of life inside and outside the workplace. Employers benefit from increased employee productivity, reduced absenteeism, and lower health care costs.

Weight control and nutrition programs are designed to educate employees about proper nutrition and weight loss, both of which are critical to good health. Information from the medical community has clearly indicated that excess weight and poor nutrition are significant risk factors in cardiovascular disease, diabetes, high blood pressure, and cholesterol levels. Over time, these programs should give employees better health, increased morale, and improved appearance. For employers, these programs should result in improved productivity and lower health care costs.

Companies can contribute to employees' weight control and proper nutrition by sponsoring memberships in such weight-loss programs as Weight Watchers. Sponsoring companies may also reinforce weight-loss programs' positive results through support groups, intensive counseling, competitions, and other incentives. Companies sometimes actively attempt to influence employee food choices by stocking vending machines with nutritional food.

FINANCIAL EDUCATION Some companies have added financial education to employee benefit offerings. Financial education programs provide employees with the resources for managing personal budgets and long-term savings (e.g., for retirement). Companies are increasingly including financial education as part of the benefits program. These companies reason that financial education is a relatively low-cost benefit that helps employees plan current and future (retirement) budgets.

STUDENT LOAN REPAYMENT ASSISTANCE Average student loan debt for undergraduate education has been rising. Various estimates place loan amounts in the $30,000 to $40,000 range. Many companies are giving thought to offering student loan repayment assistance benefits although only about 5 percent of companies currently offer this benefit.[44] The goal of student loan repayment assistance benefits is to promote recruitment and retention of recent college graduates as well as to help reduce stress levels. Concerns arise that new employees with substantial debt may actively consider employment elsewhere for higher pay, possibly undermining productivity. Aetna, an insurance company, is experimenting with different approaches to providing student loan repayment assistance.[45] The company matches an employee's loan payment up to $2,000 annually over five years for a total benefit equaling $10,000. Other program design options include stipends and loan refinancing arrangements. PwC's "Student Loan Paydown" benefit awards students $100 each month for up to six years.[46]

PET INSURANCE Approximately 5,000 companies offer a pet insurance benefit to recruit and retain talent by recognizing the strong bond between people and their pets.[47] As veterinary medicine advances, so do the available treatments and procedures for serious health ailments. Pet insurance, like human health insurance, provides access to comprehensive medical care that would otherwise be beyond the reach of most individuals. Among the large companies offering pet insurance benefits are Microsoft, Levi-Strauss, Xerox, and Yahoo.

LEGISLATION PERTINENT TO DISCRETIONARY BENEFITS

9-3. Summarize legislation that pertains to discretionary benefits.

Many laws guide the design and implementation of discretionary employee benefits practices. In Chapter 2, we reviewed the relationship between core compensation and the National Labor Relations Act, the Fair Labor Standards Act, and key antidiscrimination laws such as Title VII of the Civil Rights Act of 1964. These laws also have bearing on discretionary benefits practice in a more general way. Here we review additional key laws that influence discretionary employee benefits practice: The Internal Revenue Code (IRC), the Employee Retirement Income Security Act of 1974 (ERISA), and the Pension Protection Act of 2006.

Internal Revenue Code

As noted previously, the IRC is the set of regulations pertaining to taxation in the United States (e.g., sales tax, company [employer] income tax, individual [employee] income tax, and property tax). Taxes represent an essential source of revenue to fund federal, state, and local government programs. The Internal Revenue Service (IRS) is the government agency that develops and implements the IRC and levies penalties against companies and individuals who violate the IRC. Since the early 1900s, the federal government has encouraged employers to provide retirement benefits to employees with tax breaks or deductions. In other words, the government allowed employers to exclude retirement plan payments from their income subject to taxation. This "break" reduced the amount of a company's required tax payments. In general, the larger the contributions to retirement plans, the greater the reduction in the amount of taxes owed to the government. The IRC also permits employees to make contributions to benefits such as health care and retirement plans on a pretax basis. Earlier in the chapter we discussed 401(k) plans. The tax deductibility of benefits costs also requires that employers meet requirements set forth by the Employee Retirement Income Security Act (ERISA), which we discuss next.

Employee Retirement Income Security Act of 1974 (ERISA)

The **Employee Retirement Income Security Act of 1974 (ERISA)** was established to regulate the implementation of various employee benefits programs, including medical, life, and disability programs, as well as pension programs. The essence of ERISA is protection of employee benefits rights.

ERISA addresses matters of employers' reporting and disclosure duties, funding of benefits, the fiduciary responsibilities for these plans, and vesting rights. Companies must provide their employees with straightforward descriptions of their employee benefit plans, updates when substantive changes to the plan are implemented, annual synopses on the financing and operation of the plans, and advance notification if the company intends to terminate the benefits plan. The funding requirement mandates that companies meet strict guidelines to ensure having sufficient funds when employees reach retirement. Similarly, the fiduciary responsibilities require that companies not engage in transactions with parties having interests adverse to those of the recipients of the plan and not deal with the income or assets of the employee benefits plan in the company's own interests.

As noted, tax incentives encourage companies to offer retirement programs. Some of the ERISA Title I and Title II provisions set the minimum standards required to qualify pension plans for favorable tax treatment. **Qualified plans** entitle employers and employees to substantial tax benefits. Employers and employees specifically do not pay tax on their contributions within dollar limits that differ for defined benefit and defined contribution plans. In addition, the investment earnings of the trust in which plan assets are held are generally exempt from tax. Finally, participants or beneficiaries generally do not pay taxes on the value of retirement benefits until they receive distributions. A company's failure to meet any of the minimum standard provisions "disqualifies" pension plans from receiving favorable tax treatment. **Nonqualified plans** refer to pension plans that fail to meet at least one of the minimum standard provisions. Qualified plans possess 13 fundamental characteristics. Table 9-4 lists these characteristics. We will briefly discuss four of the more fundamental standards next—participation requirements, coverage requirements, vesting rules, and nondiscrimination rules.

Participation requirements apply to pension plans. Employees must specifically be allowed to participate in pension plans after they have reached age 21[48] and have completed 1 year of service (based on 1,000 work hours).[49] These hours include all paid time for performing work and paid time off (e.g., vacation, sick leave, and holidays). **Coverage requirements** limit the freedom of employers to exclude employees. Qualified plans do not disproportionately favor highly compensated employees.[50] The IRS specifies the criteria for highly compensated employee status. We will review these criteria in Chapter 11 on executive compensation. **Vesting** refers to an employee's nonforfeitable rights to retirement plan benefits.[51] There are two aspects of vesting. First, employees are always vested in their contributions to pension plans. Second, companies must grant full vesting rights to employer contributions on one of the following two schedules: **cliff vesting** or **6-year graduated schedule**. Cliff vesting schedules must grant employees 100 percent vesting after no more than 3 years of service. That is, after 3 years of participation in the pension plan, an employee has the right to receive all the contributions plus interest on the contributions made by the employer. This schedule is known as cliff vesting because leaving one's job prior to becoming vested under this schedule is tantamount to falling off a cliff—an employee loses all the accrued employer contributions. On the other hand, companies may use a gradual vesting schedule. The 6-year graduated schedule allows workers to become 20 percent vested after 2 years and to vest at a rate of 20 percent each year thereafter until they are 100 percent vested after 6 years of service. **Nondiscrimination rules** prohibit employers from discriminating in favor of highly compensated employees in contributions or benefits, availability of benefits, rights, or plan features.[52] In addition, employers may not amend pension plans so that highly compensated employees are favored.

TABLE 9-4 Characteristics of Qualified Retirement Plans

- Participation requirements
- Coverage requirements
- Vesting rules
- Accrual rules
- Nondiscrimination rules
- Key employee and top-heavy provisions
- Minimum funding standards
- Social Security integration
- Contribution and benefit limits
- Plan distribution rules
- Qualified survivor annuities
- Qualified domestic relations orders
- Plan termination rules and procedures

Pension Protection Act of 2006

The **Pension Protection Act (PPA)** was designed to strengthen employee rights and is an amendment to ERISA. The PPA focuses on bettering employee rights in at least two ways. The first consideration applies to defined benefit plans and the second applies to defined contribution plans.

DEFINED BENEFIT PLANS First, this law should strengthen the financial condition of the **Pension Benefit Guaranty Corporation (PBGC)**, which is a self-financed corporation established by ERISA to insure private-sector defined benefit plans. Companies that offer defined benefit plans are required to pay an insurance premium to protect retirement income promised by these retirement plans. Companies that underfund these plans pay substantially higher costs for insurance protection because they are at greater risk for not having the funds to pay promised retirement benefits. The PPA aims to strengthen the PBGC financial condition by making it more difficult for companies to skip making premium payments. Finally, the PPA raises the amount that employers can contribute to pension funding with tax advantages, creating an additional incentive to adequately fund pension plans.

DEFINED CONTRIBUTION PLANS The PPA makes it easier for employees to participate in defined contribution plans. Millions of workers who are eligible to participate in their employers' defined contribution plans do not contribute to them. In 2017, only 32 percent with access to a defined contribution plan chose to participate.[53] There are a variety of reasons why employees choose not to participate; however, a prominent reason is that most individuals feel they do not have sufficient knowledge about how to choose investment options that will help them earn sufficient money for retirement. In addition, once employees make the decision to participate in these plans and have been making regular contributions, they are not likely to stop. With these issues in mind, the PPA enables companies to enroll their employees automatically in defined contribution plans and provides greater access to professional advice about investing for retirement. Also, this Act requires companies to offer multiple investment options to allow employees to select how much risk they are willing to bear.

DESIGNING AND PLANNING THE BENEFITS PROGRAM

9-4. Discuss the fundamentals of designing and planning the benefits program.

As noted earlier, discretionary benefits can work strategically by offering protection programs, paid time off, and services. As they plan and manage employee benefits programs, HR professionals should keep these functions in mind. There is probably no single company that expects its employee benefits program to meet all these objectives. Company management, along with union representatives as appropriate, must therefore determine which objectives are the most important for a workforce.

Many experts argue that employee input is essential to developing a successful program. Such input helps companies target the limited resources they have available for employee benefits to those areas that best meet employees' needs. For example, if a company's workforce includes mostly married couples who are raising young children, family assistance programs would probably be a priority. By involving employees in program development, they are most likely to accept and appreciate the benefits they receive. Companies can involve employees in the benefits determination process in such ways as surveys, interviews, and focus groups. Fundamental design issues include:

- Who receives coverage
- Financing of benefits
- Employee choice
- Cost containment
- Communication

Employers can ascertain key information from employees that can be useful in designing these programs. The areas of input emphasize employees' beliefs about other employers' benefits offerings and employees' thoughts about the value of the benefits they receive.

Determining Who Receives Coverage

Companies decide whether to extend benefits coverage to full-time and part-time employees or to full-time employees only. As shown in Table 9-1, part-time workers have much less access to benefits than full-time employees.

Another scope issue companies must address is employees' status. In many companies, employees' initial term of employment (usually shorter than 6 months) is deemed a **probationary period**, and companies view such periods as an opportunity to ensure that they have made sound hiring decisions. Many companies choose to withhold discretionary employee benefits for all probationary employees. Companies benefit directly through lower administration-of-benefits costs for these employees during the probationary period.

Financing

Human resource managers must consider how to finance benefits. In fact, the available resources and financial goals may influence, to some extent, who will receive coverage. Managers may decide among noncontributory, contributory, and employee-financed programs or some combination thereof. **Noncontributory financing** implies that the company assumes total costs for each discretionary benefit. Under **contributory financing**, the company and its employees share the costs. Under **employee-financed benefits**, employers do not contribute to the financing of discretionary benefits. Most benefit plans today are contributory, largely because the costs of benefits have risen so dramatically. In 2017, the percentage of employees who were required to contribute to funding the following benefits is as follows: Life insurance (6 percent), long-term disability (7 percent), short-term disability (16 percent), and health insurance (95 percent).[54] On average, the employee share of the contributions for health insurance was 33 percent.

Employee Choice

Human resource professionals must decide on the degree of choice employees should have in determining the set of benefits they will receive. If employees within a company can choose from among a set of benefits, as opposed to all employees receiving the same set of benefits, the company is using a **flexible benefits plan** or **cafeteria plan**. Companies implement cafeteria plans to meet the challenges of diversity, as discussed earlier. Although there is limited evidence regarding employees' reactions to flexible benefits, the existing information indicates benefit satisfaction, overall job satisfaction, pay satisfaction, and understanding of benefits increased after the implementation of a flexible benefits plan.[55] Many of these outcomes are desirable because they are known to lead to reduced absenteeism and turnover.

Cafeteria plans vary,[56] so only the two most common will be discussed here. Flexible spending accounts (FSAs) permit employees to pay for certain benefits expenses (e.g., health care or child care) with pretax dollars. Each year, employees elect the amount of salary-reduction dollars they wish to allocate to this kind of plan. Employers then use this money to reimburse employees for expenses incurred during the plan year that qualify for repayment. IRS regulations limit the amount an employee may set aside each year in their FSA. In 2018, an employee was eligible to contribute up to $2,650 for his or her own medical expenses. For dependent care FSA accounts, the limit was $5,000.

Core plus option plans extend a preestablished set of such benefits as medical insurance as a program core, which is usually mandatory for all employees. Beyond the core, employees may choose from an array of benefits options that suit their personal needs. Companies establish upper limits of benefits values available to each employee. If employees do not choose the maximum amount of benefits, employers may offer an option of trading extra benefits credits for cash. Table 9-5 illustrates the choices of a typical core plus plan.

Cost Containment

Overall, HR managers today try to contain costs. As indicated earlier, the rise in health care costs is phenomenal, so employee benefits now account for a substantial percentage of total compensation costs incurred by companies. In 2017, total employee benefits accounted for 31.7 percent.[57]

TABLE 9-5 Core Plus Option Plan

The core plus option plan contains two sets of benefits: core benefits and optional benefits.

All employees receive a minimum level of core benefits:

- Term life insurance equal to one times annual salary
- Health protection coverage (e.g., indemnity plan, self-funded, HMO, PPO) for the employee and dependents
- Disability insurance

All employees receive credits equal to 4 to 7 percent of salary, which can be used to purchase optional benefits:

- Dental insurance for employee and dependents
- Vision insurance for employee and dependents
- Additional life insurance coverage
- Paid vacation time up to 10 days per year

If an employee has insufficient credits to purchase the desired optional benefits, he or she can purchase these credits through payroll deduction.

Discretionary benefits costs accounted for nearly 25 percent. The current amount has risen dramatically over the past few decades. This increase would not necessarily raise concerns if total compensation budgets were increasing commensurably. As we discussed in Chapter 8, the growth in funds available to support all compensation programs has stagnated. Consequently, employers face difficult trade-offs between employee benefits offerings and increases in core compensation.

Communication

Earlier, we noted that employees often regard employee benefits as an entitlement. Thus, it is reasonable to infer that employees are not aware of their value. In fact, employees are either not aware of or undervalue the employee benefits they receive. Given the significant costs associated with offering employee benefits, companies should try to convey to employees the value they are likely to derive from having such benefits. For example, a personal benefits summary, displayed in Table 9-6, is a useful approach. A benefits communication plan is therefore essential. An effective communication program should have three primary objectives:[58]

- To create an awareness of and appreciation for the way current benefits improve the financial security and the physical and mental well-being of employees
- To provide a high level of understanding about available benefits
- To encourage the wise use of benefits

Companies have traditionally used printed brochures to summarize the key features of the benefits program and to help potential employees compare benefits offerings with those of other companies they may be considering. When new employees join the company, initial group meetings with benefits administrators or audiovisual presentations can detail the elements of the company's benefits program. Shortly after group meetings or audiovisual presentations (usually within a month), new employees should meet individually with benefits administrators, sometimes known as "counselors," to select benefits options. After employees select benefits, the company should provide them with personal benefits statements that detail the scope of coverage and value of each component. Beyond these steps, companies may update employees on changes in benefits (i.e., reductions in or additions to benefits choices or coverage) with periodic newsletters.

Contemporary information sources include a company's intranet. An intranet is a useful way to communicate benefits information to employees on an ongoing basis beyond the legally required written documents. In an era of the paperless office, employees are less likely to have written materials readily available. Employees can review general information about the benefits program whenever they want. For example, Table 9-7 lists general information about the kinds of benefits options available at the University of Illinois. In the online version of such a list, each item (e.g., announcements, benefits directory) would contain a hyperlink that leads to more detailed information.

TABLE 9-6 Sample Personal Statement of Benefits

A PERSONAL BENEFITS STATEMENT FOR:	SSN: *xxx-xx-xxxx*
John Doe	Marital Status: *Single*

Date of Birth: *04/10/61*

REVIEW OF YOUR CURRENT BENEFIT CHOICES

As of March 2018, our records indicate you have chosen the following benefits (rates may change July 1, 2018):

MEDICAL

For you:

   PERSONAL CARE HMO

For your dependent(s):

   NONE

Employer's monthly contribution:

   For you: *$285.00*

   For your dependent(s): *None*

Your monthly contribution: *$37.50*

DENTAL

QUALITY CARE DENTAL PLAN

Your monthly contribution: *$9.50*

Employer's annual contribution:

For you: *$110.00*

For your dependent(s): *None*

DEPENDENTS

You have chosen to cover the following dependent(s) under your Health Plan:

No Dependents

LIFE INSURANCE

As a full-time employee, you receive employer-paid life insurance equal to your annual salary. If you work part-time, your employer-paid amount is less. When you retire at age 60 or older, you still receive $5,000 worth of employer-paid life insurance.

Employer's monthly contribution for your employer-paid life insurance:

Basic life ($90,000): $32.50

Your monthly contribution for the following optional coverage:

For you *(None): None*

Spouse life	*(None):*	*None*
Child life	*(None):*	*None*

Accidental Death and Dismemberment:

(None):   None

FLEXIBLE SPENDING ACCOUNTS

You are enrolled in the following plan(s):

Dependent Care Assistance Plan

Annual deduction	*Not Enrolled*

Medical Care Assistance Plan

Annual deduction	*Not Enrolled*

DOLLAR VALUE OF YOUR BENEFITS

Your total annual compensation is your salary or retirement payment plus the value of employer-paid medical, dental, and life insurance coverage.

Employer-paid medical insurance coverage for you:	*$3,420.00*
Employer contribution for medical insurance coverage for your dependent(s):	*None*
Employer-paid dental insurance coverage for you and your dependent(s):	*$110.00*
Employer-paid life insurance coverage for you:	*$390.00*
Total Value of Your State-Paid Benefits:	*$3,920.00*

THE BENEFITS AND COSTS OF DISCRETIONARY BENEFITS

Discretionary benefits, like core compensation, can contribute to a company's competitive advantage for the reasons discussed earlier (e.g., tax advantages and recruiting the best-qualified candidates). Discretionary benefits can also undermine the imperatives of strategic compensation. Companies that provide discretionary benefits to employees as entitlements are ultimately less likely to promote competitive advantage than companies that design discretionary employee benefits programs to fit the situation.

9-5. Explain the benefits and costs of discretionary benefits.

   Management can use discretionary benefit offerings to promote employee behaviors that have strategic value. For instance, when employees take advantage of tuition reimbursement programs, they are more likely to contribute to the strategic imperatives of product or service differentiation or cost reduction. Knowledge acquired from job-relevant education may enhance

TABLE 9-7 Menu of Employee Benefit Options

This section is designed to provide detailed information regarding your benefits as a University of Illinois employee. It will give you a comprehensive explanation of each benefit and the resources you will need to initiate enrollment, make changes, or find answers to questions regarding your benefits.

Please select from the following categories:

- *Announcements*—Provides announcements of upcoming sign-up periods or events and updated information relating to your benefits.
- *Benefits Directory*—Provides a listing of staff members, including addresses, phone numbers, and e-mail addresses for the Benefits Service Center and each campus.
- *Benefit Choice*—Benefit Choice is an annual open enrollment period that allows employees to make changes to their state of Illinois health, dental, and life insurance coverages, and enroll or re-enroll in flexible spending accounts.
- *Benefit Forms*—Provides links to printable and online benefit forms.
- *Benefits Statement*—Provides a statement outlining your current benefit enrollments and instructions for accessing that information.
- *Benefits Summary*—Provides a detailed, comprehensive description of each benefit plan and its provisions.
- *Frequently Asked Questions*—Provides a list of commonly asked questions relating to your benefits.
- *Leave Information*—Provides time off related information for such benefits as family medical leave, sick leave, and vacation leave.
- *Retirement Planning Seminars*—Provides dates and sign-up information.

the creative potential of employees, as well as their ability to suggest more cost-effective modes of work. On the other hand, deferred profit sharing plans may contribute to companies' strategic imperatives by instilling a sense of ownership in employees and a drive to help position the company to earn significant profits over the long run.

A company can use discretionary benefits to distinguish itself from the competition. In effect, competitive benefits programs potentially convey the message that the company is a good place to work because it invests in the well-being of its employees. Lucrative benefits programs will presumably attract a large pool of applicants that include high-quality candidates, positioning a company to hire the best possible employees.

Finally, the tax advantage afforded companies from offering discretionary benefits have strategic value. In effect, the tax advantage translates into cost savings to companies. These savings can be applied to promote competitive advantage. For example, companies pursuing differentiation strategies may invest these savings into research and development programs or employee development. Companies pursuing lowest-cost strategies may be in a better position to compete because these savings may enable companies to lower the prices of their products and services without cutting into profits.

PREPARING FOR EXAMS/QUIZZES

Chapter Summary by Learning Objectives

Learning Objective 9-1. *Discuss the origins of discretionary benefits.* A variety of social and economic factors contributed to companies' adoption of discretionary employee benefit practices. For example, the federal government provided tax incentives to companies that offered benefits. Wage freezes during World War II prompted companies to offset those freezes with new or enhanced benefits.

Learning Objective 9-2. *Explain the three categories of discretionary benefits.* The three categories of discretionary benefits include protection programs, paid time off, and services. An example of a protection program is life insurance. Vacation is one among many paid time off benefits. Wellness programs provide important services to employees' health and welfare.

Learning Objective 9-3. *Summarize legislation that pertains to discretionary benefits.* A host of laws influence the design and implementation of discretionary benefit practices, including the Internal Revenue Code, the Employee Retirement Income Security Act, and the Pension Protection Act.

Learning Objective 9-4. *Discuss the fundamentals of designing and planning the benefits program.* Benefit program design entails consideration of many factors including who is eligible to participate, financing of benefits, employee choice in determining benefits, cost containment methods, and communication plans.

Learning Objective 9-5. *Explain the benefits and costs of discretionary benefits.* Discretionary benefits are an essential component of the total compensation system. When designed properly, discretionary benefit practices can help promote behaviors through promoting wellness, financial security, work-life balance, and so forth.

Key Terms

welfare practices   213
short-term disability insurance   214
long-term disability insurance   214
short-term disability   214
preexisting condition   215
preeligibility period   215
elimination period   215
exclusion provisions   215
long-term disability   215
life insurance   215
term life insurance   216
whole life insurance   216
universal life insurance   216
retirement programs   216
pension plan   216
defined benefit plans   216
defined contribution plans   217
company match   217
Internal Revenue Code (IRC)   217
annual addition   217
Section 401(k) plans   218
Roth 401(k) plans   218
Section 403(b) plans   218
Section 457 plans   218

profit sharing plans   218
deferred profit sharing plans   218
hybrid plans   218
cash–balance plans   218
Sick leave   220
Vacation   220
integrated paid time off policies   220
paid time off banks   220
Parental leave   221
sabbatical leaves   221
volunteerism   222
employee assistance programs (EAPs)   222
family assistance programs   222
flexible scheduling and leave   223
day care   223
educational assistance   223
tuition reimbursement programs   223
transportation services   223
outplacement assistance   224
wellness programs   224
smoking cessation   225

stress management   225
weight control and nutrition programs   225
Employee Retirement Income Security Act of 1974 (ERISA)   226
qualified plans   227
nonqualified plans   227
participation requirements   227
coverage requirements   227
vesting   227
cliff vesting   227
6-year graduated schedule   227
Nondiscrimination rules   227
Pension Protection Act (PPA)
Pension Benefit Guaranty Corporation (PBGC)   228
probationary period   229
noncontributory financing   229
contributory financing   229
employee-financed benefits   229
flexible benefits plan   229
cafeteria plan   229
core plus option plans   229

Discussion Questions

9-1. Many compensation professionals are faced with making choices about which discretionary benefits to drop because funds are limited and the costs of these benefits continually increase. Which benefits would you *most likely* eliminate? Which would you *least likely* eliminate? Explain your rationale.

9-2. What are your beliefs about whether discretionary employee benefits should be an entitlement or something earned based on job performance? Explain.

9-3. Assume that you are an HRM professional whose responsibility is to develop a brochure for conveying the value of your company's benefits program to potential employees. Your company has asked you to showcase the benefits program in a manner that will encourage recruits to join the company. Which features would you showcase to prospective and current employees? Explain.

9-4. Conduct some research to identify examples of innovative benefit practices. A useful starting point is an Internet search using phrases such as "best companies to work for." What are some of the more innovative benefits practices that you found? Explain.

9-5. Are employees more likely to favor defined contribution plans over defined benefit plans? How about employers? Explain your answers.

PREPARING FOR MY CAREER

Compensation in Action

Many employees feel entitled to certain benefits that they consider to be the positive consequence of organizational membership. While some benefits are required by law, it will be up to the organization to decide on other benefits that are offered and administered. As a line manager or HR professional, you *might* oversee creating a benefits program, but you will *certainly* be called on to interpret policy to meet the requests of employees. Whether you are dealing with the creation or interpretation of benefits, you will want to have access to accurate information so your organization's offerings serve as true benefits for employees and not a source of frustration and ambiguity.

Action checklist for line managers and HR—helping employees understand and fully utilize benefits

HR takes the lead

- Ensure that the employee benefits handbook is up to date and accurate. Depending on the employee population, both an online version and a hard copy of the manual should be accessible.
- Create workshops to help employees understand the unique aspects of the benefits offered by the organization—highlight confusing aspects and aspects that are not well known.
- While many companies now have call centers that answer benefits questions for employees, seek to stay up to date on company policies and legal requirements so that, when more complex benefits issues arise (e.g., long-term disability, sabbaticals, and outplacement services), the questions can be dealt with in a sensitive and timely manner.

Line managers take the lead

- Suggest ways to keep the "explaining your benefits" portion of new employee orientation engaging and interesting. The session should be conducted by HR (or the benefits specialist).
- Keep track of the most common benefits questions that arise. Seek to be educated by HR on the specifics of these specific policies so responses can be given quickly and accurately.
- When changes to benefits are made, call employees together to discuss rationale and what can be done to make full use of the existing benefits.

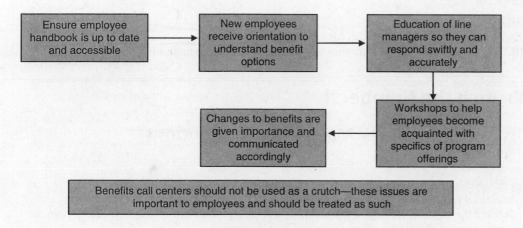

Cases

Case 1: Employee Benefits That Matter

Wayne McGraw greeted Robert Peters, his next interviewee, warmly. Robert had an excellent academic record and appeared to be just the kind of person Wayne's company, Beco Electric, was seeking. Wayne is the university recruiter for Beco and had already interviewed six graduating seniors at Centenary College.

Based on the application form, Robert appeared to be the most promising candidate to be interviewed that day. He was 22 years old and had a 3.6 grade point average with a 4.0 in his major field, industrial management. Robert was not only the vice-president of the Student Government Association, but also activities chairman for Kappa Alpha Psi, a social fraternity. The reference letters in Robert's file revealed that he was both active socially and a rather intense and serious student. One of the letters from Robert's employer during the previous summer expressed satisfaction with Robert's work habits.

Wayne knew that discussion of benefits could be an important part of the recruiting interview. But he did not know which aspects of Beco's benefits program would appeal most to Robert. The company has an excellent profit-sharing plan, although 80 percent of profit distributions are deferred and included in each employee's retirement account. Health benefits are also good. It also has long-term care insurance. The company's medical and dental plan pays a significant portion of costs. A company lunchroom provides meals at about 70 percent of outside prices, although few managers take advantage of this. Employees get one week of paid vacation after the first year and two weeks after two years with the company. Two weeks are provided each year for sick leave. In addition, there are 12 paid holidays each year. Finally, the company encourages advanced education, paying for tuition and books in full, and under certain circumstances, allowing time off to attend classes during the day. It also provides scholarships for dependents.

Questions:

9-6. What aspects of Beco's benefits program are likely to appeal to Robert? Explain.

9-7. In today's work environment, what additional benefits might be more attractive to Robert? Explain.

9-8. What aspects of Beco's benefits program would likely be the least appealing to Robert? Discuss.

Case 2: Ethics Dilemma: A Poor Bid

You are vice-president of HR for a large construction company, and your company is bidding on an estimated $2.5 million public housing project. A local electrical subcontractor submitted a bid that you realize is too low because labor costs have been incorrectly calculated. It is obvious to you that benefits amounting to more than 30 percent of labor costs have not been included. In fact, the bid was some $30,000 below those of the other four subcontractors. However, accepting it will improve your chance of winning the contract for the big housing project.

Questions:

9-9. As a compensation professional, what would you do?

9-10. What factor(s) in this ethical dilemma might influence a person to make a less-than-ethical decision?

Crunch the Numbers!

Calculating Employer Matching Contributions

Companies decide whether to institute matching contributions. Ones that offer matching contributions do so for numerous reasons, including recruitment and retention of the most qualified individuals. Also, companies choose the formulas for making contributions and setting maximum contribution limits. Here are three common approaches for determining matching contributions:

- **Full match:** The employer fully matches an employee's contribution to the 401(k) account up to an amount set by law. For illustrative purposes, an employee earning $50,000 annually contributes $2,000 to her 401(k). Then, the company's matching contribution equals $2,000.
- **Fixed dollar match**: The employer deposits $1 for every $1 the employee contributes up to a specified limit, for instance, 5 percent of pay. One employee contributes 3 percent of her $100,000 pay equaling $3,000: (3 percent × $100,000). The employer contributes the same amount. Another employee contributes 10 percent of his $100,000 pay equaling $10,000: (10 percent × $100,000). In this case, the company deposits $5,000: (5 percent × $100,000) because the plan specifies a 5 percent matching contribution maximum.
- **Variable dollar match:** The employer's contribution decreases as an employee's contribution increases. For example, an employer might deposit $1 for every $1 on the first 3 percent of pay contributed by the employee, and 50 cents per dollar on the next 3 percent of pay. An employee who earns $100,000 annually contributes 6 percent to the 401(k) plan, equaling $6,000: (6 percent × $100,000). The employer contributes a total of $4,500: [($1 × (3 percent × $100,000)) + ($0.50 × (3 percent × $100,000))].

Now, let's calculate the employer's matching contributions for three employees, Amanda, Shiyu, and Onkar, using each method. Amanda earns $35,000 annually and does not contribute anything to the 401(k) plan. Shiyu earns $125,000 annually and contributes 7 percent of pay to the 401(k) plan. Onkar earns $80,000 annually and contributes 2 percent of pay.

Questions:

9-11. *Full match:* What is the employer's contribution for (a) Amanda, (b) Shiyu, and (c) Onkar?

9-12. *Fixed dollar match*: 75 cents per each $1 employee contribution. What is the employer's contribution for (a) Amanda, (b) Shiyu, and (c) Onkar? What is the total contribution (employee's contribution plus employer's contribution) to each employee's 401(k) account: (d) Amanda, (e) Shiyu, and (f) Onkar?

9-13. *Variable dollar match*: $1 per each $1 employee contribution on the first 2 percent of pay and 75 cents per $1 employee contribution for the next 3 percent of pay. What is the employer's contribution for (a) Amanda, (b) Shiyu, and (c) Onkar? What is the total contribution (employee's contribution plus employer's contribution) to each employee's 401(k) account: (d) Amanda, (e) Shiyu, and (f) Onkar?

Working Together: Team Exercise

In small groups of three or four, come up with specific answers to the following questions. Talk through your perspectives with team members. Be prepared to share your ideas with the class.

Think about your work and non-work goals for the next five and ten years. Discuss these goals with group members and put together a list based on each member's response.

Questions:

9-14. What are some of the various work and non-work goals after graduating from school for each time frame? Briefly describe them.

9-15. What are two employee benefits that will support the attainment of these goals during each time frame? Explain.

Endnotes

1. U.S. Bureau of Labor Statistics, *Employer Costs for Employee Compensation—March 2018*, (USDL-18-0944), 2017, accessed July 15, 2018, http://www.bls.gov.
2. Kerry Jones, "The Most Desirable Employee Benefits," *Harvard Business Review* (February 15, 2017), accessed March 30, 2018 at http://www.hbr.org.
3. Employee Benefits Research Institute, "Pension Plans" (Chapter 4), *Fundamentals of Employee Benefits Programs* (Washington, D.C.: Employee Benefits Research Institute, 1997).
4. U.S. Bureau of Labor Statistics, *Welfare Work for Employees in Industrial Establishments in the United States*, 1919, Bulletin # 250, 119–123.
5. U.S. Bureau of Labor Statistics, *National Compensation Survey: Employee Benefits in the United States, March 2017,* (Bulletin 2787), accessed February 14, 2018, http://www.bls.gov.
6. Loren M. Solnick, "The Effect of the Blue Collar Unions on White Collar Wages and Benefits," *Industrial and Labor Relations Review,* 38 (1985): 23–35.
7. T. Alan Lacey, Mitra Toossi, and Kevin S. Dubina, "Projections Overview and Highlights, 2016-26," *Monthly Labor Review,* (October 2017): 1-26.
8. Joseph J. Martocchio, *Employee Benefits: A Primer for the Human Resource Professional,* 6th ed. (Burr Ridge, IL: Irwin/McGraw-Hill, 2018).
9. U.S. Bureau of Labor Statistics, *National Compensation Survey: Employee Benefits in the United States, March 2017,* (Bulletin 2787), accessed February 14, 2018, http://www.bls.gov.
10. U.S. Bureau of Labor Statistics, *National Compensation Survey: Employee Benefits in the United States, March 2017,* (Bulletin 2787), accessed February 14, 2018, http://www.bls.gov.
11. Ibid.
12. Ibid.
13. Ibid.
14. Ibid.
15. Stephanie L. Costo, "Trends in Retirement Plan Coverage Over the Last Decade," *Monthly Labor Review*, February, 2006: 58–64.
16. U.S. Bureau of Labor Statistics, *National Compensation Survey: Employee Benefits in the United States, March 2017,* (Bulletin 2787), accessed February 14, 2018, http://www.bls.gov.
17. Costo, "Trends in Retirement."
18. U.S. Bureau of Labor Statistics, *National Compensation Survey: Employee Benefits in the United States, March 2017,* (Bulletin 2787), accessed February 14, 2018, http://www.bls.gov.
19. Michael Rapoport, "Longer Lives Hit Companies with Pension Plans Hard," *The Wall Street Journal* (February 23, 2015), accessed February 25, 2015, http://www.wsj.com.
20. I.R.C. §415(c).
21. Thomas Heath, "The 401(k) Match Is Back, and It's Getting Bigger," *The Washington Post* (July 18, 2017), accessed February 21, 2018, http://www.washingtonpost.com.
22. I.R.C. §404(a)(3).
23. 26 Code of Federal Regulations §§1.401(a)(4)-8(c)(3)(I).
24. FullContact, "Amazing Benefits for Amazing Employees," 2018, accessed February 18, 2018, https://www.fullcontact.com/about/careers/denver/.
25. Paul Schrodt, "12 Companies with the Most Luxurious Employee Perks," *CNN Money* (October 9, 2017), accessed March 30, 2018, http://money.cnn.com.
26. Michael M. Markowich, *Paid Time-Off Banks* (Phoenix, AZ: WorldatWork Press, 2007).
27. U.S. Bureau of Labor Statistics, *National Compensation Survey: Employee Benefits in the United States, March 2017,* (Bulletin 2787), accessed February 14, 2018, http://www.bls.gov.

28. WorldatWork, *Survey of Paid Parental Leave in the United States (May)* (Scottsdale, AZ: WorldatWork, 2017).

29. Ibid.

30. WorldatWork, *Summary of Paid Parental Leave in the United States (May)* (Scottsdale, AZ: WorldatWork, 2017).

31. Kate Harrison. "The Most Popular Employee Perks of 2014," *Fortune* (February 19, 2014), accessed March 12, 2015, http://www.fortune.com.

32. Colleen Kane, "Go Ahead, Take That Long Vacation," *Fortune* (March 16, 2015), accessed February 18, 2018, http://www.fortune.com.

33. Society for Human Resource Management, *2017 Employee Benefits: Remaining Competitive in a Challenging Talent Marketplace,* (Alexandria, VA: Society for Human Resource Management, 2017).

34. Sarah Halzack, "Paid Time Off for Volunteering."

35. Ryan Scott, "The Best Volunteer Programs Do This," *Forbes* (June 15, 2015), accessed February 18, 2018, http://www.forbes.com.

36. U.S. Bureau of Labor Statistics, *National Compensation Survey: Employee Benefits in the United States, March 2017*, (Bulletin 2787), accessed February 14, 2018, http://www.bls.gov.

37. Katie Lobosco, "McDonald's Boosts Tuition Benefits Because of the New Tax Law," *CNN Money* (March 29, 2018), accessed March 30, 2018, http://www.money.cnn.com.

38. Katie Thomas, "Companies Get Strict on Health of Workers," *The New York Times* (March 25, 2013), accessed February 7, 2015, http://www.NYTimes.com.

39. Jen Wieczner, "Your Company Wants to Make You Healthy," *The Wall Street Journal* (April 8, 2013), accessed January 15, 2015, http://www.wsj.com.

40. U.S. Equal Employment Opportunity Commission, *EEOC Lawsuit Challenges Orion Energy Wellness Program and Related Firing of Employee.* (Press release, August 20, 2014), accessed March 12, 2015, http://www.1.eeoc.gov.

41. Katherine Baicker, David Cutler, and Zirui Song, "Workplace Wellness Programs Can Generate Savings," *Health Affairs* 29 (2010): 304–311, https://doi.org/10.1377/hlthaff.2009.0626.

42. Sara Zellner and Lawrence Bowdish, "Smoking Linked to $278 Billion in Losses for U.S. Employers," *Gallup* (September 26, 2013), accessed February 18, 2018, http://www.gallup.com.

43. Michael Blanding, "Workplace Stress R1esponsible for up to $190B in Annual U.S. Healthcare Costs," *Forbes* (January 26, 2015), accessed February 18, 2018, http://www.forbes.com.

44. Society for Human Resource Management, "Tips for Launching a Student-Loan Repayment Benefit," (October 2, 2017), accessed February 18, 2018, https://www.shrm.org/resourcesandtools/hr-topics /benefits/pages/launching-student-loan-repayment-benefit.aspx.

45. Amanda Eisenberg, "Number of Employers Offering Student Loan Repayment Benefit Grows," (2017), accessed February 18, 2018, http://Ebn.Benefitsnews.Com, p. 2.

46. Katie Lobosco, "New Employee Perk: $100 a Month For Your Student Loans," *CNN Money* (October 9, 2017), accessed March 30, 2018, http://www.money.cnn.com.

47. Susan Jenks, "Pet Insurance Is the Latest Work Perk," *The New York Times* (June 7, 2017), accessed February 21, 2018, http://www.nytimes.com.

48. I.R.C. §§410(a)(1), 410(a)(4); Treas. Reg. §1.410(a)-3T(b); ERISA §202(a).

49. I.R.C. §410(a)(3), Treas. Reg. §1.410(a)-5, 29 C.F.R. §2530.200b-2(a), ERISA §202(a)(3).

50. I.R.C. §414(q).

51. I.R.C. §§411(a)(2), 411(a)(5); Treas. Reg. §1.411(a)-3T; ERISA §203(a).

52. I.R.C. §401(a)(4).

53. U.S. Bureau of Labor Statistics, *National Compensation Survey: Employee Benefits in the United States, March 2017*, (Bulletin 2787), accessed February 14, 2018, http://www.bls.gov.

54. Ibid.

55. Alison E. Barber, Randall B. Dunham, and Roger A. Formisano, "The Impact of Flexible Benefit Plans on Employee Satisfaction." (Paper presented at the fiftieth annual meeting of the Academy of Management, San Francisco, CA, 1990).

56. Joseph J. Martocchio, *Employee Benefits*, 6th ed.

57. U.S. Bureau of Labor Statistics, *Employer Costs for Employee Compensation, September 2017*, (December 15, 2017) (USDL: 17-1646), accessed January 3, 2018, http://www.bls.gov.

58. Joseph J. Martocchio, *Employee Benefits*, 6th ed.

Legally Required Benefits

Today, legally required benefits represent a significant cost to companies. In 2017, companies spent an annual average of $5,470 per employee to provide legally required benefits.[1] For the same period, these benefits accounted for 7.9 percent of the employers' total payroll costs. That percentage will rise substantially because the Patient Protection and Affordable Care Act of 2010 *now* requires employers to offer health insurance to their employees. Adding health insurance as a component of legally required benefits propels the annual average cost to approximately $10,100. This figure amounts to more than 15.6 percent of total compensation costs. Given limited increases in compensation budgets, the costs of legally required benefits slowly cut into an employer's discretion in setting pay level and pay mix. A continuation of this trend could place companies at a competitive disadvantage.

ORIGINS OF LEGALLY REQUIRED BENEFITS

Legally required benefits historically provided a form of social insurance. Prompted largely by the rapid growth of industrialization in the United States in the early nineteenth century and the Great Depression of the 1930s, initial social insurance programs were designed to minimize the possibility that individuals who became unemployed or severely injured while working would become destitute. In addition, social insurance programs aimed to stabilize the well-being of

10-1. Discuss the origins of legally required benefits.

dependent family members of injured or unemployed individuals. Furthermore, early social insurance programs were designed to enable retirees to maintain subsistence income levels. These intents of legally required benefits remain intact today.

Workers' compensation insurance came into existence during the early decades of the twentieth century, when industrial accidents were very common and workers suffered from occupational illnesses at alarming rates.[2] The first constitutionally acceptable workers' compensation law was enacted in 1911. By 1920, all but six states had instituted workers' compensation laws.[3] State workers' compensation laws are based on the principle of liability without fault[4] (i.e., an employer is liable for providing benefits to employees that result from occupational illnesses or injuries, regardless of fault). Another key principle of workers' compensation laws is that employers should assume costs of occupational injuries and accidents. These expenses presumably represent costs of production that employers can recoup through setting higher prices.

Income discontinuity caused by the Great Depression led to the Social Security Act to protect families from financial devastation in the event of unemployment. The Great Depression of the 1930s was a time when many businesses failed and masses of people became chronically unemployed. During this period, employers shifted their focus from maximizing profits to simply staying in business. Overall, ensuring the financial solvency of employees during periods of temporary unemployment and following work-related injuries promoted the well-being of the economy and contributed to some companies' ability to remain in business. These subsistence payments specifically contributed to the viability of the economy by providing temporarily unemployed or injured individuals with the means to contribute to economic activity by making purchases that resulted in demand for products and services. The Social Security Act of 1935 also addresses retirement income and the health and welfare of employees and their families. Many employees could not meet their financial obligations (e.g., housing expenses and food) daily, and most employees could not retire because they were unable to save enough money to support themselves in retirement. Furthermore, employees' poor financial situations left them unable to afford medical treatment for themselves and their families.

Until recently, employers offered health insurance on a discretionary basis. President Barack Obama maintained that every American should have health insurance. The Patient Protection and Affordable Care Act (PPACA), enacted on March 23, 2010, is a comprehensive law that mandates that employers with 50 or more employees offer health insurance to employees (the employer mandate or shared responsibility). Employers with less than 50 employees buy insurance from their State exchanges or http://healthcare.gov. Monetary penalties are assessed for failure to meet the law's insurance mandates.

CATEGORIES OF LEGALLY REQUIRED BENEFITS

10-2. Summarize the four main categories of legally required benefits.

There are four categories of legally required benefits:

- social security programs (Social Security Act of 1935 provided for unemployment insurance and old age insurance. A 1939 change in the law added survivor benefits and benefits for the retiree's spouse and children. In 1956 disability benefits were added, and, Medicare was added in 1965),
- workers' compensation (various state compulsory disability laws),
- unpaid family and medical leave (Family and Medical Leave Act of 1993), and
- health insurance (Patient Protection and Affordable Care Act of 2010).

All provide protection programs to employees and their dependents.

Social Security Programs

The Social Security Act established the following programs:

- Unemployment insurance
- Old Age, Survivor, and Disability Insurance (OASDI)
- Medicare

Each of those programs will be reviewed in turn.

UNEMPLOYMENT INSURANCE The Social Security Act founded a national federal–state unemployment insurance program for individuals who become unemployed through no fault of their own. Each state administers its own program and develops guidelines within parameters set by the federal government. States pay into a central unemployment tax fund administered by the federal government. The federal government invests these payments, and it disburses funds to states as needed to pay benefits. The unemployment insurance program applies to virtually all employees in the United States, except for most agricultural and domestic workers (e.g., housekeepers).

Individuals must meet several criteria to qualify for unemployment benefits. Unemployment itself does not necessarily qualify a person, although these criteria vary somewhat by state. Those applying for unemployment insurance benefits must have been employed for a minimum period. This **base period** tends to be the first four of the last five completed calendar quarters immediately prior to becoming unemployed. In addition, all states require sufficient previous earnings during the base period, which is determined by each state. Other criteria are listed in Table 10-1.

Individuals who meet the eligibility criteria receive weekly benefits. Because the federal government places no limits on a maximum allowable amount, the benefits amount varies widely from state to state. Most states calculate the weekly benefits as a specified fraction of an employee's average wages during the highest calendar quarter of the base period. Unemployed individuals usually collect unemployment insurance benefits for several weeks. The average duration of benefits has ranged between 12 and 18 weeks. The average duration refers to the mean number of weeks for which unemployment insurance claimants collect benefits under regular state programs. Provisions are in place to provide extended benefits during periods of high unemployment, which was the case during and following the 2007–2009 recession.

Unemployment insurance benefits are financed by federal and state taxes levied on employers under the **Federal Unemployment Tax Act (FUTA)**. State and local governments as well as not-for-profit companies (e.g., American Cancer Association) are generally exempt from FUTA, although some states have elected to participate in this program. Employer contributions amount to 6.2 percent of the first $7,000 earned by each employee (i.e., the taxable wage base). FUTA specifies $7,000 as the minimum allowable taxable wage base. Relatively few states' taxable wage base is as low as the FUTA-specified minimum. In 2018, states' taxable wage bases ranged from $7,000 in Arizona, California, Florida, and Puerto Rico to $47,300 in Washington. Some states do require employee contributions.

OLD AGE, SURVIVOR, AND DISABILITY INSURANCE OASDI contains a few benefits that were amended to the Social Security Act following its enactment in 1935. Besides providing retirement income, the amendments include survivors' insurance (1939), and both disability insurance and Medicare (1965). The phrase *old age* in the title refers to retirement benefits. Virtually all U.S. workers are eligible for protections under the OASDI and Medicare programs.

OLD AGE BENEFITS Individuals may receive various benefit levels upon retirement, or under survivors' and disability programs, based on how much credit they have earned through eligible payroll contributions. They earn credit based on **quarters of coverage**, which each equal three consecutive months during the calendar year. In 2018, a worker earned credit for one quarter of

TABLE 10-1 Eligibility Criteria for Unemployment Insurance Benefits

To be eligible for unemployment insurance benefits, an individual must:

- Not have left a job voluntarily
- Be able and available for work
- Be actively seeking work
- Not have refused an offer of suitable employment
- Not be unemployed because of a labor dispute (exception in a few states)
- Not have had employment terminated because of gross violations of conduct within the workplace

coverage for each quarter in which she made at least $1,320 of Social Security taxable income. This figure is based on the average total wages of all workers as determined by the Social Security Administration (SSA). Workers may earn up to four quarters of coverage credit each year. Individuals become **fully insured** when they earn credit for 40 quarters of coverage, or 10 years of employment, and remain fully insured during their lifetime.

An individual who has become fully insured must meet additional requirements before receiving benefits under the programs. Under the retirement program, fully insured individuals may choose to receive benefits as early as age 62, although their benefit amounts will be permanently reduced if elected prior to full retirement age. Congress instituted changes in the minimum age for receiving full benefits. It increased the full retirement age from age 65 for people born in 1938 or later because of higher life expectancies. The age for collecting full Social Security retirement benefits is gradually increasing to age 67 in 2022.

SURVIVOR BENEFITS The SSA calculates survivors' benefits based on the insureds' employment status and the survivors' relationship to the deceased. Dependent, unmarried children of the deceased and a spouse of the deceased who is caring for a child or children may receive survivors' benefits if the deceased worker was fully insured. A widow or widower at least age 60 or a parent at least age 62 who was dependent on the deceased employee is entitled to survivors' benefits if the deceased worker was fully insured.

DISABILITY BENEFITS The SSA pays benefits to seriously disabled workers and family members. Social Security pays only for total disability. Disability under Social Security is based on a person's inability to perform work done before becoming disabled and the inability to adjust to other work because of the medical condition. The disability must also last, or be expected to last, for at least one year or to result in death.

Disability benefits are available to disabled workers who are unable to work because of a serious medical or mental impairment that lasts at least 12 months. Seriously disabled workers are eligible to receive disability benefits if they meet two criteria. First, the worker must have accumulated at least 40 credits. Second, the worker must have earned at least 20 credits of the last 40 calendar quarters in the last 10 years ending with the year of disablement.

Younger workers need fewer quarters of coverage because they have fewer years to accumulate them. For example, workers ages 21–31 may qualify with half as many credits between age 21 and becoming disabled. Becoming disabled at age 29 requires credit for four years of employment (equivalent to 16 credits based on earning four credits per year) since the eight-year period beginning at age 21.

☛ **FYI**

The average monthly OASDI benefits in 2018 were:

- Old Age: $1,404
- Survivor: $1,336
- Disability Insurance: $1,197[5]

MEDICARE The Medicare program serves nearly all U.S. citizens age 65 or older by providing insurance coverage for hospitalization, convalescent care, and major doctor bills. The Medicare program includes five separate features:

- *Medicare Part A*—Hospital insurance
- *Medicare Part B*—Medical insurance
- *Medigap*—Voluntary supplemental insurance to pay for services not covered in Parts A and B
- *Medicare Part C: Medicare Advantage*—Choices in health care providers, such as through HMOs and PPOs
- *Medicare Part D: Medicare Prescription Drug Benefit*—Prescription drug coverage

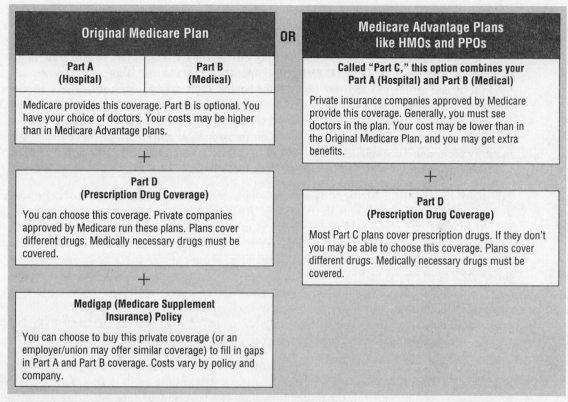

FIGURE 10-1 Options for Receiving Medicare Benefits

Source: Based on U.S. Department of Health and Human Services, (2011), *Medicare & You.* Available: *www.medicare.gov*, accessed February 14, 2011.

Most individuals who are eligible to receive protection under Medicare may choose to receive coverage in one of two ways. A person may receive coverage under the original Medicare Plan or Medicare Advantage Plans as illustrated in Figure 10-1.

The original Medicare Plan is a fee-for-service plan that is managed by the federal government. We will discuss the features of fee-for-service plans later in this chapter. Participants in fee-for-service plans possess the choice to receive care from virtually any licensed health care provider or facility. On the other hand, Medicare Advantage Plans offer a variety of insurance options, including health maintenance organizations, preferred provider organizations, Medicare special needs plans, and Medicare medical savings account plans (MSA). Medicare Advantage Plans are run by private companies subject to strict regulations specified in the Medicare program. Restrictions pertain to pricing of the different plans.

MEDICARE PART A COVERAGE This compulsory hospitalization insurance covers both inpatient and outpatient hospital care and services. Social Security beneficiaries, retirees, voluntary enrollees, and disabled individuals are all entitled. Both employers and employees finance **Medicare Part A** benefits through payroll taxes of 1.45 percent on all earnings, to be noted shortly.

Examples of Part A coverage include:

- Inpatient hospital care in a semiprivate room, meals, general nursing, and other hospital supplies and services.
- Skilled nursing facility care, including semiprivate room, meals, skilled nursing and rehabilitative services, and supplies for up to 100 days per year. Examples of skilled nursing care include physical therapy after a stroke or serious accident.

Individuals who meet the eligibility criteria do not pay a premium for Part A coverage; however, those who do not meet the eligibility criteria paid a monthly premium up to $422 in 2018.

MEDICARE PART B COVERAGE This voluntary supplementary medical insurance covers 80 percent of medical services and supplies after the enrolled individual pays an annual deductible for services furnished under this plan. Part B helps pay for physicians' services and for some medical services and supplies not covered under Part A. **Medicare Part B** pays for medical care such as doctors' services, outpatient care, clinical laboratory services (e.g., blood tests and urinalysis) and some preventive health services (e.g., cardiovascular screenings and bone mass measurement). Part B also provides ambulance services to a hospital or skilled nursing facility when transportation in any other vehicle would endanger a person's health.

Part A coverage automatically qualifies an individual to enroll in Part B coverage for a monthly premium. The premium amounts will be revised annually. In 2018, monthly Part B premiums ranged from $134 to $428.60, based on income level.

MEDIGAP INSURANCE Medigap insurance supplements Part A and Part B coverage and is available to Medicare recipients in most states from private insurance companies for an extra fee. Most Medigap plans help cover the costs of coinsurance, copayments, and deductibles. Federal and state laws limit the sale of these plans to up to 10 different standardized choices that vary in terms of the level of protection. For example, some policies cover costs not covered by the original Medicare plan.

Some insurance companies offer Medicare Select plans. **Medicare Select plans** are Medigap policies that offer lower premiums in exchange for limiting the choice of health care providers. Three states (Massachusetts, Minnesota, and Wisconsin) do not subscribe to this system for offering Medigap insurance. Separate rules apply in these states.

MEDICARE PART C COVERAGE–MEDICARE ADVANTAGE The Balanced Budget Act of 1997 established Medicare+Choice—renamed to **Medicare Advantage** in 2004 as a third Medicare program—as an alternative to the original program (Parts A and B). The Medicare Advantage program, informally referred to as Part C, provides beneficiaries the opportunity to receive health care from a variety of options, including private fee-for-service plans, managed-care plans, or medical savings accounts. Fee-for-service plans provide protection against health care expenses in the form of cash benefits paid to the insured or directly to the health care provider after receiving health care services. These plans pay benefits on a reimbursement basis. Medicare Parts A and B are based on fee-for-service plans. As we will discuss later in this chapter, managed-care plans often pay a higher level of benefits if health care is received from approved providers.

MEDICARE PRESCRIPTION DRUG BENEFITS The passage of the Medicare Prescription Drug, Improvement, and Modernization Act of 2003 (also known as the Medicare Modernization Act of 2003 for short) instituted a prescription drug benefit for Medicare program participants. Commonly referred to as Part D, the drug benefit was first offered in 2006. Medicare covers a percentage of prescription drug costs after a calendar year deductible of $405 in 2018, up to $3,750. After that, expenditures up to $5,000 are not covered by Medicare. This coverage gap is known as the "donut hole" because Medicare contributes to the payment of approved prescription medications for amounts outside the $3,750–$5,000 range less the annual deductible. While in the "donut hole," the insured pays more for prescription medications. The amount for which the insured is responsible while in the donut-hole range is decreasing each year until it reaches no more than 25 percent of the medication cost after 2020.

FINANCING OASDI AND MEDICARE PROGRAMS Funding for OASDI and Medicare programs requires equal employer and employee contributions under the **Federal Insurance Contributions Act (FICA)**.[6] FICA requires that employers pay a tax based on their payroll; employees contribute a tax based on earnings, which is withheld from each paycheck. The **Self-Employment Contributions Act (SECA)**[7] requires that self-employed individuals contribute to the OASDI and Medicare programs, but at a higher tax rate. In either case, the tax rate is subject to an increase each year to fund OASDI programs sufficiently.

OASDI PROGRAMS The largest share of the FICA tax funds OASDI programs. In 2018, of the total 7.65 percent FICA tax, 6.20 percent was set aside. Self-employed individuals contributed 15.30 percent, of which 12.40 percent was set aside for the OASDI program. OASDI taxes are subject to a **taxable wage base**. Taxable wage bases limit the amount of annual wages or payroll cost per employee subject to taxation. The taxable wage base may also increase over time to account for increases in the cost of living. In 2018, the taxable wage base was $128,400 for the OASDI portion of the FICA tax. Annual wages, payroll costs per employee, and self-employed earnings above the taxable wage base are not taxed.

MEDICARE PROGRAMS The **Medicare tax**, or **hospital insurance tax (HI)**, a portion of FICA, supports the Medicare Part A program. Employers, employees, and self-employed individuals contribute 1.45 percent. Self-employed individuals contribute double the amount, or 2.9 percent. The Medicare tax is not subject to a taxable wage base. All payroll amounts and wages are taxed.

According to the Social Security Administration, many people believe that the Social Security taxes they pay are held in interest-bearing accounts set aside by the federal government to meet their own future retirement income needs. To the contrary, the Social Security system represents a pay-as-you-go retirement system. In other words, Social Security taxes paid by today's workers and their employers are used to pay the benefits for today's retirees and other beneficiaries. There is ongoing debate within the U.S. Congress regarding how to shore up these programs for future generations.

Workers' Compensation

Workers' compensation insurance programs, run by states individually, are designed to cover expenses incurred in employees' work-related accidents. Maritime workers within U.S. borders and federal civilian employees are covered by their own workers' compensation programs. The maritime workers' compensation program is mandated by the **Longshore and Harborworkers' Compensation Act**, and federal civilian employees receive workers' compensation protection under the **Federal Employees' Compensation Act**. Thus, workers' compensation laws cover virtually all employees in the United States, except for domestic workers, some agricultural workers, and small businesses with fewer than a dozen regular employees.[8]

WORKERS' COMPENSATION OBJECTIVES AND OBLIGATIONS TO THE PUBLIC Six basic objectives underlie workers' compensation laws:[9]

- Provide sure, prompt, and reasonable income and medical benefits to work-accident victims or income benefits to their dependents, regardless of fault.
- Provide a single remedy and reduce court delays, costs, and workloads arising out of personal injury litigation.
- Relieve public and private charities of financial drains.
- Eliminate payment of fees to lawyers and witnesses as well as time-consuming trials and appeals.
- Encourage maximum employer interest in safety and rehabilitation through appropriate experience-rating mechanisms.
- Promote frank study of causes of accidents (rather than concealment of fault), reducing preventable accidents and human suffering.

Employers must fund workers' compensation programs according to state guidelines. Participation in workers' compensation programs is compulsory in all states except for New Jersey, Oklahoma, and Texas, where employers are not required to provide workers' compensation insurance (with limited exceptions such as businesses that hold construction contracts with the government). Self-insurance, another funding option allowed in the majority of states, requires companies to deposit a surety bond, enabling them to pay their own workers' claims directly.[10] Many companies select self-insurance because it gives employers more discretion in administering their own risks. Nevertheless, self-insured companies must pay their workers the same benefits as those paid by state funds or private insurance carriers.

The following Watch It! video describes the California Healthcare Foundation's approach to ensuring workplace safety. Efforts to promote workforce safety, by making it everyone's responsibility, may lead to fewer workers' compensation claims. In addition, an employer's use of wellness programs, many of which we discussed in Chapter 9, can play an instrumental role in promoting workplace safety.

HOW WORKERS' COMPENSATION COMPARES TO SOCIAL SECURITY BENEFITS Workers' compensation differs from Social Security disability insurance and Medicare in important ways. Workers' compensation pays for medical care for work-related injuries beginning immediately after the injury occurs; it pays temporary disability benefits after a waiting period of three to seven days; it pays permanent partial and permanent total disability benefits to workers who have lasting consequences of disabilities caused on the job; in most states, it pays rehabilitation and training benefits for those unable to return to preinjury careers; and it pays benefits to survivors of workers who die of work-related causes. Social Security, in contrast, pays benefits to workers with long-term disabilities from any cause, but only when the disabilities preclude work. Social Security also pays for rehabilitation services and for survivor benefits to families of deceased workers. Social Security begins after a five-month waiting period and Medicare begins 29 months after the onset of medically verified inability to work.

RECENT TRENDS IN WORKERS' COMPENSATION In recent years, workers' compensation claims have risen dramatically in terms of both numbers of claims and claim amounts. The increased prevalence of repetitive strain injuries resulting from the use of keyboards has contributed to this trend. In March 2018, workers' compensation cost nearly 18 percent of all legally required benefits.[11] The proportion in industries that generally pose substantial worker hazards spent a greater proportion of their legally required benefits dollars to provide workers' compensation insurance. For example, this proportion was approximately 34 percent in the construction industry.

FINANCING WORKERS' COMPENSATION PROGRAMS Workers' compensation laws specify the permissible methods of funding. Employers generally subscribe to workers' compensation insurance through private carriers or, in some instances, through state funds. A third funding option, self-insurance, requires companies to deposit a surety bond, enabling them to pay their own workers' claims directly.[12] Many employers select self-insurance when available because it gives them greater discretion in administering their own risks. Nevertheless, self-insured companies must pay their workers the same benefits paid by state funds or private insurance carriers. In most states, the insurance commissioner sets the maximum allowable workers' compensation insurance premium rates for private insurance carriers.

Family and Medical Leave

The **Family and Medical Leave Act of 1993 (FMLA)** aims to provide employees with job protection in cases of family or medical emergency. The basic thrust of the act is guaranteed leave, and a key element of that guarantee is the right of the employee to return either to the position he or she left when the leave began or to an equivalent position with the same benefits, pay, and other terms and conditions of employment. The passage of the FMLA reflects a growing recognition that many employees' parents are becoming older, rendering them susceptible to a serious illness or medical condition. Older parents are likely to require frequent (if not constant) attention for an extended period while ill, which can be difficult for their adult children.

The passage of the FMLA also recognizes the increasing prevalence of two-income families and the changing roles of men regarding child care. Both heterosexual and homosexual partners are now more likely to work full time and share family responsibilities, including child rearing. Much like older parents, children can also become seriously ill, requiring parents' attention. The FMLA also enables fathers to take paternity leave to care for their newborn babies. Until the passage of the FMLA, men did not have protection comparable to what women receive under the Pregnancy Discrimination Act.

Title I of the FMLA states:

> An eligible employee is entitled to 12 unpaid work weeks of leave during any 12-month period for three reasons: because of the birth or placement for adoption or foster care of a child; because of the serious health condition of a spouse, child, or parent; or because of the employee's own serious health condition. Leave may be taken for birth or placement of a child only within 12 months of that birth or placement.
>
> . . . family leave provisions apply equally to male and female employees: "A father, as well as a mother, can take family leave because of the birth or serious health condition of his child; a son as well as a daughter is eligible for leave to care for a parent."

The minimum criteria for eligibility under this act include the following: Eligible workers must be employed by a private employer or by a civilian unit of the federal government. Eligible workers must also have been employed for at least 12 months by a given employer. Finally, eligible workers have provided at least 1,250 hours of service during the 12 months prior to making a request for a leave. Employees who do not meet these criteria are excluded, as are those who work for an employer with fewer than 50 employees within a 75-mile radius of the employee's home. The FMLA does not explicitly define "hours of service." As a result, many disgruntled employees have filed lawsuits against employers' definitions of hours of service.

Employers may require employees to use paid personal, sick, or vacation leave first as part of the 12-week period. If an employee's paid leave falls short of the 12-week mandated period, then the employer must provide further leave—unpaid—to total 12 weeks. While on leave, employees retain all previously earned seniority or employment benefits, though employees do not have the right to add such benefits while on leave. Furthermore, while on leave, employees are entitled to receive health insurance benefits. Finally, employees may be entitled to receive health benefits if they do not return from leave because of a serious health condition or some other factor beyond their control.

The first major revisions to the FMLA were instituted in January 2009. The changes created leave opportunities for military families and required employees to adhere to stricter guidelines for taking leave. Relatives of seriously injured members of the military may take up to 26 weeks off from work to care for their injured military family members. In addition, relatives of members of the National Guard or reserves who are called to active duty may receive up to 12 weeks of leave to attend military programs (official send-off of the family member's troop), arrange child care, or make financial arrangements. Nonmilitary workers who claim to have chronic health conditions (e.g., ongoing back pain) must see their doctor at least twice per year for documentation.

A more recent revision effective March 27, 2015, incorporates a broader definition of spouse. Eligible employees in legal same-sex marriages will be able to take FMLA leave to care for their spouse or family member, regardless of where they live. This will ensure that the FMLA will give spouses in same-sex marriages the same ability as heterosexual spouses to fully exercise their FMLA rights.

One final comment about family and medical leave warrants mention. As discussed, the FMLA provides *unpaid* leave. On September 23, 2002, the California governor signed legislation that allows employees to take partially paid family leave beginning after July 1, 2004. This paid family leave program allows workers to take up to six weeks off to care for a newborn, a newly adopted child, or an ill family member. Under this law, employees are eligible to receive 55 percent of their wages during their absence.

State and Local Paid Leave Laws

Since the passage of the FMLA, several states and local governments have instituted laws which mandate that employers furnish paid family and sick leave. As of July 2018, six states plus the District of Columbia have paid family leave laws: California, Massachusetts, New

Jersey, New York, Rhode Island, and Washington. For instance, the New Jersey Family Leave Act permits up to six weeks of paid leave amounting to two-thirds of wages (subject to a cap). The Rhode Island Temporary Caregiver Insurance Program established four weeks of paid leave to care for a family member and up to 30 weeks of paid leave for a worker's own disability. In recent years, a multitude of local governments have enacted paid family leave benefits. For instance, New York City's law provides up to six weeks of fully paid family leave for nonunion workers employed by the city.

Paid sick leave has become a requirement in some states. State laws governing paid sick leave specify the criteria for what constitutes illness. For example, California law mandates how employees accrue and use paid sick leave benefits. Employers must include a carryover provision for unused sick leave from one calendar year to the next. Some cities have joined in. For example, Seattle requires that employers with 5 to 49 employees provide five paid sick days per year, and additional days for larger employers. In San Francisco, employers with 10 or more employees must provide 9 paid sick days and 5 sick days in companies with fewer than 10 employees.

Health Insurance

Health insurance covers the costs of a variety of services that promote sound physical and mental health, including physical examinations, diagnostic testing, surgery, hospitalization, psychotherapy, dental treatments, and corrective prescription lenses for vision deficiencies. The **Patient Protection and Affordable Care Act of 2010 (PPACA)** is a comprehensive law that mandates health insurance coverage and sets minimum standards for insurance. (We will discuss health insurance design alternatives in the next section of this chapter.) PPACA mandates that companies with at least 50 employees offer affordable health insurance under the law.

Many provisions of the law will have a broad impact on employment-sponsored health insurance plans that do not have grandfathered status. PPACA distinguishes between health plans that existed prior to the March 23, 2010, enactment date and those that come into existence afterward. Individual and group health plans already in existence prior to enactment are referred to as **grandfathered plans**. New health plans (or preexisting plans that have been substantially modified after March 23, 2010) are referred to as **nongrandfathered plans**. Grandfathered plans could lose this status if at least one of the following modifications were made:

- Elimination of all or substantially all benefits to diagnose or treat a condition.
- Increase in a percentage cost-sharing requirement (e.g., raising an individual's coinsurance requirement from 20 percent to 25 percent).
- Increase in a deductible or out-of-pocket maximum by an amount that exceeds medical inflation plus 15 percentage points.
- Increase in a copayment by an amount that exceeds medical inflation plus 15 percentage points (or, if greater, $5 plus medical inflation).
- Decrease in an employer's contribution rate towards the cost of coverage by more than 5 percentage points.
- Imposition of annual limits on the dollar value of all benefits below specified amounts.[13]

Reducing or eliminating coverage for one or more "essential benefits" will cause a grandfathered plan to lose this status. Essential health benefits must include items and services within at least the following 10 categories:

- Ambulatory patient services
- Emergency services
- Hospitalization
- Maternity and newborn care
- Mental health and substance use disorder services, including behavioral health treatment
- Prescription drugs
- Rehabilitative services and devices

- Laboratory services
- Preventive and wellness services and chronic disease management
- Pediatric services, including oral and vision care

Companies that fail to offer health care plans are subject to a penalty. The monthly penalty amount for employees who do not have coverage is approximately $180 and about $280 per month for failing to offer affordable, minimum-value coverage. These penalties are assessed per full-time employee not appropriately covered (excluding the first 30 employees) monthly. The penalty is larger if the company fails to offer affordable, minimum-value coverage. The formula is complex and is subject to modification based on possible legislative rule changes and experience. Oftentimes, a company's decision whether to offer health care plans is called "pay or play." Companies that do not offer health-care plans or ones that follow the minimum standards specified in the PPACA must pay. Those that offer health care plans that meet or exceed minimum standards are said to play.

The PPACA instituted requirements that health plans remove annual dollar limits on most health benefits as well as eliminated preexisting condition clauses altogether. (We review both features later in this chapter.) Also, in 2018, a Cadillac tax provision was scheduled to take effect, but, its implementation has been delayed until 2020. The **Cadillac tax** will apply to high-cost employer-sponsored health plans.

Plans that cost more than $10,200 annually for single coverage and $27,500 for family coverage are subject to the Cadillac tax, and these limits are subject to change from year to year. The tax equals 40 percent of the amount that exceeds those limits. For example, if a plan for single coverage costs $14,000, the employer would pay 40 percent of $3,800 ($14,000 minus $10,200), or $1,520 for each covered individual (excluding the first 30 employees). The tax was intended to be a disincentive for employers to provide overly rich health benefits, and the cost of the health plan is one way to assess the level of benefits. For clarification, **single coverage** extends benefits only to the covered employee. **Family coverage** offers benefits to the covered employee and qualified dependents.

HEALTH INSURANCE PROGRAM DESIGN ALTERNATIVES

Employers usually enter a contractual relationship with one or more insurance companies to provide health-related services for their employees and, if specified, employees' dependents. An **insurance policy** refers to a contractual relationship between the insurance company and the beneficiary. The insurance policy specifies the amount of money the insurance company will pay, for such services as physical examinations. Employers pay insurance companies a negotiated amount, or **premium**, to establish and maintain insurance policies. In this chapter, the term *insured* refers to employees covered by the insurance policy.

10-3. Describe fee-for-service plans, traditional managed-care approaches, and more recent consumer-driven approaches to providing health care coverage.

☛ **FYI**

The average monthly premium for employer-sponsored health insurance varies by economic sector (private vs. public) and coverage (single vs. family):

Private Sector
- Single Coverage: $433.91
- Family Coverage: $1,060.25

Public Sector
- Single Coverage: $536.13
- Family Coverage: $1,131.28[14]

There is a variety of health care plan design alternatives. The U.S. Bureau of Labor Statistics provides four questions to help distinguish among them:

- Is the plan an indemnity or prepaid plan? **Indemnity plans** reimburse the patient or the provider as medical expenses occur or afterward. **Prepaid plans** pay medical service providers a fixed amount based on the number of people regardless of services received.
- Does the plan have a network? A **network** is a specific group, composed of doctors, hospitals, suppliers, and clinics, that has contracted to provide services for an agreed rate.
- Does the plan allow people to receive nonemergency care outside the network? This question identifies how restrictive the plan is regarding choice of medical providers.
- Does the plan have more than two levels of coverage? This question determines if this plan is a point-of-service plan, which generally has several reimbursement levels depending on where enrollees receive services.

We review the alternative plan designs shown in Figure 10-2.

Fee-For-Service Plans

Fee-for-service plans provide protection against health care expenses in the form of a cash benefit paid to the insured or directly to the health care provider after the employee has received health care services. These plans pay benefits on a *reimbursement basis*. Three types of eligible

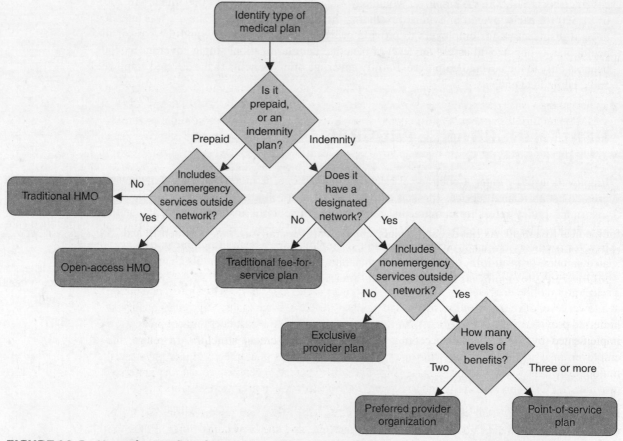

FIGURE 10-2   How the National Compensation Survey Determines the type of Medical Plan Employers Offer

Source: U.S. Bureau of Labor Statistics, "Understanding Health Plan Types: What's In a Name?" *Pay and Benefits* (Volume 4, No. 2), January 2015.

health expenses are hospital expenses, surgical expenses, and physician charges. Under fee-for-service plans, the insured may generally select any licensed physician, surgeon, or medical facility for treatment, and the insurance company reimburses the insured after medical services are rendered. These plans generally do not rely on networks of health care providers.

Managed-care Approach

The **managed-care approach** emphasizes cost control by limiting an employee's choice of doctors and hospitals. Four common managed care plans are *health maintenance organizations* (HMOs), *exclusive provider organizations* (EPOs), *preferred provider organizations* (PPOs), and *point-of-service* (POS) plans.

HEALTH MAINTENANCE ORGANIZATIONS HMOs are sometimes described as providing prepaid medical services, because fixed periodic enrollment fees cover HMO members for all medically necessary services only if the services are delivered by health care providers in the designated network and approved by the HMO. HMOs generally provide inpatient and outpatient care, emergency room care, as well as services from physicians, surgeons, and other health care professionals. Most medical services are either fully covered or, in the case of some HMOs, participants are required to make copayments, which we take up later in the chapter. Another type of HMO is the **open-access HMO**. These are prepaid plans and require the use of network health care providers with one exception. In open-access HMO plans, emergency care outside the network is covered, which is not the case for traditional HMO plans. HMOs generally do not cover expenses incurred in emergency rooms outside the designated network unless deemed by medical experts as a life-or-death matter.

HMOs designate some of their physicians, usually general or family practitioners, as primary care physicians. HMOs assign each member to a primary care physician or require each member to choose one. **Primary care physicians** determine when patients need the care of specialists. HMOs use primary care physicians to control costs by significantly reducing the number of unnecessary visits to specialists. As primary care physicians, doctors perform several duties.

HMOs require that patients make copayments. **Copayments** refer to the nominal payments an individual makes as a condition of receiving services. The most common HMO copayments apply to physician office visits, hospital admissions, prescription drugs, and emergency room services. Office visits are nominal amounts, usually $15 to $50 per visit. Hospital admissions and emergency room services are higher, ranging between $50 and $500 for each occurrence. Mental health services and substance abuse treatment require copayments as well. Inpatient services require copayments that are not higher in amount than copayments for hospital admissions for medical treatment. As flat dollar amounts, copayments generally average between 15 and 25 percent of the service provider (e.g., surgeon) charge for the service (e.g., surgical procedure).

PREFERRED PROVIDER ORGANIZATIONS Under a **preferred provider organization (PPO)**, a select group of health care providers agrees to furnish health care services to a given population at a lower level of reimbursement than is the case for fee-for-service plans. Physicians qualify as preferred providers by meeting quality standards, agreeing to follow cost containment procedures implemented by the PPO, and accepting the PPO's reimbursement structure. In return, the employer, insurance company, or third-party administrator helps guarantee provider physicians' minimum patient loads by furnishing employees with financial incentives to use the preferred providers. PPOs provide lower reimbursements for services outside preferred networks.

EXCLUSIVE PROVIDER ORGANIZATIONS An **exclusive provider organization (EPO)** is a variation of a PPO. EPOs operate similarly to PPOs, but these systems differ. EPOs are more restrictive than PPO plans. EPOs offer reimbursement for services provided within the established network. Exceptions to this rule include medical emergencies or the need for a medical specialty not contained in the provider network. Compared to HMOs, EPOs do not require having a primary care physician.

POINT-OF-SERVICE PLANS A **point-of-service plan (POS)** combines features of fee-for-service plans and HMOs. Employees pay a nominal copayment for each visit to a designated network of physicians. In this regard, POSs are like HMOs; however, employees possess the option to receive care from health care providers outside the designated network of physicians and they pay somewhat more for this choice. This choice feature is common to fee-for-service plans.

Features of Health Care Plans

Health care plans share a few features in common. These include:

- Deductible
- Coinsurance
- Out-of-Pocket Maximum
- Preexisting Condition Clauses
- Lifetime and Yearly Limits

Managed care plans share several features in common with fee-for-service plans, including out-of-pocket maximums, preexisting condition clauses, and lifetime and yearly limits. Again, HMOs differ from fee-for-service plans in three important ways. First, HMOs offer prepaid services, while fee-for-service plans operate on a reimbursement basis. Second, HMOs include the use of primary care physicians as a cost-control measure. Third, coinsurance rates are generally lower in HMO plans than in fee-for-service plans. PPO plans include features that resemble fee-for-service plans or HMO plans. Features most like fee-for-service plans are out-of-pocket maximums and coinsurance, and those most like HMOs include the use of copayments. Preexisting condition clauses, and lifetime and yearly limits are like those in fee-for-service and HMO plans. PPOs contain deductible and coinsurance provisions that differ somewhat from other plans.

DEDUCTIBLE The **deductible** is an amount an insured must pay for services before health insurance benefits become active. Over a designated period, employees must pay for services (i.e., meet a deductible) before insurance benefits become active. The deductible amount can vary widely based on the plan specifics, ranging anywhere from a few hundred dollars to a few thousand dollars. Deductible amounts may also depend on annual earnings, expressed either as a fixed amount for a range of earnings or as a percentage of income.

COINSURANCE Insurance plans feature coinsurance, which becomes relevant after the insured pays the annual deductible. **Coinsurance** refers to the percentage of covered expenses paid by the insured. Most indemnity plans stipulate 20 percent coinsurance. This means that the plan will pay 80 percent of covered expenses, whereas the insured is responsible for the difference, in this case, 20 percent.

OUT-OF-POCKET MAXIMUM As noted earlier, health care costs are on the rise. Despite generous coinsurance rates, the expense amounts for which individuals are responsible can be staggering. These amounts are often beyond the financial means of most individuals. Thus, most plans specify the maximum amount the insured must pay per calendar year or plan year, known as the **out-of-pocket maximum** provision. The purpose of the out-of-pocket maximum provision is to protect individuals from catastrophic medical expenses or expenses associated with recurring episodes of the same illness. Out-of-pocket maximums are usually stated as a fixed dollar amount and apply to expenses beyond the deductible amount. Individuals often have lower annual out-of-pocket maximums than family coverage. For example, the out-of-pocket maximum might be limited to $4,500 for single coverage and $9,000 for family coverage. As an illustration, an insurance plan specifies a $200 deductible. An individual is responsible for the first $200 of expenses plus additional expenses (e.g., coinsurance or copayments) up to $800 per year for a total of $1,000 (i.e., the out-of-pocket maximum).

PREEXISTING CONDITION CLAUSES A **preexisting condition** is a condition for which medical advice, diagnosis, care, or treatment was received or recommended during a designated period preceding the beginning of coverage. Prior to the Patient Protection and Affordable Care Act, insurance plans oftentimes excluded preexisting conditions from coverage. Insurance companies chose to impose preexisting conditions to limit their liabilities for serious medical conditions that predate an individual's coverage. The Patient Protection and Affordable Care Act eliminated preexisting condition clauses altogether, including those once specified in grandfathered plans.

LIFETIME AND YEARLY LIMITS At one time, most health care plans specified lifetime limits and yearly limits. **Lifetime limits** refer to the maximum amount a plan would include if a person receives coverage. **Yearly limits** refer to the maximum amount a plan would cover each year. Neither is permitted under PPACA for either grandfathered or nongrandfathered plans. Until the passage of the PPACA, employers could purchase health plans with lower lifetime and yearly limits at correspondingly lower costs.

Specialized Insurance Benefits

Employers often use separate insurance plans to provide specific kinds of benefits. Benefits professionals sometimes refer to these plans as **carve-out plans**. Carve-out plans are set up to cover dental care, vision care, prescription drugs, mental health and substance abuse, and maternity care. Specialty HMOs or PPOs usually manage carve-out plans based on the expectation that single-specialty practices may control costs more effectively than multispecialty medical practices. We will focus on prescription drug plans and mental health and substance abuse plans because of the rampant inflation in prescription drug costs and the increased recognition that mental health disorders may hinder worker productivity.

PRESCRIPTION DRUG PLANS **Prescription drug plans** cover the costs of drugs. These plans apply exclusively to drugs that state or federal laws require to be dispensed by licensed pharmacists. Prescription drugs dispensed to individuals during hospitalization or treatment in a long-term care facility are not covered by prescription drug plans. Insurance companies specify which prescription drugs are covered, how much they will pay, and the basis for paying for drugs.

Three kinds of prescription drug programs are currently available to companies who choose to provide these benefits to employees. The first, **medical reimbursement plans** reimburses employees for some or all the cost of prescription drugs. These programs are usually associated with self-funded or independent indemnity plans. The second kind of plan, often referred to as a **prescription card program**, operates similarly to managed care programs because it offers prepaid benefits with nominal copayments. The name arose from the common practice of pharmacies requiring the presentation of an identification card. Prescription card programs limit benefits to prescriptions filled at participating pharmacies, like managed care arrangements for medical treatment.

The third type of plan, a **mail order prescription drug program**, dispenses expensive medications used to treat chronic health conditions such as human immunodeficiency virus (HIV) or such neurological disorders as Parkinson disease. Health insurance companies specify whether participants must receive prescription drugs through mail order programs or locally approved pharmacies. Cost is the driving factor for this decision. Mail order programs offer a cost advantage because they purchase medications at discounted prices in large volumes.

MENTAL HEALTH AND SUBSTANCE ABUSE Approximately 20 percent of Americans experience some form of mental illness (e.g., clinical depression) at least once during their lifetimes.[15] Nearly 20 percent develop a substance abuse problem. As a result, insurance plans provide mental health and substance abuse benefits designed to cover treatment of mental illness and chemical dependence on alcohol and legal and illegal drugs. Delivery methods include fee-for-service plans and managed care options. Employee assistance programs (EAPs) represent a portal to taking advantage of employer-sponsored mental health and substance abuse treatment options. EAPs help employees cope with personal problems that may impair their personal lives or job performance, including alcohol or drug abuse, domestic violence, the emotional impact of AIDS and other diseases, clinical depression, and eating disorders.

Mental health and substance abuse plans cover the costs of a variety of treatments, including prescription psychiatric drugs (e.g., antidepressant medication), psychological testing, inpatient hospital care, and outpatient care (e.g., individual or group therapy). Mental health benefits amounts vary by the type of disorder. Psychiatrists and psychologists rely on the *Diagnostic and Statistical Manual of Mental Disorders (DSM-5)* to diagnose mental disorders based on symptoms, and both fee-for-service and managed care plans rely on the *DSM-5* to authorize payment of benefits.

Consumer-Driven Health Care

Managed care plans became popular alternatives to fee-for-service plans mainly to help control the costs of health care. As has been discussed, managed care plans by design impose substantial restrictions on an employee's ability to make choices about from whom they could receive medical treatment, the gatekeeper role of primary care physicians, and the level of benefits they could receive based on designated in- and non-network providers. Despite these cost-control objectives, health care costs have continued to rise dramatically over the years while also restricting employee choice. The average cost to provide employer-sponsored health insurance increased nearly 35 percent between 2008 and 2018.

According to the U.S. Bureau of Labor Statistics, companies further sought ways to control the costs of health insurance. Increasingly, companies are adopting a **consumer-driven health care plan (CDHP)** approach. This approach refers to the objective of helping companies maintain control over costs while also enabling employees to make wise choices about their health care. CDHPs combine a pretax payment account with a high-deductible health plan. **High-deductible health insurance plans (HDHPs)** require substantially higher deductibles compared to managed care plans and traditional fee-for-service plans. What exactly distinguishes an HDHP from traditional health care plans? There are two factors, which appear in the following FYI: deductible and out-of-pocket maximums.

☛ FYI

High-deductible health plans had the following minimum deductible and maximum out-of-pocket limits in 2018:

Single Coverage
- Deductible: $3,400
- Out-of-Pocket: $6,550

Family Coverage
- Deductible: $6,750
- Out-of-Pocket: $13,300[16]

The idea of consumer-driven health care received substantially greater attention than ever before under the Bush administration (President George W. Bush) and the Republican-led Congress, who favored greater employee involvement in their medical care and reductions in the cost burden for companies to help maintain competitiveness in the global market. The **Medicare Prescription Drug, Improvement and Modernization Act of 2003** added section 223 to the IRC, effective January 1, 2004, to permit most companies to establish **health savings accounts (HSAs)** for employees who are enrolled in an HDHP to help pay for medical expenses. It is important to note that HSAs are not available for any other type of health care plan.

The sum of an employer's and employee's contribution to an HSA cannot exceed the high-deductible health plan's annual deductible. Employers may require employees to contribute to these limits. An unused balance at the end of the year carries over to the next year and the employee owns the account and its holdings following termination or retirement from the company. Beginning at age 65, HSA holders may use these funds for retirement income.

Employers may consider using two other health accounts to help defray the costs of medical care: health reimbursement arrangements and flexible spending accounts. Employers establish **health reimbursement arrangements (HRAs)** that reimburse employees for health care expenses. Only the employer is permitted to fund HRAs and there is no allowable maximum contribution limit. As with HSAs, employees can carry over unused balances into subsequent years.

The establishment of flexible spending accounts preceded the era of consumer-driven health care by decades. The IRS established flexible spending accounts in the 1970s as part of flexible benefit plans because employers were increasing the annual deductible amounts and coinsurance rates in response to higher health plan premiums. These increases were proving to be particularly burdensome to employees. **Flexible spending accounts (FSAs)** permit employees to pay for specified health care costs that are not covered by an employer's insurance plan. Prior to each plan year, employees elect the amount of pay they wish to allocate to this kind of plan. Employers then use these moneys to reimburse employees for expenses incurred during the plan year that qualify for repayment.

Qualifying expenses include an individual's out-of-pocket costs for medical treatments, products, or services related to a mental or physical defect or disease, along with certain associated costs, such as health plan deductibles or transportation to get medical care. However, health, life, and long-term care (for example, nursing home or in-home assistance) premiums paid for by an employer or through an employee's pretax salary reductions generally do not qualify for reimbursement under a health FSA. Other exclusions include medical expenses reimbursed through health insurance plans and the costs of purely cosmetic procedures that enhance appearance but are not related to treating a disease or defect. Over-the-counter products are qualified expenses if they are used to diagnose, treat, alleviate, or prevent a disease or ailment, such as blood sugar monitoring kits for diabetic patients or crutches and bandages for someone with a serious leg injury.

A noteworthy drawback of FSAs is the "use it or lose it" provision. FSAs require employees to estimate the amount of money they think they will need for eligible medical expenses in the coming year, but that is often challenging because it is difficult to predict medical needs and to estimate the costs of health care. Employees lose contributions to their FSAs when they overestimate the cost of medical needs, because employees are not permitted to carry balances nor be reimbursed for unused balances remaining at the end of the year.

In summary, we reviewed consumer-driven health care approaches, including high-deductible health plans. We also described savings accounts or arrangements that are often associated with consumer-driven approaches. Table 10-2 summarizes the key features of HSA, HRA, and FSA accounts.

ADDITIONAL HEALTH CARE LEGISLATION

Besides PPACA, a variety of laws influence employer-sponsored health care offerings. We review two of the key laws in chronological order: The Consolidated Omnibus Budget Reconciliation Act of 1985 and the Health Insurance Portability and Accountability Act of 1996.

10-4. Summarize two additional key laws pertaining to legally required benefits.

Consolidated Omnibus Budget Reconciliation Act of 1985 (COBRA)

The **Consolidated Omnibus Budget Reconciliation Act of 1985 (COBRA)** was enacted to provide employees with the opportunity to continue receiving their employer-sponsored medical care insurance temporarily under their employer's plan if their coverage otherwise would cease because of termination, layoff, or other change in employment status. COBRA applies to a wide variety of employers, with exemptions available only for companies that normally employ fewer than 20 workers, church plans, and plans maintained by the U.S. government. COBRA is an amendment to the Employee Retirement Income Security Act of 1974.

Under COBRA, individuals may continue their coverage, as well as coverage for their spouses and dependents, for up to 18 months. Coverage may extend for up to 36 months for spouses and dependents facing a loss of employer-provided coverage because of an employee's death, a divorce or legal separation, or certain other qualifying events, which include employee termination, retirement, and layoff. Table 10-3 displays the maximum continuation period for qualifying events.

Companies are permitted to charge COBRA beneficiaries a premium for continuation coverage of up to 102 percent of the cost of the coverage to the plan. The 2 percent markup reflects a charge for administering COBRA. Employers that violate the COBRA requirements are subject to an excise tax per affected employee for each day that the violation continues. In addition,

TABLE 10-2 Comparison of Various Pretax Savings Accounts and Relationship to High-Deductible Health Plan

Type of account	Pretax employee contribution allowed	Employer contribution allowed	Rollover allowed	May the assets in the fund be used for investing purposes?		Must the account be linked with a HDHP?	
				Yes/ No	If yes, what investments are allowed?	Yes/ No	If yes, what plan limits constitute a Qualified HDHP?
Health savings account (HSA)	Yes	Yes	Yes	Yes	The individual may use the assets in the fund to invest in any individual retirement account.	Yes	Minimum deductible: Self—$3,400 Family—$6,750 Max. annual out-of-pocket amount: Self—$6,550 Family—$13,300 Based on Internal Revenue Service limits for 2017.
Health reimbursement arrangement (HRA)	No	Yes	Yes	No	The funds may only be used for qualified medical expenses.	No	—
Flexible spending account (FSA)	Yes	Yes	No	No	The funds may only be used for qualified medical expenses.	No	—

Adapted from S. G. Yi, "Consumer-Driven Health Care: What Is It, and What Does It Mean for Employees and Employers?" *Compensation and Working Conditions* (online), U.S. Bureau of Labor Statistics, http://www.bls.gov/opub/mlr/cwc/consumer-driven-health-care-what-is-it-and-what-does-it-mean-for-employees-and-employers.pdf, October 25, 2010.

plan administrators who fail to provide required COBRA notices to employees may be personally liable for a civil penalty for each day the notice is not provided.

Health Insurance Portability and Accountability Act of 1996 (HIPAA)

The **Health Insurance Portability and Accountability Act of 1996 (HIPAA)** contains three main provisions. The first provision is intended to guarantee that employees and their dependents that leave their employer's group health plan will have ready access to coverage under a subsequent employer's health plan, regardless of their health or claims experience. The second provision sets limits on the length of time that health plans and health insurance issuers may impose preexisting health conditions and identify conditions to which no preexisting condition may apply. As noted previously, since the passage of the Patient Protection and Affordable Care Act, preexisting condition clauses were eliminated. The third provision protects the transfer, disclosure, and use of health care information.

10-5. Discuss the main benefits and costs of legally required benefits.

THE BENEFITS AND COSTS OF LEGALLY REQUIRED BENEFITS

Employee benefits are unlike most bases for monetary compensation (e.g., merit, pay-for-knowledge, and incentives). Under these programs, the amount of compensation employees receive varies with their level of contributions to the company. Instead, benefits tend to emphasize social adequacy. Under the principle of social adequacy, benefits are designed to provide

TABLE 10-3 COBRA Continuation Requirements

Qualifying Events	Maximum Continuation Period
Employee	
a. Termination of employment for any reason, including termination of disability benefits and layoff (except for gross misconduct)	18 months[a]
b. Loss of eligibility due to reduction in work hours	18 months
c. Determination by the Social Security Administration (SSA) of disability that existed at time of qualifying event	18 months
Dependent	
a. Loss of dependent child status	36 months
b. Employee's death, divorce, or legal separation	36 months
c. Spouse (entitled to Medicare)	36 months

[a] This 18-month period may be extended for all qualified beneficiaries if certain conditions are met in cases where a qualified beneficiary is determined to be disabled for purposes of COBRA.

subsistence income to all beneficiaries regardless of their performance in the workplace.[17] Thus, although humanitarian, legally required benefits do not directly meet the imperatives of competitive strategy. Legally required benefits, however, may contribute indirectly to competitive advantage by enabling individuals to remain participants in the economy.

Nevertheless, legally required benefits may be a hindrance to companies in the short term because these offerings require substantial employer expenditures (e.g., contributions mandated by the Social Security Act and various state workers' compensation laws). Without these mandated expenditures on compensation, companies could choose to invest these funds in direct compensation programs designed to boost productivity and product or service quality.

How can HR managers and other business professionals minimize the cost burden associated with legally required benefits? Let's consider this issue for both workers' compensation and unemployment insurance benefits. In the case of workers' compensation, employers can respond in two ways. The first response is to reduce the likelihood of workers' compensation claims. The implementation of workplace safety programs is one strategy for reducing workers' compensation claims. Effective safety programs include teaching safe work procedures and safety awareness to employees and supervisors. Another strategy for reducing workers' compensation claims is health promotion programs that include inspections of the workplace to identify health risks (e.g., high levels of exposure to toxic substances) and then to eliminate those risks.

The second employer response is to integrate workers' compensation benefits into the rest of the benefits program. Because of the rampant cost increases associated with workers' compensation, several state legislatures have considered integrating employer-sponsored medical insurance and workers' compensation programs. This "24-hour" coverage would specifically roll the medical component of workers' compensation into traditional employer-provided health insurance. Some companies have already experimented with 24-hour coverage. For instance, Polaroid Corporation found cost advantages associated with integrating medical insurance and workers' compensation: reduced administrative expense through integration of the coverages, better access to all employee medical records, and a decrease in litigation.[18]

Use of 24-hour coverage is not widespread for many reasons.[19] Many insurance companies view this approach as complicated. In addition, some companies are concerned that this coverage would cost them in unanticipated ways.

Employers also can contain their costs for unemployment insurance. As discussed earlier, the amount of tax employers contribute to providing unemployment insurance depends partly on their experience rating. Thus, employers can contain costs by systematically monitoring the reasons they terminate workers' employment and avoiding terminations that lead to unemployment insurance claims whenever possible. For example, it is common for companies to employ workers on a full-time basis when they experience increased demand for their products or services. Adding full-time workers is reasonable when companies expect that the higher demand will last for an extended period (e.g., more than two years); however, when demand is lower in the short term, companies usually reduce their workforce through layoffs. Unless the laid-off employees immediately find employment, they will file claims with their local employment security office for unemployment insurance. Their claims contribute to the companies' unemployment experience rating and, thus, their cost expenditures.

PREPARING FOR EXAMS/QUIZZES

Chapter Summary by Learning Objectives

Learning Objective 10-1. *Discuss the origins of legally required benefits.* Legally required benefits provide a form of social insurance. Various benefits arose out of undesirable social, work, and economic conditions as well as former President Barack Obama's call for all Americans to possess health insurance protection.

Learning Objective 10-2. *Summarize the four main categories of legally required benefits.* There are four main categories of legally required benefits: Social Security programs (retirement, survivor and disability insurance, and Medicare under the Social Security Act of 1935), workers' compensation (various state compulsory disability laws), unpaid family and medical leave (Family and Medical Leave Act of 1993), and health insurance (Patient Protection and Affordable Care Act).

Learning Objective 10-3. *Describe fee-for-service plans, traditional managed care approaches, and more recent*

consumer-driven approaches to providing health care coverage. Alternative health insurance design options include fee-for-service plans, various managed care plans, and consumer-driven health care.

Learning Objective 10-4. *Summarize two additional key laws pertaining to legally required benefits.* Additional legislation influences legally required benefit practices, including the Consolidated Omnibus Budget Reconciliation Act of 1985 (COBRA) and the Health Insurance Portability and Accountability Act of 1994 (HIPAA).

Learning Objective 10-5. *Discuss the main benefits and costs of legally required benefits.* Legally required benefits are costly to employers; however, they do provide advantages. Legally required benefits such as health insurance can promote a productive workforce. From a societal perspective, these benefits provide a form of social insurance and contribute to work–life balance.

Key Terms

base period   241
Federal Unemployment Tax Act
    (FUTA)   241
quarters of coverage   241
fully insured   242
Medicare Part A   243
Medicare Part B   244
Medigap   244
Medicare Select plans   244
Medicare Advantage   244
Federal Insurance Contributions Act
    (FICA)   244

Self-Employment Contributions Act
    (SECA)   244
taxable wage base   245
Medicare tax   245
hospital insurance tax (HI)   245
Longshore and Harborworkers'
    Compensation Act   245
Federal Employees' Compensation
    Act   245
Family and Medical Leave Act of 1993
    (FMLA)   246
health insurance   248

Patient Protection and Affordable Care
    Act of 2010 (PPACA)   248
grandfathered plans   248
nongrandfathered plans   248
Cadillac tax   249
single coverage   249
family coverage   249
insurance policy   249
premium   249
indemnity plans   250
prepaid plans   250
network   250

Discussion Questions

10-1. Except for the Patient Protection and Affordable Care Act, the remaining legally required benefits were conceived decades ago. What changes in the business environment and society might affect the relevance or perhaps the viability of any of these benefits? Discuss your ideas.

10-2. Describe the principles of fee-for-service plans and managed care plans. What are the similarities and differences?

10-3. What are some of the choices an employer may make to help control health care costs? Explain.

10-4. In what ways may legally required benefits have contributed to an employee entitlement mentality regarding discretionary benefit offerings? Explain your rationale.

10-5. How do legally required benefits relate to a company's competitive advantage? And, which benefit do you feel is most impactful? Explain.

PREPARING FOR MY CAREER

Compensation in Action

To both employees and employers, legally required benefits can, at first glance, appear to be a burden. These costs mean that less capital will be devoted to investments or available for expenditures in other areas. However, by thoroughly understanding the principles behind the establishment of these laws, they will be viewed as less of a burden and more of a benefit. As HR and line managers, you will have the responsibility of educating employees about the broader array of benefits options, as well as protecting the company from liabilities associated with a failure to comply with certain legally mandated benefits.

Action checklist for line managers and HR—protecting the company and educating employees

HR takes the lead

- Benchmark other companies to see how flexible benefit plans are chosen and administered. This flexibility will empower employees and will likely lead to positive work-related outcomes (e.g., reduced absenteeism and low turnover).
- Involve employees in the discussion as the benefits plan is adjusted to better align the cost of the benefits plan and its attractiveness to employees.

- Make recommendations on wellness programs and other benefits that support and enhance legally required benefits (which could also decrease overall cost for the company; e.g., health care). Assess the cost up front and provide justification for the cost by comparing it to potential future costs.

Line managers take the lead

- Ensure that all employees are properly trained on equipment and that the work environment is safe. This will serve as a preventative measure against certain benefits that have a cost to employee and employer (e.g., workers' compensation).
- Seek education on certain legally required benefits that are likely to be encountered (e.g., FMLA). Become comfortable with talking about these issues; dealing sensitively with these issues when they are brought up by employees may mitigate the risk of employees filing a grievance on how their legally granted right was compromised (akin to "bedside manners" with hospitals).
- Work with HR to create a communication plan that clearly demonstrates the benefits of the plan, describes how to take full advantage of its benefits, and increases awareness and appreciation.

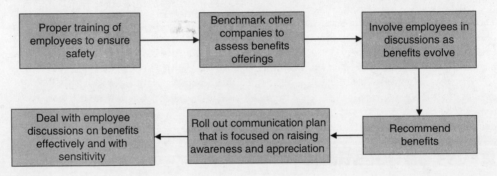

Cases

Case 1: Social Security and Retirement Planning at Taylor Foods

As Gavin Jackson leaves the monthly professional luncheon for human resource executives in his area, he starts to consider how the information he learned will affect his company, Taylor Foods. The program speaker provided an update on the Social Security system and how challenges in financing the system may affect organizations. As the director of human resources at this large food-processing and distribution company, Gavin must plan the retirement benefits for the organization's employees. Gavin had been aware that the Social Security system is in trouble, but now has some clear ideas about how it will affect both the retirement benefits offered by Taylor Foods and the retirement plans of its employees.

Gavin learned that the current Social Security system is unstable and that the future of benefits to be provided is uncertain. The Old-Age, Survivor, and Disability Insurance (OASDI), which provides retirement benefit payments to retired workers, is under a strain. Retirement benefits comprise a majority of the payments made by the Social Security system, and the instability of the system suggests that current workers may not be able to rely on the Social Security system as it exists today to support them in retirement. Gavin knows that this information affects the retirement benefit planning at Taylor Foods.

The speaker also noted that employees retiring in the relatively near future may base their retirement decisions to some extent on the Social Security benefits available to them. While employees may receive their retirement benefits from Social Security starting at age 62, the amount is reduced if they haven't reached the full retirement age, which is determined based on year of birth. For example, the age for full retirement is 67 for anyone born in 1960 or later. Further, the system contains other incentives to encourage individuals to delay retirement. This is important to Taylor Foods, as the age at which employees plan to retire affects the company's human resource planning process. Annually, Gavin creates staffing plans that include estimates for turnover of employees, and employee retirements are included in those estimates. This information, coupled with a current downturn in the economy, leads Gavin to believe that Taylor Foods may experience a lower level of turnover as employees delay retirement.

Gavin is considering both issues as he considers retirement benefits, as well as staffing planning at Taylor Foods. While the company currently offers a competitive retirement plan, he knows that he needs to reexamine the benefits in the context of his new understanding of the Social Security system. He also needs to consider how employees planning to delay retirement will affect the organization and the human resource planning process.

Questions:

10-6. How does the instability of the Social Security system affect retirement benefit planning at Taylor Foods? (*Note*: You may find it helpful to consider the material on retirement plans in Chapter 9.)

10-7. Should Gavin consider the possibility of employees delaying retirement in the company's human resource planning process?

10-8. What do you recommend? Why?

Case 2: Ethics Dilemma: Go with the High-Deductible Health Plan

The employee benefits staff at auto parts manufacturer Simpson Automotive is preparing estimates of the costs of health plans that will be offered soon. Most options will be substantially more expensive because employees and family members received health care. The higher priced options include the fee-for-service plan, the HMO, and the PPO plans. Only the price of the high-deductible plan will remain the same.

The team of employee benefits analysts completed their evaluation in time for meeting with Yufei Wang, director of Human Resources, to discuss pricing. Lead analyst Nolan Hedrick announced that the total insurance costs will be 15 percent higher next year. He went on to explain that the cost estimate assumes that employees will remain in their current plans. Finally, Nolan indicated that 90 percent of employees are enrolled in the costly fee-for-service, HMO, and PPO plans because out-of-pocket costs are much lower than for the high-deductible plan.

Yufei anxiously replied, saying that the employee benefits budget for next year will be cut by 10 percent and, consequently, the higher health insurance costs are unsustainable. Nolan indicated that the best possible prices were negotiated with the insurance companies, but high employee utilization led to higher prices. Yufei pondered the cost concerns and came up with a solution: Encourage employees to switch to the high-deductible plan in exchange for a $1,000 bonus and those who do not will forfeit receiving a bonus and cost-of-living pay increase, the first offered after a five-year pay freeze.

Questions:

10-9. As a compensation professional, what would you do?

10-10. What factor(s) in this ethical dilemma might influence a person to make a less-than-ethical decision?

Crunch the Numbers!

Calculating Federal Insurance Contributions Act (FICA) Taxes

In this chapter, we learned that FICA mandates that employers deduct taxes from employees' pay each pay period to fund the OASDI and Medicare programs. Calculate the tax amounts for the following individuals:

Employee	Annual Salary Paid Monthly	Employer
Ana	$250,000	Self
Roberto	$90,000	Johnson Manufacturing
Maria	$120,000	Johnson Manufacturing
Jim	$50,000	Self

Questions:

10-11. How much do the employer and employee pay *in total* for OASDI each monthly pay period for (a) Ana, (b) Roberto, (c) Maria, and (d) Jim? How much do the employer and employee pay for Medicare each monthly pay period for (a) Ana, (b) Roberto, (c) Maria, and (d) Jim?

10-12. How much does the employer pay in total for OASDI each monthly pay period for (a) Ana, (b) Roberto, (c) Maria, and (d) Jim? (*Remember that for self-employment, the individual and the employer are one and the same.*)

10-13. If the taxable wage base were to increase to $135,000, how much do the employer and employee pay *in total* for OASDI each monthly pay period for (a) Ana, (b) Roberto, (c) Maria, and (d) Jim?

Working Together: Team Exercise

In small groups of three or four, come up with specific answers to the following questions. Talk through your perspectives with team members. Be prepared to share your ideas with the class.

The chapter provides concise summaries of complex legally required benefits. Extend your knowledge about them by conducting some research on one of the benefits you found most interesting.

Questions:

10-14. What are some of the facts and ideas that you learned? Describe them.

10-15. Which fact or idea about the benefit did you find most surprising? Explain.

Endnotes

1. U.S. Bureau of Labor Statistics, *National Compensation Survey: Employee Benefits in the United States*, (Bulletin 2787). (2017), accessed March 15, 2018, at http://www.bls.gov.
2. Foster Rhea Dulles and M. Dubofsky, *Labor in America: A History* (Arlington Heights, IL: Harlan Davidson, 1993).
3. George E. Rejda, *Social Insurance and Economic Security* (Upper Saddle River, NJ: Prentice Hall, 1994).
4. U.S. Chamber of Commerce, *2018 Analysis of Workers' Compensation Laws* (Washington, DC: U.S. Chamber of Commerce, 2018).
5. U.S. Social Security Administration, *Fact Sheet: Social Security Changes* (2018), accessed March 15, 2018, http://www.bls.gov.
6. 26 U.S.C. §§3101–3125.
7. 26 U.S.C. §§1401–1403.
8. Ibid.
9. Jeffrey V. Nackley, *Primer on Workers' Compensation* (Washington, DC: Bureau of National Affairs, 1987).
10. Ibid.
11. U.S. Bureau of Labor Statistics, *Employer Costs for Employee Compensation,* March 2018, (USDL: 18-0944). (2018), accessed July 15, 2018, at http://www.bls.gov.
12. Nackley, *Primer on Workers' Compensation.*
13. U.S. Department of Labor, "FAQs about the Affordable Care Act Implementation: Part II," (2015), accessed July 1, 2015, http://www.dol.gov.
14. U.S. Bureau of Labor Statistics, *National Compensation Survey: Employee Benefits in the United States*, (Bulletin 2787). (2017), accessed March 15, 2018, at http://www.bls.gov.
15. U.S. Surgeon General, *Epidemiology of Mental Illness*, (2011), accessed February 22, 2011, http://www.surgeongeneral.gov/library/mentalhealth/chapter2/sec2_1.html.
16. Internal Revenue Service. Rev. Proc. 2017-37, accessed March 14, 2018, https://www.irs.gov/pub/irs-drop/rp-17-37.pdf.
17. Joseph J. Martocchio, *Employee Benefits: A Primer for Human Resource Professionals* (6th ed.). (Burr Ridge, IL: Irwin/McGraw-Hill, 2018).
18. N. C. Tompkins, "Around-the-clock Medical Coverage." *HR Magazine* (June 1992), 66–72.
19. Laurence C. Baker and Alan B. Krueger, *Twenty-Four-Hour Coverage and Workers' Compensation Insurance*. (1993). Working paper, Princeton University Industrial Relations Section.

CONTEMPORARY STRATEGIC COMPENSATION CHALLENGES

Where We Are Now:

PART IV, EMPLOYEE BENEFITS, explained the most widely used employee benefits practices and approaches to planning the employee benefits program. We have studied the context for compensation, concepts for awarding pay increases, tools for structuring core compensation (base pay and pay increases), and employee benefits, rounding out the principles and practices for building strategic total compensation systems. Now we turn to contemporary strategic compensation challenges. Our focus will be on two important strategic employee groups: executives and the flexible workforce. Many principles and practices for compensating these two employee groups differ from what we applied to the clear majority of employee groups.

In **PART V, WE WILL COVER**

CHAPTER 11 COMPENSATING EXECUTIVES

CHAPTER 12 COMPENSATING THE FLEXIBLE WORKFORCE

11

Compensating Executives

Executive compensation practices in U.S. companies have received substantial attention in the press. Questions about whether executives' compensation packages are tied to company performance is among the major issues. As we will see, executive pay practices have raised concerns that many executives receive lucrative compensation and benefits even when company performance falls below shareholder expectations. Many critics have questioned whether such practices may interfere with some executives' motivation to achieve excellent performance. Other concerns have been voiced by labor unions, which focus on social injustice given the substantial gap in pay between executive and nonexecutive employees, particularly when executive-level management chooses to limit labor through extensive reductions-in-force of nonexecutive employees.

CONTRASTING EXECUTIVE PAY WITH PAY FOR NONEXECUTIVE EMPLOYEES

11-1. Explain the difference between executive pay and pay for nonexecutives.

From an economic standpoint, the chief executive officer (CEO) is the seller of his or her services, and the compensation committee is the buyer of these services. Under classic economic theory, a reasonable price is obtained through negotiations that are at arm's length between an informed seller and an informed buyer. An awkward situation can result when the CEO hires a professional compensation director or compensation consultant. In this case, the compensation consultant who makes the recommendation to the compensation committee works for the CEO. In theory, the CEO hires the consultant to perform an objective analysis of the company's executive pay package and to make whatever recommendations the consultant feels are appropriate. This relationship has the potential to promote a conflict of interest because of the perceived pressure for the consultant to protect the CEO's financial interests. The irony is that the consultant is often viewed as representing the shareholders' interests. In a sense, the buyers of the CEO's services are the shareholders and their representatives, the compensation committee of the board of directors. They tend to act upon the compensation consultant's recommendation.[1]

It is possible that applying such practices to executives contradicts the main assumptions of performance-based pay, as discussed in Chapters 3 and 4. *Successful performance* triggers merit and incentive awards and the *degree of success* determines the amount of award. After all, pay-for-performance applies to most nonexecutive employees in U.S. companies. In some instances, executives are rewarded even after they have not performed well, with multimillion dollar awards contingent on their leaving the company. It is not surprising that those instances are often referred to as *pay-for-nonperformance* or, more harshly, *pay-for-failure*, and have become increasingly more common events in the world of executive compensation.[2]

DEFINING EXECUTIVE STATUS

It is important to define executive status because it is not an arbitrary designation. In fact, the Internal Revenue Code (IRC), which is the tax code of the United States, provides criteria to guide us in the definition of executives as these are key employees and highly compensated employees.

11-2. Define executive status.

Who Are Executives?

Virtually all the components of executive compensation plans provide favorable tax treatment for both the executive and the company. Who are executives? From a tax regulation perspective, the IRC recognizes two groups of employees who play a major role in a company's policy decisions: key employees and highly compensated employees. The IRC uses "key employees" to determine the necessity of top-heavy provisions in employer-sponsored qualified retirement plans that cover most nonexecutive employees. As an aside, a plan is said to be top-heavy if the accrued benefits or account balances for key employees exceed 60 percent of the accrued benefits or account balances for all employees. For clarity, an accrued benefit is the amount that a participant has earned under the plan's terms at a specified time.

The IRC uses "highly compensated employees" for nondiscrimination rules in employer-sponsored health insurance benefits. Although these two designations were created for federal tax rule applications, employees in both groups typically participate in executive compensation and benefits plans.

Key employees and highly compensated employees hold positions of substantial responsibility. Figure 11-1 illustrates the placement of key employees in a typical organizational structure. Although titles vary from company to company and in pay structures, CEOs, presidents, executive vice presidents, vice presidents of functional areas (e.g., human resources), and the directors below them usually meet the criteria for key employees.

Key Employees

The term **key employee** means any employee who at any time during the year is:[3]

- An officer having annual pay of more than $175,000, *OR*
- an individual who for 2018 was either of the following:

   a. A 5 percent owner of the employer's business.
   b. A 1 percent owner of the employer's business whose annual pay was more than $150,000.

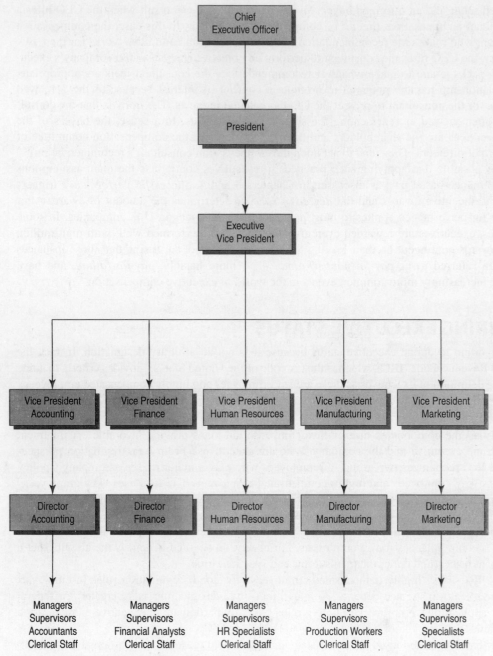

FIGURE 11-1 Examples of Key Employees

U.S. Treasury Regulations define the term *officer* used in this definition of key employees:[4]

Generally, the term officer means an administrative executive who is in regular and continued service. The term officer implies continuity of service and excludes those employed for a special and single transaction. An employee who merely has the title of an officer but not the authority of an officer is not considered an officer for purposes of the key employee test. Similarly, an employee who does not have the title of an officer but has the authority of an officer is an officer for purposes of the key employee test.

Highly Compensated Employees

The IRC defines a **highly compensated employee** as one of the following:[5]

- A 5 percent owner at any time during the year or the preceding year, *OR* for the preceding year,
- the employee had compensation from the employer in excess of $120,000 in 2018, *AND*
- if the employer so chooses, the employee was in the top-paid group of employees where top-paid employees are the top 20 percent most highly compensated employees.

We have pointed out the complexity of defining executive status. It is worth stepping aside for a moment to consider the real-world challenges of executives. In the Watch It! video, you will hear about the challenges that Microsoft's CEO Satya Nadella is facing in changing its direction in software applications to become more competitive with other companies.

EXECUTIVE COMPENSATION PACKAGES

Executive compensation has both core and employee benefits elements, much like compensation packages for other employees; however, one noteworthy feature distinguishes executive compensation packages from nonexecutive compensation packages. Executive compensation packages emphasize long-term or deferred rewards over short-term rewards. The main components of executive compensation include (we describe the components here and defer examples to later in this chapter):

11-3. List the components of executive compensation packages.

- Current or annual core compensation
- Deferred core compensation: equity agreements
- Deferred core compensation: separation agreements
- Clawback provisions
- Employee benefits: enhanced protection program benefits and perquisites

---

☛ FYI

There have been changes in CEO compensation pay mix (2010 and 2016, respectively):

- Stock Awards: 32.0% and 47.4%
- Stock Options: 17.7% and 14.0%
- Base Salary: 14.2% and 11.3%[6]

Components of Current Core Compensation

Executive current core compensation packages contain two components: annual base pay and bonuses.

BASE PAY Base pay is the fixed element of annual cash compensation. Companies that use formal salary structures may have specific pay grades and pay ranges (Chapter 8) for nonexempt employees and exempt employees, including supervisory, management, professional, and executive jobs, except for the CEO.

Chief executive officer jobs do not fall within formal pay structures for two reasons. First, the work done by CEOs is highly complex and unpredictable. It is not possible to specify discrete responsibilities and duties. The choice of competitive strategy by CEOs and other executives and the influence of external and internal market factors make it impossible to describe a CEO's job. Second, setting CEO compensation differs dramatically from the rational processes compensation professionals use to build market-competitive pay structures (Chapter 7). We will discuss agency theory, tournament theory, and social comparison theory later as explanations for setting CEO compensation.

In most cases, annual base pay represents a relatively small part of a CEO's total compensation for two reasons. First, it typically takes years before the fruits of a CEO's strategic initiatives are realized. Second, the IRS limits the amount of annual salary a company may exclude as a business expense. Only the first $1 million annually for an executive's pay may be excluded from the company's income tax liability if the pay is not deemed to be pay-for-performance.[7] Base pay would fall under this rule. This ruling was put into place to keep companies from boosting CEO annual pay to astronomical levels for the purposes of tax savings.

BONUSES Bonuses represent single pay-for-performance payments companies use to reward employees for achievement of specific, exceptional goals. As discussed in previous chapters, compensation professionals design bonuses for merit pay programs (Chapter 3), gain-sharing plans and referral plans (Chapter 4), and sales incentive compensation programs (Chapter 8). Bonuses also represent a key component of executive compensation packages.

Companies' compensation committees recommend bonus awards to boards of directors for their approval (as we will discuss later in this chapter). Four types of bonuses are common in executive compensation:

- Discretionary
- Performance-contingent
- Predetermined allocation
- Target plan

As the term implies, boards of directors award **discretionary bonuses** to executives on an elective basis. They weigh four factors in determining the amount of a discretionary bonus: company profits, the financial condition of the company, business conditions, and prospects for the future. For example, boards of directors may award discretionary bonuses to executives when a company's position in the market is strong.

Executives receive **performance-contingent bonuses** based on the attainment of specific performance criteria. The performance appraisal system for determining bonus awards is often the same appraisal system used for determining merit increases or general performance reviews for salary (Chapter 3).

Unlike the previous executive bonuses, the total bonus pool for the **predetermined allocation bonuses** is based on a fixed formula. The central factor in determining the size of the total bonus pool and bonus amounts is company profits.

The **target plan bonuses** ties bonuses to executives' performance. The bonus amount increases commensurately with performance. Executives do not receive bonuses when their performance falls below minimally acceptable standards. The target plan bonus differs from the predetermined allocation bonus in an important way: Predetermined allocation bonus amounts are fixed, regardless of how well executives perform.

SHORT-TERM INCENTIVES Companies award short-term incentive compensation to executives to recognize their progress toward fulfilling competitive strategy goals. Executives may participate in current profit sharing plans and gain sharing plans. Whereas short-term objectives reward nonexempt and lower-level management employees for achieving major milestone work objectives, short-term incentives applied to executives are designed to reward them for meeting intermediate performance criteria. The performance criteria relate to the performance of a company as dictated by competitive strategy. Change in the company's earnings per share over a 1-year period, growth in profits, and annual cost savings are criteria that may be used in executives' short-term incentive plans.

Short-term incentive compensation programs usually apply to a group of select executives within a company. The plan applies to more than one executive because the synergy that results from the efforts and expertise of top executives influences corporate performance. The board of directors distributes short-term incentive awards to each executive based on rank and compensation levels. Thus, the CEO will receive a larger performance award than will the executive vice president, whose position is lower in the company's structure than the CEO's position.

For example, let's assume that the CEO and executive vice president of a chain of general merchandise retail stores have agreed to lead the corporation as the lowest-cost chain of stores in the general merchandise retail industry. The CEO and executive vice president establish a five-year plan to meet this lowest-cost competitive strategy. The vice president of compensation recommends that the company adopt a gain sharing program to reward top executives for contributing to the cost reduction objective. After one year, the complementary decisions made by the CEO and executive vice president have enabled the corporation to save $10,000,000. The board of directors agrees that the executives' collaborative decisions led to noteworthy progress toward meeting the lowest-cost strategy and award the CEO 2 percent of the annual cost savings ($200,000) and the executive vice president 1 percent ($100,000).

Components of Deferred Core Compensation

Deferred compensation refers to an agreement between an employee and a company to render payments to an executive at a future date. Deferred compensation is a hallmark of executive compensation packages. As an incentive, deferred compensation is supposed to create a sense of ownership, aligning the interests of the executive with those of the owners or shareholders of the company over the long term. The rationale for creating an ownership stake for the executive is explained by agency theory, which we will discuss later in this chapter. Broadly speaking, there are two general types of deferred compensation plans. The first, **equity plans**, provides an executive with ownership stakes in the company through a variety of mechanisms, including various stock option plans and stock purchase plans. The second, **separation agreements**, guarantees that an executive will receive a lucrative compensation package upon employment termination.

The prevalent way in which companies create ownership interests, also known as equity interests, is by making the executive an owner of the company. Company stock ownership or stock options create an equity interest in the company.

Equity Agreements

Company stock and stock options provide the foundation for equity agreements. **Company stock** represents the total equity of the firm. **Company stock shares** represent equity segments of equal value. Equity interest increases positively with the number of stock shares. Stocks are bought and sold every business day in a public stock exchange. The New York Stock Exchange is among the best-known of the stock exchanges. Table 11-1 lists basic terminology pertaining to stocks.

Companies design executive stock compensation plans to promote an executive's sense of ownership of the company. A sense of ownership should presumably motivate executives to strive for excellent performance. Stock value generally increases with gains in company performance. A company's stock value rises in response to reports of profit gains; however, factors outside executives' control often influence stock prices despite executives' performance. For example, forecasts of economy-wide recession, increases in the national unemployment rate, and threats to national security or political instability are often associated with declines in stock value.

Five forms of deferred (stock) compensation include:

- Stock options
- Restricted stock and restricted stock units
- Stock appreciation rights
- Phantom stock plans
- Employee stock purchase plans

STOCK OPTIONS Broadly, there are two types of stock options—incentive stock options and nonstatutory stock options. **Incentive stock options** entitle executives to purchase their companies' stock in the future at a predetermined price. The predetermined price usually equals the stock price at the time an executive is granted the stock option. In effect, executives are

TABLE 11-1 Employee Stock Terminology

Stock option. A right granted by a company to an employee to purchase a number of stocks at a designated price within a specified period of time.

Stock grant. A company's offering of stock to an employee.

Exercise of stock grant. An employee's purchase of stock, using stock options.

Disposition. Sale of stock by the stockholder.

Fair market value. The average value between the highest and lowest reported sales price of a stock on the New York Stock Exchange on any given date. The Internal Revenue Service specifies whether an option has a readily ascertainable fair market value at grant. An option has a readily ascertainable fair market value if the option is actively traded on an established stock exchange at the time it is granted.

purchasing the stocks at a discounted price. Executives generally exercise their option to purchase the stock after the price has increased dramatically. An executive receives **capital gains** as the difference between the stock price at the time of purchase and the lower stock price at the time an executive receives the stock option. Executives receive income tax benefits by participating in incentive stock option plans. They are not required to pay tax on the capital gains until they sell their stock shares. The tax rate for such transactions is called the capital gains rate. It is typically substantially lower than the executive's ordinary income tax rate, further adding incentive value to incentive stock options. If the stock price at the time of disposition was lower than at the time of the stock option grant, the executive would experience a **capital loss**.

Much like incentive stock options, companies award stock options to executives at discounted prices. In contrast to incentive stock options, **nonstatutory stock options** do not qualify for favorable tax treatment. Executives pay income taxes on the difference between the discounted price and the stock's fair market value at the time of the stock grant, not at the time of disposition, and they do so at their ordinary income tax rate. They do not pay taxes in the future when they choose to exercise their nonstatutory stock options.

Nonstatutory stock options do provide executives an advantage. Executives' tax liability is ultimately lower over the long term: Stock prices generally increase over time. As a result, the capital gains will probably be much greater in the future when executives exercise their options rather than when their companies grant these options.

RESTRICTED STOCK PLANS, RESTRICTED STOCK UNITS, AND PERFORMANCE STOCK AWARDS Under **restricted stock plans**, a company may grant executives stock options at market value or discounted value, or they may provide stock. Under restricted stock plans, executives do not have any ownership control over the disposition of the stock for a predetermined period, often many years. This predetermined period is known as the vesting period, much like vesting rights associated with employer-sponsored retirement plans (Chapter 9). Alternatively, companies may provide executives with restricted stock units. **Restricted stock units** are shares of company stock that are awarded to executives at the end of the restriction period.

Similar to restricted stock plans and restricted stock units in terms of the vesting period, a company may choose to add to the vesting period a performance criterion for determining whether to award stock options or stock units. This type of equity agreement is referred to as a **performance plan**. A company's board of directors determines the performance criteria. For example, a company's earnings per stock share is often used. Coca-Cola Company recently modified its executive-level and top-management equity agreements to follow performance plan standards. These leaders will receive fewer stock shares, but additional performance share units. One of the main reasons for this change is shareholders' dissatisfaction with the company's weak performance in the U.S. market.[8]

STOCK APPRECIATION RIGHTS **Stock appreciation rights** provide executives income at the end of a designated period, much like restricted stock options; however, executives never have to exercise their stock rights to receive income. The company simply awards a bonus payment to executives based on the difference in stock price between the time the company granted the stock rights at fair market value to the end of the designated period, permitting the executives to keep the stock. Executives pay tax on any income from gains in stock value occurring between the time the stock is granted to the CEO and when they exercise their stock rights,[9] presumably after retirement when their tax rates are lower.

PHANTOM STOCK PLANS A **phantom stock** plan is a compensation arrangement whereby boards of directors promise to pay a bonus in the form of the equivalent of either the value of company shares or the increase in that value over a period. Phantom stock plans are similar to restricted stock plans because executives must meet specific conditions before they can convert these phantom shares into real shares of company stock.[10] There are generally two conditions. First, executives must remain employed for a specified period, usually several years. Second, executives must retire from the company. Upon meeting these conditions, executives receive income equal to the increase in the value of company stock from the date the company granted the phantom stock to the conversion date. Phantom stock plans provide executives with tax advantages. Executives pay taxes on the capital gains after they convert their phantom shares to real shares of company stock during retirement.

EMPLOYEE STOCK PURCHASE PLANS A company may choose to offer a formal employee stock purchase plan that allows participating employees to purchase stock after a designated period. In anticipation of making a stock purchase, employees set aside money through payroll deduction for this specific purpose during the offering period, which is the point in time when they may purchase the employer's stock based on the money set aside in their accounts. The span of time over which employees are permitted to contribute to their accounts is referred to as the **offering period**. Companies have the option of setting up employee stock purchase plans as qualified or nonqualified. To qualify for favorable tax treatment, companies' plans must meet several criteria. For example, all full-time employees with two or more years of service must be allowed to participate.

Separation Agreements

GOLDEN PARACHUTES Most executives' employment agreements contain a golden parachute clause. **Golden parachutes** provide pay and benefits to executives after a termination that results from a change in ownership or corporate takeover, that is, the merger or combining of two separate companies.[11] Approximately 80 percent of Standard & Poor's 500 companies offer golden parachute packages to CEOs who are replaced due to corporate takeover.[12] For example, Yahoo Inc. was taken over by Verizon Communications Inc. in 2017. Yahoo CEO Marissa Mayer's golden parachute payout totaled $187 million. The various components included stock options ($85 million), Yahoo stock shares ($77 million), and restricted stock units ($25 million).[13] Boards of directors often include golden parachute clauses for at least three reasons. First, golden parachutes limit executives' risks in the event of these unforeseen events. Second, golden parachutes promote recruitment and retention of talented executives. Third, if a takeover bid would benefit the company, it is possible that a CEO would work against it to save his or her job.

Companies benefit from golden parachute payments because they can treat these payments as business expenses. This means that companies can reduce their tax liability by increasing the parachute amount. The total value of golden parachutes came to exceed executives' annual income levels by far. Public outcry led to government-imposed intervention that limited tax benefits to companies. Companies may generally receive tax deductions on golden parachutes.

PLATINUM PARACHUTES In an ideal world, CEOs will perform on an exemplary basis, making decisions to drive up company profits. As you know, we do not live in a perfect world, sometimes, CEOs do not perform their jobs well and companies lose out on profit opportunities. After a period of unsatisfactory performance as determined by shareholders and other company executives, CEOs may be terminated even before the expiration of their employment contracts. Many companies reach agreements with CEOs to terminate employment, awarding a platinum parachute as an incentive. **Platinum parachutes** are lucrative awards that compensate departing executives with severance pay, continuation of company benefits, and even stock options. Companies typically use platinum parachutes to avoid long legal battles or critical reports in the press, essentially by paying off a CEO to give up his or her post. For example, FOX News Chairman Roger Ailes reportedly received a platinum parachute package worth $40 million after being forced out of his job following sexual harassment claims. Apart from this example, it is important to reiterate that golden parachutes became common when hostile corporate takeovers were occurring in large numbers during the 1980s and 1990s. As such activity slowed down, many companies continued to offer golden parachutes, but extended the use for a CEO's termination for other reasons, such as poor performance. For this purpose, it is common to see the terms golden parachute and platinum parachute used interchangeably.

Clawback Provisions

Clawback provisions in CEO employment contracts allow boards of directors to take back performance-based compensation if they were to subsequently learn that performance goals were not actually achieved, regardless of whether the CEO was responsible for performance falling short of target levels. Increasingly, these provisions are becoming more common because of the increasing scrutiny of CEO compensation packages by the public and shareholders, particularly since the global financial crisis in the late 2000s. For example, Wells Fargo clawed back $75 million from two executives after the company's scandal over fraudulent bank accounts came to light.[14] Government agencies may also follow suit. For instance, Department of Veterans Affairs (VA) Eric Shinseki rescinded a monetary bonus from Sharon Helman, Director of the Phoenix VA system.[15] Shinseki acted on allegations of falsified data on delays in doctor appointments, and the death of some veterans which occurred while awaiting care.

 FYI

In a survey of 2,500 large companies, the percentage of CEOs who are terminated has risen:

- 2007 – 2011: 3.9%
- 2012 – 2016: 5.3%[16]

Employee Benefits: Enhanced Protection Program Benefits and Perquisites

Executives receive discretionary benefits like other employees; however, executives' discretionary benefits differ in two ways. First, protection programs include supplemental coverage that provides enhanced benefit levels. Second, the services component contains benefits exclusively for executives. These exclusive executive benefits are known as **perquisites** or **perks**.

ENHANCED PROTECTION PROGRAM BENEFITS Supplemental life insurance and supplemental executive retirement plans distinguish protection programs for executive employees from protection programs for other employees. As discussed in Chapter 9, employer-provided life insurance protects employees' families by paying a specified amount to an employee's beneficiaries upon an employee's death. Most policies pay some multiple of the employee's salary (e.g., benefits paid at twice the employee's annual salary). In addition to regular life insurance, executives receive **supplemental life insurance** protection that pays an additional monetary benefit. Companies design executives' supplemental life insurance protection to meet two objectives.[17] First, supplemental life insurance increases the benefit to designated beneficiaries upon the executives' deaths. Life insurance programs may be designed to provide greater benefits than standard plans usually allow. Second, these programs provide executives with favorable tax treatments.

Supplemental retirement plans are designed to restore benefits restricted under qualified plans. In Chapter 9, we discussed some of the characteristics of qualified plans. A qualified plan generally entitles employees to favorable tax treatment of the benefits they receive upon their retirement. Any investment income that is generated in the pension program is not taxed until the employee retires.

The IRS limited the annual earnings amount for determining qualified plan benefits to $275,000 in 2018 (indexed for inflation, in increments of $5,000). In general, any annual earnings greater than this level cannot be included in defined benefit plan formulas or the calculation of annual additions to defined contribution plans. In addition, the IRS limits the annual benefit amounts for defined benefit plans to the lesser of $220,000 in 2018, indexed for inflation, or 100 percent of the highest average compensation for three consecutive years.[18] For example, an executive's three highest annual salaries are $690,000, $775,000, and $1,100,000. The average of these three highest salaries is $855,000. Of course, $220,000 is less than $855,000; therefore, an executive's retirement income based on the company's qualified pension plan cannot exceed $220,000 adjusted for inflation.

A supplemental retirement plan can make up this difference. For illustrative purposes, let's assume that the annual benefit under a qualified pension plan is 60 percent of the final average salary for the past 15 years of service, which is $400,000. Based on this formula, the executive should receive an annual retirement benefit of $240,000 ($400,000 × 60 percent). This annual benefit exceeds $220,000 (the statutory limit for qualified retirement plans). Because of the statutory limit, companies may offer a supplemental executive retirement plan that provides the difference between the value derived from the pension formula ($240,000) and the statutory limit ($220,000). In this example, the executive would receive a supplemental annual retirement benefit of $20,000.

PERQUISITES Executive perquisites are an integral part of executive compensation. Perquisites cover a broad range of benefits, from free lunches to the free use of corporate jets. Table 11-2 lists common executive perks. Perquisites serve at least four purposes. First, these benefits recognize executives' attained status. Membership in an exclusive country club reinforces executives' social status. Second, executives use perks for personal comfort or as a business tool. For example, a company may own a well-appointed cabin in Vail, Colorado. Executives may use the cabin for rest and relaxation or as a place to court new clients or close a lucrative business deal. Arranging relaxing weekends in Vail benefits executives and their families and provides executives opportunities to develop rapport with prospective clients. Third, the use of corporate aircraft may be considered a security measure for executives who are public figures.[19] The CEOs from many Fortune 100 companies have this perk.[20] Promoting security goes beyond the use of corporate jets. Twenty of the Fortune 100 CEOs received security benefits exceeding $100,000.[21] The cost ranged from as low as $284 for Phillips 66 CEO to more than $1.5 million for Amazon.com's and Oracle's CEOs.[22] Fourth, particular perks, such as having a chauffeur or tax and financial planning services, permit executives to have fewer distractions, providing for more opportunities to attend to work matters.

Despite the rationale for providing lucrative perks, many companies have begun scaling back offerings. For example, John Flannery, CEO of General Electric, instituted several cost-cutting measures shortly after assuming this leadership role. Flannery eliminated the company car program for top executives, grounded the fleet of six corporate jets, and canceled an annual three-day, invitation-only retreat for executives. Established as an internal networking event for GE executives, many of the activities were focused on leisure such as golfing and fishing.[23]

It is possible that companies will provide cash in lieu of perquisites because of stricter reporting requirements by the Securities and Exchange Commission. Particularly after the corporate scandals at Enron and other corporations, company shareholders expect management to display greater accountability for the nonbusiness use of such company property as corporate jets. Since 2008, companies have had to report perks valued at $10,000 or more apiece.

A survey of executive compensation practices in Fortune 500 companies revealed that a significant number of companies, about 85 percent, offer executive perks. But this is fewer than in the past.[24] Between 2008 and 2013, the percentage of companies offering three or more executive

---

TABLE 11-2 Common Executive Perks

- Company cars
- Supplemental life insurance
- Legal services (e.g., income tax preparation)
- Recreational facilities (e.g., country club and athletic club memberships)
- Security detail (protection)
- Travel perks (e.g., use of corporate jet)

perks dropped from 60 percent to 33 percent. In the same time frame, the number of companies that eliminated executive perks altogether jumped from 6 percent to 15 percent. The prevalence of fewer perks offerings may be due to greater economic uncertainties and the recent requirement that companies report perks valued at $10,000 or more apiece. Greater shareholder scrutiny is also a contributing factor, as more emphasis is placed on performance-based rewards.

PRINCIPLES AND PROCESSES FOR SETTING EXECUTIVE COMPENSATION

11-4. Discuss the principles and processes of setting executive compensation.

We discussed the processes compensation professionals use to reward performance (e.g., merit pay and alternative incentive pay methods) and acquisition of job-related knowledge and skills (e.g., pay-for-knowledge and skilled-based pay) in previous chapters. Although pay-for-performance is the public rationale for setting executive compensation, reality is often quite different. Three alternative theories explain the principles and processes for setting executive compensation: agency theory, tournament theory, and social comparison theory. We will begin by discussing the key players in setting executive compensation.

The Key Players in Setting Executive Compensation

Different individuals and groups participate in setting executive compensation. They include compensation consultants, compensation committees, and boards of directors. Each plays a different role in setting executive compensation.

EXECUTIVE COMPENSATION CONSULTANTS Executive compensation consultants usually propose several recommendations for alternate pay packages. Executive compensation consultants are often employed by large consulting firms that specialize in executive compensation or advise company management on a wide variety of business issues. The regulations involving executive compensation plans are extremely complex. To understand them fully requires expertise often found in leading executive compensation and benefits consulting firms. Some of the leading and most well-respected firms in this area include the following:

- Frederic W. Cook & Company (www.fwcook.com)
- Pearl Meyer & Partners (www.pearlmeyer.com)
- William M. Mercer (www.mercer.com)
- Willis Towers Watson (www.willistowerswatson.com)

Consultants make recommendations about what and how much to include in executive compensation packages based on strategic analyses, which entail an examination of a company's external market context and internal factors. Examples of external market factors include industry profile, information about competitors, and long-term growth prospects. Financial condition is the most pertinent internal factor regarding executive compensation. Strategic analyses permit compensation consultants to see where their client company stands in the market based on external and internal factors. Strong companies should be able to devote more financial resources to fund lucrative executive compensation programs than weaker companies. Often, executive compensation consultants find themselves in conflict-of-interest situations:

> Ostensibly, compensation consultants were hired by the CEO to perform an objective analysis of the company's executive pay package and to make whatever recommendations the consultant felt were appropriate. In reality, if those recommendations did not cause the CEO to earn more money than he was earning before the compensation consultant appeared on the scene, the latter was rapidly shown the door.[25]

Executive compensation consultants' professional survival may depend on recommending lucrative compensation packages. Recommending the most lucrative compensation packages will quickly promote a favorable impression of the consultant among CEOs, leading to future consulting engagements.

Since 2008, the Securities and Exchange Commission rulings require companies to include the identity of the consulting firm in public disclosure statements. This ruling has created concerns about possible conflicts of interest for consulting firms that also provide consulting services in other areas (e.g., performance management and change management) for the same client firms. Executive compensation consulting represents just one of many possible areas of management consulting. The conflict potentially arises when a consultant intentionally recommends a more-lucrative-than-warranted executive compensation package in the hope of gaining management favor and additional other management consulting opportunities. Of course, compensation consulting firms are concerned about the public image of possible conflicts of interest and have considered a variety of practices to ensure the integrity of their recommendations to client firms. For example, there has been some speculation that executive consulting practices will be spun off into independent businesses. Many companies are concerned about their own public image and have instituted policies to prevent compensation consultants from conducting other work for management.

BOARD OF DIRECTORS A **board of directors** represents shareholders' interests by weighing the pros and cons of top executives' decisions. Boards of directors have approximately 15 members. These members include CEOs and top executives of other successful companies, distinguished community leaders, well-regarded professionals (e.g., physicians and attorneys), and possibly a few top-level executives of the company.

Boards of directors give final approval of the compensation committee's recommendation. Some critics of executive compensation have argued that CEOs use compensation to co-opt board independence.[26] CEOs often nominate candidates for board membership, and their nominations usually lead to candidates' placement on the board. Board members receive compensation for their service to the boards. It's common for a board member to earn more than $50,000 per year plus a fee ($10,000 or more) for each board meeting attended. Along with monetary and stock compensation, companies are using such benefits as medical insurance, life insurance, and retirement programs to attract top-notch individuals to join boards of directors. In general, board members' failure to cooperate with CEOs may lead either to fewer benefits or their removal.

The board determines the pay of the CEO. But who determines the pay of the outside directors? Here, a sort of formal Japanese Kabuki has developed. The board of directors determines the pay of the CEO, and for all practical purposes, the CEO determines the pay of the board of directors. Is it any accident, then, that there is a statistical relationship between how highly the CEO is paid and how highly his outside directors are paid?[27]

As we will discuss shortly, recent changes in Securities and Exchange Commission rulings and the passage of the Dodd-Frank Act have increased the transparency of how executives are compensated, as well as board members' accountability for approving sound executive compensation packages—supportive of shareholders' best interests.

COMPENSATION COMMITTEE Board of directors members within and outside the company make up a company's **compensation committee**. Outside board members serve on compensation committees to minimize conflict of interest. Thus, outside directors usually are the committee's membership majority.

Compensation committees perform three duties. First, compensation committees review consultants' alternate recommendations for compensation packages. Second, compensation committee members discuss the assets and liabilities of the recommendations. The complex tax laws require compensation committees to consult compensation experts, legal counsel, and tax advisors. Third, based on these deliberations, the committee recommends the consultant's best proposal to the board of directors for its consideration.

Theoretical Explanations for Setting Executive Compensation

Three prominent theories describe the processes related to setting executive compensation: agency theory, tournament theory, and social comparison theory. The following discussion provides concrete interpretations of these theories. In addition to the works cited throughout this chapter, several excellent scholarly journal articles provide full explanations of these theoretical frames as applied to executive compensation.[28]

AGENCY THEORY Ownership is distributed among many thousands of shareholders in such large companies as Microsoft, General Electric, General Motors, and IBM. For example, owning at least one share of stock in IBM bestows ownership rights in IBM. Each shareholder's ownership is quite small, amounting to far less than 1 percent. Inability to communicate frequently or face to face to address business concerns is a major disadvantage of thousands of shareholders.

Under **agency theory**, shareholders delegate control to top executives to represent their ownership interests; however, top executives usually do not own majority shares of their companies' stocks. As a result, executives usually do not necessarily share the same interests as the collective shareholders. These features make it possible for executives to pursue activities that benefit themselves rather than the shareholders. The actions of executives on behalf of their own self-interest are known as the **agency problem**.[29] Executives may specifically emphasize the attainment of short-term gains (e.g., increasing market share through lower costs) at the expense of long-term objectives (e.g., product differentiation). Boards of directors may be willing to provide executives generous annual bonuses for attaining short-term gains.

Shareholders negotiate executive employment contracts with executives to minimize loss of control. Executive employment contracts define terms of employment pertaining to performance standards and compensation, specifically current and deferred compensation and benefits. The main shareholder objective is to protect the company's competitive interests. Shareholders use compensation to align executives' interests with shareholders' interests. As discussed earlier, boards of directors award company stock to align executives' interests with shareholders' interests.

TOURNAMENT THEORY **Tournament theory** casts lucrative executive compensation as the prize in a series of tournaments or contests among middle- and top-level managers who aspire to become CEOs.[30] Winners of the tournament at one level enter the next tournament level. In other words, an employee's promotion to a higher rank signifies a win, and more lucrative compensation (e.g., higher base pay, incentives, enhanced benefits, and perks) represents the prize. The ultimate prize is promotion to CEO and a lucrative executive compensation package. The chance of winning competitions decreases dramatically as employees rise through the ranks: There are fewer positions at higher levels in corporate hierarchical structures. Figure 11-2 depicts a visual representation of CEO compensation as a tournament.

SOCIAL COMPARISON THEORY According to **social comparison theory**, individuals need to evaluate their accomplishments, and they do so by comparing themselves to similar individuals.[31] Demographic characteristics (e.g., age or race) and occupation are common comparative bases. Individuals tend to select social comparisons with people who are slightly better than themselves.[32] Researchers have applied social comparison theory to explain the processes for setting executive compensation.[33]

As we discussed earlier, compensation committees play an important role in setting executive compensation, and compensation committees often include CEOs from other companies of equal or greater stature. Based on social comparison theory, compensation committee members probably rely on their own compensation packages and the compensation packages of CEOs in companies of equal or greater stature to determine executive compensation.

EXECUTIVE COMPENSATION DISCLOSURE RULES

11-5. Summarize the executive compensation disclosure rules and the reasons why they have been established.

Disclosure of executive compensation components and engagement of shareholder opinion set executive compensation practices apart from compensating other employee groups. Two laws, in particular, are responsible for these requirements: the Securities and Exchange Act of 1934 and the Wall Street Reform and Consumer Protection Act of 2010 (Dodd-Frank Act).

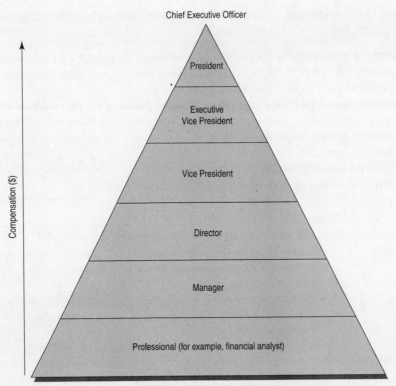

FIGURE 11-2 CEO Compensation as a Tournament

Securities and Exchange Act of 1934

Companies that sell and exchange securities (e.g., company stocks and bonds) on public stock exchanges are required to file a wide variety of information with the **Securities and Exchange Commission (SEC)**, including executive compensation practices. One of the main goals is to help prospective investors understand the financial matters of importance to themselves. The SEC is a nonpartisan, quasi-judicial federal government agency with responsibility for administering federal securities laws. The **Securities Exchange Act of 1934** applies to the disclosure of important company financial information as well as information about executive compensation practices. Each year, companies are required to file a Form 10-K, which contains a detailed picture of a company's business, the risks it faces, and the operating and financial results for the fiscal year. In addition, the 10-K includes management's perspective on their business results and what is influencing them.

Companies are also required to complete a **Definitive Proxy Statement** under Section 14A of the Securities Exchange Act, typically referred to as a DEF 14A. It reveals detailed information about the compensation of the CEO and **Named Executive Officers (NEOs)**, who generally are the four most highly compensated officers after the CEO. Within the DEF 14A, companies must disclose multiple types of information, which are listed in Table 11-3. The information should be presented in narrative and tabular form. The narrative is referred to as the **Compensation Discussion and Analysis (CD&A)** and it must present an unambiguous explanation of all executive compensation information contained in the tables. Disclosing detailed information about executive compensation should increase the accountability of company boards of directors for executive compensation policies and decisions. Failure to comply with SEC reporting rules can lead to hefty monetary penalties. For example, Polycom Inc. paid the SEC $750,000 to settle civil charges that the company failed to report when a CEO used nearly $200,000 for personal perks.[34]

The following are a table and a graphic found in the 2018 Walt Disney Company's definitive proxy statement. The first table describes the composition of the executive compensation structure, including pay-for-performance elements, compensation levels, and compensation mix.

TABLE 11-3 Securities and Exchange Commission Disclosure Requirements for Executive Compensation

- Stock option and stock appreciation right tables
- Long-term incentive plan table
- Pension plan table
- Performance graph comparing the company's stock price performance against a market index and a peer group
- Report from the compensation committee of the board of directors explaining compensation levels and policies
- Description of the directors' compensation, disclosing all amounts paid or payable
- Disclosure of certain employment contracts and golden parachutes

Pay for Performance	Provide a strong relationship of pay to performance through: • A performance-based bonus tied to the achievement of financial performance factors and an assessment of each executive's individual performance against other performance factors • Equity awards that deliver value based on stock price performance and, in the case of performance-based stock units, whose vesting depends on meeting performance targets
Competitive Compensation Levels	Provide compensation opportunities that take into account compensation levels and practices of our peers, but without targeting any specific percentile of relative compensation
Compensation Mix	Provide a mix of variable and fixed compensation that: • Is heavily weighted toward variable performance-based compensation for senior executives • Uses short-term (annual performance-based bonus) and longer-term performance measures (equity awards) to balance appropriately incentives for both short- and long-term performance

The following graphic displays the target total direct compensation mix for the CEO. Ninety-two percent of CEO target compensation is considered performance based.

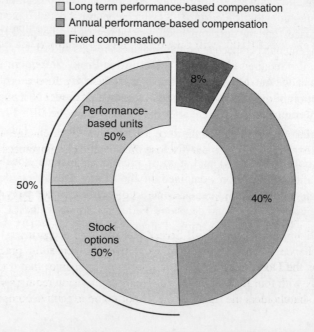

Long term performance-based compensation
Annual performance-based compensation
Fixed compensation

8%

Performance-based units 50%

50%

Stock options 50%

40%

There are additional tables contained within the DEF 14A, but the most important here is the Summary Compensation Table,[35] which discloses compensation information for the CEO and the four most highly paid executives over a 3-year period. As you can see in Table 11-4, the Summary Compensation Table for the Walt Disney Company covers the compensation paid to the named executive officers during the past completed fiscal year and the two preceding fiscal years. The table contains two main subheadings: annual compensation and long-term compensation. Salary refers to annual salary (i.e., base pay), stock and equity compensation, change in pension value, and "All Other Compensation," which is a catchall column to record other forms of compensation. Information in this column must be described in a footnote.

DEF 14As must be filed each year in advance of the annual meeting of the board of directors and company shareholders. This information is available to the public through a company's annual report, which can be found on its website. Also, the SEC offers a database on its site (http://www.sec.gov) referred to as EDGAR, which contains all of the required filings. EDGAR stands for *E*lectronic *D*ata *G*athering *A*nalysis *R*etrieval.

In 2008, the SEC unveiled additional rules for disclosing executive compensation. These rules require that companies reveal how much executives are paid, making such previously hard-to-find information as pension and estimated severance package totals transparent. Although the new rules represent a substantial improvement in pay disclosure, the SEC made a revision that resulted in a less-meaningful disclosure of stock options.

In 2009, the SEC chairperson announced further changes in the disclosure of executive compensation in a company's Summary Compensation Table. The change pertains to the reported value for stock options and stock awards. The SEC disclosure rules show components of compensation previously hidden as well as provide clarity into elements of compensation already disclosed. The most significant changes follow:

Total. The Summary Compensation Table of a company's proxy will now have a column that adds up and displays the total compensation an executive received for the previous year. In the SEC pay database this year, this is labeled SEC Total.

Change in Pension Value and Nonqualified Deferred Compensation. This column in the Summary Compensation Table shows the increase in actuarial value to the executive officer of all defined benefit pension plans and earnings on nonqualified deferred compensation plans.

All Other. This column captures compensation that does not fit in any other column of the Summary Compensation Table, including perquisites and other personal items (e.g., aircraft usage, car service, and club memberships). Each item of compensation included in All Other that exceeds $10,000 will now be separately identified and quantified in a footnote.

Pension Benefits. The new rules require companies to disclose the present value of accumulated pension benefits, showing the total lump sum amount of money an executive would receive in retirement.

Severance Benefits. Companies must disclose any termination or change-in-control agreements with executives. They must disclose the specific circumstances that will trigger payment and the estimated total payments and benefits provided for each circumstance.

Wall Street Reform and Consumer Protection Act of 2010 (Dodd-Frank Act)

President Barack Obama signed the **Wall Street Reform and Consumer Protection Act of 2010** to further enhance the transparency of executive compensation practices. Also, commonly referred to as the **Dodd-Frank Act**, it requires the companies that trade stock on public exchanges to comply with four major provisions. The first provision requires **say on pay**. Say on pay gives company shareholders the right to vote yes or no on executive compensation proposals

TABLE 11-4 2017 Summary Compensation Table

Name and Principal Position	Fiscal Year	Salary[1]	Stock Awards[2]	Option Awards	Non-Equity Incentive Plan Compensation	Change in Pension Value and Nonqualified Deferred Compensation Earnings	All Other Compensation	Total
Robert A. Iger Chairman and Chief Executive Officer	2017	$2,500,000	$8,984,191	$8,298,322	$15,200,000	—	$1,301,167	$36,283,680
	2016	2,500,000	8,828,117	8,454,674	20,000,000	$2,893,778	1,205,827	43,882,396
	2015	2,548,077	8,862,741	8,419,823	22,340,000	1,423,047	1,319,926	44,913,614
Alan N. Braverman Senior Executive Vice President, General Counsel and Secretary	2017	1,565,000	1,878,142	1,252,020	3,600,000	56,359	95,938	8,447,459
	2016	1,549,000	1,878,037	1,252,040	5,440,000	931,443	68,431	11,118,951
	2015	1,502,692	1,847,400	1,200,012	5,532,000	395,940	216,573	10,694,617
Christine M. McCarthy Senior Executive Vice President and Chief Financial Officer	2017	1,323,077	1,950,118	1,300,000	3,450,000	852,787	70,600	8,946,582
	2016	1,287,692	1,950,106	1,300,058	4,520,000	1,104,131	36,523	10,198,510
	2015	869,712	1,003,783	652,018	4,310,000	155,346	79,194	7,070,053
Kevin A. Mayer Senior Executive Vice President and Chief Strategy Officer	2017	1,323,077	1,950,118	1,300,000	3,450,000	333,928	77,495	8,434,618
	2016	1,287,692	1,950,106	1,300,058	4,520,000	1,031,418	36,075	10,125,349
	2015	1,050,250	1,354,785	880,006	4,310,000	303,767	107,763	8,006,571
M. Jayne Parker Senior Executive Vice President and Chief Human Resources Officer	2017	851,154	1,320,171	880,020	1,570,000	392,107	77,112	5,090,564
	2016	826,385	1,320,122	880,052	1,815,000	711,775	51,060	5,604,394
	2015	797,077	1,354,785	880,006	1,844,000	664,810	112,388	5,653,066

[1] The amounts reflect compensation for 53 weeks in fiscal year 2015 compared to 52 weeks in fiscal 2016 and fiscal 2017 due to the timing of the end of the fiscal period.

[2] Stock awards for each fiscal year include awards subject to performance conditions that were valued based on the probability that performance targets will be achieved. Assuming the highest level of performance conditions are achieved, the grant date stock award values would be as follows:

Fiscal Year	Mr. Iger	Mr. Braverman	Ms. McCarthy	Mr. Mayer	Ms. Parker
2017	$12,447,500	$2,240,131	$2,325,983	$2,325,983	$1,574,625
2016	12,681,647	2,287,925	2,375,735	2,375,735	1,608,262
2015	12,629,785	2,250,073	1,222,575	1,650,084	1,650,084

that are contained in proxy statements, including current and deferred components and golden parachute agreements. The frequency is determined by shareholder vote. Although the say on pay provision guarantees shareholders the right to vote on executive compensation proposals, the vote is nonbinding. That is, the outcome of shareholders' voting does not overrule any compensation decision made by the company's board of directors. The nonbinding vote advises the company's board of directors of possible concerns about the structure of executive compensation packages, including excessive perks and the lack of clarity between compensation and business results.

☛ **FYI**

Of 217 S&P 500 companies holding say on pay votes in 2017, all received shareholder support:

- 95 – 100% support: 115 companies
- 90 – 94%: 67
- 70 – 89%: 27
- 50 – 69%: 8
- Below 50%: 0[36]

The second provision details independence requirements for compensation committee members and their advisors, such as compensation consultants and legal counsel. Members of compensation committees typically receive compensation for their services, and this practice is acceptable. However, possible violations of the Dodd-Frank independence requirement may arise when at least one committee member also receives compensation as a company employee. For example, a compensation committee member who also serves as the company's executive vice president may be considered violating the independence requirement. On the other hand, a compensation committee member who does not receive compensation from the company as an employee or external consultant would not violate the independence requirement.

Similarly, the Dodd-Frank Act specifies independence requirements for advisors to the compensation committee such as compensation consultants and legal counsel. A company's compensation committee must consider whether the fees charged by advisors exceed reasonable limits based on the amount of the fees as a percentage of the company's total revenue. Another consideration is whether an advisor has a business or personal relationship with committee members.

The third provision requires that companies disclose the circumstances under which an executive would benefit from a golden parachute arrangement. Specifically, disclosure is required of all agreements and understandings that the acquiring and target companies have with the executive officers of both companies.

The fourth provision requires that companies report the ratio of CEO compensation to the median compensation of its employees in SEC filings that require executive compensation disclosure. This disclosure is intended to inform shareholders when taking a "say on pay" vote. The SEC adopted this rule in August 2015, with companies being required to demonstrate compliance for their first fiscal year beginning on or after January 1, 2017.[37] The rule provides companies with flexibility in calculating this pay ratio. For instance, a company may choose the methodology for identifying its median employee and that employee's compensation. Statistical sampling of its employee population is an acceptable method. Since the rule's announcement, many companies have complained about the pay ratio rule for two reasons. First, many companies question whether this ratio provides value, particularly as a tool to compare companies. Part of this concern is based on differences in the composition of the workforces (e.g., some companies may have more highly paid employees than others). Second, calculating the pay ratio is challenging based on the complexity of statistical sampling, determining the appropriate company records to use to calculate the ratio (e.g., tax records or payroll records), and determining whether individuals are employees or contingent workers. Only employees are to be included in the calculation. (See Chapter 12.)

Say on pay is not limited to U.S. companies. OECD countries have some form of a say on pay vote.[38] As an aside, OECD stands for Organization for Economic Cooperation and Development, which is a forum of 34 democracies that promotes economic growth, prosperity, and sustainable development. Fourteen OECD countries have say on pay votes that are binding, which means that a company's board of directors must follow the outcome of the vote. Eleven countries have advisory votes, and the remainder have no say on pay provision or leave it to the discretion of shareholders whether to hold votes. Some of the countries with binding votes include Chile, Greece, Norway, and the United Kingdom. Others with advisory votes include Australia, Denmark, Indonesia, Spain, and, of course, the United States. Votes held at the discretion of boards of directors are found in Argentina, India, and Japan. Mexico, Slovenia, and Saudi Arabia, are examples of countries with no specific requirements.

EXECUTIVE COMPENSATION: ARE U.S. EXECUTIVES PAID TOO MUCH?

11-6. Briefly explain the executive compensation controversy as it relates to whether U.S. executives are paid too much.

Are U.S. executives paid too much? Popular press and newspaper accounts generally suggest that executives are overpaid. Of course, you should form your own opinion based on the following pertinent information:

- Comparison between executive compensation and other worker groups
- Strategic questions: Is pay for performance?
- Ethical considerations: Is executive compensation fair?
- International competitiveness

Comparison between Executive Compensation and Compensation for Other Worker Groups

The median annual earnings for all civilian workers was $49,630 in May 2016.[39] Among the nonexecutive employees, food preparers earned the least ($20,460) and anesthesiologists earned the most ($269,600).[40] The U.S. Bureau of Labor Statistics reports that the median annual salary for top executives was $194,350.[41] However, other surveys provide substantially higher estimates. For example, the *Wall Street Journal* reported that 2017 average annual total compensation amounts to approximately $11.6 million, representing nearly 10 percent for half of the executives and 25 percent or more for about 25 percent of them.[42] The difference in reported amounts for CEO pay is staggering, but closer consideration of sample characteristics helps to explain some of this gap. The U.S. Bureau of Labor Statistics conducts a nationwide survey of a representative sample of companies in the private and public sectors, by different ownership types, and company size. The *Wall Street Journal* report focused on the 133 largest firms, which they determined based on an analysis of proxy statements filed with the SEC.[43]

Strategic Questions: Is Pay for Performance?

There are several measures of corporate performance (Table 11-5). Are CEOs compensated commensurately with their companies' performance? It is difficult to answer just *yes* or *no* because the evidence is mixed based on decades of academic research and the compensation of executives relative to company performance; therefore, a simple statement cannot be made about the relationship between CEO pay and company performance. Shareholder returns most often describe company performance, but there are complex forces beyond the control of CEOs that may influence shareholder returns. For example, in the pharmaceutical industry, substantial investments in research to identify promising medicines require trial and error before a promising outcome occurs in the laboratory. Then lengthy clinical trials that span multiple years may show that the new medication does not cure an illness for which it was created. Such public failures often result in lower confidence in the company, which often translates into lower shareholder returns. In the intervening time, the company hires a new CEO who was not involved in

TABLE 11-5 Corporate Performance Measures

Size
- Sales
- Assets
- Profits
- Market value
- Number of employees

Growth
- Sales
- Assets
- Profits
- Market value
- Number of employees

Profitability
- Profit margin
- Return on assets (ROA)
- Return on equity (ROE)

Capital Markets
- Dividend yield
- Total return to shareholders
- Price–earnings ratio
- Payout

Liquidity
- Current ratio
- Quick ratio
- Working capital from operations
- Cash flow from operations

Leverage
- Debt-to-equity ratio
- Short-term vs. long-term debt
- Cash flow vs. interest payments

the decision to pursue the failed initiative, raising the question whether she should receive lower compensation following a decline in shareholder returns.

Nevertheless, some companies do reduce CEO pay when company performance does not meet a preestablished standard. For example, Mark Parker, Nike CEO, took a 71 percent pay cut in 2017. The company has been experiencing intense competition from Adidas and weak U.S. sales.[44] GoPro Inc., manufacturer of cameras, fell far short of its holiday sales goals, requiring a dramatic response. In addition to a 20 percent reduction in workforce, CEO Nick Woodman cut his cash compensation to $1 from the previous year's $800,000 amount.[45]

Ethical Considerations: Is Executive Compensation Fair?

Is executive compensation fair? Three considerations drive this question: companies' abilities to attract and retain top executives, income disparities between executives and other employees, and layoffs of thousands of nonexecutive employees.

ATTRACT AND RETAIN TOP EXECUTIVES Many compensation professionals and board of directors members argue that the trends in executive compensation are necessary for attracting and retaining top executives. Even though most CEOs are promoted from within, it is often the case that companies that hire new CEOs from other companies pay them substantially more than individuals who are promoted to CEO from within the company ranks. For example, median total pay for internal promotions was $7.76 million while nearly 42 percent higher for external hires, amounting to $10.99 million.[46] However, regardless of source, the typical percentage of total compensation awarded in equity plans was approximately 50 percent.

INCOME DISPARITIES Table 11-6 illustrates the marked income disparity between annual pay for various nonexecutive jobs and pay for CEOs. The typical annual earnings for the lowest-paid occupation (food preparers) amounted to a mere 0.18 percent of the average annual CEO salary and bonus in large companies. The ratio of highest-paid occupation (anesthesiologiests) to the average annual CEO salary and bonus was not much better (i.e., 2.3 percent). Said differently, the typical CEO's annual compensation was nearly 567 times greater than the typical food preparer's annual pay and approximately 43 times greater than the typical anesthesiologist's annual pay!

Labor unions continually argue that substantial pay discrepancies between CEOs and non-CEOs are socially unjust and promote economic inequality based on marked annual pay disparities noted above. The AFL-CIO often considers other comparisons such as the number of hours full-time minimum wage earners would have to work to earn just one hour of a chief executive officer's pay. For example, full-time minimum wage earners would work 1,485 hours to earn the equivalent of one hour of pay for Walmart's CEO, Michael Duke.

LAYOFFS BORNE BY WORKERS BUT NOT EXECUTIVES Millions of workers have been laid off since 1990. Between late 2008 and mid-2009 alone, more than 2 million employees lost their jobs.[47] Top management typically advances several reasons that necessitate these layoffs (e.g., global competition, reductions in product demand, technological advances that perform many jobs more efficiently than employees, mergers and acquisitions, establishing production operations in foreign countries with lower labor costs, and the steep economic downturn following the recession). A scant few executives lost their jobs, but millions of workers lost theirs in the years following the start of the 2008 economic recession. Despite near record-low unemployment rates, massive layoffs are still commonplace. For instance, Kimberly-Clark announced that 5,000 employees would lose their jobs. At the same time, CEO Thomas Falk earned $15.7 million in 2017 despite a 7.7 percent decline in stock value.

International Competitiveness

Increased global competition has forced companies in the United States to become more productive. Excessive expenditures on compensation can threaten competitive advantage. Compensation expenditures are excessive when they outpace the quality and quantity of employees' contributions.

TABLE 11-6 Selected Median Annual Nonexecutive Earnings, May 2016

Occupation	Annual Earnings ($)
Anesthesiologists	269,600
Lawyers	135,760
General and operations managers	122,090
Registered nurses	72,180
Painters, construction and maintenance	41,510
Office clerks	33,010
Teacher assistants	27,120
Combined food preparation and service workers	20,460

Source: U.S. Bureau of Labor Statistics, *Occupational Employment Wages— May 2016* (USDL: 17-0376). Accessed: March 24, 2018, at http://www.bls.gov.

In addition, compensation expenditures may be excessive when they are substantially higher than competitors' compensation outlays. Concerns about U.S. companies' competitiveness in global markets are common because of the vast differences in compensation levels between the CEOs of U.S. and foreign companies.

INTERNATIONAL COMPENSATION COMPARISONS The SEC rules require the disclosure of executive compensation in U.S. companies; however, comparable rules do not exist in many foreign countries. As a result, it is difficult to make detailed comparisons between U.S. and foreign executive compensation. Nevertheless, recent research has studied the levels and composition of CEO compensation in the U.S. and in other countries where disclosure laws necessitate reporting of CEO pay. U.S. CEOs earned the most, approximately $11.6 million. CEO pay averaged slightly more than $10 million in the United Kingdom, approximately $8 million in Germany, nearly $3.0 million in France, $2.0 million in Japan, and $5.5 million in other countries.[48] Figure 11-3 lists average CEO pay in several OECD countries. Pay mix also differed substantially among CEOs in various countries. For instance, approximately one third of CEO pay in the United States and the U.K. was based on annual salary and bonus. The proportions were much higher elsewhere (73 percent in Germany, 75 percent in France, 89 percent in Japan, and 55 percent in other countries).

UNDERMINING U.S. COMPANIES' ABILITY TO COMPETE At present, there is no evidence showing that U.S. executive compensation pay practices have undermined U.S. companies' ability to compete with other companies in the global marketplace. Might executive compensation practices undermine U.S. companies' competitiveness in the future?

On one hand, it is reasonable to predict that CEO pay will not undermine U.S. companies' ability to compete because CEO pay increased as company profits increased. On the other hand, the current wave of widespread layoffs may hinder U.S. companies' competitiveness. The U.S. companies use layoffs to maintain profits and cut costs, heightening workers' job insecurities. The remaining workers may lose their faith in pay-for-performance systems and their trust in their employers as colleagues lose their jobs and CEOs continue to receive higher compensation. Workers may not feel that working hard will lead to higher pay or job security; therefore, they may choose not to work proficiently. As a result, reduced individual performance and destabilized workforces may make it difficult for U.S. companies to compete against foreign companies.

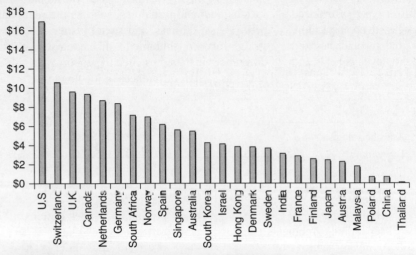

FIGURE 11-3 Average CEO Pay (in Millions)
Source: Stephani A. Mason, Ann F. Medinets, and Dan Palmon, "Say-on-Pay: Is Anybody Listening?" *Multinational Finance Journal* (2016, vol. 20, no. 4): p. 271.

PREPARING FOR EXAMS/QUIZZES

Chapter Summary by Learning Objectives

Learning Objective 11-1. *Explain the difference between executive pay and pay for nonexecutives.* Executive compensation is determined by a company's board of directors who are usually high-level executives, either within or outside the company, as well as prominent community members, such as lawyers. The recommendation for executive compensation comes from a compensation consultant, who is often hired by the CEO. Compensation for nonexecutive employees is typically based on market rates or on negotiations between union and management, and is adjusted according to performance or acquisition of new knowledge or skills.

Learning Objective 11-2. *Define executive status.* The Internal Revenue Code defines two group of employees—key employees and highly compensated employees—who are deemed to have executive status. Although the criteria differ somewhat between these two groups, both criteria are generally based on salary level and ownership stake in the company.

Learning Objective 11-3. *List the components of executive compensation packages.* Executive compensation packages include five main components: (1) current or annual core compensation and various types of deferred compensation, including (2) stock-based compensation, (3) separation agreements such as golden parachutes and platinum parachutes, (4) enhanced employee benefits and perquisites, and (5) clawback provisions.

Learning Objective 11-4. *Discuss the principles and processes of setting executive compensation.* The principles and processes for setting executive compensation are based on three theories. These include agency theory, tournament theory, and social comparison theory.

Learning Objective 11-5. *Summarize the executive compensation disclosure rules and the reasons why they have been established.* Executive compensation disclosure rules were established to protect the interests of potential and current investors (or, shareholders) of companies. Both the Securities and Exchange Act of 1934 and the Wall Street Reform and Consumer Protection Act of 2010 (Dodd-Frank Act) require extensive reporting of executive compensation amounts and the rationale for these amounts for the CEO and named executive officers, and shareholder engagement through nonbinding votes on proposed executive compensation packages.

Learning Objective 11-6. *Briefly explain the executive compensation controversy as it relates to whether U.S. executives are paid too much.* There is ongoing public controversy regarding whether executives are excessively highly compensated. The debate draws on various data and principles, such as international competitiveness, fairness, and social justice. There is not a straightforward solution to this controversy based on differences in data presented to support each side's arguments as well as differences in ideology.

Key Terms

Discussion Questions

11-1. What can be done to make the function of compensation committees consistent with shareholders' interests? Explain.

11-2. Which component of compensation is most essential to motivate executives to lead companies toward competitive advantage? Discuss your rationale.

11-3. Do you believe that say on pay should be a binding vote rather than an advisory vote? Explain.

11-4. What are the differences between enhanced benefits and perquisites?

11-5. Do you feel that executive pay is fair or unfair? Explain.

PREPARING FOR MY CAREER

Compensation in Action

Executive compensation, long under the watchful eye of the public and politicians, has been under a microscopic lens during the recent global economic crisis. Executive compensation decisions are approved in the end by the board of directors (in response to recommendations provided to them by the compensation committee of the board and external executive compensation consultants); however, line managers and HR should seek to understand the principles being applied and the compensation plans being employed. This knowledge will help as employees raise questions about executive compensation, and it will make you more aware of practices that are fair and successful versus practices that are blatantly contrary to law, thus being able to protect the company and its employees. Perhaps if line managers and HR managers had been more vigilant about these processes, the tragedies at Enron and Tyco would never have occurred.

Action checklist for line managers and HR—assessing executive compensation in your company

HR takes the lead

- Conduct an analysis of the company's culture, ideals, values, and history. Does the executive compensation plan align with those factors?
- Is the executive compensation plan balanced with regards to cash versus equity, reward versus risk, short-term versus long-term performance? An overemphasis on any one side could result in behaviors that help executives but hurt the shareholders and the company in the end.

- What severance plans are being offered? Do the platinum parachutes in your company essentially minimize all risks for executives? Will the financial windfall be so large that an executive has little reason to avoid failure?
- If you believe the practices of your organizations are not in accordance with the disclosure regulations of the SEC or the requirements outlined explicitly under the **Sarbanes-Oxley Act**, it may be necessary for you to bring this to the attention of line managers. Together you can take these concerns to the proper people inside or outside the company.

Line managers take the lead

- What are the objectives by which the executives in your company are being measured? Are these similar to the objectives by which you are measured?
- What are the long-term incentives? Is this completely tied to stock price? Ideally, the long-term plan should include multiyear stock and a cash plan. With the plan too tied to stock price (through stock options), the wrong behaviors are encouraged and shareholders suffer in the long term.

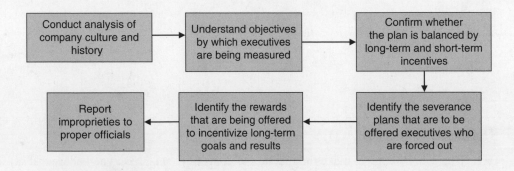

Cases

Case 1: Building an Executive Compensation Package

The executives at Safeguard Insurance are focused on continuing efforts that have brought the company significant growth in the past 15 years. Director of Human Resources Beth Frazier is considering how to provide more incentives to executives to continue this focus. Two years ago, the company went public and began selling shares of stock on the stock market. While executives were granted some stock in the company's initial public offering, Beth now wants to examine the best way to use the company's stock value in the executive compensation plan. She knows that company ownership can help incentivize executives to increase the value of the company stock, and thus the ongoing success of the company.

Safeguard Insurance is led by an executive team that includes the chief executive officer, the chief operating officer, and functional area leaders, including chief legal counsel, the director of finance, the director of operations, the director of marketing and sales, and Beth's position. There are also leaders within the different lines of business, including the director of personal lines insurance and the director of commercial lines insurance. Beth is working with the company's board of directors to examine the compensation structure of this team of leaders. In addition to a retirement plan and other basic benefits such as time off, the company offers a competitive base salary plus a bonus plan that is tied to company revenue. Beth believes that a more direct tie to the company's stock value may add just the right incentive for executives.

Since the company's stock went public, its value has been a key indicator of the overall success of the company. As the company executives are closely monitoring the company stock value, Beth believes that tying executive compensation to the stock value will provide a clear incentive for executives. If executives remain focused on increasing the overall value of the stock, they should make decisions that are in the best interest of the company. Further, both executives and the company will benefit if the value of the stock continues to increase.

Initially, Beth thought granting the executives annual incentive stock options would create the right incentive for the team. By doing so, the company would grant the executives the option to purchase stock later at the price on the date of the grant. The executives would then have an incentive to grow the stock value over time. However, a member of the board of directors suggested considering offering a phantom stock plan instead. A phantom stock plan exists when executives are compensated with hypothetical company shares rather than actual shares of company stock. Upon meeting certain conditions, executives receive income that is equal to the increase in the value of the company stock from the date that the phantom stock was granted until the conversion date.

Beth needs to conduct more research on both types of plans to formulate a recommendation for an incentive plan for executives. She must first decide if an incentive plan tied to the value of company stock is a good alternative for the company. It seems that this is a logical move to make, but Beth also needs to determine the best way to structure the plan. She thinks that the phantom stock plan may offer some advantages, but as she starts her research, she knows she needs to consider all the options.

Questions:

11-6. How does a stock option plan provide an incentive for executives?

11-7. Which plan would be better for Safeguard Insurance, the incentive stock option plan or the phantom stock plan?

Case 2: Ethics Dilemma: Resistance to Clawback CEO Severance Pay at United Airlines[49]

A recent scandal involving United Airlines' (former) CEO Jeffrey Smisek led to his termination. Smisek re-instituted an unprofitable air route between Newark International Airport and an airport in Columbia, South Carolina. Although re-establishing a money-losing air route is not unethical, Smisek made the decision outside the standard decision processes. Smisek made the decision to start up the unprofitable air route in response to a threat by David Samson, Chair of the Port Authority of New York and New Jersey, to prohibit the airline from building a hangar at the Newark Airport.

The United board of directors terminated Smisek's employment during a federal corruption investigation on other matters. Smisek received a generous severance package including cash and restricted stock totaling nearly $29 million. Outraged by this decision, a shareholder group filed a lawsuit, demanding that the United board of directors clawback Smisek's severance compensation because of the circumstances under which he was fired. United's board of directors refused, arguing that taking back Smisek's severance package would cause substantial harm to its ability to recruit and retain talent.

Questions:

11-8. As a compensation professional, what would you do?

11-9. What factor(s) in this ethical dilemma might influence a person (or group) to make a less-than-ethical decision?

Crunch the Numbers!

Comparison of Pay Within and Across Industries

As a newly hired compensation analyst, you have been asked to conduct analyses to determine differences in pay for similar jobs between two industries, the ratio of pay for similar jobs within two industries, and the ratio of pay for different jobs within an industry. The data represent annual base wages and exclude incentives or employee benefits. These data were extracted from the U.S. Bureau of Labor Statistics Occupational Employment Statistics Query System (www.bls.gov).

	Industry	
	Oil and Gas Extraction	Retail
Occupation	Annual median wage ($)	Annual median wage ($)
Chief Executives	187,199	180,360
Human Resources Managers	118,730	95,020
Accountants and Auditors	71,780	64,920
File Clerks	30,700	23,430

Questions:

11-10. By what percent does annual median pay differ between the oil and gas extraction industry and the retail trade industry for (a) chief executives, (b) human resources managers, (c) accountants and auditors, and (d) file clerks?

11-11. In the oil and gas extraction industry relative to the retail trade industry, what are the pay ratios between (a) chief executives, (b) human resources managers, (c) accountants and auditors, and (d) file clerks?

11-12. In the oil and gas extraction industry, what are the pay ratios for the chief executives job to (a) human resources managers, (b) accountants and auditors, and (c) file clerks? In the retail trade industry, what is the ratio of pay for chief executives to (d) human resources managers, (e) accountants and auditors, and (f) file clerks?

Working Together: Team Exercise

In small groups of three or four, come up with specific answers to the following questions. Talk through your perspectives with team members. Be prepared to share your ideas with the class.

The chapter revealed that executive compensation practices receive substantial public attention. Some members of the public consider executive compensation to be excessive while others consider it to be appropriate. Select two companies of your choice and conduct some research about them (conduct an internet search based on your choices).

Questions:

11-13. What are some of the issues that you identified for each company? Describe them.

11-14. Based on your knowledge of these companies, do you believe that the executive's compensation in each company is justified? (Do not be concerned with the amount. Just assume that the compensation package is lucrative). Explain.

Endnotes

1. Bruce Walters, Tim Hardin, and James Schick, "Top Executive Compensation: Equity or Excess? Implications for Regaining American Competitiveness," *Journal of Business Ethics* 14 (1995): 227–234, https://doi.org/10.1007/BF00881437.

2. Susan Adams, "The Highest-Paid CEOs Are the Worst Performers, New Study Says," *Forbes* (June 16, 2014), accessed March 24, 2018, http://www.forbes.com.

3. Internal Revenue Code, §416 (i).

4. Treas. Reg. §1.416–1, Q13.

5. Internal Revenue Code, §414 (q).

6. Matteo Tonello, "CEO and Executive Compensation Practices: 2017 Edition," Harvard Law School Forum on Corporate Governance and Financial Regulation (October 4, 2017), accessed March 24, 2018, http://corpgov.law.harvard.edu.

7. Internal Revenue Code, §162(m)

8. Mike Esterl and Joann Lublin, "Coke Scales Back Executive Equity Compensation, Bowing to Pressure," *The Wall Street Journal* (October 1, 2014), accessed February 15, 2015, http://www.wsj.com.

9. Internal Revenue Code 61, 83, 162, 451; *Treasury Regulations* 1.83.

10. Internal Revenue Code 61, 83, 162; *Treasury Regulations* 1.83.

11. Peer Fiss, "A Short History of Golden Parachutes," *Harvard Business Review* (October 3, 2016), accessed March 25, 2018, http://www.hbr.org.

12. Pradnya Joshi, "Golden Parachutes Still Very Much in Style," *The New York Times* (June 29, 2013), accessed March 31, 2015, http://www.nytimes.com.

13. Deepa Seetharaman, "Yahoo's Marissa Mayer to Reap $187 million After Verizon Deal," *The Wall Street Journal* (April 25, 2017), accessed March 25, 2018, http://www.wsj.com.

14. Stacy Cowley and Jennifer A. Kingson, "Wells Fargo to Claw Back $75 Million from 2 Former Executives," *The New York Times* (April 10, 2017), accessed March 25, 2018, http://www.nytimes.com.

15. Dennis Wagner, "Phoenix VA Chief's Bonus Rescinded Among Controversy," *The Arizona Republic* (May 22, 2014), accessed April 7, 2015, http://www.azcentral.com.

16. Dorie Meinert, "How to Reduce Unethical Behavior Among CEOs," *Society for Human Resource Management* (July 25, 2017), accessed March 24, 2018, http://www.shrm.org.

17. Joseph J. Martocchio, *Employee Benefits: A Primer for Human Resource Professionals*, 6th ed. (Burr Ridge, IL: McGraw-Hill, 2018).

18. I.R.C. §415 (b)(1)(A).

19. Sue Holloway, "Executive Perquisites," *Workspan* (March 2015), accessed March 25, 2018, http://www.worldatwork.org.

20. Paul Hodgson, "Come Fly with Them: These CEOs Spend the Most on the Corporate Jet," *Fortune* (January 27, 2015), accessed March 5, 2015, http://www.fortune.com.

21. Dan Marcec, "The 20 Largest Security Perks in the Fortune 100," *Equilar* (Press Release, January 18, 2017), accessed March 25, 2018, http://www.equilar.com.

22. Dan Marcec, "The 20 Largest Security Perks in the Fortune 100," *Equilar* (Press Release, January 18, 2017), accessed March 25, 2018, http://www.equilar.com; Claire Zillman, "Which Fortune 100 CEO Has the Biggest Security Budget?" *Fortune* (January 7, 2015), accessed March 26, 2018, http://www.fortune.com.

23. Thomas Gryta and Joann S. Lublin, "GE's New Chief Makes Cuts, Starting with Old Favorites," *The Wall Street Journal* (October 18, 2017), accessed March 25, 2018, http://www.wsj.com.

24. Minha Ahmed, "Despite the Scrutiny, Perks Remain a Key Component of Executive Rewards," *Executive Compensation Bulletin* (July 31, 2013), accessed April 3, 2015, http://www. towerswatson.com.

25. Graef S. Crystal, "Why CEO Compensation Is So High," *California Management Review*, 34 (1991): 9–29, http://dx.doi.org/10.2307/41166681.

26. Ibid.

27. Ibid.

28. Kathleen M. Eisenhardt, "Agency Theory: An Assessment and Review," *Academy of Management Review*, 14(1989): 57–74, http://doi.org/10.5465/AMR.1989.4279003; Michael Jensen and William H. Meckling, "Theory of the Firm: Managerial Behavior, Agency Costs, and Ownership Structure," *Journal of Financial Economics*, 3(1976): 305–360, http://dx.doi.org/10.1086/296060; Henry L. Tosi Jr. and Luis R. Gomez-Mejia, "The Decoupling of CEO Pay and Performance: An Agency Theory Perspective," *Administrative Science Quarterly*, 34(1989): 169–189, http://dx.doi.org/10.2307/2989894; Paul S. Goodman, "An Examination of Referents Used in the Evaluation of Pay," *Organizational Behavior and Human Performance*, 12(1974): 170–195, http://dx.doi.org/10.1016/0030-5073(74)90045-2; Edward Lazear and Sherwin Rosen, "Rank-order Tournaments as Optimum Labor Contracts," *Journal of Political Economy*, 89(1981): 841–864, http://dx.doi.org/10.1086/261010; Charles O'Reilly III, Brian

G. Main, and Graef S. Crystal, "CEO Compensation as Tournament and Social Comparison: A Tale of Two Theories," *Administrative Science Quarterly*, 33(1988): 257–274, http://dx.doi .org/10.2307/2393058.

29. Michael C. Jensen and William H. Meckling, "Theory of the Firm: Managerial Behavior, Agency Costs, and Ownership Structure," *Journal of Financial Economics*, 3(1976): 305–360, http://dx.doi .org/10.2139/ssrn.94043.

30. Edward Lazear and Sherwin Rosen, "Rank-order Tournaments as Optimum Labor Contracts," *Journal of Political Economy*, 89(1981): 841–864, http://dx.doi.org/10.1086/261010.

31. Leon Festinger, "A Theory of Social Comparison Processes," *Human Relations*, 7(1954): 117–140, http://dx.doi.org/10.1177/001872675400700202.

32. Amos Tversky and Daniel Kahneman, "Judgment and Uncertainty: Heuristics and Biases," *Science*, 185(1974): 1124–1131.

33. Charles O'Reilly III, Brian G. Main, and Graef S. Crystal, "CEO Compensation as Tournament and Social Comparison: A Tale of Two Theories," *Administrative Science Quarterly*, 33(1988): 257–274.

34. Tess Stynes, "Polycom Inc. Agrees to Pay $750,000 to Settle SEC Civil Charges," *The Wall Street Journal* (March 31, 2015), accessed April 1, 2015, http://www.wsj.com.

35. Summary Compensation Table: 17 C.F.R 229.402(b), as amended November 29, 1993, effective January 1, 1994.

36. Compensation Advisory Partners, "Say on Pay Vote Results (S&P 500)," *Compensation Advisory Partners* (May 15, 2017), accessed March 24, 2018, http://capartners.com.

37. U.S. Securities and Exchange Commission, "SEC Adopts Interpretive Guidance on Pay Ratio Rule," *Securities and Exchange Commission Press Release* (2017-172), accessed March 25, 2018, http://www.sec.gov.

38. Stephani A. Mason, Ann F. Medinets, and Dan Palmon, "Say-on-Pay: Is Anybody Listening?" *Multinational Finance Journal*, 20(2016): 273–322, https://ssrn.com/abstract=2997895.

39. U.S. Bureau of Labor Statistics, "May 2016 National Industry-Specific Occupational Employment and Wage Estimates," accessed March 22, 2018, http://www.bls.gov.

40. Ibid.

41. Ibid.

42. Theo Francis and Joann S. Lublin, "Median CEO Pay Hit Record of Nearly $12 Million in 2017, Juiced by Markets," *The Wall Street Journal* (March 21, 2018), accessed March 22, 2018, http://www.wsj.com.

43. Ibid.

44. Ahiza Garcia, "Nike CEO Takes a Pay Cut After Rough Year," *CNN Money* (July 26, 2017), accessed March 24, 2018, http://money.cnn.com.

45. Bloomberg, "GoPro Cuts 20% of Jobs, Exits Drone Division as CEO Takes Pay Cut to $1 Salary," *Orange County Register* (January 8, 2018), accessed March 24, 2018, http://www.ocregister.com.

46. Equilar, Inc., "In with the New – Compensation of Newly Hired Chief Executive Officers," (February 7, 2015), accessed March 30, 2015, http://www.equilar.com.

47. U.S. Bureau of Labor Statistics, *Mass Layoffs*; U.S. Bureau of Labor Statistics, *Extended Mass Layoffs*.

48. Equilar, Inc., "How CEO Pay Differs Around the Globe," (August 17, 2016), accessed March 24, 2018, http://www.equilar.com; Stephani A. Mason, Ann F. Medinets and Dan Palmon, "Say-on-Pay: Is Anybody Listening?" *Multinational Finance Journal*, 20(2016): 271, https://ssrn. com/abstract=2997895.

49. Gretchen Morgenson, "How Badly Must a C.E.O. Behave Before His Pay Is Clawed Back?" *The Wall Street Journal* (June 9, 2017), accessed March 24, 2018, http://www.wsj.com.

Compensating the Flexible Workforce
Contingent Employees and Flexible Work Schedules

Learning Objectives

When you finish studying this chapter, you should be able to:

12-1. Describe the four groups of contingent workers.

12-2. Discuss pay and benefits issues for contingent workers.

12-3. Summarize the three categories of flexible work schedules.

12-4. Discuss the pay and employee benefits issues for flexible work schedules, compressed workweeks, and telecommuting arrangements.

12-5. Describe unions' reactions to contingent work and flexible work schedule arrangements.

12-6. Identify strategic issues and choices companies face regarding the use of contingent workers.

Changing business conditions and personal preferences for work–life balance have led to an increase in contingent workers and the use of flexible work schedules in the United States. This chapter looks at compensation issues for contingent workers and demonstrates that compensating contingent workers is a complex proposition. Human resource (HR) and compensation professionals encounter tremendous challenges in managing pay and benefits for these individuals. Many companies employ core employees and contingent workers, often in the same jobs. To the casual onlooker, including others in the workplace, there are no visible differences; however, HR and compensation professionals must take many factors into consideration. As we will learn in this chapter, compensation professionals should be aware of the differences between core employees and contingent workers and the complexities of compensating contingent workers, particularly, pertaining to the domain of legally required benefits.

THE CONTINGENT WORKFORCE

The previous chapters addressed compensation issues for core employees. **Core employees** have full-time jobs or part-time jobs, and they generally plan long-term or indefinite relationships with their employers. In addition, all core employees were assumed to work standard schedules

12-1. Describe the four groups of contingent workers.

(i.e., fixed eight-hour work shifts, five days per week). Compensation practices differ somewhat for the flexible workforce. According to the U.S. Bureau of Labor Statistics, **contingent workers**[1] are those who do not have an implicit or explicit contract for ongoing employment. Persons who do not expect to continue in their jobs for such personal reasons as retirement or returning to school are not considered contingent workers, provided that they would have the option of continuing in the job were it not for these reasons. Alternatively, some refer to contingent employment as 'on-demand' employment.[2] This idea relies on job security as the basis for distinguishing between contingent and noncontingent employment. Figure 12-1 details questions that determine whether workers expect their employment to continue, that is, whether their work arrangement is considered to be contingent.

Groups of Contingent Workers

There are four distinct groups of contingent workers:

- Part-time employees
- Temporary and on-call employees
- Leased employee arrangements
- Independent contractors, freelancers, and consultants

 FYI

The prevalence of flexible work arrangements in companies varies:

- Standard part-time workers: 5%
- Temporary employees: 1.3%
- On-call workers: 3.5%
- Leased workers: 3.0%
- Independent contractors: 12.9%[3]

PART-TIME EMPLOYEES The Bureau of Labor Statistics defines a part-time worker as an individual who works fewer than 35 hours per week.[4] The Bureau also distinguishes between two kinds of part-time employees: voluntary and involuntary. A **voluntary part-time employee** *chooses* to work fewer than 35 hours per regularly scheduled workweek. In some cases, individuals supplement full-time employment with part-time employment to meet financial obligations.

Some workers, including a small but growing number of professionals, elect to work part-time as a lifestyle choice. These part-timers sacrifice pay, and possibly career advancement, in exchange for more free time to devote to family, hobbies, and personal interests. They often have working partners or spouses whose benefits, generally including medical and dental insurance, extend coverage to family members.

Involuntary part-time employees work fewer than 35 hours per week because they are unable to find full-time employment. Involuntary part-time work represents a substantial share of all part-time employment. There is a commonly held but inaccurate stereotype of involuntary part-time workers as being low skilled and uninterested in career advancement. To the contrary, many involuntary part-time workers hold entry-level career-track jobs.[5] Although we have discussed voluntary and involuntary part-time work as part of the contingent workforce, it is important to emphasize that many core workers negotiate part-time schedules with employers.

Table 12-1 lists the specific reasons for part-time work and the number of individuals who work part-time, defined as fewer than 35 hours weekly, for each reason. The table also shows those who usually work on a full-time or part-time basis for economic reasons, the majority of the workers who were employed on a part-time basis because of slack work or business conditions, and those who could only find part-time work. We can reasonably say that those individuals are probably working part-time on an involuntary basis. Noneconomic reasons explain approximately 80 percent of those who usually work part-time. Most of those workers indicate

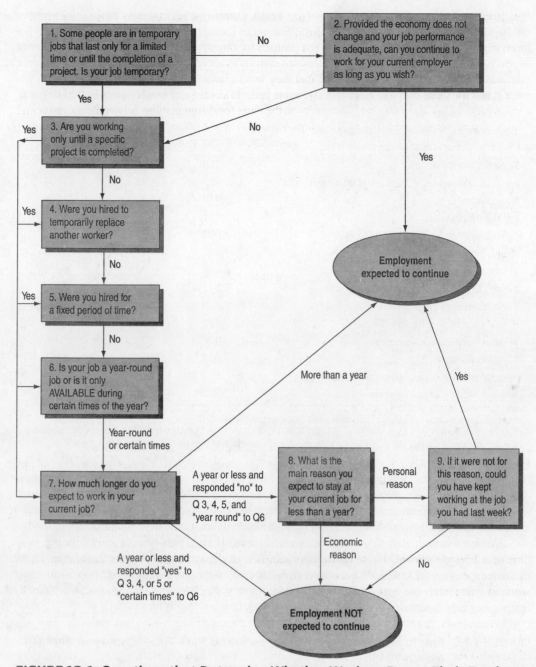

FIGURE 12-1 Questions that Determine Whether Workers Expect Their Employment to Continue

Source: Polivka, A. E. (1996). Contingent and alternative work arrangements, defined. *Monthly Labor Review, 119(10),* p. 5.

that they usually work part time because they are in school or training, or are retirees whose Social Security retirement benefit requirements place a limit on additional earnings. The average weekly hours worked for individuals who usually work part-time based on economic reasons was 22.7 hours and 19.9 hours for noneconomic reasons.

Companies may experience advantages and disadvantages from employing part-time workers. Flexibility is the key advantage. Most companies realize a substantial cost savings because they offer few or no discretionary benefits. In addition, companies realize cost savings for benefits that are linked to hours worked (e.g., retirement plan contributions). Table 12-2 shows

TABLE 12-1 Reasons for Working Less than 35 Hours per Week, February 2018 (Numbers in Thousands)

Reasons for Working Less than 35 Hours	Total	Usually Work Full-Time	Usually Work Part-Time
Total, 1 to 34 hours	35,266	9,631	25,634
Economic reasons	5,331	1,500	3,831
Slack or casual work or business conditions	3,501	1,225	2,246
Could only find part-time work	1,509	—	1,509
Seasonal work	228	152	76
Job started or ended in the middle of week	93	93	—
Noneconomic reasons	29,935	8,131	21,804
Child-care obstacles	1,051	87	964
Other family or personal obligations	5,009	570	4,439
Health or medical limitations	977	—	977
In school or training	6,464	77	6,572
Retired or Social Security limit on earnings	2,842	—	2,842
Vacation time or personal day	3,138	3,138	—
Holiday, legal, or religious obligation	796	796	—
Weather-related curtailment	421	421	—
All other reasons	9,052	3,042	6,010
Average weekly hours, economic reasons	23.0	23.9	22.7
Average weekly hours, noneconomic reasons	21.3	25.1	19.9

Note: Dash indicates no data or data that does not meet publication criteria.
Source: U.S. Bureau of Labor Statistics. (March 9, 2018). *Labor Force Statistics from the Current Population Survey*. Accessed March 28, 2018, at *http://www.bls.gov/web/empsit/cpseea25.htm*.

employers' costs for providing various discretionary benefits and legally required benefits to full-time and part-time employees. Employers save a considerable amount of money in the areas of paid leave, insurance, and legally required benefits. In Chapter 9 we discussed that a greater percentage of full-time workers receive employee benefits than part-time workers.

Companies also save on overtime pay expenses. Hiring part-time workers during peak business periods minimizes overtime pay costs. As we discussed in Chapter 2, the Fair Labor Standards Act of 1938 (FLSA) requires that companies pay nonexempt employees at a rate equaling one and one-half times their regular hourly pay rates. Retail businesses save by employing part-time sales associates during the peak holiday shopping season.

TABLE 12-2 Employers' Hourly Costs for Full- and Part-Time Employee Benefits, March 2018

Benefit	Full-Time ($)	Part-Time ($)
Total hourly benefits costs	12.72	3.72
Paid leave	3.05	0.52
Supplemental pay	1.68	0.27
Insurance	3.41	0.80
Retirement and savings	1.63	0.36
Legally required benefits	2.95	1.78

Source: U.S. Bureau of Labor Statistics. (2018). *Employer Costs for Employee Compensation, March 2018*. USDL: 18-0944. Accessed July 22, 2018, at *http://www.bls.gov*.

Job sharing is a special kind of part-time employment agreement. Two or more part-time employees perform a single full-time job. These employees may perform all job duties or share the responsibility for particular tasks. Some job sharers meet regularly to coordinate their efforts. Job sharing represents a compromise between employees' needs or desires not to work full-time and employers' needs to staff jobs on a full-time basis. Both employers and employees benefit from the use of job sharing. Table 12-3 lists some of the benefits of job sharing to employers and employees.

TEMPORARY AND ON-CALL EMPLOYEES Companies traditionally hire temporary employees for two reasons. First, temporary workers fill in for core employees who are on approved leaves of absence, including sick leave, vacation, bereavement leave, jury duty, and military leave. Second, temporary workers offer extra sets of hands when companies' business activities peak, during such times as the holiday season for retail businesses or summer for amusement parks. Temporary employees perform jobs on a short-term basis usually measured in days, weeks, or months.

Companies have been hiring temporary workers for three additional reasons. First, temporary employment arrangements provide employers the opportunity to evaluate whether legitimate needs exist for creating new positions. Second, temporary employment arrangements give employers the opportunity to decide whether to retain particular workers on an indefinite basis. "The temp job is often what one university placement director calls the 'three-month interview'—and a gateway to a full-time job and perhaps a new career."[6] In effect, the temporary arrangement represents a probationary period, during which employers observe whether workers are meeting job performance standards. As a corollary, such temporary arrangements provide workers the chance to decide whether to accept employment on a full-time basis after they have had time to "check things out." Third, employing temporary workers is often less costly than employing core workers because temporary workers are less likely to receive costly discretionary benefits.

Companies hire temporary employees from a variety of sources. The most common source is a **temporary employment agency**. In the past, most temporary employment agencies traditionally placed clerical and administrative workers. However, now many temporary agencies also place workers with specialized skills (e.g., auditors, computer systems analysts, and lawyers). Temporary agencies are becoming more common; there has been an expansion into blue collar work. For example, jobs in transportation and material moving and production now account for approximately 42 percent of the temporary employment industry.[7]

 FYI

Temporary employment agencies employ more than three million employees during an average week.[8]

TABLE 12-3 Benefits of Job Sharing

Benefits to Employers

- Maintenance of productivity because of higher morale and maintenance of employee skills
- Retention of skilled workers
- Reduction or elimination of the training costs that result from retraining laid-off employees
- Greater flexibility in deploying workers to keep operations going
- Minimization of postrecession costs of hiring and training new workers to replace those who found other jobs during layoff
- Strengthening employees' loyalty to the company

Benefits to Employees

- Continued employee benefits protection
- Continued employment when the likelihood of unemployment is high
- Maintenance of family income
- Continued participation in qualified retirement programs

Companies generally establish relationships with temporary employment agencies based on several factors. First, companies consider agencies' reputations as an important factor, judging reputations by how well agencies' placements work out. Some agencies place a wide range of employees, yet others specialize in one type of placement (e.g., financial services professionals). When companies plan to hire a variety of temporary workers, it is often more convenient to work with agencies that do not specialize. Companies should ultimately judge these agencies' placement records for each type of employee.

Second, companies also should consider agencies' fees. Cost is a paramount consideration for companies that are pursuing lowest-cost competitive strategies. Temporary agencies base fees as a percentage of their placements' pay rates. The percentage varies from agency to agency. The competition among temporary agencies fortunately keeps these rates in check.

Although temporary employees work in a variety of companies, their legal employers are the temporary employment agencies. Temporary employment agencies take full responsibility for selecting temporary employee candidates and determine candidates' qualifications through interviews and testing. Many temporary agencies train candidates to use such office equipment as fax machines, e-mail, and spreadsheet and word processing software programs, particularly for clerical and administrative jobs. Temporary employees receive compensation directly from the agency.

Companies may hire temporary employees through other means. For example, some companies hire individuals directly as temporary workers. Under **direct hire arrangements**, temporary employees typically do not work for more than one year. In addition, the hiring companies are the temporary workers' legal employers. Thus, companies take full responsibility for all HR functions that affect temporary employees, including performance evaluation, compensation, and training.

On-call arrangements are another method for employing temporary workers. On-call employees work sporadically throughout the year when companies require their services. Companies can schedule workers for several days or weeks in a row. Some unionized skilled trade workers are available as on-call employees when they are unable to secure permanent, full-time employment. These employees' unions maintain rosters of unemployed members who are available for work. When employed, on-call workers are employees of the hiring companies. Thus, the hiring companies are responsible for managing and implementing HR policies, including compensation.

LEASED EMPLOYEE ARRANGEMENTS **Lease companies** employ qualified individuals and place them in client companies on a long-term basis. Most leasing companies bill the client for the direct costs of employing the workers (e.g., payroll, benefits, and payroll taxes) and then charge a fixed fee. Lease companies base these fees on either a fixed percentage of the client's payroll or a fixed fee per employee.

Leasing arrangements are common in the food service industry. ARAMARK is just one example of a leasing company that provides cafeteria services to client companies. ARAMARK staffs these companies' in-house cafeterias with cooks, food preparers, and checkout clerks. These cafeteria workers are employees of the leasing company, not the client company. Leasing companies also operate in other industries, including security services, building maintenance, and administrative services. Lease companies and temporary employment agencies are similar because both manage all HR activities. Thus, lease companies provide both wages and benefits to their employees. Lease companies and temporary employment agencies differ in an important respect, however. Lease company placements generally remain in effect for the duration of the lease company's contract with the host company.

INDEPENDENT CONTRACTORS, FREELANCERS, AND CONSULTANTS **Independent contractors, freelancers,** and **consultants** (the term *independent contractor* will be used in this discussion) establish working relationships with companies on their own rather than through temporary employment agencies or lease companies. Traditionally, independent contractors typically possess specialized skills that are in short supply in the labor market. Companies select independent contractors to complete particular projects of short-term duration (i.e., usually a year or less). In recent years, technology has created opportunities for an emerging group of independent contractors who become connected with prospective customers through smartphone apps. For example, Uber Technologies has created a smartphone app that allows customers to arrange automobile transportation with the company's independent contractors. Uber's independent contractors use their own vehicles to transport customers to destinations of their choice, such as from a hotel to an airport. The cleaning service, Handy, connects customers with independent contractors who provide household services, facilitated by a smartphone app. There have been challenges to classification of workers as independent contractors. We will consider some of the challenges later.

Independent contractors operate in the so-called gig economy. (Gig is an informal term for a temporary job.) One estimate places the number of gig workers at 34 percent of the workforce and that number is expected to rise to 43 percent by 2020.[9] According to the U.S. Bureau of Labor Statistics, gigs are more common in some occupations than in others. Typically, a job that entails one task, such as data analysis, lends itself well to a gig arrangement. The following is a list of occupations and jobs that are often associated with the gig economy.[10]

- **Arts and design**. Many occupations in this group, including musicians, graphic designers, and craft and fine artists, offer specific one-time services or customized products, which makes them good candidates for gig work.
- **Computer and information technology**. Web developers, software developers, and computer programmers are among the occupations in this group in which workers might be hired to complete a single job, such as to create a small-business website or a new type of software.
- **Construction and extraction**. Carpenters, painters, and other construction workers frequently take on individual projects of short duration, a hallmark of gig jobs.
- **Media and communications**. The services of technical writers, interpreters and translators, photographers, and others in this group are often project-based and easy to deliver electronically, fueling a market for gig workers.
- **Transportation and material moving**. Ridesharing apps have helped to create opportunities for workers who provide transportation to passengers as needed, and on-demand shopping services have led to gig jobs for delivery drivers.

Until now, we have been examining compensation issues of *employees* in this and previous chapters. Independent contractors are not *employees* of a company. *Black's Law Dictionary* defines an *employee* as "a person in the service of another under any contract of hire, express or implied, oral or written, where the employer has the power or right to control and direct the employee in the material details of how the work is to be performed."[11] An *independent contractor* is one who, "in the exercise of an independent employment, contracts to do a piece of work according to his own methods and is subject to his employer's only as to the end product or final result of his work."[12] There are three legal tests to determine a worker's status: the common-law test, the economic realities test, and a hybrid test that incorporates various elements of both tests. We will review the first two tests and their relationships to pay and to benefits for independent contractors later in this chapter. Table 12-4 contains a brief description of each test as well as the federal laws under which the test has been applied by courts of laws to determine a worker's status.

Reasons for U.S. Employers' Increased Reliance on Contingent Workers

Structural changes in the U.S. economy have contributed to the rise of contingent employment:

- Economic recessions
- International competition
- Shift from manufacturing to a service economy

ECONOMIC RECESSIONS Many companies layoff segments of their workforces during economic recessions as a cost-control measure. Following economic recessions, some companies restore staffing levels with permanent employees. Many companies are increasingly restoring staffing levels with contingent workers. Since the early 1970s, the U.S. economy experienced several

TABLE 12-4 Tests for Determining Whether a Worker Is an Employee

Test	Description	Laws under which test has been applied by courts
Common-law test [used by Internal Revenue Service (IRS)]	Employment relationship exists if employer has right to control work process, as determined by evaluating totality of the circumstances and specific factors	Federal Insurance Contributions Act Federal Unemployment Tax Act Income tax withholding Employment Retirement and Income Security Act National Labor Relations Act Immigration Reform and Control Act (IRS test)
Economic realities test	Employment relationship exists if individual is economically dependent on a business for continued employment	Fair Labor Standards Act Title VII Age Discrimination in Employment Act Americans with Disabilities Act Family and Medical Leave Act (likely to apply)
Hybrid test	Employment relationship is evaluated under both common-law and economic reality test factors, with a focus on who has the right to control the means and manner of a worker's performance	Title VII Age Discrimination in Employment Act Americans with Disabilities Act Family and Medical Leave Act (likely to apply)

Source: Charles J. Muhl, "What Is an Employee? The Answer Depends on the Federal Law," *Monthly Labor Review* (January 2002), p. 6.

economic recessions. These repeated recessions have shaken employers' confidence about future economic prosperity. Staffing segments of workforces with contingent workers represents a form of risk control because employers save on most discretionary benefits costs. In addition, companies can terminate contingent workers' services more easily: These employment relationships are explicitly tentative. Both the host employer and the workers understand that these engagements are of limited duration. As a rule, companies rebuild the core employee workforce following the end of economic recessions; however, this has not been the case since the recession that took place during the years 2007–2009. Much anecdotal evidence suggests that the noteworthy damaging effect of the recession on business activity has shaken the confidence of many businesses even after a decade has past. Some companies are hedging against uncertainty by relying on, in part, leaner staffing levels of core employees. It is also possible that companies are choosing to employ more part-time workers because of lower compensation costs for this workforce segment.

INTERNATIONAL COMPETITION International competition is another pertinent structural change. American companies no longer compete just against each other. Many foreign businesses have demonstrated the ability to manufacture goods at lower costs than their American competitors. As a result, successful American companies have streamlined operations to control costs. Where possible, U.S. companies' streamlining aims to lower labor costs, oftentimes by reducing the number of core employees and using contingent workers as an alternative. Greater reliance on contingent workers in U.S. operations can be explained by the lower wages and salaries in many other countries.[13]

THE SHIFT FROM MANUFACTURING TO A SERVICE ECONOMY The service sector refers to six broad divisions of industries: transportation, communication, and public utilities; wholesale trade; retail trade; finance, insurance, and real estate; services; and government. Manufacturing companies' (e.g., automobile makers and textiles) employment declined substantially during the past several years,[14] and economic forecasts predict a loss of jobs in the federal government and manufacturing industry through 2026.[15] During this period, a steady decrease in employment in manufacturing industries is expected to be offset by a substantial rise in employment in the construction industry and service sectors such as professional and business services as well as health care and social assistance.[16] Service sector employment is expected to add approximately 10.5 million new jobs to the economy by 2026.[17] In addition, contingent workers typically find employment in service businesses, which are more labor intensive than capital intensive (e.g., heavy manufacturing equipment).

PAY AND EMPLOYEE BENEFITS FOR CONTINGENT WORKERS

Compensation practices for contingent workers vary. We will discuss these practices shortly. Nevertheless, all parties involved in employing or hosting contingent workers possess liability under federal and state laws, including:

12-2. Discuss pay and benefits issues for contingent workers.

- Overtime and minimum wages required under the FLSA
- Paying insurance premiums required under state workers' compensation laws
- Nondiscriminatory compensation and employment practices under the
  - Employee Retirement Income Security Act of 1974 (ERISA)
  - National Labor Relations Act (NLRA)
  - Title VII of the Civil Rights Act of 1964
  - Americans with Disabilities Act of 1990 (ADA)
  - Age Discrimination in Employment Act (ADEA)
- Patient Protection and Affordable Care Act of 2010 (PPACA)

Temporary employment agencies and leasing companies that place workers in clients' firms are liable under these laws. In addition, the client company may also be liable. "The fact that a worker is somebody else's employee while he or she is on your premises, or performing services for the business, is not necessarily a defense to alleged violations of federal and state labor laws including Title VII of the Civil Rights Act, the Fair Labor Standards Act, and the Americans with Disabilities Act."[18]

Part-Time Employees

Companies that employ part-time workers are the legal employers, as is the case for core employees. Compensating part-time employees poses the following challenges for employers:

- Should companies pay part-time workers on an hourly basis or a salary basis?
- Do equity problems arise between core employees and part-time employees?
- Do companies offer benefits to part-time workers?

PAY Part-time employees earn less, on average, than core employees. In March 2018, part-time workers in private industry earned an average $14.14 per hour, whereas full-time employees earned $26.69 per hour.[19] Full-time management and professional employees earned $42.75 per hour, whereas their part-time counterparts earned $33.54 per hour. Full-time production workers earned substantially more than their part-time counterparts ($18.66 per hour versus $12.40 per hour). Full-time service employees similarly earned more than part-timers ($13.64 per hour versus $10.76 per hour).[20]

Companies often expect salaried part-time employees to do much more than their fair share of the work because the effective hourly pay rate decreases as the number of hours worked increases. An explicit agreement pertaining to work–hour limits can minimize this problem. An agreement similarly may specify explicit work goals. On the other hand, companies may avoid this problem by paying part-time employees on an hourly basis. Part-time and full-time employees may perceive the situation as inequitable under certain circumstances. For example, equity problems may arise when salaried full-time employees and hourly part-time employees work together. It is possible that highly skilled full-time employees might effectively be underpaid relative to less-skilled part-time employees performing the same work (i.e., full-time employees' "hourly" pay rate will be lower when they perform more and better work in a shorter period than less-skilled part-time workers).

EMPLOYEE BENEFITS Companies generally do not provide discretionary benefits to part-time employees; however, benefits practices for part-time workers vary widely according to company size as well as between the private and public sectors. In March 2017, approximately 38 percent of part-time employees had access to retirement benefits compared to 81 percent of full-time employees.[21] As noted earlier, fewer part-time workers had access to medical care benefits.

Employers are not required to offer protective insurance (e.g., medical, dental, vision, or life insurance) to part-time employees even with the PPACA; however, part-time employees who do receive health insurance coverage under employer-sponsored plans are entitled to protection under the Consolidated Omnibus Budget Reconciliation Act (COBRA). As discussed in Chapter 10, COBRA provides employees the opportunity to continue receiving employer-sponsored health care insurance coverage temporarily following termination or layoff. Employees who qualify for COBRA protection receive insurance coverage that matches the coverage level during employment.

Employers may be required to provide qualified retirement programs to part-time employees.[22] Part-time employees who meet the following two criteria are eligible to participate in qualified retirement programs:

- Minimum age of 21 years
- Completion of at least 1,000 hours of work in a 12-month period (i.e., "year of service")

Special considerations apply to seasonal employees' eligibilities for qualified retirement benefits because most seasonal employees do not meet the annual service pension eligibility criterion. Maritime industries, such as fishing, represent seasonal employment, and fishermen are seasonal employees. The U.S. Department of Labor defines 125 service days as the "year of service" for maritime workers. Part-time and seasonal employees cannot be excluded from pension plans if they meet the U.S. Department of Labor's "year of service" criterion.

Temporary Employees

Temporary employment agencies are the legal employers for temporary employees. Temporary employment agencies are, therefore, responsible for complying with federal employment legislation with one exception, workers' compensation, which we will address shortly. Compensating temporary employees poses challenges for companies.

- Do equity problems arise between core employees and temporary employees?
- How do the FLSA overtime provisions affect temporary employees?
- Do companies offer temporary workers benefits?
- Who is responsible for providing workers' compensation protection: the temporary agency or the client company?

PAY In 2017, temporary workers earned an average hourly rate of $17.44 while full-time workers earned $23.86.[23] Pay rates varied widely by occupation and workers' particular qualifications. Equity problems may (or may not) arise where core and temporary employees work together. On one hand, temporary employees may work diligently because they know that their assignments in client companies are explicitly of limited duration. In addition, frequent moves from one company to the next may limit workers' opportunities or desires to build careers with any of these companies. Furthermore, temporary workers may neither take the time nor have the time to scope out pay differences because their engagements are brief (i.e., anywhere from one day to a few weeks). These temporary employees are, therefore, not likely to perceive inequitable pay situations.

On the other hand, some temporary employees may not work diligently because they did not choose temporary employment arrangements. Individuals who lose their jobs because of a sudden layoff and who have few core job alternatives are most susceptible. Pay differences between these temporary employees and core employees are likely to intensify perceptions of inequity.

It is important to distinguish between temporary employees and seasonal employees for determining eligibility under the FLSA minimum wage and overtime pay provisions. Companies hire temporary employees to fill in as needed. This means that companies may hire temporary employees at any time throughout a calendar year; however, seasonal employees work during set regular periods every year. Lifeguards on New England beaches are seasonal employees because they work only during the summer months when people visit beaches to swim. Summer camp counselors are also seasonal employees.

The FLSA extends coverage to temporary employees. Temporary employment agencies must, therefore, pay temporary workers at least the federal minimum wage rate. In addition, the FLSA requires employers to provide overtime pay at one and one-half times the normal hourly rate for each hour worked beyond 40 hours per week. Host companies are responsible for FLSA compliance if temporary employment agencies are not involved, as in the case of direct hire or on-call arrangements.

Some seasonal employees are exempt from the FLSA's minimum wage and overtime pay provisions.[24] The FLSA itself, as drafted, does not explicitly address minimum wage and overtime pay practices for seasonal employees; however, professional legal opinions were added as needed to resolve ambiguities and guide practice. The opinions pertain to specific employers' questions about the act's scope of coverage (e.g., the applicability of FLSA overtime and minimum wage provisions to seasonal amusement park workers). Professional opinions do not automatically generalize to all seasonal employees. For example, all amusement or recreational establishment employees are covered by the FLSA's minimum wage and overtime pay provisions when the establishments operate at least seven months per year; however, youth counselors employed at summer camps are generally exempt from the FLSA minimum wage and overtime pay provisions.

EMPLOYEE BENEFITS Anecdotal evidence indicates that companies typically do not provide discretionary benefits to temporary employees. This information should not be surprising. As we discussed earlier, many companies employ temporary workers to minimize discretionary benefits costs; however, temporary employees (and seasonal workers) are eligible for qualified pension benefits if they meet ERISA's minimum service requirements for seasonal and part-time employees, as discussed earlier.

The **dual employer common law doctrine** establishes temporary workers' rights to receive workers' compensation.[25] According to this doctrine, temporary workers are employees of both temporary employment agencies and the client companies. The written contract between the employment agency and the client company specifies which organization's workers' compensation policy applies in the event of injuries.

Leased Workers

Designating leased employees' legal employers is less clear than it is for part-time and temporary employees. Leasing companies are the legal employers regarding wage issues and legally required benefits; however, leasing companies and client companies are the legal employers regarding particular discretionary benefits. Compensating leased employees is, therefore, complex.

- Do leased employees receive discretionary benefits?
- Who is responsible for providing discretionary benefits: the leasing company or the client company?

PAY In May 2017, leased employees who worked on a full-time basis typically earned $1,077 per week; part-time leased workers earned $322.[26] These data are the most recent available at the time of publication. The U.S. Bureau of Labor Statistics infrequently publishes pay information for contingent worker groups. Previously, the data were collected in 2005. However, it is possible to adjust these rates for inflation using the BLS's *CPI Inflation Calculator* (http://data.bls.gov /cgi-bin/cpicalc.pl). Factors other than inflation may have an influence on these estimates, among them, the changing skill composition of the leased workforce, economic recession, and so forth. Therefore, the inflation-adjusted estimates may be biased because making adjustments on these other factors is not straightforward.

EMPLOYEE BENEFITS Both pension eligibility and discretionary benefits are key issues. Leased employees are generally entitled to participation in the client companies' qualified retirement programs; however, the leasing company becomes responsible for leased employees' retirement benefits when the **safe harbor rule**[27] requirements are met. Table 12-5 lists the safe harbor rule requirements.

Another section of the Internal Revenue Code (IRC) influences companies' discretionary benefits policies (excluding retirement benefits) for leased employees.[28] Under this rule, client companies are responsible for providing leased employees with group medical insurance, group life insurance, educational assistance programs, and continuation coverage requirements for group health plans under COBRA.

Independent Contractors, Freelancers, and Consultants

The Bureau of Labor Statistics reported that full-time independent contractors earned $851 weekly in 2017. Companies are neither obligated to pay the following on behalf of independent contractors, freelancers, and consultants:

- Federal income tax withholding;
- Overtime and minimum wages required under the FLSA (however, employers are obligated to pay financially dependent workers overtime and minimum wages);
- Insurance premiums required under state workers' compensation laws, except where states explicitly require that companies maintain workers' compensation coverage for all workers regardless of whether they are independent contractors;

nor are companies required to provide protection under the following laws, which we addressed in previous chapters:

- Protection under the Employee Retirement Income Security Act of 1974 (ERISA),
- Family and Medical Leave Act,
- National Labor Relations Act (NLRA),
- Title VII of the Civil Rights Act of 1964,
- Americans with Disabilities Act (ADA).

Following Table 12-4, the courts rely on three tests to determine whether a worker qualifies as an employee. We will focus on the common-law test and the economic realities test.

COMMON-LAW TEST Common law is developed by judges through court proceedings that decide individual cases. At issue is whether the employer has the **right to control** based on IRC criteria. According to the Internal Revenue Service (IRS), evidence of the degree of control and independence fall into three categories:

- Behavioral: Does the company control or have the right to control what the worker does and how the worker does his or her job?

TABLE 12-5 Safe Harbor Rule Requirements

- The leased employee must be covered by the leasing company's pension plan, which must (1) be a money purchase plan with a nonintegrated employer contribution rate for each participant of at least 10 percent of compensation, (2) provide for full and immediate vesting, and (3) allow each employee of the leasing organization to immediately participate in such a plan; and
- Leased employees cannot constitute more than 20 percent of the recipient's "nonhighly compensated workforce." Nonhighly compensated workforce means the total number of (1) nonhighly compensated individuals who are employees of the recipient and who have performed services for the recipient for at least one year, or (2) individuals who are leased employees of the recipient (determined without regard to the leasing rules).

Source: I.R.C. §414(n)(5).

- Financial: Are the business aspects of the worker's job controlled by the payer? (These include things like how the worker is paid, whether expenses are reimbursed, who provides tools/supplies, etc.)
- Type of Relationship: Are there written contracts or employee type benefits (i.e., pension plan, insurance, vacation pay, etc.)? Will the relationship continue and is the work performed a key aspect of the business?[29]

These questions are based on 10 factors used to determine whether a worker is an employee. Table 12-6 lists the 10 specific criteria of this common-law test. Companies must consider all of these factors when making a determination about a worker's status. There is not an absolute criterion to determine whether workers meet the criteria under this test.

ECONOMIC REALITIES TEST The **economic realities** test is most significantly applied in the context of the Fair Labor Standards Act.[30] Its focus is on the determination of whether employees are financially dependent. Table 12-7 lists the criteria to determine whether workers are financially dependent on the employer. For example, are exotic dancers entitled to minimum wage under FLSA? A nightclub's owners claimed that the exotic dancers were not eligible because they were independent contractors:

- The exotic dancers could perform whenever and wherever they wanted.
- The club had no control over the manner of performance.
- The exotic dancers must furnish their own costumes.

A federal district court ruled that the nightclub's exotic dancers were entitled to minimum wage because they were economically dependent on the nightclub.[31] The exotic dancers were economically dependent on the nightclub for the following reasons:

- The club owners set hours in which the exotic dancers could perform.
- The club owners issued guidelines on exotic dancers' behavior at the club.
- The club owners deducted 20 percent from the tips of each exotic dancer to cover administrative costs.

TABLE 12-6 Factors Used to Determine a Worker's Status under the Common-Law Test

Factor	Worker is an employee if—	Worker is an independent contractor if—
Right to control	Employer controls details of the work	Worker controls details of the work
Type of business	Worker is not engaged in business or occupation distinct from employer's	Worker operates in business that is distinct from employer's business
Supervision	Employer supervises worker	Work is done without supervision
Skill level	Skill level need not be high or unique	Skill level is specialized, is unique, or requires substantial training
Tools and materials	Employer provides instrumentalities, tools, and location of workplace	Worker provides instrumentalities and tools of workplace and works at a site other than the employer's
Continuing relationship	Worker is employed for extended, continuous period	Worker is employed for specific project or for limited time
Method of payment	Worker is paid by the hour, or other computation based on time worked is used to determine pay	Worker is paid by the project
Integration	Work is part of employer's regular business	Work is not part of employer's regular business
Intent	Employer and worker intend to create an employer-employee relationship	Employer and worker do not intend to create an employer-employee relationship
Employment by more than one firm	Worker provides services only to one employer	Worker provides services to more than one business

Source: Muhl, C. J. (2002). What is an employee? The answer depends on the Federal law. *Monthly Labor Review* (January), p. 7.

The economic realities test and common-law test are similar.[32] The common-law test focuses on whether the economic reality, as informed by various factors, is that a worker depends on someone else's business for continued employment. If there is such dependence, then the worker is classified as an employee; otherwise, the worker is classified as an independent contractor.

In recent years, there has been a spate of protests and lawsuits by a variety of independent contractors over their status with the companies for which they provide services. Many claim that companies misclassify them as independent contractors when, in fact, they maintain that they are employees. For example, FedEx was found to have misclassified several delivery-truck drivers as independent contractors. A court ruled that the drivers were employees, not independent contractors, because FedEx required them to wear company uniforms, drive company trucks, and maintain an appearance specified in company policy.

Some companies such as Handy, which provides housecleaning and handyman services, appear to have created negative sentiments among many of their independent contractors. For example, individuals who had performed cleaning services filed a class action suit against Handy. The plaintiffs argued that they were entitled to minimum wage and other legal protections because they did not possess control over their work. One of the lead plaintiffs expressed the following sentiment: "We are not robots; we are not a remote control; we are individuals."[33]

Uber has been the subject of lawsuits initiated by its drivers, which Uber classifies as independent contractors. Uber defends its classification of drivers by maintaining that it is not a transportation company, but, instead, a technology company that established a platform for connecting drivers with passengers.[34] Some courts have upheld Uber's classification of drivers while some others have concluded that Uber drivers are employees based on right to control criteria. For instance, Uber sets fares, imposes minimum performance standards, and a code of conduct for conducting business with riders.

In 2018, the California Supreme Court rendered a decision (Dynamex v. Superior Court of Los Angeles County) that makes it more difficult for employers in California to classify workers as independent contractors. Dynamex provides delivery and courier services. In 2004, the company reclassified its drivers from employees to independent contractors. Rulings in various courts of law were consistent. Dynamex drivers are indeed employees because their services are essential to the company's activities. Dynamex subsequently challenged the lower court rulings, but was unsuccessful in its attempts to maintain delivery drivers' status as independent contractors.

The so-called ABC test, which resulted from the California Supreme Court ruling, requires companies to prove that their workers are independent contractors based on meeting three criteria: First, workers provide service uninhibited from the company's control. Second, the service

TABLE 12-7 Factors Used to Determine a Worker's Status under the Economic Realities Test

Factor	Worker is an employee if—	Worker is an independent contractor if—
Integration	Worker provides services that are a part of the employers regular business	Worker provides services outside the regular business of the employer
Investment in facilities	Worker has no investment in the work facilities and equipment	Worker has a substantial investment in the work facilities and equipment
Right to control	Management retains a certain type and degree of control over the work	Management has no right to control the work process of the worker
Risk	Worker does not have the opportunity to make a profit or incur a loss	Worker has the opportunity to make a profit or incur a loss from the job
Skill	Work does not require any special or unique skills or judgment	Work requires a special skill, judgment, or initiative
Continuing relationship	Worker has a permanent or extended relationship with the business	Work relationship is for one project or a limited duration

Source: Muhl, C. J. (2002). What is an employee? The answer depends on the Federal law. *Monthly Labor Review* (January), p. 8.

is outside the company's core business (for example, a food service worker in a hospital). Third, the worker also provides service to other companies. Dynamex failed to provide compelling evidence that supports this standard. As a result, many companies' classifications will be held to stricter standards, possibly leading to changing the status of some workers from independent contractor to employee. Reclassification will greatly increase employment costs for many companies, the costs of affordable health insurance coverage and social security taxes.

FLEXIBLE WORK SCHEDULES: FLEXTIME, COMPRESSED WORKWEEKS, AND TELECOMMUTING

Many companies now offer employees flexible work schedules to help them balance work and family demands. Flextime and compressed workweek schedules are the most prominent flexible work schedules used in companies. Flexible work schedule practices apply to both core employees and contingent employees. Telecommuting arrangements have become increasingly popular and commonplace. Research shows that employees highly value flexibility as a workplace policy, as do many progressive employers. For example, Patagonia is a designer of outdoor clothing and gear for a variety of sports. The following Watch It! video showcases Patagonia's flexible work policies and the company's culture that strongly favors work–life balance. Employees may take time off with pay to take care of a sick child as needed. The only requirement is that employees are expected to complete their work assignments.

12-3. Summarize the three categories of flexible work schedules.

 FYI

The prevalence of flexible work arrangements varies:

- Telework (occasional/part-time): 89% of companies surveyed
- Flextime: 86%
- Telework (full-time remote): 61%
- Shift flexibility: 51%
- Compressed workweek: 45%
- Job sharing: 12%[35]

Flextime Schedules

Flextime schedules allow employees to modify their work schedules within specified limits set by the employer. Employees adjust when they will start work and when they will leave. Flextime, however, generally does not lead to reduced work hours. For instance, an employee may choose to work between 10 A.M. and 6 P.M., 9 A.M. and 5 P.M., or 8 A.M. and 4 P.M.

All workers must be present during certain workday hours when business activity is regularly high. This period is known as **core hours**. The number of core hours may vary from company to company, by departments within companies, or by season. Although employees are relatively free to choose start and completion times that fall outside core hours, management must carefully coordinate these times to avoid understaffing. Some flextime programs incorporate a **banking hours** feature that enables employees to vary the number of work hours daily as long as they maintain the regular number of work hours on a weekly basis.

Employers can expect three possible benefits from using flextime schedules. First, flextime schedules lead to less tardiness and absenteeism. Flexibly defining the workweek better enables employees to schedule medical and other appointments outside work hours. As a result, workers are less likely to be late or miss work altogether.

Second, flexible work schedules should lead to higher work productivity. Employees have more choice about when to work during the day. Individuals who work best during the morning hours may schedule morning hours, and individuals who work best during the afternoons or evenings can choose these times. In addition, possessing the flexibility to attend to personal matters on their own time should help employees focus on doing better work.

Third, flexible work schedules benefit employers by creating longer business hours and better service. Staggering employees' schedules should enable businesses to stay open longer hours without incurring overtime pay expenses. In addition, customers should perceive better service because of expanded business hours. Companies that conduct business by telephone on national and international bases are more likely to be open during customers' normal operating hours in other time zones.

Two possible limitations of flexible work schedules are increased overhead costs and coordination problems. Maintaining extended operations leads to higher overhead costs, including support staff and utilities. In addition, flexible work schedules may lead to work coordination problems when some employees are not present at the same time.

Compressed Workweek Schedules

Compressed workweek schedules enable employees to perform their work in fewer days than a regular 5-day workweek. As a result, employees may work four 10-hour days or three 12-hour days. These schedules can promote companies' recruitment and retention successes by:

- Reducing the number of times employees must commute between home and work
- Providing more time together for dual-career couples who live apart

Telecommuting

Telecommuting represents an alternative work arrangement in which employees work at home or at some other location besides the office. Telecommuters generally spend part of their time working in the office and the other part working at home. This alternative work arrangement is appropriate for work that does not require regular direct interpersonal interactions with other workers (e.g., accounting, systems analysis, and telephone sales). Telecommuters stay in touch with coworkers and superiors through e-mail, telephone, and faxes. Table 12-8 summarizes the variety of possible telecommuting arrangements.

Potential benefits for employers include increased productivity and lower overhead costs for office space and supplies. Telecommuting also serves as an effective recruiting and retention practice for employees who strongly desire to perform their jobs away from the office. Employers may also increase the retention of valued employees who choose not to move when their companies relocate.

TABLE 12-8 Alternative Telecommuting Arrangements

- *Satellite work center.* Employees work from a remote extension of the employer's office that includes a clerical staff and a full-time manager.
- *Neighborhood work center.* Employees work from a satellite office shared by several employers.
- *Nomadic executive office.* Executives who travel extensively maintain control over projects through use of telephone, fax, and e-mail.
- *Employees sometimes work entirely outside the office.* Others might work off-site only once a month or 2–3 days a week.
- *Telecommuters can be full- or part-time employees.*
- *Telecommuting arrangements can be temporary or permanent.* A temporarily disabled employee may work at home until fully recovered. A permanently disabled employee may work at home exclusively.

Source: Adapted from Bureau of National Affairs, Telecommuting (2005). *Compensation & Benefits.* Available: *www.bna.com*, accessed March 7, 2005.

Employees find telecommuting beneficial. Telecommuting enables parents to be near their infants or preschool-age children and to be home when older children finish their school days. In addition, telecommuting arrangements minimize commuting time and expense, which are exceptional in such congested metropolitan areas as Boston, Los Angeles, and New York City as travel time may increase threefold during peak "rush hour" traffic periods and parking and toll costs can be hefty (monthly parking rates alone often exceed thousands of dollars per car). Finally, employees' involvement in office politics will be reduced, which should promote higher job performance.

Telecommuting programs may also lead to disadvantages for employers and employees. Some employers are concerned about not having direct contact with employees, which makes conducting performance appraisals more difficult. Employees sometimes feel that work-at-home arrangements are disruptive to their personal lives. In addition, some employees feel isolated because they do not personally interact as often with coworkers and superiors.

Flexible Work Schedules: Balancing the Demands of Work Life and Home Life

Some U.S. companies use flexible work schedules to help employees balance the demands of work and home. Flextime, compressed workweeks, and telecommuting should provide single parents or dual-career parents the opportunity to spend more time with their children. Flextime gives parents the opportunity to schedule work around special events at their children's schools. Compressed workweeks enable parents on limited incomes to save on day care costs by reducing the number of days at the office. Parents can benefit from telecommuting in a similar fashion. Likewise, dual-career couples living apart also benefit from flexible work schedules. Compressed workweeks and telecommuting reduce the time partners or spouses have to spend away from each other.

PAY AND EMPLOYEE BENEFITS FOR FLEXIBLE EMPLOYEES

The key pay issue for flexible work schedules is overtime pay. The main employee benefits issues are paid time-off benefits and working condition fringe benefits.

12-4. Discuss the pay and employee benefits issues for flexible work schedules, compressed workweeks, and telecommuting arrangements.

Pay

In many cases, "flexible" employees work more than 40 hours during some weeks and fewer hours during other weeks. The FLSA requires that companies compensate nonexempt employees at an overtime rate equal to one and one-half times the normal hourly rate for each hour worked in excess of 40 hours per week. The overtime provisions are based on employees working set hours during fixed work periods. How do FLSA overtime provisions apply to flexible work schedules?

Let's assume the following flexible work schedule: An employee works 40 hours during the first week, 30 hours during the second week, and 50 hours during the third week. Although this employee worked 40 hours per week, on average, for the 3-week period ([40 + 30 + 50 hours]/ 3 weeks), is that employee entitled to overtime pay for the additional 10 hours worked during the third week?

Some employees' weekly flexible schedules may fluctuate frequently and unpredictably according to such nonwork demands as chronically ill family members. Unpredictable flexible schedules make overtime pay calculations difficult. It is possible that companies may make inadequate or excessive overtime payments. A Supreme Court ruling (**Walling v. A. H. Belo Corp.**)[36] requires employers to guarantee fixed weekly pay for employees whose work hours vary from week to week:

- The employer typically cannot determine the number of hours employees will work each week.
- The workweek period fluctuates, with both greater and less than 40 hours per week.

This pay provision guarantees employees fixed weekly pay regardless of how many hours they work, and it enables employers to control weekly labor cost expenditures. The use of compressed workweek schedules may lead to differences in overtime practices in some states. Whereas the federal government bases overtime pay on a weekly basis, some states use other time bases to determine overtime pay eligibility. Table 12-9 lists maximum hour provisions for select states. As you can see, there is wide variation in daily overtime practices.

Employee Benefits

Flexible workweek schedules have the greatest impact on paid time off benefits. Many companies determine employees' paid time-off according to their pay period, i.e. weekly, fortnightly, or monthly. The determination of paid vacation and sick leave for employees on standard work schedules is relatively straightforward; however, flexible employees work fewer hours some months and more hours during other months. This variability complicates companies' calculations of paid time-off benefits.

Another issue is the treatment of paid time-off for holidays. Under standard work schedules, the vast majority of employees work five 8-hour days from Monday through Friday. For example, all employees take Thanksgiving Day off (a Thursday) with pay. Under flexible schedules, some employees may not be scheduled to work on Thursdays. As a result, standard-schedule employees receive 1 day off with pay during Thanksgiving week, and some flexible employees work their regular schedules, missing a paid day off from work. Companies must establish policies that provide flexible workers with comparable paid time off benefits or alternative holidays. Such policies are necessary to maintain equity among employees; however, scheduling alternative holidays may lead to coordination problems for small companies: Companies with small staffs may not have enough employees to cover for flexible workers during their alternative holiday time off work.

An employee benefits issue known as **working condition fringe benefits** applies to telecommuters. Employers are likely to provide telecommuters with the necessary equipment to perform their jobs effectively while off-site: computers, printers, photocopy machines, and sundry office supplies. In addition, some employers provide similar equipment to employees who wish to work additional hours outside their regular work schedules during the evenings or weekends. This arrangement does not qualify as telecommuting.

The IRS treats the home use of office equipment and supplies as employees' taxable income when the use falls outside established telecommuting relationships; however, employees are not

TABLE 12-9 Maximum Hours before Overtime for Selected States

Alaska

Under a voluntary flexible work hour plan approved by the Alaska Department of Labor, a 10-hour day, 40-hour workweek may be instituted with premium pay after 10 hours a day instead of after 8 hours.

California

Any work in excess of 8 hours in one workday and any work in excess of 40 hours in one workweek and the first 8 hours worked on the seventh day of work in any one workweek shall be at the rate of one and one-half times the regular rate of pay. Any work in excess of 12 hours in one day and any work in excess of 8 hours on any seventh day of a workweek shall be paid no less than twice the regular rate of pay. California Labor Code Section 510. Exceptions apply to an employee working pursuant to an alternative workweek adopted pursuant to applicable Labor Code sections and for time spent commuting.

Oregon

Premium pay required after 10 hours a day in nonfarm canneries, driers, or packing plants and in mills, factories, or manufacturing establishments (excluding sawmills, planing mills, shingle mills, and logging camps).

Rhode Island

Time and a half premium pay for work on Sundays and holidays in retail and certain other businesses is required under two laws that are separate from the Fair Labor Standards Act minimum wage provision.

Washington

Premium pay is not applicable to employees who request compensating time off in lieu of premium pay.

Source: U.S. Department of Labor. (2018). *Minimum Wage Laws in the States*. Available: *http://www.dol.gov/whd/minwage/america. htm#footnote*, accessed March 22, 2018.

taxed when the home use of employer-provided equipment falls within established telecommuting relationships. Under this condition, the IRS treats the home use of employer-provided equipment as a working condition fringe benefit.

UNIONS' REACTIONS TO CONTINGENT WORKERS AND FLEXIBLE WORK SCHEDULES

Unions generally do not support companies' use of contingent workers and flexible work schedules. Most union leaders believe that alternative work arrangements threaten members' job security and are prone to unfair and inequitable treatment. The most common concerns include:

- Employers exploit contingent workers by paying them lower wages and benefits than core employees.
- Employers' efforts to get cheap labor will lead to a poorly trained and less skilled workforce that will hamper competitiveness.
- Part-time employees are difficult to organize because their interests are centered on activities outside the workplace. Part-time workers are, therefore, probably not good union members.
- Part-time employment erodes labor standards: Part-time workers are often denied employee benefits, job security, and promotion opportunities. Increasing part-time employment would promote inequitable treatment.
- Temporary employees generally have little concern about improving the productivity of a company for which they will work for only a brief period.
- Unions' bargaining power becomes weak when companies demonstrate their ability to perform effectively with temporaries.
- The long days of compressed workweeks or flextime could endanger workers' safety and health, even if the workers choose these long days themselves.
- Concerns about employee isolation, uncompensated overtime, and company monitoring in the home are among the reasons unions have been reluctant to permit telecommuting by their members.

Unions' positions against contingent employment are unlikely to change because this practice undermines efforts to secure high wages and job security for members; however, some unions, particularly in the public sector, have begun to accept the use of flexible work schedules. The benefits of these arrangements (e.g., increased productivity and lower absence rates and tardiness) strengthen unions' bargaining power.

12-5. Describe unions' reactions to contingent work and flexible work schedule arrangements.

STRATEGIC ISSUES AND CHOICES IN USING CONTINGENT AND FLEXIBLE WORKERS

What role do contingent workers and flexible work schedules play in promoting competitive advantage? These work arrangements, when properly applied, can ultimately contribute to meeting the goals of cost control and product or service innovation; however, the rationale for the appropriateness of contingent employment and flexible work schedules differs according to these objectives.

A cost control objective requires firms to reduce output costs per employee. Contingent employment saves companies considerable amounts of money because they do not give these workers most discretionary benefits or they provide less generous amounts of such benefits.

Employers' use of well-trained contingent workers also contributes through reduced training costs; however, not all contingent workers know company-specific work practices and procedures. Company-specific training represents a significant cost to companies. Companies that do not employ contingent workers long enough to realize the productivity benefits from training undermine cost control objectives. Company-sponsored training may seem to contradict the lowest-cost imperative in the short term.

12-6. Identify strategic issues and choices companies face regarding the use of contingent workers.

The following factors can increase short-term costs:

- Costs of training materials and instructors' professional fees
- Downtime while employees are participating in training
- Inefficiencies that may result until employees master new skills.

A longer-term perspective, however, may lead to the conclusion that contingent work arrangements support the lowest-cost imperatives. Over time, productivity enhancements and increased flexibility should far outweigh the short-run costs if companies establish track records of high productivity, quality, and exemplary customer service. Flexible schedules should also contribute to lowest-cost imperatives. Strong evidence indicates that employees on flexible work schedules exhibit higher productivity and lower absenteeism than employees with fixed work schedules.[37]

A product and service innovation objective requires creative, open-minded, risk-taking employees. Compared with cost control objectives, companies that pursue differentiation strategies must take a longer-term focus to attain their preestablished objectives. Both arrangements should contribute to innovation; however, systematic studies that demonstrate these relationships are lacking. Contingent employment probably is appropriate because companies will benefit from the influx of "new" employees from time to time who bring fresh ideas with them. Over the long run, contingent employment should minimize problems of **groupthink**, which occurs when all group members agree on mistaken solutions because they share the same mind-set and view issues through the lens of conformity.[38] In recent years, companies have joined or established contractor exchanges to boost innovative capacity. Consumer Products company Procter & Gamble (P&G) created Connect + Develop—a network of external scientific and marketing talent from which the company draws to promote innovation. The company maintains that more than 35 percent of its new products originated from outside P&G, and 45 percent of the initiatives in its product development portfolio have external origins.[39] Also, P&G reports that since the Connect + Develop initiative, the company increased research and development productivity by nearly 60 percent.

Flexible work schedules should also promote differentiation strategies for two reasons. First, flexible work schedules enable employees to work when they are at their physical or mental best. Some individuals are most alert during morning hours, whereas others are most alert during afternoon or evening hours because of differences in biorhythms. Second, flexible work schedules allow employees to work with fewer distractions and worries about personal matters. The inherent flexibility of these schedules allows employees to attend to personal matters as needed.

PREPARING FOR EXAMS/QUIZZES

Chapter Summary by Learning Objectives

Learning Objective 12-1. *Describe the four groups of contingent workers.* Contingent workers are those who do not have an implicit or explicit contract for ongoing employment. The four categories of contingent workers are (1) part-time employees, (2) temporary workers, (3) leased employees, and (4) independent contractors, freelancers, and consultants.

Learning Objective 12-2. *Discuss pay and benefits issues for contingent workers.* There are a variety of issues that distinguish contingent workers' pay and benefits from core workers' pay and benefits. Some include the difference in level of pay and who is responsible for providing benefits. There are substantial differences in these practices among the categories of these workers and with whom the responsibility falls for providing pay and benefits.

Learning Objective 12-3. *Summarize the three categories of flexible work schedules.* The three categories of flexible work schedules are (a) flextime schedules, (b) compressed workweek schedules, and (c) telecommuting.

Learning Objective 12-4. *Discuss the pay and employee benefits issues for flexible work schedules, compressed workweeks, and telecommuting arrangements.* In general, there are not likely to be substantial differences in pay and benefits between workers with flexible schedules and fixed work schedules. FLSA overtime pay requirements apply to nonexempt workers assigned to flexible work schedules, but overtime pay determination is more challenging for the flexible workforce. Every state possesses standards for ensuring compliance with the overtime pay provision for the flexible workforce. Depending on the arrangement, there stand to be challenges calculating vacation accrual and how to address paid holidays when a worker's schedule would not coincide with a holiday. For telecommuting, companies must be familiar with rules pertaining to working condition fringe benefits.

Learning Objective 12-5. *Describe unions' reactions to contingent work and flexible work schedule arrangements.* Unions generally do not favor contingent or flexible work arrangements. For example, they believe that employers may exploit contingent workers by paying them lower wages and benefits than core employees. Also, they express concerns that workers in telecommuting arrangements may not be fully compensated for all of the extra hours they may contribute to work activities.

Learning Objective 12-6. *Identify strategic issues and choices companies face regarding the use of contingent workers.* Contingent work arrangements, when properly applied, can ultimately contribute to meeting the goals of cost control and product or service innovation; however, the rationale for the appropriateness of contingent employment and flexible work schedules differs according to these objectives. A cost control objective requires firms to reduce output costs per employee. Contingent employment saves companies considerable amounts of money because they do not give these workers most discretionary benefits or they provide less generous amounts of such benefits. A product and service innovation objective requires creative, open-minded, risk-taking employees. Compared with cost control objectives, companies that pursue differentiation strategies must take a longer-term focus to attain their pre-established objectives. From time to time, contingent employment is appropriate because companies will benefit from the influx of "new" employees who bring fresh ideas with them.

Key Terms

core employees   293
contingent workers   294
voluntary part-time employee   294
involuntary part-time employees   294
job sharing   297
temporary employment agency   297
direct hire arrangements   298
on-call arrangements   298
lease companies   298

independent contractors   298
freelancers   298
consultants   298
dual employer common law
   doctrine   303
safe harbor rule   304
common law   304
right to control   304
economic realities   305

flextime schedules   307
core hours   307
banking hours   307
compressed workweek schedules   308
telecommuting   308
Walling v. A. H. Belo Corp.   309
working condition fringe
   benefits   310
groupthink   312

Discussion Questions

12-1.   What are some of the problems that companies are likely to face when both contingent workers and core employees work in the same location? Does it matter whether contingent workers and core employees are performing the same jobs? Explain your answer.

12-2.   What are some of the possible drawbacks for companies that employ temporary workers? Do you believe that these drawbacks outweigh the cost savings? Explain.

12-3.   What arguments can be made in favor of using compressed workweek schedules for companies that pursue lowest-cost strategies? What are the arguments against using compressed workweek schedules in such situations? Explain.

12-4.   What impact will flexible work schedules have on employees' commitment to their employers? On employee productivity? On company effectiveness? Explain.

12-5.   Should companies limit telecommuting arrangements to some job groups rather than to all groups? Explain.

PREPARING FOR MY CAREER

Compensation in Action

Both companies and people adopt strategies to achieve the professional outcomes they desire. As those desired outcomes shift, so too do the strategies. The use of a flexible workforce (in the form of temporary workers or contractors) is one method for companies to deal with the changing needs of the company. At the individual level, changes in family demands and career priorities may prompt employees to seek flexible work arrangements that allow them to balance various demands. You will likely have the challenge of managing both of these scenarios as a line manager or HR professional. There will be factors that must be assessed to ensure the company continues to operate at a high level, while at the same time providing a work arrangement that meets the needs of the people who are critical to the company's success. By understanding the needs of the employer and the employee, you will be prepared to manage the situation in a way that allows both parties to meet their goals.

Action checklist for line managers and HR—leveraging flexibility to address changing needs

HR takes the lead

- Identify various options (e.g., part-time employees, temporary workers, and contractors) that may be employed to meet the pressing business factors.
- Survey current employees to gain insight on the value placed on flexible work arrangements. Assess whether these types of desired arrangements might support the needs of the business and what associated costs and cost savings would be with the offering of the arrangement.
- Ensure that compensation and benefits being offered to flexible workers are in accordance with provisions outlined by FLSA and other legally mandated standards.

Line managers take the lead

- Identify business factors that may make the use of flexible workers a necessity (e.g., predictable season of increased customer demand, layoffs to cut headcount, and desire to employ lowest-cost strategy).
- Recognize which jobs may be carried out by some type of flexible work arrangement (e.g., telecommuter and temporary worker) and work with HR to identify which arrangement works best for those jobs.
- After plan is in place and successful arrangements have been realized, work with HR to create a communication plan outlining these successes in order to further promote the feasibility and validity of these types of arrangements. Produce online testimonial videos that speak to the value these arrangements offer to the business and its people.

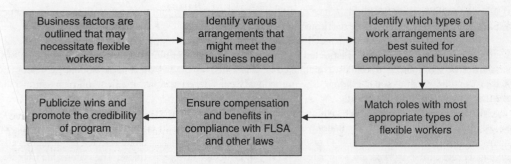

Cases

Case 1: Telecommuting at MedEx

Harry Davis just finished interviewing a candidate to fill another medical billing specialist opening. As the human resources manager for MedEx, a medical billing company, Harry is concerned about the high turnover rate for the specialists. Turnover is very costly for the company, and Harry is trying to identify ways to lower the turnover rate. The candidate he just interviewed asked Harry if any of the specialists worked from home. Harry informed him that they do not right now, but telecommuting may be an option in the near future.

MedEx employs more than medical billing specialists in its office located in a busy downtown metropolitan area. Each specialist works on a group of specific accounts, coding medical records and entering them into the computer system. The specialist position requires an intense 3-week training program to learn the coding system, but once they are proficient at their work, the specialists work independently on their assigned accounts.

In an attempt to identify the cause of the high turnover rate, Harry asked the specialists to complete an employee survey that asked about their satisfaction with their pay, benefits, and working conditions. In general, the employees indicated satisfaction with pay levels and benefits, but were not satisfied in some other areas. In the "comments" section of the survey, several employees noted challenges in getting to work each day. Some mentioned heavy traffic that caused long commutes, while others noted the high cost of parking downtown. Further, many employees noted high stress levels due to trying to balance their work and personal responsibilities.

When asked for specific ideas on how to improve the work environment, more than half of the specialists noted the option to telecommute as a desirable benefit. Because the specialists work independently, telecommuting is a feasible option. The specialists would need to work in the office at least 1 or 2 days per week in order to get updates on their accounts, but it would be possible for the employees to work from home the other days. Harry now must carefully consider whether to recommend offering the telecommuting option.

Questions:

12-6. Would offering telecommuting as an option benefit MedEx? How?

12-7. Are there any disadvantages or challenges in offering telecommuting?

12-8. What do you recommend MedEx do? Why?

Case 2: Ethics Dilemma: Cost Savings at the Expense of Employees

Business has never been better at Walden's Home Appliance store. The company has been experiencing a surge in demand for refrigerators, dishwashers, and ovens, which has led to a substantial increase in staffing in the warehouse department. Melinda Carson, Director of Human Resources, focused on employing full-time warehouse employees (more than 35 weekly hours). Warehouse workers lift boxed appliances and often find themselves placing them on delivery trucks. The work pace is speedy because Walden's guarantees an on-time delivery or gives customers whose deliveries are late ten percent off the total purchase price.

Several employees experienced back injuries requiring medical treatment and paid time-off. Many of the injuries could have been avoided if Melinda scheduled safety training. The significant injury rate resulted in rapidly rising health insurance premiums as well as higher paid time off. A further consequence was an increase in late deliveries, resulting in price reductions.

Dirk Smith, Walden's Chief Financial Officer, became alarmed. Recognizing that these cost increases were the result of HR issues, he instructed Melinda to find a solution that would result in significant cost savings or be terminated. Melinda was panicked because she was paying off a large student loan debt and had just purchased an expensive home. She immediately considered options, focusing on plans that would reduce costs in the shortest period.

Melinda presented the best cost-savings proposal to Dirk, which he accepted: Upon return to work, all previously injured employees' weekly hours were reduced to no more than 25 even though they were completed recovered from their injuries and able to resume to normal duties. This change alone resulted in substantial cost savings because these workers no longer received health insurance coverage. (Note: The Affordable Care Act requires companies to provide affordable health insurance to full-time employees who work, on average, at least 30 hours per week or 130 hours per month.) To offset reduced staffing capacity, Melinda contracted with a temporary staffing agency. Melinda also negotiated provisions that required the agency to pay for temps' workers' compensation insurance and health care premiums.

Questions:

12-9. As a compensation professional, what would you do?

12-10. What factor(s) in this ethical dilemma might influence a person to make a less-than-ethical decision?

Crunch the Numbers!

Calculating the Costs of Full-Time and Part-Time Employment

In your role as a compensation analyst, you have been assigned to calculate and compare the estimated costs of hiring full-time and part-time employees in anticipation of staffing a project. It will take 100,000 work hours to complete the project, and the project must be completed within a five-workweek period. The workweek runs Monday through Friday, with the daily hours of 8 a.m.to 4 p.m. Full-time workers provide 40 hours of weekly service. Part-time workers provide 20 hours of weekly service. Assume that the hourly wage rate for full-time workers is $20, and the rate is $12 for part-time workers. Both categories of workers perform the same sets of tasks. Also, assume that costs of benefits equal the amounts displayed in Table 12-2.

Questions:

12-11. Based exclusively on employing full-time workers, (a) How many are needed to complete the project? (b) What is the estimated total cost of wages and benefits?

12-12. Based exclusively on employing part-time workers, (a) How many are needed to complete the project? (b) What is the estimated total cost of wages and benefits?

12-13. Assume that your company has asked you to calculate the cost of staffing the project with a combination of full- and part-time workers. You've already hired 225 full-time workers. (a) How many part-time workers should you hire? (b) What is the total cost of wages and benefits based on employing this mix of full- and part-time workers?

Working Together: Team Exercise

In small groups of three or four, come up with specific answers to the following questions. Talk through your perspectives with team members. Be prepared to share your ideas with the class.

Freelancer.com (http://www.freelancer.com) and *Guru.com* (http://www.guru.com) are two popular resources for posting (advertising) opportunities for freelance (contingent) work as well as searching for these opportunities. *Monster.com* is an example of a widely used resource to post full- or part-time core employment. Explore these websites and become familiar with them. Also, identify a job posting from each site for similar work.

Questions:

12-14. What are some of the key features that you found on *Freelancer.com*, *Guru.com*, and *Monster.com*? Explain.

12-15. Which jobs did you choose? Explain.

Endnotes

1. U.S. Bureau of Labor Statistics, *Contingent and Alternative Employment Arrangements, February 2005.* (USDL: 05-1433), 2005, accessed March 22, 2018, http://www.bls.gov/.

2. Anne E. Polivka and Thomas Nardone, "On the Definition of 'Contingent Work,'" *Monthly Labor Review,* 12 (1989): 9–16, http://www.jstor.org/stable/41843238.

3. U.S. Government Accountability Office, *Contingent Workforce: Size, Characteristics, Earnings, and Benefits,* (Report: GAO-15-168R), April 20, 2015, accessed March 28, 2018, http://www.gao.gov/assets/670/669766.pdf.

4. U.S. Bureau of Labor Statistics, *Glossary,* accessed March 28, 2018, http://www.bls.gov.

5. Bruce C. Fallick, "Part-time Work and Industry Growth," *Monthly Labor Review,* 122 (1999): 22–29, http://www.jstor.org/stable/41845028.

6. John Burgess, "Making It in America's New Economy." (Commencement at University of Toledo, June 11, 1994).

7. Rebecca Smith and Claire McKenna, *Temped Out: How the Domestic Outsourcing of Blue-Collar Jobs Harms American Workers* (New York: National Employment Law Project, 2014), accessed date April 22, 2018, http://www.nelp.org/content/uploads/2015/02/Temped-Out.pdf.

8. American Staffing Association, "Staffing Industry Statistics," *American Staffing Association,* accessed March 28, 2018, https://americanstaffing.net/staffing-research-data/fact-sheets-analysis-staffing-industry-trends/staffing-industry-statistics/.

9. Larry Alton, "Why the Gig Economy Is the Best and Worst Development for Workers Under 30," *Forbes* (January 24, 2018), accessed March 28, 2018, http://www.forbes.com.

10. Elka Torpey and Andrew Hogan, "Working in a Gig Economy," *Career Outlook* (May 2016), accessed March 28, 2018, http://www.bls.gov.

11. Henry C. Black, *Black's Law Dictionary,* 6th ed. (St. Paul, MN: West Publishing Company, 1991), 363.

12. Ibid: 530.

13. Jonathan Webb, "What Is Offshoring? What Is Outsourcing? Are They Different?" *Forbes* (July 28, 2017), accessed March 28, 2018, http://www.forbes.com.

14. U.S. Bureau of Labor Statistics, *Employment Projections: 2016–2026,* (USDL: 17-1429), accessed March 28, 2018, http://www.bls.gov.

15. Ibid.

16. Ibid.

17. Ibid.

18. Scott F. Cooper, "The Expanding Use of Contingent Workers in the American Economy: New Opportunities and Dangers for Employers," *Employee Relations Law Review,* 20: 525–539.

19. U.S. Bureau of Labor Statistics, *Employer Costs for Employee Compensation, March 2018,* (USDL: 18-0944), accessed July 22, 2018, http://www.bls.gov.

20. Ibid.

21. U.S. Bureau of Labor Statistics, *Employee Benefits in the United States—March 2017*, (USDL: 17-1013), accessed March 22, 2018, http://www.bls.gov.

22. Internal Revenue Code 410(a)(1).

23. U.S. Bureau of Labor Statistics, *Employer Costs for Employee Compensation, December 2017*, (USDL: 18-0451), accessed March 22, 2018, http://www.bls.gov; U.S. Bureau of Labor Statistics, *May 2016 National Industry-Specific Occupational Employment and Wage Estimates*, accessed March 22, 2018, http:/www.bls.gov.

24. Internal Revenue Code 411(b)(4)(c).

25. Bureau of National Affairs, *Employee Relations Weekly* (October 24, 1994) (Washington, DC: Bureau of National Affairs).

26. U.S. Bureau of Labor Statistics, *Contingent and Alternative Employment Arrangements, May 2017*. (USDL: 18-0942), 2018 accessed July 22, 2018, http://www.bls.gov/.

27. Internal Revenue Code 414(n)(5).

28. Internal Revenue Code 414(n)(1)(2)(3).

29. Internal Revenue Service, *Independent Contractors (Self-Employed) or Employees?* accessed March 3, 2015, http://www.irs.gov.

30. Charles J. Muhl, "What Is an Employee? The Answer Depends on the Federal Law," *Monthly Labor Review* (January 2002): 3–11. http://www.jstor.org/stable/41845245.

31. Rebecca Davis O'Brien, *Are Exotic Dancers Employees or Independent Contractors?*, (December 2, 2014), accessed March 1, 2015, http://www.wsj.com; *Martin v. Priba Corp.*, USDC N. Texas, No. 3:91-CV-278-G (11/6/92).

32. Charles J. Muhl, "What Is an Employee? The Answer Depends on the Federal Law," *Monthly Labor Review* (January 2002): 3–11, http://www.jstor.org/stable/41845245.

33. Lauren Weber and Rachel Silverman, "On-demand Workers: 'We Are Not Robots'," *The Wall Street Journal* (January 27, 2015), accessed January 28, 2015, http://www.wsj.com.

34. Omri Ben-Shahar, "Are Uber Drivers Employees? The Answer Will Shape the Sharing Economy," *Forbes* (November 15, 2017), accessed March 28, 2018, http://www.forbes.com.

35. WorldatWork, *Trends in Workplace Flexibility (October)* (Scottsdale, AZ: WorldatWork, 2017).

36. *Walling v. A. H. Belo Corp.*, 316, U.S. 624, 2WH Cases 39 (1942).

37. Boris B. Baltes, Thomas E. Briggs, Joseph W. Huff, and George A. Neuman, "Flexible and Compressed Workweek Schedules: A Meta-analysis of Their Effects on Work-related Criteria," *Journal of Applied Psychology*, 84(4), 1999: 496–513, http://dx.doi.org/10.1037/0021-9010.84.4.496.

38. Clovis R. Shepherd, *Small Groups* (San Francisco, CA: Chandler, 1964).

39. Larry Huston and Nabil Sakkab, "Connect and Develop: Inside P&G's New Model for Innovation," *Harvard Business Review* (March 2006), accessed March 28, 2018, http://www.hbr.org.

Where We Are Now:

PART V, CONTEMPORARY STRATEGIC COMPENSATION CHALLENGES, explained the principles and practices for compensating executives and the flexible workforce. Until now, we studied compensation principles and practices employed by U.S. companies in the United States context. Compensation practices outside the United States require your attention because companies are becoming increasingly global in their reach. Now, we turn to the principles and practices of expatriate compensation and employee benefits in addition to a review of compensation and benefits in a sample of countries around the world.

In **PART VI, WE WILL COVER**

CHAPTER 13 COMPENSATING EXPATRIATES

CHAPTER 14 PAY AND BENEFITS OUTSIDE THE UNITED STATES

13 Compensating Expatriates

International compensation programs have strategic value as U.S. businesses continue to establish operations in such foreign locales as Pacific Rim countries, Eastern Europe, and Mexico. The general trend for expanding operations overseas serves as just one indicator of the globalization of the economy. U.S. companies place professional and managerial (U.S. citizen) employees overseas to establish and operate satellite plants and offices. Although there are many glamorous aspects about working overseas, the glamour comes at the price of personal and, sometimes, professional sacrifices. Compensation takes on strategic value by providing these employees minimal financial risk associated with working overseas, as well as lifestyles for them and their families comparable to their lifestyles in the United States. Multinational companies develop special compensation packages to help compensate for the personal sacrifices international assignees and their immediate families make. These sacrifices are associated with cultural variations that affect their lifestyle.

Successful international assignments increase an organization's global footprint, boost its sales and market presence, and grow its talent pool.[1] The cost of failure is high in terms of missed business development. Also, failed assignments could lead to the turnover of otherwise high-performing employees.

FYI

One survey reported that the cost of a three-year international assignment can easily exceed $3 million.[2] Surprisingly, another survey revealed that 76 percent of companies do not compare the actual vs. estimated cost at the end of an assignment; and, substantially more companies (94 percent) do not measure the program's return on investment.[3]

COMPETITIVE ADVANTAGE AND HOW INTERNATIONAL ACTIVITIES FIT IN

The presence of U.S. companies in foreign countries is on the rise. You might forget that you are in China while taking a taxi ride through the streets of Beijing: Establishments for U.S. companies such as McDonald's and Starbucks Coffee are common sights. In addition, many large U.S. companies such as General Motors have manufacturing establishments there.

13-1. Discuss competitive advantage and how international activities fit in.

Several factors have contributed to the expansion of global markets. These include free trade agreements such as the **North American Free Trade Agreement (NAFTA)**. The U.S. has free trade agreements in effect with 20 countries. Some of the agreements are bilateral (i.e., between two countries such as the U.S. and Singapore) and others are multilateral agreements (i.e., between more than two countries such as the U.S., Canada, and Mexico). Additional factors include the unification of the European market, and the gradual weakening of Communist influence in Eastern Europe and Asia.

Lowest-Cost Producers' Relocations to Cheaper Production Areas

Many U.S. businesses have established manufacturing and production facilities in Asian countries and in Mexico because labor is significantly less expensive than it is in the United States. There are two key reasons for the cost difference. First, labor laws do not bestow substantial employee bargaining power in Asian countries or in Mexico, where the governments possess extensive greater control over workplace affairs. Second, some Asian and South American governments historically have not extended significant employee rights based on fewer and less potent employment laws in comparison to the U.S.

Differentiation and the Search for New Global Markets

Nestlé products are well known worldwide because the company aggressively introduced them throughout numerous countries. Nestlé products worldwide could distinguish themselves from competing companies by taking on new business initiatives that depart from "business as usual" and meet specific market needs.

For Nestlé, "business as usual" started as manufacturing and marketing food products such as baby foods and cereal in the United States. As a departure from business as usual (from its origins), the company operates outside the U.S., using its global brand identity while, at the same time, using local ingredients.

Globally, the company's strategy focuses on entry into developing markets before competitors do. In those markets, Nestlé works toward establishing a sizable customer base by selling products which appeal to the local population. Then, the company limits its market share to many small niche markets. According to Nestlé, the company strives to ascertain at least 85 percent of market share in each location.[4] This approach has enabled Nestlé to take as much as 85 percent of the market for instant coffee in Mexico, 66 percent of the market for powdered milk in the Philippines, and 70 percent of the market for soups in Chile.

How Globalization Is Affecting HR Departments

The globalization of business requires that companies send employees overseas to establish and operate satellite plants and offices. Companies naturally must invest in the development of appropriate human resource (HR) practices. International business operations are destined to fail without the "right" people.[5] HR professionals must be certain to identify the selection criteria that are most related to successful international work assignments. For example, do candidates possess adequate cultural sensitivity? Do they believe that U.S. customs are the only appropriate way to approach problems? Are candidates' families willing to adjust to foreign lifestyles?

Another key HR function is training. Expatriates must understand the cultural values that predominate in foreign countries; otherwise, they risk hindering business. For example, one of Procter & Gamble's Camay soap commercials was successful in the United States, but the Japanese perceived the very same commercial that aired in Japan to be rude. The commercial depicted a man barging into the bathroom on his wife while she was using Camay soap. Japanese cultural values led Japanese viewers to judge this commercial as offensive. The Japanese deemed the commercial as acceptable after Procter & Gamble modified the commercial to show a woman using Camay soap in privacy. Language proficiency is another critical focus. For instance, many languages rely on nouns that can be feminine or masculine. In Italian, the word 'the' is either 'il' or 'gli' (masculine), or 'la' or 'le' (feminine). Not using these words appropriately could undermine an expatriate's credibility and ability to get work done. Many other topics include differences in negotiation style and interpersonal exchanges such as gestures for greetings (hand shaking versus bowing). In the Watch It! video, Chris Denars, a senior talent recruiter at CH2MHill, discusses the benefits of international assignments as well as the challenges that are faced in preparing for them.

Companies' investments in cross-cultural training vary. Some companies provide release time from work to take foreign-language courses at local colleges or universities. Globally focused, progressive companies, specifically among many, GE and McDonald's, run corporate universities that offer preparation for overseas assignments.

The use of international assignments is an important issue addressed by companies located in countries across the world. Approximately 86 percent of companies offer short-term assignments (typically, less than 12 months) and 97 percent offer long-term assignments (up to five years).[6] A multitude of large consulting firms (e.g., Mercer, www.mercer.com) conduct extensive research for client companies to ensure the most effective deployment of expatriates worldwide. Such consulting firms focus on pay and benefits issues for expatriates, labor law, and useful information to help expatriates select and train local country nationals. For example, "The most sophisticated companies are trying to integrate international programs with talent management programs," said ORC Worldwide Executive Vice President Geoffrey W. Latta: "These companies understand the importance of integrating international experience with local talent, particularly if the company wants to become a true leader among global organizations."[7] A recent survey reveals that 54 percent of companies that have associated their global mobility program to the organization's talent management programs consider global assignments a component of their organization's talent development initiatives.[8] GE Crotonville is an exemplar of this approach, educating management- and executive-level employees to take on challenge assignments around the world.

Complexity of International Compensation Programs

The development and implementation of international compensation programs typically pose four challenges to companies that U.S. compensation programs do not have to consider. First, successful international compensation programs further corporate interests abroad and encourage employees to take foreign assignments. Second, well-designed compensation programs minimize financial risk to employees and make their and their families' experiences as pleasant as possible. Third, international compensation programs promote a smooth transition back to life in the United States upon completion of the international assignment. **Repatriation** is the process of making the transition from an international assignment and living abroad to a domestic assignment and living in the home country. Fourth, sound international compensation programs promote U.S. businesses' lowest-cost and differentiation strategies in foreign markets.

PRELIMINARY CONSIDERATIONS

We must take some basic issues under advisement before examining the elements of international compensation programs. Compensation professionals must distinguish among host country nationals (HCNs), third country nationals (TCNs) (to be discussed next), and expatriates as compensation recipients with their own unique issues. In addition, compensation professionals should consider such matters as terms of the international assignment, staff mobility, and equity because these factors pertain directly to the design elements of international compensation programs.

13-2. Describe and explain preliminary considerations compensation professionals should take under advisement before designing international compensation programs.

Host Country Nationals, Third Country Nationals, and Expatriates: Definitions and Relevance for Compensation Issues

There are three kinds of recipients of international compensation:

- Host country nationals (HCNs)
- Third country nationals (TCNs)
- Expatriates

We will define these recipients as employees of U.S. companies doing business in foreign countries; however, these definitions also apply to employees of non-U.S. companies doing business in foreign countries.

Host country nationals (HCN) are foreign national citizens who work in U.S. companies' branch offices or manufacturing plants in their home countries. Japanese citizens working for General Electric in Japan are HCNs.

Third country nationals (TCN) are foreign national citizens who work in U.S. companies' branch offices or manufacturing plants in foreign countries—excluding the United States and their own home countries. Australian citizens working for General Motors in the People's Republic of China are TCNs.

Expatriates are U.S. citizens employed in U.S. companies with work assignments outside the United States. U.S. citizens employed in CitiBank's London, England, office are expatriates.

Our primary focus is on compensation for expatriates. Following an extensive discussion of expatriate compensation, we will consider some of the challenges compensation professionals face when compensating HCNs and TCNs.

As a reminder, our focus is on U.S. companies, and these definitions reflect this focus. Other countries can be the focus as well. For example, let's define HCN, TCN, and expatriate from the Australian perspective. BHP, an Australian company, conducts business worldwide in such countries as the People's Republic of China and the United States. A Chinese citizen who works for BHP in Shanghai is an HCN. A U.S. citizen who works for BHP in Shanghai is a TCN. An Australian citizen who works for BHP in Shanghai is an expatriate.

HR professionals construct international compensation packages based on three main factors:

- Term of international assignment
- Staff mobility
- Equity: pay referent groups

Term of International Assignment

The term of the international assignment is central in determining compensation policy. Short-term assignments (i.e., usually less than one year in duration) generally do not require substantial modifications to domestic compensation packages; however, extended assignments necessitate features that promote a sense of stability and comfort overseas. These features include housing allowances, educational expenses for children, and adjustments to protect expatriates from paying "double" income taxes (i.e., U.S. federal and state taxes as well as applicable foreign taxes).

Staff Mobility

Companies must also consider whether foreign assignments necessitate employees' moving from one foreign location to another (e.g., from Beijing, China, to the Special Economic Zone in China or from England to Brazil). Such moves within and across foreign cultures can disrupt expatriates' and their families' lives. Staff mobility comes at a price to companies in the form of monetary incentives and measures to make employees' moves as comfortable as possible.

Equity: Pay Referent Groups

Well-designed U.S. compensation programs promote equity among employees: Employees' pay is commensurate with performance or knowledge attainment. Expatriates are likely to evaluate compensation, in part, according to equity considerations. Many U.S. companies use domestic employees as the pay referent groups when developing international compensation packages because virtually all expatriate employees eventually return to the United States.

Some companies use local employees as the pay referent groups for long-term assignments because they wish to facilitate expatriates' integration into foreign cultures. As we discuss later, Mexican managerial employees' compensation packages include base pay and such cash allowances as Christmas bonuses. On the other hand, the main components of U.S. managerial employees' compensation packages include base pay and long-term incentives. U.S. expatriates working in Mexico on long-term assignments are likely to have compensation packages that are similar to Mexican managerial employees' compensation packages.

COMPONENTS OF INTERNATIONAL COMPENSATION PROGRAMS

13-3. List the main components of international compensation programs.

The basic structure of international compensation programs is similar to the structure of domestic compensation programs. The main components include base pay and employee benefits. The inclusion of nonperformance-based incentives and allowances distinguishes international compensation packages from domestic compensation packages. Table 13-1 lists the main components of international compensation programs.

Setting Base Pay for U.S. Expatriates

U.S. companies must determine the method for setting expatriates' base pay. Final determination should come only after companies carefully weigh the strengths and limitations of alternative methods. In addition, the purchasing power of base pay is an important consideration.

TABLE 13-1 U.S. Expatriates' Compensation Package

Core Compensation
- Base pay
- Incentive compensation
- Foreign service premium
- Hardship allowance
- Mobility premium

Employee Benefits
- Standard benefits
- Protection programs
- Paid time off

Enhanced Benefits
- Relocation assistance
- Educational reimbursement for expatriates' children
- Home leave and travel reimbursement
- Rest and relaxation leave allowance

Purchasing power affects standard of living. The following quote from a U.S. expatriate stationed in Italy captures the essence of purchasing power for expatriates: "Does the euro in Italy purchase as much fruits and vegetables today as it did yesterday?" Two key factors influence purchasing power: the stability of local currency and inflation, both of which we discuss shortly.

METHODS FOR SETTING BASE PAY U.S. companies use one of three methods to calculate expatriates' base pay:

- Home country-based method
- Host country-based method
- Headquarters-based method

Home Country-Based Method The **home country-based pay method** compensates expatriates the amount they would receive if they were performing similar work in the United States. Job evaluation procedures enable employers to determine whether jobs at home are equivalent to comparable jobs in foreign locations based on compensable factors. How does location create differences in jobs that are otherwise considered equal? One example may be that foreign-language skills are probably essential outside English-speaking countries. Adjustments to expatriates' pay should reflect additional skills.

The home country-based pay method is often most appropriate for expatriates. Equity problems are not very likely to arise because expatriates' assignments are too short to establish local national employees as pay referents. Instead, expatriates will base pay comparisons on their home country standards. In general, the home country-based pay method is most suitable when expatriate assignments are short and local nationals performing comparable jobs receive substantially higher pay. As we discussed earlier, expatriates may rely on local cultural norms over extended periods as the standard for judging the equitableness of their compensation.

Host Country-Based Method The **host country-based method** compensates expatriates based on the host countries' pay scales. Companies use various standards for determining base pay, including market pricing, job evaluation techniques, and jobholders' past relevant work experience. Other countries use different standards. For instance, the Japanese emphasize seniority. Expatriates' base pay will be competitive with other employees' base pay in the host countries, and companies may be seen as more legitimate employers by following local norms.[9]

The host country-based method is most suitable when assignments are of long duration. As we noted previously, expatriates are then more likely to judge the adequacy of their pay relative to their local coworkers rather than to their counterparts at home. In addition, sacrificing large incentive payments for host-country pay standards is reasonable when promotional opportunities are made available for employees upon return from international assignments.[10]

Headquarters-Based Method The **headquarters-based method** compensates all employees according to the pay scales used at the headquarters. Neither the location of the international work assignment nor home country influences base pay. This method makes the most sense for expatriates who move from one foreign assignment to another and rarely, if ever, work in their home countries. This system is administratively simple because it applies the pay standard of one country to all employees, regardless of the location of their foreign assignment or their country of citizenship.

PURCHASING POWER Decreases in purchasing power lead to lower standards of living. Expatriates quite simply cannot afford to purchase as many goods and services as they could before, or they must settle for lower quality. Diminished purchasing power undermines the strategic value of expatriates' compensation because top-notch employees are probably not willing to settle for lower standards of living while stationed at foreign posts. In addition, changes in the factors that immediately influence standard of living (i.e., the stability of currency and inflation) are somewhat unpredictable. This unpredictability creates a sense of uncertainty and risk. As we will discuss later in this section, most U.S. companies use the balance sheet approach to minimize this risk.

Currency Stabilization Most U.S. companies award expatriates' base pay in U.S. currency, not in the local foreign currency; however, foreign countries as a rule do not recognize U.S. currency as legal tender. Expatriates must therefore exchange U.S. currency for local foreign currency based on daily exchange rates. An **exchange rate** is the price at which one country's currency can be swapped for another.[11] Exchange rates are expressed in terms of foreign currency per U.S. dollar or in terms of U.S. dollars per unit of foreign currency. For example, on March 29, 2018, the exchange rate for the Chinese yuan was 6.29 yuan renminbi for each U.S. dollar. It is also possible to receive fewer units of foreign currency for each U.S. dollar exchanged. On the same day, the exchange rate was 0.71 British pound sterling for each U.S. dollar exchanged.

Government policies and complex market forces cause exchange rates to fluctuate daily. Exchange rate fluctuations have direct implications for expatriates' purchasing power. For example, let's start with the previous exchange rate of 6.29 Chinese yuan renminbi per U.S. $1. In addition, the exchange rate was 8.27 Chinese yuan renminbi per U.S. dollar on December 31, 1999. This example illustrates a decline in the exchange rate for Chinese money. U.S. expatriates experience lower purchasing power because nowadays they receive less Chinese yuan renminbi for every U.S. dollar they exchange.

Inflation **Inflation** is the increase in prices for consumer goods and services. Inflation erodes the purchasing power of currency. Let's assume that ABC Corporation did not award pay increases to its expatriates stationed in Egypt in 2016. Expatriates' purchasing power remains unaffected if there isn't any inflation (and reduced exchange rate) during the same period. These expatriates, however, had lower purchasing power because inflation was approximately 13.8 percent.[12]

Incentive Compensation for U.S. Expatriates

In the United States, companies offer incentives to promote higher job performance and to minimize dysfunctional turnover, which results when high performers quit their jobs. International compensation plans include a variety of unique incentives to encourage expatriates to accept and

> **☞ FYI**
>
> The World Bank publishes inflation annual rates for several countries and is one of the few sources for this information. For example (negative values indicate a decrease in annual inflation):
>
> - Angola: 34.7%
> - China: 2.0%
> - Germany: 0.5%
> - Japan: −0.1%
> - Venezuela: 254.9%
> - Switzerland: −0.4%[13]

remain on international assignments. These incentives also compensate expatriates for their willingness to tolerate less desirable living and working conditions. The main incentives are foreign services premiums, hardship allowance, and mobility premiums.

FOREIGN SERVICE PREMIUMS Foreign service premiums are monetary payments above and beyond regular base pay. Companies offer foreign service premiums to encourage employees to accept expatriate assignments. These premiums generally apply to assignments that extend beyond one year. The use of foreign service premiums is widespread.

Companies calculate foreign service premiums as a percentage of base pay, and these premiums range between 10 and 30 percent of base pay. The percentage amount increases with the length of the assignment. Larger amounts are sometimes necessary when there is a shortage of available candidates. Companies disburse payment of the foreign service premium over several installments to manage costs and to "remind" expatriates about the incentive throughout their assignments.

Employers that use foreign service premiums should consider the possible drawbacks. First, employees may misconstrue this premium as a regular permanent increase to base pay, and resentment toward the employer may develop following the last installment. Second, foreign service premiums may not have incentive value when employers make several small installments rather than fewer large installments. Third, employees may feel as if their standard of living has declined when they return to the United States because they no longer receive this extra money.

HARDSHIP ALLOWANCES The **hardship allowance** compensates expatriates for their sacrifices while on assignment. Specifically, these allowances are designed to recognize exceptionally hard living and working conditions at foreign locations. Employers disburse hardship allowances in small amounts throughout the duration of expatriates' assignments. It is easy for expatriates to lose sight of the foreign service premiums and hardship allowances because they appear as relatively small increments to their paychecks. Companies should take care to communicate the role of these payments.

Companies offer hardship allowances at exceptionally severe locations only. The U.S. Department of State has established a list of hardship posts where the living conditions are considered unusually harsh. Most multinational companies award hardship allowances to executive, managerial, and supervisory employees. Hardship allowances range from 5 percent to 35 percent of base pay (i.e., the greater the hardship, the higher the premium). The U.S. Department of State uses three criteria to identify hardship locations:

- Extraordinarily difficult living conditions (e.g., inadequate housing, lack of recreational facilities, isolation, inadequate transportation facilities, and lack of food or consumer services)

TABLE 13-2 Hardship Locations, Differentials, and Danger Pay, Effective March 29, 2018

Country Name	Post Name	Rate (%)
AFGHANISTAN	Kabul	35
CHINA	Beijing	15
INDIA	Mumbai	25
IRAQ	Baghdad	30
KENYA	Wangige	20
MEXICO	Mexico City, D.F.	15
PHILIPPINES	Manila	15
RUSSIA	Saint Petersburg	15
TAIWAN	Taipei	0
VENEZUELA	Caracas	30

Source: A complete listing of current locations with hardship differential for federal civilian employees can be found in Section 920 of the Department of State *Standardized Regulations (Government Civilians, Foreign Areas)*, available from the Superintendent of Documents, U.S. Government Printing Office, Washington, DC 20402. Available: *http://aoprals.state.gov/Web920/hardship.asp*, accessed March 29, 2018.

- Excessive physical hardship, including severe climates or high altitudes and the presence of dangerous conditions affecting physical and mental well-being
- Notably unhealthy conditions (e.g., diseases and epidemics, lack of public sanitation, and inadequate health facilities)

The U.S. Department of State has deemed more than 150 places as hardship locations. Table 13-2 lists examples of hardship locations and recommended hardship differentials.

MOBILITY PREMIUMS Mobility **premiums** reward employees for moving from one assignment to another. Companies use these premiums to encourage employees to accept, leave, or change assignments—usually between foreign posts or between domestic positions to ones in a foreign country. Expatriates typically receive mobility premiums as single lump sum payments.

Establishing Employee Benefits for U.S. Expatriates

Benefits represent an important component of expatriates' compensation packages. Companies design benefits programs to attract and retain the best expatriates. In addition, companies design these programs to promote a sense of security for expatriates and their families. Furthermore, well-designed programs should help expatriates and their families maintain regular contact with other family members and friends in the United States.

Benefits fall into three broad categories: protection programs, paid time off, and services. Protection programs provide family benefits, promote health, and guard against income loss caused by such catastrophic factors as unemployment, disability, or serious illnesses. Paid time off provides employees such paid time off, such as vacation. Service practices vary widely. Services provide such enhancements as tuition reimbursement and day care assistance to employees and their families.

Just like domestic employee benefits packages, international employee benefits plans include such protection programs as medical insurance and retirement programs. In most cases, U.S. citizens working overseas continue to receive medical insurance and participate in their retirement programs.

International and domestic plans are also similar in that they offer paid time off; however, international packages tend to incorporate more extensive benefits of this kind, which we will discuss later. Moreover, international employee benefits differ from domestic compensation regarding the types of allowances and reimbursements. For international assignees, these payments are designed to compensate for higher costs of living and housing, relocation allowances, and education allowances for expatriates' children.

Employers should take several considerations into account when designing international benefits programs, including:[14]

- Total remuneration: What is included in the total employee pay structure (e.g., cash wages, benefits, mandated social programs, and other perquisites)? How much can the business afford?
- Benefit adequacy: To what extent must the employer enhance mandated programs to achieve desired staffing levels? Programs already in place and employees' utilization of them should be critically examined before determining what supplementary programs are needed and desirable.
- Tax effectiveness: What is the tax deductibility of these programs for the employer and employee in each country, and how does U.S. tax law treat expenditures in this area?
- Recognition of local customs and practices: Companies often provide benefits and services to employees based on those extended by other businesses in the locality, independent of their own attitude toward these same benefits and services.

International employee benefits packages contain the same components as domestic employee benefits packages and enhancements. U.S. expatriates receive many of the same standard benefits as their counterparts working in the United States. Expatriates also receive enhanced benefits for taking overseas assignments.

STANDARD BENEFITS FOR U.S. EXPATRIATES Protection programs and paid time off are the most pertinent standard benefits.

Protection Programs We previously discussed legally required protection programs and discretionary protection programs. Let's consider the application of each kind to the international context.

Equal employment opportunity laws apply to U.S. expatriates: Title VII of the Civil Rights Act of 1964, the Age Discrimination in Employment Act, the Americans with Disabilities Act, and the Equal Pay Act. Additionally, expatriates continue to participate in the main Social Security programs (i.e., retirement insurance, benefits for dependents, and Medicare). The Family and Medical Leave Act also applies to expatriates; however, state workers' compensation laws generally do not. Instead, U.S. companies can elect to purchase private insurance that provides equivalent protection.

Discretionary protection programs provide family benefits, promote health, and guard against income loss caused by such catastrophic factors as unemployment, disability, or serious illnesses. U.S. companies provide these protection programs to expatriates for the same reasons they do in the United States (i.e., as a strategic response to workforce diversity and to retain the best-performing employees). Withholding these benefits from expatriates would create a disincentive for employees to take international assignments.

Paid Time Off Standard paid time off benefits include annual vacation, holidays, and emergency leave.

Expatriates typically receive the same annual vacation benefits as do their domestic counterparts. These benefits are particularly common among expatriates with relatively short-term assignments. Companies do not provide expatriates extended regular vacation leave because expatriates are likely to perceive the removal of these benefits on their return to domestic assignments as punitive; however, U.S. companies must comply with foreign laws that govern the amount of vacation awarded.

Expatriates generally receive paid time off for foreign national or local holidays that apply to their foreign locations. Foreign holiday schedules may provide fewer or more holidays than the United States. In addition, some countries require employers to provide all employees paid time off for recognized holidays. In the United States, companies offer paid holidays as a discretionary benefit or as set in collective bargaining agreements.

Paid leave for personal or family emergencies is also a component of most expatriate compensation packages. Such emergencies may include critically ill family members or their deaths in the United States or in the foreign posts. Most companies provide paid emergency leave, but some companies provide unpaid leaves of absence. In either case, companies cover travel expenses between the foreign post and the United States.

ENHANCED BENEFITS FOR U.S. EXPATRIATES Enhanced benefits for U.S. expatriates include:

- Relocation assistance
- Education reimbursements for expatriates' children
- Home leave benefits and travel reimbursements
- Rest and relaxation leave and allowance

Relocation Assistance Relocation assistance payments cover expatriates' expenses to relocate to foreign posts. Table 13-3 lists the items most commonly covered under relocation assistance programs. Relocation assistance is generally large enough to pay for major expenses. Companies usually base these payment amounts on three main factors: distance, length of assignment, and rank in the company.

Education Reimbursements for Expatriates' Children Expatriates typically place their children in private schools designed for English-speaking students. Tuition in foreign countries is often more expensive than tuition for private U.S. schools. U.S. companies choose to reimburse expatriate children's education for two reasons. First, some foreign public schools may not be comparable to U.S. public school curricula. Second, most U.S. children do not speak foreign languages fluently. Thus, they cannot enroll in foreign public schools.

Home Leave Benefits and Travel Reimbursements Companies offer home leave benefits to help expatriates manage the adjustment to foreign cultures and to maintain direct personal contact with family and friends. As the name implies, **home leave benefits** enable expatriates to take paid time off in the United States. Home leave benefits vary considerably from company to company. The length and frequency of these leaves usually depend on the expected duration of expatriates' assignments (i.e., longer assignments justify longer home leaves). In

TABLE 13-3 Relocation Assistance Payments

The relocation allowance or reimbursement provides employees with money for:
- Temporary quarters prior to departure because the expatriate's house has been sold or rented
- Transportation to the foreign post for employees and their families
- Reasonable expenses incurred by the family during travel
- Temporary quarters while waiting for delivery of household goods or while looking for suitable housing
- Moving household goods to the foreign post
- Storing household goods in the United States

addition, expatriates must serve a minimum period at the foreign post before they are eligible for home leave benefits (i.e., anywhere from 6 to 12 months). Companies offer these extended benefits along with the standard paid time off benefits.

Companies compensate expatriates while they are away on home leave. In addition, most companies reimburse expatriates for expenses associated with travel between the foreign post and the United States. These reimbursements apply to expatriates and to family members who live with expatriates at foreign posts. Companies typically reimburse the cost of round-trip airfare, ground transportation, and accommodations while traveling to and from the foreign post.

Rest and Relaxation Leave and Allowance Expatriates who work in designated hardship foreign locations receive rest and relaxation leave benefits. Rest and relaxation leave represents additional paid time off. Progressive employers recognize that expatriates working in hardship locations may need extra time away from the unpleasant conditions to "recharge their batteries." Rest and relaxation leave benefits differ from standard vacation benefits because companies designate where expatriates may spend their time. For example, many U.S. companies with operations in China's Special Economic Zone designate Hong Kong as an acceptable retreat because it is relatively close by and has many amenities not present in the Special Economic Zone (e.g., diverse ethnic restaurants and Western-style entertainment).

Rest and relaxation leave programs include allowances to cover travel expenses between the foreign post and the retreat location. Companies determine allowance amounts based on such factors as the cost of round-trip transportation, food, and lodging associated with the designated locations. Allowances usually cover most costs. The U.S. Department of State publishes per diem schedules for various cities. Location and family size determine per diem amounts.

BALANCE SHEET APPROACH FOR U.S. EXPATRIATES' COMPENSATION PACKAGES

Most U.S. multinational companies use the balance sheet approach to determine expatriates' compensation packages. The **balance sheet approach** provides expatriates the standard of living they normally enjoy in the United States. Thus, the United States is the standard for all payments.

The balance sheet approach has strategic value to companies for two important reasons. First, this approach protects expatriates' standards of living. Without it, companies would have a difficult time placing qualified employees in international assignments. Second, the balance sheet approach enables companies to control costs because it relies on objective indexes that measure cost differences between the U.S. and foreign countries. We will discuss these indexes shortly.

13-4. Discuss the balance sheet approach for U.S. expatriates' compensation packages.

The use of the balance sheet approach is most appropriate when:

- The home country is an appropriate reference point for economic comparisons.
- Expatriates are likely to maintain psychological and cultural ties with the home or base country.
- Expatriates prefer not to assimilate into the local foreign culture.
- The assignment is of limited duration.
- The assignment following the international assignment will be in the home country.
- The company promises employees that they will not lose financially while on foreign assignment.

Companies that use the balance sheet approach compare the costs of four major expenditures in the United States and the foreign post:

- Housing and utilities
- Goods and services
- Discretionary income
- Taxes

Employees receive allowances whenever the costs in the foreign country exceed the costs in the United States. Allowance amounts vary according to the lifestyle enjoyed in the United States. In general, individuals with higher incomes tend to live in more expensive homes, and they are in better positions to enjoy more expensive goods and services (e.g., designer labels versus off-brand labels). Higher income also means higher taxes.

Where do U.S. companies obtain pertinent information about costs for foreign countries? U.S. companies may rely on three information sources. First, they can rely on expatriates who have spent considerable time on assignment or foreign government contacts. Second, private consulting companies (e.g., Willis Towers Watson) or research companies (e.g., Bureau of National Affairs) can conduct custom surveys. Third, most U.S. companies consult the *U.S. Department of State Indexes of Living Costs Abroad, Quarters Allowances, and Hardship Differentials*, which is published quarterly. It is the most cost-effective source because it is available at no charge in libraries with government depositories as well as at www.state.gov.

Housing and Utilities

Employers provide expatriate employees with **housing and utilities allowances** to cover the difference between housing and utilities costs in the United States and in the foreign post. The U.S. Department of State uses the term **quarters allowances**. Table 13-4 displays pertinent information from the U.S. Department of State's quarters allowances.

The quarters allowances table contains three main sections: the survey date, exchange rate, and annual allowance by family status and salary range. The survey date is the month when the Office of Allowances received housing expenditure reports.

The exchange rate section includes three pieces of information: effective date, foreign unit, and number per U.S. dollar. We reviewed the concept of exchange rate earlier. It is expressed as the number of foreign currency units given in exchange for the U.S. dollar.

Table 13-4 contains information on family status and salary range. The term *single* is self-explanatory. The term *rate* refers to rank within a company. Roughly, these are senior management, middle management, and entry-level management. In Beijing, the quarters allowance is $65,600 for single expatriates who are members of senior management. In Taipei, the allowance is $23,100.

TABLE 13-4 Quarters Allowances, 2018 (in U.S. Dollars)

Country and City	Family Status	Rate (Senior)	Rate (Middle)	Rate (Entry-Level)
BELGIUM:	*Family*	45,000	42,000	37,800
Brussels	*Single*	42,000	39,500	33,100
CANADA:	Family	53,000	47,000	41,500
Montreal	Single	49,500	41,500	37,000
CHINA:	*Family*	71,200	65,000	58,200
Beijing	*Single*	65,600	58,200	58,200
MEXICO:	Family	47,900	45,000	41,400
Mexico City	Single	46,800	41,400	37,200
TAIWAN:	*Family*	23,100	23,100	19,100
Taipei	*Single*	23,100	23,100	19,100

Source: U.S. Department of State. *Annual Living Quarters Allowance in U.S. Dollars* (*Rates Effective: 03/18/2018*). Washington, DC: U.S. Government Printing Office. Accessed March 29, 2018, at http://www.state.gov.

The term *family* refers to two-or-more-person families, including married couples and domestic partnerships. Employees with larger families living with them at the foreign posts receive supplements. Families of two to three persons receive a 10 percent supplement, families of four or five persons receive a 20 percent supplement, and families of six or more persons receive a 30 percent supplement.

Goods and Services

Expatriates receive **goods and services allowances** when the cost of living is higher in that country than it is in the United States. Employers base these allowances on **indexes of living costs abroad**, which compare the costs (U.S. dollars) of representative goods and services (excluding education) expatriates purchase at the foreign location with the cost of comparable goods and services purchased in the Washington, D.C., area. The indexes are place-to-place cost comparisons at specific times and currency exchange rates.

Discretionary Income

Discretionary income covers a variety of financial obligations in the United States for which expatriates remain responsible. These expenditures are usually of a long-term nature. Companies typically do not provide allowances because expatriates remain responsible for them despite international assignments. Table 13-5 lists examples of discretionary income expenditures.

Tax Considerations

All U.S. citizens working overseas for U.S. corporations are subject to the Federal Unemployment Tax Act (FUTA).[15] Expatriates continue to pay U.S. income taxes and Social Security taxes while on assignment. The Internal Revenue Service (IRS) taxes U.S. citizens' income, regardless of whether they earn income in the United States or while on foreign assignment.[16] Expatriates must also pay income taxes to local foreign governments based on the applicable income tax laws. Paying taxes to both the U.S. government and foreign governments is known as "double" taxation.[17] The Internal Revenue Code (IRC) includes regulations that address taxation issues.

EMPLOYER CONSIDERATIONS: TAX PROTECTION AND TAX EQUALIZATION Under the balance sheet approach, companies choose between two approaches to help address concerns of double taxation:

- Tax protection
- Tax equalization

A key element of both tax protection and tax equalization methods is the **hypothetical tax**. Employers calculate the hypothetical tax as the U.S. income tax based on the same salary level, excluding all foreign allowances. Under **tax protection**, employers reimburse expatriates for the difference between the actual income tax amount and the hypothetical tax when

TABLE 13-5 Discretionary Income Expenditures

- Pension contributions
- Savings and investments
- Insurance payments
- Equity portion of mortgage payments
- Alimony payments
- Child support
- Student loan payments
- Car payments

the actual income tax amount—based on tax returns filed with the IRS—is greater. Expatriates simply pay the entire income tax bill when the taxes are less than or equal to the hypothetical tax. Expatriates realize a tax benefit whenever actual taxes amount to less than the hypothetical tax because they will have paid lower income taxes on their overseas assignments than on assignments in the United States.

Under **tax equalization**, employers take the responsibility for paying income taxes to the U.S. and foreign governments on behalf of expatriates. Tax equalization is a process that ensures that the tax costs incurred by an expatriate approximate the cost of taxes had he or she remained at home. Under tax equalization, the expatriate neither suffers significant financial hardship nor realizes a financial windfall from the tax consequences of an international assignment. Tax equalization starts with the calculation of the hypothetical tax. Based on this hypothetical tax amount, employers deduct income from expatriates' paychecks that total the hypothetical tax amounts at year end. Employers reimburse expatriates for the difference between the hypothetical tax and actual income tax, whenever the actual income tax amount is less. Expatriates reimburse their employers whenever the actual income tax amount exceeds the hypothetical income tax amounts.

Of the two approaches, employers stand to benefit more from the tax equalization approach. Expatriates receive equitable treatment regardless of their location and do not keep the unexpected tax gain from being posted in countries with income tax rates lower than in the United States. As a result, employers should have an easier time motivating expatriates to move from one foreign post to another. In addition, companies save money by not allowing expatriates to keep tax windfalls.

REPATRIATION PAY ISSUES

13-5. Describe repatriation issues.

Special compensation considerations should not end with the completion of international assignments. Effective expatriate compensation programs promote employees' integration into their companies' domestic workforces. Returnees may initially view their domestic assignments as punishment because their total compensation decreases. Upon return, former expatriates forfeit special pay incentives and extended leave allowances. Although most former expatriates understand the purpose of these incentives and allowances, it often takes time for them to adjust to "normal" compensation practices. Many expatriates may not adjust very well to compensation-as-usual because they feel their international experiences have made them substantially more valuable to their employers. Their heightened sense of value may intensify when former expatriates compare themselves with colleagues who have never taken international assignments. Two consequences are likely. First, former expatriates may find it difficult to work collaboratively with colleagues, which can undermine differentiation objectives. Second, strong resentments may lead former expatriates to find employment with competitors. Adding insult to injury, competitors stand to benefit from former expatriates' international experiences.

 FYI

A survey of companies revealed that 75 percent of companies start the repatriation planning process three to six months prior to an expatriate's return to the home country.[18]

Companies can actively prevent many of these problems by the following two measures. First, companies should invest in former expatriates' career development. Career development programs signal that companies value returnees. In addition, former expatriates may view their employers' investments in career development as a form of compensation, reducing the equity problems described earlier. Second, companies should capitalize on expatriates' experiences to gain a better understanding of foreign business environments. In addition, former expatriates can contribute to the quality of future international assignments by conveying what did and did not work well during their assignments.

PREPARING FOR EXAMS/QUIZZES

Chapter Summary By Learning Objectives

Learning Objective 13-1. *Discuss competitive advantage and how international activities fit in.* The presence of companies in foreign countries is on the rise. There are a variety of reasons for this trend, which relate to lowest-cost producers' relocations to less expensive production areas and differentiation and the search for new global markets. This trend also has implications for the role of the HR department and changes in the design of compensation packages.

Learning Objective 13-2. *Describe and explain preliminary considerations compensation professionals should take under advisement before designing international compensation programs.* There are important preliminary considerations before establishing an international compensation program. These include understanding the differences between HCNs, TCNs, and expatriates. In addition, companies must determine the term of international assignment, staff mobility, and pay referent groups.

Learning Objective 13-3. *List the main components of international compensation programs.* International compensation components require choices about methods for setting base pay and employee benefits, and, in doing so, recognize the role of purchasing power of currencies in other countries and other standard-of-living issues.

Learning Objective 13-4. *Discuss the balance sheet approach for U.S. expatriates' compensation packages.* The balance sheet approach provides expatriates the standard of living they normally enjoy in the United States. Many considerations include housing and utilities costs, costs of goods and services, discretionary income, and taxation laws in other countries.

Learning Objective 13-5. *Describe repatriation issues.* Repatriation addresses an expatriate's return to the home country, and a company anticipating readjustment to working and living at home, differences work compared to the international assignment, and changes in the compensation package.

Key Terms

Discussion Questions

13-1. What are the strengths and weaknesses of the following methods for establishing base pay in international contexts: home country-based pay, headquarters-based pay, and host country-based pay? Explain.

13-2. Do you believe that pay-for-performance is appropriate in all countries? Explain.

13-3. Should U.S. companies increase base pay (beyond the level that would be paid in the United States) to motivate employees to accept foreign assignments? Explain.

13-4. Allowances and reimbursements for international assignments are costly. Should companies avoid international business activities? Explain. If you answer *no*, what can companies do to minimize costs?

13-5. Of the many reimbursements and allowances that U.S. companies make for employees who take foreign assignments, which one is the most essential? Discuss your reasons.

PREPARING FOR MY CAREER

Compensation in Action

International assignments can be one of the most rewarding experiences during an employee's career. However, along with the excitement and novelty of living in a different part of the world comes the reality of dealing with new customs, living in different communities, and arranging a lifestyle in a way that makes the experience logistically enjoyable. As an HR manager or line manager, you will likely deal with expatriate employees on several occasions. By asking the right questions, establishing sound and consistent policy, and working to meet the requests and needs of the individual employee (within established guidelines), you can take steps to maximize the employee experience, that in the long run, could prove to have significant value to the company.

Action checklist for line managers and HR—maximizing the experience of expatriate employees

HR takes the lead

- Identify what type of training or other areas of preparation are necessary prior to the employee beginning the expatriate assignment.
- Sit down with the employee to discuss that may need to be considered prior to the employee beginning the assignment (e.g., family needs, pets, and expectations of employee).
- With compensation specialists, align the individual needs of the employee with the policies already in place in the company. For example, if the expatriate will be compensated on a home country-based pay method, are foreign service premiums necessary to "sweeten the deal?" Is the host country an area where hardship allowance will be awarded? Will the employee have a spouse or children who will need special benefits (e.g., private schooling and language lessons)?

Line managers take the lead

- Establish a pipeline of talented employees who are ready for an international assignment. As these opportunities arise, work with HR to identify which of those employees match up best with the specific opportunities.

- Partner with other line managers who have had experience working with expatriates to understand the ideal length of time for the assignment, and what issues should be considered to guarantee successful transition into the assignment (this should include discussions with domestic line managers and host country managers).
- Work with HR to keep the expatriate employee connected to operations in the United States; prior to repatriation, establish a plan to keep the employee engaged through experiences wherein he or she can use the critical skills acquired during the assignment (e.g., mentoring an employee preparing for a similar experience). Accurately communicate changes in compensation and other areas which could be of concern to the employee so that appropriate expectations are established.

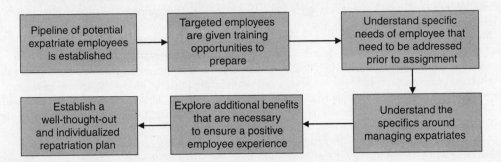

Cases

Case 1: Jenkins Goes Abroad

Jenkins Consulting is a national firm that helps companies improve their performance and effectiveness by advising on all aspects of business management and operations. Companies hire consultants from Jenkins Consulting for a variety of projects such as assisting with company-wide cost reduction initiatives or revenue growth initiatives, improving supply-chain management, and/or improving individual departments such as information technology. Jenkins employs consultants in 200 offices across the United States and will soon expand its operations internationally.

A company located in the United Kingdom has hired Jenkins for a major project that will be based at the company's headquarters in London. Jenkins will assist the company with an organization-wide effort to restructure and reposition the company to succeed in a more competitive market. To complete this project, Jenkins will assign five full-time consultants for a period of approximately two years. Because of the significant time commitment, Jenkins has decided to relocate the selected consultants to the United Kingdom for the duration of the project.

Dale Kugar, the human resource director at Jenkins, must prepare to transition the consultants to the new assignment. This is the company's first exposure to expatriate management, and Dale needs to ensure that the consultants who move to the United Kingdom for the project are compensated appropriately. His intention is to have the consultants maintain their current benefits, including health care insurance, retirement savings, and paid time off. However, he must make a recommendation on any changes to each consultant's salary.

Dale has a few concerns as he prepares his recommendation. First, the United Kingdom is currently experiencing a high level of inflation. The value of the American dollar compared to the British pound is low. That is, the consultant's U.S. salary will not have the same purchasing power in the United Kingdom as it does at home. He is also concerned about the consultants' interest in taking on the international assignment. Some of the consultants he spoke to about the assignment are concerned about the impact the assignment will have on their career. Because this is Jenkins' first international experience, the consultants are concerned that being out of the country for two years may affect their future career opportunities because they will not have regular interactions with the firm partners who make decisions on promotions. These concerns weigh heavily on Dale's mind as he starts to draft his recommendation.

Questions:

13-6. How should Dale approach the determination of the consultant's salaries as expatriates?

13-7. Should Jenkins offer any incentive compensation or additional benefits to the expatriates? Why or why not?

Case 2: Ethics Dilemma: Request Approved, then Denied

Jennifer Smith is an operations manager at Get It to You, which is based in Cleveland, Ohio. The company provides same-day letter and package delivery service within metropolitan areas throughout the United States. Get It to You is expanding operations to metropolitan areas in several countries, starting with Caracas, Venezuela. Jennifer reluctantly agreed to take the three-year expatriate assignment after several operations managers refused it.

About six months before departure, Steven Brown, director of Human Resources, discussed the terms of the assignment, including Jennifer's new salary, housing allowance, food allowance, annual cost-of-living adjustment, and relocation bonus. Jennifer expressed concern that the allowances were too low given the exorbitant cost of living in Caracas, and she expressed that the modest bonus was misaligned with the personal sacrifices she would make. She went on to propose substantially higher amounts and indicated that she would refuse the assignment if her request was denied. Steven indicated that her terms exceeded policy limits, but he would seek written authorization from the company's CEO, Juanita Jimeno.

As promised, Steven spoke with Juanita to seek approval; however, she was angered by Jennifer's demands and was inclined to deny them. At the same time, the board of directors was pressuring Juanita to launch global operations. The launch was already several months behind schedule. As a result, Juanita reluctantly agreed to Jennifer's terms. Steven requested written confirmation, which he did not receive following several attempts. In the meantime, Jennifer moved to Caracas to begin her assignment after Steven assured her that everything was set. Eventually, Juanita refused to provide written authorization after the board of directors instructed her to institute cost savings measures. Get It to You profits were expected to fall well below the forecasted level. Nevertheless, Steven made one more appeal. This time, Juanita expressed concern that she would lose her job if she granted the request.

13-8. As a compensation professional, what would you do?

13-9. What factor(s) in this ethical dilemma might influence a person to make a less-than-ethical decision?

Crunch the Numbers!

Calculating an Expatriate's Base Pay and Incentives

One of your colleagues will be taking a one-year work assignment in Beijing, China. As a compensation analyst, you must prepare an estimate of her new base pay and incentive payments. Her base pay is being increased 5 percent from her current $75,000 because the assignment will require additional responsibilities. Your colleague will be awarded a 20 percent foreign service premium, a 15 percent hardship allowance, and a quarters allowance equal to $58,200.

Questions:

13-10. Calculate your colleague's new base pay rate.

13-11. Calculate the (a) foreign service premium, (b) hardship allowance, and (c) quarters allowance.

13-12. Based on your calculations for the previous questions, how much will your colleague receive for her one-year assignment in Beijing, China?

Working Together: Team Exercise

In small groups of three or four, come up with specific answers to the following questions. Talk through your perspectives and come up with a team response. Be prepared to share your ideas with the class.

As a group, choose a country you would like to learn more about. Assume that you work for a software development company that is planning to open a customer service center in your chosen country. The center is scheduled to open there next year and a team of home-country employees will spend six months in the new location supervising the center's opening. None of the team members have visited the country before. A translator will accompany the team. Your job is to prepare this team for the cultural transition.

13-13. What are two important topics that you will address with the team? Explain the rationale for your choices.

13-14. What did you find most unique about the destination country?

Endnotes

1. Kenneth Burgess and Neil M. Carson, "How Prepared Are Expatriates for Global Assignments?" *Workspan* (February 2017): pp. 32–40.
2. Society for Human Resource Management, "Introduction to the Global Human Resources Discipline," (March 7, 2017), accessed March 31, 2018, http://www.shrm.org.
3. Roy Maurer, "Half of Employers Report Not Tracking Global Mobility Costs," *Society for Human Resource Management* (July 15, 2016), accessed March 31, 2018, http://www.shrm.org.
4. Jaffery, "Nestle – International Strategy," Blog (April 8, 2013), accessed March 29, 2018, https://blogs.baruch.cuny.edu/mgt4880nestle/2013/04/08/nestle-international-strategy/.
5. Sylvia Vorhauser-Smith, "Global Mobility: A Win-Win for You and Your Employer," (October 31, 2013), accessed January 30, 2015, http://www.forbes.com.
6. KPMG International, *Global Assignment Policies and Practices Survey: 2017 Results* (2017), accessed March 29, 2018, https://assets.kpmg.com/content/dam/kpmg/xx/pdf/2017/10/2017-gapp-survey-report.pdf.
7. WorldatWork, "Companies Are Leveraging International Assignments to Better Compete Globally," accessed July 7, 2007, http://www.worldatwork.org.
8. KPMG International, *Global Assignment Policies and Practices Survey: 2017 Results.*
9. Yoshio Yanadori, "Paying Both Globally and Locally: An Examination of the Compensation Management of a US Multinational Finance Firm in the Asia Pacific Region," *The International Journal of Human Resource Management, 22,* 2011: pp. 3867–3887. https://doi.org/10.1080/09585192.2011.610972.
10. Morgan Crosby, "Knowing When to Use a Host-Based Compensation Program," *Workspan* (July 2013): pp. 27–30.
11. Glenn G. Munn, Ferdinand Lawrence Garcia, and Charles J. Woelfel, *Encyclopedia of Banking and Finance*, (Chicago, IL: St. James Press, 1991).
12. The World Bank, "Inflation, Consumer Prices (Annual %)," *The World Bank*, accessed March 29, 2018, https://data.worldbank.org/indicator/FP.CPI.TOTL.ZG.
13. Ibid.
14. Mary E. Horn, *International Employee Benefits: An Overview,* (Brookfield, WI: International Foundation of Employee Benefit Plans, 1992).
15. *Internal Revenue Code*, Section 306(c), paragraph 3306(j).
16. ORC Worldwide, "Savings Initiatives in Expatriate Programs Underway," accessed June 14, 2009, http://www.orcworldwide.com.
17. Ibid.
18. KPMG International, *Global Assignment Policies and Practices Survey: 2017 Results.*

Pay and Benefits Outside the United States

The current state of globalization has resulted in a high level of interconnections between the economies of various parts of the world. U.S. employers will increasingly conduct business with entities in a variety of other countries as former underdeveloped parts of the world experience tremendous growth in economy, trade, and standard of living. In addition, the move from traditional manufacturing to knowledge- and service-based employment also means that jobs, as well as markets, are more likely to be dispersed geographically. As the need for employers to interact globally increases, HR management professionals are going to have increased opportunities to develop compensation and benefits programs for U.S. employees in foreign assignments, as well as for indigenous employees in foreign offices of the parent company.

It is essential that compensation professionals know the basic legal employment context and the minimum statutory employment standards of the country where they propose to do business, just as we've discussed throughout this book for U.S. employment (e.g., recall the Fair Labor Standards Act of 1938). After that, compensation professionals may consider the norms for competitive pay and benefits needed to attract the desired talent.

In this chapter, we will provide a glimpse of the wide variation in compensation and benefits practices across several regions of the world. We will start off each review with a brief treatment of governmental structure, norms, and historical events that help shed light on pay and benefits. For each country, we will peruse statutory minimum wage rates. Next, we will consider such basic benefits issues as paid time off, protection programs (including retirement and health care), and stand-out benefits regions. We will note where such protection programs as retirement and health care are required by the government or offered at the discretion of the employer.

In some instances, we will find that other countries impose stricter control over terms of compensation than is the case in the United States. Compensation requirements in other countries may place some drag on the flexible and entrepreneurial characteristics of small- and medium-sized enterprises (SMEs) that are establishing a global presence early in their life cycles. The Watch It! video describes the global strategy of DLP, Inc., which is an SME in the business of manufacturing catheters and surgical tubing. As you read this chapter, keep in mind the impact compensation requirements in other countries may have on DLP's competitiveness.

PERTINENT CONCEPTS FOR QUANTIFYING ECONOMIC ELEMENTS IN THE DISCUSSION OF PAY AND BENEFITS OUTSIDE THE UNITED STATES

When discussing compensation in other countries, it is important to note some of the important concepts and measures. First, the **gross domestic product (GDP)** describes the size of a country's economy. Size is expressed as the market value of all final goods and services produced within the country over a specified period. The GDP is typically calculated by the country's national statistical agency. **GDP per capita** generally indicates the standard of living within a country: The larger the per capita GDP, presumably the better the standard of living. Table 14-1 lists GDP per capita for the countries reviewed in this chapter. These figures represent each

14-1. Explain the pertinent concepts for quantifying important economic elements in the discussion of pay and benefits outside the United States.

TABLE 14-1 Per Capita Expenditures, Labor Force Size, and Hourly Compensation Costs by Country

Country	Per Capita GDP ($)	Per Capita Healthcare ($)	Labor Force Size (millions)	Hourly Compensation Costs ($)
United States	59,500	10,200	160.4	39.03
Canada	48,100	5,200	19.5	30.08
Mexico	19,500	1,200	54.5	4.38
Brazil	15,500	1,300	111.6	7.98
Germany	50,200	5,800	45.9	43.18
India	7,200	1,100	521.7	1.60
People's Republic of China	16,600	860	806.7	4.11

Notes: The per capita GDP is expressed in U.S. dollars and adjusted for the PPP exchange rate. Hourly Compensation Costs are in U.S. dollars. Hourly compensation costs (2016 actual data, except 2014 actual data for India and People's Republic of China): Conference Board (December 2017). *International Comparisons of Hourly Compensation Costs in Manufacturing*, 2016, accessed March 31, 2018 at https://www.conference-board.org/ilcprogram/index.cfm?id=38269.

Source: All data (excluding hourly compensation costs) are based on per capita GDP and labor force size (2016 estimates): Central Intelligence Agency (2018). *The World Factbook*, accessed March 31, 2018 at *https://www.cia.gov/library/publications/the-world-factbook/index.html.*

nation's GDP at **purchasing power parity (PPP) exchange rates**. That is, these figures indicate the worth of all goods and services produced in the country valued at prices prevailing in the United States. This is the measure most economists prefer when looking at per capita welfare and when comparing living conditions or use of resources across countries.

Second, the **per capita expenditure on health care** (the sum of Public Health Expenditure and Private Expenditure on Health) is another important measure. This measure helps compensation professionals understand the standard of health care, addressing an important element of discretionary and legally required benefits. This figure will be stated in the discussion of each country's benefits.

☞ FYI

The three countries with the highest per capita expenditure on health care:

- United States
- Switzerland
- Luxembourg

The three countries with the lowest per capita expenditure on health care:

- Latvia
- Turkey
- China[1]

Third, hourly compensation costs are important as well. We examined hourly compensation costs—wages and salaries and a variety of employee benefits—in previous chapters. Other countries publish these data, but there are sometimes methodological differences that make cross-country comparisons difficult. For many years, until 2012, the U.S. Bureau of Labor Statistics provided data that compared the hourly compensation costs in the manufacturing sector within several countries, making it easier to compare costs across countries. Since then, the Conference Board began publishing hourly compensation costs in the manufacturing setting, relying on much of the same methodology used in previous years by the U.S. Bureau of Labor Statistics. These data are reported in Table 14-1 in U.S. dollars.

NORTH AMERICA

14-2. For North America (Canada and Mexico), summarize key facts about wage and salary, paid time-off benefits, and protection programs.

This section takes a brief glance at the employment relationship and employee benefits in Mexico and Canada. Both countries and the United States are part of a trade bloc known as NAFTA—the North American Free Trade Agreement. According to the Office of the United States Trade Representative, formed on January 1, 1994, NAFTA called for the elimination of duties and the phasing out of tariffs over a period of 14 years.[2] Trade restrictions were removed under NAFTA from such industries as motor vehicles and automotive parts, computers, textiles, and agriculture. In addition, the treaty also delineated the removal of investment restrictions between the three countries. Because of supplemental agreements signed in 1993, worker and environmental protection provisions were added.

The labor side of NAFTA is the North American Agreement on Labor Cooperation (NAALC). This was created to promote cooperation between trade unions and social organizations to champion improved labor conditions. There has been a convergence of labor standards in North America because of NAALC. The impact on wages in the three countries has been positive. Real wages have increased since the passage of NAFTA, with Mexico seeing the greatest boost.[3]

This section will present a brief overview of the employment relationship in Canada and Mexico and some basic wage and salary, and employee benefits required by law in these countries.

Canada

According to the Central Intelligence Agency's *CIA World Factbook*, Canada is a constitutional monarchy that is also a parliamentary democracy and a federation consisting of 10 provinces and 3 territories.[4] With a per capita gross domestic product (GDP) of $48,100 and 19.5 million people in the labor force, the Canadian economy is very similar to that of the United States' market-based economy. Even though Canada has enjoyed a trade surplus and balanced budgets for many years, concern and debate have recently grown over the increasing cost of the publicly funded health care system.

Employment law researchers report that the basic rule of Canadian law holds that labor and employment law fall within the exclusive jurisdiction of the provinces.[5] Thus, both individual and collective employment relationships are controlled at the province level. Federal legislation cannot override provincial laws, even when the industry or employer primarily conducts business overseas (except in the cases where the industries are expressly assigned to federal jurisdiction). The origins of the common law governing individual employment contracts are in the English Statute of Labourers of 1562, which established working hours and wages. This statute was eventually repealed in the early nineteenth century, but it became part of the English common law and later became part of the common law governing all the provinces other than Quebec. Quebec has the Civil Code of Quebec, which came into effect in 1866. A modernized version of the Civil Code came into effect on January 1, 1994.

WAGE AND SALARY [6] Canada does possess a statutory minimum wage law. At the federal level, there is an obligation placed upon provincial governments to establish minimum rates of pay by or under an act of the legislature. The jurisdiction defined by province determines the minimum hourly rate. In 2018, Nova Scotia had the lowest minimum wage rate (i.e., $10.85). The highest rate (i.e., $15.00) was in Alberta and Ontario.

PAID TIME OFF BENEFITS Canadian employment law holds that employees are entitled to between 6 and 10 annual paid holidays based on provincial law as well as two weeks' paid vacation time along with a sum of money as vacation pay (increasing to three weeks after six years of employment).[7] The amount of vacation pay is equal to 4 percent (based on two weeks of vacation) and 6 percent (based on three weeks of vacation). There are slight variations from province to province. Law provides for up to 17 weeks of maternity leave. Also, an employee who assumes the care of a newborn or newly adopted child is entitled to parental leave of up to 63 weeks.[8] The Canadian government most recently introduced compassionate care leave, which provides up to 26 weeks of paid leave (55 percent of pay) to care for a seriously ill family member. For the purposes of this leave, family members include spouse, common law partner, children, and parents.[9]

PROTECTION BENEFITS

Pensions and Retirement Benefits Canada has two state pension plans: one for Quebec residents only and one for the rest of Canada. Outside of Quebec, the plan is referred to as the Canada Pension Plan, and it provides benefits similar to U.S. Social Security benefits. Both plans are funded by matching contributions from employers and employees, and both are fully portable upon employment changes, much like 401(k) plans in the United States. In addition to the public plans, many employers provide supplementary pension plans that are regulated by provincial or federal legislation that establishes minimum funding standards; specifies the types of investments that the plans may make; and deals with such matters as portability, benefit vesting, and locking-in contributions. Employers frequently have different plans for executive, managerial, and other employees.

Health and Disability Benefits Medical and basic hospital care in Canada is paid for by provincial medical insurance plans with compulsory coverage for all residents and funding revenue derived from both general federal taxation and from provincial taxes, and the system is governed by the Canada Health Act. This act establishes criteria and conditions for health insurance plans that must be met by provinces and territories for them to receive full federal cash transfers in support of health.[10] Even though public health plans normally do not provide employed persons with prescription drugs except while they are hospitalized, additional benefits are provided by private supplementary insurance through employers, including dental and vision care. Employers also provide long- and short-term disability benefits for sickness or injury as part of a benefits package. These programs are governed by federal and provincial law. Canada's per capita expenditure on health (the sum of Public Health Expenditure and Private Expenditure on Health), based on the country's PPP exchange rate, was $5,200 in 2017.[11]

Mexico

Mexico is a federal republic,[12] and Mexican labor law is based on the Constitution of the United Mexican States adopted in January 1917.[13] The *CIA World Factbook* reports that Mexico's labor force was nearly 52.9 million people and its per capita GDP was $19,500.[14] Its free-market economy is composed of a mix of new and old industry as well as agriculture, which are both increasingly becoming dominated by the private sector. The "Labor and Social Security" article of the constitution is still in effect.[15] Employment relationships in Mexico fall under the Federal Labor Law, which was last revised in January 1997 and clearly defines the terms *worker* and *employer* for individual employment. Some of the employee benefits ensured under federal jurisdiction in Mexico will be discussed shortly.

WAGE AND SALARY The Mexican government requires that two minimum wage rates be applied. The first, general minimum wage, applies to all workers, and the amount depends on the region of the country—Zone A or Zone B. In 2018, the daily minimum wage rate was 88.36 pesos.[16]

The second is the occupational minimum wages that are higher than the general minimum wages. Similar to the U.S. General Schedule (Chapter 3), occupations that require greater skill, knowledge, and experience are compensated at higher rates. For example, a sales clerk employed in a pharmacy had a minimum wage of 99.99 pesos per day while a graphic journalist had a minimum wage of 236.28 pesos per day.[17]

PAID TIME OFF BENEFITS Mexican employment laws stipulate certain paid time off benefits for all employees, as reported in publications on international employment laws.[18] Workers are entitled to paid time off during public holidays, and workers required to work during a mandatory holiday are entitled to double pay. Female employees are entitled to maternity leave (six weeks of leave prior to giving birth and six weeks of leave after birth on full salary). Maternity leave can also be extended with half pay for as long as necessary and does not affect seniority rights. Employees are entitled to six vacation days after being employed for one year and to two more days for each subsequent year, up to the fifth year, with two additional days every five years thereafter. Employers must pay workers a vacation premium equivalent to 25 percent of the salary earned during scheduled vacation days; vacations must be taken on the date indicated by the employer, within the six months following the end of the work year.

PROTECTION BENEFITS

Social Security Social Security programs in Mexico are administered by the Mexican Social Security Institute, which protects employees in the matters of occupational accidents and illnesses, maternity, sicknesses, incapacitation, old age, retirement, survivor pensions, day care for children of insured workers, and social services.[19] The system is financed by contributions from workers, employers, and the government, with contributions based on salary levels, and with workers earning minimum salary exempt from making contributions, whereas employers bear the bulk of the contributions to the different insurance funds.[20]

The benefits for employees are laid out as follows.[21] Workers with at least 52 weeks' worth of payments into the system who withdraw are entitled to continue making voluntary payments. Should they return to salaried employment again, they may return to the system and maintain all benefits, which may be in cash or in kind. Cash benefits take the form of transfer payments in the early stages of illness or incapacitation, depending on the medical condition and its effects on work and pensions. In-kind benefits take the form of medical attention, including surgery and medicines, hospitalization services, and so forth.

Pensions and Retirement Benefits The U.S. Social Security Administration (SSA) Office of Policy reports that effective July 1, 1997, all workers must join the mandatory individual account system, slowly replacing the former social insurance system.[22] At retirement, employees covered by the social insurance system before 1997 can choose to receive benefits from either the social insurance system or from the mandatory individual account system.

Health Benefits Medical services are normally provided directly to patients (including old-age pensioners covered by the 1997 law) through the health facilities of the Mexican Social Security Institute. Benefits include general and specialist care, surgery, maternity care, hospitalization or care in a convalescent home, medicines, laboratory services, dental care, and appliances; they are payable for 52 weeks, but in some cases, they may be extended up to 104 weeks.[23] Mexico's per capita expenditure on health was $1,200.[24]

Other Benefits A national system of worker housing exists, paid for by employer contributions in the form of a payroll tax fixed at 5 percent, and helps workers obtain sufficient credit for the acquisition of houses. Workers not employed after age 50 are entitled to receive the full balance of contributions made in their name to the housing fund.

 FYI

The United States is the only country without national laws that mandate paid time off for vacation and public holidays. Kuwait's government mandates 43 paid time off days annually (30 paid vacation and 13 paid public holidays).[25]

SOUTH AMERICA

According to the International Monetary Fund's World Economic Outlook Database, Brazil, Argentina, Colombia, and Chile are the largest economies in South America.[26] Venezuela and Peru are experiencing economic development as well. On the other hand, Argentina, Chile, and Uruguay have the best human development index (HDI)—a comparative measure of life expectancy, literacy, and standard of living measured by the United Nations,[27]—and Venezuela has large oil reserves that have turned the nation into an important player in world trade. The biggest trade bloc in South America used to be Mercosur, or the Southern Common Market, which was composed of Argentina, Brazil, Paraguay, Uruguay, and Venezuela as the main members and Bolivia, Chile, Colombia, Ecuador, and Peru as associate states.[28] The second-biggest trade bloc was the Andean Community of Nations, made up of Bolivia, Colombia, Ecuador, Peru, Venezuela, and Chile. These two trade blocs merged as of a declaration signed on December 8, 2004, at the Third South American Summit, and they formed one large trade bloc known as the South American Community of Nations, which plans to model itself on the European Union.[29] This section will take a brief look at one of the largest economies in South America, Brazil.

The *CIA World Factbook* reports that Brazil is a federal republic with a workforce of 111.6 million and a per capita GDP of $15,500 in 2016.[30] The *Consolidation of Labor Laws (Consolidação das Leis do Trabalho)* accords many employee benefits the status of fundamental

14-3. For South America (Brazil), summarize key facts about wage and salary, paid time-off benefits, and protection programs.

constitutional rights, and in general the employment relationship in Brazil is highly regulated by statute. For example, Brazilian law states that all benefits habitually granted by the employer, whether expressly or tacitly, are considered part of the employee's salary for all legal purposes and cannot be abolished. The status of employment contracts is based on the country's legal principle of continuity. This principle applies to all employment contracts, written and oral.

WAGE AND SALARY Brazil does impose a minimum wage. In accordance with the Federal Constitution, the minimum wage rate is nationally uniform and set by law. The minimum wage is fixed by a provisional measure, namely an act of the executive having the force of law, in accordance with Article 62 of the Federal Constitution and placed before Congress for conversion into law. In 2018, the monthly minimum wage was 969 R$ (Real), representing a decrease from 979 R$ in 2017.[31]

PROTECTION BENEFITS

Social Security The social security system that went into effect in 1991 details various benefits for workers in Brazil.[32] Comprehensive social security benefits are provided by law to all workers regarding retirement for illness, old age, or length of service; death benefit pensions; assistance during imprisonment of worker; savings fund; social services; professional rehabilitation assistance; work accident payments; maternity leave payments; family salary support; accident insurance; and sick leave benefits.

Pensions The U.S. SSA Office of Policy reports that social insurance in Brazil is provided to persons employed in industry, commerce, and agriculture; domestic servants; some categories of casual workers; elected civil servants; and the self-employed.[33] There is also voluntary coverage for students, housewives, the unemployed, and other categories, as well as a special system for public-sector employees and military personnel. The monthly benefit is equal to 70 percent of average earnings plus 1 percent of average earnings for each year of contributions, up to a maximum of 100 percent. Employees contribute 8 to 11 percent of gross earnings based on earnings level. Voluntary contributors and members of cooperatives contribute 20 percent of declared earnings. These contributions also finance sickness and maternity benefits and family allowances. In general, employers are required to contribute 20 percent of payroll.

Health Benefits In Brazil, medical services are provided directly to patients in rural and urban areas through the Unified Health System, and they include such benefits as general, specialist, maternity, and dental care; hospitalization; medicines (some cost sharing is required); and necessary transportation.[34] Brazil's per capita expenditure on health in 2016, based on the country's PPP exchange rate, was $1,300.[35]

EUROPE

14-4. For Europe (Germany), summarize key facts about wage and salary, paid time-off benefits, and protection programs.

The European Union (EU) is a unique international organization that aims at becoming an economic superpower, while still retaining such quintessential European practices as high levels of employment, social welfare protection, and strong trade unions.[36] Even though the EU has its own legal powers and performs executive, legislative, and judicial functions like any other governing body, it has limited authority in labor and employment laws. Although the EU does not attempt to harmonize the employment laws of member states, under the laws of all member states employers must provide employees with a written document about the terms of the employment contract. The concept of "employment at will" does not exist in the EU as it does in the United States. The EU makes use of Directives and Community Legislations to ensure that some minimum standards are adopted by member states. All member states either have specific legislation or unfair dismissal or general civil code provisions that apply to termination of employment contracts.

The EU Web site reports that community labor law was designed with the aim of ensuring that the creation of the single market did not result in a lowering of labor standards or distortions in competition.[37] The law has also been increasingly called upon, however, to play a key role in making it easier for the EU to adapt to evolving forms of work organization. Based on Article 137 of the treaty, the Community shall support and complement the activities of the member states in social policy. It defines minimum requirements at the EU level in the fields of working and employment conditions and regarding the information and consultation of workers. Improving living and working conditions in member states depends on national legislation, but also to a large extent on agreements concluded by the social partners at all levels (i.e., country, sector, and company). This section will briefly present some of the basic employee benefits practices in the EU member state of Germany.

Germany is a federal republic and its economy is the largest in Europe as indicated by a per capita GDP of $50,200, according to the *CIA World Factbook*.[38] The German labor force has about 45.9 million workers. The integration of the former East German economy is a strain on the overall economy of unified Germany, and unemployment rates have been very high. Germany has recently been pushing such labor market reforms as increasing the retirement age and increasing female workforce participation. There have been increasing concerns about the aging workforce and high unemployment bankrupting the Social Security system, but for now Germany has managed to bring the deficit to within the EU debt limit. Germany's employment laws provide considerable voice to labor and job security to employees; the German Civil Code provides numerous statutes that deal with individual employment as well as collective agreements.

WAGE AND SALARY Minimum wage in Germany is established through the collective bargaining process. In Germany, there are two types of collective agreements. First, association agreements are made between trade unions and employers' associations. Second, company agreements are made between trade unions and individual employers. An extension of either type of agreement to other sectors or employers may be granted upon request of at least one party to the collective agreement.

As an example, the agreement for the metalworking industry in Baden-Württemberg has been selected because it concluded a new pay framework agreement (ERA-Eckentgelt) in 2003, and in February 2018, concluded a collective agreement fixing the projected percentage increases in minimum wage for the next 27 months. The German government does not mandate a minimum wage, except for construction workers, electrical workers, janitors, roofers, painters, and letter carriers, set by collective bargaining agreements in other sectors of the economy and enforceable by law.

PAID TIME OFF BENEFITS Employees cannot be required to work on official holidays, which range from 10 holidays per year in northern Germany to 13 in southern Germany. The statutory minimum vacation has been set at 24 working days (or four weeks because Saturdays are counted). Younger workers have a right to a vacation of 25–30 working days; disabled workers have an additional five days of vacation. There is minimum six-month employment eligibility for vacation. Under the terms of the Maternity Leave Law, time away from work because of maternity leave or other limits on work by pregnant women and mothers must be counted as time worked for determining entitlement to vacation time. Employees may take 5 days annually or 10 days every two years (under individual state level statutes) as paid holidays for continuing education purposes at only state-approved institutions. The employee retains a job if he is drafted for military duty or called for military exercises with a suspended employment relationship. The employee should receive regular pay during illness for a period of six weeks.

Expectant mothers can take six weeks' leave before the due date and eight weeks after giving birth. During this time, the employee must be paid at least their average salary or wages calculated based on the last 13 weeks before commencement of leave. An employee can request up to three years of child-rearing leave. Employers must guarantee return to the same job following completion of this leave. Any payments for child-rearing leave are made solely by the national health authority.

PROTECTION BENEFITS

Pensions Germany has a statutory pension system analogous to the Social Security system in the United States. In addition, employers offer the company pension plan and a tax-favored investment plan. Employees have three different sources for their pension benefits: statutory pension insurance, company pension plans, and private life insurance.

Health Insurance German laws stipulate guidelines for minimal health welfare of workers. For blue-collar workers (and some white-collar workers), mandatory state health insurance premiums are borne 50 percent by the insured and 50 percent by the employer. The employer is required to collect the employees' contributions and to pay the entire amount to the appropriate collector. Employees whose income exceeds a certain amount can opt out of the state plan and purchase private health insurance. In such cases, employees may request that the employer's health insurance contribution be included in their salary. Germany's per capita expenditure on health in 2016, based on the country's PPP exchange rate, was $5,800.[39]

☛ FYI

Annual salary budget increase amounts vary by country:

- Australia: 3.2%
- Brazil: 8.3%
- India: 10.5%
- Japan: 2.5%
- Singapore: 4.0%[40]

ASIA

14-5. For Asia (India and the People's Republic of China), summarize key facts about wage and salary, paid time-off benefits, and protection programs.

In 2017, China was the largest economy in Asia, followed by India and Japan.[41] Asia has several trade blocs, including the Asia-Pacific Economic Cooperation, Asia-Europe Economic Meeting, Association of Southeast Asian Nations, and South Asian Association for Regional Cooperation. Given the wide variation and diversity in the world's largest and most populous continent, however, there is no unifying economic body like the EU or NAFTA that represents all the countries of Asia. This section will examine a representative sample of the relatively more developed and developing economies in Asia: India and China. A bloc of countries that is not examined here, but that nonetheless deserves mention because considerable jobs are being outsourced there, are those in Southeast Asia: Thailand, Vietnam, Singapore, Malaysia, Philippines, Cambodia, and Laos. These economies are seeing a current influx of foreign investment, although they are not close to the countries discussed here in terms of annual growth rates.

India

According to the *CIA World Factbook*, India is a democratic federal republic with a diverse economy ranging from traditional farming to high-technology industries.[42] India's labor force is quite large with 521.7 million individuals with a per capita GDP of $7,200. The Indian economy, though steadily growing at a close to 5 percent annual rate, is plagued with income disparity and developmental challenges similar to China. More than half of India's output is created with less than one-quarter of its labor force, and services are the major source of economic growth. Strong economic growth combined with easy consumer credit and a real estate boom is fueling inflation concerns, and the huge and growing population poses fundamental social, economic, and environmental problems. Basic constitutional legislation governs the employment relationship for all employees, ensuring equality of opportunity to public employment and prohibition of child labor.

The Directive Principle of State Policy has statutes that affect various aspects of the employment relationship (e.g., working conditions and participation in management).[43] Some of the key employee benefits provided by employers in India are provident fund, gratuity (bonus), pension (i.e., either defined benefit or defined contribution), housing, car, loans, life insurance protection for dependents, health and disability benefits, medical benefits for employees and their families, and leave encashment. The Employees' Provident Fund Organization is one of the world's largest Social Security programs. Gratuities apply to most employees in India, and these are funded through employer contributions totaling 4.5 percent of payroll.[44]

There are wide variations between the public and private sectors, with the Ministry of Labour and labor laws governing employment relationships in the public sector and with more employer discretion allowed in the private sector. In addition, all blue-collar employees and factory workers are governed under existing labor laws.

WAGE AND SALARY Minimum wage is fixed by a dual authority system. Minimum wage rates are determined by the government for certain sectors, and a collective agreement determines others. Minimum wage rates may be set in accordance with the Minimum Wages Act 1948 for occupations that are largely nonunionized or have little bargaining power. This act applies throughout India, including the provinces of Jammu and Kashmir. Schedules 1 and 2 of the act set forth the occupations for which applicable central and regional governments may set minimum wage rates. The central government sets minimum wages for 45 different occupations, including agricultural work, construction, road maintenance work, mine work, railway work, and stone breaking or crushing work. In addition, states have set minimum wages for 1,232 different occupations in their respective regions. Minimum wage rates apply only to those scheduled occupations that have more than 1,000 employees working in the applicable state. For example, in Delhi, the minimum wage rate ranged between 513 and 677 rupees per day in 2018.[45] The wage rate varies by the level of job skill and industry.

PAID TIME OFF BENEFITS[46] Workers employed in privately owned factories, mines, and plantations are entitled to one day off for every 20 days worked during the previous year. Typically, this accrual method provides 12 days off with pay each year. These rules do not apply to workers employed in government-owned factories or railroads. Paid leave policies are usually determined by states and industries where local governments set the number of minimum required days off and companies choose whether to offer additional paid time-off benefits. Local governments also determine the number of paid holidays, varying between 15 and 20 days.

Leave is usually calculated for each year based on the number of days worked in the previous year, and if a worker does not take all the accumulated leave, a maximum of 30 days can roll over to the succeeding calendar year. There is no statutory provision for paternity leave, but maternity leave is allowed in the form of paid time off and a possible medical bonus. All employees get paid time off for various public and national holidays.

PROTECTION BENEFITS

Pensions[47] The first and current laws regarding pensions were passed in 1952 (employees' provident funds), with amendments in 1972 (payment of gratuities), 1976 (employees' deposit-linked insurance), and 1995 (employees' pension scheme and the national social assistance program). Pension benefits include provident funds with survivor (deposit-linked) insurance and pension funds, gratuity schemes for industrial workers, and a social assistance system. In 2004, a voluntary old age, disability, and survivors' benefits scheme was enacted. This program is part of the Unorganized Sector Social Security scheme for employees and self-employed persons earning up to 15,000 rupees or less but without mandatory coverage, and it was introduced as a pilot program in 50 districts. Contributions are income-related and flat-rate. Coverage includes employees (such as casual, part-time, and daily wage workers and those employed through contractors) with monthly earnings of 15,000 rupees or less working in establishments with a minimum of 20 employees in one of the 182 covered industries (the establishment remains covered even if the number of employees falls below 20).

Employees covered by equivalent occupational private plans may contract out. Voluntary coverage exists for employees of covered establishments with monthly earnings up to $15,000 rupees, with the agreement of the employer and for establishments with less than 20 employees if the employer and most of the employees agree to contribute. Provident fund contributions include 12 percent of basic wages (10 percent of basic wages in five specified categories of industry) in covered establishments with less than 20 employees and some other specific cases.

Health Benefits The SSA reports that state governments arrange for the provision of medical care on behalf of the Employees' State Insurance Corporation.[48] Services are provided in different states through social insurance dispensaries and hospitals, state government services, or private doctors under contract. Benefits include outpatient treatment, specialist consultations, hospitalization, surgery and obstetric care, imaging and laboratory services, transportation, and the free supply of medications, dressings, artificial limbs, aids, and appliances. The duration of benefits is from three months to one year, according to the insured's contribution record. India's per capita expenditure on health, based on the country's PPP exchange rate, was $1,100 in 2016.[49]

People's Republic of China

The People's Republic of China (PRC), as reported by the *CIA World Factbook*, is a communist state characterized by a fast-growing economy that has shifted over the past couple of decades from a centrally planned system to a more market-oriented one.[50] The country's labor force has approximately 806.7 million people and a per capita GDP of $16,600. One of the key challenges for the government has been to sustain adequate job growth for tens of millions of workers laid off from state-owned enterprises, migrants, and new entrants to the workforce.

The PRC Labor Law was established in 1995, resulting in a break from the traditional "iron rice bowl" system of employment, with a shift from state-owned enterprises to private ones, a move that has given rise to new employment relationship issues.[51] Under the older welfare system, the workforce was considered the property of the state, and such benefits as housing, medical, and retirement schemes were payable directly by the state-owned enterprises to the employees. Since the introduction of the PRC Labor Law, the employment relationship is now defined by individual contracts.[52]

WAGE AND SALARY According to China's Labor Act, 1994, the state possesses the responsibility to implement a system of guaranteed minimum wages. There is no national minimum wage rate in China; instead, minimum wage rates are set by region. Separate standards are stipulated by provincial, regional, and municipal peoples' governments for their respective region and reported to the State Council for consent. The provisions concerning minimum wages apply to enterprises, private nonenterprise entities, individual industrial and commercial households with employees (the employing entities), and the laborers who have formed a labor relationship with them. The minimum wage rate varies by region. In 2017, the monthly minimum wage was highest in Shanghai at 2,300 yuan, and lowest in Guangxi Province at 1,000 yuan.[53] The minimum wage has increased significantly in recent years, in part, to reduce social inequality and to boost domestic consumption (i.e., those within China purchasing goods and services originating within China). Some companies have expressed concerns that continued increases in the minimum wage threaten the long-term viability of the company, particularly now that China's economic growth is less than it was in previous years.[54]

PAID TIME OFF BENEFITS[55] The length of an employer-approved medical treatment period generally depends on employee age and period of service and can range from 3 to 24 months. During this period, the salary paid to the employee may not be less than 80 percent of the local minimum wage. Employees who have worked for 1 to 10 years are entitled to paid annual leave of 5 days. Employees who have worked 10 to 20 years are entitled to paid annual leave of 10 days, and those with more than 20 years of experience are entitled to 15 days. Employees receive time off for 11 public holidays each year. Employees who have worked for more than one year are entitled to "home leave" if they do not live in the same place as their spouse or parents. Employees earn normal wages during this period, and employers are obligated to pay all travel expenses for employees visiting their spouse and for unmarried employees visiting their parents. Women are entitled to no less than 90 days of maternity leave starting 15 days prior to birth.

PROTECTION BENEFITS

Pensions The Office of Policy of the SSA reports that there has been a new law to decouple the employment relationship from the social insurance system, setting up a unified basic pension system.[56] The system now has social insurance and mandatory individual accounts, and provincial and city or county social insurance agencies and employers do adapt central government guidelines to local conditions. Coverage includes employees in urban enterprises and urban institutions managed as enterprises and the urban self-employed. In some provinces, coverage for the urban self-employed is voluntary. (Urban enterprises comprise all state-owned enterprises, regardless of their location.) Old-age provision in rural areas is based mainly on family support and through community and state financial support. Pilot schemes in the form of individual accounts, supported at the town and village level and subject to preferential support by the state, operate in some rural areas. Employees of government and communist party organizations, and of cultural, educational, and scientific institutions are covered under a government-funded, employer-administered system. Enterprise-based pension systems cover some employees (including the self-employed) in cities. The pension system is transforming further. The Chinese government is implementing a plan to make pensions uniform and it is expected to be in place sometime in 2020.[57]

An employee contribution to mandatory individual accounts is 8 percent of gross insured earnings. (The contribution rate is higher in some provinces.) The minimum earnings for employee contribution and benefit purposes are equal to 60 percent of the local average wage for the previous year. The maximum earnings for employee contribution and benefit purposes vary. Employer contribution to mandatory individual accounts is up to 20 percent of insured payroll based on local regulations. The contribution is taken from the total contribution made to basic pension insurance. Central and local government subsidies are provided to city and council retirement pension pools as needed.

Health Insurance[58] There is a unified medical insurance system with all employers and workers participating. Employers contribute 6 percent of payroll to the system, whereas employees contribute 2 percent of their salary. Health insurance is based on a Basic Medical Insurance Fund consisting of a Pooled Fund and Personal Accounts. Employees' contributions go directly to their personal accounts and 30 percent of employer contributions are paid into this account. Covered workers receive medical benefits at a chosen accredited hospital or clinic on a fee-for-service basis. The individual account is used to finance medical benefits only, up to a maximum equal to 10 percent of the local average annual wage. The social insurance fund reimburses the cost of the medical benefit from 10 to 400 percent of the local average annual wage, according to the schedule. Medical treatment in high-grade hospitals results in lower percentage reimbursements, and vice versa. Reimbursement for payments beyond 400 percent of the local average annual wage must be covered by private insurance or public supplementary schemes. Contract workers receive the same benefits as permanent workers. Per capita expenditure on health based on the country's PPP exchange rate, was $860 in 2016.[59]

PREPARING FOR EXAMS/QUIZZES

Chapter Summary by Learning Objectives

Learning Objective 14-1. *Explain the pertinent concepts for quantifying important economic elements in the discussion of pay and benefits outside the United States.* The pertinent concepts for quantifying important elements in the discussion of pay and benefits outside the United States include gross domestic product (GDP), GDP per capita, purchasing power parity exchange rate, and per capita expenditures on health care.

Learning Objective 14-2. *For North America (Canada and Mexico), summarize key facts about wage and salary, paid time-off benefits, and protection programs.* There are many similarities and differences in wage and salary, paid time off benefits, and protection programs between Canada and Mexico. For example, minimum wage rates vary by geographic regions in both countries. In Mexico, certain occupations have minimum wage rates assigned to them that also vary by geographic region.

Learning Objective 14-3. *For South America (Brazil), summarize key facts about wage and salary, paid time-off benefits, and protection programs.* Among the compensation and employee benefits structures in Brazil, the minimum wage rate is uniform and set by law.

Learning Objective 14-4. *For Europe (Germany), summarize key facts about wage and salary, paid time-off benefits, and protection programs.* Among the compensation and employee benefits structures in Germany, the minimum wage rate is set through the collective bargaining process.

Learning Objective 14-5. *For Asia (India and the People's Republic of China), summarize key facts about wage and salary, paid time-off benefits, and protection programs.* There are many similarities and differences in wage and salary, paid time-off benefits, and protection programs between India and China. For example, in India, minimum wage is set by collective bargaining where unions are dominant or set by the government law for occupations with little bargaining power, such as agricultural workers. In China, there are several minimum wage rates based on geographic location. These rates are set by local and regional governments. In recent years, China has increased the minimum wage rates dramatically to reduce social inequality and to boost domestic consumption.

Key Terms

gross domestic product (GDP)   341
GDP per capita   341
purchasing power parity (PPP) exchange rates   342
per capita expenditure on health care   342

Discussion Questions

14-1. What are the main differences between the minimum pay regulations in the United States (Chapter 2) and one other country's practices discussed in this chapter? How do these differences affect companies' ability to compete with other companies worldwide?

14-2. What are the main differences between retirement systems in the United States (considering legally required and discretionary programs) and one other country discussed in this chapter? Does it appear that the costs of retirement programs are creating burdens for competitive advantage?

14-3. What are the main differences between paid time-off practices in the United States and one other country discussed in this chapter?

14-4. What are the main differences between health care systems in the United States (Chapter 10) and one other country discussed in this chapter? Does it appear that the costs of health care programs are creating burdens for competitive advantage?

14-5. What is the purchasing power exchange rate and how is it helpful to compensation professionals whose work spans multiple countries?

PREPARING FOR MY CAREER

Compensation in Action

With companies operating seamlessly across borders, employees will come to expect you (their line managers and HR managers) to respond to their compensation and benefits needs accordingly. You will need to carefully educate managers who have supervisory responsibility for employees in other parts of the world. Because there are differences in laws and social norms among countries, the expectations of the employment exchange can be radically different. While it isn't the expectation that managers know the details of employment law in every country around the world, it will be your responsibility to equip them with the resources necessary to provide educated answers to questions the employees may raise, and to do so with sensitivity to the perspective and expectations of those employees who are many time zones away.

Action checklist for line managers and HR—seamless and sensitive strategies for a global workforce

HR takes the lead

- Be familiar with the laws and norms of all countries in which there are client group operations; read reports on these countries, deal with employment experts specializing in these areas, and talk with other HR professionals who are native to the location. Educate line managers about the pertinent high-level particulars of these laws.
- As the company seeks to expand into emerging markets in which minimal business has been conducted in the past, proactively seek out information on employment laws, events of historical significance, societal values, and general employee expectations.
- Identify areas of difference that could potentially cause conflict between line mangers in the United States and their employees who are natives of the locales in which they work (e.g., paid leave in France).

Line managers take the lead

- Be a visible presence in areas of the world where there are direct reports (set a predictable schedule that allows you to travel to these locations consistently). This presence will ensure better awareness of, and exposure to, compensation and benefits laws that may be radically different from those in the United States.
- Work with HR to provide a packet of information that can be shared with other managers. This packet would include specifics that should be taken into serious consideration as other line managers work with employees in certain countries. HR could elaborate on this packet by turning it into various training sessions for managing employees across the globe.

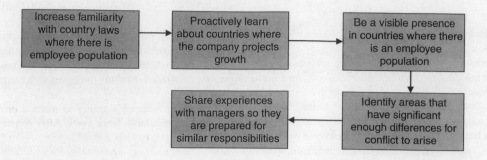

Cases

Case 1: Expanding Internationally at Suds Microbrewery

As the director of Human Resources at Suds Microbrewery, Ellie Gomez has helped successfully open 20 new brewery locations across the United States in the past 10 years. Suds Microbrewery is a successful chain that was started with one location in the Midwest and quickly grew. Suds brews several variations of their award-winning beers at each location and ships to restaurants and retail outlets within a short radius of each brewery. Thus, company growth requires opening new breweries. They've had success in the twenty major markets they have entered thus far in the United States, and are now ready to expand internationally. The company's market research has identified Canada and the United Kingdom as the company's first international locations. While Ellie is now an expert in opening a new location, she knows that hiring employees in different countries will create a lot of new challenges.

The company has secured locations in Toronto and London and Ellie is in the process of determining the staffing plan for each new brewery. While a staff from another brewery will help open the new locations and train the new employees, Suds plans to hire local nationals to staff each brewery. Ellie has a lot of research to do to understand local labor markets and how to recruit the right staff, but she knows the total compensation package that the company offers will be important. She has started to explore local pay rates but needs to also outline the employee benefits package to offer at each location. This is a new challenge for Ellie as all the U.S. locations have the same benefits package.

The U.S. locations offer standard benefits to all full-time employees. The U.S. benefits offerings include a company paid health insurance option which employees can enroll in after one month of employment. To support the retirement savings of workers, the company offers a 401(k) retirement plan with a match of employee contributions of up to 5 percent of the employee's annual pay. The employees also receive six paid vacation days plus seven paid holidays each year.

Ellie knows that it is important to establish a compensation and benefits package that is not only comparable to the U.S. offerings, but is also competitive with the offerings of competitors in the local market where the new breweries will open. Several of the employees at the new locations, managers in particular, will talk to employees at U.S. locations and thus they will have an opportunity to compare compensation and benefits. Ellie is aware, however, that employer practices are generally different in these countries. Health insurance, retirement benefits, and time-off requirements may be regulated by law. Before Ellie can begin to make recommendations, she must first conduct research to understand what is required in each country, and how the requirements compare to Suds' current offerings.

Questions:

14-6. What are some challenges Ellie is going to face in creating the new benefits packages for the international locations?

14-7. What are some general recommendations for Ellie as she plans these benefits offerings?

Case 2: Ethics Dilemma: Underpaying Workers at Serenity Resorts

U.S.-based Serenity Resorts started with humble beginnings in 1985 when it opened its first full-service resort in a small Arizona community. Success led the company to open several more resorts throughout the

United States. Initially, guests traveled across the United States to vacation at Serenity. Before long, guests traveled from around the world to stay at the various locations. Serenity's leadership decided to begin international expansion, beginning with building a resort in a small island nation off the coast of France. The goal was to create a local experience for travelers from other countries. Staffing the resort with country nationals was essential to providing that experience.

Construction of the resort far exceeded the budget, threatening Serenity's ability to make a profit. Serenity's leadership considered ways to reduce operation costs, particularly, labor costs. After construction began, the country's minimum wage unexpectedly increased 15 percent because of high annual inflation, creating further pressures on profitability. The country's economy also stood to lose substantial tax revenue if the resort were to fail.

Both Serenity's executives and local government officials met to discuss the dilemma. Following local laws would make it difficult for sufficient cost reductions. The locale's labor standards chief hinted that he would "look the other way" if Serenity paid workers less than minimum wage. In exchange, Serenity would have to make annual payments directly to the chief.

Serenity's chief financial officer calculated the cost savings based on substandard wages. Also, companies are required to make a two percent contribution to each worker's pension based on annual income. Serenity's total pension contributions would be significantly less at the lower pay rates, thus creating further savings. Deducting the annual payment to the labor chief would still allow Serenity to achieve profitability after two years. Serenity's chief operations officer decided to accept the labor chief's proposal.

Questions:

14-8. As a compensation professional, what would you do?

14-9. What factor(s) in this ethical dilemma might influence a person to make a less-than-ethical decision?

Crunch the Numbers!

Comparing the Rates of Change in GDP Per Capita for Select Countries

The following table contains GDP per capita for five countries over a 10-year period between 2007 and 2016. You want to know the rate of change in GDP within countries for specific time periods.

GDP per capita

Converted to Current U.S. Dollars				
Year	United States	Australia	Singapore	Denmark	Italy
2007	48,061	40,991	39,223	58,487	37,698
2008	48,401	40,644	39,721	64,322	40,640
2009	47,001	42,472	38,577	58,163	36,976
2010	48,373	51,874	45,699	58,041	35,846
2011	49,790	62,245	53,166	61,753	38,334
2012	51,450	67,635	54,431	58,507	34,814
2013	52,787	67,708	56,029	61,191	35,370
2014	54,898	62,099	56,336	62,548	35,396
2015	59,649	56,408	53,629	53,012	30,171
2016	57,638	49,775	52,962	53,578	30,661

Source: World Bank, *GDP Per Capita (Current US$)*, accessed April 1, 2017 at https://data.worldbank.org/indicator/NY.GDP.PCAP.CD?locations=US.

Questions:

14-10. What is the five-year change in GDP per capita (2007–2011) for (a) the United States, (b) Australia, (c) Singapore, (d) Denmark, and (e) Italy?

14-11. What is the five-year change in GDP per capita (2012–2016) for (a) the United States, (b) Australia, (c) Singapore, (d) Denmark, and (e) Italy?

14-12. State whether the rate of change for the more recent five-year period (2012–2016) was lower or higher than the rate of change for the earlier five-year period (2007–2011) in each country: (a) the United States, (b) Australia, (c) Singapore, (d) Denmark, and (e) Italy.

Working Together: Team Exercise

In small groups of three or four, come up with specific answers to the following questions. Talk through your perspectives with team members. Be prepared to share your ideas with the class.

This chapter described the basic structure of various countries in terms of government organization, minimum wage, pension, health care, and paid time off requirements. Select a country of your choice (excluding countries discussed in this chapter). Conduct some research on your chosen country. Use sources that you find in an internet search as well as some of the resources listed in the endnotes.

14-13. For your chosen country, what have you learned about the structure of its government? How does the governmental structure compare to another country of your choice (any country discussed in this chapter)? Explain.

14-14. For your chosen country, what have you learned about the minimum wage and benefits requirements? How do these practices compare to the country (of the same country within this chapter that you considered in question 14-13)? Explain.

Endnotes

1. Organization for Economic Cooperation and Development, "Health Spending," OECD Data, accessed April 1, 2018 at https://data.oecd.org/healthres/health-spending.htm; Central Intelligence Agency, *The World Factbook,* accessed March 31, 2018, https://www.cia.gov/library/publications/the-world-factbook/index.html.

2. Office of the U.S. Trade Representative, *North American Free Trade Agreement (NAFTA),* accessed March 31, 2018, https://ustr.gov/trade-agreements/free-trade-agreements/north-american-free-trade-agreement-nafta.

3. Lorenzo Caliendo and Fernando Parro, *Estimates of the Trade and Welfare Effects of NAFTA* (working paper 18508), (Cambridge, MA: National Bureau of Economic Research, 2012, revised December 2014).

4. Central Intelligence Agency, *The World Factbook,* accessed March 31, 2018, http://www.cia.gov/library/publications/the-world-factbook/index.html.

5. Roy L. Heenan and Thomas E. F. Brady, in William L. Keller & Timothy J. Darby, *International Labor and Employment Laws*, Vol. I (2003), 21-2–21-6.

6. Information in this chapter about minimum wage policy was found on the International Labour Organization Web site. ILO Database on Conditions of Work and Employment Laws. ILO, Geneva, accessed March 31, 2018, http://www.ilo.org/dyn/travail/travmain.home.

7. Government of Canada. *Vacation and General Holidays*, accessed March 31, 2018, https://www.canada.ca/en/employment-social-development/programs/laws-regulations/labour/interpretations-policies/vacation-pay.html.

8. Government of Canada. *Maternity-related Reassignment and Leave, Maternity Leave and Parental Leave*, accessed March 31, 2018, https://www.canada.ca/en/employment-social-development/ services/labour-standards/reports/maternity-leave.html.

9. Government of Canada. *EI Compassionate Leave – Overview,* accessed March 31, 2018, https://www.canada.ca/en/services/benefits/ei/ei-compassionate.html.

10. Health Canada. *Canada's Health Care System*, accessed March 31, 2018, https://www.canada .ca/en/health-canada/services/health-care-system/reports-publications/health-care-system/ canada.html.

11. Central Intelligence Agency, *The World Factbook,* accessed March 31, 2018, http://www.cia.gov/ library/publications/the-world-factbook/index.html.

12. Ibid.

13. Nestor de Buen Lozano and Carlos de Buen Unna, in William L. Keller & Timothy J. Darby, *International Labor and Employment Laws*, 2nd ed. (2003), Vol. I, Chapter 22, p. 1.

14. Central Intelligence Agency, *The World Factbook,* accessed March 31, 2018, http://www.cia.gov/ library/publications/the-world-factbook/index.html.

15. Nestor de Buen Lozano and Carlos de Buen Unna, *International Labor,* Chapter 22, p. 1.

16. Anthony Harrup, "Mexico to Raise Minimum Wage above Inflation," *The Wall Street Journal* (November 21, 2017), accessed March 31, 2018, http://www.wsj.com.

17. WageIndicator, "Minimum Wage in Effect from 01-12-2017 to 30-11-2018," accessed March 31, 2018, https://wageindicator.org/main/salary/minimum-wage/mexico.

18. Nestor de Buen Lozano and Carlos de Buen Unna, *International Labor,* Chapter 22, p. 60.

19. Nestor de Buen Lozano and Carlos de Buen Unna, *International Labor,* Chapter 22, p. 67.

20. Nestor de Buen Lozano and Carlos de Buen Unna, *International Labor,* Chapter 22, p. 68.

21. Ibid.

22. U.S. Social Security Administration, *Social Security Programs throughout the World: The Americas, 2017 – Brazil,* 2017, accessed March 31, 2018, https://www.ssa.gov/policy/docs/progdesc/ ssptw/2016-2017/americas/mexico.pdf.

23. U.S. Social Security Administration, *Social Security Programs throughout the World: The Americas, 2017 – Mexico,* 2017, accessed March 31, 2018 at https://www.ssa.gov/policy/docs/progdesc/ ssptw/2016-2017/americas/mexico.pdf.

24. Central Intelligence Agency, *The World Factbook*, accessed March 31, 2018, http://www.cia.gov/ library/publications/the-world-factbook/index.html.

25. Wikipedia, "List of Minimum Annual Leave by Country," accessed April 1, 2018, https://en.wikipedia.org/wiki/List_of_minimum_annual_leave_by_country.

26. International Monetary Fund, *World Economic Outlook Database*, accessed March 31, 2018, http://www.imf.org/en/data.

27. United Nations, *Human Development Index and Its Components* (2017), accessed April 1, 2018, http://hdr.undp.org/en/reports/global/hdr2017/chapters/en/.

28. Bilaterals.org, *North & South America*, accessed March 31, 2018, https://www.bilaterals .org/?-Americas.

29. BBC News, "S America Launches Trading Bloc," *BBC News* (December 9, 2004), accessed March 31, 2018, http://news.bbc.co.uk/2/hi/business/4079505.stm.

30. Central Intelligence Agency, *The World Factbook*, accessed March 31, 2018, http://www.cia.gov/ library/publications/the-world-factbook/index.html.

31. Jay Forte, "Brazil Reduces 2018 Minimum Wage Forecast to R$969," *The Rio Times* (August 16, 2017), accessed April 1, 2018, http://www.riotimesonline.com.

32. U.S. Social Security Administration, *Social Security Programs throughout the World: The Americas, 2017 – Brazil,* accessed March 31, 2018, https://www.ssa.gov/policy/docs/progdesc/ ssptw/2016-2017/americas/brazil.pdf.

33. Ibid.

34. Ibid.

35. Central Intelligence Agency, *The World Factbook*, accessed March 31, 2018, http://www.cia.gov/ library/publications/the-world-factbook/index.html.

36. Jeff Kenner, in William L. Keller & Timothy J. Darby, *International Labor and Employment Laws*, 2nd ed. Vol. I (2003), 1-1–1-2.

37. Europa, *Labour Law*, accessed March 31, 2018, http://ec.europa.eu/social/main.jsp?catId=157.

38. Central Intelligence Agency, *The World Factbook*, accessed March 31, 2018, https://www.cia.gov/library/publications/the-world-factbook/index.html.

39. Ibid.

40. WorldatWork, "WorldatWork Salary Budget Survey: Top-Level Results," (July 11, 2017), accessed April 1, 2018, http://www.worldatwork.org.

41. International Monetary Fund, *Report for Selected Countries and Subjects*, accessed March 31, 2018, http://www.imf.org/external/index.htm.

42. Ibid.

43. Ravi Singhania, in William L. Keller & Timothy J. Darby, *International Labor and Employment Laws*, 2nd ed. (2003), Vol. II, 24-10–24-13.

44. U.S. Social Security Administration, *Social Security Programs throughout the World: Asia and the Pacific, 2016*, accessed March 31, 2018, https://www.ssa.gov/policy/docs/progdesc/ssptw/2016-2017/asia/india.pdf.

45. Paycheck.in, *Minimum Wage India 2017 – Current Minimum Wage Rate India*, accessed March 31, 2018, https://paycheck.in/main/salary/minimumwages.

46. Paycheck.in, *Maternity and Work – India*, accessed March 31, 2018, https://paycheck.in/main/salary/maternity-and-work.

47. U.S. Social Security Administration, *Social Security Programs throughout the World: Asia and the Pacific, 2016*, accessed March 31, 2018, https://www.ssa.gov/policy/docs/progdesc/ssptw/2016-2017/asia/india.pdf.

48. Ibid.

49. Central Intelligence Agency, *The World Factbook*, accessed March 31, 2018, http://www.cia.gov/library/publications/the-world-factbook/index.html.

50. Ibid.

51. Andreas W. Lauffs, et al., in William L. Keller & Timothy J. Darby, *International Labor and Employment Laws*, 2nd ed. (2003), Vol. I, 31–35.

52. Ibid.

53. Alexander Chipman Koty and Zhou Qian, "A Complete Guide to 2017 Minimum Wage Levels across China," *China Briefing* (November 15, 2017), accessed April 1, 2018, http://www.china-briefing.com.

54. Bloomberg News, "China's Workers Are Saying Goodbye to Double-Digit Pay Raises," (June 19, 2017), accessed April 1, 2018, http://www.bloomberg.com.

55. International Labour Organization, *Working Conditions Laws Database*, accessed April 3, 2015, http://www.ilo.org/dyn/travail/travmain.home.

56. U.S. Social Security Administration, *Social Security Programs throughout the World: Asia and the Pacific, 2016*, accessed March 31, 2018, https://www.ssa.gov/policy/docs/progdesc/ssptw/2016-2017/asia/india.pdf.

57. Ibid.

58. Ibid.

59. Central Intelligence Agency, *The World Factbook*, accessed March 31, 2018, http://www.cia.gov/library/publications/the-world-factbook/index.html.

EPILOGUE

CHALLENGES FACING COMPENSATION PROFESSIONALS

EPILOGUE: Challenges Facing Compensation Professionals

Learning Objectives

When you finish studying this chapter, you should be able to:

E-1. Explain the issues associated with a possible increase to the federal minimum wage rate.

E-2. Summarize the trends in performance appraisal and the relationship to compensation practices.

E-3. Describe the compensation–productivity gap issue.

E-4. Discuss the gender pay gap.

E-5. Explain the issue of pay transparency.

Thus far in *Strategic Compensation*, we have considered a story about the fundamentals of employee compensation and benefits programs and the building blocks and structural elements that make them. The book's approach to studying compensation arms professionals with the knowledge to make compensation decisions more effectively that fit well with companies' competitive advantages. There is much more to consider besides the fundamentals. In this epilogue, we will briefly examine five key issues among many more that have created persistent challenges for compensation and HR professionals. These issues have influenced and will continue to influence the story about compensation system design and practice. How these issues will *ultimately* change compensation strategy and practices remains to be seen.

- Possible increases to the federal minimum wage rate
- Performance appraisal trends
- Compensation–productivity gap
- Gender pay gap
- Pay transparency

POSSIBLE INCREASE TO THE FEDERAL MINIMUM WAGE RATE

In Chapter 2, we described the three central provisions of the Fair Labor Standards Act: minimum wage, overtime pay, and child labor. Over the years, many public campaigns have called for increasing the federal minimum wage rate. There have been at least as many public campaigns advocating for maintaining the status quo. We have watched them play out on the political stage in Washington D.C., and within states and cities across the United States.

E-1. Explain the issues associated with a possible increase to the federal minimum wage rate.

The federal hourly minimum wage rate ($7.25) has remained the same since 2009; however, we learned in Chapter 2 that many states and the District of Columbia have higher minimum wage rates than the federal level. Many recent efforts within states such as New York and in cities such as Chicago have led to substantial rises in those areas' minimum wage rates. The New York City rate rose to $15 at the end of 2018 and by 2021, the state rate will match New York City's current level.

Within some states, pushes for higher local minimum wage rates have taken hold. For example, in Los Angeles, unions successfully lobbied for a minimum wage rate for hotel workers—the lowest paid in the city—to $15.37 in 2017. Concerns about layoffs are evident. However, one study found municipalities with higher pay did not suffer job losses among low-wage restaurant workers.[1] This study also found that restaurants often instituted modest price increases to avoid layoffs. Further, the study showed that higher wages often resulted in lower turnover because of higher wages.

Not all economists believe that legislating a higher minimum wage will be harmless to the economy. Many argue that increasing the minimum wage will have negative ripple effects throughout the U.S. economy. These arguments are based on the economic principles of supply and demand. In this context, raising the minimum wage could lead to increases in the price of goods and services as companies try to offset higher labor costs. As the prices of goods and services increase, consumers are more likely to buy less. In turn, reduced demand for goods and services stand to cut into profits, which may lead to cost reductions in the form of layoffs rather than further price increases.

Much scholarly research supports this conclusion. An exhaustive review of recent research concluded that approximately 85 percent of minimum wage studies provide strong evidence of negative employment effects resulting from minimum wage laws.[2] However, a study by the Congressional Budget Office indicates mixed outcomes. On one hand, an increase in the minimum wage rate to $10.10 would likely lead to the loss of 500,000 low-skilled jobs. On the other hand, raising the minimum wage would raise pay of nearly 1 million workers to above the federal poverty levels.[3] Some of the loss in labor would be offset by lower cost automation. In the fast food industry, for example, labor-cost saving alternatives include online ordering and touch-screen kiosks.

Beyond legislation, many retailers, as we discussed in Chapter 2, have chosen to raise the minimum starting wage rate. As noted there, large retailers are finding it increasingly more difficult to hire well-qualified workers at lower pay rates, particularly since the unemployment rate has declined. For instance, retailer Target announced that it would raise the pay for all its U.S. employees to at least $11 per hour, rising to $15 per hour by 2020.[4] Coupled with higher starting pay rates, others are offering bonuses and paid family leave.

Notwithstanding these broader dynamics, compensation professionals face the challenge of managing pay inequities between a company's employees who are distributed across municipality or state lines where minimum wage rates differ. In addition, rising minimum wage rates stand to compress pay structures that include minimum wage jobs. Compression in this context occurs when a higher minimum wage rate boosts the pay range minimum rate. Unless all the pay rates are increased commensurately, the reduced pay differences effectively understate the relative value of higher paying jobs, creating opportunities for more highly paid employees to feel pay inequity.

Compensation professionals also face the challenge of planning budgets. Dozens of states are considering possible increases to their minimum wage rates. Political debates, business and labor lobbying efforts, and politicians' interest in boosting re-election chances create uncertainty about whether minimum wage rates will increase, and, if increased, by what amount.

Finally, increases in the minimum wage force companies to reconsider its total compensation offerings. Coupled with higher starting pay rates, Wal-Mart offered seniority-based cash bonuses and now provides paid family leave. It is likely that many smaller companies or companies of any size that are losing ground, will not follow Wal-Mart's or Target's initiatives. Higher compensation costs, in the short-term at least, could further jeopardize financial viability. Alternatively, choosing to increase starting pay rates does not necessarily lead to higher total compensation budgets. For example, a company could choose to offset the cost of a higher minimum wage by eliminating one or more benefits that employees do not fully utilize.

TRENDS IN PERFORMANCE APPRAISAL

E-2. Summarize the trends in performance appraisal and the relationship to compensation practices.

In recent years, many HR professionals, business executives, and employees have questioned the value of traditional annual performance appraisal methods. A survey by Deloitte University revealed that 78 percent of HR professionals said that performance management is important or very important.[5] However, only eight percent of the respondents stated that their performance management process drove business results.[6] Some firms have transitioned to ongoing reviews that entail more frequent, developmental feedback, often making pay raise and promotion decisions separately. For instance, Kris Duggan, CEO of the information technology company BetterWorks maintains, "When evaluating who gets promotions, raises, and bonuses, it has to be done in a more subjective manner, taking into account the competitive rate for the market, the amount of time since the last raise, what sorts of customer or internal relationships have been developed, and how well the employee is executing on his or her objectives."[7]

☛ **FYI**

A survey of more than 10,000 companies revealed that 71 percent are re-evaluating current performance appraisal practices, upgrading them, or have already updated them during the previous three years.[8]

By September 2015, 51 large firms transitioned to systems without ratings.[9] Many more are contemplating the same. Several other firms have modified their performance appraisal methods. General Electric (GE), once known for using forced ranking systems, stopped using them. At GE, employees who were rated in the bottom 10 percent of the performance distribution were either encouraged to leave or fired. Instead, the company now expects 200,000 salaried employees and managers to share frequent feedback via a mobile app called PD@GE.[10] Janice Semper, a GE human resource executive, maintained that eliminating ratings "led to more meaningful, richer conversations that were not getting distracted by . . . a label."[11] Goldman Sachs Group Inc. has taken the rating less approach even further by providing real-time feedback to employees.[12]

Adobe Systems had used a forced ranking system for many years until 2012.[13] The company estimated that managers spent a total of 80,000 hours conducting annual reviews.[14] Nowadays, the company provides extensive training to educate employees and managers about how to conduct more frequent "check-in" meetings. Donna Morris, senior vice president of human resources, described check-ins as " . . . a 180 [-degree turn] in terms of giving people the material they need to improve their performance and change course."[15] Morris added: "It completely changes how employees feel about their jobs and opportunities. Feedback is now viewed as a gift." Adobe also deemed the new approach as successful based on an analysis of involuntary and voluntary turnover. Adobe saw a 30 percent increase in the number of employees who left the company voluntarily and a 50 percent increase in the number of employees who left involuntarily.[16]

Some companies recognize the value of frequent feedback and elements of a rating system. For instance, IBM uses technology to facilitate more frequent performance reviews. IBM uses the Checkpoint app to set short-term goals and managers provide quarterly feedback on their progress. For the ratings portion, managers evaluate every employee on five criteria—business results, impact on client success, innovation, personal responsibility to others, and skills. Diane Gherson, chief human resource officer at IBM, said: "In the old system, there was one score. People [got] sort of obsessed by that."[17] In addition, she spoke highly of the five-factor rating: "It leads to a much richer, more balanced discussion."

Other companies making changes encourage employees to seek feedback. For example, J.P. Morgan Chase & Co. offers feedback programs that permit employees to request mini interviews following the completion of a project.[18] Employees may interview either with their boss or colleagues.

Despite some companies' shifts away from traditional performance appraisal methods, these practices are far from extinction. One survey revealed that roughly 90 percent of firms worldwide use performance ratings. Many of the companies use both qualitative and quantitative (performance ratings) approaches. In addition, these firms rely on ratings as a factor in pay raise decisions.[19] For example, Facebook utilizes a formula to limit opinions in determining pay raise amounts.[20] This process involves a formula, so managers have no discretion in compensation decisions. The goal is for managers to focus on what they can specifically measure and allows the company to manage pay using compensation expertise.

There are many reasons that companies maintain the status quo. Perhaps most noteworthy is the lack of executive-level support for change. For example, Intel Corporation executives were worried that sacrificing ratings would draw healthy tension out of a workplace.[21] In addition, others were concerned that managers may not possess sufficient skills to use performance discussions effectively. There is merit to this concern. In some cases, managers displayed difficulties explaining job performance to employees as well as clearly describing specific steps for improvement.[22] Perhaps managers have become accustomed to using traditional ratings. Without them, they may have difficulty framing the discussion.[23] At Facebook, a participant of a focus group assembled to assess the use of performance ratings characterized their use as a punctuation mark because they are well-defined.[24] Ratings better enable managers to quantify pay increase differences.

THE COMPENSATION-PRODUCTIVITY GAP

The **compensation–productivity** gap refers to the difference between real hourly compensation and labor productivity. The U.S. Bureau of Labor Statistics defines **labor productivity** as real output per hour worked (i.e., how efficiently labor is used in producing goods and services).[25] There are many possible factors affecting labor productivity growth, including changes in technology, capital investment, capacity utilization, use of intermediate inputs, improved managerial skills or organization of production, and improved skills of the workforce.

E-3. Describe the compensation–productivity gap issue.

In the United States, pay has not been keeping up with productivity. Productivity growth promotes rising living standards in the following manner. Increases in productivity growth indicate companies' investments in capital equipment and information technology. Examples of capital equipment include new manufacturing facilities, research and development labs, and sales distribution centers. Examples of information technology include structured databases containing expert information to help end users make informed decisions in complex situations. For instance, physicians may access databases to help them diagnose health conditions based on patients' symptoms and health histories. Another example occurs in the marketing field where information systems enable companies to identify customers for new products and services based on a variety of factors, including household income and purchasing history.

Since the 1970s, real hourly compensation has lagged labor productivity growth as shown in Figure E-1.[26] The growth of productivity and real hourly compensation in the nonfarm business sector (which accounts for three-fourths of output and employment in the total U.S. economy) was comparable until 1973. The annual change in productivity averaged 2.8 percent and real hourly compensation growth averaged 2.6 percent during the 1947–1973 period. In 1973–1979,

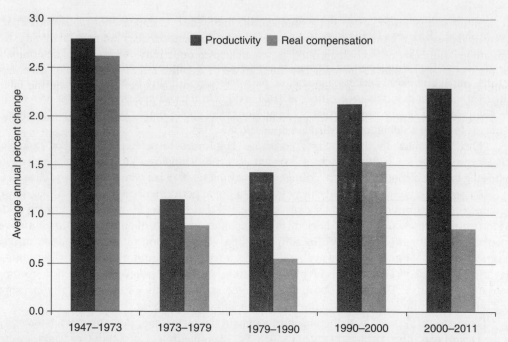

FIGURE E-1 Productivity Growth and Real Hourly Compensation Growth, Selected Years, 1947–2011

Source: U.S. Bureau of Labor Statistics.

the annual averages were at 1.1 and 0.9 percent, respectively. Real hourly compensation growth failed to keep pace with accelerating productivity growth over the past three decades, and the gap between productivity growth and compensation growth widened. Hence, during 2000–2011, average annual growth in productivity and real compensation equaled 2.3 percent and 0.9 percent, respectively. Not shown in Figure E-1 is the continued trend through mid 2018.

The compensation–productivity gap is evident in most industries, but the magnitude of the gap varies by industry as shown in Figure E-2. For the period 1987–2015, the gap is most

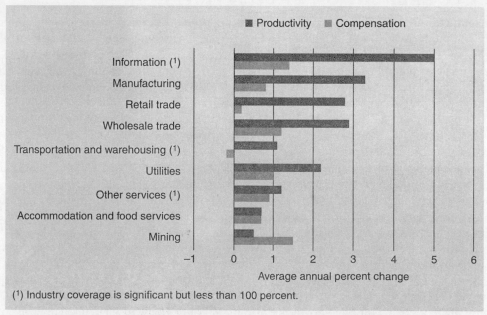

(1) Industry coverage is significant but less than 100 percent.

FIGURE E-2 Productivity and Compensation by Sector, 1987–2015

Source: U.S. Bureau of Labor Statistics.

substantial in the information and manufacturing industries. Compensation and productivity grew at approximately the same rate in the accommodation and services industry. In mining, the growth in compensation far outpaced the growth in labor productivity. An important determinant of the gap is labor share of income. The **labor share of income** refers to the part of economic output that goes to workers as compensation in return for their labor.[27] Declines in the labor share widen the gap between these two measures, while increases narrow the gap.[28]

The compensation–productivity gap undoubtedly poses challenges for compensation professionals who develop and implement pay-for-performance systems, especially, merit pay. As discussed in Chapter 3, under merit pay programs, employees earn permanent merit increases based on job performance. A widening compensation–productivity gap undermines the intent of pay-for-performance. Meanwhile, years of small annual merit pay increase budgets have lagged productivity increases. This problem is exacerbated when rises in the cost of living further erode the value of merit pay increases.

GENDER PAY GAP

The **gender pay gap** refers to the proportion of women's earnings relative to men's earnings. Women earn substantially less than men. A gender-based pay gap has endured for over 150 years.[29] Figure E-3 shows the trend in the size of the gender pay gap. Although the pay gap has decreased in recent decades, it is still substantial. In 1979, the gap was 62.3 percent, or women earned about 62.3 cents for every $1 that men earned and by 2016 that had improved to 81.9 percent.[30]

E-4. Discuss the gender pay gap.

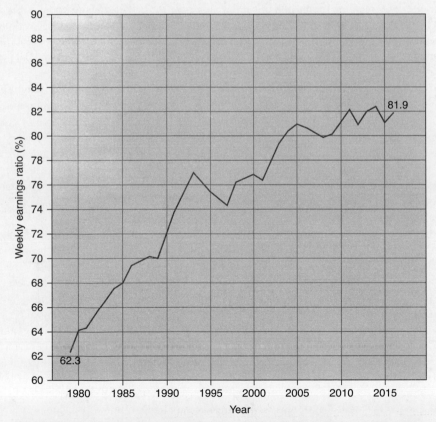

FIGURE E-3 Gender Earnings Ratio by Weekly Earnings, 1979–2016
Source: U.S. Bureau of Labor Statistics, "Earnings and Earnings Ratios," *1979–2016 Current Population Survey, U.S. Bureau of Labor Statistics,* accessed April 13, 2018, at http://www.bls.gov.

Through the years, the gap has been the subject of discussion and heated debates at all levels of government, in legal circles, HR departments, and in executive board rooms. Academic and public policy researchers have studied the gender pay gap from various perspectives, including social stratification, social justice, illegal discrimination, and economics. These perspectives are complex and many are intertwined. As a starting point, it is useful to consider the underlying causes of the gap and what compensation professionals can do to eliminate any pay gap that is attributable to gender. One remedy is to provide equal pay for equal work. Another is to provide comparable pay for comparable worth. Some academic and public policy researchers advanced the idea of comparable worth. **Comparable worth** has been a part of an ongoing societal debate regarding the pay differentials between men and women who perform similar, but not identical work. We will review the comparable worth debate here and its relationship to compensation practices.

Paula England, a renowned sociologist, has written extensively about the Comparable Worth debate.[32] For the purposes of this discussion, only a summary of the key issues based on her work are presented.

An important question in this debate is, *Why are jobs that are typically held by women paid substantially less than comparable jobs that men tend to occupy?* Many comparable worth advocates argue that discrimination against women explains this pay differential. Two contextual factors contribute to this discrimination:

- Increase in employment among women
- Segregation of women from men in the work place based on jobs and industry

Since World War II, U.S. women have joined the work force in increasing numbers, both out of economic need, and increased opportunities for jobs and higher wages. Single or divorced mothers have had to support themselves financially, and many women entered the work force during the 1970s when economic recessions resulted in the temporary layoffs for their husbands.

Besides economic need, the number of employment opportunities for women rose. This growth resulted from a restructuring of the economy that produced declining employment in both agriculture and manufacturing, and increases in service industries such as food service, retail sales, and the health industry.

Job segregation also influences comparable worth. Relatively few jobs in the United States are substantially integrated by gender. Essentially, comparable jobs held by women have been devalued compared to men.[33] Devaluation explains how two similar occupations, janitors (mostly men) and housekeepers (mostly women), have different pay scales. The female-dominated job, housekeeping, has lower pay than male-dominated janitorial work. Janitors have median weekly earnings of $574 for men and $481 for women; housekeeper earnings were $508 for men and $439 for women.[34]

Many comparable worth advocates believe that two compensation practices—job evaluation and compensation surveys—represent the media through which discrimination against women operates. Job evaluation per se is not discriminatory. In fact, many comparable worth advocates argue that the use of a single job evaluation system that reflects the complete range of female- and male-dominated jobs can establish the "true" worth of jobs based on content.[35] However, the use of multiple job evaluation systems to evaluate jobs may be discriminatory where one system is applied to male-dominated jobs, and the other is applied to female-dominated jobs.

Take the point rating system for example. Let's assume that two point rating programs are developed, one for service jobs that are generally held by women—maid service, food service—and the other for service jobs that are generally held by men—janitorial, maintenance. In addition, both systems are based on the four universal compensable factors—skill, effort, responsibility, and working conditions (Chapter 2), and the same descriptions for these compensable factors apply to each group of jobs. Job evaluators may consciously or unconsciously underrate the degree of compensable factors for the female-dominated jobs relative to the male-dominated jobs.

Compensation surveys also have been implicated as culprits in pay disparity between men and women holding jobs of comparable worth. Specifically, comparable worth advocates (among others) argue that market rates are biased against women. In *Lemons v. The City and County of Denver*[36], Lemons claimed that her job as a nurse—a female-dominated job—was illegally paid less than comparable jobs held predominantly by men. In fact, Lemons argued that nursing required more education and skill than some of the male-dominated jobs, and so should be paid at a higher rate despite market factors—the fact that the male-dominated jobs generally earned higher rates in the local labor market. She also argued that local labor markets were inherently biased against women, and, therefore, should not be a legitimate basis for establishing pay rates. The court disagreed with her charge on the basis that *Title VII* (Chapter 2) did not focus on equalizing market disparities.

More recently, asking job candidates to reveal salary history has been implicated in perpetuating the gender pay gap, and legislation in some cities (e.g., New Orleans and Pittsburgh) and states (California and Massachusetts) have banned this and related practices. The Massachusetts' Pay Equity Act prohibits companies from inquiring about an applicant's pay history on job applications, interviews, and during pay negotiations. Companies are also prohibited from asking previous employers to verify pay amount prior to making a job offer. This law does have the potential to reduce the pay gap. For example, let's say that an employer's policy is to offer a salary that is 10 percent higher than the applicant's previous salary. And, for this illustration, a female applicant making $50,000 would receive a salary offer of $55,000 under the company's policy. A male applicant whose current salary is $75,000 would receive a salary offer of $82,500, thus, perpetuating the pay gap. Prohibiting questions about salary history helps companies to focus on the market value of the job (Chapter 7), but this is easier said than done. Sue Holloway, director of Executive Compensation Strategy for WorldatWork, characterizes this difficulty: "The idea of having to craft a total rewards offer without salary history information can be daunting . . . When hiring managers and recruiters are educated and reliable compensation data on market rates and pay ranges, the need for a candidate's salary history diminishes."[37]

Notwithstanding the passage of legislation in many areas, others failed to pass in Minnesota, Mississippi, and Washington. Many HR professionals are debating the merits of a salary history ban. Some are not convinced that such policies will significantly reduce the gender pay gap. Two prevalent reasons for this position are that companies already have pay systems that monitor for pay equality; and, the gender pay gap is much smaller than widely reported statistics that do not necessarily taking into account differences in jobs and job holder qualifications.[38]

Still, some companies voluntarily attempt to reduce the pay gap by prohibiting salary negotiations. These actions are based on the belief that most men are presumably better negotiators than women and women tend to ask for less money than their male counterparts.[39] Examples of companies that prohibit salary negotiations or requesting salary history include Alameda Electrical Distributors as well as Reddit.

☛ **FYI**

A survey of companies revealed the following about the likelihood of adopting a salary history ban adoption:

- Extremely likely: 12%
- Somewhat likely: 28%
- Somewhat unlikely: 19%
- Extremely unlikely: 14%
- Not considering adoption: 28%[40] (sums to more than 100 percent due to rounding error)

PAY TRANSPARENCY

E-5. Explain the issue of pay transparency.

Pay transparency refers to the extent to which companies make available information about one or more elements of the compensation system, including all employees' pay or the formula for all pay decisions, pay grades and ranges, and the process and criteria for setting base pay and pay increase amounts. Revealing all information is full transparency; sharing less information refers to partial pay transparency. Choosing to reveal no information is synonymous with pay secrecy. Perspectives about the merit of pay transparency vary. It is common to find ones that advocate for pay transparency or pay secrecy exclusively. Many companies are cautious about revealing information, believing that pay transparency can create as much or more damage as good.[41]

☛ FYI

A survey of employees in several countries responded in the following way to the statement: I have a good understanding of how people are compensated at all levels in my company:

- All countries: 56%
- Canada: 71%
- United Kingdom: 61%
- United States: 60%
- Netherlands: 56%
- France: 52%
- Switzerland: 49%
- Germany: 43%[42]

Starting with good, transparent policies can promote motivation and higher performance over the long run by sharing information about the processes or formulas used to determine pay and pay increases throughout the company. A study by PayScale found "that one of the top predictors of employee sentiment, including 'satisfaction' and 'intent to leave,' was a company's ability to communicate clearly about compensation."[43] Transparency alone is insufficient to reap these benefits. Companies must go beyond written words to full-on engagement of employees as valuable contributors and providing opportunities for their development.

On the flip side, (partial) pay transparency may compromise motivation and performance. Consider a company's decision to publish partial information about pay structures, including pay grades, the jobs within each grade, and the corresponding pay ranges. An employee can easily see their place within the pay structure; however, knowledge of placement in the structure alone will likely lead to questions and concerns about unfair treatment. Armed with pertinent knowledge, employees may take the initiative to strive for better performance and to ask for performance feedback more regularly.

A downside of transparency is the biases with which we judge comparative information. Individuals often believe that their performance or contributions are higher than they are. A study of engineers found that nearly half judged themselves to be within the top five percent of their peers and 92 percent (including the previous group) believed that they were in the top quartile of performance.[44] Self-flattering assessments may lead to complacency or unrealistic expectations that they should be paid more.

The absence of pay transparency often raises questions about the legality and fairness of the gender pay gap. As we discussed earlier, not all gender pay gaps are illegal; the absence of information may raise suspicions. When employees share information about their pay with coworkers, any gender pay differential will be scrutinized. In the absence of information about decisions that led to the differences are revealed, the differential may be seen as potentially discriminatory. Many companies are reluctant to disseminate employees' pay to protect privacy and information about their status in the organization. For instance, lower pay for equal work could be due to a track record of mediocre or poor performance.

Sometimes, companies choose to withhold pay information for the sake of convenience. Kevin F. Hallock, dean of the Industrial and Labor Relations School at Cornell University, said that transparency "is too disruptive, and not worth it." Also, he pointed out that many companies choose not to reveal pay information because they "aren't very good at explaining to employees why they're being paid what they're paid, or what they must do to earn more."[45]

PREPARING FOR EXAMS/QUIZZES

Chapter Summary by Learning Objectives

Learning Objective E-1. *Explain the issues associated with a possible increase to the federal minimum wage rate.* There are discussions occurring on the national stage about the possibility of raising the federal minimum wage rate. While such changes will be welcome news to a large segment of the labor force, there are possible consequences, such as higher unemployment.

Learning Objective E-2. *Summarize the trends in performance appraisal and the relationship to compensation practices.* Traditional performance appraisal methods have come under scrutiny for a variety of reasons. Many companies have set aside traditional performance appraisal approaches for continuous performance discussions; others have introduced hybrid methods that combine features of ratings and continuous discussions. Criticisms of traditional methods do not signal the extinction of this approach. While new approaches show promise, they are not without limitations, including how to determine pay increase amounts based on qualitative feedback and managers having difficulty framing the performance discussion.

Learning Objective E-3. *Describe the compensation–productivity gap issue.* The compensation–productivity gap refers to the difference between hourly compensation and labor productivity. For decades, increases in compensation have lagged increases in productivity, and it is prevalent in most industries. This gap poses challenges for compensation professionals who strive to establish pay-for-performance programs that motivate employees. The challenge is greater because of small merit pay increase budgets and the rising cost of living.

Learning Objective E-4. *Discuss the gender pay gap.* The gender pay gap refers to the proportion of women's earnings relative to men's earnings. Women earn substantially less than men. The pay gap was 81.9 percent in 2016. Besides illegal pay discrimination, a variety of other factors captured in the comparable worth debate are believed to contribute to the gender pay gap. Compensation practices thought to contribute to the gap is job evaluation, market pay surveys, and asking job candidates for their salary history. In recent years, some cities and states have passed legislation that prohibits asking job candidates for their salary history. There are differences in opinion among compensation and HR professionals about the utility of the ban.

Learning Objective E-5. *Explain the issue of pay transparency.* Pay transparency refers to the extent to which companies make available information about one or more elements of the compensation system, including all employees' pay or the formula for all pay decisions, pay grades and ranges, and the process and criteria for setting base pay and pay increase amounts. There are a variety of pros and cons of sharing compensation information and these vary, in part, by how much information companies share with employees.

Key Terms

compensation–productivity gap 363	labor share of income 365	comparable worth 366
labor productivity 363	gender pay gap 365	pay transparency 368

Discussion Questions

E-1. Discuss at least one advantage and one disadvantage of increasing the minimum wage. Consider this action's impact on the company.

E-2. What are some of the considerations associated with changing from the use of employee ratings to continuous discussions in appraising employee performance?

E-3. From a total compensation perspective, what can companies do toward minimizing the negative impact of the compensation–productivity gap? (Note: Please think of something other than providing permanent pay increases.)

E-4. Do you agree or disagree with comparable worth advocates' perspectives on the gender wage gap? Explain.

E-5. Should companies make their pay systems transparent? Explain.

E-6. This chapter discusses five important issues that will shape compensation professionals' work for years to come. Which one of these issues stands to create the greatest uncertainty for compensation professionals? Explain.

Endnotes

1. Arindrajit Dube, T. William Lester, and Michael Reich, "Minimum Wage Effects across State Borders: Estimates Using Contiguous Counties," *Review of Economics and Statistics*, 62 (2010): 945–964.

2. David Neumark and William Wascher, *Minimum Wages and Employment: A Review of Evidence from the New Minimum Wage Research*, National Bureau of Economic Research Working Paper No. 12663 (January 2007).

3. Congressional Budget Office, *The Effects of a Minimum-Wage Increase on Employment and Family Income*, Publication 4856, Washington, D.C.: Congress of the United States, 2014.

4. M. Boyle, (2017), "Target Will Raise Hourly Wage to $11 to Counter Wal-Mart," *Bloomberg (September 25)*, accessed January 8, 2018, http://www.bloomberg.com.

5. Jeff Schwartz, Laurence Collins, Heather Stockton, Darryl Wagner, and Brett Walsh, "Rewriting the Rules for the Digital Age: 2017 Deloitte Global Human Capital Trends," Deloitte University Press (2017), accessed March 3, 2017, http://www2.deloitte.com/us/en/pages/human-capital/articles/introduction-human-capital-trends.html.

6. David Schatsky and Jeff Schwartz, "Leading in the New World of Work: Global Human Capital Trends," Deloitte University Press (2015), accessed February 27, 2017, http://www2.deloitte.com/au/en/pages/human-capital/articles/global-human-capital-trends-2015-leading-new-world-work.html.

7. Dana Wilke, "If the Annual Performance Review Is on the Way Out, What Can Replace It?" *Society for Human Resource Management* online (December 7, 2015), accessed February 15, 2017, http://www.shrm.org/resourcesandtools/hr-topics/employee-relations/pages/performance-reviews-dead.aspx.

8. Jeff Kauflin, "Hate Performance Reviews? Good News: They're Getting Shorter and Simpler," *Forbes* (March 9, 2017), accessed April 12, 2018, http://www.forbes.com.

9. David Rock and Beth Jones, "Why More and More Companies Are Ditching Performance Ratings," *Harvard Business Review* online (September 8, 2015), accessed February 15, 2017, http://www.hbr.org.

10. Rachel Emma Silverman, "GE Does Away with Employee Ratings," *The Wall Street Journal* online (July 26, 2016), accessed March 9, 2017, http://www.wsj.com.

11. Ibid.

12. Liz Hoffman, "Goldman Goes beyond Annual Review with Real-Time Employee Feedback," *The Wall Street Journal* (April 21, 2017), accessed April 12, 2018, at http://www.wsj.com.

13. Jeff Kauflin, "Hate Performance Reviews? Good News: They're Getting Shorter and Simpler," *Forbes* (March 9, 2017), accessed April 12, 2018, http://www.forbes.com.

14. Graham Kenny, "Fixing Performance Appraisal Is about More Than Ditching Annual Review," *Harvard Business Review* (February 2, 2016), accessed March 2, 2017, http://www.hbr.org.

15. David Burkus, "How Adobe Scrapped Its Performance Review System and Why It Worked," *Forbes* (June 1, 2016), accessed March 13, 2017, http://www.forbes.com.

16. Ibid.

17. Claire Zillman, "IBM Is Blowing Up Its Annual Performance Review," *Fortune* (February 1, 2016), accessed February 28, 2017, http://www.fortune.com.

18. Rachel Feintzeig, "The Never-Ending Performance Review," *The Wall Street Journal* (May 9, 2017), accessed April 12, 2018, http://www.wsj.com.

19. "The Measure of a Man," *The Economist* (February 20, 2016), accessed March 13, 2017, http://www.economist.com.

20. Lori Goler, Janelle Gale, and Adam Grant, "Let's Not Kill Performance Evaluations Yet," *Harvard Business Review* (November 2016), accessed April 14, 2018, http://www.hbr.org.

21. Rachel Feintzeig, "The Trouble with Grading Employees," *The Wall Street Journal* (April 21, 2015), accessed March 1, 2017, http://www.wsj.com.

22. Rachel Emma Silverman, "GE Does Away with Employee Ratings," *The Wall Street Journal* (July 26, 2016), accessed March 13, 2017, http://www.wsj.com.

23. Jenna McGregor, "This Big Change Was Supposed to Make Performance Reviews Better. Could It Be Making Them Worse?" *The Washington Post* (June 7, 2016), accessed March 9, 2017, http://www.washingtonpost.com.

24. Lori Goler, Janelle Gale, and Adam Grant, "Let's Not Kill Performance Evaluations Yet," *Harvard Business Review* (November 2016), accessed April 14, 2018, http://www.hbr.org.

25. Michael Brill, Corey Holman, Chris Morris, Ronjoy Raichoudhary, and Noah Yosif, "Understanding the Labor Productivity and Compensation Gap," *Beyond the Numbers: Productivity*. Vol. 6, No. 6 (U.S. Bureau of Labor Statistics, June 2017): 1–14.

26. U.S. Bureau of Labor Statistics, (February 24, 2011), *TED: The Editor's Desk. The Compensation-Productivity Gap*, accessed April 9, 2011, *www.bls.gov*; S. Fleck, J. Glaser, and S. Sprague (2011). "The Compensation-Productivity Gap. A Visual Essay," *Monthly Labor Review*, January, 57–69.

27. Michael D. Giandrea and Shawn A. Sprague, "Estimating the U.S. Labor Share," *Monthly Labor Review,* U.S. Bureau of Labor Statistics (February 2017), accessed April 11, 2018, http://www.bls.gov.

28. Ibid.

29. Claudia Goldin, *Understanding the Gender Gap: An Economic History of American Women*. New York: Oxford University Press, 1990.

30. Women's Bureau of the U.S. Department of Labor (1993). *Facts on Working Women*. Washington, D.C.: Government Printing Office.

31. U.S. Bureau of Labor Statistics, "Earnings and Earnings Ratios," *1979–2016 Current Population Survey, U.S. Bureau of Labor Statistics*, accessed April 13, 2018, http://www.bls.gov.

32. Paula England, *Comparable Worth: Theories and Evidence*. New York: Aldine De Gruyter (1992).

33. Asaf Levanon, Paula England, and Paul Allison, "Occupational Feminization and Pay: Assessing Causal Dynamics Using 1950–2000 U.S. Census Data," *Social Forces*, Volume 88, Issue 2, 1 December 2009, 865–891.

34. U.S. Bureau of Labor Statistics, "Median Weekly Earnings of Full-Time Wage and Salary Workers by Detailed Occupation and Sex," *Current Population Survey* (2017), available April 15, 2018, http://www.bls.gov.

35. National Committee on Pay Equity (1987). *Job evaluation: A tool for pay equity*. Washington, D.C.: Author.

36. *Lemons v. City and County of Denver* (1980, F. 2d 228).

37. Melissa Sharp Murdock, "Banning the Use of Salary History in Job Offers Proves Less Difficult than Anticipated," *Worldatwork* (press release, March 20, 2018), accessed April 19, 2018, http://www.worldatwork.org.

38. Jenna McGregor, "Employers Don't Think Bans on Asking about Salary History Will Achieve Goal, Survey Says," *LA Times* (November 17, 2017), accessed April 19, 201, http://www.latimes.com.

39. Susan Milligan, "Salary History Bans Could Reshape Pay Negotiations," *Society for Human Resource Management* (February 16, 2018), accessed April 19, 2018, http://www.shrm.org.

40. "Quick Survey on Salary History Bans (U.S.)," *Worldatwork*, accessed April 19, 2018 at https://www.worldatwork.org/dA/9abc8ad414/salary-history-bans.PDF.

41. Todd Zenger, "The Case against Pay Transparency," *Harvard Business Review* (September 30, 2016), accessed April 15, 2018, http://www.hbr.org.

42. "Employee Perceptions of Talking Pay," *Glassdoor® Global Salary Transparency Survey*, accessed April 15, 2018, http://www.glassdoor.com.

43. Lydia Frank, "What Is Pay Transparency & Why Does It Matter?" *PayScale.com* (2017), accessed April 15, 2018, http://www.payscale.com.

44. Todd Zenger, "The Downside of Full Pay Transparency," *The Wall Street Journal* (April 13, 2017), accessed April 15, 2018, http://www.wsj.com.

45. Sue Shellenbarger, "Open Salaries: The Good, the Bad and the Awkward," *The Wall Street Journal* (January 12, 2016), accessed April 15, 2018, http://www.wsj.com.

Glossary

360-degree performance appraisals incorporate several sources of pertinent information to give a more complete (and presumably) less biased assessment of job performance. Examples of pertinent sources include supervisors, coworkers, and clients.

6-year graduated schedule allows workers to become 20 percent vested after two years and to vest at a rate of 20 percent each year thereafter until they are 100 percent vested after six years of service.

Abilities are enduring attributes of the individual that influence performance.

Ability based on Equal Employment Opportunity Commission guidelines, refers to a present competence to perform an observable behavior or a behavior that results in an observable product.

Accrual rules specify the rate at which participants accumulate (or earn) retirement benefits.

Affirmative action refers to a written document that states a company's goals to recruit and hire underrepresented minorities.

Age Discrimination in Employment Act of 1967 (ADEA) protects older workers age 40 and over from illegal discrimination.

Agency problem describes an executive's behavior that promotes his or her self-interests rather than the interests of the company owners or shareholders.

Agency theory provides an explanation of executive compensation determination based on the relationship between company owners (shareholders) and agents (executives).

Alternation ranking a variation of simple ranking job evaluation plans, which orders all jobs from lowest to highest, based on alternately identifying the jobs of lowest and highest worth.

Americans with Disabilities Act of 1990 (ADA) prohibits discrimination against individuals with mental or physical disabilities within and outside employment settings, including public services and transportation, public accommodations, and employment.

Annual addition is the annual maximum allowable contribution to a participant's account in a defined contribution plan, including employer contributions allocated to the participant's account, employee contributions, and forfeitures allocated to the participant's account.

Annual salary is one type of base pay. Employees earn salaries for performing their jobs, regardless of the actual number of hours worked. Companies generally measure salary on an annual basis.

Annuities are a series of payments for the life of the participant and beneficiary. Annuity contracts are usually purchased from insurance companies, which make payments according to the contract.

Atonio v. Wards Cove Packing Co. a Supreme Court case, ruled that plaintiffs (i.e., employees) in employment discrimination suits must indicate which employment practice created disparate impact and demonstrate how the employment practice created disparate impact (intentional discrimination).

Baby boom generation refers to the generation of people born between 1946 and 1964.

Balance sheet approach provides expatriates the standard of living they normally enjoy in the United States.

Banking hours refers to a feature of flextime scheduling that allows employees to vary the number of hours they work each day as long as they work a set number of hours each week.

Base pay represents the monetary compensation employees earn on a regular basis for performing their jobs. Hourly pay and salary are the main forms of base pay.

Base period is the minimum period of time an individual must be employed before becoming eligible to receive unemployment insurance under the Social Security Act of 1935.

Basic skills information describes developed capacities that facilitate learning or the more rapid acquisition of knowledge.

Behavioral encouragement plans are individual incentive pay plans that reward employees for such behavioral accomplishments as good attendance or safety records.

Behavioral systems are a type of performance appraisal method that requires raters (e.g., supervisors) to judge the extent to which employees display successful job performance behaviors.

Behaviorally anchored rating scales (BARS) are a specific kind of behavioral system based on the critical incident technique (CIT). These scales are developed in the same fashion with one exception. For the CIT, a critical incident would be written as "the incumbent completed the task in a timely fashion." For the BARS format, this incident would be written as, "The incumbent is expected to complete the task in a timely fashion."

Benchmark jobs are positions found outside the company that provide reference points against which the values of jobs within the company are judged.

Bennett Amendment allows employees to charge employers with Title VII violations regarding pay only when the employer has violated the Equal Pay Act of 1963.

Bias errors happen in the performance evaluation process when the rater evaluates the employee based on the rater's negative or positive opinion of the employee rather than on the employee's actual performance.

Board of directors represents shareholders' interests by weighing the pros and cons of top executives' decisions. Members include chief executive officers and top executives of other successful companies, distinguished community leaders, well-regarded professionals (e.g., physicians and attorneys), and a few of the company's top-level executives.

Boureslan v. Aramco a Supreme Court case in which the Supreme Court ruled that federal job discrimination laws do not apply to U.S. citizens working for U.S. companies in foreign countries.

Brito v. Zia Company a Supreme Court ruling, deemed that the Zia Company violated Title VII of the Civil Rights Act of 1964 when a disproportionate number of protected-class individuals were laid off on the basis of low performance-appraisal scores. Zia Company's action was a violation of Title VII because the use of the performance-appraisal system in determining layoffs was indeed an employment test. In addition, the court ruled that the Zia Company had not demonstrated that its performance appraisal instrument was valid.

Broadbanding is a pay structure form that leads to the consolidation of existing pay grades and pay ranges into fewer, wider pay grades.

Cadillac tax was established by the Patient Protection and Affordable Care Act of 2010 (PPACA). Employers that offer health plans that exceed designated dollar amounts will be required to pay a tax equal to 40 percent of the amount that exceeds the designated dollar amounts. The tax was intended to be a disincentive for employers to provide overly rich health benefits, and the cost of the health plan is one way to assess the level of benefits.

Cafeteria plan See *flexible benefits plan.*

Capital refers to the factors that enable companies to generate income, higher company stock prices, economic value, strong positive brand identity, and reputation. There is a variety of capital that companies use to create value, including financial capital (cash) and capital equipment (state-of-the-art robotics used in manufacturing). Employees represent a specific type of capital called *human capital.*

Capital gains refers to the difference between the company stock price at the time of purchase and the lower stock price at the time an executive receives the stock options when the stock price at disposition is higher.

Capital loss refers to the difference between the company stock price at the time of purchase and the lower stock price at the time an executive receives the stock options when the stock price at disposition is lower.

Carve-out plans are insurance plans that offer specific kinds of benefits such as dental care, vision care, prescription drugs, mental health and substance abuse treatment, and maternity care.

Cash–balance plans represent a cross between traditional defined benefits and defined contributions retirement plans. The rate of monetary accumulation slows as the employee's years of service increase.

Central tendency represents the fact that a set of data clusters around or centers on a central point. Central tendency is a number that represents the typical numerical value in a data set.

Certification ensures that employees possess at least a minimally acceptable level of skill proficiency upon completion of a training unit. Certification methods can include work samples, oral questioning, and written tests.

Civil Rights Act of 1964 is a major piece of federal legislation designed to protect the rights of underrepresented minorities.

Civil Rights Act of 1991 shifted the burden of proof of disparate impact from employees to employers, overturning several 1989 Supreme Court rulings.

Classification plans particular methods of job evaluation, place jobs into categories based on compensable factors.

Clawback provisions are provisions in CEO employment contracts that allow boards of directors to take back performance-based compensation if they were to subsequently learn that performance goals were not actually achieved, regardless of whether the CEO was responsible for performance falling short of target levels.

Cliff vesting enables employees to earn 100 percent vesting rights after no more than three years of service.

Coinsurance refers to the percentage of covered expenses paid by the insured. Most commercial plans stipulate 20 percent coinsurance. This means that the insured will pay 20 percent of covered expenses, whereas the insurance company pays the remaining 80 percent.

Collective bargaining agreement refers to a written document that describes the terms of employment approved by management and employees during negotiations. It codifies the terms and conditions of employment regarding rates of pay and pay adjustments, hours of work, or other working conditions of employees.

Commission is a form of incentive compensation, based on a percentage of the product or service selling price and the number of units sold.

Commission-only plans are specific kinds of sales compensation plans. Some salespeople derive their entire income through commissions.

Commission-plus-draw plans award sales professionals commissions and draws.

Common law is developed by judges through court proceedings that decide individual cases.

Common review date is the designated date when all employees receive performance appraisals.

Common review period is the designated period (e.g., the month of June) when all employees receive performance appraisals.

Company match refers to the amount of money an employer may choose to contribute to a defined contribution plan for an employee's contributions.

Company stock represents the total equity or worth of the company.

Company stock shares represent equity segments of equal value. Equity interest increases with the number of stock shares held.

Compa-ratios index the relative competitiveness of internal pay rates based on pay range midpoints.

Comparable worth has been a part of an ongoing societal debate regarding the pay differentials between men and women who perform similar, but not identical work.

Comparison systems a type of performance-appraisal method, require that raters (e.g., supervisors) evaluate a given employee's performance against other employees' performance attainments. Employees are ranked from the best performer to the poorest performer.

Compensable factors are job attributes (e.g., skill, effort, responsibility, and working conditions) that compensation professionals use to determine the value of jobs.

Compensation Compensation budgets are blueprints that describe the allocation of monetary resources to fund pay structures.

Compensation committee a group that contains board of director members within and outside a company. Compensation committees review executive compensation consultants' alternate recommendations for compensation packages, discuss the assets and liabilities of the recommendations, and recommend the consultant's best proposal to the board of directors for its consideration.

Compensation Discussion and Analysis (CD&A) contained within the definitive proxy statement (DEF 14A), must present an unambiguous explanation of all executive compensation information contained in the tables.

Compensation plans represent the selection and implementation of pay level and pay mix policies over a specified time period, usually one year.

Compensation–productivity gap refers to the difference between real hourly compensation and labor productivity.

Compensation strategies describe the use of compensation practices that support HR and competitive strategies.

Compensation surveys involve the collection and subsequent analysis of competitors' compensation data.

Competency refers to an individual's capability to orchestrate and apply combinations of knowledge and skills consistently over time to perform work successfully in the required work situations.

Competitive advantage Competitive advantage describes a company's success when the company acquires or develops capabilities that facilitate outperforming the competition.

Competitive business strategy refers to the planned use of company resources—financial capital, equipment capital, and human capital—to promote and sustain competitive advantage. The time horizon for strategic decisions may span multiple years.

Compressed workweek schedules enable employees to perform their full-time weekly work obligations in fewer days than a regular 5-day workweek.

Consolidated Omnibus Budget Reconciliation Act of 1985 (COBRA) was enacted to provide employees with the opportunity to continue receiving their employer-sponsored medical care insurance temporarily under their employer's plan if their coverage would otherwise cease due to termination, layoff, or other change in employment status.

Consultants See *independent contractors*.

Consumer-driven health care plan refers to an employer-sponsored program that shifts a greater amount of the responsibility to employees for selecting health care providers.

Consumer Price Index (CPI) indexes monthly price changes of goods and services that people buy for day-to-day living.

Content Model a model of O*NET that lists six categories of job and worker information. Job information contains the components that relate to the actual work activities of a job (i.e., information that HR professionals should include in the summary and duties sections of job descriptions). Worker information represents characteristics of employees that contribute to successful job performance.

Contingent workers engage in explicitly tentative employment relationships with companies.

Contrast errors occur when a rater (e.g., a supervisor) compares an employee to other employees rather than to specific explicit performance standards.

Contributory financing implies that the company and its employees share the costs for discretionary benefits.

Copayments represent nominal payments individuals make for office visits to their doctors or for prescription drugs.

Core compensation describes the monetary rewards employees receive. There are seven types of core compensation: two forms of base pay hourly pay (or wage) and salary, seniority pay, merit pay, incentive pay, cost-of-living adjustments (COLAs), and pay-for-knowledge and skill-based pay.

Core employees possess full-time jobs, and they generally plan long-term or indefinite relationships with their employers.

Core hours as applied to flextime schedule, are the hours when all workers must be present.

Core plus option plans establish a set of benefits (e.g., medical insurance) as mandatory for all employees who participate in flexible benefits plans.

Cost-of-living adjustments (COLAs) represent periodic base pay increases that are based on changes in prices, as indexed by the consumer price index (CPI). COLAs enable workers to maintain their purchasing power and standard of living by adjusting base pay for inflation.

Cost leadership strategy or lowest-cost strategy focuses on gaining competitive advantage by being the lowest-cost producer of a product or service within the marketplace, while selling the product or service at a price advantage relative to the industry average. Lowest-cost strategies require aggressive construction of efficient-scale facilities and vigorous pursuit of cost minimization in areas such as operations, marketing, and human resources.

Coverage requirements limit an employer's freedom to exclude employees from qualified plans. Tests to determine whether coverage requirements are met include the ratio percentage test and the average benefit tests.

Critical incident technique (CIT) a specific kind of behavioral system, requires job incumbents and their supervisors to identify performance incidents—on-the-job behaviors and behavioral outcomes—that distinguish successful performance from unsuccessful performance. The supervisor then observes the employees and records their performance on these critical job aspects.

Cross-departmental models a kind of pay-for-knowledge program, promote staffing flexibility by training employees in one department with some of the critical skills they would need to perform effectively in other departments.

Cross-functional skills information indicates developed capacities that facilitate performance of activities that occur across jobs.

Current profit sharing plans award cash to employees, typically on a quarterly or annual basis.

Davis–Bacon Act of 1931 established employment standards for construction contractors holding federal government contracts valued at more than $2,000. Such contractors must pay laborers and mechanics at least the prevailing wage in their local area.

Day care refers to programs that supervise and care for young children and elderly relatives when their regular caretakers are at work.

Deductible is the out-of-pocket expense that employees must pay before dental, medical, or vision insurance benefits become active.

Deferred compensation refers to an agreement between an employee and a company to render payments to an employee at a future date. Deferred compensation is a hallmark of executive compensation packages.

Deferred profit sharing plans plans place cash awards in trust accounts for employees. These trusts are set aside on employees' behalf as a source of retirement income.

Defined benefit plans guarantee retirement benefits specified in the plan document. These benefits usually are expressed in terms of a monthly sum equal to a percentage of a participant's preretirement pay multiplied by the number of years he or she has worked for the employer.

Defined contribution plans require that employers and employees make annual contributions to separate retirement fund accounts established for each participating employee, based on a formula contained in the plan document.

Definitive proxy statement [DEF 14(A)] companies must file this statement under Section 14a of the Securities Exchange Act. This statement is typically referred to as a DEF 14A, revealing detailed information about the compensation of the chief executive officer (CEO) and named executive officers (NEOs), who are the four most highly compensated executives after the CEO. Within the DEF 14A, companies must disclose multiple types of information about compensation. This information should be presented in narrative and tabular form. The narrative is referred to as the Compensation Discussion & Analysis (CD&A) and it must present an unambiguous explanation of all executive compensation information contained in the tables.

DEF 14A See *definitive proxy statement.*

Deliberate and knowing torts are a type of tort that entails an employer's deliberate and knowing intent to harm at least one employee. See also *torts.*

Dental insurance provides reimbursement for routine dental checkups and particular corrective procedures.

Depth of knowledge refers to the level of specialization, based on job-related knowledge, an employee brings to a particular job.

Depth of skills refers to the level of specialization, based on skills, an employee brings to a particular job.

Differentiation strategies focus on product or service development that is unique from those of its competitors. Differentiation can take many forms, including design or brand image, technology, features, customer service, and price.

Direct hire arrangements refer to companies' recruitment and selection of temporary workers without assistance from employment agencies.

Discretionary benefits are benefits that employers offer at their own choice. These benefits fall into three broad categories: protection programs, paid time off, and services.

Discretionary bonuses are awarded to executives on an elective basis by boards of directors. Boards of directors weigh four factors in determining discretionary bonus amounts: company profits, the financial condition of the company, business conditions, and prospects for the future.

Discretionary income covers a variety of financial obligations in the United States for which expatriates remain responsible.

Disparate impact represents unintentional employment discrimination. It occurs whenever an employer applies an employment practice to all employees, but the practice leads to unequal treatment of protected employee groups.

Disparate treatment represents intentional employment discrimination, occurring whenever employers intentionally treat some workers less favorably than others because of their race, color, sex, national origin, or religion.

Distribution refers to the payment of vested retirement benefits to participants or beneficiaries.

Dodd-Frank Act See *Wall Street Reform and Consumer Protection Act of 2010*.

Draw is a subsistence pay component (i.e., to cover basic living expenses) in sales compensation plans. Companies usually charge draws against commissions that sales professionals are expected to earn.

Dual capacity is a legal doctrine that applies to the relationship between employers and employees. Specifically, a company may fulfill a role for employees that is completely different from its role as employer.

Dual employer common law doctrine establishes temporary workers' rights to receive workers' compensation. According to this doctrine, temporary workers are employees of both temporary employment agencies and the client companies. The written contract between the employment agency and the client company specifies which organization's workers' compensation policy applies in the event of injuries.

Early retirement programs contain incentives designed to encourage highly paid employees with substantial seniority to retire earlier than they planned. These incentives expedite senior employees' retirement eligibility and increase retirement income. In addition, many companies include continuation of medical benefits.

Economic Growth and Tax Relief Reconciliation Act of 2001 created tax benefits for individuals and companies in various ways (e.g., increasing the amount companies and employees can contribute to qualified retirement plans on a pretax basis).

Economic realities help companies determine whether employees are financially dependent on them.

Economic recession refers to a general slowdown in economic activity. Evidences of economic recessions include reduced gross domestic product (GDP) and increased unemployment rates.

Education based on Equal Employment Opportunity Commission guidelines, refers to formal training.

EEOC v. Chrysler a district court ruling, deemed that early retirement programs are permissible when companies offer them to employees on a voluntary basis. Forcing early retirement upon older workers represents age discrimination.

EEOC v. Madison Community Unit School District No. 12 a circuit court ruling, sheds light on judging whether jobs are equal based on four compensable factors: skill, effort, responsibility, and working conditions.

Elimination period refers to the minimum amount of time an employee must wait after becoming disabled before disability insurance payments begin. Elimination periods follow the completion of the preeligibility period.

Employee assistance programs (EAPs) help employees cope with personal problems that may impair their job performance (e.g., alcohol or drug abuse, domestic violence, the emotional impact of AIDS and other diseases, clinical depression, and eating disorders).

Employee benefits include any variety of programs that provide paid time off (e.g., vacation), employee services (e.g., transportation services), and protection programs (e.g., life insurance).

Employee-financed benefits do not require the employer to finance discretionary benefits because employees bear the entire cost.

Employee Retirement Income Security Act of 1974 (ERISA) was established to regulate the establishment and implementation of various fringe compensation programs. These include medical, life, and disability insurance programs, as well as pension programs. The essence of ERISA is the protection of employee benefits rights.

Employee stock option plans represent one type of companywide incentives. Companies grant employees the right to purchase shares of company stock.

Employee's anniversary date represents the date an employee began working for his or her present employer. Employees often receive performance appraisals on their anniversary dates.

Equal Employment Opportunity Commission (EEOC) a federal government agency, oversees and enforces various employment laws that guard against illegal discrimination including Title VII of the Civil Rights Act of 1964.

Equal Pay Act of 1963 requires that men and women should receive equal pay for performing equal work.

Equity plans refers to a type of deferred compensation that is designed to provide an executive with an ownership stake in the company through a variety of mechanisms, including stock plans.

Equity theory suggests that an employee must regard his or her own ratio of merit-increase pay to performance, as similar to the ratio for other comparably performing people in the company.

Errors of central tendency occur when raters (e.g., supervisors) judge all employees as average or close to average.

Exchange rate is the price at which one country's currency can be swapped for another's.

Exclusion provisions are the particular conditions that are ineligible for coverage. For example, most disability insurance plans do not provide coverage for disabilities that result from self-inflicted injuries.

Exclusive provider organization (EPO) is a variation of a PPO. EPOs operate similarly to PPOs, but these systems differ. EPOs are more restrictive than PPO plans.

Executive compensation consultants propose recommendations to chief executive officers and board of director members for alternate executive compensation packages.

Executive Order 11246 requires companies holding contracts (worth more than $50,000 per year and employing 50 or more employees) with the federal government to develop written affirmative action plans each year.

Executive Order 11478 prohibits employment discrimination on the basis of race, color, religion, sex, national origin, handicap, and age (401 *FEP Manual* 4061).

Executive Order 11935 prohibits employment of nonresidents in U.S. civil service jobs (401 *FEP Manual* 4121).

Executive orders influence the operation of the federal government and companies that are engaged in business relationships with the federal government.

Exempt refers to an employee's status regarding the overtime pay provision of the Fair Labor Standards Act of 1938 (FLSA). Administrative, professional, and executive employees are generally exempt from the FLSA overtime and minimum wage provisions.

Expatriates are U.S. citizens employed in U.S. companies with work assignments outside the United States.

Experience and training information describes specific preparation required for entry into a job plus past work experience contributing to qualifications for an occupation.

Extrinsic compensation includes both monetary and nonmonetary rewards.

Fair Labor Standards Act of 1938 (FLSA) addresses major abuses that intensified during the Great Depression and the transition from agricultural to industrial enterprises. These include substandard pay, excessive work hours, and the employment of children in oppressive working conditions.

Fairpay Rules specify the criteria for distinguishing between work that is not exempt from the overtime pay provision of the Fair Labor Standards Act.

Family and Medical Leave Act of 1993 (FMLA) requires employers to provide employees 12 weeks of unpaid leave per year in cases of family or medical emergency.

Family assistance programs help employees provide elder care and child care. Elder care provides physical, emotional, or financial assistance for aging parents, spouses, or other relatives who are not fully self-sufficient because they are too frail or disabled. Child care programs focus on supervising preschool-age dependent children whose parents work outside the home.

Family coverage offers health insurance benefits to the covered employee and his or her family members as defined by the plan (usually, spouse and children).

Federal constitution forms the basis for employment laws.

Federal Employees' Compensation Act mandates workers' compensation insurance protection for federal civilian employees.

Federal government oversees the entire United States and its territories. The vast majority of laws that influence compensation were established at the federal level.

Federal Insurance Contributions Act (FICA) taxes employees and employers to finance the Social Security Old-Age, Survivor, and Disability Insurance Program (OASDI).

Federal Unemployment Tax Act (FUTA) mandates employer contributions to fund state unemployment insurance programs.

Fee-for-service approach provides protection for three types of medical expenses: hospital expenses, surgical expenses, and physician's charges.

Fiduciaries are individuals who manage employee benefits plans and pension plan funds.

First-impression effect occurs when a rater (e.g., a supervisor) makes an initial favorable or unfavorable judgment about an employee and then ignores or distorts the employee's actual performance based on this impression.

Flexible benefits plan allows employees to choose a portion of their discretionary benefits based on a company's discretionary benefits options.

Flexible scheduling and leave allows employees to take time off during work hours to care for relatives or react to emergencies.

Flexible spending accounts (FSAs) benefits that permit employees to pay for certain expenses (e.g., child care) with pretax dollars.

Flextime schedules allow employees to modify work schedules within specified limits set by the employer.

Forced distribution is a specific kind of comparison performance appraisal system in which raters (e.g., supervisors) assign employees to groups that represent the entire range of performance.

Foreign service premium is a monetary payment awarded to expatriates above their regular base pay.

Forfeitures are amounts from the accounts of employees who terminated their employment prior to earning vesting rights.

Freelancers See *independent contractors*.

Free-rider effect occurs when employees of lower ability, skill, and effort benefit equally as employees of higher ability, skill, and effort in group incentive plans. The free-rider effect can lead to resentment and turnover of stronger contributors because weaker contributors are getting a "free ride."

Fully insured refers to an employee's status in the retirement income program under the Social Security Act of 1935. Forty quarters of coverage lead to fully insured status.

Gain sharing describes group incentive systems that provide participating employees an incentive payment based on improved company performance, whether for increased productivity, increased customer satisfaction, lower costs, or better safety records.

Gender pay gap refers to the proportion of women's earnings relative to men's earnings. Women earn substantially less than men.

General Schedule (GS) classifies federal government jobs into 15 classifications (GS-1 through GS-15), based on such factors as skill, education, and experience levels. In addition, jobs that require high levels of specialized education (e.g., a physicist), significantly influence public policy (e.g., law judges), or require executive decision making are classified in three additional categories: Senior Level (SL), Scientific & Professional (SP) positions, and the Senior Executive Service (SES).

Generalist may be an executive, performs tasks in a variety of HR-related areas. The generalist is involved in several, or all, of the compensation functions such as building job structures, market competitive pay systems, and merit pay structures.

Generalized work activities information describes general types of job behaviors occurring on multiple jobs.

Golden parachutes executive deferred compensation that provides pay and benefits to executives following their termination resulting from a change in ownership or corporate takeover.

Goods and services allowances compensate expatriates for the difference between goods and services costs in the United States and in the foreign post.

Government Employee Rights Act of 1991 protects U.S. Senate employees from employment discrimination on the basis of race, color, religion, sex, national origin, age, and disability (401 *FEP Manual* 851).

Graduated commissions increase percentage pay rates for progressively higher sales volume in a given period.

Grandfathered plans are health plans that were in effect prior to the implementation date (March 23, 2010) of the Patient Protection and Affordable Care Act of 2010.

Great Depression refers to the period during the 1930s when many businesses failed and many workers became chronically unemployed.

Green circle rates represent pay rates for jobs that fall below the designated pay minimums.

Gross domestic product (GDP) describes the size of a country's economy. Size is expressed as the market value of all final goods and services produced within the country over a specified period. The GDP is typically calculated by the country's national statistical agency.

GDP per capita generally indicates the standard of living within a country: The larger the GDP per capita, presumably the better the standard of living.

Group incentive programs reward employees for their collective performance, rather than for each employee's individual performance.

Groupthink occurs when all group members agree on mistaken solutions because they share the same mind-set and view issues through the lens of conformity.

Hardship allowance compensates expatriates for their sacrifices while on assignment.

Headquarters-based method compensates all employees according to the pay scales used at the headquarters.

Health insurance covers the costs of a variety of services that promote sound physical and mental health, including physical examinations, diagnostic testing (X-rays), surgery, and hospitalization. Companies can choose from four broad classes of plans: fee-for-service plans, managed care plans, point-of-service plans, and consumer-driven health care.

Health Insurance Portability and Accountability Act of 1996 (HIPAA) contains three main provisions. The first provision is intended to guarantee that employees and their dependents that leave their employer's group health plan will have ready access to coverage under a subsequent employer's health plan, regardless of their health or claims experience. The second provision sets limits on the length of time that health plans and health insurance issuers may impose preexisting health conditions and identify conditions to which no preexisting condition may apply. As noted previously, since the passage of the Patient Protection and Affordable Care Act, preexisting condition clauses were eliminated. The third provision protects the transfer, disclosure, and use of health care information.

Health Maintenance Organization Act of 1973 (HMO Act) encouraged the use of HMOs as an alternative approach to delivering health care services.

Health maintenance organizations (HMOs) are sometimes described as providing "prepaid medical services" because fixed periodic enrollment fees cover HMO members for all medically necessary services, as long as the services are delivered or approved by the HMO. HMOs represent an alternative to commercial and self-funded insurance plans.

Health reimbursement arrangements (HRAs) reimburse employees for health-care expenses. Only the employer is permitted to fund HRAs and there is no allowable maximum contribution limit. As with health savings accounts, employees can carry over unused balances into subsequent years.

Health savings accounts (HSAs) are established by employers for employees as a source to cover eligible health care costs. Employees, employers, or both may make contributions to fund these accounts. HSAs have advantages relative to other types of medical savings accounts (flexible spending accounts and health reimbursement accounts). HSAs are portable, which means that the employee owns the account balance after the employment relationship ends. Also, HSAs are subject to inflation-adjusted funding limits.

High-deductible health insurance plans (HDHPs) require substantial deductibles and low out-of-pocket maximums.

Highly compensated employee is defined by the Internal Revenue Service as an officer. The term key 'employee' means any employee who at any time during the year is an officer having annual pay of more than $175,000, *OR* an individual who for 2018 was either of the following: a 5 percent owner of the employer's business or a 1 percent owner of the employer's business whose annual pay was more than $150,000.

Home country-based pay method compensates expatriates the amount they would receive if they were performing similar work in the United States.

Home leave benefits enable expatriates to take paid time off in the United States.

Horizontal knowledge refers to similar knowledge (e.g., record keeping applied to payroll applications and record keeping applied to employee benefits).

Horizontal skills refer to similar skills (e.g., assembly skills applied to lawn mowers and assembly skills applied to snow blowers).

Hospital insurance tax (HI) supports the Medicare Part A program. Also known as *Medicare tax.*

Host country-based method compensates expatriates based on the host countries' pay scales.

Host country nationals (HCNs) are foreign national citizens who work in U.S. companies' branch offices or manufacturing plants in their home countries.

Hourly pay is one type of base pay. Employees earn hourly pay for each hour worked.

Housing and utilities allowances compensate expatriates for the difference between housing and utilities costs in the United States and in the foreign post.

Human capital as defined by economists, refers to sets of collective knowledge, skills, and abilities (KSAs) that employees can apply to create value for their employers. Companies purchase the use of human capital by paying employees an hourly wage or salary and providing benefits such as paid vacation and health insurance. See also *human capital theory.*

Human capital theory states that employees' knowledge and skills generate productive capital known as human capital. Employees can develop knowledge and skills from formal education or on-the-job experiences.

Human resources strategies specify the use of multiple HR practices to reinforce competitive business strategy. These statements are consistent with a company's competitive strategy.

Hybrid plans are retirement plans that combine features of defined benefit and defined contribution plans.

Hypothetical tax is the U.S. income tax based on the same salary level, excluding all foreign allowances.

Illegal discriminatory bias occurs when a supervisor rates members of his or her race, gender, nationality, or religion more favorably than members of other classes.

Improshare is a specific kind of gain sharing program that rewards employees based on a labor hour ratio formula. A standard is determined by analyzing historical accounting data to find the number of labor hours needed to complete a product. Productivity is then measured as a ratio of standard labor hours and actual labor hours.

Incentive effect refers to a worker's willingness to work diligently to produce more quality output than simply attending work without putting in the effort.

Incentive pay or variable pay is defined as compensation, other than base wages or salaries, that fluctuates according to employees' attainment of some standard (e.g., a preestablished formula, individual or group goals, or company earnings).

Incentive stock options entitle executives to purchase their companies' stock in the future at a predetermined price. The predetermined price usually equals the stock price at the time an executive receives the stock options. Incentive stock options entitle executives to favorable tax treatment.

Income annuities distribute income to retirees based on retirement savings paid to insurance companies in exchange for guaranteed monthly checks for life.

Indemnity plans refer to traditional health insurance plans in which the insurance company agrees to pay a designated percentage of the costs for health insurance procedures and the insured (i.e., recipient of the insurance benefit) agrees to pay a designated percentage.

Independent contractors are contingent workers who typically possess specialized skills that are in short supply in the labor market. Companies select independent contractors to complete particular projects of short-term duration—usually a year or less.

Indexes of living costs abroad compare the costs (U.S. dollars) of representative goods and services (excluding education) expatriates purchase at the foreign location and the cost of comparable goods and services purchased in the Washington, DC, area. Companies use these indexes to determine appropriate goods and service allowances.

Individual incentive plans reward employees for meeting work-related performance standards (e.g., quality, productivity, customer satisfaction, safety, and attendance). Any one or a combination of these standards may be used.

Inflation is the increase in prices for consumer goods and services. Inflation erodes the purchasing power of currency.

Insurance policy refers to a contractual relationship between the insurance company and beneficiary. It specifies the amount of money that the insurance company will pay for such particular services as physical examinations.

Integrated paid time off policies enable employees to schedule time off without justifying the reasons.

Integrity Staffing Solutions, Inc. v. Busk et al. a U.S. Supreme Court ruling in which security screenings were not deemed to be a compensable activity when this activity is not an integral part of an employee's job description.

Interests represent individuals' liking or preference for performing specific jobs.

Interindustry wage differentials represent the pattern of pay and benefits associated with characteristics of industries. Interindustry wage differentials can be attributed to a number of factors, including the industry's product market, the degree of capital intensity, the profitability of the industry, and unionization of the workforce.

Internal Revenue Code (IRC) is the set of federal government regulations pertaining to taxation in the United States (e.g., sales tax, individual income tax, corporate income tax).

Internally consistent compensation systems clearly define the relative value of each job among all jobs within a company. This ordered set of jobs represents the job structure or hierarchy. Companies rely on a simple, yet fundamental, principle for building internally consistent compensation systems: Jobs that require greater qualifications, more responsibilities, and more complex duties should be paid more highly than jobs that require lesser qualifications, fewer responsibilities, and less complex job duties.

Intrinsic compensation reflects employees' psychological mind-sets that result from performing their jobs, for example, experiencing a great feeling from the belief that one's work matters in the lives of others.

Involuntary part-time employees work fewer than 35 hours per week because they are unable to find full-time employment.

Job analysis is a systematic process for gathering, documenting, and analyzing information in order to describe jobs.

Job-based pay compensates employees for jobs they currently perform.

Job content refers to the actual activities that employees must perform in the job. Job content descriptions may be broad, general statements of job activities or detailed descriptions of duties and tasks performed in the job.

Job-content evaluation an approach to evaluating job worth, takes skill, effort, responsibility, and working conditions into account.

Job control unionism refers to a union's success in negotiating formal contracts with employees and establishing quasi-judicial grievance procedures to adjudicate disputes between union members and employers.

Job descriptions summarize a job's purpose and list its tasks, duties, and responsibilities, as well as the skills, knowledge, and abilities necessary to perform the job at a minimum level.

Job duties a section in job descriptions, describe the major work activities and, if pertinent, supervisory responsibilities.

Job evaluation systematically recognizes differences in the relative worth among a set of jobs and establishes pay differentials accordingly.

Job leveling refers to corrections that companies can make for differences between their jobs and external benchmark jobs. These corrections are based on subjective judgment rather than on objective criteria.

Job-point accrual model a type of pay-for-knowledge program, provides employees opportunities to develop skills and learn to perform jobs from different job families.

Job sharing is a special kind of part-time employment agreement. Two or more part-time employees perform a single full-time job.

Job structures formally recognize differences in job characteristics that enable compensation managers to set pay accordingly.

Job summary a statement contained in job descriptions, summarizes the job based on two to four descriptive statements.

Job titles listed in job descriptions, indicate job designations.

Just-meaningful pay increase refers to the minimum pay increase that employees will see as making a substantial change in compensation.

Key employee as defined by the Internal Revenue Service (IRS), includes any employee who, during the current year, is an officer of the employer having an annual pay of more than $175,000, *or* an individual who for 2018 was either of the following: a 5 percent owner of the employer's business or a 1 percent owner of the employer's business whose annual pay was more than $150,000. These dollar amounts are indexed for inflation in increments of $5,000.

Knowledge based on Equal Employment Opportunity Commission guidelines, refers to a body of information applied directly to the performance of a function. Similarly, according to O*NET, knowledge refers to organized sets of principles and facts applying in general domains.

Labor hour ratio formula used in determining the payouts in Improshare plans, refers to a standard determined by analyzing historical accounting data to find the number of labor hours needed to complete a product. Productivity is then measured as a ratio of standard labor hours and actual labor hours.

Labor productivity as defined by the U.S. Department of Labor, is the real output per hour worked (i.e., how efficiently labor is used in producing goods and services).

Labor share of income refers to the part of economic output that goes to workers as compensation in return for their labor.

Lease companies employ qualified individuals and place them in client companies on a long-term, presumably "permanent" basis. Lease companies place employees within client companies in exchange for fees.

Ledbetter v. Goodyear Tire & Rubber Co. a court case in which a female employee named Ledbetter sued Goodyear Tire & Rubber Co. after she learned that some male employees with the same job had been paid substantially more than her over a period of several years. Ledbetter claimed that the statute of limitation period began when each discriminatory pay decision was made and communicated to her. She argued that multiple pay decisions were made over the years each time Goodyear endorsed each paycheck, making each paycheck a separate act of illegal pay discrimination.

Legally required benefits are protection programs that attempt to promote worker safety and health, maintain family income streams, and assist families in crisis. The key legally required benefits are mandated by the following laws: the Social Security Act of 1935, various state workers' compensation laws, the Family and Medical Leave Act of 1993, and the Patient Protection and Affordable Care Act of 2010.

Leniency error occurs when raters (e.g., supervisors) appraise an employee's performance more highly than it really rates, compared with objective criteria.

Licensing information describes licenses, certificates, or registrations that are used to identify levels of skill or performance relevant to occupations.

Life insurance protects employees' families by paying a specified amount to employees' beneficiaries upon employees' deaths. Most policies pay some multiple of the employees' salaries.

Lifetime limits Lifetime limits refer to the maximum amount a plan would include if a person receives coverage. Lifetime limits are not permitted since the passage of the Patient Protection and Affordable Care Act.

Lilly Ledbetter Fair Pay Act enables a female employee to file a charge of illegal pay discrimination within 180 days following receipt of a paycheck in which she feels that she may be discriminated against.

Line employees are directly involved in producing companies' goods or service delivery. Assembler, production worker, and sales employee are examples of line jobs.

Local governments refer to municipal or county-level organizations that provide public services and ensure that the rights of citizens and employees are upheld in accordance with pertinent laws and regulations.

Longevity pay systems reward employees with periodic additions to base pay according to employees' length of service in performing their jobs.

Longshore and Harborworkers' Compensation Act mandates workers' compensation insurance protection for maritime workers.

Long-term disability initially refers to illnesses or accidents that prevent an employee from performing his or her "own occupation" over a designated period. The term *own occupation* applies to employees based on education, training, or experience. After the designated period elapses, the definition becomes more inclusive by adding the phrase "inability to perform any occupation or to engage in any paid employment." The second-stage definition is consistent with the concept of disability in workers' compensation programs.

Long-term disability insurance provides benefits for extended periods of time anywhere between 6 months and life.

Lorance v. AT&T Technologies a Supreme Court case, limited employees' rights to challenge the use of seniority systems to only 180 days from the system's implementation date.

Lump sum distributions refer to single payments of benefits. In defined contribution plans, lump sum distributions equal the sum of the vested amount of all employee and vested employer contributions and interest on this sum.

Mail order prescription drug program dispenses expensive medications used to treat chronic health conditions.

Malemployment occurs when job holders possess greater education, skills, or knowledge than is required to perform their jobs.

Managed care plans emphasize cost control by limiting an employee's choice of doctors and hospitals. These plans also provide protection against health care expenses in the form of prepayment to health care providers.

Management by objectives (MBO) a goal-oriented performance-appraisal method, requires that supervisors and employees determine objectives for employees to meet during the rating period, and then employees appraise how well they have achieved their objectives.

Management incentive plans award bonuses to managers who meet or exceed objectives based on sales, profit, production, or other measures for their division, department, or unit.

Market-based evaluation an approach to market-competitive pay systems, uses market data to determine differences in job worth.

Market-competitive pay systems represent companies' compensation policies that fit the imperatives of competitive advantage. Compensation professionals build market-competitive compensation systems based on the results of compensation surveys.

Market lag policy distinguishes companies from the competition by compensating employees less than most competitors. Lagging the market indicates that pay levels fall below the market pay line.

Market lead policy distinguishes companies from the competition by compensating employees more highly than most competitors. Leading the market denotes pay levels above the market pay line.

Market match policy most closely follows the typical market pay rates because companies pay according to the market pay line. Thus, pay rates fall along the market pay line.

Market pay line is representative of typical market pay rates relative to a company's job structure.

Mean is a measure of central tendency calculated as the sum of numbers (e.g., annual salaries in the marketing department) divided by the number of salaries.

Median is the middle value in an ordered sequence of numerical data.

Medical reimbursement plans reimburse employees for some or all of the cost of prescription drugs. These plans pay benefits after an employee has met an annual deductible for the plan.

Medicare Advantage refers to a variety of health insurance coverage options for individuals eligible for Medicare protection who choose not to participate in Parts A and B. It is informally referred to as Medicare Part C.

Medicare Part A refers to compulsory hospitalization insurance that covers both inpatient and outpatient hospital care and services.

Medicare Part B is voluntary supplementary medical insurance that covers 80 percent of medical services and supplies (e.g., outpatient care, laboratory tests). Part B also provides ambulance services when other modes of transportation may endanger the patient's life.

Medicare Prescription Drug, Improvement and Modernization Act of 2003 led to changes in the Medicare program by adding prescription drug coverage and recognizing health savings accounts (HSAs).

Medicare Select plans are Medigap policies that offer lower premiums in exchange for limiting the choice of health care providers.

Medicare tax See *hospital insurance tax (HI)*.

Medigap insurance supplements Medicare Part A and Part B coverage and is available to Medicare recipients in most states from private insurance companies for an extra fee.

Mental Health Parity Act and Addiction Equity Act of 2008 is a law that requires that any group health plan that includes mental health and substance use disorder benefits along with standard medical and surgical coverage must treat them equally in terms of out-of-pocket costs, benefit limits, and practices such as prior authorization and utilization review.

Merit pay are programs that assume that employees' compensation over time should be determined, at least in part, by differences in job performance as judged by supervisors or managers.

Merit pay increase budget limits the amount of pay raises that can be awarded to employees for a specified time period. A merit pay increase budget is expressed as a percentage of the sum of employees' current base pay.

Merit pay programs reward employees with permanent increases to base pay according to differences in job performance.

Midpoint pay value is the halfway mark between the range minimum and maximum rates. Midpoints represent the competitive market rate determined by the analysis of compensation survey data.

Mobility premiums reward employees for moving from one assignment to another.

Multiple-tiered commissions increase percentage pay rates for progressively higher sales volume in a given period only if sales exceed a predetermined level.

Named executive officers (NEO) are the four most highly compensated after the CEO, and detailed information about their compensation must be disclosed in the definitive proxy statement DEF 14A.

National Labor Relations Act of 1935 (NLRA) establishes employees' rights to bargain collectively with employers on such issues as wages, work hours, and working conditions.

Negative halo effect occurs when a rater (e.g., a supervisor) generalizes an employee's negative behavior on one aspect of the job to all aspects of the job.

Network is a specific group of doctors, hospitals, suppliers, and clinics who have contracted to provide services for an agreed rate.

Nominal compensation is the face value of a dollar.

Noncontributory financing implies that the company assumes total costs for discretionary benefits.

Nondiscrimination rule prohibits employers from discriminating in favor of highly compensated employees in contributions or benefits, availability of benefits, rights, or plan features. Also, employers may not amend pension plans to favor highly compensated employees.

Nonexempt refers to an employee's status regarding the overtime pay provision of the Fair Labor Standards Act of 1938 (FLSA). Employees whose jobs do not fall into particular categories (e.g., administrative, professional, and executive employees) are generally covered by overtime and minimum wage provisions.

Non-grandfathered plans refer to health plans that were established after the implementation date (March 23, 2010) of the Patient Protection and Affordable Care Act of 2010.

Nonqualified plans are welfare and pension plans that do not meet various requirements set forth by the Employee Retirement Income Security Act of 1974 (ERISA), disallowing favorable tax treatment for employee and employer contributions.

Nonrecoverable draws act as salary because sales employees are not obligated to repay the loans if they do not sell enough.

Nonrecurring merit increases or merit bonuses are lump sum monetary awards based on employees' past job performances. Employees do not continue to receive nonrecurring merit increases every year. Employees must instead earn them each time.

Nonstatutory stock options a kind of executive deferred compensation, entitle executives to purchase their companies' stock in the future at a predetermined price. The predetermined price usually equals the stock price at the time an executive receives the stock options. Nonstatutory stock options do not entitle executives to favorable tax treatment.

North American Free Trade Agreement (NAFTA) became effective on January 1, 1994. NAFTA has two main goals: First, NAFTA was designed to reduce trade barriers among Mexico, Canada, and the United States. Second, NAFTA also set out to remove barriers to investment among these three countries.

Occupation a group of jobs, found at more than one company, in which a common set of tasks are performed or are related in terms of similar objectives, methodologies, materials, products, worker actions, or worker characteristics.

Occupational Information Network (O*NET) is a database designed to describe jobs in the relatively new service sector of the economy and to more accurately describe jobs that evolved as the result of technological advances. O*NET replaces the *Revised Handbook for Analyzing Jobs*.

Occupational requirements in O*NET include information about typical activities required across occupations. Identifying generalized work activities and detailed work activities summarizes the broad and more specific types of job behaviors and tasks that may be performed within multiple occupations.

Occupational Safety and Health Act of 1970 ensures safe and healthful working conditions for working men and women by authorizing enforcement of the standards under the act.

Occupation-specific information requirements information describes the characteristics of a particular occupation. These particular requirements are occupational skills, knowledge, tasks, duties, machines, tools, and equipment.

Offering period refers to the span in time over which employees, including executives, may purchase the employer's stock based on the money set aside in their accounts established through payroll deduction.

Older Workers Benefit Protection Act (OWBPA) the 1990 amendment to the ADEA, indicates that employers can require older employees to pay more than younger employees for health care insurance coverage. This practice is permissible when older workers collectively do not make proportionately larger contributions than the younger workers.

On-call arrangements are a method for employing temporary workers.

O*NET database See *Occupational Information Network (O*NET)*.

O*NET User's Guide provides detailed information about the O*NET job content model, its applications, and how to use the system.

Open-access HMO a prepaid plan that requires the use of network health-care providers with one exception. In open-access HMO plans, emergency care outside the network is covered, which is not the case for traditional HMO plans.

Organizational context information indicates the characteristics of the organization that influence how people do their work.

Out-of-pocket maximum provisions in medical insurance plans limit the total dollar expenditure a beneficiary must pay during any plan year. These provisions are most common in commercial medical insurance plans.

Outplacement assistance refers to company-sponsored technical and emotional support to employees who are being laid off or terminated.

Parental leave compensates new-parent employees following the birth, adoption, or foster placement of a child.

Paid time off represents discretionary employee benefits (e.g., vacation time) that provide employees time off with pay.

Paid time off banks are policies that compensate employees when they are not performing their primary work duties. Companies offer most paid time off as a matter of custom, particularly paid holidays, vacations, and sick leave.

Paired comparisons a variation of simple ranking job evaluation plans, order all jobs from lowest to highest based on comparing the worth of each job in all possible job pairs. Paired comparisons also refers to a specific kind of comparison method for appraising job performance. Supervisors compare each employee to every other employee, identifying the better performer in each pair.

Participation requirements apply to pension plans. Employees must specifically be allowed to participate in pension plans after they have reached age 21 and have completed 1 year of service (based on 1,000 work hours).

Patient Protection and Affordable Care Act of 2010 (PPACA) enacted on March 23, 2010, is a comprehensive law that requires employers to offer health insurance to employees (the employer mandate). If individuals do not have insurance through employment, they are required to purchase their own insurance (the individual mandate). In either case, monetary penalties are assessed for failure to meet the law's insurance mandates. Since the act's passage, the employer requirements have been implemented in phases. Full implementation will be completed by 2018.

Pay compression occurs whenever a company's pay spread between newly hired or less qualified employees and more qualified job incumbents is small.

Pay grades group jobs for pay policy application. Human resource professionals typically group jobs into pay grades based on similar compensable factors and value.

Pay ranges represent the span of possible pay rates for each pay grade. Pay ranges include midpoint, minimum, and maximum pay rates. The minimum and maximum values denote the acceptable lower and upper bounds of pay for the jobs within particular pay grades.

Pay structures represent pay rate differences for jobs of unequal worth and the framework for recognizing differences in employee contributions.

Pay transparency refers to the extent to which companies make available information about one or more elements of the compensation system, including all employees' pay or the formula for all pay decisions, pay grades and ranges, and the process and criteria for setting base pay and pay increase amounts.

Paycheck Fairness Act is a second key initiative in closing the pay gap between men and women. This bill strengthens the Equal Pay Act of 1963 by strengthening the remedies available to put sex-based pay discrimination on par with race-based pay discrimination. That is, employers are now required to justify unequal pay by showing that the pay disparity is not sex based, but, rather, job related. This act also prohibits employers from retaliating against employees who share salary information with their coworkers.

Pay-for-knowledge rewarding managerial, service, or professional workers for successfully learning specific curricula.

Pension Benefit Guaranty Corporation (PBGC) is a self-financed corporation established by ERISA to insure private-sector defined benefit plans.

Pension plan provides income to individuals and beneficiaries throughout their retirement. Also called *retirement program.*

Pension programs provide income to individuals throughout their retirement.

Pension Protection Act (PPA) Pension Protection Act of 2006 is supposed to help shore up the financial solvency of defined benefit plans in private sector companies and to permit employers to automatically enroll employees in defined contribution plans (e.g., 401(k) plans).

Per capita expenditure on health care refers to the sum of public health expenditure and private expenditure on health. This measure helps compensation professionals understand the standard of health care in different countries, addressing an important element of discretionary and legally required benefits.

Percentiles describe dispersion by indicating the percentage of figures that fall below certain points. There are 100 percentiles ranging from the first percentile to the 100th percentile.

Performance-contingent bonuses awarded to executives, are based on the attainment of such specific performance criteria as market share.

Performance plan refers to a type of equity agreement whereby a company's board of directors establishes performance criteria that an executive must meet before receiving a reward of stocks or stock options.

Perks See *perquisites.*

Perquisites are benefits offered exclusively to executives (e.g., country club memberships).

Person-focused pay plans a system of rewards for employees for specifically learning new curricula.

Phantom stock a type of executive deferred compensation, is an arrangement whereby boards of directors compensate executives with hypothetical company stock rather than actual shares of company stock. Phantom stock plans are similar to restricted stock plans because executives must meet specific conditions before they can convert these phantom shares into real shares of company stock.

Piecework plans individual incentive pay programs, reward employees based on their individual hourly production against an objective output standard, determined by the pace at which manufacturing equipment operates. For each hour, workers receive piecework incentives for every item produced over the designated production standard. Workers also receive a guaranteed hourly pay rate regardless of whether they meet the designated production standard.

Plan termination rules are specifications set forth by the Pension Benefit Guaranty Corporation (PBGC) regarding the discontinuation of an employer's defined benefit pension plan.

Platinum parachutes are lucrative awards that compensate departing executives with severance pay, continuation of company benefits, and even stock options.

Point factor leveling refers to a particular method of job evaluation.

Point method represents a job-content evaluation technique that uses quantitative methodology. Quantitative methods assign numerical values to compensable factors that describe jobs, and these values are summed as an indicator of the overall value for the job.

Point-of-service plan (POS) combines features of fee-for-service systems and health maintenance organizations. Employees pay a nominal copayment for each visit to a designated network of physicians; alternatively, they may receive treatment from providers outside the network, but they pay more for this choice.

Portal-to-Portal Act of 1947 defines the term hours worked that appears in the FLSA.

Positive halo effect occurs when a rater (e.g., a supervisor) generalizes employees' positive behavior on one aspect of the job to all aspects of the job.

Preadmission certification is a certification by a medical professional of a health insurance company that may be necessary before a doctor can authorize hospitalization of a policyholder. Failure to ascertain preadmission certification may lead to denial of hospitalization benefits.

Predetermined allocation bonus awarded to executives, is based on a fixed formula. Company profits are often the main determinant of the bonus amounts.

Preeligibility period spans from the initial date of hire to eligibility for coverage in a disability insurance program.

Preexisting condition is a mental or physical disability for which medical advice, diagnosis, care, or treatment was received during a designated period preceding the beginning of disability or health insurance coverage.

Preferred provider organization (PPO) one of a select group of health care providers that provides health care services to a given population at a higher level of reimbursement than under commercial insurance plans.

Pregnancy Discrimination Act of 1978 (PDA) is an amendment to Title VII of the Civil Rights Act of 1964. The PDA prohibits disparate impact discrimination against pregnant women for all employment practices.

Premium is the amount of money an individual or company pays to maintain insurance coverage.

Prepaid plans refer to most benefits offered by HMOs because fixed periodic enrollment fees cover HMO members for all medically necessary services only if the services are delivered or approved by the HMO. Also, alternative name for HMOs.

Prescription card program operates like HMOs by providing prepaid benefits with nominal copayments for prescription drugs.

Prescription drug plans cover the costs of drugs that state or federal laws require be dispensed by licensed pharmacists.

Primary care physicians are designated by HMOs to determine whether patients require the care of a medical specialist. This functions to control costs by reducing the number of medically unnecessary visits to expensive specialists.

Probationary period is the initial term of employment (usually less than 6 months) during which companies attempt to ensure that they have made sound hiring decisions. Employees are often not entitled to participate in discretionary benefits programs during their probationary periods.

Profit sharing plans pay a portion of company profits to employees, separate from base pay, cost-of-living adjustments, or permanent merit pay increases. Two kinds of profit sharing plans are used widely today: current profit sharing and deferred profit sharing.

Profit sharing pool is money earmarked for distribution to employees who participate in profit sharing plans. Companies may choose to fund profit sharing plans based on gross sales revenue or some basis other than profits.

Protection programs are either legally required or discretionary employee benefits that provide family benefits, promote health, and guard against income loss caused by such catastrophic factors as unemployment, disability, or serious illnesses.

Purchasing power parity exchange rates (PPP) indicate the worth of all goods and services produced in the country (GDP) valued at prices prevailing in the United States. This is the measure most economists prefer when looking at per capita welfare and when comparing living conditions or use of resources across countries.

Qualified plans are welfare and pension plans that meet various requirements set forth by the Employee Retirement Income Security Act of 1974; these plans entitle employees and employers to favorable tax treatment by deducting the contributions from taxable income. Qualified plans do not disproportionately favor highly compensated employees.

Quarters allowances is the U.S. Department of State term for housing and utilities allowances.

Quarters of coverage refers to each 3-month period of employment during which an employee contributes to the retirement income program under the Social Security Act of 1935.

Quartiles allow compensation professionals to describe the distribution of data, usually annual base pay amount, based on four groupings.

Range spread is the difference between the maximum and the minimum pay rates of a given pay grade.

Rating errors in performance appraisals reflect differences between human judgment processes versus objective, accurate assessments uncolored by bias, prejudice, or other subjective, extraneous influences.

Real compensation measures the purchasing power of a dollar.

Recertification ensures that employees periodically demonstrate mastery of all the jobs they have learned.

Recoverable draws act as company loans to employees that are carried forward indefinitely until employees sell enough (i.e., earn a sufficient amount in commissions) to repay their draws.

Red circle rates represent pay rates that are higher than the designated pay range maximums.

Referral plans are individual incentive pay plans that reward employees for referring new customers or recruiting successful job applicants.

Regression analysis describes the linear relationship between two variables (i.e., simple regression) or between the linear composite of multiple variables and one other variable (i.e., multiple regression).

Rehabilitation Act mandates that federal government agencies take affirmative action in providing jobs for individuals with disabilities (401 *FEP Manual* 325).

Relevant labor markets represent the fields of potentially qualified candidates for particular jobs.

Reliable job analysis method yields consistent results under similar conditions.

Relocation assistance payments cover expatriates' expenses to relocate to foreign posts.

Repatriation is the process of making the transition from an international assignment and living abroad to a domestic assignment and living in the home country.

Restricted stock plans a company may grant executives with stock options at market value or discounted value, or they may provide stock instead. Under restricted stock plans, executives do not have any ownership control over the disposition of the stock for a predetermined period, often many years. This predetermined period is known as the vesting period, much like vesting rights associated with employer-sponsored retirement plans.

Restricted stock units are shares of company stock that are awarded to executives at the end of the restriction period.

Retirement programs provide income to individuals and beneficiaries throughout their retirement. Also called *pension plans*.

Right to control test helps companies determine whether their workers are employees or independent contractors.

Right-to-work laws prohibit management and unions from entering into agreements requiring union membership as a condition of employment.

Roth 401(k) plans are similar to 401(k) plans, but differ in two notable ways: First, employee contributions are taxed at the individual's income tax rate. Second, upon retirement, withdrawals are not taxed.

Rucker plan is a particular type of gain sharing program that emphasizes employee involvement. Gain sharing awards are based on the ratio between value added (less the costs of materials, supplies, and services rendered) and the total cost of employment.

Sabbatical leaves are paid time off for professional development activities such as professional certification, conducting research, and curriculum development.

Safe harbor rule refers to compliance guidelines in a law or regulation.

Salary-only plans are specific types of sales compensation plans. Sales professionals receive fixed-base compensation, which does not vary with the level of units sold, increase in market share, or any other indicator of sales performance.

Salary-plus-bonus plans are specific types of sales compensation plans. Sales professionals receive fixed base compensation, coupled with a bonus. Bonuses are usually single payments that reward employees for achievement of specific, exceptional goals.

Salary-plus-commission plans are particular types of sales compensation plans. Sales professionals receive fixed base compensation and commission.

Sales value of production (SVOP) is the sum of sales revenue plus the value of goods in inventory. This is part of the equation to determine payout amounts in Scanlon gain sharing plans.

Sarbanes-Oxley Act of 2002 mandated a number of reforms to enhance corporate responsibility, enhance financial disclosures, and combat corporate and accounting fraud in response to corporate accounting scandals in Enron, Tyco, and other large U.S. corporations. The act established the Public Company Accounting Oversight Board (PCAOB) to oversee the activities of the auditing profession.

Say on pay gives company shareholders the right to vote yes or no on executive compensation proposals, including current and deferred components, including golden parachute agreements, at least once every 3 years. Although the say on pay provision guarantees shareholders the right to vote on executive compensation proposals, the vote is nonbinding.

Scanlon plan is a specific type of gain sharing program that emphasizes employee involvement. Gain sharing awards are based on the ratio between labor costs and sales value of production.

Scientific management practices promote labor cost control by replacing inefficient production methods with efficient production methods.

Second surgical opinion is a feature of many health insurance plans, reducing unnecessary surgical procedures and costs by encouraging an individual to seek an independent opinion from another doctor.

Section 401(k) plans are qualified retirement plans named after the section of the IRC that created them. These plans permit employees to defer part of their compensation to the trust of a qualified defined contribution plan. Only private sector or tax-exempt employers are eligible to sponsor 401(k) plans.

Section 403(b) plans are defined contribution plans that apply to employees of public educational institutions (e.g., state colleges and universities) and private tax-exempt organizations (e.g., charitable organizations, state-supported hospitals).

Section 457 plans are defined contribution plans that apply to state government workers.

Securities and Exchange Commission (SEC) is a nonpartisan, quasi-judicial federal government agency with responsibility for administering federal securities laws.

Securities Exchange Act of 1934 applies to the disclosure of executive compensation.

Self-Employment Contributions Act (SECA) requires self-employed individuals to contribute to the OASDI and Medicare programs but at a higher tax rate than required for non-self-employed individuals.

Self-funded plans are similar to commercial insurance plans with one key difference: Companies typically draw from their own assets to fund claims when self-funded.

Self-funding refers to health insurance plans that pay benefits directly from an employer's assets.

Seniority pay systems reward employees with permanent additions to base pay periodically, according to employees' length of service performing their jobs.

Separation agreements refer to a type of deferred compensation which guarantees that an executive will receive a lucrative compensation package upon employment termination.

Services represent discretionary employee benefits that provide enhancements to employees and their families (e.g., tuition reimbursement and day care assistance).

Severance pay usually includes several months of pay following involuntary termination and, in some cases, continued coverage under the employer's medical insurance plan. Employees often rely on severance pay to meet financial obligations while searching for employment.

Short-term disability refers to an inability to perform the duties of one's regular job usually for fewer than 6 months.

Short-term disability insurance provides income benefits for limited periods of time, usually less than 6 months.

Sick leave benefits compensate employees for a specified number of days absent due to personal illness.

Signing bonuses are monetary awards given to promote recruitment and job offer acceptance. These bonuses are particularly effective when coupled with a competitive wage or salary offer.

Similar-to-me effect refers to the tendency on the part of raters (e.g., supervisors) to judge employees favorably who they perceive as similar to themselves.

Simple ranking plans specific methods of job evaluation, orders all jobs from lowest to highest according to a single criterion (e.g., job complexity or the centrality of the job to the company's competitive strategy).

Single coverage extends health insurance benefits only to the covered employee.

Skill based on Equal Employment Opportunity Commission guidelines, refers to an observable competence to perform a learned psychomotor act.

Skill-based pay used mostly for employees who do physical work, increases these workers' pay as they master new skills.

Skill blocks model a kind of pay-for-knowledge program, applies to jobs from within the same job family. Just as in the stair-step model, employees progress to increasingly complex jobs; however, skills do not necessarily build on each other in a skill blocks program.

Skill (knowledge) blocks are sets of skills (knowledge) necessary to perform a specific job (e.g., typing skills versus analytical reasoning) or group of similar jobs (e.g., junior accounting clerk, intermediate accounting clerk, and senior accounting clerk).

Smoking cessation a particular type of wellness program that stresses the negative aspects of smoking and can include intensive programs directed at helping individuals to stop smoking.

Social comparison theory provides an explanation for executive compensation determination based on the tendency for the board of directors to offer executive compensation packages that are similar to those in peer companies.

Social Security Act of 1935 (Title IX) established three main types of legally required benefits: unemployment insurance, retirement income and benefits for dependents, and medical insurance (Medicare).

Sorting effect addresses an employee's choice to stay versus leave his or her employer for another job, presumably one without an incentive pay contingency.

Specialist may be an HR executive, manager, or non-manager who is typically concerned with only one of the areas of compensation practice.

Spillover effect refers to nonunion companies' offer of similar compensation as offered by union companies to their employees. The goal is to reduce the likelihood that nonunion workforces will seek union representation.

Spot bonuses are relatively small monetary gifts provided to employees for outstanding work or effort during a reasonably short period of time.

Staff employees support the functions performed by line employees. Human resources and accounting are examples of staff functions.

Stair-step model a type of pay-for-knowledge program, resembles a flight of stairs. The steps represent jobs from a particular job family that differ in terms of complexity. Skills at higher levels build upon previous lower-level skills.

Standard deviation refers to the mean distance of each salary figure from the mean (i.e., how larger observations fluctuate above the mean and how small observations fluctuate below the mean).

State governments local governments enact and enforce laws that pertain exclusively to their respective regions (e.g., Illinois and Michigan).

Stock appreciation rights a type of executive deferred compensation, provide executives income at the end of a designated period, much like restricted stock options; however, executives never have to exercise their stock rights to receive income. The company simply awards payment to executives based on the difference in stock price between the time the company granted the stock rights at fair market value to the end of the designated period, permitting the executives to keep the stock.

Stock options describe an employee's right to purchase company stock.

Straight commission is based on a fixed percentage of the sales price of the product or service.

Strategic analysis entails an examination of a company's external market context and internal factors. Examples of external market factors include industry profile, information about competitors, and long-term growth prospects. Internal factors encompass financial condition and functional capabilities (e.g., marketing and human resources).

Strategic compensation refers to the design and implementation of compensation systems to reinforce the objectives of both HR strategies and competitive business strategies. Compensation and benefits executives work with the lead HR executive and the company's chief financial officer (CFO) to prepare total compensation strategies.

Strategic decisions support business objectives.

Strategic management entails a series of judgments, under uncertainty, that companies direct toward achieving specific goals.

Stress management is a specific kind of wellness program designed to help employees cope with many factors inside and outside their work that contribute to stress.

Strictness errors occur when raters (e.g., supervisors) judge employee performance to be less than what it is when compared against objective criteria.

Supplemental life insurance protection represents additional life insurance offered exclusively to executives. Companies design executives' supplemental life insurance protection to increase the value of executives' estates, bequeathed to designated beneficiaries (usually family members) upon their death, and to provide greater benefits than standard plans usually allow.

Supplemental retirement plans offered to executives, are designed to restore benefits restricted under qualified plans.

Tactical decisions support competitive strategy.

Target plan bonus awarded to executives, is based on executives' performance. Executives do not receive bonuses unless their performance exceeds minimally acceptable standards.

Tax equalization is one of two approaches (the other is tax protection) to provide expatriates tax allowances. Employers take the responsibility for paying income taxes to the U.S. and foreign governments on behalf of the expatriates.

Tax protection is one of two approaches (the other is tax equalization) to provide expatriates tax allowances. Employers reimburse expatriates for the difference between the actual income tax amount and the hypothetical tax when the actual income tax amount—based on tax returns filed with the Internal Revenue Service—is greater.

Taxable wage base limits the amount of annual wages or payroll cost per employee subject to taxation to fund OASDI programs.

Team-based (or small-group) incentive plans a small group of employees shares a financial reward when a specific objective is met.

Telecommuting represents alternative work arrangements in which employees perform work from home or some other location besides the office.

Temporary employment agency company that places individuals in client companies as employees on a temporary basis.

Term life insurance is the most common type of life insurance offered by companies; provides protection to an employee's beneficiaries only during a limited period based on a specified number of years or maximum age. After that, insurance automatically expires.

Third country nationals (TCNs) are foreign national citizens who work in U.S. companies' branch offices or manufacturing plants in foreign countries—excluding the United States and their home countries.

Time-and-motion studies analyze the time it takes employees to complete their jobs. Factory owners used time-and-motion studies and job analysis.

Title I of the Americans with Disabilities Act of 1990 (ADA) requires that employers provide reasonable accommodation for disabled employees. Reasonable accommodation may include such efforts as making existing facilities readily accessible, job restructuring, and modifying work schedules.

Title VII of the Civil Rights Act of 1964 indicates that it shall be an unlawful employment practice for an employer to discriminate against any individual with respect to compensation, terms, conditions, or privileges of employment because of such individual's race, color, religion, sex, or national origin.

Torts are laws offering remedies to individuals harmed by the unreasonable actions of others. Tort claims usually involve state law and are based on the legal premise that individuals are liable for the consequences of their conduct if it results in injury to others. Tort laws involve civil suits, which are actions brought to protect an individual's private rights.

Tournament theory provides an explanation for executive compensation determination based on substantially greater competition for high-ranking jobs. Lucrative chief executive compensation packages represent the prize to those who win the competition by becoming chief executives.

Trait systems a type of performance-appraisal method, require raters (e.g., supervisors or customers) to evaluate each employee's traits or characteristics (e.g., quality of work, quantity of work, appearance, dependability, cooperation, initiative, judgment, leadership responsibility, decision-making ability, and creativity).

Transportation services represent energy-efficient ways to transport employees to and from the workplace. Employers cover part or all of the transportation costs.

Tuition reimbursement programs promote employees' education. Under a tuition reimbursement program, an employer fully or partially reimburses an employee for expenses incurred for education or training.

Two-tier pay structures reward newly hired employees less than established employees on either a temporary or permanent basis.

Underemployment refers to employees who wish to work full-time but are forced to work part-time for economic reasons, such as poor business conditions or inability to find a job, both of which are common problems during economic recessions.

Universal compensable factors based on the Equal Pay Act of 1963, include skill, effort, responsibility, and working conditions.

Universal life insurance provides protection to employees' beneficiaries based on the insurance feature of term life insurance and a more flexible savings or cash accumulation plan than is found in whole life insurance plans.

Vacation refers to paid time off for reasons other than illness, holidays, parental leave, or formally designated paid-time off.

Valid job analysis method accurately assesses each job's duties or content. In this regard, we are referring to a particular type of validity—content validity.

Value-added formula is the difference between the value of the sales price of a product and the value of materials purchased to make the product. This is part of the equation to determine payout amounts in Rucker gain sharing plans.

Variable pay See *incentive pay*.

Variation represents the amount of spread or dispersion in a set of data.

Vertical knowledge refers to knowledge traditionally associated with supervisory activities (e.g., performance appraisal and grievance review procedures).

Vertical skills are those skills traditionally considered supervisory skills (e.g., scheduling, coordinating, training, and leading others).

Vesting refers to employees' acquisition of nonforfeitable rights to pension benefits.

Vietnam Era Veterans Readjustment Assistance Act applies the principles of the Rehabilitation Act to veterans with disabilities and veterans of the Vietnam War (401 *FEP Manual* 379).

Violations of an affirmative duty are violations taking place when an employer fails to reveal the exposure of one or more workers to harmful substances or when the employer does not disclose a medical condition typically caused by exposure.

Voluntary part-time employee chooses to work fewer than 35 hours per regularly scheduled workweek.

Volunteerism refers to giving of one's time to support a meaningful cause. More and more companies are providing employees with paid time off to contribute to causes of their choice.

Wage See *hourly pay*.

Wall Street Reform and Consumer Protection Act of 2010 enhances the transparency of executive compensation practices. Also commonly referred to as the Dodd-Frank Act.

Walling v. A. H. Belo Corp. is a court ruling that mandates employers to guarantee fixed weekly pay for employees whose work hours vary from week to week when certain conditions are met.

Walsh–Healey Public Contracts Act of 1936 mandates that contractors with federal contracts meet guidelines regarding wages and hours, child labor, convict labor, and hazardous working conditions. Contractors must observe the minimum wage and overtime provisions of the FLSA. In addition, this act prohibits the employment of individuals younger than 16 and convicted criminals. Furthermore, it prohibits contractors from exposing workers to any conditions that violate the Occupational Safety and Health Act.

Weight control and nutrition programs a particular type of wellness program, are designed to educate employees about proper nutrition and weight loss, both of which are critical to good health.

Welfare practices were generous endeavors undertaken by some employers, motivated to minimize employees' desire to seek union representation, to promote good management, and to enhance worker productivity.

Wellness programs promote employees' physical and psychological health.

Whole life insurance is a type of life insurance that provides protection to employees' beneficiaries during employees' employment and into the retirement years.

Work context information describes physical and social factors that influence the nature of work.

Work styles are personal characteristics that describe important interpersonal and work style requirements in jobs and occupations.

Worker characteristics refer to ability, interests, and work styles.

Worker requirements represent the minimum qualifications and skills that people must have to perform a particular job. Such requirements usually include education, experience, licenses, permits, and specific abilities such as typing, drafting, or editing.

Worker specifications a section in job descriptions, lists the education, skills, abilities, knowledge, and other qualifications individuals must possess to perform the job adequately.

Workers' compensation refers to state-run insurance programs that are designed to cover medical, rehabilitation, and disability income expenses resulting from employees' work-related accidents.

Workforce characteristics refer to variables that define and describe the general characteristics of occupations that may influence occupational requirements.

Working condition fringe benefits refer to the work equipment (e.g., computer) and services (e.g., an additional telephone line) employers purchase for telecommuters' use at home.

Working conditions are the social context or physical environment in which work will be performed.

Yearly limits refer to the maximum amount a plan would cover each year. Yearly limits are not permitted since the passage of the Patient Protection and Affordable Care Act.

Author Index